For Carrie,
Merry Christmas
with love —
    from Tom and Candy

December 25, 1974

THE LAST ATTACHMENT

IRIS ORIGO

THE LAST ATTACHMENT

*The story of Byron and Teresa Guiccioli
as told in their unpublished letters
and other family papers*

CHARLES SCRIBNER'S SONS

NEW YORK

CONTENTS

The serial numbers following certain words in the text refer to the Notes which are to be found at page 492 *et seq.*

INTRODUCTION

I have lived in far countries, abroad, or in the agitating
world at home . . . so that almost all I have written has
been mere passion – passion, it is true, of different kinds,
but always passion: for . . . my *indifference* was a kind of
passion, the result of experience, and not the philosophy
of nature.

BYRON

THREE years after Byron's death, the Contessa Teresa Guiccioli – the object of the poet's last, longest and perhaps deepest
attachment – wrote to Barry that his letters to her were 'a
treasure of goodness, affection and genius, which for a hundred
reasons I cannot now make public'.[1] Thirty years later, however,
roused to indignation by reading Leigh Hunt's malicious book,
Lord Byron and his Contemporaries, she told John Murray that she did
not care what the consequences to her own reputation might be,
'so long as none of the documents and letters are lost, which can
reveal the great and kind heart of Lord Byron in its true light'.[2]
And finally, on her deathbed in Italy in 1873, she is said to have
expressed to her sister-in-law her desire that *all* her papers should
be published. 'The more Byron is known,' she said, 'the better he
will be loved.'[3]

Since then seventy-five years have passed. And now, owing to
the courtesy of Count Carlo Gamba, Teresa's great-nephew, – to
whom she left her villa at Settimello and all its contents –
Teresa's papers and treasures have at last come to light. The
treasures – Byron's 'relics', as she called them – still lie in the
carved mahogany box in which Teresa kept them. There is the
locket containing her hair, and hung on a chain of her hair, which
Byron was wearing when he died, and which Augusta Leigh sent
back to her; there is another locket, containing Byron's hair,
which he gave to Teresa when he sailed for Greece. There,
too, carefully wrapped up by Teresa, with an inscription in
her writing, lies a curious, moving assortment of objects: a piece
of the wall-hangings of the room in Palazzo Gamba where Byron
used to visit Teresa, Byron's handkerchief and a fragment of one
of his shirts, – and a crumbling rose-leaf, with the branch of a tree
and a small acorn, from Newstead Abbey. Finally there is a fat
little volume bound in purple plush: the copy of *Corinne* in
which he wrote his famous love-letter to Teresa in Bologna.

The papers in this collection have proved to be as exciting and
interesting a hoard as the most exacting biographer could hope
for. They include, not only 149 of Byron's love-letters, mostly in

Italian, to Teresa, and some of her answers, but Teresa's 'Vie de Lord Byron', – her unpublished account of his life in Italy, which she wrote in her old age and thought too intimate to be published during her lifetime. In addition there are the documents of the Guiccioli lawsuits, containing a complete account of the complicated circumstances which led to Teresa's separation from her husband, and there are Pietro Gamba's letters to his sister from Greece, besides many other letters to her from Shelley, Lady Blessington, Lamartine, John Murray and others. In short, we have at last – with all the gaps filled in by information at which, until now, it was only possible to guess – the full story of Byron and Teresa Guiccioli.

It is not – this must be admitted – a wholly pleasant story, and it is one which it is difficult to tell impartially. There is a temptation to take sides: either to portray Byron as an unscrupulous cad, seducing a pretty young woman who had fallen desperately in love with him, laughing at her in his letters to his friends, and gradually cooling off, to leave her abandoned and alone; or, alternatively, to depict Teresa as a designing minx, who, tired of her elderly husband and her dreary provincial life, flung herself at Byron's head until he was perforce obliged to turn a fugitive love-affair into a 'romance in the Anglo fashion'. Or else the whole affair could be presented in the manner of the Goldonian Comedy – with the audience's sympathy focused on the two lovers, and with Count Guiccioli (the avaricious, calculating husband) as the villain, Fanny Silvestrini as the obliging confidante, Count Ruggero as the noble father, and Pietro as the young gallant. Even the minor parts could be allotted – the venal priest, the maid, the Moorish page-boy, – and, in the pine-forest of Ravenna, the chorus of conspirators.

But now, with these new papers before us, none of these simplified versions will do. The actors too often speak out of part – and the story that emerges is too full of discrepancies and inconsistencies. Besides, there are a few minor points which, to my mind, even now remain obscure. I am still not quite certain about the motives of Count Guiccioli; I do not know what Byron meant by his letter on page 184; I am not always sure when Teresa is, or is not, speaking the truth. The reader, too, must guess and draw his own conclusions. I have merely attempted to fill in the background – to complete the story with passages from Byron's other letters at the time or from the accounts of his contemporaries, and to give such information as seemed necessary about the people, the setting and the local history. But I have carefully refrained from adding any imaginary details or touches of 'local colour': any information that the book contains can be confirmed by some record.

For it is the papers themselves – the scribbled, passionate love-letters, the painstaking police reports, the formal ecclesiastical decrees, the gossip of observant contemporaries – that must tell the story. They provide a singularly intimate and unvarnished account of the daily life of this little group of people, 130 years ago. Their passionate protestations, their jokes, their retractions and lies, their plans and disappointments, all that constituted the most private aspect of their lives – these are now laid before us in merciless detail. Now, after more than a century, we can follow the negro page carrying Teresa's notes to Byron up the staircase of Palazzo Guiccioli, or stand with the groom Morelli, watching by the front door to warn the lovers of the Count's return. We can look out from Teresa's balcony in Palazzo Lanfranchi in the moonlight – and Mary Shelley's carriage is clattering up the Lungarno, and she is calling out, 'Sapete alcuna cosa di Shelley?' We are in Teresa's sitting-room in Casa Saluzzo, and Byron comes in, very cross, and gives her an unpleasant letter for Mary – and when he has gone out again, she turns it over and over and peers at the seal, and does not dare to look inside. We are with Byron – bored and flat and sad – on the *Hercules* in Leghorn harbour, and Pietro Gamba is standing over him with a pen, to make him write to Teresa his last meagre note of farewell.

Here is the story of two passionate, unstable human beings – one of them a great poet, and a very odd man – the other a young woman of quite exceptional vitality and strength of will. They loved each other; they quarrelled; they trampled ruthlessly on whatever stood in their way. Of the two of them it was, curiously enough, Byron who occasionally played the moralist. Teresa, for all her convent-school training, appears to have been unaware throughout that any moral problem was involved. They committed themselves, and they drew back again. One of them was often disloyal, the other sometimes insincere. Each of them in turn – Byron in Ravenna, Teresa in the English circle in Pisa – had to conform, for the other's sake, to the ways of a bewildering and alien society. As time wore on, one of them became plaintive, the other exasperated. But at all times they were quite extraordinarily alive. They galvanized everyone who came near them. In these letters, they are living still.

Moreover, these papers light up a facet of Byron's character which, until now, has been unfamiliar: they show him living in an *Italian* setting. And the extent to which these new surroundings affected and changed him appears in a manner which is not only interesting, but sometimes disconcerting.

Byron himself, indeed, tried to tell his friends about it: 'Now I have *lived* among the Italians, – not *Florenced* and *Romed* and Galleried and Conversationed it for a few months, and then home again – but been of their families, and friendships and feuds, and loves and councils, and correspondence, in a part of Italy least known to foreigners; and have been amongst them of all classes, from the Conte to the Contadino.'⁴ But neither his friends at the time, nor his biographers, paid much attention to all this. His life in Ravenna has been treated merely as a part of the whole paraphernalia of conspiracy and romance in which the histrionic side of his nature delighted: one more scene in the great Italian performance, like the quarrels with the Fornarina, or the swim across the Venetian Lagoon. But now it has become apparent that this was not the whole truth. If in Venice he was still the 'Englishman in Italy', a foreigner playing a part, in Ravenna he had been 'inoculated into a family. This', he added, 'is to see men and things as they are.'⁵

It is. But it can only be achieved at a price. In this case, it implied nothing less than a partial change of personality – a change which no reader who compares Byron's Italian letters with his English ones, can feel to be for the better. It is not that they are written in bad Italian. Although they are the letters of a foreigner, they are also unmistakably those of a man of letters, and they contain certain amusing indications as to where and how he learned his Italian: a Dantesque expression or a quotation from Tasso stand beside a Venetian phrase, straight from the mouth of the Fornarina, or a piece of Romagnolo dialect. What is disconcerting about these early letters is that their elaboration of phrase and conventionality of idiom are matched by an almost equal, a wholly un-Byronic, conventionality of *sentiment*. At first, indeed, this is so marked that one is inclined to wonder whether this is not merely Byron overplaying his part; perhaps, in his desire to be the perfect *Cavalier Servente* in the Italian manner, he has copied some phrases outright from a polite letter-writer's manual of Venice – or has allowed not only single words (as he frankly admits), but whole sentences, to be suggested by Lega Zambelli, the priest turned secretary. 'Sentiment, the most beautiful and fragile thing in all our existence.' 'How much happier than I is this letter, which in a few days will be in your hands – and perhaps even will be brought close to your lips.' 'When I weep, my tears are from the heart, and are of blood.' These are not sentences which, if we encountered them without a signature, we should ever guess to be Byron's. As the correspondence goes on, it is true, such sentences become less frequent. Not only does he gain a greater ease in the use of the Italian language, but he allows himself a lighter touch, more recognizably his own. 'It would suit me better to be with you in a desert, than without you in Mahomet's paradise, which is considerably more agreeable than ours.' – 'I kiss you more often than I have ever kissed you – and this (if Memory does not deceive me) should be a fine number of times, counting from the beginning.' – But still, I think the reader will agree that the writer of these letters is an unfamiliar Byron.

For one thing, he is more deeply involved. If the adventure started like many others, with a mixture of physical attraction and contempt – if, indeed, he was faintly irritated, as well as flattered, by this new silly young woman who threw herself at his head – the relationship very soon changed, and held him. Its progress is revealed in these letters. But here, too, it is curious to note that the feeling, although quite unmistakably genuine, is all within the Italian convention of the period. Passion, jealousy, storms, reconciliations, protestations of eternal fidelity ('your friend and lover forever', is the most frequent signature) – it is all, to English ears, curiously *formal*. What is odd in these earlier letters, too, is a total absence of his usual flippancy and irony — with which, however, he made sufficiently free in his letters *about* the affair, to his friends at home. Teresa did not either like or understand irony; and though occasionally, in the later letters, Byron does laugh at her, it is as one smiles at a child, who will not share the joke.

What is the explanation of all this? I think it is to be found in Teresa's own character. Teresa was in some ways – like Caroline Lamb and Augusta – a *silly* woman; but she was not a stupid one; and she had all the strength of a one-track mind. From the moment that her passion for Byron held her, she knew what she wanted, and it was a foregone conclusion that she would get it. She persuaded her father, a simple and upright country gentleman, that nothing was wrong in her relations with Byron, long after the evidence of his senses must have told him the contrary. She defeated the complicated manœuvres, and stood up to the brutality and violence, of her husband. She imposed an acceptance of the situation (however much people might gossip behind her back) on the whole tight little society of Ravenna, and even on her own correct, affectionate, family circle. And finally, she imposed her will upon Byron himself. He struggled, he grumbled, he tried to laugh at her; but in the end, he did what she wanted. 'I have come, I have gone – I have come back, I have remained – it is more than a year that I have done nothing but obey you in every respect.' Moreover she succeeded in shaping this relationship according to *her* standards, *her* view of life. For in such cases it is always the narrower, but more positive, purpose that wins.

There is an interesting account, in the diary of one of the most assiduous of Byron's Venetian friends, the Cavaliere Mengaldo, of how he once visited Byron's 'Casino' at Santa Maria Zobenigo. What shocked him, although he was himself no Puritan, was the casualness of Byron's affairs. 'Je fus effrayé de son horrible système!' The Latin convention in the pursuit of pleasure, as in domesticity, is a strict one – and it was Byron's refusal to conform to it that so profoundly scandalized his Venetian observers. But in the end he too was caught. A girl of nineteen, by her very limitations, her unawareness of any other world than that familiar to her, translated their passion into the only language that she knew – and her lover (first, we suspect, as a joke, a *tour de force*, then in all seriousness – and finally, as a habit) made it his language, too. He became – this was what shocked and disconcerted Mrs. Hunt and Mary Shelley so much – Italianized.

What was the quality in Teresa which – in spite of her inexperience, her lack of sensitiveness and her silliness – enabled her to achieve all this? It hardly seems worth while to examine in detail the controversy about her looks. From her contemporaries we have, on the one hand, such distressing adjectives as 'chumpy' and 'fubsy' – while, on the other hand, Shelley thought her 'very pretty', Lady Blessington, 'decidedly handsome . . . Her complexion delicately fair, her hair of rich golden tint, her bust and arms exquisitely beautiful'; and Lord Malmesbury, 'handsome, with a brilliant complexion' and 'a profusion of auburn hair'. Undoubtedly, at the time she met Byron, we must grant her brilliancy of colour and complexion – what the Victorians called 'bloom' – fine eyes and teeth, and beautiful arms and bust. But her legs were too short. The real point, however, is not what her looks were, but what Byron thought of them. He thought her 'fair as sunrise – warm as noon'* – as pretty as Caroline Lamb and much gentler – and endearingly funny, too, in her sky-blue riding-habit and her hat like Punch's.

But in any case, the strength of physical attraction is not dependent only – or even chiefly – upon looks. Teresa and Byron *suited* each other – as to that there can be no question. Every line of the correspondence confirms this; even in the later phase, when weariness and exasperation had crept in, there remain the little jokes of physical intimacy, half-unintelligible to any reader but one – and the pervading sense that, whatever else went wrong, *that* remained all right.

But even the most delightful physical relation is not, by itself, enough; the evenings, as Byron wrote at La Mira, always seem longer than the nights. What else was it in Teresa that attracted him so strongly? I think it was her sheer vitality, her youthful high spirits. To self-conscious, complex human beings, there is something extremely restful in the company of people less highly organized than themselves – and Teresa possessed to the full not only the freshness and zest of youth, but a certain childlike ruthlessness, a quality which Byron always found attractive. Life with her was uncomplicated, gay and exciting. If she sometimes talked affected nonsense, it was the kind of nonsense that he found diverting – perhaps even, at first, a little touching; – and then it was leavened by so unlimited an admiration, so unrestrained a devotion! 'Mio Byron!'

In some ways Byron's love for Teresa more closely resembled his feeling for Augusta, than what he felt for any other woman – and perhaps it was just for this reason that their relationship lasted for so long. To both Augusta and Teresa he showed the same half-humorous, half-mocking tenderness; with both of them he found the release from self-consciousness that brought him gaiety and peace. For Byron did not want women to understand him: Annabella had understood him, and what had that led to? He wanted them to amuse him. 'I ask nothing of a woman but to make me laugh,' he had brutally told his wife in the first days of their marriage. 'I can make Augusta laugh about anything. No one makes me happy except Augusta.'[7] And to Augusta herself, he wrote about Teresa: 'She has a good deal of *us*, too. I mean that turn for ridicule like Aunt Sophy and you and I and all the B.s.'[8] Teresa's absurdities, too, were just the kind that Augusta would enjoy: 'She is an equestrian, too, but . . . she can't guide her horse – and he runs after mine – and tries to bite him – and then she begins screaming in a high hat and sky-blue riding-habit – making a most absurd figure.'[9] She was as silly as Augusta – and amoral, too, in very much the same way. Like her, she could not really believe that anything was wrong that did not cause anyone any pain – and she continued to be kind, even to the people she was deceiving. Byron used, in writing to her, the same symbol, the +, that he had used with Augusta. 'Ah,' he had said on one occasion, showing Augusta this mark in Annabella's presence, 'if she knew what *that* means.'[10] And to Teresa, after making use of this symbol for the first time, he wrote, 'There can be few crosses more holy for us than these.'

But Teresa, for all this, was only partly like Augusta. She had, as I think these papers show, far greater *staying power*: she had more guts, and – for all her sentimentality – more sense. It is now

necessary, I think, to reconsider the previous estimate of her. 'The
nice, pretty girl without pretensions, good hearted and amiable',
of Mary Shelley's description, is evidently not enough; and still
less Leigh Hunt's 'buxom parlour-boarder, composing herself
artificially into dignity and elegance'.[11] (For Teresa had snubbed
Mrs. Hunt.) 'Stupid,' says Miss Mayne, 'at once insensitive and
sentimental . . . so obtuse that he could not shake her off.'[12]
'Insincere,' says her husband's grandson, Alessandro Guiccioli,
'with more calculation than sentiment, cold, selfish and comfort-
loving.'[13] In all these opinions there is, perhaps, a grain of truth.
But I think that Drinkwater was nearer to it when he spoke of
Teresa as 'a woman of more quality and character than history
has commonly realized', – and above all when he said, of Byron's
love for her, 'He talked at times as if this was not so, but then he
talked at times as if everything was not so that was . . . He had,
on the whole, a more genuine and lasting respect for her than he
had for any other woman in his life.'[14]

These new papers confirm this assertion. Byron's early letters
have a quite unmistakable note of genuine passion; and as, in the
later letters, passion fades, it is replaced by a semi-conjugal bond
of half-humorous, resigned acceptance. Teresa's answers show,
in the midst of much flowery rhetoric and exasperating romanticism, an equal passion, and unexpected flashes of both insight
and shrewdness. They show, above all, an unquestioning, disinterested devotion, which, in the long years in which she survived
him, continued to manifest itself in a fierce and irrepressible
loyalty. Leigh Hunt, in his spiteful record of his own grievances,
professed to believe that, during the last year at Pisa and Genoa,
Byron found this devotion so cloying that Teresa at last became
aware that he was tired of her. 'In the course of a few months,
she seemed to have lived as many years.'[15] Mr. Harold Nicolson
clearly implies that by then she had become nothing but an
obstacle and a burden. I think that the truth was rather more
complicated than this. To Lady Blessington, before leaving for
Greece, he admitted that he was 'worn out in feelings' – but at the
same time he added, perhaps not without a wry smile, that if he
and Teresa could be married, they would be 'cited as an example
of conjugal happiness'. This passage, in Teresa's own copy of
Lady Blessington's book, is heavily underscored – and in the
margin she has written 'God bless him!'

The letters of Byron and Teresa, as well as the greater part of
the 'Vie de Lord Byron', are almost wholly concerned with the

two lovers' personal affairs, and throw but little light on the other side of Byron's life in Ravenna: – his part in the Italian revolutionary movement. But in the other sources I have consulted – the minute and detailed police reports of the day, the archives of the Vatican and of Venice, Bologna, Ravenna, Florence, Forlì and Pisa, the contemporary Memoirs of the Carbonari, and the works of Italian scholars, – a good deal of information about Byron's political activity has come to light. This new information suggests that his part in the Romagna rising was greater than has generally been realized – and was actuated by very much the same motives as his expedition to Greece. Had he remained in Italy a few years longer and met a *Sanfedista* bullet in the insurrection of 1831, he might have been the hero of the Italian war of independence, instead of that of Greece. As it is, his activities in Italy have always been slightly slurred over, or dismissed, while his Greek venture has been thrown into the limelight.

One reason for this comparative neglect is that the whole emphasis of his biographers, in writing of his life in Ravenna, has always been upon his liaison with Teresa – or upon his literary work during this period. Another reason is that the documents about the Carbonari are in Italian and are not easy to find. Moreover the most interesting, for British readers, has disappeared. This was Byron's own account of the Carboneria, and of his share in the Romagna insurrection – the notes, presumably, which he had in mind when he wrote in 1821: 'Some day or other, if dust holds together, I have been enough in the Secret (at least in this part of the country) to cast perhaps some little light upon the atrocious treachery which has replunged Italy into Barbarism.'[16] These notes, together with some others on more personal matters, he handed over in July 1823, as he was sailing from Leghorn, to his Venetian friend Mengaldo – presumably not liking to put such dangerous papers into the hands of the Gambas, who were about to return to the Romagna. Mengaldo, however, burned the whole envelope, unopened, 'on the shores of the Adriatic' – and with it, all that Byron could have told us about the secrets of the Carbonari.[17]

But, even without these notes, it is now possible to form a fairly accurate picture both of the activities of the Carbonari in the Romagna and of the degree to which Byron shared in them. Various Italian writers have taken some pains to prove – on quite insufficient evidence – that Byron's participation in the Italian struggle for liberty was a mere consequence of his having been, as they affirm, a Freemason. They attempt to link up his activity in

the Romagna with his previous meetings with the Liberal intel-
lectuals in Milan (Pellegrino Rossi, Lodovico di Breme, Silvio
Pellico) and, on the other hand, with his subsequent venture in
Greece. This was also the line taken in the reports of the Austrian
and Papal police, which described the English Mylord as a sinister
emissary of England, seeking to extend English Liberal influence
(like Lord Bentinck in Sicily) in order to sap the power of the
Holy Alliance all over the Continent.

All this, however, presupposes a complete misconception of
Byron's attitude to public matters. He was in politics a dilettante,
an aristocrat at odds with society, an intellectual with a strong
partiality for liberty. But this partiality was not attached to any
definite political structure: it was merely a personal taste. As
Bertrand Russell pertinently remarks, 'the freedom he praised was
that of a German Prince or a Cherokee Chief, not the inferior sort
that might conceivably be enjoyed by ordinary mortals'.[18] When
he found himself, as he did in the Romagna, in a country ruled by
a despotic and oppressive government, his sympathies went out,
in typically English and amateurish fashion, to that section of
society which was oppressed, while at the same time, in Italy as in
Greece, his historical imagination was fired by the idea of a
renascence of the two great nations of the past. 'Only think, a free
Italy! Why, 'tis the very poetry of politics.'[19] But it was in him –
although leavened by the practical common sense which he
showed again in Greece* – a poet's vision, not a statesman's.

In actual prosaic fact, the risings in the Romagna were not a
very important episode. The anxious police spies who opened
Byron's letters and dogged his footsteps were correct in considering
him one of the moving spirits of the conspiracy; but the plan was
wholly dependent on concerted action in the South, and it fizzled
out the moment the Neapolitan army was dispersed. Nevertheless
Byron was right in saying that 'the more selfish calculation ought
never to be made on such occasions. . . .'

'It is not one man nor a million, but the *spirit* of liberty that
must be preserved. The waves which dash upon the shore are,
one by one, broken, but the *ocean* conquers nevertheless. It overwhelms the Armada, it wears the rock. In like manner, whatever
the struggle of individuals, the great cause will gather strength.'[20]

Mr. Harold Nicolson has gone so far as to affirm that, if Byron
had deserted the Hellenic cause, there would have been no

* 'If there was one quality that characterized Byron more than another, it was his
solid common sense.' – Disraeli.

Navarino. It would perhaps be rash to make a similar claim for the poet's influence on the Risorgimento – largely because he did not have the good fortune to die in Italy. But certainly in Italy, as in Greece, the results of Byron's intervention were entirely disproportionate to the immediate achievement: he came to be 'more important as a myth, than as he really was'.[21] The rising in which he took part was only a minor affair, but it was one of the first faint rumblings which, all over Europe, heralded the great revolutionary storm of 1848; and Byron's name is still remembered by Italians, as that of a friend of Italy and of her freedom.

Finally, the part that Byron played in Italy was important to *himself*. One of the ingredients was, of course, a certain pleasure in the whole *mise en scène*: he enjoyed the encounters in the Pineta with the bands of conspirators who cheered him as he rode by; he enjoyed the 'camaraderie' of their banquets – slightly spurious, for what would he have said if his friendship with them had entailed his giving up a single one of his privileges as 'Pari d'Inghilterra'? He remained with them, too, the 'Cherokee Chief'. He liked to write home about the danger of receiving a stiletto in his back, about secret plots and documents, and weapons concealed in his cellar.

And beneath all this, there was something more. The motive which underlay the Italian venture and the Greek one was the same: a desire for rehabilitation in the eyes of his fellow-countrymen. The 'tremulous web of sensitiveness' which Moore had already noted – the constant preoccupation with English opinion which Lady Blessington was to observe★ – is already evident in the pages of the *Ravenna Journal*. The smallest scrap of news from England, indeed, the slightest breath of approval or criticism, had for Byron a *reality* which nothing in his life abroad ever acquired. In vain did he declare that he had shaken off the dust of the country which had misunderstood and insulted him; in vain did he achieve fame and success all over the Continent. Never could he rid himself of the nagging conviction that the only true criterion of fame and success, the only true achievement, lay in the opinion of Englishmen, at home. Always he remained what he called himself in signing the visitor's book in the Armenian monastery at Venice: 'Lord Byron, inglese.'

This constant preoccupation with English opinion is, perhaps,

★ 'Tremblingly alive to the censure or opinions of persons for whom he entertains little respect.' 'Byron seems to take a pleasure in censuring England and its customs, yet it is evident to me that he rails at it and them as a lover does at the failure of his mistress ... Why talk so much and so constantly of his country, if he felt that indifference, nay, hatred to it which he professes?' LADY BLESSINGTON, *The Idler in Italy*, p. 167.

B

the key to all his public behaviour abroad. 'If I live,' he told Lady
Blessington (and Teresa has marked the passage in the margin),
'and return from Greece with something better and higher than
the reputation or glory of a poet, opinions may change, as the
successful are always judged favourably of in our country; my
laurels may cover my faults better than the bays have done.'²²
For Byron had to the full the intellectual's admiration for the man
of action. 'A man', he told Teresa, 'ought to do more for society
than write verses.' And elsewhere he had written: 'If I live ten
years longer, you will see, however, that it is not over with me –
I don't mean in literature, for that is nothing; and it may seem
odd enough to say, I do not think it my vocation.'²³ When in the
Ravenna Journal, on his thirty-third birthday, he deplores the passing of the years, not 'so much for what I have done, as for what I
might have done,'²⁴ it was not of literary achievement that he was
thinking. It was – at Ravenna as at Missolonghi – a 'nobler aim'.
The Italian venture – undertaken with a similar mixture of
motives, a similar irresolution and conflict, fraught with a similar
exasperation with the people whose cause he was defending – was
the prelude to the Greek tragedy.

My deepest gratitude is due to Conte Carlo Gamba for his
permission, not only to consult and transcribe Contessa Guiccioli's papers, which form the basis of this book, but to examine
her books and treasures, and to visit her villa at Settimello.

In addition to the Gamba papers, I have consulted a number of
other unpublished papers, which are listed in Appendix I. For
permission to examine these, I am indebted first of all to Mon-
signor Mercati, Prefect of the Archivio Segreto of the Vatican
Library, for allowing me to consult the documents of the 'Sacra
Rota', and to the Committee and Librarian of the Keats-Shelley
Memorial in Rome, Signora Vera Cacciatore, for letting me make
use of books and unpublished papers in that library; to the
Trustees and to the Librarian of the Pierpont Morgan Library in
New York, for permission to quote from several letters of Byron's,
Contessa Guiccioli's and Alexander Scott's. I also wish to express
my warm gratitude to Conte and Contessa Pasolini dall'Onda,
who have allowed me to quote passages from papers in their
family archives at Ravenna and to borrow some rare books from
their library, and who have helped me with much interesting
information.

For permission to publish the majority of the unpublished

Byron letters I am grateful and indebted to the Legal Personal Representative of Lord Byron's estate.

I should also like to thank Lord Abinger for permission to quote from several unpublished letters from Contessa Guiccioli to Mary Shelley and a letter from Pietro Gamba to Teresa Guiccioli.

Especially I wish to say how deeply I am indebted – in common with many other students of Byron – to Sir John Murray and to Mr. John Grey Murray, for their permission to consult the inexhaustible Byron archives in Albemarle Street.

The more important books I have consulted are listed in the Bibliography. I must, however, express my especial indebtedness to those recent scholars whose brilliant treatment of some of the episodes described in my book, has smoothed the way for me: in particular to Mr. Harold Nicolson, M. André Maurois and Mr. Peter Quennell. Mr. Nicolson's *The Last Journey*, indeed, illuminates so vividly the whole background of the Greek adventure that, in annotating Pietro Gamba's letters from Greece, I have not attempted to do anything more than follow in his footsteps.

I am most grateful to Professor Leslie A. Marchand for drawing my attention to some interesting material, for reading my typescript and for many valuable suggestions, and to Mr. Percy Lubbock and Mr. W. H. Hughes for their willing ears and their constructive criticism.

Finally and above all I wish to thank my friend Elsa Dallolio for her patient and generous help in sharing every task, even the most tedious, for her indefatigable researches, and for the unfailing support of her intuition and judgment.

THE LAST ATTACHMENT

I cannot exist without some object of attachment.
> Byron to Lady Melbourne, 1813

I can hope no more to inspire attachment, and I trust never again to feel it.
> Byron to Hoppner, 1819

PROLOGUE

On ne saurait s'y prendre de trop de façons, et
par trop de bouts, pour connaître un homme.
SAINTE-BEUVE

'ON the happy occasion of the Espousals arranged and concluded between the Cavaliere Commendatore Alessandro
Guiccioli and the Contessa Teresa Gamba Ghiselli
daughter of Conte Ruggero, both of this city, it has been thought
desirable to put on record the dowry assigned by Conte Ruggero
to his aforesaid Daughter, as well as to establish the rules that will
govern their future union. . . .

In view of this Marriage Conte Ruggero Gamba Ghiselli,
having come before this Notary Public and in the presence of
Witnesses . . . has assigned and made over to his Daughter
Contessa Teresa the dowry of scudi 4500. . . .

The Cavaliere promises and guarantees to his Spouse the
Contessa in case of her Widowhood – which God avert – a decent
and comfortable provision from the Guiccioli Fortune, so long as
she lives a Widow's life, and the interest on her dowry remains
with the Guiccioli family. . . .'[1]

This marriage contract, drawn up in the little provincial town
of Ravenna in the Romagna, on January 20th, 1818, is the
beginning of the story.

Forty years lay between the bride and bridegroom,[2] and they
had met for the first time three months before, when the bride had
just come home from school. The second of Count Gamba's five
pretty daughters, she was, by all accounts, the most attractive,
and moreover the prize pupil of S. Chiara, the new-fangled convent school at Faenza – which had been opened during the recent
French domination. Here – although she was something of a
little hoyden, quick-tempered and vain and, her schoolfellows
whispered, extremely ambitious[3] – Teresa had received an
education exceptional for a girl of her time. The Abbess, Madre
Rampi, – a woman of great character – had decided to create a
model establishment, in which girls (almost as if they were boys)
would be given *une éducation forte*, comprising not only an
appreciation of the classic authors of their own language, but a
thorough training in the arts of eloquence and rhetoric. The
school, indeed, was closed a few years later by the Church, on the
grounds that so much learning was dangerous for women; but
meanwhile its pupils had learned how to hold a conversation about

23

Dante or Petrarch, and how to write letters in a style from which every trace of simplicity and naturalness was eliminated. Moreover at home Teresa had also enjoyed the teaching of her brother's professor, Paolo Costa, who had imparted to her, as well as a love of literature, the rudiments of philosophy. She was, in short, a very well-educated young lady indeed, and aware of it; and perhaps this helped her to face with equanimity the prospect of marriage with a man who, whatever his faults (and it is not likely that much of the gossip had reached her ears), was known to be the wittiest and most cultivated man in Ravenna, who had been a friend of Alfieri's, and was a patron of the theatre. Teresa, her sisters whispered enviously, would have her own box at the Opera – had not the Ravenna theatre been restored largely at the Count's expense? – she would have a fine house, with many servants in livery, including two 'mori' in rich Oriental costumes, with pistols and daggers at their belts; she would drive in the Carnival cavalcade in a coach-and-six preceded by outriders with blue and white feathers in their caps. Besides, says the Count's grandson, 'my grandfather was a handsome man, vigorous, rich, intelligent, agreeable in conversation, skilled in seduction, of fine manners and illustrious family'.⁴ What more could a girl desire? And so, on a late autumn evening of the year 1817, a curious little scene took place in the drawing-room of Palazzo Gamba.

A gentle, blushing girl of eighteen – with a poor figure, but a brilliant complexion and a mass of lovely auburn hair, stood in the middle of the room, curtsying, as her father introduced her to a rigid elderly man with red hair and whiskers, whom she had never seen before. The room was ill-lit, and the future bridegroom was short-sighted.

Without a word, he took a candle in his hand, and with a faint smile on his thin lips he slowly walked round the girl, examining her points 'as if about to buy a piece of furniture'.⁵ The next day the bargain was concluded.

———————

The bridegroom, according to all accounts, was an expert in bargains, and – since this was his third marriage – presumably knew what he required. To form a picture of his character it will perhaps be fairest to turn first to the evidence of a completely impartial observer – one who had nothing to do with the Byron affair – the Vice Legate of Ravenna, who in 1827 sent a report about the Count to the Head of the Austrian police.

'The Cavaliere Guiccioli', the report begins, 'belongs to one of the patrician families of this city. Possessed of uncommon talents

and a subtle intelligence, he was given an education suitable to
his rank. While still young he lost his Father, who left him only
a moderate fortune, and that in poor condition. He then married
the Contessa Placidia Zinanni, who made up for the disparity of
her age – much greater than that of the Cavaliere – and for her
physical imperfections, by a very large dowry.'•

This dowry her husband immediately put to good use, 'in such
a manner as to attain the level of the other good families of the
city'; while for his wife's instruction – and subsequently, for that
of her successors – he prepared a series of 'maxims', enlightening
her as to the behaviour he expected of her:

'Let her determine always to be a solace to me, and never a
trouble; she should therefore always be cheerful with me, annoy
no one in the house, ask politely for anything she wishes, but
accept in silence any refusal.

Let her be satisfied with modest amusements and suitable
provision.

Let her be true and frank, so that she will have no mysteries
from me, and that I may always see into her heart, but let her be
prudent in handing on my confidences to others.

Let her be docile and ready to execute all my directions.

Let her be faithful and beware of any appearances to the
contrary.'

Of his own side of the contract nothing is said – and we shall see
later on how he interpreted it.

In 1797 the Napoleonic Army and its revolutionary ideas
invaded the Romagna; and Count Guiccioli began to play a part
in the public life of the Province. Many of the Ravenna patricians
– among them Count Ruggero Gamba, Teresa's father – at once
ardently and sincerely adhered to the Jacobin cause. They set up
in the Piazza a Tree of Liberty – a thirty-foot pole painted with
the national colours, and crowned with a Republican bonnet and
a laurel wreath – and burned at the foot of it the 'Golden Book'
containing their own titles of nobility, while making speeches
'full of high-sounding phrases'.⁷ Others – like Monaldo Leopardi
of Recanati, the poet's father, who wrote of Napoleon that it was
'too great an honour for such a blackguard that a gentleman
should rise to see him pass' – shut themselves up in their palaces or
in their country-houses until the storm had passed.⁸ But the most
prudent – and Count Guiccioli was their leader – trimmed their
sails to the wind. 'The only alternative now left to a gentleman',

he wrote in his notebook, 'is either to have his head cut off by the *canaille*, or to put himself at their head; I prefer the second.'•

His decision bore immediate fruit. When the Romagna was united to the Provinces of the Cisalpine Republic, Guiccioli was made President of the Central Administration of the Province; he became a deputy of the Cisalpine Council; he attended Napoleon's coronation in Milan cathedral. Then, in 1814, after the fall of Napoleon, the French left the Romagna; and a rumour was spread that the English intended to create in Italy an independent State.* The extreme Republicans rejoiced, but more prudent citizens, like Guiccioli, bided their time – and indeed, within a few weeks, the Pope himself was in Ravenna on his way back to Rome. The same crowd which had danced round the Tree of Liberty now unharnessed the Papal coach and drew it in triumph down the Corso, while hundreds thronged, in tears, to ask for the Pope's blessing and kiss his foot; and a Papal Edict published at Cesena promised 'happiness to His faithful subjects'. Before the year was out, the Papal Government – entrusted to two Cardinal Legates, one with his See at Ravenna, the other at Forlì – was firmly re-established in the Romagna.

And in this return to the old order, too, Count Guiccioli found himself at home. Always a correct and conventional churchman and an upholder of 'law and order', besides possessing an elegant tongue and a sharp wit, he was soon upon excellent terms with the prelates of the Cardinal's court. He had, however, his troubles. In his attempts to restore the family fortunes, he had bought a great deal of land, with insufficient cash to pay for it; he had recourse to borrowing; and soon he found himself involved in a very unpleasant lawsuit (the first of many) with a certain Domenico Manzoni, a rich landowner of Forlì. Manzoni won the case, and Guiccioli was shut up for several months in the prisons of Castel Sant'Angelo in Rome.

When he came out again, he continued 'through the practice of a careful economy', to add successfully to his fortune – but the sudden and mysterious assassination of Manzoni caused some unpleasant rumours to be circulated, which were still current gossip in Venice five years later.

'They are liberal with the knife in R^a', wrote Byron with some gusto to Hobhouse, 'and the Cavaliere Conte G. – is shrewdly suspected of two assassinations already, one of a certain Mazzoni

---

* FARINI, op. cit., p. 46. 'These rumours were spread in every corner where the English set foot, and were backed up by proclamations, promises and speeches by the principal actors in the scene, among whom Count Bentinck deserves special mention.'

[*sic*], who had been the cause of Count G.'s being put in the castle
of St. Angelo for some dispute or other, the which Mazzoni [*sic*],
soon after G.'s release, was stabbed going to the theatre and killed
upon the spot, *nobody knows by whom* – and the other, of a com-
missary who had interfered with him. These are but *dicerie* and
may be true or not.'[10]

The chief interest of this story – true or false – lies in the light it
throws upon the Count's popularity and reputation. And, indeed,
as the story goes on, it does not become prettier.

'During his marriage', says the Vice Legate's report, 'with the
aforesaid Contessa Placidia, he used to keep in his house a series
of maids, whom he seduced and then changed and sent away,
according to circumstances and to the greater or lesser resentment
of his wife.' One of these, Angelica Galliani, 'a young woman of
some attractions' – (her grandson tells us that she had a beautiful
figure, very white skin, dark hair and large 'resigned' eyes) –
presented him, in due course, with no less than six illegitimate
children – until at last even the Contessa Placidia was moved to
protest. He then established his wife in a remote and lonely
country-house from which she did not return until very shortly
before her death, in time to make a will in his favour. And once
again (although again without evidence) the unpleasant words of
'murder' and 'poison' were murmured by the Count's numerous
enemies, while a letter written by the Archbishop of Ravenna,
Antonio Codronchi, reveals the writer's opinion of the recent
widower.

'The Cavaliere Guiccioli, who has come here to prevent the
confiscation of all the property he has bought, but not wholly
paid for, came to call on me, and spoke, with honey on his lips, of
the loss of his wife, which he considers an act of Providence, to
enable him to regularize his position. I answered him as he
deserved, and told him of the infamy with which he has covered
himself in the eyes of all citizens of Ravenna present and future.
With one of his usual little laughs he accepted it all, patiently.'[11]

He then married Angelica, – and succeeded in legitimizing
some of his children – not without the help (according to a contemporary) of Cardinal Malvasia himself, who used openly to
boast of the fine ring presented to him by Guiccioli as a reward for
his intervention.* But in 1817 Angelica died, too – apparently
not much regretted by her spouse, since, on the very night of her

* FARINI, op. cit., p. 72. It should however be said that Farini was a violent anti-
clerical, and as such only too glad to spread any little story of this kind.

death, he attended the theatre at Forlì[¹²] – leaving him with seven children, of whom the eldest, Ferdinando, was only twelve.

And so it was that the Cavaliere again required a bride.

For the first few months, in spite of the forty years that lay between the bride and the bridegroom, the marriage went smoothly enough. We have the letters that Teresa wrote to her husband when, just before and after their marriage, he had to be away for a few days; and even discounting the formal 'eloquence' of a pupil of S. Chiara, they are something more than duty letters.[¹³] 'My adorable husband and friend,' the first one begins, 'it is not two hours since you left, and already I feel the weight of our separation . . . I shall not see you for ten days . . . With these words I went to sleep last night with these I wake up this morning.' And again: 'You are all my soul, you are the greatest good I have on earth and I feel that I could not live without you. My family's love has become nothing for me, since you have become my husband.' She sends him a kiss 'as different from the one I sent my brother as fire is from light'. She implores him to look after himself well, to 'beware of the Rimini *scirocco*, of the heat, of the return journey at night', – she reminds him that: 'on your welfare depends that of your Spouse and all her happiness'. She shows the greatest anxiety about a letter of hers that has been delayed, 'for fear that you might accuse me of negligence'; she tells him that her time has been spent only 'in keeping company with my old grandmother, and in playing on my instrument', and in the evening, 'a short walk, and conversation with old men and priests'. Finally she is at pains to show him that his bride, although young, can be economical: 'I have still kept the five scudi untouched, and hope that when you return, you will be satisfied with my economy. I am telling you this, so that you may know how much I care to please you, even in little things.' What could be more edifying and reassuring?

But soon a different note appears. Count Guiccioli's careful 'economy', of which his biographer speaks with so much praise, extended itself, it would seem, to the minutest details of housekeeping; and now, in going over the accounts, he handed over to the servants some matters which Teresa considered to be in her own province. He made her look a fool, she complained with childish petulance, in front of the servants. 'From now onwards, I shall not take the risk of interfering in any domestic matter without a sign from you . . . feeling sure that it is all the same to you whether I am there or not.' The intimate *tu* of the first letters gave place to the formal *voi*; without a doubt the rigidity and monotony of the daily routine, and the duty and self-effacement required of her, had begun to weigh upon her spirits. Moreover, her relations with her large family of step-children (even though they were mostly at school) were not going too well. 'I do not believe much in Ferdinando's welcome,' she wrote of the eldest boy, who was very little younger than herself, 'but will defend myself as best I can.' Finally, in a sentence whose meaning is not quite clear, there is a curious foreshadowing of the future. She was writing to her husband about a letter she had received from the *Direttrice* of her old school. 'On one point', she wrote, 'she seems to be of your opinion – that is, as regards Cavalier Serventi.'[14] Was the young wife already demanding one?

Beneath the surface of this marriage – a typical marriage of convenience, it would seem, between April and December – there is an occasional glimpse of something darker, more sinister – an aspect which becomes evident as the story unfolds itself. The bird and the snake – that is the obvious image. Here is a man 'skilled in seduction', as his own grandson described him, a man whose acquisitiveness in later years reached 'the point of mania', so that one of his peasants said that there was a part of his land which he would never visit, because 'he could not bear to see his boundaries', a man whose rapacity, moreover, sprang 'not so much from love of money as lust of power'. That is his own family's opinion. 'A gloomy, intriguing, proud, generous man', says one report of the Austrian police; 'a sordid, miserly spirit', says another report – not so completely in contradiction with the first as might appear, since the generosity only showed itself in cases where, as in the restoration of the theatre, the benefactor could add thereby to his own prestige and power. A 'man of property' – whose need to dominate and love of intrigue extended itself into his family life.

I think it is not too much to maintain that Teresa was tied to her husband by a bond in which there was fascination as well as fear. I think that this rigid, eccentric, ironic old man, with suave formal manners, made use of his experience to gain, by a mixture of sensuality and violence, an evil and strange hold over his young bride. In the 'Vie', in her letters, as in her statement to the members of the 'Sacra Rota' (the Vatican tribunal), we find the same expressions constantly recurring: 'his *strange* habits' – 'his eccentricity'. After her return to him in 1826, no longer an inexperienced child, but a woman who had been for four years Byron's mistress, Teresa spoke of the impossibility of being 'as vilely complaisant' as he required; she told of nights when she had to lock herself up into her room and he attempted to batter down the door;[15] she said that the reasons which led her to ask for a second separation were 'of so vile a nature'[16] that she could not speak of them except to her lawyer, or in confession. I cannot see in this only a calculating woman's effort to get back her freedom, with as large an allowance as possible; nor do I believe, had that been the case, that she would have had the support of her step-children, – who themselves were so unhappy in their father's house that, after Teresa's departure, her stepson Ignazio helped his sisters to run away![17]

And yet when, several years later, Teresa looked back, her remarks about her husband have, in spite of everything, a curiously exculpatory accent. 'A man who cannot be judged like another', she called him, 'an eccentric', 'a man of great intelligence'[18] – and finally, after his death, she wrote: 'I have always attributed his behaviour towards me to natural and invincible eccentricity, rather than to perfidiousness.'[19] Only two months after her first separation from him, and at the height of her affair with Byron, Teresa was sending her husband a letter of condolence on the death of his eldest son, writing: 'Indirectly, may I not still do you some good?' And when, after their second separation, his eyesight gave him trouble, she consulted famous oculists for him in Paris and London. Perhaps the best comment is the one that Teresa herself wrote to Byron, on the subject of his relations with *his* wife: 'The human heart is very complicated – and I fear I shall never be able to understand it.'

The year 1818, which introduced Teresa to matrimony, was Byron's second year in Venice. Too much has been said else-where of his Venetian period to go over the ground again here. His own letters, and the accounts of his friends, have described the state of bitterness and despair in which he arrived there, and the immediate spell which the city – 'the greenest island of my imagination' – cast over him. They have described the great, bare rooms of the Palazzo Mocenigo, and the long procession of beautiful mistresses, queer animals and curious British visitors that passed through them; they have portrayed Marianna Segati and 'Mme la Boulangère', and all the lesser figures of his Venetian masquerade. Every episode, too, has been told and retold: the midnight swims in the Grand Canal, the rides on the Lido, the studious hours in the library of the Armenian monastery. It has all been noted with the pomposity of Hobhouse – the censorious-ness of the Hoppners – the hero-worship of Shelley – the geniality of Moore. But it has all been seen only through *English* eyes.

It may be amusing, for a change, – since every life has as many facets as it has observers – to watch Mylord for a moment through another peep-hole, that of his Italian acquaintances.

Byron was no longer a novelty in Venetian society by the end of 1818; but, in the journalistic sense, he was always 'news'. Wherever he went there was a rustle of chatter. Always there was a fresh story to tell about *l'Anglico Mylord* – so rich, so beautiful, so dissipated, so generous, so irascible. To a lady who dared to criticize one of his verses, he said he wished he could drown her in the sea – and as to his horsemanship, that was an even more tender subject. One day at Florian's Café a young man permitted himself to show some amusement in describing Byron's style of riding, and at once Byron slapped his face.[20] Another sure way of arousing one of his sudden fits of rage was to attempt any translation of his work; a poor young Venetian began to translate 'Manfred', – and promptly Byron offered him whatever price he could obtain for what he had done, provided he would throw it into the fire. Some bargaining ensued, brought to an end by Byron's threat that, if the translator would not accept the sum he offered, he would exchange it for a horsewhip.* 'Lord Byron', Teresa wrote in the 'Vie', 'always dissuaded people from translating his poems. He said that it was quite enough to see his elucubrations dressed up in English garb but that to see them also in fancy-dress, was extremely disagreeable to him.'[21]

But Byron could be as generous as he was high-handed. A young girl with a bundle of manuscripts which had been refused by every Venetian publisher, somehow managed to get into the Palazzo Mocenigo and began to tell him her story. While she was talking, Byron was scribbling something; then he changed the subject, and she thought her appeal had failed; but as she rose to say goodbye, he put a piece of paper in her hand: it was a cheque for several pounds. The house and press of a Venetian printer having been destroyed by fire, Byron headed the poor man's subscription list with £150. A singer, the Cortesi, had a benefit night; the most generous gift she received was Byron's purse, containing 50 golden napoleons. No wonder the Venetians chattered! 'It is said that he has an income of 120,000 pounds sterling. And moreover his poems are paid by his editor at a pound a verse, a sum which he uses to help a noble friend who has lost his fortune.'[22]

* To Hoppner, Byron wrote about this translation: 'As I did not write *to* the Italians, nor *for* the Italians, nor *of* the Italians . . . I confess I wish that they would let me alone . . . Our modes of thinking and writing are so unutterably different, that I can conceive no greater absurdity than attempting to make any approach between the English and Italian poetry of the present day.' *L.J.*, IV, p. 205.

It is said, it is said . . . what was not said? The eyes and ears of
the Venetians were not less sharp, and their curiosity hardly less
keen, than that of his fellow-countrymen at Geneva who had kept
watch upon his garden with a telescope. In Venice, as elsewhere,
he was a menagerie animal, a rhinoceros at the ball. After nights
spent in unbelievable debaucheries, they whispered, he would
leap from his bed, seize the sword which he always kept by his
side, and, clad only in his night-shirt, would fence with the
window-curtains! He breakfasted on a dish of rice, with a glass of
water and vinegar; he supped on a snipe, with a glass of tea, two
raw eggs and a biscuit. He was growing whiskers because someone had told him that without them he looked like a musician.
When he went for his daily ride, a small crowd was always waiting
on the quay, beside the Jewish Cemetery, watching for his return.
He could not bear to see a woman eating (this was true). He had
never seen the Piazza San Marco (so as not to be watched limping
across it) except from the windows of Casa Cicognara or Casa
Michiel. So the chatter went on. A great deal of it is to be found
in the *Cronaca* of Count Francesco Rangone, a literary nobleman
and an industrious gossip of Ferrara, – whose acquaintance Byron
was to make a little later on in Bologna, but who, even before they
had met, amused himself with collecting as many stories about
him as he could, and setting them down under the title: '*Peep at
a very cultivated and rich, but strange Mylord.*'

'He was able to attract the interest of an illustrious young lady,
both cultivated and rich, who, having refused every proposal,
desired to be united to a man of superior distinction. This she
recognized in Lord Byron. Little time was needed to arrange the
marriage, but the strange Lord, having achieved the first night,
abandoned next day the unhappy Milady, who, being enceinte,
gave birth to a little girl, who she constantly fears may be sent for
by her singular husband. Mylord Byron then – disgusted with his
own government for political reasons – left for Italy, printing his
farewell to his wife beforehand and taking with him a Little Girl,
issue of genial relations with a distinguished Damsel, whom he
abandoned with the same indifference as his wife. The respectable
Lord then established himself in Venice, bringing with him 24
servants, some dogs, parrots, monkeys and horses.'

As to the respectable Lord's character:

'He seems indisposed towards his own government and the
Austrian. He speaks freely, however, about everyone, and

dedicates his life only to study and to the pleasures of Love. Also, even as he gives free rein to his thoughts, so also does he show no restraint in satisfying his desires, and even less in telling everyone about his amorous adventures . . . Dear to the Learned, he is not less so to the Fair – alike for his riches, for an appearance not to be despised, for his charming manners and the singularity of his character.'[23]

But Rangone's information, as yet, was only second-hand, probably gathered chiefly from his brother, who was Contessa Benzoni's Cavalier Servente, and had met Byron in her salon. A more entertaining account is that left us by assuredly the most assiduous – if not, as he would have liked to think, the most intimate – of Byron's Venetian friends, Cavaliere Angelo Mengaldo. This Venetian Boswell was a stout solemn little man who had distinguished himself in the Napoleonic wars, taking part with great valour in the Russian campaign and saving the life of a fellow officer who was drowning in the Beresina – a Liberal, a Romantic, a snob, a writer of occasional verses – and, it is obvious from his diary, a quite insufferable bore. His first meeting with Byron took place in March 1818, at the house of the British Consul, Richard Hoppner, 'un Anglais pas incommode' – by which Mengaldo meant, he explains, an Englishman who, although he showed a polite contempt for all that was not English, was yet 'fairly civil' to him.[24]
But the meeting with Byron was a disappointment. 'I could have wished him a little more courteous – that is to say, that he had spoken a little more Italian.' Byron, by then, knew Italian well – but he would not take the trouble to speak it in another Englishman's house. The acquaintance, however, continued; the next entry in Mengaldo's diary describes Byron as an 'être étònnant', and soon the Cavaliere decided that nobody was so suited as he, by both circumstances and temperament, to become Byron's closest friend in Venice. Were they not both Liberals, both Romantics, both regarded with suspicion by the Austrian police? Had they not both been unhappy in their family life? Had they not both meditated – or at least talked of – suicide? So Mengaldo industriously continued to frequent every conversazione where he might hope to see the English poet – and soon met him again at Contessa Benzoni's. The conversation turned to swimming: Byron does not fail to describe his swims across the Hellespont and the Tigris; nor does Mengaldo keep silence about *his* swimming, under fire, across the Danube and the Beresina. For the first time, Byron showed some interest in his companion

c

– but now there was a contretemps. Among the guests at Contessa Benzoni's there were three other English people: a Colonel Montgomery ('of serious and rather ferocious appearance, affable but reserved') and his wife and sister. After supper, when Mengaldo was sitting beside Miss Montgomery, whom he afterwards discovered to have been a friend of Lady Byron's, he saw the poet crossing the room, and said to his neighbour, 'He is coming to speak to you.' 'He will not dare to,' replied the young woman – and as Byron stopped to speak to her, she got up and cut him dead.* Mengaldo spread the story all over Venice – it even reached Stendhal's ears, and he wrote to a friend to say that Colonel Montgomery had challenged Byron to a duel. 'La phrase de Byron avait été insignifiante, courte et archidécente; mais le souffle de ce monstre souille une beauté pâle et froide.'²⁵

Then there was Byron's and Mengaldo's famous swimming-match. The version given by the two chief protagonists (Alexander Scott, who was also with them, seems to have held his tongue) vary as much as one would expect. According to Mengaldo, they all started from the Lido, with two gondolas following them, and all three of them, having reached the Grand Canal together, started swimming down it; Mengaldo got out of the water at the Rialto, Scott at S. Felice and Byron only at S. Andrea (nearly at the end of the Grand Canal.)

But Byron in a subsequent letter to Murray says that: 'At the entrance of the Grand Canal, Scott and I were a good way ahead, and we saw no more of our foreign friend, which, however, was of no consequence, as there was a Gondola to hold his cloathes and pick him up.'²⁶

He must have told the same tale in Venice at the time, for Mengaldo notes in his diary that everyone is talking of the match – 'mais' he adds sadly, 'pas tant en ma faveur. Lord Byron n'est plus si courtois qu'il était autre-fois.' Nevertheless, as a souvenir of the swimming-match, Byron presented Mengaldo with a copy of his 'Giaour'. 'Ma fantaisie', notes the recipient, 'est fort agitée par cette lecture. Je crains que l'anglomanie ne me soit entrée dans le corps.' And then comes a pathetic postscript: 'Tout homme de génie m'enflamme et me transporte. Pourquoi ne le suis-je pas?'

---

* This was the same Colonel Montgomery who inopportunely turned up in Genoa when Byron was there. 'His pale face,' says Lady Blessington, 'flushed crimson when one of our party inadvertently mentioned that Colonel M. was at Genoa. He tried in various ways to discover whether Colonel M. had spoken ill of him to us, and displayed an ingenuity in putting his questions, that would have been amusing had it not betrayed the morbid sensibility of his mind.' LADY BLESSINGTON, *The Idler in Italy*, I, p. 330.

By the following January he is hopefully writing: 'Il me témoigne plus de familiarité que je n'aurais pu m'attendre.' The next week Byron entertains him with 'le récit très intéressant de son mariage et de son amour . . . Sa vie est aussi romanesque que le genre de ses poésies.' In February: 'Chez Lord Byron; confidences mutuelles.' During the Carnival balls they met almost every night – and now Mengaldo, convinced that he had a right to the position of Byron's closest friend, began to be jealous of Alexander Scott. 'A la redoute avec Lord Byron, mais sa première confidence me fut ravie par Scott. Il en a le droit par son ancienneté [*sic*] par sa qualité d'Anglais, et j'ose même dire par son immoralité.'

For Mengaldo, like so many of Byron's friends, was at heart a Puritan. He, too, was passing from one light love-affair to another; but he was doing so like a good Catholic, with a proper sense of sin, and like a good citizen, with order and method. Byron treated his love affairs with the same casualness as everything else; this was truly shocking. On one occasion, on their way back from riding on the Lido, Mengaldo accompanied him to his *Casino*.[27] This was the pleasure-house where Byron entertained his 'Chorus of the Nine Muses' – the Venetian women whom the Fornarina's jealousy would not allow to enter the Palazzo Mocenigo – and it was here that only a few months later he must have taken Teresa. We do not know what Mengaldo saw there, but we do know that he was deeply shocked: 'Je fus effrayé de son horrible système.' A few weeks later Byron allowed himself 'mille plaisanteries' with la Pallerini, a *première danseuse* with whom Mengaldo himself was in love. ('Elle vous arrache les larmes, les cris de joie, de désespoir, d'étonnement, de frayeur.') And then Madame Hoppner, that snake in the grass, had a conversation with him: 'Découvertes sur le caractère de Lord Byron, très défavorables à lui.' It was Byron's peculiar lot to cause practically all his friends to turn into preachers or governesses. Madame de Staël lectured him about his private life at Coppet; Mr. Hobhouse in Albania; Mr. Hoppner on the Lido; Lady Blessington in Genoa. And now even the Cavaliere Mengaldo took it upon himself to improve him. Walking up and down the Riva degli Schiavoni, he told the noble Lord that he would be able to do much more for Italy if he first reformed his own morals. But it was not a success: 'L'amitié de Lord Byron pour moi s'allentit: mes sermons n'étaient pas de son goût.'

The friendship – if such a one-sided relationship can be so called – was over. But there was a curious sequel. When at the beginning of June Byron was leaving Venice, to follow Teresa to

Ravenna, Mengaldo came to call upon him in the early morning, to say goodbye. 'These hours were solemn ones for the friendship of the great poet of freedom and the soldier of Bonaparte.' Mengaldo gave Byron a letter of introduction to friends in Ferrara, about which Byron – having made full use of it – subsequently wrote disagreeably to Hoppner: 'Mengaldo gave me a letter for which I am grateful, which is a troublesome sensation.'[28] But at the time, he did something very odd – and most characteristic. He drew out of his pocketbook a French cross of the Légion d'Honneur, and pinned it on to his friend's chest, saying: 'It could not be in a better place.' Then he left Venice – having made at least one man happy.[29]

And then there was an equally characteristic, if regrettable, epilogue. Mengaldo, left behind in Venice, continued to deplore Lord Byron's dissolute habits; he gossiped with Contessa Benzoni; he repeated her remarks to Mrs. Hoppner. And Hoppner took up his pen and wrote a long letter to Byron attacking Contessa Guiccioli – and Byron supposed, rightly or wrongly, that Mengaldo had had a finger in the pie.

'In future I shall be less kind to them,' [Hoppner and Mengaldo] he wrote angrily to Scott – 'and you may tell Mengaldo so – a little tittle-tattling boasting parvenu – who never could forgive one's beating him in his little narrow field – as we did hollow.'[30]

If I have dwelt so long upon these very minor episodes of Byron's life in Venice, it is because they seem to me to throw some light upon the next phase of his life. They reveal to us how completely he had remained, in Venice, a foreigner. In the midst of all those inquisitive eyes, those outstretched hands, those uncompanionable companions, he was still alone. Towards the end of his time there, he was himself acutely aware of this, and showed it in an almost complete withdrawal from 'good' Venetian society. In the first year, he had assiduously frequented, for instance, the salon of Contessa Isabella Teotochi Albrizzi, who fancied herself as the Madame de Staël of Venice, and he had tried to make friends with the Italian men of letters whom he met at her house. But it was no good. Contessa Albrizzi herself was intelligent, but pretentious – the one fault Byron would never put up with – and her celebrities, in his eyes, were even worse: 'Your literary everyday man and I never went well in company – especially your foreigner, whom I never could abide. Except Giordani – and – and – and – (I really can't name any other) I do not remember a

man amongst them whom I ever wished to see twice.'[31] Giordani
was the one exception, and we know that he warmly responded to
Byron's immediate liking for him. Byron had at first refused to be
introduced to him, he told a friend in a letter, and then had only
given way on condition that their conversation should not be
'about his works, about poetry, or worst of all about the Romantics,
whom he abominates! I kept the pact and our conversations were
then so long and so intimate that the numerous assembly was
surprised and amused.' They spoke about Byron's travels, about
Italy, about politics.

'He hates and despises the French, who in 25 years have
changed their government and opinions 19 times; he hates the
English government, which tyrannizes over its own nation and
the world;, but he does not despair of the human species . . . I
found nothing in him of the arrogance of a man who had become
so famous so young; nothing of English pride; nothing of the contempt which he shows all the time to some people.' He showed
Giordani the Segati's portrait; he spoke of his wife. 'He exhorted
me to settle in Venice, so that we could see each other often.'[32]

It sounds a most successful and agreeable evening. But Giordani
did not stay in Venice; they never corresponded, and that
acquaintance, too, faded away. And the Conversazioni at the
Albrizzi's became more and more wearisome, more and more self-
consciously pedantic. Byron could not stand for ever looking at
Canova's bust of Helen, even though he thought it the most
beautiful in the world.[33] One evening he gave his arm to a young
bride, who had just arrived and wished to see the famous bust.
But she must have held her head so low, in shyness or fatigue, after
three days of marriage and two of travelling, that he did not even
notice her face, and Teresa also – for it was Teresa, on her wedding
journey – declared the next day that she had not seen her companion.[34] No foreshadowing of the future, no breath of a wing,
touched them that night.

And very soon after this evening, Byron quarrelled finally with
the Albrizzi – who insisted on including him in her absurd gallery
of literary portraits. He had seen enough, he decided, of Venetian
society – and he knew only too well what his Venetian popularity
was worth. 'As to the "adoration" of the Venetians,' he wrote
later on to Scott, 'you are, of course, laughing. I have never
counted [on] their liking – but have done them no harm – at
least not intentionally.'[35] Of Venice he was not yet tired – 'all its
disadvantages are more than compensated by the sight of a single

gondola'^{**} – but, after his early efforts to live like the Italians, he had gone back to his solitude. He rode with Hoppner and Scott at the Lido; he talked with his Armenian monks; he made love when he must. But of any equal companionship he was as deprived as if he had been living in the Sahara. He was ready, more than ready, for some deeper tie, some permanent human attachment.

The only Conversazioni to which he occasionally still went were those of Contessa Marina Querini Benzoni – but they were a very different matter from Contessa Albrizzi's.

When Byron met Marina she was approaching sixty, but her gaiety, vitality and ardour endowed her favours – which it was said she did not deny to Mylord – with a perennial freshness. At the time of the French domination, she had danced with Ugo Foscolo in the Piazza San Marco round the Tree of Liberty, dressed only in an Athenian tunic, which revealed her fine legs and thighs. But, according to Teresa, 'she was so kind, so charming and so tolerant, that no one asked her to account for what the morals of Venice had permitted to her in her youth'. After a liaison which had lasted for thirty years her Cavalier Servente, Count Giuseppe Rangone, 'still considered her as a divinity', and when, one morning, Byron inquired of him how the Contessa was today, he replied with the single word '*Rugiadosa*'.* Her *embonpoint*, however, was considerable – no doubt partly in consequence of her immoderate taste for *polenta*, which caused her, even when she went out in the 'gloomy gaiety' of her gondola, to conceal a smoking hot slice of that delicacy, which she nibbled at intervals, in her abundant bosom – a habit which earned for her the nickname of '*el fumeto*'. '*Xe quà el fumeto!*' the gondoliers would cry, as they saw her pass.† At the age of sixty she suddenly decided to marry Rangone, who was then seventy – and they enjoyed eleven more years of happiness together. Outspoken and vivacious, making no secret of her love of pleasure, gay and kind, her memory echoes to this day on the Venetian canals, in the love-song which she inspired, 'La biondina in gondoleta'. And it was at a Conversazione at her house, under her sharp and observant eye, that Byron – for one really cannot count those five minutes at the Albrizzi's – met, and fell in love with, Teresa Guiccioli Gamba.

* 'Dewy'. 'Vie', pp. 36, 37.
† 'Here comes the little smoke!' MALAMANI, *Isabella Teotochi Albrizzi, i suoi amici, il suo tempo*.

1 : VENICE

A stranger loves the Lady of the land

TERESA GUICCIOLI was very reluctant, on that April evening, to go to Casa Benzoni. She had only arrived in Venice two days before, she was tired by the journey – and she was, moreover, in deep mourning for both her mother and her sister. Her husband, as usual, had insisted on going to the theatre – 'it was for him a necessity' – but to go on to Contessa Benzoni's Conversazione seemed to her superfluous. She argued with her husband in the gondola, and finally, she tells us, gave way 'merely out of obedience', with tears in her eyes, 'making him promise that they would not stay more than a few minutes. Hardly, however, had she entered, than she saw – sitting on the sofa opposite the door, beside another young man, – a figure that seemed to her 'a celestial apparition'. 'This meeting sealed the destiny of their hearts.'*

The effect on Byron, however, seems to have been somewhat less immediate. When Contessa Benzoni wished to introduce him, he refused saying: 'You know that I do not wish to meet any more ladies; if they are ugly because they are ugly and if they are pretty because they are pretty.' It was only after a good deal of persuasion from his hostess and from Mr. Scott† – who said that surely he might make one exception, in a salon where beauty was far from common – that he gave way and allowed himself to be taken across the room and be introduced as 'Pair d'Angleterre et son plus grand poète'. 'This introduction,' says Teresa, 'placed on Byron's lips one of those charming smiles which Coleridge so much admired and called the Gate of Heaven.' He sat down beside her and they began to talk – about Venice and Ravenna, and also, says Teresa proudly, 'with enthusiasm and assurance' about Dante and Petrarch. 'But already the subject of their conversation had become an accessory,' and when Guiccioli at last came across the room to tell Teresa that the 'few minutes' of their visit had long since elapsed, 'she rose to leave as if in a dream – and on crossing the threshold of the palace she realized that she no longer felt as tranquil as she had on entering. These mysterious attractions are too shaking to the soul and make one afraid!'¹

* The account of this meeting is taken from Teresa's 'Vie de Lord Byron', pp. 41-51, which gives many more details than she supplied to Moore. The whole of the 'Vie' is written in the third person, and Teresa generally refers to herself as 'Madame la Comtesse' or even as 'la jeune dame'. She does not state the exact day of the meeting; it appears to have been on April 2nd or 3rd, 1819.

† Alexander Scott.

39

At this point Teresa's official narrative becomes somewhat vague. She speaks of meetings every evening at the theatre and afterwards at supper, of conversations always more intimate and more inexhaustible – of long gondola rides across the Lagoon – of sunsets at the Lido. 'This existence,' says Teresa, 'seemed to them entirely natural and was already becoming necessary!' But all the details are shrouded in a golden haze of romantic sentiment. Fortunately, however, we possess another document which is considerably more informative. It is Teresa's 'Confession' to her husband.*

'I then felt attracted to him', she says, after describing their first meeting, 'by an irresistible force. He became aware of it, and asked to see me alone the next day. I was so imprudent as to agree, on condition that he would respect my honour: he promised and we settled on the hour after dinner, in which you [Count Guiccioli] took your rest. At that time an old boatman appeared with a note, in an unknown gondola, and took me to Mylord's gondola, where he was waiting, and together we went to a *casino* of his. I was strong enough to resist at that first encounter, but was so imprudent as to repeat it the next day, when my strength gave way – for B. was not a man to confine himself to sentiment. And, the first step taken, there was no further obstacle in the following days.'[2]

The long absences in her gondola, Teresa explained, were rendered possible by the presence of 'a companion with whom she always went out, who had been a governess in the house and with whom she practised the French language'. This is the first appearance of another important character in the story: Fanny Silvestrini, the *confidante*. Though she may well have been a governess in Casa Guiccioli in her youth, this does not appear to have been her only profession, and at this time, most conveniently, she was the mistress of Lega Zambelli, who was Count Guiccioli's steward and who subsequently passed into Byron's service. It is her pen which relates some of the next stages of the story – and it was she who not only, with a gusto worthy of Juliet's nurse, concealed and protected those first secret meetings, but sub-

* This very curious document, which exists only in the Elliot Papers, purports to be a letter from Teresa to her husband, telling the whole story of her relationship with Byron. Its peculiar mixture of truth and lies and its remarkable skill in skating over thin ice, are characteristic, but it is difficult to account for its having been written at all, except on the supposition that Guiccioli extracted it from her, to disprove what was being said of him by the Gamba family. It is unfinished, and was apparently never made use of. It is not quoted in *I Guiccioli*, nor in any documents in the Vatican Archives.

sequently transmitted Teresa's letters to Byron. Her fluent, persuasive, interminable letters exhale an aroma of Goldonian comedy, a heavy breath of patchouli; almost we can hear the insinuating tones of her voice, in the soft Venetian dialect so suited to the language of love; we can see the abundant curves of her figure, reclining in Teresa's gondola, as she patiently waits for the two lovers who have disappeared into the little house at S. Maria Zobenigo – and the hours pass, and the sun goes down, and a little cold wind springs up over the lagoon.

During this time, according to Teresa, Byron showed occasional moods of 'melancholy and preoccupation', which she liked to attribute to his sense of duty and 'his knowledge of the human heart'. But she frankly admits that she herself was quite simply and wholeheartedly happy. 'She had known too little of life to reflect – and she gave up her soul entirely where her heart led. This Venice, without flowers, without trees, without scents, without birds, which had pleased her so little before, with its lugubrious gondolas instead of her team of horses, now seemed to her the abode of the very light of life, an earthly paradise.'³

It would appear, however, that even Byron – accustomed as he was to easy conquests – was slightly taken aback by the extreme facility and publicity of this one.

'She is pretty,' he wrote to Hobhouse on April 6th, 'but has no tact; answers aloud when she should whisper; talks of age to old ladies who want to pass for young; and this blessed night horrified a correct company at the Benzona's by calling out to me *'mio Byron'*, in an audible key, during a dead silence of pause in the other prattlers, who stared and whispered their respective *serventi*!'⁴

All the fans fluttered, and Teresa was delighted. She was far too pleased with the conquest of the most celebrated figure in Venice, to wish to keep it to herself.

Rangone, naturally, does not fail to mention such a delightful new titbit.

'The arrival of the noble Young Lady gave a new direction to Mylord's gallantries. The fair nymph was flattered by his attentions and, renouncing any attempt at decorum, made herself an object of general conversation by her unreserved behaviour. Mylord himself warned her, but Mylord himself also told everyone of her gracious favours.'⁵

Byron's private meetings, however, with Teresa, were very few in number. 'We had but ten days', he wrote to Kinnaird, 'to

manage all our little matters in', [6] and added in a later letter that
'the *essential* part of the business' had only lasted 'four continuous
days'. [7] 'Earthly Paradises', wrote Teresa sadly, 'cannot be
expected to endure.' She was suddenly informed by her husband
that they would be leaving two days later for their country estate
on the Po, and was so much dismayed that she at once hurried off,
in the company of an old family friend, to the theatre, in the hope
of meeting Byron and telling him the sad news herself. She did
indeed at once meet him in the lobby and 'almost involuntarily
followed him into his box and told him of her troubles'. 'This box',
she adds, 'was generally used by men only, and was always the
target of Venetian curiosity; one can imagine that this was
increased a hundredfold by the young lady's presence!' The opera
was Rossini's *Othello*, and 'in the midst of this atmosphere of
melody and harmonious passion . . . they realized what they were
going to lose'. [8] When, however, the Count rejoined his wife at the
theatre, he showed no traces of jealousy but invited Lord Byron to
visit them in Ravenna – and when, on the following evening, the
moment for departure arrived, it was on Byron's arm that Teresa
descended into her gondola – while once again he promised to
rejoin her as soon as possible.

'This promise', says Teresa, 'seemed doubly solemn in the
silence of the night and the starlight, and gave to both their hearts
the courage that was so badly needed.' [9] Her gondola – (for
apparently they were making the journey by night) – stole across
the lagoon in the starlight, with no sound but the faint lapping of
the gondolier's oars; 'her heart stayed behind in Venice'.

The estate to which Count Guiccioli was taking his wife, on
their way back to Ravenna, Cà Zen, had recently been bought by
him from the Zeno family and lay at the mouth of the Po, in a
desolate marsh. The great plain – frequently flooded when the
rivers broke their banks – was unshaded by a single bush or tree;
only a vast expanse of rough, tangled grass and wild marshland
stretched from the river to the lagoon. The only sound was that of
the wind and the wailing of sea-birds; the only sight, an occasional
fisherman's boat, moored beside its nets in the river. In this
melancholy setting – 'with no one to speak to, without music,
almost without books, waiting for the Count to come back from
his business expeditions' – Teresa now spent her days, remembering the delights of Venice and writing long, unhappy letters to
her lover. These, she tells us, she took to the post at the neighbouring village of Loreo – sending them, as we shall see, under
cover to the obliging Fanny Silvestrini.

We do not possess these letters. The first was forwarded to

Byron on April 13th by Fanny Silvestrini, with a note in which she said that she would bring any subsequent letter to him in person; the second was sent under cover of the following letter from Fanny.

FANNY SILVESTRINI TO BYRON[10]

[April 19th, 1819]

My Lord: The most afflicted Teresina, on leaving here, begged only one thing of me – that I should try to see Mylord, and speak to him of her, always of her – in order to bring her back more vividly to his memory. This, Mylord, is why I sought the honour of seeing you, and am seeking it again today, if I may do so without being impertinent.

Permit me also to remind you that the aforesaid Teresina is counting on a letter from you on Thursday, when she will arrive in Ravenna, and that the post leaves tomorrow at midday. I hope you will not render her expectations vain.

I enclose a second note. Awaiting your commands, pray honour me with your kindness and accept my humble duty.   FANNY

To Teresa, Fanny described at some length how faithfully she was carrying out her role as go-between.

FANNY SILVESTRINI TO CONTESSA GUICCIOLI

Venice   *April* 19th, [1819]

My dear Friend: Without any preamble let me tell you that on the morning of the 13th, M[ylord] had your note on awakening, that every day I went to the post office to fetch any others, and that only yesterday evening your other letter reached me, which now, while I am writing, should be reaching its destination. If by a man's words one may judge his heart, if it adds to your happiness to be certain of the love, the tenderness of M[ylord], I will tell you that he loves you with the greatest *enthusiasm and ardour, of which the most susceptible heart is capable.* He has sworn and declared to me, in the short time that we have seen each other, that this is not a mere flash nor a whim, but a true sentiment – and that you have made on him an impression that can *never* be erased. He vows he is completely estranged from anything that could distract him, and he is impatiently awaiting your letter, which no doubt will cheer him at his awakening. I exhort you,

I advise you, I beg you, dear Friend, to be circumspect and prudent, lest the intensity of your love betray you, and to remember that sometimes a first strong inclination may be decisive for a whole life-time. I will not write about the chatter of the idle gossips (for the affair of the Box gave them full scope). Today they have ceased talking about it – and the unconventional – male and female – are all on your side.

Today I will go out about your errands, but I fear I shall not succeed in doing anything at such prices, the gilt bronze beads especially – for they are asking not five but eight Lira a string, as you should well remember, since you were present. As to the feathers, it shall be done, and when I have fresh instructions and M[ylord] goes to Ravenna I shall be able to send you everything. I embrace you with all my heart and am, believe me, always at your service.   FANNY

And now, at last, we have Byron's first letter to Teresa. The original is enclosed, together with his next three letters, in a folder, inscribed in Teresa's hand: '4 letters from Lord Byron. First series. From our first acquaintance to his arrival in Ravenna.' On another small sheet of paper is written: 'The address I gave him to write to me in Ravenna:
            Al Signor Don Gaspare Perelli
            Ravenna.'
This obliging priest was living in Ravenna, and continued to be of considerable assistance to the two lovers, after Byron's arrival. 'By the aid of a Priest,' Byron was writing to Hoppner in June, 'a Chambermaid, a young Negro-boy, and a female friend, we are enabled to carry on our unlawful loves.'[11] Later on in the year, when Byron had gone to Bologna, we find Don Gaspare writing to him – in a half-educated style and hand – to tell him how much he would have liked to go to the great annual fair at Lugo. 'But the lack of money is keeping me in town. If you had been in Ravenna, who knows but that I might not have had some help to go to the Fair!'[12]

BYRON TO CONTESSA GUICCIOLI

Venice   *April 22nd*, 1819

My dearest Love: Your dearest letter came today and gave me my first moment of happiness since your departure. My feelings correspond only too closely to the sentiments expressed in your letter, but it will be very difficult for me to reply in your beautiful language to your sweet expressions, which deserve an answer in deeds, rather than words. I flatter myself, however, that your heart will be able to suggest to you *what* and *how much* mine would like to say to you. Perhaps if I loved you less it would not cost me so much to express my thoughts, but now I have to overcome the double difficulty of expressing an unbearable suffering in a language foreign to me. Forgive my mistakes, the more barbarous my style, the more will it resemble my Fate away from you. You, who are my only and last love, who are my only joy, the delight of my life – you who are my only hope – you who were – at least for a moment – all mine – you have gone away – and I remain here alone and desolate. There, in a few words, is our story! It is a common experience, which we must bear like so many others, for love is never happy, but we two must suffer more, because your circumstances and mine are equally extraordinary. But I don't want to think of all this, let us love

... let us love now
When love to love can give an answering vow.[1][2]

When *Love* is not *Sovereign* in a heart, when everything does not give way to him, when all is not sacrificed to him, then it is Friendship – esteem – what you will – but no longer *Love*.

You vowed to be true to me and I will make no vows to you; let us see which of us will be the more faithful. Remember that, when the time comes that you no longer feel anything for me, you will not have to put up with my reproaches; I shall suffer, it is true, but in silence. I know only too well what a man's heart is like, and also, a little, perhaps, a woman's; I know that Sentiment is not in our control, but is what is most beautiful and fragile in our existence. So, when you feel for another what you have felt for me, tell me so sincerely – I shall cease to annoy you – I shall not see you again – I shall envy the happiness of my rival, but shall trouble you no more. This however I promise you: You sometimes tell me that I have been your *first* real love – and I assure you that you shall be my last Passion. I may well hope not to fall in love again, now that everything has become indifferent to me. Before I knew you – I felt an interest in many women, but never in one only. Now I love *you*, there is no other woman in the world for me.

You talk of tears and of our unhappiness; my sorrow is within; I do not weep. You have fastened on your arm a likeness that does not deserve so highly; but yours is in my heart, it has become part of my life, of my soul; and were there another life after this one, there too you would be mine – without you where would Paradise be? Rather than Heaven without you, I should prefer the Inferno of that Great Man buried in your city, so long as you were with me, as Francesca was with her lover.

My sweetest treasure – I am trembling as I write to you, as I trembled when I saw you – but no longer – with such sweet heart-beats. I have a thousand things to say to you, and know not how to say them, a thousand kisses to send you – and, alas, how many Sighs! Love me – not as I love you – for that would make you too unhappy, love me not as I deserve, for that would be too little – but as your Heart commands. Do not doubt me – I am and always shall be your most tender lover.   BYRON

Venice   *April 22nd*, 1819
P.S. How much happier than I is this letter: which in a few days will be in your hands – and perhaps may even be brought to your lips. With such a hope I am kissing it before it goes. Goodbye – my soul.

April 23rd, 4 o'clock

At this moment two other letters of yours have come! The irregularity of the post has been a great trouble to us both – but pray – my Love, do not lose faith in me. When you do not get news from me – believe that I am dead, rather than unfaithful or ungrateful. I will answer your dearest letters soon. Now the post is going – I kiss you ten thousand times.[14]

On the superscription is added, in Byron's hand:
'Written April 22nd, 1819.
April 28th, 1820. I have re-read it in Ravenna, after a year of most singular events.'

Venice   *April 25th*, 1819
My Love: I hope you have received my letter of the 22nd, addressed to the person in Ravenna of whom you told me, before leaving Venice. -- You scold me for not having written to you in

the country – but – how could I? My sweetest treasure, you gave me no other address but that of Ravenna. If you knew how great is the love I feel for you, you would not believe me capable of forgetting you for a single instant. You must become better acquainted with me – perhaps one day you will know that although I do not deserve you – I do indeed love you.

You want to know whom I most enjoy seeing, since you have gone away, who makes me tremble and feel – not what you alone can arouse in my soul – but something like it? Well, I will tell you – it is the *old porter* whom Fanny used to send with your notes when you were in Venice – and who now brings your letters – still dear, but not so dear as those which brought the hope of seeing you that same day at the usual time. My Teresa, where are you? Everything here reminds me of you – everything is the same, but you are not here, and I still am. In separation the one who goes away suffers less than the one who stays behind. The distraction of the journey, the change of scene, the landscape, the movement, perhaps even the separation, distracts the mind and lightens the heart. But the one who stays behind is surrounded by the same things; tomorrow is like yesterday – while only She is lacking who made him forget that a tomorrow would ever come. When I go to the Conversazione, I give myself up to Tedium, too happy to suffer ennui rather than grief. I see the same faces – hear the same voices – but no longer dare to look towards the sofa where I shall not see *you* any more – but instead some old crone who might be Calumny personified. I hear, without the slightest emotion, the opening of that door which I used to watch with so much anxiety when I was there before you, hoping to see you come in. I will not speak of *much dearer* places still, for *there* I shall not go – *until* you return. I have no other pleasure than thinking of you, but I do not see how I could see again the places where we have been together – especially those most consecrated to our love – without dying of grief.

Fanny is now in Treviso – and God knows when I shall have any more letters from you – but meanwhile I have received three; you must by now have arrived in Ravenna – I long to hear of your arrival; my fate depends upon your decision. Fanny will be back in a few days – but tomorrow I shall send her a note by a friend's hand to ask her not to forget to send me your news, if she receives any letters before returning to Venice.

My Treasure – my life has become most monotonous and sad; neither books, nor music, nor *Horses* (rare things in Venice – but you know that mine are at the Lido) – nor dogs – give me any pleasure; the society of women does not attract me; I won't speak of the society of men, for that I have always despised. For some years I have been trying systematically to avoid strong passions, having suffered too much from the tyranny of Love. *Never to feel admiration*[15] – and to enjoy myself without giving too much importance to the enjoyment in itself – to feel indifference towards human affairs – contempt for many, but hatred for none, – this was the basis of my philosophy. I did not mean to love any more, nor did I hope to receive Love. You have put to flight all my resolutions – now I am all yours – I will become what you wish – perhaps happy in your love, but never at peace again. You should not have reawakened my heart – for (at least in my own country) my love has been fatal to those I love – and to myself. But these reflections come too late. You have been mine – and, whatever the outcome – I am, and eternally shall be, entirely yours. I kiss you a thousand and a thousand times – but

> What does it profit you, my heart, to be beloved?
> What good to me to have so dear a lover?
> Why should a cruel fate
> Separate those whom love has once united?*

Love me – as always your tender and faithful   B.

Teresa meanwhile – after a short stay in another of her husband's new estates near Pomposa – had arrived in Ravenna. But she says that the violent emotions of the last few weeks, her depression since her separation from Byron, and the discomfort of the journey, had so much affected her health that she fainted several times on the way, and on getting home immediately took to her bed. She then – to the alarm of her friends and relations – gave herself up to a mysterious illness, whose symptoms she poetically described as consisting chiefly of a consumptive cough (this was a hereditary ailment in her family) and of frequent swoons, 'in which her spirit skimmed over the Venetian lagoons'. On returning to consciousness, she would speak of 'melodious

---

* GUARINI, *Il Pastor Fido*: Che giova a te, cor mio, l'esser amato?
　　　　　　　　Che giova a me l'aver si caro amante?
　　　　　　　　Perchè, crudo destino,
　　　　　　　　Ne disunisci tu, s'Amor ne stringe?
　　　　　　　　　　　　　　　　　　Act III, Scene IV.

sounds, perfumes of unfamiliar sweetness, and smiles of a celestial countenance', and reproved her anxious relatives, who were gathered round her bed, for awakening her from 'such a delicious dream'.[16]

The more prosaic truth, however, is that she was having a miscarriage which had begun at Pomposa,[17] a fact she took considerable pains to conceal, by attempting to erase, both in a letter of Fanny's and in one of Byron's, the word miscarriage (which is, however, still legible in both cases) and substituting for it the word 'illness'. It is difficult to understand why she took so much trouble, since at this early date the baby could not possibly have been Byron's – unless she thought it more romantic to be suffering from consumption. Byron himself felt no such delicacy, and on May 15th he was writing to Kinnaird:

'It was my intention to have left Venice tomorrow on my journey to R[avenna] – but the lady has miscarried and her recovery seems more remote than was expected.'[18]

And in a later letter he added:

'I can't tell whether I was the involuntary Cause of the miscarriage, but certes I was not the father of the foetus, for she was three months advanced before our first passade, and whether the Count was the parent or not I can't imagine; perhaps he might.'[19]

The following letter of Fanny's enclosed two letters of Byron's written on May 3rd, one to Teresa and one to Fanny.

FANNY SILVESTRINI TO CONTESSA GUICCIOLI

Venice   *May 4th*, [1819]

My dear Friend: I was in Treviso when I received your letter with the errand about Elmetto* and also the one bringing the news of your illness. I did not answer either the one or the other, wishing to see B[yron] first, and after five days' stay here, having returned to Venice, my first care was to see him, and I found him, I assure you, most unhappy about that unpleasant accident, and immoderately in love with you, I vow, my Teresina. Then, when he only saw your letter to me of the 26th and observed that you had not mentioned two letters of his written on the 19th or 20th of last

* Teresa's dog, Elmò.

D

month, he became very ill-humoured, supposing that you had never received them, or you would have acknowledged them.

I reassured him as best I could, telling him that you would have complained openly to me; and this calmed him, and after much talk, all about you, about the journey he is planning to make, and about his love, I left him, assuring him that by the first courier he would *receive your letters*, with the acknowledgment of his. Yesterday evening, indeed, I sent one to him, so that he should have time to write to you before the post (for you know the Young Gentleman sleeps until two) and, behold, this morning he sent me this answer to forward to you, with a few lines which I enclose, so that you may see and feel in what a *fever* he is about these letters, which doubtless have been lost, although sent to the same address as the one I wrote to you on the evening of the 16th, if I am not mistaken, and which you have already acknowledged. For Heaven's Sake, my dear, ask P[erelli] about it and show all necessary prudence, so that no unpleasant accident may occur.

I have written to you by post a letter that can be shown, so that the Cavaliere,* who knows our correspondence, may not be surprised at seeing it suspended, and begin to draw conclusions. Pray write to me, if he is in a good humour with you, this interests me very much for the sake of your peace. No friend loves you as much as I do, and none will ever give you such good advice as I, because I know by experience how important is a first passion, which often shapes our whole Destiny.

As for the rest, I can again assure you that you are truly loved, that I see in him a violent passion – not affected, but real. He told me that he had already sent his horses ahead, in order to get ready for the journey, which will crown his happiness by seeing you. Do not give yourself away then, for pity's sake; be reserved in public, remember that He is the most rigid of Censors.

I will tell you, too, for your comfort, that B[yron] is truly faithful to you, because I have not failed to observe him from a distance, and nothing did I see which could make me think him guilty. He swears, indeed, that he could not be, because you are too much attached to him for him to renounce, even for a single instant, the sentiment that you have inspired in him. So be happy, my dear Teresina, and may the ghosts of jealousy and suspicion

* Guiccioli.

always keep away from you. Tell P[erelli] to be careful, for God's sake.

Today at four I shall go to B[yron] to comfort him, see how he begs me to. Be assured of my friendship and command me.

I embrace you with all my heart and am for life your affectionate friend.

BYRON TO FANNY SILVESTRINI

Venice   *May 3rd,* 1819
Just now, at home.

Teresa's letter says nothing about having received my two letters, and I am in the greatest distress. What can have happened to these letters? Pray write to her and assure her that I have not failed to keep my promise, nor in my duty – and that I love her more, much more, than my life. Perhaps your letters will be more fortunate – meanwhile here is my *third* – which you can send to the same address. Do me the very great favour of coming to me *at four o'clock* for a minute. I don't know what to say – or think – T[eresa]'s letter is of the 26th.

Forgive me this and all the other trouble I have occasioned. Ever yours

BYRON TO CONTESSA GUICCIOLI

[Venice]   *[May 3rd,* 1819]

My Soul: This time friendship has prevailed over love, and Fanny has been more fortunate than I in seeing your writing. Your very dear letter from Ravenna, however, caused me great grief by telling me that you have been *ill** although I still trust that this will not bring about other consequences; and it is in this hope that I am writing to ask you to send me more precise news about the state of your health. I attributed your illness to riding, – but you write as if there were *some other cause* and do not tell me the real reason – pray clear up the mystery, which you have not wanted to tell the doctors.

Fanny has already come back from Treviso. I am waiting for

---

* The word *'ammalata'* = ill, has been substituted by Teresa for another word which she has partially erased, and which must have been *avvortito* (for *abortito* = miscarried).

your answer to know when to undertake my journey and how to behave on my arrival. Remember that I have no other object in taking this journey but that of seeing you – and loving you. I neither seek nor want diversions – introductions – Society – all very tedious things. It would suit me better to be with you in a desert, rather than without you in Mahomet's paradise, which is considerably more agreeable than ours.

I shall seek you, you alone; if only I can see you for a few moments every day, I shall be able to spend the rest of the time with your image; if there were to be a minute in which I did not think of you, I would consider myself unfaithful. Our love and my thoughts will be my sole companions, books and horses my only distractions, except for a little trip to Rimini, in order not to break a promise made to a friend in England three years ago[20] that, if ever I should see that city, I would send him any tradition about the story of Francesca (if any such remain there) beside what is to be found in Dante. This story of a fatal love, which has always interested me, now interests me doubly, since Ravenna holds my heart.

I long to embrace you and leave the rest to fate, which cannot be cruel, so long as it leaves me your love. I kiss you with all my soul – a thousand and a thousand times – and am eternally your lover.

P.S. This is my *third* letter – to the *address given* – I trust in God that none has gone wrong.

From the last letter it would appear that Byron was only awaiting his mistress's instructions, to set off for Ravenna. But when at last they came, her plans for their meeting were so childishly imprudent and impracticable – as is shown in Fanny's next letter – that he decided to put off his departure. 'I was still required to set out;' he told Kinnaird, 'but my instructions were a little confused, and though I am really much in love, yet I see no great use in not adopting a little caution.'[21] The experienced Fanny did not fail to observe Mylord's reluctance with dismay, and hastened to send her young friend some prudent advice. She fully realized what Teresa was still too inexperienced to know, that Byron – like most libertines – was a stickler for public behaviour: 'Remember that He is your severest Censor.'

As for Byron – it is clear that he was both irritated and puzzled –

'She is the queerest woman I ever met with,' he told Kinnaird, 'for in general they cost one something one way or other, whereas by an odd combination of circumstances, I have proved an expense to *Her* which is not my custom. . . .'

But these romantic, uncontrolled love-letters were beginning to alarm him – had he got another Caroline Lamb on his hands? Teresa, he reflected, was 'much prettier and not so savage. But she has the same red-hot head, the same noble disdain of public opinion, with the superstructure of all that Italy can add to such natural dispositions'.[22] His friends, too, were urging him to be cautious. The Venetian ladies, says Teresa, were overcome by jealousy, and in their fear of losing him told tales about her to Hoppner, depicting besides, in the darkest colours, her husband's character for jealousy and violence.[23] And Hoppner was only too delighted to repeat every word of it to his friends.

Hobhouse, too, had something to say on the subject:

'If you are making love to a Romagnuola, and she only nineteen, you will have some jobs upon your hands, which will leave you few spare moments. Don't you go after that terra firma lady; they are very vixens, in those parts especially, and I recollect when I was at Ferrara seeing or hearing of two women in the hospital who had stabbed one another . . . and all *per gelosia*! Take a fool's advice for once, and be content with your Naiads, your amphibious fry; you make a very pretty splashing with them in the lagune, and I recommend constancy to the neighbourhood. Go to Romagna indeed! Go to old Nick, you'll never be heard of afterwards, except your ghost should be seen racing with Guido Cavalcanti in the wood.'[24]

So, with so many influences against her, Teresa's despairing appeals remained unanswered, and Byron stayed on in Venice.

FANNY SILVESTRINI TO CONTESSA GUICCIOLI

Venice   *May* 11*th*, 1819

My Dear and Amiable Friend: Your letter, dated the 7th of this month has saddened my heart greatly by your illness. I was expecting better news, although your postscript of the 8th consoled me a little, telling me of your improvement after the bloodletting. It is certain that mild remedies do nothing but protract the evil and weakness follows in any case, even without being caused by blood-letting, and the Cavaliere has done very well to allow what is perhaps the only remedy for inflammation. I am impatiently expecting your news and I beg you not to disappoint us.

Two hours after receiving your letter, I went to B[yron] with your enclosure, certain of giving him pleasure, and indeed he showed it in his most cordial manner towards me. I was about to read him my letter first, but he said impatiently, 'and are there no letters for me?' 'Yes,' I said, 'but wait.' – 'Well, but it is too long to wait.'

I began, but he made the excuse that he could not see by the light of a single lamp, and went to fetch another, and meanwhile, would you believe it, stole from the sofa, on which it was lying, your letter which I had set aside, and, turning away, opened it and read half of it. Then he could not but come back with the light, and I went on reading my letter, and he his.

I vow to you, my dear, that he seemed to me much affected by your illness. We spoke a great deal about both the letters, he commented a great deal on them and pulled them to pieces, but there is one passage which he simply cannot interpret – that in which you speak of the *Zinnani coming to Venice for the same purpose as the other (the inn-keeper) and for another reason which I will tell you by word of mouth and which I deplored so much that it caused me to write rather coldly by last post.* He does not know how to interpret all this and begs me to ask you for an explanation. If he does not write by this post, it is because he has already prepared a letter which, now that he has received yours, will not do at all, but he will certainly write by the next post.

Meanwhile, my dear Teresina, be very certain that *he loves you with the most intense, most vivid and most fervent love,** but not with a love that blinds him to reality, and this, I assure you, will help a great deal to shield you from the storm by which I see you excessively shaken. Listen, but remember and be certain that he loves you, and let that be enough to reassure you. He had prepared everything necessary for his departure, and not before the 20th he would already have started, but reflection and the instructions you gave him, not well suited to your circumstances, have caused him to put it off for the present, unless you can give him some more precise instructions, tempered by prudence.

* This passage has been underlined by Teresa with ink of another colour.

For instance, the inn will not do for him, nor for you either, for that woman would always be dangerous for you, not for him, and just because of this she might make scenes and compromise you, beware with whom! And secondly, to meet in the theatre would certainly be an unwise step: Love knows no precautions, especially when it burns in a young heart. You will give yourself away in the eyes of the public, and soon in those of your husband – what would happen then? The Town is small, the resources for two lovers are few, perhaps none at all, – but do not be afraid, Teresina, – if you absolutely wish it, he will come, he will come at any cost, he will come, I vow it on his behalf, for he told me that if it were a question *of seeing* you *but once, even in your convalescence, he* would certainly do it, and would thus fulfil the wishes of his own heart by following both his love and his duty.

You see, therefore, from these remarks and reflections of his, that he is aiming at your happiness and at preserving that Love which, if known, would bring about tragic consequences, and to him the most cruel of all, that of having to break off your relationship. During our talk, be sure, my dear and tender friend, I wished you to have this satisfaction, but in my heart I applauded him, for I realize that you are caught up in a great storm of passion, while he, familiar with strong emotions, desires you intensely, but more wisely, and does not wish for your destruction. But you will say that he moralizes too much, is too subtle, and I will at once silence you by saying that in spite of all this, one sign from you, and he will fly to your arms. I know for certain and must say it in honour of truth and in your honour, that he has been so full of you that he has not allowed himself any diversion, for all Byron's diversions are proclaimed by the whole of Venice; but now no one hears any more talk about him, than if he were dead in that respect, and however much I have examined his conduct, I have not been able to find him wanting in the least way. This too should console you. You, meanwhile, try to recover, so that your B[yron] may find your beauty, your freshness, and your amiability, unimpaired.

Rest in my friendship and be certain that I shall always speak to you the language of the purest sincerity. Farewell, Farewell. Your Friend.

In spite of Fanny's assurances, it was hardly true that Byron was 'not allowing himself any diversions'. He was, indeed, in the thick

of an entanglement with a noble Venetian girl of eighteen, called
Angelica, who had been locked up on a diet of 'prayers and bread
and water' by 'her flinty-hearted father'. This was a setting to
Byron's taste, and on May 18th – according to a letter to John
Murray – he was falling into the Grand Canal on a nocturnal
visit to her.

'In going, about an hour and a half ago, to a rendez-vous with
a Venetian girl . . . I tumbled into the Grand Canal . . . my foot
slipped in getting into my gondola to set out (owing to the cursed
slippery steps of their palaces) and in I flounced like a Carp, and
went dripping like a Triton to my Sea nymph.'[25]

This was the letter which Murray considered 'really too gross',
– but what is stranger – or perhaps, since it was Byron, not strange
at all – is that on the very night before this absurd incident, he was
writing a tender letter to Augusta.

'I have never ceased, nor can cease to feel for a moment that
perfect and boundless attachment which bound and binds me to
you – which renders me utterly incapable of *real* love for any other
human being – for what could they be to me after *you* . . . I can
never be other than I have been – and whenever I love anything
it is because it reminds me in some way or other of yourself. . . .'[26]

What are we to make of all this? Augusta – and this it is indeed
difficult to understand – forwarded the whole letter to Annabella,
saying:

'He is surely to be considered a *Maniac* – I do not believe any
feelings expressed are by any means permanent – only occasioned
by the passing and present reflection and occupation of writing to
the unfortunate Being to whom they are addressed. . . .'[27]

This is no place to enter into the Augusta controversy – vital as it
is – but perhaps the key to this particular letter, and to Byron's
state of mind at this time, lies in the sentence, 'Whenever I love
anything, it is because it reminds me in some way or other of
yourself'.
Was it not Teresa who sent his thoughts back to Augusta – and
the memory of Augusta, that in future would send him back to
Teresa? 'I am damnably in love . . . and nothing but hope keeps
me alive *seriously*'.[28]
But still he stayed on in Venice – and still Teresa waited.

FANNY SILVESTRINI TO CONTESSA GUICCIOLI

Venice   *May 14th* [1819]

My Sweet Friend: Here is a fresh letter for you. I do not yet know whether I shall receive any from you today; my many domestic duties have prevented me till now from going to the post, but now I will go. You will have received my letter dated the 11th. This evening B[yron] expects me, probably to talk to me about his journey, as to which I shall encourage him. . . .

He does indeed love you. Do not doubt it, my friend. I embrace you and assure you once again that I am your most faithful

FANNY

BYRON TO CONTESSA GUICCIOLI

Venice   *May 20th, 1819*

My Love: I had written you a letter to go by the last post, which I did not send because yours, which arrived on the same day, was in fact an answer to my questions about the journey we had planned. I hope that Fanny wrote to you, as I begged her to do. Your illness is causing me great anxiety and it seems to me that you have not made up your mind whether my arrival at such a moment would be quite fitting. Meanwhile I am still awaiting your news, to know whether I shall start or not. I remember you told me that in June you would be going to Bologna, – and perhaps, in view of all circumstances, our meeting there would be more convenient, not only for appearances, but also for our own happiness. Certainly there you would be less exposed to gossip than in your own town. I am writing in a great hurry and in very great agitation – but pray believe that I am always the same towards you. I love you – I cannot find words to express to what degree, – but time will prove and you yourself will see, that you have become the only object for which I live and for which I would die.

Your instructions, my Treasure, are a little confused; our first meeting is *not* to take place 'at the theatre', and 'the landlady of the Inn'– of whom you say so many nice things!! Listen, my Soul, if she is as you say, it would be necessary for me to make love to her; – Yes or no? If I do, she will have a certain right to play the Spy on us – and if *not*, she will do it out of spite, for a woman of that sort never forgives being despised.

I do not at all understand your allusions to Signora Z[inanni] whom I have not the honour of knowing, except perhaps by sight during the Carnival. How then can that woman come into our affairs? I do not know her – she does not know me – how can or could it be in her power to distress you? Yet you say you are distressed about her, without explaining the reason.

My love, I kiss you with all my soul – think of me as eternally your most tender and faithful

FANNY SILVESTRINI TO CONTESSA GUICCIOLI

Venice *May 24th*, 1819

My Friend: And why do you not write, my dear Friend? I will tell you, what I have already said, that your silence is the reason that B[yron] is not already in your arms. He had already twice settled the date of his departure, and twice put it off, always waiting for your letters. The other day, however, after posting my letter dated the 20th, I thought of sending again to the post to see if there were any letters from you, and in fact I did find one, with another inside it, which I at once took to him myself. I cannot express to you his pleasure in receiving it, he assured me that he had slept badly the night before for lack of it, and he finally settled to wait for any letters that might come today, and then to leave tomorrow, Tuesday. So there you are, my Friend, deprived for the second time of a visit you so much desire. But he will certainly come, and if we have your answer he will leave on Saturday of this week. It is therefore for you to press him in your letters; I, too, beg you to do so, so that I may see two people gay and happy.

What you will like to know is that I am writing at his writing-desk, opposite him, while he is looking through your letters, putting some aside, taking up others, in short I can only confirm to you that he loves you very much, my dear Teresina, and that you are happy to possess the heart and affections of the most amiable and most gracious person, while he on his part is happy to be loved by you, whose virtues are always recalled by him to me, with all the *enthusiasm* of love.

Farewell, my dearest Friend. I think that the postscript will please you more than the letter. Your   FANNY

P.S. [in Byron's hand]

I should have started on Wednesday, if I had had your letters. Being without them, I am still in a very ill humour and desire nothing but to receive some so as to be able to decide to start. Pray write to me, but in any case I shall leave on Saturday. – I kiss you a thousand times with my whole Heart and am eternally your most tender and faithful Lover.

FANNY SILVESTRINI TO CONTESSA GUICCIOLI

Venice *May* 28*th,* 1819

My dear Friend: God be praised, I have finally received three letters of yours at once, one for me, one from Perelli dated the 22nd, which should have come by the previous post, and another written indeed by Perelli, but dictated by you.

So, my poor Teresina, you are ill, and your very illness keeps your medicine away. Your lover, to fulfil his duty and to satisfy his love, and the desires of his heart, should already be in your arms. Three times he has got everything ready for the journey, and three times he was delayed by the uncertainties, the postponements and the vague instructions in your letters. But now he will not wait any longer. He is leaving tomorrow, as you will see from his postscript. He will stay in Bologna, awaiting there the letter you have promised, which I will send on as soon as I get it. So we agreed yesterday evening, when I took him your letter.

I cannot find words to describe to you his anxiety about your silence by the last post. When he saw me yesterday evening, he looked at me without saying a word, and I, knowing how much he needed consolation, at once gave the packet to him: he took it, with an expression of pleasure, then, shutting and opening his fine eyes, he put his hand upon his heart, as if to feel what it was saying to him, then raised his head and began slowly to open one of your letters, trying to make out the words as he came to them, one by one; finally he read them both, but *his own* with great emotion. Afterwards, he commented on them to me, as he always does, and I feel more than ever that he is not one of those ordinary *lovers* who love *thoughtlessly,* if I may say so, who love themselves, rather than the object, not caring a rap for the consequences. No, my Teresa, he unites with his love a great deal of good sense, which you must not confuse with good *manners,* or *conventionality,* still less with coldness. You will see him and will know for yourself whether I am wrong.

Hasten to get well, but even in that be prudent; forcing the pace might be bad for you. I shall not cease, my tender Friend, to give you the most salutary advice, dictated by affection and experience.

Control yourself, for Mercy's sake, before your husband and the whole of Ravenna. Do not let Love betray you, for he would be betraying himself. Do not compromise yourself, if you value your peace; do not compromise him, if he is dear to you. I implore you, my dear, to treat him in public without any partiality, as you would have treated him a year ago. Even in arranging your rendezvous, for mercy's sake measure the time, the place, the circumstances; do not lose your head – all this to avoid making yourself unhappy for ever.

Forgive me, my friend, if I annoy you with this advice; I know only too well that when one is in love and blinded, to the degree that you are, one despises any salutary counsels, and leaps forward towards one's goal. – But, no, no, for mercy's sake, you have a lot of sense and you trust me too much to refuse to listen to me. And now I have said everything; the question is whether you will keep Byron or lose him, and with him your peace and your happiness.

Since the first day I knew you, you have been a person very dear to me; but your present situation has rendered you so interesting that I do not know what I would not do for you. So accept my counsels as a token of my tenderness. Farewell.

[*The letter continues in Byron's hand*]

My Love: I hear with the greatest distress of your illness, and all the more because I had hoped to hear by today's post that you were completely recovered. However, in spite of what you write I shall leave here on Saturday the 29th. I shall go to Bologna and there wait for the letter which you say you are sending me, which Fanny will not fail to forward. My desire is equal to yours, to see you, to embrace you – and to say a thousand times that I love you. I kiss you with all my soul, and am always yours.

[*The letter continues in Fanny's hand*]

Two more lines from Fanny. As, on the eve of a journey, whatever it may be, there is a great deal to do, Mylord is very busy, and so could not write to you this morning; besides, you know his habit of getting up at 2 p.m. and the post has then gone. So he contented himself with writing these few lines under my eyes yesterday evening, leaving space for me to write. Probably he will write to you from Bologna, if indeed he does not arrive before his letter. I beg you, if any freedom of mind remains to you, which I hardly believe, to go on writing to me during his visit, so that I may know about it and rejoice if his coming, as I do not doubt, has brought health to your body and Joy and Paradise to your soul.

I must also tell you, for I am certain you will like to hear it, that Mylord has shown me* such signs of his generosity and his good heart that I have been astounded and shall always be grateful. I do not know whether it is on account of the bond of friendship which binds you and me, and since the motive springs from his love for you, I leave it to your good sense whether or not to mention it; do what you think best. Meanwhile I embrace you, my friend, and I leave your case in your own hands, be very careful. Farewell, farewell.

At last, on June 1st, Byron did get off. 'The die is cast,' he wrote to Hobhouse, 'and I must (not figuratively but *literally*) pass the Rubicon . . . Everything is to be risked, for a woman one likes.'[10] Before he had reached Padua, however, he was already regretting his decision, and was writing to Hoppner in a thoroughly bad temper. The letter, he said, which he had received from Teresa just before starting, had been more than a little disquieting.

'La G.'s instructions are rather calculated to produce an *éclat*, and perhaps a scene, than any decent iniquity . . . to go to Cuckold a Papal Count, who, like Candide, has already been "the death of two men, one of whom was a priest", in his own house, is rather too much for my modesty when there are several other places at least as good for the purpose. She says they must go to Bologna in the middle of June, and why the devil then drag me to Ravenna? . . . The Charmer forgets that a man may be whistled anywhere *before*, but that *after* – – a Journey in an Italian

---

* The letter L (for Lepri), has been written by Teresa over a word which is obviously 'me' or 'with me' (*me* or *meco*). For obvious reasons, Teresa did not want to leave on record that Fanny had been *paid* by Byron for her good services.

June is a Conscription, and therefore she should have been less liberal in Venice, or less *exigent* at Ravenna.'[30]

A marked contrast to this letter is afforded by the highly romantic poem which he was writing, in these very same days, for Teresa – the *Stanzas to the Po*.*

> River, that rollest by the ancient walls
> Where dwells the Lady of my love . . .
>
> A stranger loves the Lady of the land,
> Born far beyond the mountains, but his blood
> Is all meridian, as if never fanned
> By the black wind that chills the polar flood.
>
> My blood is all meridian; were it not,
> I had not left my clime, nor should I be,
> In spite of tortures, ne'er to be forgot,
> A slave again of love, – at least of thee.

A year later he said of these verses that they were written 'in red-hot earnest'† – and most probably, in spite of all he wrote to Hoppner – it was true.

By June 6th he was in Bologna – 'where I am settled like a sausage and shall be broiled like one if this weather continues' – and was making use of some letters of introduction which had been given to him in Venice – one to Count Marescalchi and one to Count Francesco Rangone, the literary gentleman who was collecting anecdotes about him and who wrote at once to a friend: 'Lord Byron has arrived and I am engaged in paying him my court.' But literary men – or foreign provincial noblemen, for that matter – were not companions whom Byron found enlivening, and Rangone was obliged to add to his notes about the great English poet that he was often silent in conversation, and did not appear to enjoy listening to long stories.

Byron escaped from him and went sightseeing – first to look at Domenichino's pictures and then to the cemetery, where the custodian showed him the skull of a capuchin monk ('One of my

* These verses were indubitably addressed to Teresa, and – although Byron told Kinnaird that they were written on June 1st ('I wrote them *this very day* last year, June 1st', he wrote in 1820) – they were probably *conceived* when Teresa was still at Cà Zen, which *is* on the Po.

† June 8th, 1820. Unpublished letter to Hobhouse. 'You say the Po verses are fine; I thought so little of them that they lay by me a year uncopied, but they were written in *red-hot* earnest, and that made them good.' On sending the poem to England, he had written; 'they must not be published' because they were 'written upon private feelings and passions'.

best friends – I begged his head of his brethren – I put it in lime and boiled it:') and the monument of a beautiful Princess Barberini, whose hair, after two hundred years in her grave, was still found to be intact and 'as yellow as gold'.[31]

But then it was time to drive back to the city – and still there was no news from Teresa. Why could the tiresome woman not write? Should he go on or return to Venice? The nights were oppressive and the rooms at the Albergo del Pellegrino intolerably stuffy and hot. He told Hoppner to prepare for his return. But in the morning he woke up in a different mood; he was already half way, he would go on, after all, and see what Teresa was about. On the outside cover of his letter to Hoppner he scribbled the words: 'I am just setting off for Ravenna, June 8th, 1819. I changed my mind this morning, and decided to go on.'[32]

How I have loved the twilight hour and thee.
Don Juan

IT was on the morning of June 10th that Byron's great, gaudy travelling-coach[1] – adorned with his coat of arms, and large enough to hold his bed, his travelling-library and a vast assortment of china, linen and plate – drew up at the Porta Sisi of Ravenna. The coach, the travellers were told, might proceed no further, for it was the feast of Corpus Domini, and on that day the narrow streets – shaded by great awnings which gave them the appearance of enclosed galleries – were kept clear for the passage of the procession to the cathedral square. The pavements were strewn with flower-petals, and the façades of the palaces were hung with tapestries and brocades, and adorned with gold-framed mirrors and holy pictures, and even with portraits of the owner's ancestors, so that the whole city looked like one vast drawing-room.[2]

Unwillingly, in the midst of the curious, jostling crowd, the traveller descended. His eyes fell at once upon an extremely pretty young woman – and with a flourish he asked her the way to the inn. She told him, and then – for Ravenna was a very small town, and he had lighted upon a friend of Teresa's – she at once hastened to Palazzo Guiccioli, to tell Teresa about her encounter. 'Never,' she exclaimed, 'had she met a man of such beauty.' The Countess felt assured that it could only be Lord Byron.*

Teresa was at that moment engaged in writing a letter to her lover, whom she believed to be still in Bologna, contradicting her previous pressing invitations and begging him to postpone his visit. She had had a relapse, with high fever, and feared that the difficulties of seeing each other while she was still unwell would be insuperable – and besides, she added, she did not feel she 'deserved' so great an attention. She had already written all this to Fanny Silvestrini in Venice – but had addressed her letter to Mme Francesca instead of Fanny, so that the letter had not arrived. But now that at last Byron had come, all her doubts and hesitations were forgotten.

Byron, meanwhile, had presented a letter of introduction to Count Giuseppe Alborghetti, the Secretary General of the Province, and had been civilly invited to the Count's box at the

---

* 'Vie', p. 115. The friend was Signora Geltrude Vicari, of whom more will be heard later.

theatre that evening.* On his arrival, his host inquired whether he had any acquaintances in Ravenna.

' "Yes," replied Byron, "I am very friendly with Count and Countess Guiccioli." "But alas," replied Alborghetti, "you will not be able to see the young lady, as they say she is at death's door." At this sudden and unexpected news, given so abruptly, Byron lost his head – and, unable to control his emotion, replied that if the lady should die, he hoped he would not survive her.'

The effect was all that can be imagined. 'Count Alborghetti, who had believed that Byron was attracted to Ravenna by literary interests – by Dante's tomb, the Byzantine monuments, and memories of Dryden, Boccaccio and Gaston de Foix – gaped round-eyed at the emotion of the young Lord ... Fortunately', Teresa adds, 'Count Guiccioli, who had caught sight of Lord Byron, then called on him in the box and calmed him by giving him better news.'³

Byron took up his abode in the uncomfortable little inn in the Via di Porta Sisi, which was the best that the city could afford and waited for Teresa's bidding.

The following letters, which enable us to follow the whole course of Byron's and Teresa's affairs during the next feverish two months, are enclosed in a folder inscribed in Teresa's writing: *Second Series: 19 notes from Lord Byron.*⁴ At the top of some of the letters (in Teresa's writing) is the word ost^{ble} (*ostensible* – can be shown). The explanation is also in Teresa's writing: 'Dans ces billets il y a à choisir ... des phrases seulement ... parceque ils témoignent tous de son excellent cœur et de ses sentiments de loyauté et de délicatesse.'

The first of the following letters was sent to Teresa by hand immediately after Byron's arrival – the second, later in the evening, after coming back from the theatre.

BYRON TO CONTESSA GUICCIOLI⁵

June 10th, 1819

My Treasure: Here I am, in Ravenna. If you can arrange to see me I shall be happy – if not, I have at any rate not broken my word – and I hope at least to hear that your health is better. Always.

* Conte Giuseppe Alborghetti (1776-1852) was a nobleman and writer of occasional verses, which had won him some distinction. Teresa describes him as 'a man of intelligence, and Chief of the government of the Lower Romagna in the absence of the Prince Legate'.

E

June 10th, 1819°

My Love: I have been to the theatre without finding you – and was sorry to hear that you are still weak. Your husband came to see me in the box and replied courteously to the few inquiries I dared to make at that moment. Count Z[inanni] then turned up and was so insistent that I should go to his box that I could not avoid paying that call without being rude – and I did go there for a moment.

My sweetest Soul – believe that I live for you alone – and do not doubt me. I shall stay here until I know what your wishes really are: and even if you cannot arrange to see me I shall not go away. I beseech you to command me as entirely and eternally yours. I would sacrifice all my hopes for this world and all that we believe we may find in the other – to see you happy. I cannot think of the state of your health without sorrow and tears. Alas, my Treasure! How much we endured – and shall still have to endure! And you so young – so beautiful – so good – you have had to suffer through my fault – what a thought!

I kiss you a thousand thousand thousand times with all my soul.

P.S. I sent you a note this evening by means of P[erelli]. But the bearer did not find him until midnight. I am writing now after the theatre before going to bed. I hope you will receive both.

June 11th, 1819'

My Love: Pray instruct me how I am to behave in these circumstances. I am not clear as to what it is best to do. I think of staying here until you go – and then finding a way of meeting in Bologna, and then in Ferrara. But all these plans depend upon your wishes. I have no life now, except in you. My peace is lost in any case – but I should prefer death to this uncertainty. Pray forgive and pity me. Remember that I am here because you ordered me to come – and that every moment in which I do not ... but it is useless to write. I feel inexpressibly unhappy. I do see you – but how? – in what a state?

I have tried to distract myself with this farce of visiting antiquities – it seems quite intolerably tedious – but at the moment everything else is equally displeasing. The little that interests me – Dante's tomb and a few things in the library – I have already seen with an indifference made pardonable by the state of my heart. You see that I do not go into Society – and that I only seek ways of being near to you – but how? You are so surrounded: I am a foreigner in Italy – and still more a foreigner in Ravenna – and naturally little versed in the customs of the country – I am afraid of compromising you. For myself there is little more to fear – my fate is already decided. It is impossible for me to live long in this state of torment – I am writing to you in tears – and I am not a man who cries easily. When I cry my tears come from the heart, and are of blood.

At this point (midnight) I have received your letters and the handkerchief – and I am a little calmer. I shall study to do all that you command.

I am continuing this note without changing a word – to show you what sort of an inferno I have carried in my heart since my arrival.

If you knew what it costs me to control myself in your presence! But I will not say more – let us hope that time will teach me hypocrisy. You speak of 'my sacrifices' – don't say any more – my heart is already sacrificed, and after that victim, I can offer no other. A sign from you will suffice to lead me or send me – not only to Bologna, but to the grave.

Do not mistrust me – I do not mistrust you – but the difficulties of our circumstances. I should like to hope – but – but – always a *But* – meanwhile *you* hope – and that is enough.

I thank you – I embrace you – I kiss you a thousand thousand times.

P.S. Why send me back my handkerchief? I see from the mark that it is the one I gave you on the evening before your departure. I would not give you back a *thread* of yours (which I always keep by me) to obtain an empire.*

Byron's first visit to Teresa had taken place, as the preceding letter shows, on the day after his arrival, 'although it was a Friday and he did not like to do anything important on that day'. Guiccioli himself had come to fetch him in his coach, and had accompanied him to Teresa's bedside, where she, feverish and flushed

* The handkerchief – of fine white cambric – was kept by Teresa in the box that contained her other 'relics'. Medwin gives an amusing account of the private theatricals in Pisa, in which Byron took the part of Iago. ' "Shakespeare was right", said he, after he had finished, "in making Othello's jealousy turn upon that circumstance. The handkerchief is the strongest proof of love, not only among the Moors, but all Eastern nations".' (MEDWIN, *Conversations with Lord Byron*, p. 201.)

and 'surrounded by friends and relations', was not able to speak to him alone even for a moment. 'He returned home', she tells us, 'extremely melancholy.'[8] And although during the following days he called upon her as often as twice a day – 'a frequency', she would have us believe, 'sanctioned by Italian custom and which surprised no one',[9] – his visits continued to take place in the presence of her observant relations.

That first week in Ravenna, indeed, was not a happy time. The sleepy little provincial town to which Byron was to become so much attached had, at first sight, little to offer the traveller. The members of the local nobility, to whom his letters of introduction were addressed, hastened to call upon their distinguished visitor and to take him to see their sights: Dante's tomb, the Rotonda, the great Byzantine mosaics in S. Apollinare in Classe – the fine manuscripts in the library. But Byron, at best, was not much of a sightseer – and now he was far too much preoccupied with Teresa to care about anything else. He seems, indeed, to have made this only too clear to his hosts.

'The common opinion', wrote Conte Giulio Rasponi acidly to Rangone, 'is that the Palazzo Guiccioli has impressed him more than the Rotonda and the ruins of Theodoric. In any case his stay is a good thing for the town and for the people who see him, although his manner of life and preoccupation with his affections do not often render him accessible. I have not failed to offer him my humble services in various forms, but he, very much reserved, has only made a very limited use of them.'[10]

For indeed Teresa took up all his thoughts. After reading the daily letters that he wrote to her at this time, it seems no longer possible to maintain that this was only a half-hearted relationship. Grudgingly as he had come to Ravenna – flippantly as he still wrote about the affair to his English friends – it is evident that he was now completely absorbed by Teresa. He sat up all night writing to her, in tears; he made a scene when he saw her talking to someone else; he was touchy, uncertain of himself, and so moody that everyone observed it. 'Lord Byron is staying on at Ravenna', wrote that incorrigible gossip, Rangone, to his brother in Venice. 'They tell me of his intense passion and his great melancholy.' He even reached the point of asking Teresa, in so many words, whether – if the moment should come when she would have to choose between her husband and himself, – she would elope with him.

There is in his letters not only an unmistakable note of passion, but a curious lack of self-confidence, a deep discomfort. 'I am a foreigner in Italy,' he told Teresa, 'and still more a foreigner in Ravenna, and naturally little versed in the customs of the country. I am afraid of compromising you.' All day, except in the few hours that he could be with her, he sat in the hot, dingy little inn – and wondered why he had come, and whether indeed he should stay. Did Teresa really care for him? And even if she did, what could come of it all? Everyone in Ravenna was prodigiously civil – but it was not for them that he was there. Moreover – accustomed as he was to dealing with husbands – there was something singularly disconcerting about the old Count. He, too, was only too civil – but what lay beneath his formal, half-ironic courtesy? 'I can't make him out at all,' he wrote to Hoppner, 'he visits me frequently and takes me out (like Whittington, the Lord Mayor) in a coach and *six* horses. The fact appears to be, that he is completely *governed* by her – for that matter, so am I.' The letter ends: 'My coming – going – and everything depends upon *her* entirely.'[11]

The pages of the 'Vie', at this period, are written in the form of a diary, so that it is possible to follow in detail all the ups and downs of the lovers' hopes and fears. By June 14th Teresa was better, and was up when Byron came to see her – but in the evening she was obliged to send him some bad news. The Abate Perelli, who had been the transmitter of their letters, had gone off to the country with Teresa's uncle. Byron was greatly upset, but nevertheless called on her both in the afternoon and evening – finding her, once again, surrounded by people, but better. 'Letter of devotion after leaving me,' she adds – 'a masterpiece of passion, devotion and generosity!'[12] Here is the letter which pleased her so greatly, and which ended with the suggestion that they should run away together.

BYRON TO CONTESSA GUICCIOLI[13]

June 14th, 1819

Perhaps I am mistaken – my Love – but this sudden country expedition of your uncle's with P[erelli] makes me afraid that we have been betrayed – and that P[erelli] has been taken off to the country to interrupt our correspondence. Passion makes me fear everything and everyone. If I lose you, what will become of me? Was this journey planned before my arrival – or not? If *not*, I feel very suspicious. In any case, how shall we manage to get our letters? How shall I be able to get even this one to you, without risk of a discovery which would be sad for you – and for me, fatal. In losing me you lose very little, – but I am unlikely to survive a break with you. Until now the fruits of my journey have been rather bitter – but if you are pleased, I do not regret what I am suffering – for I am suffering for your sake.

Love has its martyrs like religion – with this difference – that the victims of love lose their Paradise in this world, without reaching it in the other, while the devout of the other faith gain by the change.

Meanwhile – my Love – tell me what I am to do? Remain here? – or return to Bologna? If trouble arises there is only one adequate remedy, that is, to go away together – and for this a great Love is necessary – and some courage. Have you enough?

I can already anticipate your answer. It will be long and divinely written – but it will end in a negative.

I kiss you from my heart ten million times.

Byron was right. Teresa's answer was long, poetic and full of numerous good reasons why she should not run away with him. Nor indeed did he yet grasp, perhaps, how unheard-of a thing he was asking. The essence of *serventismo*, as he was to realize later, was that the lady should *stay* with her husband. But, after this letter of his, he had no right to complain later on that he had been inveigled into 'a romance in the Anglo fashion'. It was he who had first desired it.

BYRON TO CONTESSA GUICCIOLI[14]

June 15th, 1819

You are right – but when one can *argue* a great deal, Love is not capable of very great sacrifices. Your answer is what I expected, it does not surprise me, and that is enough. Remember that my proposal was not made for the present time. I only asked, in case the alternative arose, what you would do? You are right in your answer, and now I know what my decision must be.

What you say is very true, only it has come a little too late – for the greatest injury to . . . was already done in Venice. To go away would be the height of imprudence – a thing only to be done if we were discovered – in case you were obliged to abandon

one of us two. But forgive me if I say (now that we are speaking
of morals) that the greatest injury is in the deception, not the
desertion, of a man who is already in the condition of a great
number of husbands.

Besides, I esteem him very much – and would make friends
with him willingly – at any cost.

Returning to the *alternative* – I can tell you that I too should
lose a great deal, but I prefer you to anything else – for I love
you. But I will not speak any more of Love – now that you cannot
doubt *mine*, after I have shown you how completely I would sacrifice everything.

Meanwhile you have not answered my question – that is,
whether I shall meet your wishes by staying here – or by leaving
for Bologna.

I kiss you and am always.

Teresa, however, continued to be most exasperating. To his
question whether he was to remain in Ravenna or go away, she
merely replied with a long disquisition on *The Lament of Tasso*,
which she had just read, – insisting on being told 'the *secret* of the
suffering which produced this poem, and who was the original of
Eleonora'.[15] Byron's annoyance, which Teresa's ill-timed poetic
flights were so often to arouse in him, is expressed in his answer.

BYRON TO CONTESSA GUICCIOLI[16]

June 15th, 1819

My Soul: I speak of *Love* and you answer me about *Tasso*. I write
about *you*, and you ask me about '*Eleanora*'. If you want to render
me even more insane than he, I can assure you you are on the
way to succeeding. In fact, my dear, your inquiries seem to me
superfluous. You know, at least in part, my story, and even
without it can imagine that, in order to depict strong passions,
it is necessary to have experienced them. One of these days
(if *ever*, *ever* they occur again, which I, alas, doubt) when we are
alone, – I will tell you whether your conjectures as to the original
of the portrait are founded on truth or not. If you know what
love is – if you love me – if you feel – how can you at this moment –
seeing the state in which we find ourselves – think or speak of
imaginary things? Have we not only too much *reality*? I swear

that these last few days have been among the most unhappy of
my life. Love – doubt – uncertainty – the fear of compromising
you when I see you in the presence of others – the impossibility
of seeing you alone – the thought of losing you for ever – these
combine to destroy the few hopes that inspired me until now.

Society disturbs me – solitude terrifies me. My only consolation
is to see you recovered in health.

I am awaiting with the greatest impatience your answer to my
two letters. What shall I do?

It seems to me that your father looks at you with some suspicion –
and that naturally he does not much like to see me so near you –
and that this journey of your uncle with Perelli and the sudden
departure of your friend [amica] are not the happiest presages for
us. Meanwhile my coming to Ravenna, as I foresaw, instead of
increasing our understanding, has diminished it. Oh Venice –
Venice – *there* we were united, at least for a few hours!

P.S. Forgive me if my answer has been *too English* in the first lines
of this note – but I have not come to Italy to speak of myself and
my own doings – but rather to forget my life of *beyond the mountains* – and above all, to love you – *you*, my only and last delight.
That is why I showed impatience in answering your question
whether E. was the . . . etc. etc. . . .

But now there was a change for the better. Teresa's fever left
her, and at last the doctor allowed her to go out again. On the
evening of June 6th, at 7 o'clock, 'she came down the stairs of her
palazzo leaning on Byron's arm. He seated himself in her closed
carriage beside her; behind them, in another carriage, rode the
Count and some other friends'.[17] It was their first time alone
together, since he had come to Ravenna. They reached the great
pine-wood that lies between Ravenna and the sea, at sunset. 'The
whole world was fresh and green; the nightingales were singing,
the crickets chirping. Lord Byron was charmed by the landscape;
he seemed at once happy and melancholy.' It was on that evening,
says Teresa, as they drove home together through the forest and
watched the reflection of the sunset lights in the still pools under
the pine-trees, that she asked Byron, since he had already written
about Tasso, to write something also about Italy's greatest
poet, Dante. 'Your wishes are my commands', he replied –
and the next day began *The Prophecy of Dante*, which he dedicated
to her.[18]

> LADY! If for the cold and cloudy clime
>   Where I was born, but where I would not die,
>   Of the great Poet-Sire of Italy
> I dare to build the imitative rhyme,
> Harsh Runic copy of the South's sublime
>   THOU art the cause; and howsoever I
>   Fall short of his immortal harmony,
> Thy gentle heart will pardon me the crime.
> Thou, in the pride of Beauty and of Youth,
>   Spakest; and for thee to speak and be obeyed
> Are one; but only in the sunny South
>   Such sounds are uttered and such charms displayed,
>   So sweet a language from so fair a mouth –
> Ah! to what effort would it not persuade?

It was at this period, too, that having seen on Teresa's table Dante's *Inferno*, he read with her the verses about Paolo and Francesca. Teresa asked him whether it had ever been translated into English. 'Non tradotto, ma tradito', he replied[19] – and thereupon promised her to try his hand at a better rendering.

But still, when they were alone together, they would go over and over the same ground: what did the future hold for them? It is clear from the letters that Byron repeated his suggestion to elope with her, and that she again drew back. According to Moore, – who seems to have seen some letters which have since been lost, and to which Teresa does not refer in the 'Vie' – she 'even proposed, as a means of escaping the ignominy of an elopement, that she should, like another Juliet, "pass for dead"',[20] a proposal which must have afforded Byron some amusement. For the moment the project was shelved; but Teresa now knew – or thought she knew – how completely her lover was committed.

BYRON TO CONTESSA GUICCIOLI[21]

June 16th, 1819

My Love: Let us not talk about the subject any more now. It is enough that you cannot doubt me, knowing what I would be capable of doing for you. In any case and in all circumstances your happiness will be my only care. If a time comes of trouble and disturbance caused by our love, then you shall decide, according to your feelings. I shall not try to persuade you or to influence your choice. My '*duties*', dearest Teresa, are always the same – and it seems to me I am showing every possible eagerness to fulfil them.

Everything depends on you – my life – my honour – my love. Love me, then – my feeling for you deserves to be returned: I suffer so much in loving, that I have tried to avoid strong passions in these last three years – but in vain, as you see now. To love you is my crossing of the Rubicon and has already decided my fate.

I shall not fail to carry out all that you say – I kiss you 100000 times.

June 17*th*, 1819[11]

Yes – my Love – I am *very indifferent* to you. I have travelled here from Venice – I have been so happy after my arrival – my diversions have been so many – they cheer me so greatly – yes – you are right in this as in everything – there is no doubt as to my *indifference*. Think a little – my Treasure – and then I shall challenge anyone whatever to find in my conduct ever since I have known you the slightest thing that deserves such a reproach. I love you only too much, but in *Love, too much* is not enough. This I feel, too – for I believe that you do not love me to the degree that I long for; – and meanwhile I am very sure that my heart is more engaged than yours – but that should be so – for you deserve a love which I could neither hope for nor inspire. Such a love I feel for you – do you want proofs?

You tell me that I, and not '*riding*', have done you so much harm – this means that the cause of the illness* was a fault of mine. This is the first time that you have said this to me – and being a rather serious accusation – and seriously made – I should like to have some explanation. – If you only knew . . . but – it is useless – all I write, or say.

My Love – We have surely enough trouble without making ourselves unhappy by ill-founded suspicions and torments caused by wounded pride, perhaps unnecessarily. A slave is not more humble in the presence of his master – than I am in yours, – but do not abuse your power, for you have too much. Think only if I deserve the reproaches of your last note – and then forgive . . . *yourself* if you can.

Believe me eternally your most unchangeable and loving

---

* Under the word 'illness' the word 'abortion' can be read.

The mention of 'the hope of travelling together' in the following letter suggests that Teresa's ingenious brain was already making plans to enable her and Byron to set forth together for Venice – a plan which they did at last carry out in August. But for the time being Byron had no intention of moving from Ravenna, and he sent off to Alexander Scott, in Venice, a series of urgent letters (on June 10th, 20th and 26th) telling him to send him his saddle-horses and his carriage-horses, and to forward all his English letters. Hoppner and Scott – united in their jealousy of 'La Guiccioli' – delayed as long as they could. 'There could surely be no difficulty', wrote Byron to Scott, after waiting for ten days. 'It will be very disagreeable if he is not set off by this time.'[22] But at last his instructions were carried out – and he finally told Scott that he had 'no intention of returning to Venice for some time'. 'All has gone on very well here – as you may suppose by my stay. The Lady does whatever she pleases with me – and luckily the same things please both.'[24]

BYRON TO CONTESSA GUICCIOLI[25]

June 20th, 1819

'And you could' – What is there that you could not, my Love, if you wish it?

There can be nothing more delightful to me than the hope of 'travelling together'.

Your little note ends – or rather does *not* end – when will you tell me the rest?

As I have said to you many times, my fate is in your hands; where you are is my country – and what you say, my law. Meanwhile I am longing for the hour when I see you again – and I kiss you untiringly with all my soul.

The next of Byron's notes[26] consists only of two fragments, which have been cut out of a longer letter. It obviously refers to one of their early quarrels – possibly to the same attack of jealousy described in the following letters.

Of these attacks of jealousy Byron himself wrote to Hobhouse: 'Hitherto all had gone on *well*, with the usual *exception* of some *gelosie*, which are the fault of the climate, and of the conjunction of two such capricious people as the Guiccioli and the *inglese*.[27]

The sentences which still remain of the letter are:

'I am going to bed – and it would be better for me if my sleep (if indeed sleep is possible for me) could become eternal . . . . how to make him forget to come to you . . . . . Perhaps this is only a prologue – and you will . . . .
. . . .
But I loved you – and after having been a man well-known for his independence and strength of mind . . . . Unfortunately for me he has lost his wings. Perhaps he will find them again, at least I hope so. Farewell.'

Teresa appears rather to have enjoyed these outbursts of jealousy as tributes to her power, for Byron's next letter is headed by her: 'Billet de jalousie *magnifique – passionné – sublime mais* très injuste. Il ne me connaissait encore que depuis trop peu!!!'[20]

BYRON TO CONTESSA GUICCIOLI[21]

[no date]

'My thoughts cannot find rest in me'* – I was right then: what is that man doing every evening for so long beside you in your box? 'So we are agreed' – fine words! '*You* are agreed', it appears. I have noticed that every time I turned my head toward the stage you turned your eyes to look at that man – and this, after all that had happened today! But do not fear, tomorrow evening I shall leave the field clear to him. I have no strength to bear a fresh torment every day – you have made me despicable in my own eyes – and perhaps soon in those of others. – Have you not seen my torments? Have you not pitied them? I forgive you what you have made me suffer – but I can never forgive myself the weakness of heart which has prevented me until now from taking the only honourable step in such circumstances – that of bidding you goodbye – for ever –

Midnight

My time for sleep before I knew you.
Let me go – it is better to die from the pain of separation, than from that of betrayal – my life now is a constant agony. I have enjoyed a unique and final happiness in your arms – but – oh

---

* TASSO, *Gerusalemme Liberata*, Canto X°. The original line: '*I suoi pensieri in lui dormir non ponno*' ('His thoughts cannot find rest in him') was placed by Byron at the beginning of his *Corsair*.

God! how much those moments are costing me! – and *they* [cost]
this! – now that I am writing to you alone – completely alone. I
had no one but you in the world – and now, not having you any
more (without the heart, what is the rest?) solitude has become as
tedious as society – for that image which I pictured as so pure,
so dear, is now nothing but a perfidious and menacing shadow, –
and yet – always *yours*.

[*No date*][30]

My Love: Why not after dinner? What do I care about the
'promenade' and the 'prescription'? You well know *what* I 'like' –
every day in which we do not see and *love* each other, in deed as
in our hearts, is (at least for me) the most irreparable of losses,
one happiness the less.

Tell me *when* – ever and entirely thine

'The most irreparable of losses.' It was at this time that Byron
– already conscious of a physical decay far in advance of his years,
and of a corresponding exhaustion – was writing to Webster:

'At thirty I feel there is no more to look forward to . . . My
hair is half grey, and the Crow's-foot has been rather lavish of its
indelible steps. My hair, though not gone, seems going, and my
teeth remain by way of courtesy.'[31]

These were the times of weariness and self-distaste which Byron
– like an over-tired child at a party, who, dropping with fatigue,
yet clamours for one game more – attempted to defeat always by
the same method: some fresh sensation that would reconfirm for
him the sense of his own reality. Life had become tasteless for him,
except in the pursuit of passion. And passion brought pain – and
pain, weariness – and then he was off on the treadmill once again.

'At thirty-one', he wrote to Hobhouse in the same strain, 'so few
years, months, days, remain, that "carpe diem" is not enough. I
have been obliged to crop even the seconds, for who can trust
tomorrow? – Tomorrow, quotha! To-hour, *to-minute*. I cannot
repent me (I try very often) so much of anything I have done, as
of anything I have left undone. Alas! I have been idle and have
the prospect of early decay, without having seized every available
instant of my pleasurable years'.[32]

This was the high summer of Teresa's and Byron's passion – when Byron's fears for her health and his consciousness of his own exhaustion, only served to fan his feverish thirst. Her youth, her freshness, her vitality (in spite – or even increased by – her illness) all gave him an illusion of renewed vigour, of a last lease of life.

During all this time neither Byron nor Teresa – since they did not at the moment require her services – thought it necessary to write to Fanny. She, however, kept up an eloquent flow of tender inquiries.

'Pray,' she begged Byron, 'in an interval of rest, take a moment to remember Fanny as one who has an infinite love for Teresina, and the highest regard for Mylord.'[33]

The next week, under cover to Don Perelli, she was writing to Teresa herself:

'Your long silence is making me very anxious . . . Is it possible that you should have forgotten me? . . . My dear Friend, write if you can and tell me everything. I hope it will not be long before I see and embrace you, if the Cavaliere your Spouse does not change his mind.'[34]

But neither Byron nor Teresa answered, and early in July she was again appealing to Byron:

'I turn to you, Mylord, begging you for pity's sake to relieve me of a painful uncertainty and tell me by what illness she [Teresa] is affected and how severely.'[35]

For Teresa was still seriously ill, and as the weeks passed and her cough and fever continued, Byron's letters to his English friends lost their deliberate flippancy and revealed a deep anxiety, even if expressed with characteristic egotism:

'Thus it is with everything and everybody for whom I feel anything like a real attachment. "War, death or discord doth lay siege to them." I never even could keep alive a dog that I liked or that liked me.'[36]

To John Murray he was still franker:

'I see my *Dama* every day at the proper (and improper) hours; but I feel seriously uneasy about her health, which seems very precarious. In losing her, I would lose a being who has run great risks on my account, and whom I have every reason to love – but I must not think this possible. I do not know what I *should* do if she died, but I ought to blow my brains out – and I hope that I should.'**

It being evident that the Ravenna doctors were not doing Teresa any good, Byron prevailed upon Count Guiccioli to let him send for his own doctor from Venice, Professor Aglietti. To Alexander Scott he wrote:

'I have sent again to Venice for Dr. Aglietti – the Guiccioli is seriously ill, and her state menaces consumption – I need hardly say how this occupies and distresses me . . . If you can say anything to Aglietti to persuade him to come, in addition to what I have written – pray do — I have written at Count Guiccioli's own request, and enclosed besides a long medical statement of her case.

'Although there is no doubt on that score, yet you may tell Aglietti *I myself* will be responsible for his time, trouble and expence, etc., being reimbursed, and his coming will be to me also a great personal favour. I can say no more.'**

Professor Aglietti – who granted Byron's request and, after obtaining the permission of the Governor of Venice, at once set off for Ravenna – was a very famous doctor, and, by all accounts, a most delightful man. A poet and scholar, as well as a physician, – a doctor who openly stated that he did not believe in medicine – his enormous figure was to be seen, with his pockets bulging with books, peering into every bookshop in the streets of Venice. We are told that, before his arrival in a patient's house, the family would hastily clear away any books, pictures or old etchings in the halls and passages, since otherwise he would stand all day looking at them, instead of visiting the patient. Not that he did not take his profession seriously. He had a remarkable gift for diagnosis, and – being the kindest of men – would even call upon a serious patient as often as eight times a day. But he had little patience with feminine vapours, and if called in to such a case, would sit by the lady's bed and – while pretending to feel her pulse, – drop off for a short nap.**

His nights, at the end of his long day's work, were often spent in study, and sometimes, in the morning, the maid would find him still in his chair, where he had fallen asleep over his books. His appearance, we are told, was 'at once grave and friendly, with simple, easy manners, joined to a peculiar and sweet courtesy. He had a flexible nature, indulgent, warm in his affections, sensitive to all forms of beauty, loved by all, welcomed by all'. But his strongest quality was kindness, 'a kindness which coloured with affection his behaviour and his work as a doctor. The imagination slumbered in him, unless moved by the heart'.

Byron, who had always considered him the best doctor in Europe, was no doubt aware of this last quality too – and perhaps the great doctor's imagination was moved by the lovers' plight. We have no record of what he prescribed for Teresa (except that it included 'a complete change of regime', the application of leeches and some 'Peruvian bark' of extreme bitterness, which Byron promptly sent for from Venice) – but we do know that on his departure he left renewed hope behind him, and that Teresa and her family considered his visit to have been the turning-point in her illness, and Byron, consequently, her 'saviour'.

Before leaving Ravenna the great doctor and the famous poet – both dressed, we are told, in their best clothes (*abiti di grandissima gala*) took part in a solemn little ceremony. They drove together, in Byron's carriage, to Dante's monument – where Byron solemnly placed a volume of his own poems upon the tombstone. The contemporary who describes the scene, Filippo Mordani, adds that 'every time that the poet passed in front of that monument, he bared his head; and I myself have seen it several times'.[40]

And very soon – whether owing to Aglietti's prescriptions, to the Peruvian bark, or to the daily presence of her lover – Teresa really did begin to get better. By now, too, Byron's horses had arrived – and although the midsummer heat was intense, the two lovers rode together every evening in the Pine Forest, 'so full of pastime and prodigality.'

> Sweet Hour of Twilight! – in the solitude
>   Of the pine forest, and the silent shore
> Which bounds Ravenna's immemorial wood,
>   Rooted where once the Adrian wave flowed o'er,
> To where the last Caesarean fortress stood,
>   Evergreen forest! which Boccaccio's lore
> And Dryden's lay made haunted ground to me,
> How have I loved the twilight hour and thee![41]

Byron, now in the highest of spirits, took up his pen and wrote to tell Augusta all about it.

'I write from Ravenna – I came here on account of a Countess
Guiccioli – a Girl of Twenty married to a very rich old man of
Sixty about a year ago; with her, last winter, I had a liaison
according to the good old Italian custom – she miscarried in May
– and sent for me here – and here I have been these two months.

She is pretty – a great Coquette – extremely vain – excessively
affected – clever enough – without the smallest principle – with
a good deal of imagination and some passion. She had set her
heart on carrying me off from Venice out of vanity – and
succeeded – and having made herself the subject of general conversation has greatly contributed to her recovery. . . .

I send you a sonnet which this faithful Lady had made for the
nuptials of one of her relations in which she swears the most
alarming constancy to her husband – is not this good? – You may
suppose my *face* when she showed it to me – I could not help
laughing – one of *our* laughs. All this is very absurd – but you see
that I have good morals at bottom.

She is an equestrian too – but a bore in her rides – for she can't
guide her horse – and he runs after mine – and tries to bite him –
and then she begins screaming, in a high hat and Sky-blue riding
habit – making a most absurd figure – and embarassing me and
both our grooms – who have the devil's own work to keep her
from tumbling – or having her cloathes torn off by the trees and
thickets of the Pine forest.'[42]

But Teresa, in the true romantic tradition, scorned to chronicle
any such undignified episodes as these. *Her* account is all fine
scenery and poetry.

'They would remain for hours together,' she wrote, 'in the
deep forest shade – dismounting and seating themselves under the
great resinous pines. They walked on thyme and other scented
herbs . . . Lord Byron's delight was that of a poet, hers of a happy
young woman.'[43]

They would linger there together until the last hour of twilight,
when the vesper bell, heard faintly through the trees from the
tower of the Duomo, would call them home again.

At that moment, in Ravenna, two pages would come out on to
the marble balcony of the Palazzo del Comune, where two great
torches had been lit, and would play on their trumpets a short air
– while the faithful in the streets bowed their heads and knelt in
prayer, reciting the 'Ave Maria'.[44]

F

Ave Maria! bléssed be the hour!
The time, the clime, the spot, where I so oft
Have felt that moment in its fullest power
Sink o'er the earth – so beautiful and soft,–
While swung the deep bell in the distant tower,
Or the faint dying day-hymn stole aloft,
And not a breath crept through the rosy air,
And yet the forest leaves seemed stirred with prayer.

Ave Maria! 't is the hour of prayer!
Ave Maria! 't is the hour of Love!*

At dusk, returning home, Byron and Teresa only separated to
meet again 'at the theatre or at an assembly – *en tête-à-tête* or
in the presence of others – it little mattered, so long as they
breathed the same air.'[45]
Such behaviour, however, was more than a little conspicuous,
and there were plenty of willing tongues and pens to describe it.

'Mylord's love was becoming ever more intense, and more
noticeable in a small town. The time chosen for his calls was
especially noticed with some criticism, as coinciding with the
business or siesta times of the husband, when the wife was most at
leisure.'[46]

Count Guiccioli's numerous enemies took great pleasure in the
whole episode, and before long – indeed it is surprising that it
should not have happened sooner – one of them sent him a most
unpleasant anonymous letter. It came, Teresa tells us, on a
Friday, and her husband hastened to her room to read it to her,
and to show her the extremely scurrilous verses it contained –
which were being sung, the letter said, even by the little boys in
the streets.

Di Lord è innamorata, ognun lo sa,
La moglie del Falcon fatto Cucù,
Nè ancor s'avvede il vecchio babalà
Che ormai conviengli andar col capo in giù.

Ridono i sassi ancor della città
Del Becco e di Madonna, e molto più
Dei rimedi che Lord venir le fa
Da Venezia, da Londra e dal Perù.[47]

* *Don Juan*, III, XL, cii-ciii. 'I have known in Italy', said Byron to Dr. Kennedy
in Greece, 'a person engaged in sin, and when the vesper-bell has rung, stop and repeat
the Ave Maria, and then proceed in the sin: absolution cured all.' KENNEDY, *Conversations on Religion with Lord Byron*, p. 150.

That same evening – certainly *this* Friday was not Teresa's lucky day – some of her guests, in her own house, allowed themselves to indulge in innuendoes less coarse, but not less malicious. 'I saw him on horseback today,' said one young lady. 'Oh God, how beautiful he was! Truly the men should agree to exile him,' she added, looking pointedly at her hostess. – 'Is he married?' asked her young sister, and was answered by a long account of Byron's past adventures, furnished by another guest who had recently returned from Milan, and had heard more gossip about the poet there. 'It was not Byron's genius', adds Teresa somewhat superfluously, 'that excited public interest about him. It was his rank, his beauty, his fortune, and his mysterious reputation for strange adventures.'[48]

It was at this inauspicious moment that Byron, by a quite gratuitous piece of rudeness, got himself into trouble also with the clerical society of Ravenna. His first acquaintance there, Count Alborghetti, wrote to suggest that it would be no more than courteous for him to pay his respects to the Cardinal Legate, Malvasia – an old man of considerable distinction and learning. Byron answered civilly enough.

'I am as you know but a retired sort of being (of late years) and have been at more Mahometan than Christian Courts, besides which and though I have invariably voted in Parliament for the Catholics I am but little conversant with Cardinals. However – if – as a stranger who has been some time in Ravenna, nobody knows why – you think that I ought to pay my respects to His Eminence for whom I entertain great esteem and reverence – I will go. In that case nobody more agreeable to me personally or so proper in other respects to be my introducer as yourself. Perhaps you will do me the honour to call on me tomorrow at three – and indicate the time and manner. I could wish the *hour* to be an *Evening* one – for a Noonday presentation in the month of an Italian July in our English scarlet uniform – would be an operation of active service not necessary in time of peace to anyone but a Field Marshal.'[49]

The call, moreover in spite of the hot scarlet uniform, seems to have gone well; on July 5th Byron was writing to Kinnaird that the Cardinal was 'a fine old fellow . . . [who] has been rather loose in his youth, without being much tighter in his age. He and I took very kindly to each other.'[50]

The next stage of the acquaintance, however, was less fortunate. The Cardinal, who greatly prided himself upon the Literary

Academy, called after him the Malvasiana, which he had founded in Ravenna, decided to hold a large Conversazione, with Byron as the guest of honour. Such an invitation, in the Papal States, was practically a Royal Command – but Byron, who was already bored with behaving properly, not only refused, but found no better pretext for doing so than that the weather was too hot for going to large parties. His refusal caused all the offence that can be imagined.

'In this very moment', wrote Alborghetti in very odd English, 'the Cardinal has called on me in order to express his amazement and angry for your refusal of coming to his Society this evening. I supposed that you should have employed the pretext of health, not that of warmth, which was too little to refuse a conversation arranged and prepared on purpose for you. It is a duty of my friendship to prevent you of all that: it will be of your prudence and politeness to do what you think the best . . . You do not want [anything] of the Cardinal, and your liberty will and can not ever be forced; but the Chief of a Province, which now you live in, deserves some regards.'[51]

To all this Byron replied in a most characteristic manner.

BYRON TO CONTE GIUSEPPE ALBORGHETTI[52]

Ravenna   *July 9th*, 1819

My dear Count: I thought that I had sufficiently manifested my sincere respect for the Cardinal in paying him the first visit – and if there is any manner in which I can further testify my esteem personally, it shall be shewn. – –

But I am not a man of society nor Conversazioni – it is some years that I have given up both. With regard to the attentions necessary to be paid to the 'Chief of a Province' etc. – it cannot of course be my wish nor my interest to offend him – and I presume that such offence could only be the consequence of misconduct, and that His Eminence is of a character not to disquiet himself for such trifles as the appearance or non-appearance of a foreigner at a conversation. When at Venice last winter – I twice declined the offer of an introduction to the Vice-Roy and to the Arch-duchess Maria Louisa, made to me through the medium of the Prince of Hohenzollern and the English Consul General.

I did not find that I was supposed to have been guilty of any affront – and I am sure at least that I was far from intending it. As little do I think of displeasing His Eminence to whom I am grateful for his kindness – and for *his own proper conversation*.

I decline going into extensive society, because for these last three years I am not in the practice; indeed it distresses me – I am besides unwell, and expressed as much to you yesterday; if His Eminence thinks for a moment he must be aware that I can have no design to slight or to offend him – but the contrary.

I trust that you will do me the favour to represent as much to His Eminence and to believe me ever very truly yours obliged and obed.t Ser.t – P[ai]r d'A[ngleterre]   BYRON

To count Alborghetti
    etc. etc. etc.
P.S. I did *not* know that the Conversation was *made for me* – and I *did* say that I was *unwell in health* both to you and afterwards to the Count Zinanni.

As to this reply – for of course the whole story was at once written off to Rangone by one of his Ravenna correspondents – Rangone commented that it was written 'in a manner very clear and somewhat disobliging'. Byron remained at home with Teresa, and 'the Cardinal's Conversazione took place without Mylord'.*

It was, perhaps, natural that Byron should have been disinclined for parties that week, for the Cardinal's invitation coincided with the arrival of several distressing letters. The first of these was to Teresa from her young brother Pietro, who was completing his studies in Rome and who, having heard some of the gossip about Byron from literary friends, at once believed every word of it.

CONTE PIETRO GAMBA TO CONTESSA GUICCIOLI

So it is true, my dearest sister, that a young English Lord and Poet called Byron has made his way into your house. What I hear about him, in the aristocratic and literary society of Rome which I frequent, fills me with apprehension about the consequences that this relationship may have for you. You are so young – your experience of life is so limited – and his personal

---

* RANGONE, op. cit. His correspondent was Conte della Torre, a nobleman of Ravenna.

attractions are, so everyone says, so superior to those of most men, that I tremble for your peace. Your heart is pure – your soul is noble – and with the poetic ideas of your intellectual education you may well see in him a Petrarch, and in yourself a Laura.

I feel as if I could see into your heart, my dear little sister, but as your brother I wish also to be your protector, and to show you the rocks which surround your enchanted palace. Well, you must know that this man, whom you described to me in your last letter as an angel upon Earth, is the husband of a young woman full of innocence and affection like yourself; and, not satisfied with having abandoned her to give himself up to a life of disorder, he keeps her shut up in a Castle, of which many dark mysterious tales are told. It is even said that, in spite of his rank, he has been a Pirate during his journeys in the East.

It seems to me, therefore, my dear Sister, that before forming an intimate tie with a man so strange, and of so doubtful a reputation, you should reflect a great deal – and that is what I beg you to do – and what is particularly incumbent upon you, owing to your social position and your beauty. [53]

This was – so Teresa tells us, and we can well believe it – a most upsetting letter. She could not bear to think 'that there was anyone in the world, and especially her brother, who could harbour such thoughts about her noble friend'. 'It would have been easy for her', she remarks, 'to ask Byron what was the truth of the matter, but she felt that it would be an insult.' Moved only by 'the instinct of a child who knows by whom it is loved or not', she concealed her brother's letter, and sent him an immediate and eloquent answer.

After a preamble in which she stated that she owed the recovery of her health, after God, to Byron, who had arrived in Ravenna when she was dying, 'like an angel sent from Heaven to save me', she passed on to a complete avowal of her feelings:

'Why should I not love such a friend? The feelings I have vowed to him are stronger than all arguments, and, in loving Lord Byron as I love him, I do not think that I am offending the holy laws of God. You ask me to give up this friendship; but why? Is it because of the Count? But it is by his wish that Byron is here. Is it because of what the World will say? But this World, whose acquaintance I have scarcely made, I have I think, already appraised; I have realized its vanity, its injustice, and its incapacity to fill a Heart and Soul that has any other than frivolous and vulgar needs. Is it for fear that the World may find a chance of exercising its malice? But it seems to me, from the little I have seen of it, that it does not need any behaviour to do so. And what would the world give me in return, to make up for the sacrifice that I should make – of this friend's hand that protects me – of his high intelligence – of his great soul which will be the illumination of my life to show me the right road? Are you asking this in the name of my peace, of my happiness? But where should I henceforth find happiness without him? It seems to me that if I never saw him again, there would be no Sun left in the sky for me. . . .

As for the Gossip spread about him by his enemies in Rome, I beg you to consider it only as a fable. To keep a young and innocent spouse shut up in a Castle, as in the days of Dante and Pia de' Tolomei – is that possible in our time? And where? In England, the land of Law and Liberty?'

Such calumnies, she added, were destroyed by their own absurdity. Yet even if they came down to the simple accusation that Lord Byron had been unkind to his wife –

'Well, I do not believe it. I have had constant proofs of the extreme goodness of his Heart! Tears of mental or physical suffering make him almost ill – the dread of treading on an ant makes him go out of his way – a scene at the play, a sad story or a melodious tune bring tears to his eyes.'

Like many another woman before her, Teresa confused sensibility with kindness. But at the end she added:

'As to the causes of his separation, I will learn them and tell you what they were. You must tell me in exchange the names of your reporters, and so we shall mutually illuminate each other.'*

But hardly had Teresa sent off her answer to her brother, than a much more disruptive letter than Pietro's arrived. This one – which also arrived upon a Friday – came from Venice. It was written to Byron by Hoppner who, from the first, had realized that Byron's affair with Teresa was likely to be more serious than his other Venetian episodes, and had looked upon it with a proportionate jealousy and disapproval. For Hoppner, like so many of Byron's friends, considered himself privileged to play the part of

* 'Vie', pp. 277-83. It should perhaps once again be emphasized that all letters by herself or others quoted by Teresa, of which we have not got the original, should be taken with some caution, as they are likely to have been touched up.

Mentor; and he was encouraged in his censoriousness by his narrow-minded, sanctimonious Swiss wife – a lady of whom, to judge by the consistent politeness of his behaviour to her, Byron was more than a little afraid. It was to her unloving but supposedly maternal care that poor little Allegra was, for a time, entrusted; and it was her report of the calumnies of a dismissed maid that, in the following year, started the abominable story about Shelley and Claire which Byron had the weakness either to believe, or to pretend that he believed.

But on this occasion her influence was hardly needed – for, from the day of Byron's arrival in Ravenna, a steady stream of letters from both Hoppner and Alexander Scott had followed him, attempting with every device to bring him back to Venice. Both Hoppner and Scott, it is clear, were consumed with jealousy – and both knew that Byron's most vulnerable point was his vanity. He would be capable of almost any disloyalty, rather than let his friends believe that he was seriously involved.

At first, however, Hoppner – uncertain of Byron's state of mind, and still expecting him to return soon to Venice – confined himself to dark, mysterious hints.

'It is a thousand pities, for your sake as well as my own,' he wrote, six days after Byron's arrival in Ravenna, 'that I dare not always speak to you as I think, but, if I tell you something for your own advantage, which immediately concerns another person, you directly acquaint that third person whence you received the information, then what was intended for your good alone, becomes a means of making me hated by others. As you take any delight in saying ill-natured things, you will not be surprised at the above remark, however puzzled you may be to guess at its meaning. And puzzled you must remain, and to your own cost.'⁵⁴

Byron's only reply was to send for his horses and carriage, and Hoppner's hints became broader.

'I am glad you amuse yourself so well, but would have you take care of the stiletto. A blow in the dark costs but little to people who are accustomed to make their passions stifle any appeal their conscience might foolishly attempt to make to them.'⁵⁵

This letter, however, crossed one from Byron which firmly stated:

'I can fix no time for my return to Venice – it may be soon or late – it all depends on the *Dama* –'⁵⁶

and within the same week he was sending, in the greatest urgency and distress, for Dr. Aglietti. To this request Scott replied, with some decency: 'With the suspense of illness, I will not venture to write other nonsense that I had in store for you.'[57] But Hoppner was restrained by no such fine feelings. Of Aglietti he could only say that he was doubtless impelled by 'two very powerful motives, the hope of getting a short respite from his official fatigues, and at the same time of earning a little money to exert his best rhetorical powers'. And as to Teresa – 'It is certainly very hard upon you, having gone to Ravenna for corporeal purposes alone, to have so cruel an attack made on your sensibility.'[58]

But then Byron wrote to Scott: 'The G. is better and will get well with prudence. Our amatory business goes on *well* and daily.'[59] Hoppner could bear it no longer; it was clear that Byron was becoming hopelessly involved and that it was his duty to save him. He accordingly sent off – on July 9th – the following singularly unpleasant letter, in which, after a few sentences about the accounts of the lease of Palazzo Mocenigo – he came straight to the point.

'I am very sorry for the distress you feel on the G.'s account, not only because I think in almost every such case they are good feelings thrown away on an unworthy object; but because I have reason to think it is particularly so in the present instance. Human nature is such that our greatest pleasures are derived from, and depend upon illusion, and it is therefore the more cruel in anyone who attempts to destroy those which make another happy though but for a moment: but I really cannot with patience see you throwing yourself away upon such people. While it is merely for your amusement, and thus the impression was only to be momentary, I should never interfere with your pleasures: but to hear you talking of a serious attachment to a woman, who under her circumstances would be unworthy of it, if it were only for her breach of duty in admitting it, and who in the present instance is reported avowedly not to return it, but to have entangled you in her nets merely from vanity, is what the friendship you have honoured me with does not allow me to witness without a remonstrance.

Perhaps you will think I am taking an unwarrantable liberty with you. It is your own fault, you have had repeated proofs of the frankness of my disposition, and since notwithstanding the disagreeable things I have before said to you, you have still tolerated me, you have given me a kind of right to speak my thoughts freely to you. Were it not so, it is the duty of every

man to endeavour to aid another in distress; and I see you over-
whelmed in a passion which is in every way unworthy of you, and
for one who, when she thinks herself sure of you, will leave you in
the lurch, and make a boast of having betrayed you. It may be
that considering her present illness I ought not to say these hard
things of the lady. But this is the last opportunity I shall have to
write to you for some time. Should her disorder prove fatal, what
I have said will appear not only particularly offensive, but
ridiculous, as there will be no time to prove the truth of it: if she
recovers, which I am sure I hope she may do, you will have
leisure and opportunity to discover that if I am not right in my
opinion of the fair G., I have been greatly deceived by what is
here said about her.'[60]

It is hardly possible to imagine a letter more profoundly galling
and disturbing to a man of Byron's character. All his weakest
points – his vanity, his pride, his fear of ridicule – were simultaneously attacked. It is, indeed, surprising – and an indication
that his tie with Teresa was stronger than he liked to admit – that
this letter did not bring about an immediate breach with her. But
it did leave an aftermath of doubt, suspiciousness and wounded
vanity which damaged their relationship for a considerable time
and which manifested themselves only too clearly in the reply he
sent off, not to Hoppner himself, but to Scott. This letter, indeed,
is a completely characteristic document of Byron at his most
caddish: the mask of bravado imperfectly concealing the deep
inner disquiet and fear of ridicule. What the letter, however, does
not show, is indifference towards Teresa.

BYRON TO ALEXANDER SCOTT[61]

July 12th, 1819

My dear Scott: I enclose you Hoppner's last letter – you will
understand *why* on reading it through. All his amiable bile is
gratis – and *unasked* – now I *ask you* and whatever you say on the
subject disagreeable will not be your fault but mine. – I never
supposed that the G. was to be a despairing shepherdess – nor
did I search very nicely into her motives – all I know is that *she*
sought me – and that I have *had her* – *there and here and everywhere* –
so that if there is any fool-making on the occasion I humbly
suspect that *two* can play at that – and that hitherto the parties
have at least an equal chance. – I have no hesitation in repeating

that I *love* her – but I have also *self-love* enough to be cured by the least change or trick on her part when I know it. Pride is one's best friend on such occasions. – As to her '*vanity*' (I wish it may – there is no passion so strong) in getting me as Hoppner says – *that* might be very well in an English woman – but I don't see how *English* poetical celebrity – or rank; is to operate upon an *Italian* – besides which I have no paramount character to go upon personally – at least in Italy – if he had said '*interest*' I should have thought him nearer the mark – though I have *no right hitherto* to assert even that. As you are much more in the way of hearing the *real truth or lie* than H. perhaps you will tell me to what Gossip he alludes – at any rate -you will tell it without *mystery* and *hints* and without *bile* – so pray do – I forgive whatever may be unpleasant in the intelligence – and it may be of use to me.

Pray answer by return of *Post* – lest I should be off again. I suppose this may possibly be some *cookery* between H. and Minghaldo – if it should not – *you* are fifty times more likely to know than he is – what does he mean by '*avowedly*' – does he suppose a woman is to go and '*avow*' her likings in the Piazza?

I should think her public *disavowal* the strongest proof – at least it is thought so in most women – what think you?

She is getting well very fast – all the rest as usual – and I very truly yours.   BYRON

P.S. Comp[limen]ts to Missiaglia.*

P.S. What does H. mean by '*when she is sure of me*'?_how '*sure*'? When a man has been for some time in the habit of . . . a female – methinks it is his own fault if the being 'left in the lurch' greatly incommodes him [. . . . . .] and unless he is a sighing swain – the accounts at parting are at least equal – if the lady takes another caprice. – Ebbene? Can't we match her in that too think you? And then let her boast of her 'betraying' . . . So corroborate or contradict that Consular Diogenes.

You should give me notice in time, that I may be the first to throw up the Cards.

There has been no public exhibition for I never go out with her – except twice or thrice in the Carriage – but I 'am *not in waiting*.

* Giovan Battista Missiaglia was the proprietor of the Apollo Library and the principal publisher and bookseller in Venice.

Give me but a proof or a good *tight suspicious confirmation* and I will rejoin you directly, and – we will village at the Mira – there is a bribe for you.

Of course I was perfectly aware that there would be a grand Benzonian Controversy – and much evil said and thought on the occasion – but all this was not in Hoppner's precise department so that I am '*rimasto*'! ! ! remember *you* and *I* can say and hear anything from one another – it is in *our line* – but I never gave him the right of *hinting* and teazing me out of temper.

You will think me a damned fool – but when she was supposed in danger – I was really and truly on the point of poisoning myself – and I have got the drug still in my drawer. If Hoppner is *not* gone ask him in a friendly way from *me* what he means – but *don't* show him this letter.

Dear Scott: I have forgotten one thing which will make you laugh. The *G's* brother wrote from Rome to their father here (I saw the letter) a long dissuasion against any 'relazione' with me – because (principally) I had for *molti anni incarcerato* – confined my wife in '*un suo castello*' in England of mine out of revenge!!! Tell this to Hoppner it is a good set-off to his letter. I suspect Mengaldo and Rizzo★ in Hoppner's diatribe – but be that as it may – I will never forgive H. for his gratuitous – bilious – officious inter-meddling. – He might at least have waited till asked.

I translated the enclosed to her *today* (the 12th) you may imagine her answer – of course she would be at no loss for that none of them are. She volunteered an elopement, saying, 'then instead of being at my mercy – I shall be at yours – for you have my letters in which I have not only exposed my feelings but my name – you have every proof that a man can have of my having been in earnest – and if you desire more – try me. Besides – what do they *know* of me at Venice? – you should judge by what they say of me here – if you like hearsay better than experience.'

All this you may say to Hoppner: from me – with my sentiments on his conduct into the bargain; – he is really intolerable.

The reference in the last postscript tells us that Teresa had by now shown Pietro's letter to Byron. It would be interesting to know whether she also showed him her reply – so much more loyal than his own.

★ Conte Francesco Rizzo-Patarol was a well-known Venetian gossip.

Scott appears to have answered Byron immediately, and to have disclaimed any share in Hoppner's accusations – but unfortunately to have added that Teresa was thought 'ridiculous' in Venice – a remark more calculated to damp Byron's feelings for her than the most serious calumnies. He did, indeed, refrain from showing that particular passage to Teresa.

'If I had told her that she was called and thought an absurd woman (which I carefully avoided) *there* indeed I should have been truly Hoppnerian. – You may tell a man that he is thought libertine – profligate – a villain – but not that his nose wants blowing or that his neck-cloth is ill tied. Suppose you were to say to that coxcomb Mengaldo that he was dangerous – disaffected – a severe disciplinarian in his regiment – that he had ill-used Carlotta Aglietti* – that he had been guilty of atrocities in his retreat from Moscow . . . he would affect but feel nothing – but if you told him his father sold eggs not very fresh – he would be wrath to a degree. I do not know whether I make myself understood – but it is in the little nooks of Character – where your two tormentors play the Mosquito and the Gadfly – and where such fellows as M[engaldo] and H[oppner] distil their little drop of venom. – Now I do maintain that I have always avoided this.'⁶²

His consideration for Teresa's feelings, however, did not go so far as to prevent him from telling her of Hoppner's other charges against her – and these distressed her so much that she insisted on at once writing to Scott herself.

Byron forwarded her letter with the comment:

'You will judge for yourself – knowing the people – I make no more pretensions to any kind of judgment satisfied that I am a damned fool . . . The letter was written at the other end of the room, with several persons talking all at once – so that you may make some allowance for the difficulties of the situation, to say nothing of that of the Subject.'⁶³

After all this, Teresa's own letter is unexpectedly brief, dignified and sincere; only the writing shows the depths of her distress.

* Carlotta Aglietti was the daughter of Professor Aglietti, whom Mengaldo had wished to marry.

CONTESSA GUICCIOLI TO ALEXANDER SCOTT

Mylord:* Byron has read me some parts of your last letter, which concerns me. What feelings it has awakened in me, you can easily imagine; but it is certain that not the least of them has been my sense of how great my obligation is towards you, and how great should be my Esteem. And therefore I do not blush or fear to take the liberty of sending you these lines, indeed I feel it to be my duty. To your great kindness I hope you will add yet another favour, and it is this: to give counsels of patience to those who are condemning me for future errors.

My life, Mylord, is, I may say, only a few months old; I am certain that no action of mine, either for good or bad, can strengthen my accusers and put them in the right; I therefore am astonished at the *sublime acuteness* of those people who can see, foresee and judge the future. – But I hope to receive my justification from another judge: Time. If you could see, Mylord, with how much firmness I am saying this word and with how much longing I am invoking that Time! But you know your friend well, you can, at least in part, imagine it. What a wretch I should consider myself if I feared that, one day, so great a man would blush to have loved me! But I am as sure of myself as I am of seeing the Sun again tomorrow.

I will not trouble you any more, Mylord. Forgive the liberty that I have taken, understand me, continue your courteous offices, and say that my crime is *one only, and always will be one*.

I thank you, Mylord, and wish you every happiness, which you well deserve.

Your most obedient and affectionate servant."

In the 'Vie' Teresa makes no reference to this correspondence. She merely reports that Hoppner wrote a long letter to Byron, 'repeating the thousand slanders which Byron's stay in Ravenna had awakened in Venice. Byron was irritated and made no reply'." Four months later, however, Byron did write to Hoppner, telling him that his letter

'displeased me very much: – not that it might not be true in its statement and kind in its intention, but you have lived long enough to know how useless all such representations ever are, and must be, in cases where the passions are concerned ... Upon that subject

* 'She has Mylorded you,' commented Byron, 'taking that for granted.'

we will (if you like) be silent. You might only say what would distress me without answering any purpose whatever.'⁶⁶

To this Hoppner replied with a lame apology though not a retraction:

'It grieves me heartily that my last letter made so sore an impression on you. I had no intention to give you pain . . . However I will now say no more, lest in blundering out an excuse I chance to make what is already bad worse.'⁶⁷

Hoppner's resentment, however, was never placated. Thirty-five years after Byron's death, in 1869, he was writing:

'I regret to learn that Madame Guiccioli has made so free with my name and opinions respecting Lord Byron. I hope she does not also say I enjoyed the advantage of her acquaintance in Venice, for although I cannot absolutely say I never saw her, I can safely assert the next thing to it . . . On one of those occasions [a call of Hoppner's on Byron] while he was at his breakfast, a female crossed the room, entering it on one side and leaving it at the opposite door, in whose appearance there was nothing to attract attention, and I actually took her for one of the maids of the house, learning only from him when she had passed that it was Madame Guiccioli. . . .'*

To Scott Byron had said that 'Hoppner was really intolerable'. But, for all that, he could not dismiss the incident from his mind. All his letters at this time show how deeply it rankled – not, indeed, from any real doubt of Teresa but merely from the festering dread of appearing ridiculous.

For this, he believed, there was only one remedy – and within a fortnight of Hoppner's letter he was telling Scott that he had other diversions in view.

---

* 'I certainly did not approve', he sanctimoniously added, 'the life Lord Byron led in Venice. In a previous letter I have said he led a foolish disreputable life: on which account I well remember to have told him that he made himself ridiculous in the eyes of everyone. I have little doubt it was his disgust with the very life he was leading which made him take a dislike to Venice, and glad of the opportunity the connection he at this time formed with Madame Guiccioli offered him to quit it altogether. It was pretty evident to me that he at first cared little for her, however much his vanity may have been flattered at seeing the impression he had made on a young lady of rank in society so different from the other women he had known since his arrival in Venice; and it depended on the toss-up of a halfpenny whether he would follow her to Ravenna or return to England.' *The Athenaeum*, May 22nd, 1869.

G

'I have something besides her [Teresa] on my hands and in my eye . . . There are better things in that line – in this part of the world than at Venice – besides – like the preserve of a Manor – this part has not yet been shot over.'⁶⁸

The reference is to Geltrude Vicari, Teresa's 'confidante "in white linen", a very pretty woman, noble also as her friend', about whom he had already written to Kinnaird. 'La Geltrude is gone to Bologna, after pinching her left thigh one evening. I was never permitted to set eyes on her *not no more*.'⁶⁹ The affair seems to have been of no importance and to have been entered into merely to show off to his friends. 'There are as good fish in the sea . . .' This is, of all the aspects of Byron's character, the most unpleasant – and there is nothing to be gained by dwelling on it.

'I doubt', he added to Kinnaird about Teresa, 'her liking anything for long, except one thing, and I presume she will soon arrive at varying even that, in which case I should be at liberty to repass the Po, and perhaps the Alps, but as yet I can say nothing.'⁷⁰

Yet, even while he was writing these letters, he was already determined to settle in Ravenna, by Teresa's side, for good – and by the end of the month he found himself obliged to communicate the news to his Venetian Mentors, so as to give them the necessary instructions about his horses and his numerous houses: the Palazzo Mocenigo, the 'Casino' at S. Maria Zobenigo and the Villa Foscarini at La Mira. 'I have taken my part, which is *not* to return to Venice.' But hastily he added: 'The G.s have no influence in this, for *they do* return in Winter – to pass some time.' And at the end of the letter, after sending greetings to his Venetian acquaintances: 'You need make no secret of my intended removal; but at the same time you may state the fact – which is – that the G.s have nothing to do with it.'⁷¹ Can he really have expected to be believed?

Scott, who for a long time had been expecting this decision, and had not answered Byron's previous letters, now replied by return of post:

'Your letter, so far from making me laugh, has made me sad. It has all the melancholy tinge of a last will and testament where one is not named. Give up your houses! Discharge your servants! Oibò! I will wait for your second thoughts . . . In one of your letters to H[oppner] you say that you were disposed to think well of the Venetians till they forced you to the contrary. How can that be? What have they done? I am in the dark and love the light. I know that the V[enetians] are idle, ignorant and vicious, – so am I, but that is no reason for incurring dislike ... For my part I can assure you that I never heard the Venetians talk of your life but with respect, and when they ask after you, 'tis with the same sort of solicitude as if they were asking after one of their own, whom they wished to return.'[72]

Contessa Benzoni's letters to Byron at this time, indeed, show an affectionate and spontaneous warmth which confirms Scott's assurances.

CONTESSA MARINA QUERINI-BENZONI TO BYRON[73]

You have forgotten all your friends in Venice [the first letter begins, without any preamble]. – This is a fault towards the others, but towards Marina and Beppe, to whom you are so dear, it is almost a crime. I am seeing very little of Scott, too: Madame Dempsen, the mother of Beppe Dempsen, took him away from me, she takes him to play chess at a café. So Marina has lost her two beloved Englishmen. Write me a line about yourself, tell me if you are happy and how you are faring. I have been told that Contessa Guiccioli is not well; I am sorry; pray greet her for me. I should have liked to see your little girl, but don't dare to look for her, where she is staying. In short I have nothing by me to remind me of you but my constant friendship, which will never be altered. Many greetings from Beppe, and pray write and command me anything for your affairs here, for Beppe and I will see to it very gladly. Farewell. Farewell.

Her second letter, too, strikes a most agreeable note, after Hoppner's and Scott's acidity.

My friend: I hear that you are in a place where you are *having some* trouble. If I did not think it would make someone sad, I would tell you to come back to us. I know that in Ravenna, too, you are much loved and respected: so it should be; I have been told too a great deal about the generosity of your heart. I was not surprised, but took a great pleasure in it. You are great not only in your head but in your heart. In the head there are some

G

singularities, which are hardly ever lacking in those who possess sublime talents – but that heart of yours is perfect. All the Englishmen who come here ask me at once about Lord Byron, which Mylord doesn't care a pin about, and they know it. A great many have gone through, in this summer season, but they do not stay long. Our Hoppners are in Switzerland; now that I know them better I like them very much, all the more because they are very fond of you.

All the Venetians are off to the country. I cannot tell you any anecdote, for I do not think there is a city more silent than this one, *à quelques bavardages près*, for Venice has a fault which it had not in its natural state, *Gossip*. Madame Albrizzi has gone to Florence to get reprinted her eulogies of Canova, who will soon be in Venice and who has given me two excellent busts, in gesso, of Laura and Tasso's Eleonora.

I am glad that your dear child is in such hands, *give her a kiss* [this is written in Venetian dialect]. Here is some Venetian which is so dear to you. Pray thank Countess Guiccioli for her message, and greet her for me. At the beginning of August I shall go to the country for a few days. If you have any commands, if I can do anything for you, go on writing to Venice. Count Rangone who speaks of you always as if you were his spoilt child, clasps your hand and is very, very fond of you.

Good day, good day. I am always your

MARINA QUERINI BENZONI[74]

Meanwhile at Ravenna life went on as before – until a fresh blow fell upon the two lovers. Count Guiccioli, whether in consequence of all the gossip, or because he genuinely had business on his estates near Bologna, suddenly decided to go there – and, since his wife was now fully recovered, saw no reason why she should not go with him.

Before the following two notes were written, the date of departure had already been decided, and the lovers had settled to meet again in Bologna.

BYRON TO CONTESSA GUICCIOLI[75]

Ravenna   *August 4th*, 1819

My treasure: Remember your portrait and my heart. – Farewell. What a moment! Farewell!   BYRON

My Treasure: Your reproaches are unjust; – Alessandro and your
father being present – and I not being able then to clasp you to
my heart – I kissed your hand and hurried away, so as not to show
my suffering, which would only too clearly have revealed the
whole, whole truth! I vow that I love you a thousand times more
than when I knew you in V[enice]. You know it – you feel it.
Think, my love, of *those* moments – delicious – dangerous – but –
happy, in every sense – not only for the pleasure, more than
ecstatic, that you gave me, but for the danger (to which you were
exposed) that we fortunately escaped. The hall! Those rooms!
The open doors! The servants so curious and so near – Ferdinando
– the visitors! how many obstacles! But all overcome – it has been
the real triumph of Love – a hundred times Victor.*

 Farewell – my only Treasure – my one Hope. Farewell – I kiss
you untiringly from my heart – and am ever yours.

P.S. Send me the note about *Dante's tomb* with your name in it.
I saw it on your little table the day before yesterday, – Love me
as I love you.

 The address will be as we agreed – in case I arrive in B[ologna]
on the day suggested.

 What does a.a.a. mean in your very dear booklet?

 Do not forget to send someone to Imsom† to tell him to hand
over my letters only to someone sent by you.

 I have just received yours. I swear I will kiss nothing but *that*
remembrance of you until I see you again. Farewell!

Before going to Bologna, however, Count Guiccioli and his wife
visited their estates near Forlì – and from here the Count 'who'
according to Teresa, 'had a great deal of wit and was flattered by
the friendly manners of Lord Byron', sent Byron an invitation.
His writing – of which we possess only this example – is as rigid
and cramped as the descriptions of his bearing, and the letter
consists merely of two formal sentences, acknowledging Byron's
'delightful letter', and asking him to 'come and see this poetic
place of ours'. This, according to Teresa, was 'a great and noble

* Byron referred to these same risks in a letter to Hoppner on June 20th. 'The
local is inconvenient (no *bolts* and be d—d to them) and we run great risks (were it
not at sleeping hours after dinner) and no place but the great saloon at his own palace.'
Unpublished passage. The rest of the letter is in *L.J.*, IV, p. 318.
† Cristoforo Insom (not Imsom) was Byron's banker in Bologna.

residence, that had been an abbey and had been transformed by him [Guiccioli] into a fine summer residence'. Teresa herself was so charmed by it that, desiring extremely to show it to Lord Byron, she added to the Count's letter a second pressing note in her most romantic vein.

Come, Mylord: pray do not fear that noise or callers may disturb you – here all is nature and tranquillity. One hears no sound but that of the wind shaking the leaves of the trees, and the sweet song of birds. On Sunday morning we shall leave for Bologna, and tomorrow we shall make an excursion to Faenza, returning to Forlì at eight in the evening. So we could spend the evening together, walking in the garden, where we need not fear, as at Ravenna, the bad effects of the evening dew.[76]

To both these invitations Byron answered with a refusal.

BYRON TO CONTE ALESSANDRO GUICCIOLI[77]

Ravenna   *August 7th*, 1819

My dear Chevalier: I write my answer in English to the letter, which I had the honour of receiving from you and your consort, for fear of 'spropositi' in Italian. I am very sorry that it will not be in my power to be at Forlì tomorrow evening, as I must wait for the post of Domenica; but on Lunedì I intend to set out for Bologna, where I shall try to discover your Palazzo Savioli. My auberge will be the Pellegrino. I make no apology for troubling you in English, which you understand better than I can write in Italian, and even if you do not, I would rather be unintelligible in my own tongue than in yours. . . .

My time has passed in a melancholy manner since your departure. Ferdinando and I have been riding as usual, and he told me a sad story of Madam's losses – *un anello, una catena e dei quattrini* . . . I regretted to hear that you had *sospetti* of *Ferd.* about the scudi which disappeared: surely he would be the last person to be guilty of such a thing.

I desire my best respects to the Contessa your gentle Consort and with many thanks for your kind invitation and in the hopes of seeing you in Bologna in a few days, believe me to be very gratefully and affectionately yours.   BYRON

The lost ring to which Byron referred and about which, in his next letter, he reproached Teresa, had a very odd history. 'You ask me', wrote Rangone's diligent correspondent, Conte della Torre, 'for more anecdotes about Lord Byron,' – and proceeded to tell him that Teresa's 'anglico amante' had presented her, on the very evening of the Cardinal's Conversazione, with a valuable ring. But now a problem arose: how could she wear it in her husband's presence? Once again the help of the obliging Abate Perelli was required. He had the ring valued and brought it to Count Guiccioli, offering it to him at only one third of its value, – in order, he said, to save from ruin a poor family, whose last treasure it was. The Count hesitated; Teresa pretended to be reluctant to spend so large a sum; the priest reproved her for lack of charity; the Count, ever unable to resist a good bargain, joined forces with him – and finally bought for his wife, for one hundred scudi, a ring which, he was told, had been valued at three hundred and fifty.

And then Teresa lost it, and did not dare to tell Byron! And the whole story – which, of course, everyone in Ravenna knew except the Count – was sent off to Rangone, and carefully set down in his *Cronaca* – to be confirmed for us, after 130 years, by Byron's letters.

BYRON TO CONTESSA GUICCIOLI

Ravenna   *August 7th*, 1819

My Treasure: I have written an answer in English to A[lessandro]. I am extremely sorry not to see you again in Forlì, but very soon (on Monday or Tuesday) I hope to arrive in Bologna. I am writing in some anxiety as to the fate of this letter – for I must trust it to my Courier. I hope however that Fortune will not forsake two lovers at such a point.

So you have lost the *ring* – without saying a single word to me! This is a lack of trust which surprises and hurts me, who have never made any mysteries with *you*. I cannot say more now. I love you+++++++++* Do you understand me? For us there can be few crosses holier than these.

You cannot imagine how much our separation is distressing me. I long to see you again, but I tremble, believing myself always about to lose you – and I feel anxious – for that head of

* These crosses are the same symbol that Byron and Augusta used in writing to each other. Cf. *Astarte*, p. 58 and passim.

yours is an enigma – and *you have no heart*. I can see you reading these last words – '*Oh Fury!*' as the tyrant says in our comic plays. Alas! *no longer comic* since your departure. The theatre has become a desert – I dare not look at your box. Don't think that I am saying seriously that you have no heart. You have one – for dress? *This* was only an English compliment; an ultramontane joke. *It is my revenge* – not for the *loss of the ring*, but for showing me little trust, in keeping silence' about it.

Farewell, my dearest *Evil* – farewell, my torment – farewell, my *all* (but *not all mine!*) I kiss you more often than I have ever kissed you – and this (if Memory does not deceive me) should be a fine number of times, counting from the beginning. Meanwhile, – you can be sure of me – of my love – and of your power. 'I pray for peace.'[78] Love me – not as I love you – that would be too much for your kind heart – but as you love your *Elmò*.* Farewell. I kiss you 1000000 times with my whole heart, insatiably.

Three days later, on August 10th, the lovers met again in Bologna.

* Elmò was Teresa's dog.

3: BOLOGNA–LA MIRA–VENICE

All this comes of reading Corinne.

BYRON

'I WRITE in haste', wrote Byron to Murray on August 9th, 'tomorrow I set off for Bologna – I write to you with thunder, lightning, etc., and all the winds of heaven whistling through my hair, and the racket of preparation to boot. My "Mistress dear" who hath "fed my heart upon smiles and wine" for the last two months, set off with her husband for Bologna this morning, and it seems that I follow him at three tomorrow morning.'[1] The next day Byron was in Bologna.

On his arrival he first went to live in the *Locanda del Pellegrino*, where he had stayed in June, and after a few days he took some rooms in an eighteenth-century palazzo, in Via Galliera, quite close to Palazzo Savioli, where the Guicciolis lived. Byron's apartment, which consisted of only three or four rooms, decorated in the Empire style, looked out into a small garden, and some furniture was soon provided for it by Teresa's servants.[2] He never, however, actually lived there, since Guiccioli soon put at his disposal some rooms on the ground floor of the Palazzo Savioli, into which he moved, using the Palazzo Merendoni only as a lodging for his servants and a place to entertain his Bolognese acquaintances.

In Bologna, as in every other town he visited, Byron's daily life was observed by the police with an anxious and unceasing assiduity. In the concerto of his life in Italy, their activities resemble the part of the 'basso obbligato' – ceaselessly reiterating, however many variations the main theme may offer, its monotonous and persistent accompaniment. The archives of Venice and Bologna, of Ravenna, Florence, Pisa and Lucca, and above all of the Vatican, still contain the fruits of their researches: long, dull, often half-illiterate reports, which note the most trivial and insignificant details about the dangerous British Lord. For the Governments of Austria, of the Papal States and of Tuscany were all agreed in this: Byron was not merely a dissolute nobleman, a dilettante traveller; he was a dangerous freethinker, an emissary of Liberalism, to be kept under constant supervision. And so, wherever he went, a trail of obscure and painstaking spies followed in his wake – opening his letters, talking to his servants, watching outside his doors, noting the names of his visitors and the times at which he got up and went to bed, and interpreting these facts as best they could for the benefit of their respective

Governments. For all these spies, poor fellows, were greatly handicapped: they were so much in awe of the great Lord, that they did not dare to approach him!

'I do not conceal from Your Excellency', said a report to the Director General of Police in Rome, 'that this news [of Byron's arrival] both perplexes and embarrasses me. Byron is a man of letters, and his literary merits will attract to him the most distinguished men of learning in Bologna. This class of men has no love for the Government. Your Excellency sees, therefore, how difficult it becomes for me to exercise the necessary supervision over Mylord's private affairs.'[3]

It is, indisputably, very difficult to spy upon a man effectively under these circumstances. But in Bologna – as subsequently in Ravenna and Pisa – the Government's emissaries did their best. The most formidable of them was the Tuscan spy Giuseppe Valtancoli of Montepulciano, who was playing a double part: on the one hand, on behalf of Austria, he was to foment a rebellion in the Romagna, so as to provide a pretext for an Austrian armed intervention, and thus pave the way for the annexation of the Romagna; while at the same time he was persuading the Liberals that they would receive help from their Tuscan sympathizers, provided they consented to being annexed to the Grand Duchy. In these transactions Guiccioli – on his usual principle of keeping on good terms with both sides – seems to have taken part.[4] Valtancoli was greatly assisted by his position as an ex-Freemason, since he had once been a member of the Masonic Lodge of Pisa, and had then obtained possession of secret papers and emblems belonging to the Lodge.[5]

The question of the connection between the Freemasons and the Carboneria is an exceedingly complicated one.[6] As early as 1813, information was sent to Eugène de Beauharnais, the Grand Master of the Milanese Freemasons, about a 'semi-masonic' *corporazione de' Carbonari*, which in Naples alone already numbered 40,000 members, all of the lower classes, 'whose object is nothing less than the overthrow of the monarchic governments in Italy, in order to replace them by republics'.[7] Within the next few years the movement spread all over the country, especially in the south, where many adherents were attracted, as they had been to Freemasonry, by the complex symbolism and mysteries of the new society. Their romantic titles and complicated degrees of hierarchy, their secret rites and passwords and dark, terrifying penalties, held the appeal of the *secret*, the occult, to which, in the

Carboneria, was added a more explicitly Christian element. Its members worshipped Jesus Christ, – 'our Redeemer and our Model', as they called him in their oath of allegiance, – and they believed in a revival of Christian brotherhood. Their patron saint was S. Theobald of Brie – who, in the eleventh century, gave up his country, his high rank and his fortune to live as a charcoal-burner in the forests of Swabia. The world, in the symbolism of the Carboneria, was a Forest, and 'to rid the forest of its wolves' was to free the world from its tyrants. All the members of the order, in whatever country they lived, were 'Good Cousins', and met in lodges called 'Vendite'; all those who did not belong to the order were called 'Pagans'.

The solemn oath taken at his initiation by a new member – 'a Pagan wandering in the Forest' – included a promise to maintain complete secrecy in all matters pertaining to the Society, to 'come to the aid of all Good Cousins in their need, and to respect the honour of their families'. And it ended with the words: 'If I break my oath, let my body be torn to pieces and burned and my ashes scattered to the winds, so that my name may be a lesson to other Good Cousins, all over the earth.'[8] The member who betrayed the Order's secrets was subject to the most severe penalties: his name was inscribed, 'for general execration', in the Black Book of the Order; he was boycotted by every other member and deprived of 'fire and water', and his name, or a little effigy of his person, was burned in the presence of the assembled members – while in some cases (since it was declared to be no crime to take away the life of a traitor) he was condemned to be killed by another member of the Order, chosen by lot. Moreover penalties hardly less severe were inflicted on the Good Cousins who transgressed against the austere rules of life of the Order – the punishable crimes including conjugal infidelity, drunkenness and gambling.[9]

In 1818 a Congress of the Carboneria was held in the Palazzo Hercolani in Bologna, at which the *Costituzione Latina* was approved. This Constitution regulated the position and duties of all the branches of the Movement in Italy, whose members took a solemn oath of 'eternal hatred against all monarchies', and swore to 'give all their strength and even their lives to achieve the independence of Italy'.[10] Bologna thus became the centre of the subversive activities of Northern Italy, and when Byron, already doubly suspect as an Englishman and a Liberal, arrived there, it was perhaps not unnatural that the Austrian and Papal Governments should have regarded him with some suspicion. Great then was the satisfaction of Valtancoli, when he was able to report from Bologna on October 4th, 1819, that

'The constant watch kept by the police upon Lord Byron has led to two discoveries. The first is that his Lordship wears on his watch-chain a triangular (or rather pyramidal) seal, on the face of which are engraved three small stars; on the seal are cut the letters F.S.Y. This is the new signal adopted some months ago by the Guelph Society.'

The second 'discovery' was that a letter in the handwriting of Byron's secretary [Lega Zambelli?] addressed to a certain Alexis Gartner in Milan, contained an extract from 'a very curious and very rare work of Captain George Smith, on Jesuitical Masonry'.[11]

Thenceforth the Austrian and Papal Governments felt confirmed in their conviction: the true object of Byron's residence in Italy lay neither in his literary pursuits nor in his amorous adventures, but in the destruction of the established Government:

'The Romantici form a band that aims at the destruction of our literature, our politics, our country. Lord Byron is certainly its champion, and you deceive yourself if you believe that he is only occupied in making a cuckold of Guiccioli. He is libidinous and immoral to excess; but he soon tires of the object of his worship, and offers it as a sacrifice on the altar of his contemptuous pride. But, at the same time, in politics he is not so inconstant. Here he is an Englishman in the fullest meaning of the term. He is like a madman in his desire to ruin everything that does not belong to him, to paralyse every tendency that our society displays towards natural independence, to involve us in ruin and bloodshed, in order that at last the deserted and still smouldering States may be divided among his greedy and demoralized conspirators.'[12]

It is a curious, dark little world, that these emissaries observe through their spy-glasses. Through their eyes we can see Byron in Bologna like a figure in a distorted mirror; he walks towards us and away again, deformed and always slightly out of focus. 'He is not unknown as a man of letters, and in his own country has a reputation of being a fine poet.' He is in Bologna only in order to found a branch of the Società Romantica, and will soon be joined there, for the same purpose, by Lady Morgan and by 'Lord Kinnaird, who shot at the Duke of Wellington'. He has written for the Romantici a set of rules entitled 'Statutes of the Joyous Company'. 'He has with him a young secretary, very expert in different languages, who corresponds in English, French, Italian and German with equal facility.' (The identity of this interesting character is unknown; he can hardly have been Lega Zambelli! But a later note suggests that the reporter meant Kinnaird – who had left Italy a year before.)

'By most careful supervision it has been discovered that his [the secretary's] time is chiefly occupied in writing in various cyphers. But it is not known in what way these writings are dispatched, for they are certainly not sent to the post. There is reason to believe that English travellers, many of whom have introductions to my Lord, are charged with these dispatches.'[13]

On October 25th, when, in actual fact, Byron was at La Mira with Teresa, he is reported to be 'at the Borromean Islands in a pleasant rural retreat, occupying the country-house of his august friend the Princess of Wales'. At Lugano, on December 8th, an anonymous English traveller obligingly supplies the information that Byron's time on the Lakes was spent in circulating 'a number of copies of one of his detestable works entitled *Don Juan*, a work which attacks religion, morals and the Government – and as soon as he had distributed these copies he retired to Venice'. The traveller also told the spy 'that Lord Byron made a regular practice of changing his residence immediately after he had finished a work, so that the Italian Governments might not suspect his intentions'.[14]

So it goes on, until we sometimes almost begin to wonder whether indeed this queer distorted world is the real one. And as if this police espionage were not enough, we then discover that yet other eyes and ears were following the poet's doings in Bologna, not indeed for the same reason, but still watching and listening in ante-rooms and passages, and gleaning everything that could be gleaned secondhand, from friends or acquaintances or servants – all for the sheer love of gossip. This other observer, who spared no pains to make himself agreeable in every direct encounter with Byron, was Count Francesco Rangone, who was now able to call on him every day, and to keep a detailed account of how he spent his time.

'He is invisible', Rangone wrote, 'till three p.m. At four he goes to see his Lady, and remains there until six. He rides for an hour, always in the great Cemetery. At eight he dines, at nine goes to his Amica and remains there until midnight. He studies until dawn. What he does until three remains a mystery. He eats and drinks little. But', the Count added, 'he does not much like conversation nor seeing what is worth seeing. He lets others talk and says little. He makes himself agreeable, but his expression clearly reflects the moods of his changeable humour.'¹⁵

For indeed at this time Byron, besides being bored by Rangone, was in one of his most melancholy and tormented moods — 'the penalties', as he himself called them, 'of the life I have always lived'. 'I am out of sorts,' he wrote to Murray, 'out of nerves, and now and then (I begin to fear) out of my senses.'¹⁶ A few days after his arrival he went with the Guicciolis to the theatre, to see a performance of Alfieri's *Myrrha*, a play whose subject (the incestuous love of Myrrha for her father and her persecution by the Furies) sufficed to evoke the ghosts that haunted his own darker moods. 'The two last acts', he told Murray, 'threw me into convulsions. I do not mean by that word a lady's hysterics, but the agony of reluctant tears and the choking shudder, which I do not often undergo for fiction.'¹⁷ Poor Teresa, though sufficiently prone herself to exhibitions of sensibility, did not know what to make of it, and 'went off in the same way. I believe more from fright than any other sympathy — at least with the players; but she has been ill, and I have been ill, and we are all languid and pathetic this morning, with great expenditure of sal volatile'. Teresa, in her account of this evening, put it all down to the skill of the actress, Mme Pelzet, who played the part of Myrrha. 'Byron was affected', she wrote, 'to the point of fainting, and — unable any longer to hide his convulsions of tears and sobs — he hurriedly left the box.'¹⁸

After this upsetting evening, Teresa not unnaturally decided to go to the play very seldom — 'preferring more gentle sensations to these violent emotions', — and while the Count continued to frequent the theatre and the Bologna assemblies, she spent her evenings at home with Byron. Her rooms, on the second floor of the Palazzo Savioli, looked out on an enchanting garden, with a little fountain in its midst and a pergola of vines — and here the two lovers enjoyed the beauty of the soft summer nights. 'This sweet existence, however,' says Teresa, 'was interrupted by an expedition which the Countess was obliged to make with the Count on a visit to his estates between Bologna and Ferrara' — a place called Molinella, at the south of the Po.¹⁹ And now Byron, alone in Bologna in the stifling midsummer heat, decided to send for his small daughter Allegra* for company. It was, indeed, time for someone to concern himself with poor little Allegra. In the preceding winter, at the age of two and a half, she had been

---

* The illegitimate daughter of Byron and Claire Clairmont, who was now three years old.

entrusted to the charge of the Hoppners, who – while smugly taking full credit for 'saving' the child from the atmosphere of Palazzo Mocenigo and the immoral influence of 'Mme la Boulangère' – failed to give her what every child needs most – affection.

'She was not by any means an amiable child,' wrote Hoppner, 'nor was Mrs. Hoppner or I particularly fond of her, but we had taken her to live with us, not thinking Lord Byron's house . . . a very proper one for the infant or her nurse, a young Swiss girl, who besides, had no kind of experience as to the care of children.'[20]

A letter from Mrs. Hoppner to Mrs. Shelley, written while the child was staying with them, contains several comparisons to Allegra's disadvantage, between her and Mrs. Hoppner's own little boy. He, the letter says, was far quicker than she; his feet were always warm and hers like bits of ice, he was 'toujours gai et sautillant', and she 'tranquille et sérieuse comme une petite vieille'.

'Je crois toujours,' Mrs. Hoppner added, tightening her lips, 'que c'est très malheureux que Miss Clairmont oblige cette enfant de vivre à Venise, dont le climat est nuisible en tout au physique de la petite et vraiment, pour ce que fera son père, je trouve un peu triste d'y sacrifier l'enfant. My lord continue de vivre dans une débauche affreuse, qui tôt ou tard le mènera à la misère, puisqu'il dépense au dela de son révenu. J'envoye Allegra aussi souvent que possible lui faire visite, mais comme il n'est visible qu'après trois heures, c'est trop tard pour la petite. D'ailleurs, quand elle va voir son papa, Madame la Boulangère s'en empare, et lui donne à boire et à manger des choses qui font du mal à l'enfant. . . .'[21]

When the spring came, the Hoppners attempted to persuade Byron to send the child, who was suffering from the heat of Venice, to be educated in Switzerland – 'where her health is less exposed than it is here, and her chances of education better'.[22] But Byron would have none of it – and now, in the height of the August heat, the child was still in Venice and had just been transferred by the Hoppners from one indifferent stranger to another: first to an Italian family and then to the care of Mrs. Martens, the wife of the Danish Consul. It was at this point that Byron told Scott to send the child to join him – only to learn that her nurse had been dismissed at the beginning of June, and that there was consequently no one to travel with her.

'When I left Venice', he wrote to Scott, 'my daughter had a
Governante – of course I supposed that she had one still. Let one
be obtained (but not that foolish woman Mrs. Edgecombe on any
account) and let Allegra be sent accompanied by Edgecombe the
moment this is received. You need not be alarmed about the
"Dama" – I wish to see my child – and have her with *me* – now
that Hoppner is no longer in Venice – and her being with me will
not prevent my return.' 'I send this by express', he added at the
end of the letter – 'that Allegra may set out without loss of time –
you can surely find a proper woman to accompany her. And
Edgecombe must come too.'²³

The reference to the 'Dama' was in reply to a letter from
Alexander Scott, who had warmly approved the Swiss plan for the
child ('No female education in Italy'),²⁴ and who had now written
to expostulate about Byron's new idea.

'Allow me to tell you what I think on the subject – Allegra,
once in the hands of your "Dama" (you will not keep her at a
hotel) will be a hostage for your future conduct, and if she should
be taken to Ravenna, and if she should there be put in a convent, it
will be no easy matter to get her out again. Has the Count any
male children? Has he asked what *Dote* you mean to give her?'
Moreover, Scott added that Allegra lived in a family 'where there
are a lot of girls, all very attentive to her, and is as happy as
childhood may be.'*

This last consideration would probably not, in any case, have
weighed much with the child's Papa, and the suggestion in the first
part of the letter only reinforced his determination. On August
28th he was writing again, 'I must have her sent immediately,
with or *without* a Governante – or *Edgecombe* shall instantly quit my
service.'²⁵

At last, at the end of the month, the little girl did arrive – 'a
child of quite particular amiability', according to Rangone –
while Byron took considerable pleasure in observing her increasing
resemblance to himself. Like Augusta, he wrote, she could not
pronounce her 'r's. She was a true Byron; she had the same dimple
in her chin, the same scowl, the same white skin and soft voice, and
'particular liking of music, and her own way in everything'.²⁶
Byron sat by the fountains in the garden of Palazzo Savioli and

* August 18th, 1819. Allegra was not yet four years old, but Scott's idea was not
quite so preposterous as it might seem, for in October 1821, after Allegra had been
sent to the convent school at Bagnacavallo, a police report noted, 'It is said that
Gamba, the brother of Contessa Guiccioli, will marry Byron's child.'

watched her play. He taught her to say 'Buon di, Papà' – and then he forgot all about her again.

To pass the time he allowed Rangone to introduce to him some of the literary men of Bologna – the Abate Macchiavelli, the writer Michele Leoni, and the famous philologist Mons. Mezzofanti, 'a Master of Languages, the Briareus of parts of Speech',[27] of whom Stendhal said, 'quoique si savant, il n'est pas bête'.[28] Once again he rode out to the Cemetery and talked to his old friend the Custodian, taking a ghoulish pleasure in imagining the face of his pretty fifteen-year-old daughter, if it were divested of its flesh. He had a row, which nearly ended in a duel, with a captain of Dragoons who tried to sell him a bad horse. He wrote an exasperated letter to Murray about some requested alterations in 'Donny Johnny'. But he could not really feel much interest in anything. Teresa was away and 'as I could never live for but one human being at a time . . . I feel alone and unhappy'.[29]

'I have to do', he wrote, 'with a woman rendered perfectly disinterested by her situation in life, and young and amiable and pretty – in short as good, and at least as attentive as anything of the sex can be, with all the advantages and disadvantages of being scarcely twenty years old and only two out of her Romaguolo convent at Faenza.

But I feel – and I feel it bitterly – that a man should not consume his life at the side, and on the bosom of a woman, and a stranger; that even the recompense, and it is much, is not enough, and that this Cicisbean existence is to be condemned.

But I have neither the strength of mind to break my chain, nor the insensibility which would deaden its weight. I cannot tell what will become of me – to leave, or to be left would at present drive me quite out of my senses; and yet to what have I conducted myself?

I have, luckily, or unluckily, no ambition left; it would be better if I had, it would at least awake me; whereas at present I merely start in my sleep.'[30]

He started, but he was not roused. His melancholy, indeed, at this time had something of the unhappiness of dreams – vague, haunting and pervasive. By Moore it was described in highly romantic terms, which seemed to Teresa so apt that she transcribed them in the 'Vie'.

'That spring of natural tenderness within his soul, which neither the world's efforts nor his own had been able to chill or

H

choke up, was now, with something of its first freshness, set
flowing once more. He again knew what it was to love and be
loved – too late, it is true, for happiness, and too wrongly for
peace, but with devotion enough, on the part of the woman, to
satisfy even his thirst for affection, and with a sad earnestness, on
his own, a foreboding fidelity, which made him cling but the more
passionately to this attachment, from feeling that it would be his
last.'[31]

He tried to assuage his loneliness by visiting the Palazzo
Savioli – since Teresa had left him the keys of her rooms and of the
garden. He sat 'under a purple canopy of grapes', by the edge of
the little stone fountain, thinking of Teresa – and one day (so he
told Moore later on) 'there came suddenly into his mind such
desolate fancies, such bodings of the misery he must bring on her
he loved', that he was overtaken by a passionate fit of weeping.
Then he wandered back into the empty house and began to turn
over the books in Teresa's sitting-room. Among them was her
favourite novel, *Corinne*, which she had often read with him – and
about which, in future, he was often to laugh at her. But now he
was in no mood for mockery. He turned over its pages, marked a
passage here and there – and on the index page wrote the famous
letter which, although already familiar, must have a place in this
narrative.

My dearest Teresa: I have read this book in your garden; – my
love, you were absent, or else I could not have read it. It is a
favourite book of yours, and the writer was a friend of mine.
You will not understand these English words, and *others* will not
understand them, which is the reason I have not scrawled them
in Italian. But you will recognize the handwriting of him who
passionately loved you, and you will divine that, over a book which
was yours, he could only think of love. In that word – beautiful
in all languages, but most so in yours – *Amor mio* – is comprised
my existence here and hereafter. I feel I exist here, and I fear
that I shall exist hereafter, – to *what* purpose you will decide;
my destiny rests with you, and you are a woman, eighteen
years of age, and two out of a convent. I wish that you had staid
there, with all my heart, – or, at least, that I had never met you
in your married state.

But all this is too late. I love you, and you love me, – at least
you *say so* and act as if you *did* so, which last is a great consolation

in all events. But *I* more than love you, and cannot cease to love you.

'Think of me, sometimes, when the Alps and the ocean divide us, but they never will, unless you *wish* it.   BYRON[32]

Teresa kept among her 'relics' the book in which this letter was written, a fat little volume of very small print, bound in purple plush, with Byron's letter written in the blank spaces of the index. A number of passages are underscored in the same ink as the letter. 'I had learned to love', runs one of them, 'from the poets, but real life is not like that. There is in the realities of existence something arid, which every effort is vain to alter.'[33] Another marked passage is in the same vein. It describes how Domenichino, when poor and in prison, assuaged the tedium of his imprisonment by adorning with frescoes the walls of his cell. 'But', the writer continues, 'his sufferings were caused by exterior circumstances, his trouble was not in his soul. *When it is there, nothing can be done. The source of everything is dried up.*'[34]

Finally, at the bottom of page 92, there is a footnote in Byron's handwriting: 'I knew Madame de Staël well – better than she knew Italy, but I little thought that, one day, I should *think with her thoughts* ... She is sometimes right, and often wrong, about Italy and England; but almost always true in delineating the heart.'[35]

On her return to Bologna, Teresa asked Byron for a translation of what he had written in her book; but this he refused, as he had also previously refused to translate a note which he had written in her copy of *Jacopo Ortis*. 'Lord Byron', Teresa comments, 'never made a show of his sensibility; expressions of it only left his lips or his pen against the grain, and almost involuntarily.'[36]

And then – life at the Palazzo Savioli began again, as before.

Byron at this time was still on the most amicable terms with Count Guiccioli – and was engaged in furnishing (with furniture which he had sent for from Venice) the rooms which the Count had put at his disposal in Palazzo Savioli.

'Doubtless', says Teresa, 'one might call this imprudent, and attribute it to a great many other motives, but the truth cannot be understood without admitting first of all that the Count was a man different from others – an eccentric – seeing everything from his own particular point of view – and often very indulgent and almost generous ... One must however add to this explanation, that he not only, as a man of intelligence, found Byron agreeable

H

and was flattered by his preference and his intimacy, but that he had at the moment a particular reason to oblige him, for he was asking a favour.'[27]

The favour was a very odd one: that Guiccioli should be given, 'without salary or emolument', the post of British Vice-Consul at Ravenna. The Count's reason for wishing this post, according to Teresa, was that he was on the worst possible terms with the Papal Government, which had intervened against him in a law-suit – because, Teresa affirms, his opponent had succeeded in currying favour with the Clergy by sending to Rome 'some relics and so-called bodies of Saints'. Guiccioli believed that the post of Consul to a great foreign nation would protect him against the Papal Government and enable him to obtain various privileges – and accordingly we find Byron writing in the most pressing terms to John Murray on his behalf.

'He is a man of very large property, – noble, too, – but he wishes to have a British protection, in case of changes ... That his office might be useful, I know; as I lately sent off from Ravenna to Trieste a poor devil of an English sailor, who had remained there, sick, sorry and penniless (having been set ashore in 1814) from the want of any accredited agent able or willing to help him homewards.'[*] Moreover, he assured Murray, 'In case of accidents in Italy, he [the Count] would be no feeble adjunct – as you would think if you knew his property.'[28]

The case was pressed by Byron with unusual fervour. 'I can assure you, I should look upon it as a great obligation; but alas! that very circumstance may, very probably, operate to the contrary.' He even went so far as to suggest that he himself should be made Consul, 'that I may make him my Vice' – a suggestion which, if it had been carried out, would have added yet one more absurdity to the tangled tragi-comedy soon to be enacted in Ravenna.

But long before Murray's answer could arrive events had taken another turn. According to Teresa's subsequent account to her lawyers, Count Guiccioli, when he rented the ground-floor of his

---

[*] The sailor was a John Dodd, who having fallen from the rigging was set ashore from 'the *Nancy* Transport'. Byron not only provided him with funds for his journey to Trieste, but gave him an open letter of recommendation. 'According to the best confirmation I could obtain, his story is true and his case is a hard one. I therefore recommend him, as far as lies in my power, to the aid of his more fortunate fellow-citizens.' The letter is signed 'Byron–Peer of England' (Keats-Shelley Memorial Library, Rome).

palace to Byron, took also the opportunity of borrowing a considerable sum from his tenant. In Bologna, however, –

'since he had to make a heavy payment to the Casa Balloccanti in Brescia, and as he had already experienced Mylord's generosity, he again turned to Lord Byron for a very large sum of money. Lord Byron promised it, but having been warned by his banker, Imson, that Count Guiccioli was not acting in good faith, he excused himself from giving it, saying that his banker had not at the moment sufficient funds at his disposal.'

The Count then lost his temper and said that it was all Teresa's fault – and when she told him that she had had another relapse and must go to Venice to consult Dr. Aglietti again, he declared that he himself had to return to Ravenna on urgent business; his wife might go to Venice if she pleased, and take Lord Byron for her escort. – 'Cosa', she herself comments, 'appena credibile!'[39]

This story, credible or not, is told in a much milder form by Teresa in the 'Vie'. There she merely states that, the Count having a large payment suddenly due to a firm in Brescia,

'Lord Byron lent him, *du soir au matin*, the sum he needed – a few thousand francs, a sum insignificant to both of them and especially to Count Guiccioli, whose fortune was colossal, and far more considerable than Byron's at that time ... The Count', she adds, 'never had any other business with Lord Byron, except for the apartment which he rented to him at Ravenna in the following year.'[40]

Which of these two versions are we to believe? It is possible that Teresa exaggerated the story when, for the purpose of her lawsuit, it was to her interest to show the Count in the worst possible light. Or, on the other hand, she may have preferred, in later years, for the sake of everyone concerned, to record the less unpleasant version.

What is certain is that Guiccioli was called back to Ravenna on business, and that, whatever his motives may have been, he allowed his wife, 'in view of her delicate health, shaken by so many emotions', to set off to consult Dr. Aglietti in Venice, in Byron's company.

'You suggested', says Teresa's Confession to her husband, 'another travelling companion, but I insisted on having Byron, to whom you added my maid and the oldest servant of our house-

hold, and I promised to stay in the apartment that you ordered
Lega, then your steward, to prepare for me.'[41]

As to the opinion of the world, it is reported for us by the
Austrian spy: 'Lord B. departed suddenly with Madame Guiccioli,
who was therefore said to have been either carried off by him or
sold to him by her husband.'*

So now at last the two lovers were on the road to Venice.
Teresa in her husband's coach-and-six, with her maid and her
manservant—Byron following in his own great travelling-
carriage. 'On faisait les haltes ensemble', Teresa records—'on
descendait aux mêmes hotels'—and on the second day of their
journey, as the carriages wound their way up the slopes of the
Euganean hills, the two lovers made a romantic excursion to
Arquà, the resting-place of Petrarch. The road became steeper,
the postillions refused to proceed, and it was on foot that the two
lovers—at last free and alone—made the last stages of their
pilgrimage.
    'It was', says Teresa, in her most poetic vein, 'one of those
Italian days—all serenity, softness and splendour.—when the sky
appears to be made of sapphire and opal, and seems to wish to
come nearer to the earth, to explain its consoling mysteries.' The
path by which the lovers climbed was flanked by vineyards and
pomegranate trees, and a gentle breeze—'like that of the Earthly
Paradise'—cooled their cheeks.
    Petrarch's house, when at last they reached it—for the walk,
during which Teresa recited a number of Petrarch's verses, must
have taken some time,—was half-ruined, and the ground-floor
filled with 'domestic utensils and jars of wheat'. But the two
sightseers went on upstairs, and there were the frescoes portraying
Laura which Petrarch had caused to be painted, the chair in which
the poet died,—and even, in a niche above a door, the embalmed
body of Petrarch's cat. Of this Byron characteristically remarked
that the hearts of animals were often better than ours—and that
this animal's affection may well have put Laura's coldness to
shame. The lovers wrote their names together in the visitors'
album, Byron remarking that although he had already written his

---

* There is some uncertainty as to the precise date of their departure from Bologna.
The Austrian spy gives the date as September 12th, Teresa herself, in the 'Vie', speaks
of the 15th; while a letter from Byron to Murray is dated from Bologna on September
17th. But since they spent three days on the journey, and Fanny's letter of the 20th
shows that by then the two lovers were already settled at La Mira, it seems probable
that Byron's letter was misdated and that they left on the 12th.

name there, he wished to record it once again, beside hers.
Together they leaned out of the window, looking down over the
vineyards and orchards – and at last together they walked down
to the poet's tomb – a sarcophagus of rose-coloured marble, in
the midst of a grove of young laurel-trees, where some vill‹ ,e
children were chasing butterflies. They drank water from the
fountain, and Teresa recited yet another of Petrarch's sonnets,
while the children brought them some grapes and peaches, –
Byron taking the opportunity to remark with satisfaction that
hardly ever before, in the whole long journey, had he seen his
companion eating or drinking, and that in this she represented
'the fulfilment of one of his dreams'. Then, arm in arm, in silence,
'absorbed by the emotions of the past, the uncertainty of the
future and the strangeness of their present situation', they
descended the hill to rejoin their coach.

'I cannot linger', Teresa told Moore many years later, 'over
these recollections of happiness. The contrast with the present is
too dreadful. If a blessed spirit, while in the full enjoyment of
heavenly happiness, were sent down to this earth to suffer all its
miseries, the contrast could not be more dreadful between the
past and the present.'[42]

But, alas, even this one halcyon day was not to be left undis-
turbed, for as the lovers approached their coaches, loud cries of
anger reached their ears. A fight was in progress between their
servants and the postillions – and although Byron at once brought
it to an end, Teresa did not fail to record his annoyance 'at having
to descend from the sublime and tender heights to which his
soul had risen, to the vulgar and prosaic details of material
existence'.

They spent the night at the inn at Padua – where the innkeeper
kissed Byron's hands with such deep emotion that Teresa,
'although no sign of respect for Lord Byron could seem to her
excessive', inquired as to its cause, and learnt that in the previous
year Byron – by coming to the innkeeper's assistance in a moment
of crisis, – had re-established his fortunes and thus earned his
undying gratitude. This showed itself on the present occasion by
the most magnificent banquet that the inn could provide, and by
some music in the adjoining room – 'attentions', says Teresa,
'which touched Byron so deeply that tears came to his eyes'. But
their stay, so harmoniously begun, was to end less agreeably. As
the travellers were on the point of setting forth next morning, who
should call upon Byron, having arrived the night before at the

same inn, but Contessa Benzoni with her Cavalier Servente, Conte Rangone!

'Their expression as they came in', Byron told Teresa the next morning, 'was embarrassed and comic. They seemed uncertain whether I deserved their blame or their protection. The Countess asked me where I was going – and if you were going with me. I replied that I was going to Venice – and that my plans were uncertain, except that I would certainly not remain in Venice where so many lies had been invented against me and my friends. I added that your health was still delicate – that you were going by the Count's wishes to consult Prof. Aglietti who had lately looked after you in Ravenna; that you were accompanied by your servants and that in Venice your lodging was prepared according to the orders of the Count, who had been called back to Ravenna on business, but who, rather than leave you alone, had been delighted that I should be your escort.'[43]

'This explanation', Byron added, 'appeared only partially to satisfy his two visitors.' The whole story soon went the rounds of Venice. This liaison, it was settled by the Venetian ladies, had now broken the laws of correct Serventismo; Teresa must have lost her head completely . . . and what could her husband be thinking of? The society which had tolerated all Byron's previous sordid adventures could not accept a serious love-affair. 'You must really scold your friend,' said Contessa Benzoni to Moore soon after. 'Till this unfortunate affair he conducted himself *so* well!'[44]

The whole incident came as a shock to the two lovers, breaking in on their dreams of a whole life together, as sweet, effortless and romantic as the three days' journey. 'We were very near going off together from Padua, for France and America,' Byron told Kinnaird two months later, 'but as I had more prudence, and more experience, and knew that the time might come when both might repent, I paused and prevailed upon her to pause also.'[45] But Teresa – so she tells us – 'avait la confiance de son âge'. She could not believe that she could ever repent.

That evening, after a few hours' rest at Byron's villa at La Mira, they arrived in Venice. Here, according to Teresa's promise to her husband, they should have separated, Byron going to the Palazzo Mocenigo and Teresa to the apartment 'on one of the small canals in Venice, disagreeable on account of their exhalations', which her husband's steward, Lega Zambelli, had prepared for her in Palazzo Malipiero. On the 17th, however, Lega Zambelli was reporting to Count Guiccioli that although 'the Signora Contessina arrived safely on Tuesday evening, and had sent for him at once, she said that owing to the fatigue of the journey she would postpone her removal to the lodging which had been prepared, and would stay instead in the house of Lord Byron, who had kindly prepared an apartment.'⁴⁶

It was plain, however, to both lovers, that they could not indefinitely remain in Venice together – so, after Prof. Aglietti's examination, the following careful letter was dispatched to Teresa's husband.

My dear Alessandro: I arrived yesterday evening in Venice, in excellent condition, because the two days' journey had done me more good than any medicine . . . This morning Aglietti came, and having examined me, ordered me no drugs, but instead advised another journey and change of air. Your affairs, I feel sure, would not allow you to come with me, so Byron having offered to take me with him to the lakes of Garda and Como – a journey suitable to the season, and which he is now thinking of taking, not being much pleased with Venice, – I ask for your permission, and await its speedy arrival with the greatest anxiety.
Since I arrived in Venice I have not even gone out of the house, and shall only do so to see the girls.
Byron greets you and charges me to tell you that the English friend to whom he wrote about the Vice Consulate, etc., has answered him that he will send in a petition at once and do everything possible to obtain it. Pray answer me quickly. Greet my Papa and all friends and relations. Goodbye, my Alessandro, write soon and believe me, Your affectionate spouse   TERESA⁴⁷

To this letter Guiccioli, to Teresa's own surprise, replied 'that if this excursion could contribute to re-establishing her health, she could make it, and that, as far as he was concerned, he saw no objection'.⁴⁸ But meanwhile the lovers had already moved to Byron's villa at La Mira.
It was a most attractive place. The great Foscarini Villa on the banks of the Brenta was surrounded by a romantic 'giardino all' inglese', with little toy lakes and bridges, and a great avenue of plane trees led along the water's edge. Here, for the first time, Teresa and Byron were alone together – and one can only suppose that they were happy. In some ways, Teresa's visit to La Mira is

curiously reminiscent of another happy interlude in Byron's life:
Augusta's visit to Newstead. Teresa, indeed, and Augusta were
the only women – the only human beings, except for some children
and servants – with whom Byron was ever able to cast off every
trace of his neurotic self-consciousness. And when he was at ease,
he could laugh all day like a child, with a child's love of nicknames
and baby-talk and a schoolboy's taste for practical jokes. The
vaults of Newstead had resounded with his and Augusta's
laughter, and now it was a similar laughter that echoed in the
gardens of Villa Foscarini. Teresa was warm and gay and kind –
and she adored him – and she was young.

> Round her she made an atmosphere of life,
> The very air seemed lighter from her eyes . . .⁴⁹

When they were not laughing or love-making, they rode along
the Brenta, past the elegant Palladian villas where the Venetian
nobles spent their summers, or sat on the rustic benches, beside
the little lakes of the 'English Garden', while Byron read aloud the
romantic works of Teresa's choice or his own translation of Pulci's
Morgante Maggiore on which he was working at this time. He was
also then busy with the third Canto of *Don Juan* – 'No occupation
for him', writes Teresa, 'but just a distraction.' – and she adds that
his facility in composition was so great that he would often tell her
to go on chattering while he wrote, 'for he worked much better
while he saw her and heard her voice'. In the evenings there was
more reading aloud, or Teresa played to him on the piano he had
ordered for her, and even tried to persuade him to join her in
duets.

Only one shadow fell upon their days:– now and again a messenger would appear from Venice, bringing a letter from Count
Guiccioli, forwarded by Lega, or, later on, some disturbing letter
from Teresa's own relations – or a note from Fanny. She,
according to the 'Vie', had actually gone to La Mira with Teresa
– 'une dame Silvestrini qui lui tenait compagnie'. But if so, she
cannot have stayed there long, – for by September 20th she was
back in Venice, opening the Count's letters to Lega (and, we have
little doubt, those addressed to Teresa as well) and proffering to
Teresa her exuberant sympathy and advice.⁵⁰

'The Cavaliere has written to Lega,' Fanny wrote, 'asking him
to keep him *informed* about his wife. He asks him [Lega] to give
more detailed news of you, which he is awaiting impatiently. In
answer Lega will write to him in the most appropriate manner.'⁵¹

Fanny's letters also contained a great many domestic details. Byron had reason to believe that the clerk of the British Consulate, Edgecombe, who had been acting as his accountant, had been cheating him – and he now set Lega Zambelli, assisted by the zealous Fanny, to look into the accounts.

'The papers I enclose', writes Fanny, 'will show you how much has been stolen in seventeen days... Lega, as you may well believe, has used all possible diligence not to leave a difference of even one soldo. On the comb, as I wrote you, I found a difference of eight lire.'⁵²

Then there was Teresa's shopping. She required some white merino, and Fanny bustled off to get it from 'the Jew under the Procuratie'; she also ordered a new corkscrew for Byron, and 'some brandy of the best quality', from someone 'who will take nothing but the honour of having served me'. And she took the opportunity to put in a good word for a manservant whom Byron had dismissed:

'The poor young man, is he then to be ruined? He is so timid, discouraged, prostrated, and what can he do? You, who have been granted an excellent heart, you only can move Mylord. He will not refuse to listen to your persuasive supplications.'

All this was delightfully domestic – nor was there anything half-hearted about the gusto with which Fanny dwelled upon the thought of the two lovers in their pastoral retreat. 'So now La Mira has become for you the enchanted abode of Armida.' It was true, she remarked, that 'il Cavaliere' had written again, announcing that 'before the end of October he will be here'. But the end of October was still far away!

'I entirely approve', wrote Fanny, 'your idea of awaiting your husband *a piede fermo*... I can imagine... the nature of the letters you write to your Alessandro, and I can also imagine the effect his two letters produced on you – although he will not, I think, understand what you mean, his own feelings being so confused and so contradictory.'

But, indeed, it would not have been easy for anyone, at this time, to be sure what Teresa's letters meant. Here is the first of them, as printed in the Guiccioli Memoirs, but unfortunately incomplete.⁵³

My Dear Alessandro: I had written two letters, meaning to send
them by the last two couriers, but I have always been too late
in sending them to the post. This will make 'you laugh, but will
not surprise you much, because you know me. I have received
three letters from you in the last few days, and with this of mine
will reply to them all. It is impossible, my Alessandro, for me to
send you Valeriano – you will realize that it is not suitable for
me, in my position, to remain with one woman only. . . .

I have not seen Lepri because, as you will see from the address,
I am not in Venice but at La Mira, a delightful place, where I
have come by Aglietti's advice . . . I am going on looking after
myself under the direction of Aglietti and also of the surgeon
Campana, having had much inconvenience in the last few days
from piles, from which I am not yet quite recovered. He has,
however, reassured me on the point which interested me most,
the supposed *prolapsus uteri*, so that I am much more at ease.
Byron, who overwhelms me with kindness, greets you cordially.
By the next post I will write to you at greater length and a little
better, because at this moment I am dropping from sleep. Goodbye, my Alessandro, send me your news and be sure of your most
affectionate consort   TERESA

Alessandro, however, appears not to have been completely
reassured, and three days later, obviously with the intention of
preventing his coming to see for himself what was happening,
Teresa was writing again.

Dearest Alessandro: . . . You have seen the letter I wrote to Papa.
I am not sorry, but you must not think that not having spoken of
my health is a proof that I am well. Indeed it is now a few days
since the piles – a very tiresome ailment – have been followed by
a bad headache, and a little cough has begun again. For these
last two complaints I am advised to travel, but I am determined
not to do so without thinking it over a little. I am still at La Mira,
a delightful place, where one can very well lead, as I am doing,
a retired life, without its being at all tedious.

I cannot tell you all the attentions of Mylord. He has sent for
a pianoforte for me, some music, quantities of books, and then
[I have] his company which is of greater value than them all, so
that if only I were well, I should not know what to wish for . . .
Byron greets you and is not very pleased not to see even a simple

greeting for him in the letter you sent me recently. I am sorry
to hear you are so much annoyed. . . . [54]

Here the letter, in the incomplete version printed in the
Guiccioli Memoirs, breaks off abruptly, and we are left wondering
whether the causes of the Count's annoyance were not more
complex than we are told. For in the interval Count Ruggero
Gamba, Teresa's father, who from the first had viewed his
daughter's relationship with the English Mylord with the greatest
disapproval and who had now only realized that his daughter was
not still in Venice – had intervened. He hurried in from his
country-house to Ravenna, told Count Guiccioli roundly that he
'did not approve of allowing an inexperienced young woman to go
off alone, and still less, escorted by a young man like Lord Byron'
– and added that 'if her husband refused to join her at once, he
would go and fetch her himself'.*

Guiccioli excused himself as best he could, explaining his
indulgence as due to his wife's ill-health and his complete confidence in her honour and Lord Byron's – and added that 'as to
the world's opinion, he was entirely indifferent to it'. He did,
however, end by promising that he would go and fetch Teresa, and
meanwhile her father, still far from reassured, sent her a long letter
of warning – a letter which, in the opinion of Teresa, was 'affectionate and indulgent, in accordance with his adorable character',
but which did not attempt to conceal his anxiety, and told her of
further gossip which had reached him from his son in Rome.

'You have hardly entered the world,' Count Gamba wrote, 'but
it will make no allowance for your youth, the purity of your heart,
the innocence of your journey, or for all the circumstances which
may justify your present position. This most seductive young man
is by your side, protecting you – no doubt in a manner honourable
and worthy of you both. That may be enough to convince me,
and your husband, and your own conscience. But the world will
not be satisfied with these arguments. The retired life that you are
leading will only provide further weapons for those who may wish
to criticize your position.'†

This letter reached Teresa soon after her husband's permission
to set forth with Byron to tour the Italian Lakes, and it awakened
in her, more than any other feeling, a childish disappointment at

* 'Vie', p. 260. Teresa adds that Count Gamba had heard that 'people were talking
and attributing to him [her husband] every sort of turpitude, such as an intention of
selling me'.
† 'Vie', p. 262. This letter too only exists in Teresa's transcription of it in the 'Vie'
and should therefore, in style if not in content, be taken with some caution.

having to give up her journey – 'an excursion which her imagination painted as one of the joys which one can only hope to fulfil in heaven'. She took her father's letter into the garden, and sat there, she says, with its pages open on her lap and tears of disappointment running down her cheeks, until Byron came out and found her. He took up the letter, read it, and exclaimed:

'So they are still pursuing me all the way to Italy!' – 'But who are these persecutors?' Teresa inquired, 'and why do they treat you like this?'
'I will tell you later,' said Byron, 'but meanwhile what is necessary is to reassure your father. Answer him at once – consult your heart and your duty – and do not think of me. My destiny is subject to your will – and you know it.'⁵⁵

Teresa obeyed, and wrote to 'reassure' her father, by promising that she would remain at La Mira until her husband came to fetch her – and would give up the expedition to the Lakes.

The trouble about Teresa's reports of her conversations with Byron is that she has no ear for any style but her own. It is possible that Byron's meaning was what she conveys; it is hardly possible to believe that that is how he expressed it! It was on that same afternoon, she wrote, that Byron – with reference to the 'calumnies' that her father and brother had heard about him, sat with her for many hours in the shade of the plane trees and – in a conversation that lasted until dusk – told her the story of his marriage and separation. The whole story? It is difficult to think so. The *leitmotiv* in Teresa's version, is 'his ignorance, then and always, of the true causes of the separation'. She considered the faults of which he had then been guilty 'such as could be forgiven by any kind, religious and reasonable woman', and Annabella's subsequent silence, 'which wished to appear magnanimous', was, on the contrary, 'the most poisonous weapon that could have been used against him, opening the door to all the accusations of his adversaries'. The story of Byron's marriage, then and subsequently, remained for Teresa one of cruel injustice done to *him* – of the incomprehensible coldness and implacability of a woman he had trusted – and of hypocritical British cant. Yet it is clear, from the context, that later on – though not on that day – the story of Astarte did reach Teresa's ears, for she speaks of 'the atrocious calumny', which *then* his generous spirit could not imagine. And many years later, we find, scribbled in pencil on the back of a letter which she received during her first visit to London, after Byron's death, the following remarks:

'Lord Byron needed a companion who was not only fond of him and devoted to him, but all of whose faculties were occupied in making him happy, without his knowing it. Certainly she [Lady Byron] had something to bear – but his faults were only caprices – and where is the woman whose husband does not give her cause to exercise some virtue? Is it not said in the marriage formula that one takes one's husband for better for worse? She should have been indulgent – have been tender with this gift of God, this superior intelligence – tried to diminish the sufferings that were the result of his great gifts – and not tread him underfoot ... The most terrible injury against him is the silence and mystery about the reasons for their separation, a mystery which, since it makes any supposition possible, has even caused certain inclinations to be attributed to him, which one hesitates to reproduce in words. To confute such horrors would be unworthy of one who has known the purity, modesty and simplicity of his sentiments.'[56]

But these are the reflections of later years. The girl who listened to Byron on that September evening was moved by much simpler feelings: indignation against the injustice that had been done to her lover, pity for the pain he had endured. As they sat there together under the plane trees, England and Annabella, and the whole pack of his accusers, seemed very far away. 'Their hatred cannot harm me any more', he told her, 'so long as *you* believe in me.'[57]

There was, however, in Teresa's mind an immediate problem – and one which the letters she was now receiving made increasingly pressing: how to keep her father quiet, and her husband away, for as long as possible. It is clear from both her letters and Byron's at the time that they, like the rest of the world, were more than a little disconcerted by the Count's peculiar behaviour, however convenient.

'I can't make him [Guiccioli] out,' wrote Byron to Scott, 'conjectures are useless – we shall see. He ought to have been here last week, but delays a month longer.' As for himself – 'I do not leave these parts immediately – and am not sure that I shall leave them before Spring, being as undecided as when I saw you in Venice.'[58]

On the following day Teresa sent off to her husband a letter in which an injudicious petulance does not conceal that she is both surprised and bewildered.

... I hear from a letter of Papa's that you are displeased that I should have *left the apartment*. I do not know whether you say this for conventional reasons or *from some other motive*. But in any case, my Alessandro, rather than talk to others you might have made your complaints to me, and if they had seemed reasonable, I would have done all I could to satisfy you. But instead you either don't write at all, or merely two lines about my health and minor matters, and your own business. Which of us then is most in the wrong? This, even without speaking of many things that are not satisfactory to me, owing to the mystery in which you veil them. I enclose a letter from Prof. Campana, which he wrote to me yesterday from Venice. It will partly show you my condition, to which I can add that the cough is not at all gone yet. As I desired to know Papa's wishes as well as yours, I did not start on my journey, and now perhaps the weather and this half-cured ailment will prevent it. You will not come back until All Saints. These were not your promises when you left me. What shall I do meanwhile? I assure you that I am very much embarrassed. It was indeed necessary that I should have a *Man* and a *Friend* – like Byron – to relieve me a little in this situation, and I assure you that if, from now onwards, I am to compare Men with Him (the only person whom I see) I shall always be very dissatisfied with everyone. It is impossible to desire a better friend. ...

Accept the cordial greetings of Byron, and from me the assurances of your most affectionate Consort.**

It is not known whether this letter received any reply. The Guiccioli Memoirs say that Teresa wrote again to her husband on October 10th, but do not quote the letter; and they quote only in part the somewhat more conciliatory note which she sent him on October 23rd, when the date of his arrival was very close at hand:

'I continue to improve in health. I hope you will find me well in this respect, as you will find me in regard of other good intentions, which you almost seem to doubt, by the way you constantly persist in ignoring them. Byron wishes to be remembered to you in Friendship, and looks forward as I do to seeing you.'**

This letter, as printed in the Guiccioli Memoirs, consists only of these few lines; it is possible that the part left out, as well as the two letters omitted, may have contained references to a much more delicate matter: the new request for a loan which, at this stage of the proceedings, Guiccioli is supposed to have made to his wife's lover. The amount in question was no less than a thousand pounds, a sum which was then lying in the hands of Byron's banker in Bologna, but which the Count professed to think would be more advantageously placed in his own. Security, he added, would be given, and five per cent interest paid – as the acceptance of the sum on any other terms he would hold to be an *avvilimento*. This story we owe to Moore, who commented that although Teresa's own disinterestedness was beyond question, yet it seemed so important, 'for her lover's sake as well as her own, to retrieve, while there was yet time, their last imprudent step, that even the sacrifice of this sum . . . did not appear to me by any means too high a price to pay for it'.

But Byron would have none of it. 'Nothing could be more humorous and amusing than the manner in which, in his newly assumed character of a lover of money, he dilated on the many virtues of a thousand pounds, and his determination not to part with a single one of them to Count Guiccioli.' The three men – for Scott had joined the party after dinner – enjoyed their wine and the excellent joke – and before the night was over, Byron had laid a wager with Alexander Scott that he would 'save the lady and the money too'.[61]

This story, it is but fair to add, Teresa absolutely denies. 'What Moore said he heard in Venice can only be a misunderstanding about the little loan [the one in Bologna] or else the consequence of a joke, or a mystification of Lord Byron's.'[62]

Teresa's acquaintance with Moore on this occasion was of the slightest, and we know that, at their first meeting, he did not even think her very pretty. When he came out to La Mira, she tells us, Byron, *très ému*, begged her to come down to the drawing-room to make his guest's acquaintance.

'But Moore could only speak English, and their conversation was therefore very short, with Lord Byron as their interpreter. The two friends then left together for Venice, where Lord Byron offered Moore the noble hospitality of his own palace.'[63]

When the time came for Moore's departure, he returned to La Mira to say goodbye to Teresa. She found him in the dining-room, 'with a glass of Bordeaux in his hand – an attitude which harmonized with his gay and animated countenance'. She gave him a letter of introduction to her brother – and she also observed that Byron handed to him 'a little bag of papers. "These", Byron said, "are my Memoirs, which I am giving to Moore." One could read

on his fine countenance the most exquisite and noble sentiments.'⁶⁴
Alas, Teresa adds, that so much confidence should have been
ill-placed! She was never able to forgive Moore for what she considered his betrayal, in allowing the manuscript – 'which contained every slightest detail as to what occurred between his wife
and Lord Byron' – to be destroyed.

Teresa's letter to her brother, according to Moore himself, was
given to him open (as good manners in Italy require) – and he
therefore felt no scruple about either reading it or copying it –
adding as a half-hearted excuse that 'the greater part of it was, I
have little doubt, dictated by my noble friend'. The passage
which he quotes, however, is so like Teresa's answer to her brother
in July, that there can be no doubt as to its authorship.

'He [Moore] is a friend of Lord Byron, and much more
accurately acquainted with his history than those who have
related it to you. He will accordingly describe to you, if you ask
him, the *shape*, the *dimensions*, and whatever else you may please to
require, of *that Castle in which he keeps imprisoned a young and innocent
wife*, etc. My dear Pietro, when you have had a good laugh, do
send two lines in answer to your sister who loves you, and ever will
love you with the greatest tenderness.'⁶⁵

Teresa now felt so secure, that she could afford to laugh at her
brother's fears. Yet, had she known Byron better, she would
perhaps at this moment have begun to notice certain small danger
signals. He hung about waiting for the English post, and fretted
when it was late; he spent a long time over it when it came; he was
less attentive to her chatter; he took rather more brandy at night,
and a great deal more magnesia in the morning. And when Moore
arrived and he went off to Venice with him, it was 'with all the
glee of a schoolboy who has been given a holiday'.

Moreover – but this Teresa fortunately could not know – the
old flippant note was creeping back in his letters to his friends.

'What you say of the long evenings at the Mira, or Venice,
reminds me of what *Curran* said to Moore – "so I hear you have
married a pretty woman – and a very good creature too – an
excellent creature – pray – um – *how do you pass your evenings?*"
it is a devil of a question that, and perhaps as easy to answer with a
wife as with a mistress; but surely they are longer than the nights.'
However, he adds, 'I am all for morality now, and shall confine
myself henceforward to the strictest adultery.'⁶⁶

The truth was, of course, that Byron, once again, was beginning to get bored. Teresa was young and pretty and tender – but such continual adoration – even expressed in a language not one's own – soon became a little cloying. And her gaiety, which at first he had mistaken for a true temperamental affinity – 'we have laughs together – *our* laughs', he told Augusta – proved only to be animal high spirits, without a touch of humour. Once again tedium descended upon him.

> Men grow ashamed of being so very fond,
>   They sometimes also get a little tired,
> (But that, of course, is rare) and then despond:
>   The same things cannot always be admired,
> Yet 'tis 'so nominated in the bond',
>   That both are tied till one shall have expired.[67]

This, perhaps, was one of the passages that Byron did not translate for Teresa's benefit.

And Byron's tedium, as Moore had observed in 1816, always took the same form: it brought 'some return of this restless and roving spirit'. It was, as he penetratingly observed, 'the habit of the writer's mind to seek relief, when under the pressure of any disquiet or disgust, in that sense of freedom which told him that there were homes for him elsewhere'.[68] In 1816, and later on, in 1823, his 'roving spirit' led him to thoughts of Greece; in 1820, in Ravenna, he played with the idea of rushing off to Naples to take part in the Neapolitan revolution. And now, in the dull evenings at La Mira, he turned his mind to a 'South American project', which would take him and Allegra (but of Teresa there is no mention) to settle in Venezuela, 'and pitch my tent there for good and all'.

'I am not tired of Italy, but a man must be a Cicisbeo and a Singer in duets, and a connoisseur of Operas – or nothing – here. I have made some progress in all these accomplishments, but I can't say that I don't feel the degradation. Better be an unskilful Planter, an awkward settler, — better be a hunter, or anything, than a flatterer of fiddlers, and fan carrier of a woman. I like women – God he knows – but the more their system here developes upon me, the worse it seems, after Turkey too; here the *polygamy* is all on the female side. I have been an intriguer, a husband, a whoremonger, and now I am a Cavalier Servente – by the holy! it is a strange sensation . . . Yet,' he adds, 'I want a country and a home, and – if possible – a free one. I am not yet thirty-two years of age. – I might still be a decent Citizen, and

I

found a house, and a family as good – or better – than the former.'⁶⁹

Here is the same note that sounded in Byron's letter to Hobhouse in Bologna, two months earlier. But now, for the first time – and at a moment when passion was temporarily sated and ardour stilled – an opportunity presented itself for an honourable release. After innumerable letters and protests, Count Guiccioli at last appeared in Venice on All Saints' Day, to fetch his wife.*

His arrival, according to Teresa, was preceded by a letter to her, telling her to go and wait for him 'if Byron did not mind, at his Palazzo Mocenigo, as he himself and his son would arrive there for a two days' stay'.⁷⁰ This curious choice of residence is explained by Teresa as 'the best way to defeat Venetian gossip',⁷¹ and her father seems to have been of the same opinion, for, on October 30th, he had written to her:

'I have just left Casa Guiccioli after speaking to Alessandro, whom I have left in a good humour. He did not say anything to me about going to stay at Mylord's house, nor did I think it desirable to ask him about it. But I am glad that it will be so, and that your Husband's friendship with Byron will thus be consolidated, this being the only way of putting an end to gossip, and perhaps the only one by which the peace can still be kept.'

It is clear from what follows that Count Gamba still believed his daughter's protestations as to the platonic nature of her tie with Byron, while not unaware of the intensity of her feelings.

'I pity your state and know by experience that love is something that is felt and cannot be commanded. But you must never forget that you are a wife, and that it is your duty to make your husband happy; and that this cannot be achieved without the greatest circumspection.

Your friend's wisdom makes this very difficult task easier for you, and I am full of hope. Remember me kindly to Mylord, to whom I am much obliged.

Before leaving Venice, write down the excellent regime of that good counsellor Aglietti, and try to reacquire your former health, which your husband desires intensely, and rightly.'⁷²

* Hoppner's malicious satisfaction when this news of Guiccioli's plans reached him, was reflected in a letter to Byron: 'Count G. is a most amiable man and will, I hope, be as complaisant to his wife as Menelaus was of old to his; as the lady no doubt will be as penitent as the fair Helen is described by Homer to have been, when Paris was but out of the way.' October 30th, 1819. Unpublished letter belonging to Sir John Murray.

By the time Guiccioli arrived, Teresa was already in Venice, having hurried there to nurse Byron who had caught a severe tertian fever from getting wet in a heavy thunderstorm. During his delirium he alternatively raved that he saw his mother-in-law in the room, or composed verses against her, which he dictated to his valet, Fletcher. 'You see', he told Teresa afterwards, before destroying them, 'the truth comes out, not only in drunkenness but in delirium.'[73] 'On my senses coming back,' he wrote to Murray, '[I] found Fletcher sobbing on one side of the bed and la Contessa G. weeping on the other.'[74]

Before he was fully recovered, Count Guiccioli, accompanied by one of his sons, was also in the Palazzo. His meeting with Byron was, Teresa assures us, 'as courteous as in the past', and he told the Poet that he would be only too delighted to see him again in Ravenna, 'but that, owing to comments and gossip, an obstacle had arisen, and this obstacle was Count Gamba'.[75] He added that he was therefore obliged to appeal to Byron's honour not to return there – 'so as not to make trouble between Guiccioli and the Gamba family'. Moreover, he asked him to say nothing about all this to the Countess. 'Lord Byron did not know what to say; the Count seemed to him to be within his rights, Count Gamba also; he could only conceal his feelings and his sadness within his own heart.'[76] He had now recovered, and, in spite of Guiccioli's presence, was apparently spending his evenings with Teresa – but no longer peacefully as before. Even when the old Count's rigid figure and ironic smile was not actually before their eyes, they were very acutely conscious of his presence. One evening, when Guiccioli was at the theatre and Byron working at Don Juan, Teresa looked over his shoulder and asked what a certain passage meant. "Nothing," he replied, "but 'your husband's coming.'" She started up in a fright and said *"Oh, my God, is he coming?"* thinking it was *her own*, who either was or ought to have been at the theatre. You may suppose we laughed when she found out the mistake.'[77]

As for Byron's description of the Count's visit, it is considerably franker than Teresa's.

'At last the Cavaliere Conte Guiccioli came to Venice,' he told Kinnaird, 'where he found his wife considerably improved in health, but hating him so cordially, that they quarrelled violently. He had said nothing before, but at last, on finding this to be the case, he gave her the alternative, *him* or *me*. She decided instantly for *me*, not being allowed to have both, and the lover generally having the preference. But he had also given her a paper of rules to which he wished her to assent, all of them establishing his authority.'[78]

These rules, which the Count had prepared before his arrival, and which are referred to by Teresa in the 'Vie' as 'embarrassing proposals and requirements', form one of the oddest documents in the whole story. It was customary, indeed, in some Italian cities, for the marriage agreement to contain some clauses concerning the details of conjugal daily life — in such matters as the number of horses and carriages, the ordering of the household, the box at the theatre, the summer holidays. But these rules — like those which the Count had prepared for his two former wives — went a great deal further. From the hour of his wife's waking until her bed-time — even as to the manner of her toilet, and the way she might amuse herself during his siesta — he claimed the right to supervise and control every action, and indeed every thought, of her existence.

November, 1819.   INDISPENSABLE RULES[79]

1. Let her not be late in rising, nor slow over her dressing, nor fussy over lacing and washing, with danger of injuring herself.

2. Let her busy herself at once with those household matters which are within her competence, striving to obtain the greatest cleanliness and the best order, and all this with method, continuous diligence, patience and economy. Until she has acquired the experience that can only be got by practice and by a habit of continuous and constant diligence, patience and memory, and finally by practising the aforesaid economy, order and method, let her offer suggestions and ask for advice, but not give orders . . . Let her reflect that in so much as she neglects the care of her business and of the house, so much and more shall I neglect her. In so much as she despises practical matters and the aforesaid cares and duties, so much and more shall I feel contempt, dislike and aversion for her, who, while she is served by all, is of service to none, and while greatly increasing my burdens and anxieties, refuses to bear any part of them herself, exposing me thus to trouble and damage of every kind.

3. After midday, let her spend the time until dinner with me, in conversation and reading aloud, which she shall share with my son.

4. After dinner, when I rest, let that be her regular time for music.

5. After our drive together, in the early part of the evening,
    reading aloud as before dinner, then together to the
    theatre, then conversation and to supper and bed
    together.

Such was the Count's regulation of daily life. He then passed
on to general injunctions, designed to bring about 'that full mutual
satisfaction which is the true happiness of married couples'.

6. Let her not be too conceited or impatient, for one can only
    learn with time, experience and much reflection. Let her
    not do things casually, because a wish or an idea presents
    itself, but only because this idea, first considered and
    examined by her, and then always referred to her husband
    or to experts, is seen to be well-advised.
7. Let her accustom herself to the aforesaid prudent economy in
    household matters, and to economy and care in her
    personal concerns, for which she now, out of vanity,
    declares her contempt. Let her be content with the
    allowance of twelve monthly zecchini, the complete
    interest of her dowry received until now. I might possibly,
    in the event of finding myself overflowing with riches,
    provide something more, but at most not more than two
    hundred zecchini a year. Let the regret of refusing use-
    less requests therefore be spared me.
8. Let her not care for pomp and luxury, as her husband does
    not. Let her reflect that only a similarity of habits can
    render conjugal life agreeable . . . She can easily change
    hers, which have only lasted for a few years, but I cannot
    change mine, which have more than forty years of
    absolute and deliberate practice behind them.
9. Let her be satisfied with the rooms and furniture as they are,
    not arguing about this, nor fussing about details.

And now, at last, the Count passed on to his real purpose.

10. Let her receive as few visitors as possible.
11. Let her be always prepared to live, go away or come back, as
    best suits her husband's plans, and let her therefore keep
    her things in order, giving up her longing for travel, or
    for dwelling-places which do not suit her husband's or her
    family's arrangements.
12. Let her be completely docile with her husband. Then only
    will she be able to ask of him that any orders and com-

plaints which in any way affect her, should be
communicated directly to her and not to others.

13. She may, however, sweetly, modestly and tentatively, submit
her own views and reflections, and even answer the
arguments that I shall offer her. But if all this does not
convince her, then she shall refrain from insisting, and
yield with good will and good temper.

14. Let her have a constant and preventive care of her health,
which has been damaged by her own carelessness and
thoughtlessness, vanity and capriciousness, and let her not
be alarmed by complaints which a wise diagnosis show to
be non-existent.

The reference in this clause to recent events is unmistakable.
And now come the most significant paragraphs:

15. Let her never cause trouble between her husband and her
father, or anyone else. Let her consider him [her hus-
band] as Father, Husband, Friend and constant faithful
companion, and give no one else preference over him.

16. If she should feel inclined to do so, let her at once bring such a
relation to an end, and not trust herself; otherwise she
will be for ever condemned in the opinion of her husband,
and of a wise Society.

17. How can she always be completely sincere with her husband
with this worm gnawing at her heart? And where one
cannot be open and sincere, how is it possible to be happy
together?

The old Count does not appear to have reflected that the mode
of life suggested in the earlier part of this document would hardly
be a training in frankness and sincerity. The rest of the paper is a
series of threats as to the consequences which would attend his
wife's refusal to obey his rules. She would, he says, no longer be
considered the mistress of the house: its management would be
handed over to the servants; while his children would despise her.
She would be given no money, not having any property of her
own. Her complaints would be believed by no one, and at
her husband's death she would have difficulty in finding another.

To this document Teresa replied with greater brevity, but considerable spirit:

CLAUSES IN REPLY TO YOURS

1. To get up whenever I like.
2. Of my toilette I will not speak.
3. In domestic matters to be absolute mistress of all that is within a Lady's province.
4. I do not refuse the reading aloud with you, at which your son's presence is a matter of indifference to me.
5. To dine together as usual, but to spend the time of your rest as I please, even if it were in pulling the donkey's tail.
6. Drive together, Theatre, Conversation, bed, supper, etc., – all together, as you please.

'But all this,' she added, in a parody of her husband's clauses, 'would not be enough to live together peacefully, etc., – if you should refuse to grant me the following:

1. A horse with everything necessary for riding.
2. *To receive, without discrimination, any visitor who may come.*'

Deadlock had now been reached, and in despair of convincing his headstrong young wife, the old Count went to Byron himself.

'He actually came to *me*, crying about it, and I told him, "if you abandon your wife I will take her undoubtedly; it is my duty – it is also my inclination – in case of such extremity; but if, as you say, you are really disposed to live with, and like her as before, I will not only not carry further disturbance, into your family, but even repass the Alps; for I have no hesitation in saying that Italy will be now to me insupportable." '[80]

In all this, it will be noticed, Teresa herself was hardly consulted at all. We know that she quarrelled with her husband; we may suspect that she pleaded and argued with Byron. But storms and tears were in vain. At such times 'a disrelish more powerful than indifference' would sweep over Byron – an invincible emotional fatigue. All the crises of his past, every hour of tedium and disillusionment and remorse, weighed in the scales against her. He yielded – and, as many another man has done, gave the name of duty to what was chiefly weariness.

'What could I do? On one hand to sacrifice a woman whom I loved, for life; leaving her destitute and divided from all ties in case of my death; on the other hand to give up an *amicizia* which had been my pleasure, my pride and my passion. At twenty I should

have taken her away, at thirty, with the experience of *ten such years*!
– I sacrificed myself only; and counselled and persuaded her, with
the greatest difficulty, to return with her husband to Ravenna.'[81]

So Teresa, after all, was sent home again with her husband.
She went, she tells us, only because she felt certain that Byron
would soon follow her – and he himself wrote that he had given
her a half-promise, 'else she refused to go'.*

And now Byron was again alone – 'in a gloomy Venetian
palace . . . unhappy in the retrospect, and at least as much so in
the prospect'.[82] The alternatives, indeed, were not attractive. On
the one hand – if, after all, he stayed in Italy – he would be
obliged to take up for good the too familiar duties and pleasures of
a Cavalier Servente – or, still worse, to find himself responsible
for the destruction of Teresa's marriage, and be saddled with her
for life! But on the other hand, if he went back to England – what
would lie before him? 'I return to England with a heavier heart
than when I left it; with no prospects of pleasure or comfort.'[83]

He wrote to Teresa in one mood, to his friends in England in
another. To Teresa he said:

'You are and ever will be my first thought. But at the moment
I am in a most dreadful state, not knowing which way to decide –
on the one hand, fearing to compromise you for ever by my return
to Ravenna and the consequences of such a step, and, on the other,
dreading to lose both you and myself, and all that I have ever
known or tasted of happiness, by never seeing you more. I beg
you, I implore you, to calm yourself, and to believe that I can only
cease to love you, with my life. . . .'†

To Kinnaird, however, he was writing:

'I shall quit Italy. I have done my duty, but the country has
become sad to me; I feel alone in it; and as I left England on
account of my own wife, I now quit Italy for the wife of another.'[84]

* This promise appears to have been known even by the Austrian police, for a
report dated November 25th says: 'Byron, in order to calm the amorous agitation of
Signora Guiccioli, who refused to leave him, promised to return to see her in Ravenna;
but his only real intention is to return to England.' *Carte segrete della polizia austriaca
in Italia*, p. 207.

† This passage and another paragraph beginning 'I go to save you' are quoted by
Moore (II, p. 288) as belonging to the same letter, and very possibly Teresa told him
that it was so. But their content certainly suggests that they belonged to *two* letters;
the first written before he had made up his mind, and the second after. The originals
are not in the Gamba Papers; I have translated them from the Italian text in Moore.

As soon, however, as he had made up his mind, an unexpected contretemps delayed him. Allegra fell ill, and kind Dr. Aglietti informed him that it was the *doppia terzana* – a peculiarly virulent form of malaria. 'The poor child has the fever *daily*,' he wrote, 'all my plans . . . are lulled upon the feverish pillow of a sick infant.'[85]

Dr. Aglietti was assiduous in his care of the child, and on November 25th wrote to Byron that he now considered her well enough to travel, and that if she followed his prescriptions, she would recover her health completely in England. At the same time he asked Byron whether he could not arrange for him to receive some English books, in exchange for Italian ones, from Murray, and bade him farewell, 'with the most sincere feelings of esteem, gratitude and attachment'.[86]

Fanny, meanwhile, was sitting in Allegra's playroom and writing to Byron a note in which she offered him her services, to accompany him as far as Calais and look after the child on the journey. She promised to 'fulfil towards her all the duties of a mother', as a token 'of the sentiments of esteem, gratitude and affection that I nourish for you, Mylord'.[87] The proposal, it is hardly necessary to state, was not accepted.

Byron, however, still held to his decision; 'in Italy I will not remain a moment longer than enables me to quit it'.[88] And on November 25th he was writing Teresa a final letter of farewell.[89]

'I go *to save you*, and to leave a country which, without you, has become insupportable. Your letters to F[anny] and even to me do wrong to my motives – but in time you will see your injustice. You speak of grief; I feel it, but words fail me. Is it not enough that I must leave you – for motives of which you yourself were convinced not long ago – is it not enough that I must leave Italy, with a deeply wounded heart, after having passed all my days since your departure in solitude, sick in body and mind – but I must also have to endure your reproaches, without replying, and without deserving them. Farewell! – in that one word is comprised the death of my happiness.'[90]

It was at this time that he composed the lines which, three years later, he showed to Lady Blessington.

> Could love for ever
> Run like a river,
> And Time's endeavour
>   Be tried in vain –
> No other pleasure

With this could measure;
And as a treasure
    We'd hug the chain.
But since our sighing
Ends not in dying,
And, formed for flying,
    Love plumes his wing;
Then for this reason
Let's love a season;
But let that season be only Spring.

When lovers parted
Feel broken-hearted,
And, all hopes thwarted,
    Expect to die;
A few years older,
Ah! how much colder
They might behold her
    For whom they sigh!
When linked together
In every weather
They pluck Love's feather
    From out his wing,
He'll sadly shiver
And droop for ever
Shorn of the plumage which sped his Spring. . . .

Wait not, fond lover!
Till years are over,
And then recover
    As from a dream;
While each bewailing
The other's failing,
With wrath and railing
    All hideous seem;
While first decreasing
Yet not quite ceasing
Wait not till teasing
    All passion blight:
If once diminished
Love's reign is finished —
One last embrace then, and bid good-night!

Before showing these lines to Lady Blessington, Byron remarked,
speaking of marriage, that 'there was no real happiness to be found

out of its pale. "If people like each other so well", said he, "as not to be able to live asunder, this is the only tie that can ensure happiness – all others entail misery." ' Lady Blessington pointed out that these sentiments were somewhat at variance with those expressed in the poem. 'He laughed and said, "Recollect, the lines were written nearly four years ago; and we grow wiser as we grow older; but mind, I still say that I can only approve marriage when the persons are so much attached as not to be able to live asunder, which ought always to be tried by a year's absence before the irrevocable knot is formed." '⁹¹

Teresa's own opinion of these verses is sufficiently revealed in the following letter to John Murray:

'The song *Could Love for ever* was written at a moment of great moral and bodily suffering – when he [Lord Byron] wanted to take *the resolution* to leave Italy. This step, which he thought his duty to take, costed him the greatest sacrifice of feelings – and he wrote such verses (as occasionally he did in different circumstances) not for *publication* but only for relieving his mind and give himself the strength he wanted but which he could not find, though in the very day and hour in which they were written he was under the influence of a periodical fever – a circumstance which may sufficiently explain the indifference of such a composition, which he esteemed so unworthy of being published, that he threw it among other useless papers in a corner of his room, where having been found by chance and finally given to the public.'⁹²

But, for all this, November passed into December – and Byron was still in Venice. The more he thought about his return to England, the less assured he felt about his welcome there. Would even his friends be glad to see him? Would the scene in Lady Jersey's drawing-room be repeated?

He did not, in any case, propose to *remain* in England; perhaps, after all, he would carry out his South American scheme, or go to the Cape, 'if I don't take a much longer voyage'.⁹³ But meanwhile he and little Allegra must stay somewhere. 'I have nobody to receive me but my sister' . . . but would Augusta really want him?

His doubts were even better founded than he knew. When Augusta did at last receive his letter, stating that 'I expect to be in or near England by the New Year', and asking her to send him 'a line at Calais',⁹⁴ she was overcome by dismay.

'Luckily (or *unluckily* perhaps) I don't die easily, or I think this stroke would about finish me.' She hurried to send on Byron's letter to Annabella, asking for her advice. 'I'm sure I don't know how to address a letter to *Calais* – it being out of the question to *give him welcome* to England.'⁹⁵ A prompt reply came back to her from Lady Byron:

'The reasons which, a short time since, induced you to deliberate whether you ought to continue the correspondence . . . have infinitely more weight in the question whether any personal interview is admissible . . . Several of his letters . . . demonstrate that he has not relinquished his criminal *desires*, and I think I may add designs. It can scarcely be doubted, from the whole series of his correspondence, that you are his principal object in England . . . Consider then for yourself, whether it would be advisable to apprize him at Calais of the impossibility of your consenting to personal intercourse.'⁹⁶

All this, however, fortunately, Byron did not know – and he continued his preparations for departure. It appears to have been common knowledge in Venice that he had promised Teresa, if he could not follow her to Ravenna, to save her face by leaving the country altogether, for Alexander Scott, who had heard the story from the bookseller Missiaglia, wrote from Milan to Byron to expostulate:

'When I received this letter, I had just finished reading a chapter of Machiavelli, entitled, "In che modo i Principi debbono osservare la fede" – and though I am a Scotchman and had a religious education and am very well disposed to observe my promises on such occasions, I confess, I was not a little startled at the idea of one setting out on a long journey in Winter in order to keep one's promise. In said chapter M[achiavelli] discussing the qualities of the Lion and the Fox that ought to compound a prince, observes . . . "Non può pertanto un Signore prudente, né debbe, osservare la fede quando tale sua osservanza gli torni contro, e che sono spente le cagioni che la fecero promettere." Now I suppose your motives for promising were, to persuade the Countess to go quietly home and to win your wager, and these ends being obtained, there can be no occasion for your keeping your promise before the end of the winter.'*

But for once Byron did not seem disposed to accept such counsels – and Fanny Silvestrini, in reply to Teresa's despairing

* December 18th, 1819. Unpublished letter belonging to Sir John Murray. The quotation is from Machiavelli's *Principe*, chapter xviii. 'A prudent Prince cannot, therefore, and should not, keep his word, when to keep it is against his interests, and when the reasons that made him give it, have ceased to exist.'

requests for news, could find no better comfort than to suggest that, after all, Mylord's determination to leave Italy was, since he could not be near her, his last tribute to her power.''

'Mylord is leaving Venice, is abandoning Italy, is crossing the mountains and the sea in such a bitter season, is going to England for you, only for you, – so as not to cause you to wonder whether his not coming to Ravenna, yet still remaining in Italy or abroad, had reasons unrelated to you – and this is your great triumph. He, however, assures me, and charges me to assure you in his name, that if you continue to feel the same sentiment for him, and desire it, he is prepared to return here from London, only to see you, as he is leaving only for your sake. . . .

Do not doubt, Teresina, that you will have news of Mylord by every post, so far as I can gather it during his journey. Calm yourself, for pity's sake. Think of your health, which is dear to Mylord, I vow it, Teresina. Do not believe you have been deceived, he would not ever be capable of deceiving you; he has always been swayed by your will . . . But after all, what use is it going over the past? Do not heed the present too much, but give a great deal of thought to the future. I am writing from my heart, and no one can be a better friend to you than I.

I enclose a card of invitation that Mylord had from the Benzone. He, with dry courtesy, sent her his thanks and a message that in a few days he was leaving Venice. For all the gold in the world he would not have gone there, nor to any other place of amusement. He will go out of his house only to leave Venice, as he promised you; nor has he ever done so, everyone can testify to it . . . My Dear, B[yron] is taking Valeriano with him, as well as many of his other servants, and when he gets to Calais he will send him back with news; from him you will be able to hear about the journey, and from him too you will receive his letters, this will also be a slight consolation. I will close, impatient to hear that you are a little calmer. My Friend, Farewell again.'

At the bottom of this letter two brief lines from Byron are all that he could find to say.

My Love: At the moment – it is impossible for me to write in detail – but in time you will realize that I am and always shall be yours.

At last the date of his departure came, and once again it is Fanny who describes the scene:

'He was already dressed for the journey, his gloves and cap on, and even his little cane in his hand. Nothing was now waited for but his coming downstairs – his boxes being already on board the gondola. At this moment Mylord, by way of pretext, declares that if it would strike one o'clock before everything was in order (his arms being the only thing not yet quite ready) he would not go that day. The hour strikes and he remains. Evidently he had not the heart to go.'[98]

Within the next few days, an English post arrived which was certainly not calculated to increase his desire to return to his native land. No word from any of his friends; no word from Augusta; but, forwarded by John Murray – a copy of Blackwood's *Edinburgh Magazine* for August, containing – on the pretext of a review of the first two Cantos of *Don Juan*, to which it referred as a 'filthy and impious poem' – a virulent attack upon his private life.

'For impurities there might be some possibility of pardon . . . for impiety there might at least be pity . . . but for offences such as this . . . which speak the wilful and determined spite of an unrepenting, unsoftened, smiling, sarcastic, joyous sinner – for such diabolical, such slavish vice, there can be neither pity nor pardon.'[99]

'Such outrageous license', commented Byron to Murray, 'is overdone and defeats itself.'[100] But the trouble was, that not only feelings were at stake. Murray wanted to apply to the Lord Chancellor for a copyright for *Don Juan* – but, Byron warned him, 'You will recollect that if the publication is pronounced against, on the grounds you mention, as *indecent* and *blasphemous*, that *I* lose all right in my daughter's *guardianship* and *education* . . . It was so decided in Shelley's case'.[101]

All this brought back to Byron the recollection of all that he most hated, most had reason to dread, in England. Why should he, after all, return to 'a country where I neither like nor am liked'?

And while he was still uncertain, Teresa played her trump card. Exhausted by all she had been through, by the rapid passage from joy to despair, from freedom to renewed imprisonment – unutterably bored in the grim solitude of Palazzo Guiccioli, with her husband even more embittered and suspicious than before – uncertain, above all, whether she would ever, once he had crossed the Alps, see her lover again, – she had another serious relapse.

It is not necessary to wonder, as some of Byron's biographers have done, whether this illness was merely a pretext to recall her lover. Many of the Gambas had consumptive tendencies – and this is, of all illnesses, the one most easily revived by distress and anxiety of mind. Teresa's attack was so serious that her whole family became alarmed. Her father hastened to her bedside – and, while admitting that unhappiness over Byron's departure was the chief cause of her relapse, she succeeded in persuading him that their relations were still platonic, and that there was no reason why Lord Byron should not come, 'Like anyone else, to spend the winter in Ravenna – and to be near the sea and the fine pine-forest which he loved so well.'[102]

Was the Count wholly convinced? We shall never know. What is certain is that he yielded to his daughter's persuasions – re-enforced by her illness and her tears – and wrote to Byron as she requested. 'Her father (who had, all along, opposed the *liaison* most violently till now) wrote to me to say that *he* begged me to come and see her – and that her husband had acquiesced, in consequence of her relapse.'*

So at last Byron reached a decision. To Augusta (no doubt to her great relief) he wrote: 'The health of my daughter Allegra, the cold season, and the length of the journey, induce me to postpone for some time a purpose (never very willing on my part) to revisit Great Britain.'[103] To Murray: 'I have changed my mind, and shall not come to England. The more I contemplate, the more I dislike the place and the prospect.'[104] And to Kinnaird: 'I shall go again to Ravenna; anything better than England.'[105]

But to Teresa, in Ravenna, he wrote the letter for which, in all these weary weeks, she had been waiting.

'F[anny] will have told you, *with her usual sublimity*, that Love has won. I have not been able to find enough resolution to leave the country where you are, without seeing you at least once more: – perhaps it will depend on *you* whether I ever again shall leave you. Of the rest we shall speak. You should now know what is more conducive to your welfare, my presence or my absence. I am a citizen of the world – all countries are alike to me. You have always been (since we met) *the only object of my thoughts*. I believed that the best course, both for your peace and for that of your family, was for me to leave, and to go *very far away*; for to

* *L.J.*, IV, p. 396. To Moore, dated January 2nd, 1820. The world's opinion is recorded for us by Rangone: 'The complaisant husband seemed disposed to make a complete break, but a loan, procured through his wife's good offices, produced a reversal of feeling, – and the Cavaliere went quietly to stay with Mylord and his own wife, and then took them both home.'

remain near and *not* approach you, would have been impossible for
me. But you have decided that I am to return to Ravenna. I shall
return – and do – and be – what you wish. I cannot say more.'[106]

On Christmas Eve Byron – welcomed with infinite joy by
Teresa and with great cordiality by all her relations – was once
again in Ravenna.

4 : RAVENNA AGAIN

Brunello is his name that hath the ring,
Most lewd and false, but politike and wise.
(ARIOSTO, 'Orlando Furioso', translated
by Sir John Harington)

'IT will depend on you', Byron had written to Teresa, 'whether I ever again shall leave you.' Little did he know, as he wrote those words, how true they would prove. 'I have not decided anything', he wrote to Hoppner in January, 'about remaining at Ravenna. I may stay a day, a week, a year, all my life; but all this depends upon what I can neither see nor foresee. I came because I was called, and will go the moment that I perceive what may render my departure proper. My attachment has neither the blindness of the beginning, nor the microscopic accuracy of the close to such *liaisons*; but "time and the hour" must decide upon what I do.'[1]

Yet, however much he might try to preserve – in the sight of others, and even in his own – an illusion of freedom, Byron's return to Ravenna had been the turning-point. The moment when he handed Teresa over to her husband in Venice had been the last one at which, as he himself soon came to realize, he could decently have made a break with her; henceforth he was committed. On his first public appearance in Ravenna, at a party on New Year's Eve, in the house of Teresa's uncle, Marchese Cavalli, where 'there were between two and three hundred of the best company I have seen in Italy', he found himself welcomed by the whole of Teresa's family as one of themselves.

'The G.'s object appeared to be to parade her foreign lover as much as possible, and, faith, if she seemed to glory in the Scandal, it was not for me to be ashamed of it. Nobody seemed surprised; – all the women, on the contrary, were, as it were, delighted with the excellent example. The Vice Legate, and all the other Vices, were as polite as could be; – and I, who had acted on the reserve, was fairly obliged to take the lady under my arm, and look as much like a Cicisbeo as I could on so short a notice.'[2]

'He was received', says Teresa in the 'Vie', 'with the greatest cordiality, like a friend who has come home again.'[3] She says that the party was the first assembly of the season – it being then the custom in Ravenna for the families of the nobility to join an association, whose members held the assemblies of the year in turn, during Advent and Lent, in their respective houses. The first

party of each year was given in the house of the most recent bride,
– who, in this case, happened to be Teresa's cousin, the young
Marchesa Clelia Cavalli* – and the hostess then decided who her
successor should be on the following night. There were refresh-
ments, cards and conversation, and the young people danced in
the adjoining room.⁴

All this mild provincial life was very entertaining – for a while.
The cage was charmingly gilded, and now Teresa expected her
tame poet to sing in it. She says of him that 'il voyait tout en beau, –
except the inn in which he was lodged, although it was the best in
the town. He attempted to find lodgings elsewhere but failed –
and 'it was then', says Teresa, 'that Count Guiccioli offered him
the apartment on the first floor of his *palazzo*' – while the Guicciolis themselves remained on the ground floor.

'After some hesitation, and probably even encouraged and
urged by the Countess, Lord Byron accepted. Certainly,' Teresa
adds, 'the offer might appear strange. It was so, indeed, but
people were accustomed to consider the Count *an eccentric*, and
after a few days they stopped talking about it.'†

But Teresa can hardly have believed this herself – or expected
us to believe it. They went on talking – and have indeed been
doing so ever since. In *I Guiccioli* the arrangement is explained as
being part of a deliberate scheme of Teresa's husband, 'while in
the depths of his heart his plans were maturing', to discover what
his wife's relationship with Byron really was. 'For while in public
nothing transpired on his impassive countenance, he exercised a
secret and untiring espionage.'⁵

'The world', Teresa said in a later statement to her lawyers,
'talked a great deal and my father was upset, but Guiccioli found
it to his own advantage; and so Lord Byron entered our house and

* It was in honour of this lady that Byron – 'repeatedly urged to do so by the
Countess G.' – had written a sonnet; assuredly with his tongue in his cheek.
'A noble Lady of the Italian shore
Lovely and young, herself a happy bride,
Commands a verse and will not be denied ...
A sweeter language and a luckier bard
Were worthier of your hopes, Auspicious Pair!
But – since I cannot but obey the Fair,
To render your new state your true reward
May your fate be like *Hers* and unlike *Mine*!
Ravenna, July 31st, 1819.

† 'Vie', p. 335. Byron's inn, although bearing the name of 'Imperiale', was indeed
of the most modest description, consisting only of six rooms. These he afterwards
used for his servants.

was there constantly and confidentially in our company – Guiccioli
even asking Mylord to take me to the Theatre in public, so as to
be free to pursue his own amusements.'⁶

'Lord Byron thus became what was called her Cavalier Servente, a position which', so Teresa affirmed, 'did not in the least
expose him to criticism, since it was allied, or could be allied, to
the most immaculate and respected reputation of all three people
concerned.'⁷

As to public opinion in Ravenna, it is again recorded by
Rangone:

'The respected Lord looked for an apartment, but, finding none,
accepted the noble suggestion of the Cavaliere to come and stay
in his own house to square their accounts. And so dogs, monkeys,
house-servants, a little girl – said to be his offspring by a girl in
London – and Mylord, took up their abode in this most delightful
new inn ... Lord became an accomplished Cavalier; he took a
box at the theatre for himself and his household, gave a gratuity to
the impresario, was generous on benefit nights, distributed money
to the poor, helped the suffering – in fact, made himself popular
with everyone.'⁸

Whatever may have been the motive of the Count in coming to
this arrangement, that of Teresa and Byron requires no
elucidation. But, in spite of this favourable beginning, the next
few months were not a happy period.

'Lord Byron', Teresa herself admitted, 'began to play his role
[of Cavalier Servente] with pleasure, indeed, but not without
laughing at it a little ... One would almost have thought that he
was a little ashamed – that in showing himself kind he was making
an avowal of weakness and being deficient in that virility of soul
which he admired so much ... This', she firmly added, 'was a
great fault of Lord Byron's.'*

* 'Vie', p. 353. An Italian sonnet of the period gives a portrait of a typical *cavalier
servente*:

> Femmina di costumi e di maniere
> E di esercizi sol maschio e di sesso,
> Non marito, non celibe, ma spesso
> L'uno e l'altro per genio e per mestiere.
> Supplemento diurno il cui dovere
> E' di star sempre all'altrui moglie appresso,
> Ed ha per patto e complemento espresso
> Noiarsi insieme le giornate intiere. ...
> > CLEMENTE BONDI (1742-1821)

Besides, daily life in the Palazzo Guiccioli was far from easy. Here they were again under the same roof – but how differently the time passed, compared with those golden autumn days at La Mira! Now they were dependent for their few snatched hours together on anxious stolen meetings during the Count's siesta, or on the nights when he went to the theatre or to a Conversazione without his wife. Sometimes the Count was suave and courteous, sometimes curt and morose. But always, in the background, his presence made itself felt – formidable, inscrutable, perpetually observant.

When the two lovers could not meet, they wrote to each other – hasty, scribbled notes, carried from one floor of the palazzo to the other by Teresa's maid or one of the negro pages.* Many of these notes concern a series of quarrels – of which the causes, seen at a distance, are extremely slight: the dismissal of a maid, Teresa's jealousy of Geltrude Vicari, Byron's jealousy of an old friend; Teresa's childish resentment because Byron failed to sit beside her the whole evening during her game of cards. There are references, too, to disagreements between Byron and his host: on one occasion about a carriage and some furniture which Byron had ordered from Florence; on another about the engagement of a celebrated prima donna at the opera. All this seems very trivial, but Byron's letters to Teresa reveal something rather different from the usual reproaches, fair or unfair, of an angry lover. They show, first of all, a growing uneasiness about Teresa's character. Byron was under no illusion about his own weaknesses – but disingenuousness was not one of them, and it is plain that Teresa's lack of frankness caused him much disquiet. He complained that he could not 'extract a word of truth' from her; he implored her to behave in a manner 'unequivocal, even in appearances'. Her lack of sincerity distressed him so much that he tried to find excuses for it by considering it, not as an individual, but a national, trait. He wrote of 'the sincerity that unfortunately cannot exist in the present conditions of Italian morals' – of 'social morals fatal to a foreigner who loves an Italian woman'.

It appears probable that the Puritan in Byron – 'the little Scottish Calvinist', – as Maurois said – 'who never lost his respect for purity' – felt more than a little uncomfortable in the situation in which he now found himself. He minded it, precisely in proportion to the depth of his feelings for Teresa. It was not only that he was, as Teresa herself admits, 'a little ashamed' of his role of

---

* One of these pages – Teresa's messenger – came from East Africa; the other, who was faithful to Guiccioli, from the coast of Guinea. Both wore 'rich oriental costumes, with pistols and daggers at their belt'. *I Guiccioli*, I, p. 68.

Cavalier Servente. What must have been even more disquieting was something at which it is only possible to guess, and which the letters – though they hint at it – never explicitly state. This was Teresa's very curious relationship with her husband. I think the evidence in these letters, in Teresa's subsequent statements to her lawyers and to her parish priest, in her step-children's letters to her later on, and in her own family's attitude to the whole question of her separation, points to something very unpleasant in Guiccioli's influence over her. Moreover, this hold, which was founded on cold-blooded calculation, seems to have been exceedingly strong; at the time of Byron's return to Ravenna, she had not by any means shaken it off.

From the available evidence it would seem that in the early days of the liaison, when Guiccioli was still hoping to gain some advantages, in prosperity or prestige, from Byron's friendship, he gave Teresa every reason to believe that he would cause no trouble – and that when, after La Mira, she was presented with a definite choice, she was not only distressed, but completely taken aback. As to Byron's return to Ravenna, a very curious sidelight is thrown on it by the following sentence in one of his letters. 'All this would already be over,' he tells Teresa, 'if that man [Guiccioli] had allowed me to leave in December of last year. He not only *wished* me to come – but he said to me with his own lips that I ought not to go away – this being too far-fetched a remedy.'

In the face of such a statement, is it not permissible to suppose that, when Guiccioli offered Byron an apartment in his house for the *second* time (the first was at Bologna) Teresa had reason to think that all might again go smoothly?* She only gradually came to realize that her husband was playing a very tortuous game – on the one hand trying to see of how much use the English Mylord could be to him – but on the other, spying on the lovers, so that, if he decided that a separation would suit his books better, he would have the necessary evidence to get rid of her. But, as she began to realize all this, Teresa must have been in a very difficult position indeed. That she really loved Byron is indisputable, and that at any moment she would have been willing to throw everything else overboard for him. But this correspondence shows that she had every reason to doubt whether Byron wanted matters to come to that point.

In this dilemma Teresa must have attempted, at least in the first months of this year, to conciliate her alarming, inscrutable husband until, as we shall see, he tried to make her ask Byron for another loan – at which point she stood firm, with considerable courage. But in smaller matters, she would sometimes give Byron an impression of complicity with Alessandro against him. This is, I think, the most probable explanation of the underlying note of tormented uneasiness in Byron's letters. There must have been moments in which, in this foreign country, this strange society, caught up in these unfamiliar conventions, he felt himself completely at sea – and when it must have seemed to him that Teresa, too, was on the other side.

The next two letters, written only a few days after Byron's arrival in Ravenna, were enclosed in a folder on which Teresa has written:

'Two very unjust notes, caused by

1. my having taken and kept in my service a maid who, he had been told, was not respectable, and whom Count G. wished to keep near me to spy on me.

2. my having received and conversed in a familiar manner with an old family friend (aged 60) Count R * * * who had always treated me as a daughter, and

3. my having suggested that a woman friend, who had been dear to me in the past, was rather flighty, and, above all, that she had tender feelings for him.'

About the first accusation Teresa added later on that 'Shortly before taking possession of his apartment in Palazzo Guiccioli, Lord Byron had learned that one of the maids was an intriguing woman who had always caused trouble in every house where she had been'. In addition he believed that Guiccioli was keeping this maid in the house as his own mistress, and to spy upon Teresa.

'Lord Byron begged his friend to send her away ... The Countess did so, but the Count, hearing that she had done so on Byron's advice, insisted on the woman's remaining; and expressed his will as master of the house, in a manner wounding both to Lord Byron and the Countess.'[10]

Byron's feelings on the subject were so strong, that he even at first refused to enter Palazzo Guiccioli until the maid, whom he referred to as 'Teresa the Second', had left it; and indeed he did not move there until the end of January – although without having gained his point.

As to the lady mentioned in the third accusation – Geltrude Vicari – Byron's high moral tone about her, though possibly justified in regard to this particular incident, is slightly invalidated by a letter of his to Augusta, in the previous summer:

'I fell a little in love with her intimate friend – a certain Geltruda (that is, Gertrude) who is very young and seems very well disposed to be perfidious – but, alas! – *her* husband is jealous – and the G. also detected me in an illicit squeezing of hands – in consequence of which the friend was whisked off to Bologna for a few days – and since her return I have never been able to see her but twice – with a dragon of a mother-in-law and a barbarous husband by her side – besides my own dear precious Amica who hates all flirting but her own. – But I have a Priest who befriends me – and the Gertrude says a good deal with her great black eyes, so that perhaps – '[11]

Perhaps Teresa was not so unjustified in her jealousy, after all!

BYRON TO CONTESSA GUICCIOLI

January 3rd, 1820

My Friend: You must do as you think best – I have not dictated what you should do – I replied when you reproached me for calling on the Vicari, – 'that it was less improper for me to visit your most intimate friend than for you to retain in your house a woman like Teresa, kept for so many years, for *one reason* – and now – according to all appearances – for *another*.

If you had not begun by reproaching me about a most innocent matter, I should have gone away without saying a single word on the subject. Nevertheless I now believe, as I always have believed – from outward signs – from what I have suspected – and heard – that that woman and her former lover have deceived you for their own purposes.

The familiarities of that man may be innocent – but decent they are not – even this evening, when you thought I was reading the manuscript that A[lessandro] put into my hands, I observed, by the fire, certain things that do not suit me. You will know well enough what I mean, without my saying any more.*

You would have done better to let me go away from you before I came here; since my arrival I have enjoyed pleasures that only you can give me – but on the other hand I have suffered very much in seeing you, in my opinion, either degraded or weak.

---

* Teresa, in her note about this letter, wished to make the future reader believe that this accusation referred to a family friend; but subsequent letters make it seem probable that Byron meant Count Guiccioli.

There is a mystery about these things that I cannot understand; – a morality without principle – a love without faith – and a friendship without esteem or trust – these have unfortunately shown themselves lately to such a degree that it has been impossible for me to extract a word of truth from a person for whom I have given up everything.

If you can reconcile your code as a lady with your defence of the aforesaid woman who is now in your service; if you can reconcile your love for me with the liberties you have permitted to another man in my presence; and your most sincere (or most affected) friendship with the Vicari with the way in which you spoke of her to me tonight – I shall admit that you are a lady of great gifts – but no longer my friend.

Your A[lessandro] accused me this evening of indecision. *He* accused *me* – very fine! *He*, after all the scenes in Venice – all his plans to travel to Vienna – to Florence – to change his country – to send his sons to school, then to England – to break off your relationship – really, that is fine! What does he want? That I, a foreigner, far from my own country and from the manners and customs and ways of thought and behaviour of my fellow-countrymen – that I should decide things for the people of another land!

Since I have known you I have lived *for you* – and *with you* – is this indecision? If I see my country in danger of destruction – some of my friends arrested – others on the point of being involved in civil war – my family without support – much of my property none too safe – in the conditions prevalent under this insecure government – if in such a moment it seems to you or to others that I am upset – does this deserve the name of indecision? – For I must consider that I have left everything in such a state – for a woman who not only does not love me, – but never . . . [page torn and a line missing] . . . loved. – I cannot deny your gifts and your beauty; you write eloquent notes; in your physical attributes you are . . . all that one can desire . . . [the page is torn and the rest of the letter is missing.]

January 4th, 1820

In reply to your letter of this morning, I can only say that we do not understand each other. If you had not reproached me for paying a brief and most unimportant call on a friend of yours, very dear to you six months ago – and as I believe still dear *now* –

I should never have thought of mentioning what seemed to me little to your credit, in a well-ordered household. For the rest I cannot be the bearer of your communications to C.R. either for good or evil, and I will not in any way enter into the affairs of those two creatures. As to receiving people in your house – why not everybody? – then it would have no importance. Meanwhile, it would matter little to me who comes or goes, if you showed the sincerity that unfortunately cannot exist in your circumstances, in the present state of Italian morals. Only I should like to tell you that when you give such a gracious and friendly welcome to your friend, it is difficult for me to guess that in that very moment you are hating her most. I have nothing more to say about this hardly pleasant subject.

I am very sorry to hear that you have not felt well this evening, and I hope that tomorrow you will be better.

I have been with Lega to the Bacinetti apartment, of which I do not think the accommodation convenient – the position I like – but in those quarters it would be impossible for me to live with my family – without almost rebuilding the house.

Pray believe that I feel as I have always felt towards you – and do not attribute unworthy motives to me – such as trying 'to test you'. I say what I feel; I have not come here for such trivial reasons. I do not put great faith in a fine style, nor in eloquent notes – which no one can do better than you – but in honest deeds, in sincerity – with women as with men friends – and in a conduct which is unequivocal even in appearances. I am etc. etc.*

6 *o'clock* – [no date, but as it enclosed the preceding note, it must be January 4th.]

I wrote you the enclosed letter before receiving yours – Lega having returned only this moment from the port. This will confirm my feelings and my resolution, which was and is unalterable.

Anyway T[eresa]† will not lose much (except your good graces, which I would mind losing much more than she would). As to her interests, I will do all that can be done until she finds another place, and will do so very willingly. I am not seeking *vengeance* – or to cause pain – but only that that woman should not be near

* In the whole of this letter Byron uses the formal *voi* instead of the intimate *tu*.
† The name of the maid whom Byron wished to be dismissed, was also Teresa.

you, not only for [your] sake and mine, but for all the other
people you know. I have given orders to Lega – he will see to
everything.

'You say that A[lessandro] told you that I "did not love you". I
do not know what he means, but I know that I said to his face –
that even if he did not want you, I was *fond of you* and would be
for ever. Can one say more to a husband? As to the rest – you
know whether I *loved* you – and how – and how much – even in
the last and greatest troubles – and *oppressed with fever* – I was your
lover – as I shall be on my deathbed, at least while I have the
same strength in me.'*

'I will come.[11] I think I have done justice to those qualities
which really are yours – and as to the faults I have told you about
(perhaps with too much frankness) you have those in common
with a whole nation – and with social morals fatal to a foreigner
who loves an Italian woman.'

                                                January 10*th*, 1820
My love: Pray explain what A[lessandro] said this evening about
the membership for the assemblies – I don't understand very well –
the thing may be a Romagnole politeness or a discourtesy. I most
certainly should not have become a member myself, if the presence
of Alessandro and of Cristino R. had not reassured me as I was
doing it. In any case I consider myself at least the equal of the
members as to *birth*, which is not within our control, and also as
to everything else, which is. Pray instruct me for my guidance –
for I do not want to demean myself – not even for your sake, – but
in all that you desire (feeling certain that you would not desire
anything that could mortify your friend) I am and always shall
be yours (as you say) *eternally*.

P.S. I vow I should vastly prefer not to go to these assemblies –
and only thought of going because you wished it.[12]

* This letter consists of two fragments, which have been cut out of a longer letter.
They bear no date, but are enclosed in a folder on which is written (in another
handwriting than Teresa's) 'January 3rd and 4th, 1820'. On the back of the letter is
written in Byron's own hand: 'This was the postscript to my last letter – but I did
not send it.'

Forgive this Inn's paper[14]
My Love: I am sorry that I cannot go with you – but I am not feeling well this evening – and then this removal requires my own particular attention – which you will understand well enough, knowing the character of my people. I am thinking of coming to you in a few minutes, but I do not want you to give up the Conversazione of C[lelia] C[avalli] on my account. I am

It was at about this time that two letters from Venice recalled to Byron's memory the existence of Fanny Silvestrini, who, from the moment that she ceased to be of use to him, was regarded by him with increasing distaste. It appears that 'that chaste lady, Madame Lega' (the expression is Hoppner's) had been sent by Byron to Hoppner with a message about the forwarding of his furniture. To Hoppner – no longer able to express his disapproval directly to Byron himself – this was a godsent opportunity, and he first, as he admitted in a letter to Byron, refused to receive the lady at all, and then kept her waiting for some hours in a cold hall.

'If I could have believed', wrote Fanny, 'that he could be so indiscreet and absolutely uncivil to me, I should indeed have spared myself the trouble of waiting unnecessarily in a very cold waiting-room, on the ground floor and without a chair, in icy cold, tired from the long walk, and in my present condition. Nevertheless I returned the next day at the time he condescended to establish, and he received me, standing, in the same room, without greeting me either when I came or went, and hardly condescending to tell me that he would see to everything; but I assure you, Mylord, with an air and a tone that you, Mylord, would certainly not have used with the least of your servants.

I cannot see the reason of such behaviour towards me. You, who have always shown so much goodness towards me, then came into my mind, and the comparison rendered odious to me the temporary presence of the most inurbane Mr. Opner.'[15]

Fanny did not add that, while Hoppner was still upstairs, she – according to Hoppner's account – 'bounced into our drawing-room, saying she was not accustomed to be kept waiting in a hall, and I understand was so angry at my usage, that she actually tore her veil!'[16]

Byron and Teresa were both far too much preoccupied with their own affairs to pay much attention to this story. Byron's next letters refer to further disagreements between him and his host.

January 17th, 1820

My Love: Elisei has confirmed what you said about the 'prima donna'* in connection with me, but was already convinced that it was not true – and I asked him once more, warmly, to contradict that bit of gossip everywhere – and he promised to, very gladly.

I have not seen Giulio Rasponi – when I do I shall say the same thing to him too. I did not come to see you, because you had gone out calling, and then A[lessandro] did not find the key of the box – so what was to be done? Do you want me to come at 6 or not – and how shall I behave with regard to the assembly? A[lessandro] seemed to me in a bad humour. Believe that I am in *deeds* what you are in *words* – Your *'lover for ever'*

Yes – and *if not* – I will pay the journey here – and back to F[lorence] with something more for their pains – but I wish to reserve for myself the right to refuse, in case the landau does not correspond to the description. A[lessandro] is a buffoon – who does not know what he wants or says when he is in a raging temper. Tell him so.[17]

[page torn] 31*st*, 1820[18]

You have heard your father talk about that woman – and if you will not listen to him or to your friend, it is enough to listen to the town. She has caused trouble in every household where she has been.

I asked Ferdinando to whisper in *your ear* – perhaps he misunderstood.

The other evening I gave you my *word of honour* not to go into any house where that woman is – and in my country this counts for more than an oath. As to the rest – everyone is master in his own house, and no one more than A[lessandro]. He will do what he likes and will be right. I have told *you* – even in the presence of Count Ruggero. Do you think there is any difference of opinion between us about your defence of this woman? Ask him.

I am not trying to humiliate anyone – but neither your honour nor mine will allow me to be silent when I see things to which I

* The 'prima donna' was Mme Pasta and it was about her engagement that Byron had quarrelled with Count Guiccioli. According to Teresa, Byron had expressed to Guiccioli – who was at the head of the Ravenna Theatre Committee – a warm admiration for the talent of Mme Pasta, and had undertaken to contribute two hundred pounds sterling for her engagement. See also Byron's letter of March 30th.

will not give their *real* name, so as not to use words which might offend you. The imprudence of Ferdinando was my fault, – in part – but I had no other way at the time of communicating with you – and I thought he would tell you at a more suitable moment what was only repeating a resolution already taken and explained a long time ago.

My intention was not to offend either A[lessandro] or anyone, but I do not regret having done everything possible at any cost – to prevent the continuance of an imprudence which would have ended dishonourably.

One must do what one must – and not only what is agreeable – and this I have done. I am and shall be your most humble servant and friend.

7 o'clock

My Love: It is difficult to foresee how this affair may end. In any case you can always be certain of my most sincere, my most passionate love. You are in a position to know better than I what A[lessandro's] ideas are. I have sent Lega to tell him that neither Papa nor the Rasponi had spoken to me or sent me a message about the matter – as is the case.

Of the woman I retain my opinion and my resolution – since the reasons are constantly increasing against my entering any house inhabited by this fine Helen of the new Trojan war. You know that the name of *Paris* in Greek is *Alexander* – as you saw in Monti's translation of Homer.

What will happen to you – I don't know – what will happen to me, now and always – depends almost completely on you, and on the degree and constancy of your love for me. I did not come to R[avenna] to give you up – but circumstances – chance – and *death* are the rulers of men; we shall see, in time, the unfolding of our destiny.

I kiss you 100.000 times – my dearest.

February 1st, 1820

I am awaiting with impatience – my Love – your letter, which must decide a great deal – perhaps everything – for me. I am so convinced of being right in my resolution – that even should it cost me my happiness – I hold firm. The recent predilection of A[lessandro] in favour of the person in question I cannot well understand. In Venice he had quite the opposite opinion – and if you remember, expressed it in very plain language. My reasons I have already explained – I have no others – but I shall not repeat them here again. I have no right to say more than I have already said either to you or to him – but I am also my own master to go or not to go into a house where someone lives whom I deem to be evil in every way; especially when it is a case (as recently it has been) of my occupying part of the same house.

Pray tell me your decision once for all; – if, after all that I have endured, I am to be sacrificed, I am sorry that it is not to be for a better reason – and for a subject more deserving than this kept woman; but what will be, will be. Remember that I have come twice to Ravenna to please you – that *I loved you with all my heart* – and that I shall go away not owing to a whim of my own, nor from fatigue, nor from a failure of the slightest part of the love I have always felt and *always shall feel* for you – but because I realize that to remain in a town where I should only see you very seldom, would be worse than separation – for both of us.

Pray answer me and at once – if you can – for I have orders to give to Lega, and do not fail to explain to Papa and to your brother that our relation is not ending through any instability on my part.

6 o'clock

My Love: Last night I said 'perhaps' – and although for many reasons besides the love I feel for you, I should like to see you in your own house – I cannot suddenly resolve to take a step that seems to me cowardly, and which I am sure, after the first moments, which cause *everything to be forgotten*, I should never forgive myself for having taken in view of all the circumstances that have been the cause and the accompaniment of this disagreement. I leave to the fair Helen all the advantages of her worthy triumph. I have promised, and I shall certainly keep my word, not to try any more to get rid of her either directly or indirectly – and this conduct is the only possible course – since only A[lessandro] has a true right to dismiss her. I have thought about it all night – but in spite of all my love for you — I cannot suddenly reconcile myself to going back to a house where she is living. – Perhaps in time it will be possible – but now – it would be buying too dearly the pleasure of returning to your arms.

We shall see each other at the assembly, I hope – I shall go punctually at 7. A[lessandro] wanted me to give him an answer this morning – but I am still too tormented to do it. I could do it easily – my Heart would only too gladly dictate it – but *afterwards?*

Meanwhile we shall see each other at the assembly. Believe me ever and always yours

But in spite of all this – it was Byron who yielded. 'Teresa the second' remained in Guiccioli's household; Byron, with Allegra and all his menagerie, moved into the apartment on the first floor – and harmony appeared to be restored.

February 7th

My Love: The Guiccioli revolution is the consequence of the revolution in Spain, and the good humour of A[lessandro] is caused by his having read the supplement to the *Lugano Gazette*. What a good thing Politics are in this world! Enough – so long as the good news is not contradicted next Sunday – for then I am afraid that the despotism of Ferdinand VII and of Teresa II would come to life again – indeed the Maid has more talent than his Catholic Majesty – and is so much the more dangerous.

As you wish – Miss Biron will be at your orders – but – but – never mind.

I will come to you whenever you wish. To go to the assembly without you would be neither suitable nor pleasurable – at least for me. I do not want to disappoint you, but if that is what you fear, it would be quite easy to stay at home together; the assembly itself is the most indifferent and tedious affair. I went to the others because you wished me to, and for no other reason.

Come – if you will – for the child; she is already dressed. Believe me with all my soul always and entirely. Your lover forever

Teresa was to 'come for the child'. For now the Ravenna Carnival was in full swing, and 'Miss Biron' – not yet four years old – was to drive with Teresa down the Corso in her coach-and-six – preceeded by outriders with blue and white feathers in their caps – as part of the gay cavalcade. Byron, too, would follow in his gaudy post-coach, sometimes bringing with him an English guest,

L

William Bankes, the explorer, with whom he 'buffooned very merrily'.

'There is,' Byron wrote, 'to a foreigner, a mixture of mystery and hilarity in the general burst from everyday cares, that renders a Carnival peculiarly attractive . . . Grave and gay, old and young, handsome and those who might be called so by courtesy, were all abroad, laughing, flirting, tormenting, pleasant and sometimes pleasing . . . It is at this periodical Saturnalia that all ranks are jostled, and mingled and delighted, and all this without fear, observance or offence . . . Curiosity is always excited, sometimes Passion, and occasionally Pleasure. Life becomes for the moment a drama without the fiction.'[19]

These were the aspects of his life in Ravenna that Byron wholeheartedly enjoyed, – taking part, with childlike gusto, in the mild social diversions of the little country town – not, indeed very unlike the life he might have led in Nottingham, but still enhanced for him by a sense of novelty and freedom. Here, he told Hoppner, he had found

'Conversazioni . . . and much better ones than any at Venice . . . small games at hazard . . . other card tables, and as much talk and coffee as you please . . . There is to be a theatre in April, and a fair, and an opera, and another opera in June, besides the fine weather of nature's giving, and the rides in the Forest of Pine.'[20]

He was freed, besides, from the constant menace of English tourists which had hung over him in Venice, – and from the painful self-consciousness, now defiant, now propitiatory, which the presence of his fellow-countrymen awakened in him. Here his only guests were of his own choosing. At the end of April came Sir Humphry Davy, the great Irish scientist, 'much pleased with the *primitive Italian* character of the people, who like Strangers because they see so few of them'.[21] Teresa exercised her charms upon him, but overreached herself by asking, when he was talking about Mount Vesuvius, whether 'there was not a similar volcano in Ireland?' – and continued, with childish pertinacity, to insist that she was right, until Byron guessed that she meant Mount Hecla in Iceland. After their guest's departure she implored Byron: 'Pray beg him to give me something to dye my eyebrows black – I have tried a thousand things and the colour *will* come off.'

'All this', commented her lover, 'with the greatest earnestness; and what you will be surprised at, she is neither ignorant nor a fool, but really well educated and clever. But they speak like children, when first out of their convents; and after all, this is better than an English blue-stocking.'*

Better than a blue-stocking, perhaps – yet not wholly satisfactory. Byron's little notes to Teresa at this time are affectionate, teasing, familiar – but there is in them an underlying note of both condescension and uneasiness. Besides, he was sometimes, already, more than a little bored. Even before the Carnival was over, he had discovered that the Ravenna parties – once their first novelty had worn off – were as tedious as provincial parties anywhere else. In a way, indeed, they were worse; for at least at home he had never been deprived of 'good talk', while in this respect the Conversazioni in Ravenna were 'not Society at all'.

'They go to the theatre to talk and into company to hold their tongues. The *women* sit in a circle, and the men gather into groups, or they play at dreary *Faro* or *Lotto Reale* for small sums.'²²

To his friends in England, indeed, he still swaggered about the great houses where he was received as the *amico di casa* or *amico di cuore*, and boasted how completely he had settled into regular *serventismo*.

'I double a shawl with considerable alacrity; but have not yet arrived at the perfection of putting it on the right way; and I hand in and out, and know my post in a Conversazione and theatre; and play at cards as well as a man can do who of all the Italian pack can only distinguish *Asso* and *Re*.'²³

All this had been a game, but soon it had become a game that was a little tedious; and then – it suddenly ceased to seem worth playing at all. More and more, in his great rooms in the Palazzo Guiccioli, where the fox and monkey fought with each other and Allegra screamed in a fit of babyish passion, Byron began to feel himself alone. 'A foreigner', he had called himself, writing to Teresa in such a moment, 'far from the moral customs and ways of thought and behaviour of my fellow-countrymen', – and this

---

* *L.J.*, V, p. 24. Byron had a particular dislike of any show of learning in women. 'Our age', he wrote to Kinnaird, 'is an affected age and when affectation prevails the *fair* sex – or rather the *blue* – are always strongly tinctured with it. A little learning may be swelled to an ominous size by artifice. Madame de Staël, I grant, is a clever woman; but all the other *madams* are not Staëls.' September 17th, 1820. From an unpublished letter, to be published in *Byron, a Self-Portrait*, the new 2-volume edition of Byron's correspondence, Murray, London.

sense of having come into a world entirely alien, now grew daily upon him.

'Their moral is not your moral,' he told Murray, 'their life is not your life . . . The Conventual education, the Cavalier Servitude, the habits of thought and living are so entirely different, and the difference becomes so much more striking the more you live intimately with them, that I know not how to make you comprehend a people, who are at once temperate and profligate, serious in their character and buffoons in their amusements, capable of impressions and passions which are at once *sudden* and *durable*. . . .'[24]

Was it of Teresa that he was thinking? She, too, had succumbed to a passion that was *sudden* and *durable*. Would he, her Cavalier Servente, be able to stay the course?

'Their system has its rules, and its fitnesses, and decorums, so as to be reduced to a kind of discipline or game at hearts, which admits few deviations, unless you wish to lose it . . . They exact fidelity from a lover as a debt of honour; while they pay the husband as a tradesman, that is, not at all. You hear a person's character, male or female, canvassed, not as depending on their conduct to their husbands or wives, but to their mistress or lover. And – and – that's all.'[25]

Yes, that was all. So long as Byron had made love in Venice to women of no repute – to a gondolier's daughter or a Fornarina – the difference between the Italian background and his own had only given a touch of exotic colour, of heightened intensity, to his adventure. For in superficial relations it is variety and brilliance that is pleasing. It is only when the heart is involved, that the lover begins to seek not the alien and exciting, but the familiar and kind.

And this was precisely what, in Teresa, he did not find. She was pretty, she was passionate, she was – in spite of all her faults of taste – a lady. But she was not, as at first he had hoped, an animal of his own species. This, too, he was beginning to feel, was but one more encounter of strangers. But by the time he had fully realized this, a habit – which is responsible for more lasting ties than passion – had been formed.

BYRON TO CONTESSA GUICCIOLI

Your little head is heated now by that damned novel – the author of which has been – in every country and at all times – my evil Genius.[16]

As for the rest, I vow I don't know what I have done to you. Zinnantina's Tuda was not there – and you know the Zinanni – so what is it?

I am not riding today – so when you can – or wish – I am here and. ever and entirely yours.

'The note is copied from some French book. The sentences are coupled together like horses of different colours – and form a rather singular team. – "Besoin" does not need an *e* at the end. Dieu *sait* and not *"sais"* (as you write) that you are a very bad child and a very naughty O . . . . Your fidelity is like your progress in this new language, vacillating. . . . .*
Bon soir – bon repos – *bonne nuit* is not F[rench].'

My Love for Ever: We shall be meeting. I have not got the Letters of the Maintenon – who was a devout wh . . . – and not a merry one like Clemilda – so I can't even understand what the aforesaid Clemilda can want with such a book. If I had it – I would certainly send it you.

I have read the 'few lines' of your note with all due attention – they are written with your usual eloquence, which you will never lose, until you lose – not a Heart, but *Corinne*.

There was, now, some further unpleasantness with Guiccioli – this time about some money which Byron had advanced for the engagement of a prima donna – Mme Pasta – for the Ravenna opera.†

March 3rd, 1820
'*He is my creditor.*' How? And if it were so, since he has been paid 200 scudi – is that not a reason the more for giving me a receipt? He should not have signed any obligation – but these are

_____

* Two lines erased or torn. The last words legible are '. . . and rash vows, like this evening's breeze'.

† See letter of January 17th. Byron had already advanced half the sum he had promised (two hundred pounds), but Guiccioli wanted to take the credit for the whole transaction himself, and therefore refused to give him a receipt – hence Byron's very natural annoyance. 'Vie', p. 372.

trifles. Let us come to the facts. The sum that I have to pay to the Comune – or to the Deputies – is 400 scudi. I have acknowledged it, and I do so very gladly, with all possible pleasure. Of this, the sum of 200 scudi has already been paid – for which He refuses me a receipt – for reasons which I do not understand and do not want to understand. I am quite ready to pay the whole sum tomorrow – and among other reasons for this – not to let Count Guiccioli be placed under an obligation on my behalf – but if I pay, I shall once again ask for a receipt – the first duty of anyone who *receives* anything, even from one of his own peasants.

On this occasion it was to Teresa that Byron complained – but a sense of unease and mistrust was once again clouding their relationship.

BYRON TO CONTESSA GUICCIOLI

Very naughty 'O'.[27] – I should like to know what that paper was, which you were reading just now, after getting back from the Conversazione – and which you would not show me. It looked very much like contraband. Think of a good excuse at once and send me the most probable lie you can invent.

And by the next day, another violent quarrel – this time provoked by Teresa's jealousy – had broken out. Only a few days earlier Byron had told Murray that Italian women 'are extremely tenacious, and jealous as furies; not permitting their lovers even to marry if they can help it, and keeping them always close to them in public as in private whenever they can'.[28] The incident to which the following letters refer must have confirmed this opinion, but he would hardly have taken so seriously Teresa's threat of breaking with him on so very slight a pretext, unless this quarrel had been one of many. One may, indeed, surmise that some of these storms were deliberately provoked by Teresa – who had enough *intelligence du cœur* to know that tedium was, in Byron, her greatest enemy. 'His misfortune', Annabella had noted in her Journal many years before, 'is a passion for excitement . . . It is the tedium of a monotonous existence that leads beings of this type, even when they have a good heart, along the most dangerous paths . . . The love of tormenting comes from this source.'[29] But Annabella, who analysed so neatly, could not act on her conclusions. Teresa, with less reasoning, but a quicker instinct, provoked the storm that broke the tedium, and changed the tormentor into the tormented.

M[arch] 4th, 1820

Your imagination is too active – To have sent you a book which you have wanted to see for some time, is not surprising and is no reflection on you.

'You will not see me again.' Why – What have I done to you? It is true that I did not stay by your side during cards this evening at the C[avalli]'s, because you put yourself in a corner where there was not room for your friend – for reasons which perhaps you know better than I. But this does not seem to me a sufficient reason to end a friendship of some duration and many trials.

If I have been guilty towards you – you can find it out. In a small town one can find out the truth, when one wishes either to speak evil or to hear it.

If you are serious in your resolution – I am not a man who will be importunate – but I require you *to repeat* this resolution in *cold blood* in writing – then I shall draw my own conclusions. Remember only that *you* want this, and not I.

March 5th, 1820

I have sent twice for a reply to my last night's letter. At least, whatever your decision may be, I think that in justice to me you should tell me, for my guidance, your definite decision and the reasons for it. I have a duty towards your father, with whom – before taking the steps which I must take if you are really determined to hold me to this very strange decision – I must speak for a moment.

Remember always that you are the one who wants to break off our relationship – and not I – and that I have never wronged you in word, or deed or thought.

[Paper torn] . . . . In case you really are resolved . . . because – I shall not importune you any more and shall leave at a moment's notice.

I am nevertheless always your friend and lover*

It would be better to tell me tonight – anything is better than this uncertainty.

I left because the evening showed signs of becoming very long –

---

* 'Amico ed amante.' 'A.a. in e.' 'amico ed amante in eterno' (friend and lover for ever) became Byron's and Teresa's regular signature to each other.

and I saw Papa – who did not look as if he would be leaving soon. Pray tell me what you have to say now instead of tomorrow – because – I too have my own reasons for wanting to know, and have some things to decide before Saturday.³⁰

P.S. Luigi has come back saying that you have gone to bed. You will say what suits you, – but pray say it soon – for I will not be exposed any longer to the caprices either of husbands or of 'amiche' who take a pleasure in being as ungracious as possible.

My Love:³¹ You count on the power that you have had over me until now and over my actions – my thoughts – my heart – to make me believe this – and everything else you want – and that is most convenient to you: now and for ever. I do not say that you will not succeed now, because you have already succeeded only too often – but I warn you that a moment will come when your [arts]* will be in vain.

It is better that we should not see each other again tonight – tomorrow perhaps we can talk more quietly. – I am inclined to believe what you say – but I also have my suspicions sometimes, and you, who are at least equally suspicious, ought rather to pity than blame me. – I beg you not to come to me now – because to see each other at this moment could do nothing but increase my grief. Tomorrow I shall see you and we will talk.³²

So the spring wore on – with Byron's spirits 'unequal – now high, now low'.³³ To Harriette Wilson, who wrote at this time to ask whether he was 'tolerably happy', he replied:

'In answer to your wish that I should tell you if I was "happy", perhaps it would be a folly in any human being to say so of themselves, particularly a man who has had to pass through the sort of things which I have encountered; but I can at least say that I am not miserable, and am perhaps more tranquil than ever I was in England.'³⁴

He told Kinnaird that he had been

'changing my sea-residence for a land house, much as a Triton would on coming ashore. I have had to buy me a landau in lieu

* Word torn out.

of a Conch or Gondola, to get me horses, to alter my tarpaulin liveries into terra firma fashions, and to leave nothing of the Sea about us but the crest on my carriage, a Mermaid, as you may remember. I have brought me furniture, and new saddles, and all that from Milan, and chairs and tables from various parts of the Globe, at some cost and great trouble.'[85]

His health was suited by his long daily rides in the Pineta, and he was working hard; having completed the *Prophecy of Dante*, of which Teresa corrected the proofs,* and the translation of *Francesca da Rimini*, he had now started his Venetian tragedy, *Marino Faliero*. About this he later wrote to Murray: 'I never wrote or copied *an entire Scene of that play* without being obliged to *break off* – *to break* a commandment, to obey a woman's, and to forget God's.'[86] And to Teresa he wrote: 'It was written by your side, and in moments assuredly more tragic for me as a man than as a writer – because *you* were in distress and danger.'

But indeed, the emotional storms of the next few months only contributed to his intellectual fertility. Violent passions, even painful, gave him the enhanced sense of his own existence, which is the spring of all creative energy. 'The great object of life', he wrote, 'is sensation – to feel that we exist, even though in pain. It is this "craving void" which drives us ... to intemperate, but keenly felt pursuits of any description, whose principal attraction is the agitation inseparable from their accomplishment.'

And, within the next few weeks, the events that took place within the walls of Palazzo Guiccioli, were sufficiently dramatic to satisfy even Byron's need for sensation. A peculiar intensity was given them – not only by the character of the chief protagonists, but by the nature of the society which played the part of chorus: a society as observant, gossipy and censorious as that of any other provincial town – but, in addition, one in which political feeling – since it was allied to religious prejudice – ran as high as in Ireland, say, in the time of the 'Black and Tans'. Moreover, as in Ireland, this political animus was extended into every branch of private life. When Byron first arrived in Ravenna – only five years after the departure of the French and the restoration of Papal rule – the town was divided into two mutually suspicious camps; the Clerical and the Liberal. The first centred round the Palazzo dell'Arcivescovado, close to the Cathedral Square; for there lived the Cardinal Legate, the Pope's representative, whose

* 'While I am scribbling to you, they [the proofs] are corrected by one who passes for the prettiest woman in Romagna.' (*L.J.*, V, p. 16, April 23rd, 1820.)

power it is hardly possible to overestimate.* The spiritual power and the temporal, the administration of justice and finance, the control of the police, the direction of education, the welfare of the poor – all these were in his hands – or rather in the hands of the large number of ambitious, crafty and frequently corrupt minor prelates and employees who formed his court.[37] The greater part of the taxes ended in the pockets of these 'administrators', or in 'pensions' to religious bodies; and bribery and corruption were so much the acknowledged order of the day, that the clerk of one Comune frankly presented to his Gonfaloniere the following account:

> For one *magna-magna* scudi
> For another *magna-magna* scudi . . .

saying that, as he did not know how to spell the names of all the people who received the bribes ordered by the Gonfaloniere, this seemed to him the most suitable expression for them!†

'Tout le monde vole, tout le monde est content, et cependant maudit les prêtres,' commented Stendhal, and added that a friend of his had said to him: 'Demain Sa Sainteté peut me jeter dans les cachots de Saint Leo et confisquer ma fortune: cela sera cruel, mais non pas *injuste*; il n'y a aucune loi qui le défende.'[38]

Nevertheless, the Clerical party of Ravenna, in the eyes of many of the old-fashioned aristocracy, still represented stability and order; and its members regarded with the gravest suspicion, as traitors to their religion and their class, the new-fangled Liberals, like Teresa's father, who openly regretted the days of the French occupation and dreamed of a free and independent Italy. But every day, as the injustice and incompetence of the Papal regime became more and more apparent, their numbers were increasing. It was whispered that in the other cities of the Romagna, too, there was a similar discontent. Secret societies sprang up all over the province, and in every class of society: spies and informers hurried to the Cardinal's palace; priestly quills painstakingly wrote out report after report to Rome – and, from the pulpit, violent diatribes attacked the new ideas, harbingers of 'a false, un-Christian brotherhood'.

It is doubtful whether Byron, when he first came to Ravenna, was interested in, or even aware of, these local politics, which were

---

* 'Le gouvernement', wrote Stendhal of the Romagna at this period, 'est sous le droit divin. C'est une persécution exercée par les bigots et les nobles. . . Le Pape n'est rien moins qu'un imbécile; il est ultra comme un chien, ainsi que Consalvi; mais il veut *la sua pace*.' Stendhal, *Correspondance inédite*, I, p. 141. March 28th, 1820.

† FARINI, op. cit., p. 71. *Magna-magna*, literally 'eat-eat'.

indirectly to influence the course of his own life. Certainly he did not take any trouble to conciliate the Clerical faction – and, as has been described, he rebuffed the first advances made to him by the Cardinal, when invited to his Conversazione, making it clear that he preferred to make love in private, rather than conversation in public. On his second visit, however, he heard more of the political talk of the Gamba family, and saw for himself the misrule from which the country was suffering. His sympathies were awakened, and when, in the spring, the first signs of trouble began to show themselves, he commented on them in his letters to England (read, of course, by the police) in a tone hardly calculated to please the representatives of law and order. 'We are on the verge of a row here', he told Murray with gusto. 'The police is all on the alert, and the Cardinal glares pale through all his purple. . . .'
The walls of the town had been covered during the night with posters.

'They must have been all night about it, for the "Live republics", "death to popes and priests", are innumerable and plastered over all the palaces; ours has plenty. There is "down with the Nobility", too – they are down enough already, for that matter. ... I vaticinate a *row* in Italy – in which case I don't know that I won't have a finger in it. I dislike the Austrians and think the Italians infamously oppressed.'[39]

He was even more convinced of this a few weeks later, when the local Papal police actually dared to interfere with his household:

'[They] have petitioned the Cardinal against my liveries, as resembling too nearly their own lousy uniform ... My liveries are of the colours conforming to my arms, and have been the family hue since the year 1066 ... I have directed my ragamuffins ... to defend themselves, in case of aggression; and, on holidays and gaudy days, I shall arm the whole set.'[40]

Some time before this – though without Byron's knowledge – the Archbishop of Ravenna had thought it worth while to trouble Cardinal Consalvi, the Secretary of State in Rome, with a report on another member of Byron's household, his steward Antonio Lega Zambelli. This man, who had previously been in Count Guiccioli's service and was Fanny Silvestrini's lover, was an unfrocked Priest who, according to the Archbishop, 'forgetting his priestly character entirely, has abandoned his ecclesiastical robes,

giving himself up to a wholly secular life'. Now, the Archbishop
complained, he had come back 'as the secretary of the Englishman
Mylord Byron, who seems inclined to settle in Ravenna. The
arrival of this Priest, and his *wholly* secular clothing and manners,
have not failed to excite talk which is most prejudicial to the
Ecclesiastical Order,' and therefore the Archbishop requested the
Cardinal to send him 'his superior and wise suggestions and
decisions on the subject'.[41]

It is probable that, in all this, the government's real interest lay
not in the servant but in his master. Now that trouble was
indubitably brewing, Byron's presence in the Romagna had
become most undesirable – but to ask a foreigner of his rank to
go away, unless there were some very definite charges against him,
was manifestly impossible. Could not some indirect, yet equally
efficacious way, be found? Monsignor Marini,* one of the most
able and ambitious young prelates of the Cardinal's entourage,
and a great friend of Guiccioli's, thought that it should not be too
difficult. It was gently insinuated to the old gentleman that a
situation which, until then, had preserved a semblance of
decorum, was becoming too unseemly, that Mylord was now the
true master of Palazzo Guiccioli. Was it not time for the Count to
intervene?

It is not certain to what an extent Guiccioli was really influenced
by these remarks. The rest of the evidence suggests that his plans
had been maturing for some time; but it is of course possible that
– since he was a violent-tempered man, as well as a crafty one –
some unpleasant insinuation at one of Mons. Marini's evening
parties caused him to take action. What we do know is that on the
morning of April 2nd, Teresa sent an agitated note to Byron.
Early that morning, she wrote, before she was up, her husband
had forced open her writing-desk, and had read, one by one, all
the letters it contained. Fortunately, she added, they held nothing
which could provide him with weapons against Byron. She ended
her letter with the declaration: 'I will die, before I cease to be your
true friend!'†

And now the Count decided to change his tactics. For some
time, according to Teresa, his ill-humour and 'strangeness' had

---

* Mons. Pietro Marini, by birth a Roman, had come to Ravenna with the previous
Legate, Cardinal Malvasia, as assessor and governor of Ravenna, and had founded
with him a literary Academy known as the Malvasiana. He then entered upon an
ecclesiastical career and lived to become Governor of Rome (a post from which he
was removed for excessive despotism), a Cardinal and Legate of Forlì.

† This letter is quoted by Teresa in the 'Vie' (pp. 376-8), but the edges of the pages
on which it is written have unfortunately been nibbled by mice, so that none of the
sentences are complete.

been increasingly marked, and finally, one evening in the middle of May, when he returned home and found Mylord, as usual, in Teresa's company, he made, for the first time, a violent scene.

'The Count went straight up to him [Byron] and said to him that the visits he had once allowed had now become displeasing to him, and that he begged him to discontinue them. Lord Byron had enough self-control to listen fairly calmly – and after replying, with noble pride, a few words signifying that he would defer to his host's age and the fact that he was in his house, he went upstairs again. The scenes which took place after his departure upset and frightened the Countess so much by their violence, that on the following morning she sent for her father – and after confiding to him all that had occurred, she declared to him that it was impossible for her to live with the Count any longer, and begged for his permission to return and live under his protection.'[42]

At this point the story again takes an unexpected turn. From the whole of Count Gamba's behaviour until now, it would have seemed probable that he would tell his daughter roundly to attend to her wifely duties and send Byron away; but, instead, he at once agreed to her request and dispatched a formal petition to Pope Pius VII, asking that Teresa should be granted a decree of separation, on the ground that it had become 'utterly impossible for her to live any longer with so exacting a husband'.[43] This petition was forwarded and recommended to the Pope by Teresa's maternal grandmother, Countess Cecilia Machirelli Giordani – 'a lady of the highest merit', says Teresa, 'for whom the Pope had a very great friendship'. The Pope, indeed, Gregorio Chiaramonti, was an old family friend; he had officiated, as Bishop of Imola, at the wedding of Teresa's parents, and had stayed with her grandmother at the family palazzo at Pesaro. He was therefore naturally prepossessed in favour of the family, and – according to Teresa – remarked on receiving the petition: 'such a request, made by Count Gamba on his daughter's behalf, and recommended by Countess Cecilia, cannot be anything but just.'*

Here is Count Gamba's petition:

* 'The father of the Signora', – said Guiccioli, in referring to this petition of Gamba's when he himself appealed, later on, to Leo XII – 'instead of persuading her to fulfil her duties towards her husband and dissuade her from vice and immoral conduct, did not shrink from stating to Pius VII (of happy memory) a number of falsehoods.' Elliot Papers.

Most Holy Father: Ruggero Gamba of the city of Ravenna, most humble petitioner of Your Holiness, with the most profound veneration states that in the past year, 1818, he gave his daughter Teresa in marriage to Signor Cavaliere Alessandro Guiccioli, of the same city. In the short space of one year the Cavaliere has behaved so strangely and heaped so many insults upon his unhappy bride, that it has become wholly impossible for her to live any longer with so exacting a Husband, and she is obliged, in the opinion of the whole city, to seek a complete separation.

In this state of affairs the petitioner humbly appeals to Your Holiness, beseeching that the Cav. Guiccioli may be ordered to pay a suitable allowance to his wife (the aforesaid daughter) in accordance with the position of her husband, in order that she may live suitably, as befits her birth and position. By the grace, etc., etc.[44]

Guiccioli's scene with Byron took place about the middle of May, and indeed on May 15th Byron was writing to Harriette Wilson:

'I am at "this present writing" in a scrape (not a pecuniary one, but personal, about one of your ambrosial sex) which may probably end this very evening. Don't be frightened. The Italians don't fight: they stab a little now and then; but it isn't that, it is a divorce and separation; and as the aggrieved person is a rich noble and old, and has had a fit of discovery against his moiety, who is only twenty years old, matters look menacing.'[45]

For meanwhile the Count's spies had not been idle. No less than eighteen of his servants – ranging from his accountant and major-domo to the cook, the maids, the coachman, one of the Moors (the other was faithful to Teresa) and even two blacksmiths and carpenters – were now engaged in spying upon his wife – and later on he required all of them to sign a written statement, which he forwarded to the Pope.[46] This evidence affirmed that until the middle of May 'perfect harmony' had reigned between Teresa and her husband, 'who had constantly showed to his Lady Consort all the attentions of a most loving husband' – and that the servants 'never saw any act that was not in harmony with their mutual respect for each other'. The cause of a change in Guiccioli was attributed by them all, according to their testimony, only to 'the jealousy that the Cavaliere felt for the Englishman Lord Byron, who was then no more admitted to call upon the lady'.

'She, who until then had sometimes been seen to go upstairs secretly to the rooms rented and inhabited by Mylord, then began to go there almost daily, during the two hours after dinner, when her husband was resting. She gradually ceased from going to church, to parties, to the "trottata"[47] and to the theatre with her husband, and "instead made use of the theatre hours to join Mylord in his rooms, taking care to be warned of her husband's return by one of her own footmen, Luigi Morelli, who used to stand on guard outside the house door". This man was dismissed by Guiccioli on this account, but was immediately taken into Byron's service instead, and "continued to do the best he could".'

In addition the two carpenters testified to having seen Teresa in Mylord's rooms, while her husband was asleep downstairs. And, according to another statement, 'the blacksmith was one day called, by order of the Countess, and was ordered to remove the lock from a certain room, which he did in the presence of Lord Byron and of the Countess'. The 'certain room' was the one leading into Byron's bedroom, and the smith was ordered to change the lock of that door, because a second key was in Count Guiccioli's hands. But later on in the day, 'the Count having returned, he found the said door open, and the lock removed. He then ordered the smith to replace the lock. At the sound of the hammering, Lord Byron and Contessa Teresa appeared on the other side of the door'.[48]

The trouble was now beyond mending. By May 20th, Byron was writing to Murray:

'The Contessa G. is on the eve of being divorced on account of our having been taken together *quasi* in the fact, and, what is worse, that she did not *deny* it: but the Italian public are on our side, particularly the women – and the men also, because they say that *he* had no business to take the business up now, after a year of toleration. The law is against him, because he slept with his wife after her admission. . . .'[49]

A few days later he continued the story:

'There will probably be a separation between them, as her family, which is a principal one, by its connections, are very much against *him*, for the whole of his conduct; – and he is old and obstinate, and she is young and a woman, determined to sacrifice everything to her affections. I have given her the best advice, viz. to stay with him, – pointing out the state of a separ-

ated woman . . . and making the most exquisite moral reflections,
– but to no purpose. She says "I will stay with him, if he will let
you remain with me. It is hard that I should be the only woman
in Romagna who is not to have her *Amico*".'⁵⁰

During all this time life at Palazzo Guiccioli must have been
very odd indeed. Although Shelley wrote of Byron's 'splendid
apartments' and Byron himself described them to his friends in
much the same strain, Palazzo Guiccioli was in fact a not particularly spacious town-house, with a single staircase. Here
Byron, Guiccioli, Teresa, and all their numerous servants – not
to mention Allegra, the dogs, the cats, the monkey, the peacock,
the guinea-hens and the Egyptian crane – must have met several
times a day. Then they would retire to their separate apartments –
the Count and his wife quarrelling downstairs and Byron sulking
upstairs, while love-letters were carried up and down by Morelli
and the negro page, and the servants took sides and spied and
whispered – and the Pope's answer still delayed.

And now we can again follow the story in Byron's letters to
Teresa. The next group of thirteen notes were enclosed in a
folder on which Teresa had written '*Avant*' or '*Après l'abboccamento*' – that is, before or after the interview (between Byron
and Guiccioli). They are not dated, but they all plainly belong
to the late spring and early summer of 1820, since the first refers
to the opening of Teresa's writing-desk by her husband on April
2nd, and the last two to the Papal decree of July 6th, which
allowed Teresa to leave her husband.

These notes enable us to follow all the stages of Byron's behaviour, after he had realized that a choice was now inevitable:
that he must either make a permanent break with Teresa herself –
or be left with her on his hands. Faced with this alternative
Byron – as he had already done five months before in Venice –
made a last attempt to go away. 'There cannot be any remedy',
he told her, 'but my departure.' His 'exquisite moral reflections'
on the subject were based on the most conventional of arguments:
'With me you would be unhappy and compromised in the eyes
of the world. With your husband you would be, if not happy, at
least respectable and respected.' I do not think we need see in all
this only the last efforts of a reluctant lover to free himself.
Byron's conventionality was genuine, and he probably believed
every word of these remarks. If he had played for so many years
the rebel's part, it was because society, to his mind, had not been
kind to him. But he never questioned – as Shelley did – the
essential validity of the social laws. He wrote to Moore of himself

and Teresa as 'those who are in the wrong – the lady and her lover'. Moreover, he very much disliked, in women, the spectacle of uncontrolled behaviour. He had had enough of being the centre of violent scenes in public. His mother had flung the tongs at him in the presence of his friends; Caroline Lamb had tried to cut her veins at Lady Heathcote's ball; the Fornarina had slashed his picture with a bread-knife. But what he *liked* in women – or thought he liked – was the gentleness of the antelope, the timidity of the gazelle; and when he was looking for a wife, nothing could have been more conventional than the considerations that had inspired his choice. Teresa had done herself great harm in the first period of their liaison – as Fanny had tried to tell her – by the headlong impulsiveness of her behaviour. And now, for the last time, Byron tried to bring her to her senses – to make her realize how serious, how *lasting*, the consequences of her decision would be. 'A woman requires a great deal of character, the truest friendship, and the profoundest and *untiring* love . . . to decide on a course so disadvantageous.'

But it was no good. Teresa merely cried – complained that he did not really love her – and held more strongly to her determination. 'I see how it will end; she will be the sixteenth Mrs. Shuffleton.'[51]

The first of these notes refers to Guiccioli's search in his wife's writing-desk.

BYRON TO CONTESSA GUICCIOLI
Avant

My Love[52] The skeleton key – that is why I wanted my letters in my own hands *for the present* – and nevertheless you violently insulted me, because of my request. Pray look after the letters that are shut up in your writing-desk (with the music that was at La Mira) for something might be found there, if not of *mine* – yet something that you would not like.

My opinion is still the same – but if there is no remedy – I assuredly shall do my duty. Of my love you cannot doubt, and perhaps the greatest proof has been – that I prefer to sacrifice myself, rather than you.

Believe me ever and entirely

P.S. Your illness seems to me only *skin-deep* – when shall we see each other – tomorrow?

Remember – do not sign anything for that arch-scoundrel.

Avant

My Love: I do not esteem him and I do not fear him – he will do as he pleases. For my part I feel love and a duty towards you – but I do not wish to influence your decision in any way. After having done what he has done – no vileness – no wickedness – on his part would surprise me – or anyone else.*

Talk to your friends and relations and as you decide – so also will decide your

Avant

My love + 'Women! Women! Who can guess . . .† etc.' – What do you want me to do about it? You do not realize – he never does anything without a reason – and this is only the beginning. – I repeat to you that there is not and cannot be any remedy but my departure.

Of my love be assured – but I cannot understand how a love can be *true* that sacrifices the beloved object. With me you would be unhappy and compromised in the eyes of the world; with your husband you would be, if not happy, at least respectable and respected. So I see no alternative except a separation, which sooner or later would in any case have to come. I want to save you – even at the price of your – unjust – hatred – which however, in time, would give place to a feeling of gratitude.

Of what can you accuse me? I have come, I have gone – I have come back, I have remained. It is more than a year that I have done nothing but obey you in every respect – so long as it was possible to reconcile your welfare with your wishes, – and now that I see that this is no longer possible, – I shall take the only course that can be either reasonable or honourable.

I shall come to you this evening – and we will talk. Believe me ever and wholly your true friend and lover.

Avant

My love + I will come – but when and how? – If you do not fear for yourself, we must think of your family – for it is really against

---

* The reference is presumably to Guiccioli's breaking open Teresa's writing-desk.
†   'Donne, donne, eterni Dei!
             Chi vi arriva a indovinar?'
             (Women, women! – Eternal Gods!
             Who can ever guess your wishes?)
                         ROSSINI, *Barbiere di Siviglia*, Act I, Scene 7.

them that these things are directed – Against myself (apart from what I feel for you) they cannot do anything – but it would not be very heroic of me to compromise you all without sharing in the danger. So I would like to be instructed beforehand – how to behave – and for this purpose I should like to speak to Papa.

Indeed it is better for you in every way to be with A[lessandro], in six months you will think so too – and will be assured that I have been your *true* and sacrificed friend.

. . . .

You accuse me – I do not deserve it – and you know it. The time for deciding was before leaving V[enice], to which unhappy place you will remember how, and how much, I implored you not to force me to return. Behold the consequences!*

Avant

My love + What do you want me to reply? He has known – or ought to have known, all these things for many months – there is a mystery here that I do not understand, and prefer not to understand. Is it only now that he knows of your infidelity? †
What can he have thought – that we are made of stone – or that I am *more* or *less* than a man? I know of one remedy only – what I have already suggested, *my departure*. *It would be a great sacrifice*, but rather than run into things like this every day it becomes necessary – almost a duty – for me not to remain any longer in these parts.

He says that it is impossible for him to tolerate this relationship any longer – I answer that he *never* should have tolerated it. Assuredly it is not the happiest condition, even for me, to be exposed to his scenes, which come too late, now. But I shall do what a gentleman should do, that is, not cause disturbance in a family. All this would already be over – if that man had allowed me to leave in December of last year. – He not only *wished* me to *come*, but he said to me with his own lips that I ought not to go away – 'This being too far-fetched a remedy'.‡

* The above are two fragments of a letter, of which the rest has been destroyed, but which from the context appears to belong to this period.
† Teresa has tried to change this sentence to 'is suspicious of your fidelity'.
‡ This is an interesting sidelight on the events of the previous December, when Byron – at Count Gamba's request, and – it would now appear – not only with Count Guiccioli's consent, but his approval – returned to settle in Ravenna.

M

In these circumstances we shall not see each other tonight.
Always and *all yours*!

Avant

My love + As things are now it is better *not* to come – just now –
out of prudence. If He is in earnest – he will do everything
possible (according to his nature – and for revenge) not to let
you obtain any *allowance*. In this you must not *give way* – not so
much for the thing in itself, but on account of your reputation.

He assuredly has some end in view – he is a man who cannot
be trusted for a moment.

I fancy that it has always been his intention to make the matter
end like this, and that he made me come the *second time* on purpose.

Speak to Papa – and then (or before) we will talk. Do you
want me to take you to the theatre or not? Tell me.

If the matter ends with your separation from him – (which I
do not wish – though, on the other hand, it would not surprise
me) we shall make our decision, – and I shall do all that should
be done in the circumstances. –

I am only sorry for you – and just because *I love you*; I am sorry
too for your family, – For me – it doesn't matter – if I can help
in any way to make you less unhappy. –

Now I feel doubly the burden of not being free to render you
greater justice in the eyes of the world* – and also to assure your
independence after my death – in case (as I hope) you should
survive me. But I shall manage somehow to overcome this
difficulty.

I will come to you after changing when I come back from the
Pineta.

Believe me always and wholly your friend and lover.

Avant

My Love + I shall not go to any place of amusement – until this
affair is finished one way or the other. I shall ride, because that
is exercise – in a solitary place – and not in order to be seen.

* Byron, as early as July 1819, had written to Augusta: 'If you see my Spouse –
do pray tell her that I wish to marry again; and as probably she may wish the same,
is there no way in *Scotland*? without compromising her immaculacy? – cannot it be
done there by the husband solely?' *Astarte*, p 291.

If A[lessandro] wants to speak to me, let him – but assuredly I shall have very little to say in reply. If, after suffering the insult of his requiring separate rooms – owing to his mad folly – you go back to yielding to his false blandishments and dotardly caresses, it is you who will be to blame, and your weakness of character will be more confirmed than ever. However do what suits you – so long as I know it for my own guidance. I am

Byron's fear, that his liaison might be used by the Papal Government as a political weapon against the whole Gamba family, was justified by events, although not until some time later. But for the present, public opinion in Ravenna was wholly on Byron's and Teresa's side:

'All the world are implicated, including priests and cardinals. The public opinion is furious against *him*, because he ought to have cut the matter short at *first*, and not waited twelve months to begin.'[53]

Yet during the last weeks, according to Teresa, Guiccioli was seeking daily interviews with Byron, and it must have been after one of these meetings that the preceding letter was written.

By now Byron had justifiably reached the conclusion that the Count was 'a man who cannot be trusted for a moment', and who had a secondary motive for practically everything he said or did. Moreover there was another unpleasing aspect to the affair – one which Byron, to his credit, never hinted at in his letters to his English friends. This was the financial one. We have seen that the Count had borrowed money from Byron in Bologna, and had hoped to avoid repaying it by letting him occupy, rent free, the upper floor of the Ravenna palazzo. But, not content with this arrangement, he had attempted, during the spring, to obtain yet another loan from his guest. This, indeed, had been the beginning of all the trouble.

'Guiccioli having continued his plans for making money,' says a statement of Teresa to her lawyers, 'and the Countess having naturally refused to be his intermediary, and moreover her delicate health requiring precautions which inconvenienced him, he began to be estranged and to become insufferable'.[54]

In Rangone's *Cronaca* the story is told in even plainer terms:

'Suddenly the Cavaliere suggests to his wife to ask Byron for another 4.000 scudi. She refuses – out of honest motives. The Cavaliere insists, is estranged from his wife – and requires that Lord shall move out of the house and see her no more. In vain. Mylord remains, to work off his credit; and continues to visit the lady as much as he likes.'[55]

The *Cronaca* is not, of course, wholly reliable, being tinged with a mixture of provincial curiosity, envy and spite; nevertheless it is interesting to know that this was the general opinion in Ravenna at the time. And that the same opinion was held by the Government is shown by a report subsequently sent to the Austrian police in Venice by the Vice Legate of Ravenna, Conte Lavinio De Medici Spada:

'So long as the Guiccioli's avaricious and sordid mind nourished hopes of the Lord's guineas, there was no trouble; but when these faded, owing to his Wife's refusal to help him – since love of Byron had not destroyed in her the sense of honour and delicacy which her husband had never known – then, pretending to have just become aware of their relationship, he showed some resentment, which led to his separation.'[56]

The following note from Byron to Teresa would appear to relate to one of the many unpleasant scenes which were taking place at this time in Palazzo Guiccioli.

BYRON TO CONTESSA GUICCIOLI

It is just because I love you so much – that I cannot be patient where money matters are involved – especially with *him*. I would make any sacrifice for you – but in that case I want you to myself – entirely and now – all these things belittle me in my own opinion.

To him I cannot give way. He treats me with the insolence that he would show to one of his servants, and I will not bear such things any longer. I will submit to the opinion of any gentleman, that in this affair he has been equally lacking in courtesy and good faith – but enough!

Farewell, I kiss you

Avant

My Love+ Only this was lacking to complete our unhappiness!* I am, however, not surprised. And in these circumstances I shall not be allowed to visit you.

But most of all I am distressed by the last words of your note. They would be unjust at any time, and now more than ever. I always advised you for your good – and on seeing that it was useless, finally gave way to your wishes – and for this you now reproach me. In spite of this, I am constantly, and shall ever be

    Your ever most sincere and loving friend

After the Interview

My Love +++ The usual inconclusive business – and inconcludable, if there be such a word.

He proposed that I should *go away* (saying that this is the *general desire* and opinion – and that his friend Marini is surprised that I should stay to cause trouble in the life of a family) or else that I should use my influence over you to persuade you to detach yourself from *me* and to love *him* – and also that I should attach myself, as soon as possible, to *another*.

As to separation – he says that he does not want it – not being disposed to 'lose the woman' – to disgust his relations – and, above all, to *pay* an allowance. He does not want to cut the figure, he says, of a 'complacent cuckold' – and he charges me to persuade you that true love is *conjugal* love. I am using his own words. – He says that, my love not being a first passion – like yours – I should not behave like this, etc. etc. He does not want this – he does not want that – and does not know what he does want – but meanwhile he does not want us to love each other – which however I always shall.

The preceding letter shows that the long prepared *abboccamento* between Guiccioli and Byron had taken place at last – and the Count had made a final attempt to persuade Byron to go away. He had been taking legal advice, and had discovered that for Teresa to obtain a separation, by which he would have to pay her

---

* The reference in this letter is to an attack of erysipelas from which Teresa was suffering. On May 24th Byron was writing to Moore: 'I should have retreated, but honour, and an erysipelas which has attacked her, prevent me – to say nothing of love, for I love her most entirely, though not enough to persuade me to sacrifice everything to a frenzy.' (*L.J.*, V, p. 32.)

alimony, would not suit his books at all. If he had set spies on his wife and her lover, if he had so assiduously watched them himself all these long months, it had certainly not been in order to be forced to return his wife's dowry and pay her a handsome allowance.

The interview with Byron having failed, Count Guiccioli took up his pen and wrote a long letter to his wife's brother, Pietro Gamba, in Rome, telling him the whole story. This letter was shown later on by Pietro to Teresa, and by her to Byron, to whom it seemed so curious that he sent Murray a copy of it. 'Remember', he added, 'that Guiccioli *is telling his own story*, true in some things and very *false* in the details . . . *You* want to know *Italy*', he continued. 'There's more than Lady Morgan can tell me in these sheets, if carefully perused.'[57]

But meanwhile old Count Gamba had taken action. To the petition on his daughter's behalf, which he had already sent to the Pope, he now added a personal letter to Cardinal Rusconi, the Papal Legate in Ravenna.* In his letter, of which the original draft was preserved by Teresa, he not only protested against the 'calumnies' which Guiccioli was spreading about him – to the effect that Teresa's closest relations were encouraging her illicit love-affair – but referred, in a passage which someone – perhaps Teresa – has subsequently tried to erase, to his son-in-law's attempt to 'prostitute' his daughter.

In reading this significant letter it should be borne in mind that it was not addressed to the Vatican, but to a prelate actually living on the spot and by birth a citizen of Bologna, who would be fully aware whether Gamba's statements as to 'public opinion' were accurate or not. The draft among the Gamba papers is only a fragment, on which Teresa has written: 'Part of the original of a letter from Count Ruggero Gamba to His Eminence the Legate Rusconi in 1820.'[58]

June 23rd [1820]

'. . . Now it is truly surprising that the Cavaliere should attempt to put part of the blame due to him upon my shoulders by his calumnies. I say frankly, calumnies, for if he had believed what he now attempts to make others suspect, why did he then invite Lord to Ravenna, and in his own house, too? In either of the

---

* Cardinal Antonio Lamberto Rusconi, of a noble family of Bologna, was born in 1743. He joined the Franciscan Order, was made Cardinal in 1816, and had just been sent to Ravenna as a successor to the first Legate, Cardinal Malvasia, who had died in September 1819.

two cases, be he in good faith or bad, does he not by this admit himself to be the blackguard which the world considers him? I hope that your Eminence will recognize him to be one – and that will suffice me. For if I wished, by words, deeds or writings, to prove how he attempted, for vile financial considerations, to prostitute, sell* and disgrace my daughter and make her unhappy, I could show it with the greatest clearness; but the extremely delicate nature of the subject obliges me to keep silent, avoiding the scandal of public controversy; so that, satisfied by public opinion, I am willing to trust myself to the conscience and justice of my superiors, among whom I recognize in your Most Reverend Eminence my defender, my judge, my . . .'

Here the letter breaks off. It would be interesting to know whether it was Teresa who destroyed the missing parts of this document. In the 'Vie' she makes no reference to this letter.

Nor did Count Gamba confine himself to writing letters: he sought out his son-in-law and challenged him to a duel. It seems to me that not enough attention has been given, in considering this story, to this very odd behaviour. Here is an honest and simple country gentleman, whose uprightness has never been called into question, and who until now had shown the most correct and natural disapproval of his daughter's liaison. It is probable that his letter to Byron, suggesting his return to Ravenna, was written in good faith, believing his daughter's protestations of a platonic relationship. But, when at last the storm broke, and no further doubt could remain in his mind, what was his course of action? First he sent a petition to the Pope for a decree of separation – then he wrote the letter to the Cardinal – and finally he challenged to a duel, not his daughter's lover, but her husband!† Is this not overwhelming evidence that what Teresa at last told him about her husband's behaviour, shocked him so deeply as to place him, – against all his principles and preconceptions – completely on her side?

With Byron, however, even at this point, Teresa does not seem to have been completely frank. A curious and not wholly comprehensible letter of his at this time which Teresa destroyed in part, suggests that his suspicions had been reawakened about the nature of Teresa's relations with her husband. Was Guiccioli's

* The words 'prostitute' and 'sell' are legible in the copy of the letter in the Archives of the Sacra Rota.

† 'Yes, challenged him,' wrote Teresa in a marginal note to her copy of Moore's Life, 'and he would not have done so, if Count Guiccioli was not in the wrong and had not slandered and ill-treated me.'

hold upon her, he wondered, still so strong that she was in con-
nivance with him even now? At this point he does indeed seem
to have come very near to leaving Teresa for ever; and his letter,
although not wholly explicit, reveals a most profound disquiet.

BYRON TO CONTESSA GUICCIOLI

I had not the slightest suspicion, but your *anxiety* – your violence
– awakened in me not *suspicion*, but *certainty*. The motive must be
very strong – to shed *blood* in defence of a matter generally
indifferent and known to all the world . . . Do you think that I am
like . . . . vanity and indign . . . . I blush for what I have
suffered – for what you have seen me suffer on your account
. . . . Ever perfidious Italy . . . . to hide. . . .
I had the weakness to love you – I shall find strength to overcome a love of which everyone anticipated the consequences. I
am not surprised, but feel degraded. [five words erased] Farewell,
one day you will know what you sacrificed. . . . .

[on the back of the page]

This was written last night – I am sending it to show you to
what a state you have brought me. Even in A.'s presence I could
not control myself.*

With his friends in England, however, Byron kept up his old
flippant tone – referring to the duel as 'a superfluous valour, for
he [Guiccioli] don't fight, though suspected of two assassinations'.
He added that he had been warned, in consequence, not to take
such long rides in the Pine Forest, alone and unarmed.

'They say here that he will have me taken off, it is the custom . . .
They pop at you from behind trees, and put a knife into your back
in company, or in turning a corner, while you are blowing your
nose. He may do as he pleases, I only recommend him not to miss,
for if such a thing is attempted, and fails, he shan't have another
opportunity, "Sauce for the goose is sauce for the gander" . . .
I have taken no precaution (which indeed would be useless)
except taking my pistols when I ride out in the woods every
evening . . . A man's life is not worth holding on such a tenure as
the fear of such fellows.'⁵⁹

* What is left of this undated letter is in three fragments. Teresa appears first to
have destroyed another page of the letter; then she cut several passages out of this
page; and finally she put the remaining fragments into a folder entitled: '*Unjust
letters – to be destroyed!*'

Undoubtedly Byron, who had plenty of nervous courage, was tickled in his sense of the picturesque by this idea, and enjoyed writing to all his friends about it. But it is doubtful whether the danger was ever very real – and the Guiccioli Memoirs mock at it as 'a flight of poetic fancy, another dream of a foreigner who knew little about us and was imbued with the romantic tales of a school that imagined the Italy of 1819 to be unchanged from that of the Borgias and the Farnese'.[60]

It was now evident to Byron that there was no hope of a reconciliation between Teresa and her husband, or of a tolerable life for her in his company. And at this critical juncture, it must be admitted, Byron behaved correctly. 'Now I can hesitate no longer. He may abandon you, but I never shall.' If we still catch a glimpse of his inner misgivings in his last warnings to go slowly, to speak first to her Papa, we can hardly consider them unnatural. Even now Teresa was only twenty-one – a headstrong young woman who knew nothing of the world beyond Ravenna, Venice and the convent of S. Chiara. Byron, as he told her, felt immeasurably her elder – 'centuries older in experience'. He felt old, flat and sad; he embarked upon this new, permanent relationship with few illusions. But for the first time, he called himself her *husband*. Teresa, at last, had won.

BYRON TO CONTESSA GUICCIOLI

Après

Promesse ! ! ! ! d'être mon Époux!![*]

My Love+My honest behaviour and my advice were what they were because I did not wish to hurry you – and put you in a situation where the greatest reciprocal sacrifices would be needed. A woman requires a great deal of character, the truest friendship, and the profoundest – and *untiring* love – proved often and for long – to decide on a course so disadvantageous in every way, and irrevocable for all the rest of her life. But as that man has persecuted you in words and deeds for injuries to which no one has *contributed*, and which no one has protected – more than he – now I can hesitate no longer. – He may abandon you – but I *never*. – I have *years* more than you in age – and as many *centuries* in sad experience; I foresee troubles and sacrifices for you, but they will be *shared*; my love – my duty – my honour – all these and

* This heading, with its exclamation marks, was written by Teresa.

everything should make me forever what I am *now*, your lover friend and (when circumstances permit) your *husband*.

P.S. Don't commit yourself for several *reasons* – which I have explained to you in part by word of *mouth*, but if he goes ahead I shall not fail you.

Speak to Papa first.

Après

My Love+Yes, – I hope to see you this evening – and very quickly recovered – calm yourself – and believe what I have always said. It was a real sacrifice for me – but nevertheless it was my duty to show you the consequences of your resolution.

I have two letters – one from Paris, the other from Bologna. The address of the French letter will make you laugh. Here they are.

Always and entirely your most loving friend

Après la decision

My Love+++I have always said to you – that I did not wish to hurry things – but that once the matter was settled – you could command me. Now that we have reached this point, you will see that I have no fear or hesitation – and never have hesitated, except on *your account*. P. will have told you what I said about your affairs. I am not going to the Corso today – for I do not want to enjoy any diversion while my friend still is in the slightest trouble. Au revoir when you wish.

Believe me ever entirely yours

My Love+in 20 minutes I shall be free – and you can do what you think best.

I don't know what else to say to you – you will not hear reason and are committing yourself, for ever.

But . . . . . . I am

At last, after two long months of waiting, the Pope's answer came. On July 6th, Byron had written to Murray, returning to the swagger of some of his earlier letters:

'I have been the cause of a great conjugal scrape here – which is now before the *Pope* (seriously, I assure you) and what the decision of His Sanctity will be no one can predicate... The husband is the greatest man in these parts, with 100.000 Scudi a year, but he is a great Brunello in politics and private life – and is shrewdly suspected of more than one murder. The relatives are on my side because they dislike him. We wait the event.'*

By July 12th the news had come.

'The Pope has pronounced *their separation*. The decree came yesterday from Babylon – it was *she* and *her friends* who demanded it, on the ground of her husband's (the noble Count Cavalier's) extraordinary usage. *He* opposed it with all his might because of the alimony, which has been assigned,† with all her goods, chattels, carriage, etc., to be restored by him. In Italy they can't divorce. He insisted on her giving me up, and he would forgive everything, – even the adultery, which he swears that he can prove by "famous witnesses". But in this country, the very courts hold such proofs in abhorrence, the Italians being as much more delicate in public than the English, as they are more passionate in private. The friends and relatives, who are numerous and powerful, reply to him – "You, yourself, are either fool or knave, – fool, if you did not see the consequences of the approximation of these two young persons – knave, if you connived at it. Take your choice, – but don't break out (after twelve months of the closest intimacy, under your own eyes and positive sanction) with a scandal which can only make you ridiculous and her unhappy.

He swore that he thought our intercourse was purely amicable, and that *I* was more partial to him than to her, till melancholy testimony proved the contrary. To this they answer, that 'Will of *this* Wisp' was not an unknown person, and that *Clamosa Fama* had not proclaimed the purity of my morals; – that *her* brother, a year ago wrote from Rome and warned him that his wife would infallibly be led astray by this *ignis fatuus*, unless he took proper measures, all of which he neglected to take, etc., etc. Now he says that he encouraged my return to Ravenna, to see *in quanti piedi d'acqua siamo* and he has found enough to drown him in.'*¹

When Teresa, twelve years later, read this letter in Moore's *Life*, she was very much upset. 'This word adultery is *cruel*,' she

* *L.J.*, V, pp. 47-8. To Murray, July 6th, 1820. 'There has not been such a row in Romagna', he told Hobhouse on the same day, 'these hundred years.'
† Byron told Kinnaird that the alimony was of 'twelve hundred crowns a year... a handsome allowance for a lone woman in these parts, almost three hundred pounds sterling a year, and worth about a thousand in England'. Unpublished letter, of July 20th, 1820, see n. 59, p. 503.

wrote in the margin, 'and could at least be sostituted [*sic*] by another less odious.'

'All his manner of expressing himself', she added, 'is the biggest proof how his own imagination could represent him the things in a quite different light than to others. He is almost always wrong in everything he says about the separation, which had not its source in jealousy or love, (which were but pretexts for Count G.) but in incompatibility of the temper and in the ill conduct of the Count, which will be proved one day or other.'⁶²

The Pope's decree, dated July 6th, 1820, stated unequivocally that Teresa was granted her separation because it was 'no longer possible for her to live in peace and safety with her husband'. The decree was sent to Countess Cecilia Machirelli Giordani at Pesaro, and from there was forwarded to Count Gamba at Filetto. Gamba at once sent it to his daughter, together with a letter to Teresa from Cardinal Rusconi, clearly explaining the conditions under which she would be allowed to return to her father's house.

July 14th, 1820

Most Illustrious Lady! His Holiness having been informed that your Ladyship has found herself in circumstances in which she can no longer live in peace and safety with her Husband, Cav. Alessandro Guiccioli, His Holiness has benignly condescended to authorize me to permit you to leave your Husband's House and to return to the House of your Father, Count Ruggero Gamba; so that you may live there in such laudable manner as befits a respectable and noble Lady separated from her Husband.

Further the Holy Father, in order that Your Ladyship may not be deprived of the necessary provisions and all that is requisite for the noble and decorous state of a Lady, condescends to assign you one hundred scudi a month, which shall be paid by the Husband in such manner and means as the integrity and providence of the Holy Father directs and shall be conveyed to you in future by the Cardinal Legate, the present writer, in fulfilment of the Sovereign Command.

Furthermore, it is the considered and express wish of the Holy Father that Your Ladyship, in leaving your Husband's house, shall take with her such linen, clothing and other objects as appertain to the decent adornment of a married Lady, as well as all that may be required for bed and board, following an inventory of these objects, to be signed by both parties, excepting valuables which your Ladyship did not bring with her to her Husband's House, and which she received as gifts on the occasion of her Wedding.

The Cardinal Legate, in communicating these Sovereign decrees, consigns them with the truest and most distinguished esteem.   A. CARD. RUSCONI[63]

To this letter Teresa at once replied:

Ravenna   *July* 15th, 1820

Most Reverend Eminence: the favour accorded me by the Clemency of the Holy Father gives me back the peace I had lost and assures me a comfortable subsistence. Meanwhile, to avoid any unpleasant gossip or any other disagreeable consequences, I am going to the country with my Father, where I shall quietly await the instructions and benevolence of your Most Reverend Eminence.

I have the honour to kiss your Holy Purple.

Your Most Reverend Excellency's most humble, devoted and obedient Servant   TERESA GUICCIOLI *née* GAMBA[64]

It was only on the following day that the news was sent by the Cardinal to Alessandro Guiccioli, together with a copy of the Pope's Order, and an injunction 'not to delay in executing these Sovereign Orders'. The Count asked for a copy of the letter sent to Teresa, and of her answer, both of which were sent to him, but at the same time he was firmly told that 'any objections, or any steps he might care to take in the matter' should be addressed directly to Rome, since, the Order having been given directly by His Holiness, the Ravenna Legation would be unable to interfere in the matter.[65]

Count Guiccioli, however, was not so easily discouraged. He immediately gathered together his eighteen servants, drew up for their signature their evidence against Teresa, which has already been quoted, and sent it off to Rome. He also persuaded twelve of his most respectable fellow-citizens, – including some of the judges of the Ravenna Legation – five members of the Criminal Court, a parish priest, and the family doctor – to sign another document, testifying – almost in the same words as the servants – that Guiccioli 'had always shown to his Lady Consort every attention of a most loving husband', that he and his wife had

always been seen together 'at the carriage parade or in the Corso,
at the Conversazioni, and in Church', and that the only cause of
the interruption of this domestic harmony had been Guiccioli's
jealousy of Lord Byron, whose lease he had then tried to break'.
And finally – the italicizing is Guiccioli's – that *never had the
Cavaliere been an exacting husband* ("indiscreto marito") *and even in the
last period had shown her every due respect*.⁶⁶ His case, which was
sustained with equal vehemence by his children's advocate after
his death – was based on the assertion that a justified jealousy of
Byron was his *only* quarrel with his wife; in all other respects he
had been an admirable husband.

At the end of the whole strange story, and also taking into
consideration Count Guiccioli's later behaviour to his wife, when
she returned to him after Byron's death, we are forced to the conclusion that neither his version nor Teresa's hold the whole truth:
the real key, perhaps, lay simply in Guiccioli's cold-blooded
avarice. His wife was to him a piece of property like any other –
and, like other property, should be made to prove a good invest-
ment.⁶⁷ Being a man of an unusually strong will, he did at first
gain a great hold over her; but when he attempted to use this for
his own ends he encountered, where Byron was concerned, an
unexpected resistance. Teresa, with regard to Byron, was
totally and whole-heartedly disinterested. This Guiccioli could
not forgive.

But before the news of the Pope's decree reached Count Guiccioli, Teresa was already safely in her father's country-house. Her
last day in Palazzo Guiccioli – July 15th – must have been a
singularly unpleasant one. She already had in her pocket a letter
from her father, enclosing Cardinal Rusconi's, and telling her –
'in order to avoid a violent scene or scandal' – to meet him outside
the town that afternoon. But Guiccioli – possibly guessing that
something was afoot – had given orders that none of the horses
were to be taken out that day. Both husband and wife, however,
kept up, in the presence of their household, a formal appearance
of harmony, and during dinner – according to the servant's
evidence – 'the Cavaliere himself served his Wife, as is customary
with a Lady, and they made conversation on indifferent matters,
with the courteous manners characteristic of both of them'.⁶⁸

Two hours later – the faithful Morelli having succeeded in
hiring a coach – Teresa stole out of Palazzo Guiccioli – for ever –
and, accompanied only by her maid and Morelli, met her father
on the road to Filetto. 'Thus', she wrote, 'took place the
separation of which Lord Byron was the occasion, rather than the
cause.'⁶⁹

5 : FILETTO

When a man hath no freedom to fight for at home,
Let him combat for that of his neighbours.

BYRON

COUNT GAMBA'S country-house, Filetto, lay some fifteen
miles south-west of Ravenna, in a wide, unbroken plain. It
was a green land, rich in water. In Teresa's day a wide
strip along the coast was still given up to the great pine-forest –
'full of pastime and prodigality' – which stood in the midst of
marshes and lagoons, the home of every sort of water-fowl – and,
further inland, the fields were intersected by a network of canals
and streams, flowing between grassy banks broad enough for a
carriage to drive along. Beside one of these rivers, the Montone,
and surrounded by a wide lawn, framed by an avenue of old
olive-trees, stood Count Gamba's villa, a pleasant, spacious house
built at the end of the seventeenth century. A wide double outer
stairway of grey stone led up to the vast saloon on the first floor,
which was open to the roof. The bedrooms of the second floor
looked down on it, from windows and doors giving on to an upper
gallery, so that when, on hot summer nights, these doors stood
open, their occupants could talk agreeably with each other from
their beds.* A mixture of old-fashioned splendour and discomfort marked the furnishing: beds and walls were hung with red
damask, and there was an abundance of great Renaissance arm-
chairs, of family portraits and holy pictures and *prie-Dieu*. But the
stone floors were bare, there were few fire-places, and little protection for the chilly mists which, on autumn evenings, would
creep up from the river. It was a summer house, and indeed it was
chiefly in the summer that the Gambas lived there, in patriarchal
fashion – a large, cheerful, easy-going family, devoted to each
other and to their country pursuits. 'They might well', wrote
Lord Malmesbury, 'have been called the Osbaldistones of Italy.
They were all sportsmen according to their knowledge, which
consisted of hunting a slow pointer, who stood woodcock and
partridge equally well, through the forests and vineyards.'¹ They
also shot duck and snipe in the marshes, rode in the forest and
fished in the river; they took an active interest and pride in the
management of their estates; they entertained their country neighbours, and, as will appear, they came to find this secluded country-
house a most convenient centre for their conspiratorial activities.

* Young Lord Fitzharris, when he visited Teresa there in 1828, was somewhat taken
aback by this 'Italian sans-façon' – and no less by the perpetual presence of Don
Giovanni, 'a domestic Levite'. MALMESBURY, *Memoirs of an ex-Minister*, I, p. 32.

191

Here Teresa had lived as a child – sharing her brothers' and sisters' sports, riding with her father to visit the outlying farms, reading her poetry-books and dreaming her romantic dreams, – and here, after two years of married life, she now returned.*

The terms of the Pope's decree required, as we have seen, that she should live in her father's house 'in such a laudable manner as befits a respectable and noble lady separated from her husband', and this her father very naturally interpreted as meaning that Lord Byron should not be constantly in her pocket.

'She returns to her father's house,' wrote Byron, 'and I can only see her under great restrictions – such is the custom of the country. The relations behave very well. I offered any settlement, but they refused to accept it, and swear she *shan't* live with G. (as he has tried to prove her faithless) but that he shall maintain her.' ²

Byron, on his side – in spite of all that had occurred, – remained in the Palazzo Guiccioli – and, although the Count sent him notice to quit, firmly refused to move.

For nearly two months, according to Teresa, the lovers did not meet. They did, however, exchange letters – brief on Byron's part and long on Teresa's – every two or three days. Byron's letters, which Teresa kept with meticulous care, had changed very greatly from those that he was writing to her a year before, or even during the spring at Palazzo Guiccioli. The note of frustrated passion and uncertainty has disappeared, giving place to an affectionate but faintly condescending ease, – and also, it must be admitted, to a certain dullness. Teresa has become his 'gossip', his 'duck'; he tells her that he is preparing Villa Bacinetti for 'the two little girls, – Allegra and you'; he teases her about her age and laughs at her long sentimental letters. There is a good deal about the servants, a little Ravenna gossip; there are numerous half-veiled allusions to their love-making, and excuses for his delayed visits – and there really is not much else.

As to Teresa's answers, only three of this period have been preserved – but a later letter of Byron's, at the time of his move to Pisa, declared that they were at least five hundred.³ It had taken him, he complained, at least two hours to sort and tie them up. Two of the letters which still remain, however – the one about *Adolphe* and the one about Byron's *Farewell* — throw a new light upon their relationship. They show a Teresa both shrewder and

* The villa was completely destroyed by the Germans, who blew up most of the houses and farms on the canal banks in 1944. Nothing now remains but a few steps of the great staircase. The chapel, too, where Count Ruggero Gamba was buried, was partially destroyed and looted.

more independent than she has yet appeared; devotedly attached to Byron, and yet capable, on occasion, of standing up to him; sentimental, but no longer blind.

The first of Byron's letters to Filetto – written on the day after Teresa's departure – describes Guiccioli's ill-humour on discovering that his wife had departed. It was taken to her by two of Byron's most trusted servants, his cook Valeriano, and Luigi Morelli. The folder containing her letters is inscribed by Teresa: 'Le désir et le devoir de faire connaitre sous cet aspect de bonté, de raison, de vrai sentiment de cœur Ld. B., peut seul faire vaincre la répugnance qu'on eprouve a mettre le monde dans la confidence'.

BYRON TO CONTESSA GUICCIOLI

Ravenna   *July 15th*, 1820

My Love+Hardly had you left than the whole town knew of your departure. – I went for my usual ride and upon my return was informed that the Pig of St. Stephen* (you know that St. Anthony had a similar one, but blessed, and cleaner than the animal in question) had appeared with a fairly black and surly snout, which I do not think will become any more cheerful tomorrow, when he learns the consequences to his pocket. He is now at the theatre – his solace and delight. I send you Valeriano, begging you to keep him with you for the present – for *my satisfaction* – as well as Luigi – until we know something more. Don't trouble yourself to answer, but do not humiliate me by sending back Valeriano, whom I trust very much. I am expecting your news and *superior orders*. – I will do what you wish – but I hope that in the end *we may be happy*. – Of my love you cannot doubt – let yours continue. – Remember me to Count G[amba] your father and I am always your most

P.S. It is said that A[lessandro] cuts a poor figure. Write to me in the finest style of Santa Chiara. Very naughty O.+++++++ Be very careful!!

* S. Antonio Abate, as opposed to St. Anthony of Padua, was always depicted in the company of a pig. Byron's reference is to Guiccioli, who was a Cavaliere di S. Stefano (Knight of St. Stephen). Teresa seems subsequently to have felt that it was in somewhat bad taste, for she has tried to erase the words 'pig' and 'animal' writing over these words the letters 'N.N.'

N

Ravenna *July* 17*th*, 1820

My Love,+++Your dearest letter was brought to me by P. yesterday evening. – He is leaving almost at once – so I have only a few minutes in which to answer you; but you will forgive me. – What people are thinking – what they are saying – it would be difficult for me to guess, as I do not go about, nor shall I do so, except for my usual rides on horseback, until we two are able to go into Society together. – I have refused to go to the theatre – as I did when you were still here. – Papa will be able to give you private and political news; of the latter we know nothing more. – The Lugano Gazette says that, our Queen having rejected every peace proposal, the House of Lords has begun the trial.* I would not have troubled you with so much had you not asked for '*political news*'. – P. will tell you what he thinks about my *visits* just now – but if you are not convinced, I will obey you – as I should. – I write in very great haste. – Keep Valeriano without compunction – I have found a temporary under-cook who is marvellously successful with trifles – *ducks* (without onions – I expect you said it as a joke) and even with cakes – so I am not fasting. –

I have finished the tragedy⁴ – now comes the work of revision– and I have no copyist. –

Meanwhile I keep busy – and in the hope of finding you again with a love still not much inferior to mine, I shall always be your +++

P.S. *Sandri* says the decree 'is a bestial decree' – this is the consequence of not having given that wretch the 60 scudi he asked for. That is what men are like – if you do not help them they hate you – and if you do they hate you the more for having had the power and means of doing so. Louis XIV of France was right in saying that every time he granted a favour, 'he made a hundred men discontented, and one ungrateful'.

But as to Sandri – I shall find a way of punishing him. There is a certain . . . . ? no? – I feel as if I could hear it. *Ricordati di me che son la Pia.*

Lega greets you humbly – he is being scolded a good deal by his amiable master. Elisei makes the round of the boxes without

* This was the trial, before the House of Lords, of Queen Caroline, who was accused of adultery with her Italian courier, Bergami. Most of the witnesses were Italian grooms or servants, and it was believed that many of them had been bribed. The trial – which aroused great popular feeling against King George IV – lasted from June to November, and ended with the Queen's acquittal. See p. 245.

getting any nearer to the 'desired nest' – some assemblies are being given for Donzelli, but not as good as they were for the Morandi and the Cortesi.* – I have sent the medicine to the Cardinal, and if he takes it properly it will do him good – I think. But I told him to send for the surgeon Rima before taking it. –

Yesterday a priest of Faenza was assassinated – and a factor of Alessandro's. –

Tomorrow the theatre ends – but you knew that before you left. – Goodbye +++

Ravenna   *July* 18*th,* 1820

My Love+Truly I know nothing, since I see no one but Elisei on my usual rides – and he is now too busy about an accident of his own to think about us or about his country. Jumping with me yesterday in the fields, he fell with his horse – and hurt an eye – not very badly – but enough to disfigure him in society for a few days. The worst of it is, that [Elisei] being a great horseman in his own opinion (and rightly, for he rides well), by chance a great many spectators in carriages were present and witnessed his misadventure – consequently his pride has been no less injured than his eye. – His cap – his clothes – and all his equipment down to [illegible – paper torn] – his spurs were also halfspoiled by the fall, which was rather heavy. Fortunately for him there was some grass and no stones.

Your letter has given me the first news about A[lessandro]'s conversation with the Cardinal and Alborghetti. – From this you will realize that I know nothing about what you say and ask – this is all gossip that will not last more than a few days. – It would be a fine thing if you could not have a servant because he served me before going to you!†

Guiccioli told Lega this morning that he did not want to pursue the lawsuit about *the house* – I have replied that it was for him to bring it to an end.

About our separation I don't know what to say to you – you know what I want – but the decision must depend on you and on

* Domenico Donzelli was an opera singer. The reference is to the benefit night for the singer, Rosa Morandi, a week before (on July 11th) who was honoured in a most sensational manner, with the streets of the city illuminated, fireworks, a 'golden rain in the theatre'. Carolina Cortesi was also an opera singer.

† Teresa had written saying that she had heard there had been gossip in Ravenna because she had taken into her service the two men servants (Luigi and Valeriano) whom Byron had sent to her.

your family. For my part (if you will) we will live together and send A. and his alimony to . . . . .*

I have not been very well these days, owing to the great heat, but am better today.

Thank you *very* much for your roses which are still fresh – I *kissed* them and at once put them in fresh water.

You are afraid for me – I don't know why – but what can I do about it? – What will be, will be – and one place is not safer than another. Look after yourself well – this matters much more to me than myself, or anything that can happen to me. Papa will keep you informed about the gossip (if there is any) but remember that it will be over in a month, whether it is good or bad. – This evening is Donzelli's benefit night, but I have not gone to it – pray love me and believe me your most sincere and loving +++ ++++++

Ravenna   *July 23rd*, 1820

My Love: I don't think you have done right in present circumstances in sending Luigi back – and it won't be much use – I shall send him off again this evening.

You need not be afraid of violence against me – you *yourself* have more to fear from your *husband*, this I *know* – and therefore I beg you to keep your servants always about your person – when you go out. – As to the news, Luigi will give you all of it – domestic and political. – I don't know anything. – A Papal guard has been wounded, a comedy has arrived, that is all that I have learnt in these days.

I am writing in a great hurry, so as not to keep the servant waiting. – Elisei has recovered from his wound, but not from his wounded pride. – I do not know what else to say, except that *I love you – and I shall always love you* – but when we shall see each other again, it is not in my power to decide. – With a twister like the Cavaliere one can know nothing – and count on nothing – He turns round and round like a clown, and as effectively.

I am well, except for a little pain in one hand – from having fired an over-primed pistol the day before yesterday in the Pine-forest. –

I am sending you some other books – and am always your most sincere and loving.

* The paper has perished or has purposely been torn.

Ravenna   *July 24th*, 1820

My Love: Don't be afraid – I assure you that it was only for amusement that I discharged my pistols in the Pineta and not in self-defence against an assassin – my servants had overcharged them and I suffered a little pain in one hand – which is already gone. –

I have sent away three servants, because, instead of doing their duty, they went to the tavern – a little before midnight – an insufferable thing – leaving eight horses, harness, three carriages, etc., at that time of night with nobody to look after them – But if you want me to – I shall have to forgive them. –

You are not obliged, my love, to read all those books – I thought you were like me – I like sometimes to read one book and sometimes another, a few pages at a time, – and change frequently, that is, change *books* – but nothing else except *linen* – since I am the essence of fidelity. – I wrote to you yesterday in a bad humour; – not seeing you has upset me – and a thousand other things – little things, but tiresome, household matters; the heat, etc.

I have no particular news from England – the Gazettes are full of our blessed Queen – it is a fine thing that in this world one cannot be loved in peace – without all this fuss! – Her Majesty has put the morals of my very moral country in great danger and scandal.[5] They seem deteriorated already, for I read in the Gazette of an Irish lady of 37 who has run away with a young Englishman of 24 – leaving behind a husband of 50 and a daughter of 16.

I kiss you ten thousand times + + + and console myself with the thought that in any case we shall see each other soon.

Love me – I am always yours

Ravenna   *July 26th*, 1820

My Love+ + + + + I at once sent a message to Giulio Rasponi about the villeggiatura* but he says that Countess Capra wants it for herself – and that he cannot do it without her consent.– Very naughty O – so you have become a huntress, but it is not a good beginning to kill the poor dogs. – You cannot desire me and want me back more than I do you – Love stings me very much,

* Teresa had been urging Byron to take a villa in the country, so as to avoid the dangers of contracting fever in the Ravenna midsummer air – and also, no doubt, so as to bring him nearer to her. But the danger of fever was real – a form of malaria – and before the summer was over poor little Allegra had caught it.

without counting the cake [some words erased] but let us hope that soon we shall be able to arrange something – the Cavaliere is spreading rumours – that you have been here to visit me – (would it were so!) – that he has found some letters of mine that he has had impounded – that he wants to sue me – and a *thousand other* fantastic designs. One thing is certain – he is seeking (and in some people finding) witnesses to say that he did not seem to be *ill-treating* you. – But who can ever know! Neither the public nor one's friends – for these are family matters, at home.*

The Play is here but I have not been to it. I have been riding – and firing pistols – I read and write – that is all!

This separation from you inconveniences me greatly – you understand.

Lega tells me that Fanny has produced another bastard – a boy – whom I believe she is to present to the Venice hospital – I advised him to send Aspasia too, – it would be one ugly . . . . the less in that not over beautiful family. –

The other 'cadreghe'† (this is not a word of Santa Chiara's but of St. Mark's) have come from Forli with some other stuff – fine – but they want too much money and Lega has had to take some furious scoldings.

Pray forgive all this nonsense and believe me your most + + + +

P.S. Yes, my Duck – I have understood you – with all your + + + poor child! I hope that we shall fulfil all these wishes of ours very soon – have a little more patience.

Ravenna   *July* 29*th*, 1820

My Love + + + + I like your ˹little brother very much – he shows character and talent – Big eyebrows! and a stature which he has enriched, I think, at your expense – at least in those . . . . do you understand me?‡ His head is a little too hot for revolutions – he must not be too rash.

If A[lessandro] wants to make peace, I hope he will give you a *constitution* first – that being now the fashion with tyrants.

I am sending you a letter from Monaco, from a certain Baronessa Miltitz, who wants to correspond with me, she must be a mad literary lady – do you want me to answer her? –

---

* The reference is to the evidence that Guiccioli had sent off to Rome the day before and shows how very well-informed everyone in Ravenna was, about everyone else's affairs! See chapter IV, p. 189.
† 'Chairs', in Venetian dialect.
‡ Byron is presumably referring to his lady's legs, which were rather short.

There is some hope of Villa Colombani – I shall do everything possible, as you know, to get it. – I am writing in the greatest haste – for Papa is leaving in a few minutes. – Lega is here – I am using him as a dictionary – when I need a word – I ask him. Pray continue your love for me – and always believe me your most sincere and loving + + + + +

Pietro Gamba had returned from Rome – bringing with him a breath of youth, of patriotism and of disinterested enthusiasm. 'Pierino' is, indeed, perhaps the most sympathetic figure in the whole story. A gentle, handsome young man – feminine in the quickness of his enthusiasms and intuitions, but with plenty of courage and enterprise – he possessed a desire for adventure and a passion for the abstract idea of liberty, equal to Byron's own. 'A very fine, brave fellow', was Byron's own later description of him. '(I have seen him put to the proof) and wild about liberty.'[1]

So far Pietro has only appeared 'off-stage' – writing to warn Teresa of the dangers of her liaison, and sending anxious letters of protest to his father and brother-in-law. But beneath his moralizing, it is possible to discern more than a little curiosity about the wicked English Lord, – traveller and pirate, seducer and adventurer, – against whom he was warning his sister. And when, still divided between disapproval and curiosity, he at last returned to Ravenna, he too, like the rest of the family, succumbed to the Byron charm. From that day, until his premature death in Greece, he remained Byron's enthusiastic, disinterested – and unfailingly unpractical – disciple. Moreover he possessed to a remarkable degree a quality which Byron, since he himself was devoid of it, seldom elicited from his friends: a simple and uncritical loyalty.

To Byron Pietro's arrival upon the scene must have been exceedingly refreshing. He liked, indeed, the whole Gamba stock. He was attracted by their manners, by their physical appearance, and by a certain warmth and naturalness that was common to them all. Teresa describes his affection for her little sisters, who used sometimes, in Ravenna, to drive out with her into the Pineta to watch Byron shooting. 'Byron caressed them affectionately, and said that he liked *le beau sang* of the family; he felt as if he had become part of it.'[2] Pietro, too, was exceedingly like his sister – with the further advantage of not belonging to 'the absurd race of women' – and of taking his romance (for he, too, was a romantic) in a different way. The boy's enthusiasm, the quick flush that mounted to his cheeks as soon as he was excited – his headlong speech, his candour, his disarming modesty – these were qualities that Byron had not encountered for a long time. They took him back to the first friendships of his youth – with Long, with Clare. In a few days he was treating Pietro with the half-humorous, half-impatient affection of an elder brother. They rode together in the forest; they practised marksmanship and fencing; they planned the overthrow of Austria and the banishment of the barbarians. For although Byron might smile with Teresa at her 'little brother's' hot head, his own was hardly much cooler. What he and Pietro dreamed of together was 'the very *poetry* of politics' [9] – the fulfillment, after so many centuries, of the Italian 'unquenched longing after independence'. Now, at last, they believed that longing would find expression in action.

'There is THAT brewing in Italy', Byron wrote to Murray, 'which will speedily cut off all security of communication, and set all your Anglo-travellers flying in every direction ... I shall, if permitted by the natives, remain to see what will come of it, and perhaps to take a turn with them, ... for I shall think it by far the most interesting spectacle and moment in existence, to see the Italians send the Barbarians of all nations back to their own dens. I have lived long enough among them to feel more for them as a nation than for any other people in existence.' [10]

The revolutionary movement, however, which was arousing such high hopes, was still – as Byron was well aware – in an exceedingly chaotic state. 'They want Union and they want principle', [11] wrote Byron of his fellow-conspirators – and he was only echoing the thoughts of their own leaders. 'Liberi non sarem,' cried Manzoni, 'se non siam uni.' [12] And Foscolo, writing in 1821 to the Countess of Albany, had bitterly ascribed all the troubles of his fellow-countrymen to their not knowing themselves what they really wanted.

'It seems as if their intellectual energies were sharpened only for chatter, for discontent with everything and everyone ... Experience has not been able to hammer into their wooden heads the old tale, as old, I believe, as Adam, which is: that the man who does not know what he wants must resign himself to doing what others want. Our nobles want and do not want the omnipotence of the priests; the priests want the Inquisition, but do not want the monks; the monks hope to reacquire a hold over men's consciences, but fear the competition of the Jesuits; the well-off want well-paid jobs, but want to pay only a third of the taxes, and the people want bread that only costs three halfpence a pound. And each of them believes that the rulers of Europe have taken arms in order to redress his individual wrongs!'[18]

During the early part of the spring Byron had been too much absorbed in his own private life to pay much attention to the state of the country, but since in Italy no matter is so personal that it does not become tinged with politics, both Liberals and Clericals had taken sides in his affairs – Monsignor Marini influencing Guiccioli, as we have seen, to bring matters to a head and get this dangerous foreigner out of the city, and the Liberals protecting him. It is improbable that Byron himself was aware of the amount of intriguing that was going on – although in one letter to Teresa he did suggest that some of the slanders were aimed against her family, on political grounds, as well as against herself. But his natural sympathies were with the Liberals – and when Pietro Gamba arrived – fresh from Rome and Naples and bearing news of the progress of the rising in the South – he was already prepared to become something more than a detached and amused spectator.

'We are here', he wrote to Murray, 'upon the eve of evolutions and revolutions. Naples is revolutionized, and the ferment is among the Romagnuoles, by far the bravest and most original of the present Italians, though still half savage. Buonaparte said the troops from Romagna were the best of his Italic corps, and I believe it. The Neapolitans are not worth a curse, and will be beaten if it comes to fighting: the rest of Italy, I think, might stand.'[14]

The Neapolitan rising, which was to awaken such disproportionate hopes in the Liberals all over Italy, was, as events proved, a very minor episode: a farce rather than a tragedy. While the Carboneria, in Sicily and Calabria, had become a genuine popular movement, in Naples it was merely a party, consisting almost entirely of the prosperous but discontented middle classes. Some of its members were well-to-do bourgeois who resented the Bourbons' taxes, but the greater part were veterans of the Napoleonic wars, who wanted promotion, or provincial clerks and prelates who required better jobs, to whom must be added a small handful of genuine Liberal idealists and some mere adventurers. The Bourbon government against which they were plotting was perhaps the weakest, most suspicious and most inefficient in Europe; it was also, as it soon showed, the most timid.

The rising began on the smallest possible scale: on the evening of July 2nd a little group of deserters – two lieutenants and 127 cavalry troopers, accompanied by a priest – Don Menichini – and twenty civilians, marched out of the barracks of the little town of Nola along the road which leads to Avellino, crying 'Long live God!' 'Long live the King!' 'Long live the Constitution!' King Ferdinand Ist of Naples happened to be at sea, on the way to meet his son in Sicily; and the news of this very mild insurrection terrified him so much, that it was only with the greatest difficulty that he was persuaded to return home. He said, however, that he dared not send any of his generals against the rebels, because he did not trust their loyalty; the generals said that they themselves did not trust their soldiers; the soldiers certainly did not trust their generals; and thus four days passed, during which the original handful of insurgents was joined by other groups from Avellino and the neighbouring cities, who put themselves under the command of the magniloquent and theatrical Napoleonic veteran, General Guglielmo Pepe. By now the king and the Government were thoroughly frightened, and when, on the night of July 5th, five Carbonari made their way to the Palace in Naples, asked to speak to the king and demanded a Constitution within two hours, they immediately obtained what they wanted. The Constitution was proclaimed the next morning, and General Pepe's 'army' – now swollen by all the rabble of the province – triumphantly made its entry into Naples, headed by the 'sacred squadron' of the Nola deserters, while Don Menichini, clothed as a priest, but carrying arms and adorned with all the insignia of the Carbonari, was followed by 7000 civilians. The king, meanwhile, lay trembling in bed in his palace; and three-coloured cockades (of the colours of the Carboneria, red, blue and black) made by the royal princesses themselves, were distributed to the crowd. Within a few days there was a reception at Court, at which the chief rebels, notably General Pepe, kissed the king's hand; sonnets were written by Don Menichini, and copies of his portrait sold by thousands in the streets of Naples. On October 1st the Neapolitan Parliament (consisting almost entirely of members of the middle class – priests, lawyers and small landowners, all Carbonari) was opened. Such was the revolution which the Carbonari of the North regarded as the dawn of liberty and independence – such the army on which they counted, to oppose the power of Austria.

The first news of these events was brought back to the Romagna, with many details not to be found in the Gazettes, by Pietro Gamba and an advocate of Faenza called Cicognani* – and at

* Avvocato Cicognani had been sent from Faenza to Naples to find out the intentions of the Neapolitans with regard to the Romagna, and to tell them of the preparations that were being made to rise against the Government, as soon as the Neapolitan army arrived. On his return he was one of the leaders of the Romagna conspirators. PIERANTONI, *I Carbonari dello Stato Pontificio*.

once the Romagnoli conspirators were roused to fresh hopes – and sporadic acts of violence. By midsummer Byron was writing:

'Here there are as yet but the sparks of the volcano; but the ground is hot, and the air sultry. Three assassinations last week here and at Faenza – an anti-liberal priest, a factor and a trooper last night, – I heard the pistol-shot that brought him down within a short distance of my own door. There had been quarrels between the troops and people of some duration: this is the third soldier wounded within the last month. There is a great commotion in people's minds, which will lead to nobody knows what.'[15]

In these activities the Gamba family was deeply involved. Count Ruggero Gamba, indeed, was an old hand at revolutions. After the departure of the French in 1814 he had gone for a while into exile, and on his second return home he had become a leading spirit of the Romagna branch of the Carbonari, together with his son Pietro and his nephew Antonio Cavalli. Both he and Pietro were considered by the Austrian and Papal governments *pecore segnate* (black sheep), and were under police supervision. And now Byron – already sufficiently suspect – joined them, and was soon made the head of one of the local bands, that of the *Cacciatori Americani*.

'The "*Mericani*", of whom they call me the "Capo" (or chief) means "Americans", which is the name given in Romagna to a part of the Carbonari, that is to say, to the *popular* part, the *troops* of the Carbonari. They were originally a society of hunters in the forest, who took that name of Americans, but at present comprise some thousands, etc.; but I shan't let you further into the secret, which may be participated with the postmasters.'[16]

Byron's band – the *Cacciatori Americani* – belonged to the third and popular section of the Ravenna Carbonari, which was also known as 'la turba'. All over the country, within the last two years, such bands of conspirators had been springing up – many of them with high-flown names suggesting a direct link with the Freemasons, such as the '*Guelfi*', '*Adelfi*', '*Maestri Perfetti*', '*Latinisti*', and '*Massoni Riformati*'. Then there were the '*Figli di Marte*', the '*Ermolaisti*', the '*Fratelli Artisti*', the '*Illuminati*'; at Cesena the '*Difensori della Patria*' (Defenders of their Country), at Forlì the '*Figli dell'Onore*' (Sons of Honour), and at Ravenna itself the '*Società degli Amici del Dovere*' (Society of the Friends of Duty).[17]

By the spring of 1820 it was said that over 15,000 men were secretly enrolled in the Romagna.

In reading the history of the Carbonari, it is impossible not to observe the marked similarities between the conspirators of that day and the Partisans of the recent war. In the 1820s as in the 1940s a sincere purpose was often obscured by bombastic rhetoric, and fine plans brought to nought by a muddled execution. There was a similar conspiratorial setting, a similar enthusiasm, a similar volume of talk. In both periods genuine patriots were fighting beside mere political agitators, fools or scoundrels, and deeds of true heroism alternated with behaviour that was both foolish and purposeless.

Perhaps, after all, it is not so very astonishing. All conspiracies, whenever they may take place, seem to affect their adherents in much the same way – or perhaps it would be truer to say, that all conspiracies attract to themselves the same kind of human beings. 'The temperament of conspirators', wrote an acute Italian historian of the last century, 'greatly resembles that of lovers. It is not their fault, but the fault of their profession. Their vision is restricted, and generally it is also falsified – for the object of their passion occupies them entirely. In this object resides all good, beauty and truth; everything else is evil, false and ugly.'[18] Like lovers, too, they live in a twilight world of secret meetings and whispered passwords, where everything is a little more vivid, a little more intense, than reality. They meet behind locked doors, or in lonely woods at nightfall, always on the watch for an enemy footstep, scanning each man's face to guess if he may be a spy. Their sense of proportion is seldom equal to their courage; each scrap of news, every vague rumour, takes on a fictitious importance; all colours are intensified, all shadows blackened. Each little band becomes an army, each ruler a villainous tyrant. Moreover, the conspirator, in every period, has a dangerous satisfaction: the sense of secret power. The very complication of his life – spying and counter-spying, lying and treachery, opening of letters and listening at doors, but all done for 'the good cause' – these things lead even a little man to feel that he is a great one.

Here is a description, – by an 'old Carbonaro of Ravenna', Primo Uccellini – of the ceremony by which he, as a mere schoolboy, was admitted into one of the local branches of the Society.

'It was in 1818, that is, the time when the Carboneria was flourishing everywhere. Italy was a hotbed of sects which had various names, but all aimed at the same goal: the abolition of absolute monarchy. In Ravenna the Carboneria was divided into three branches: the first was given the name of *Protettrice* (Protectress), because it controlled the others; the second that of *Speranza* (Hope) because it was composed chiefly of young students; and the third, because it included a mixture of all sorts of people, mostly workmen, and was the most prepared for action, was named *Turba* (Mob).'[19]

Uccellini, who had already, although only a schoolboy, written some fiery verses against tyranny, was admitted into the branch called *Speranza*, and was taken one night into the house of the head of the local lodge, where he was at once blindfolded.

'An imposing voice asked me various questions, and when I had given my word that I was prepared for any sacrifice for my country's good, and wished to take an active part in the overthrow of *Tyranny*, I was made to place my hand on a naked dagger, and take the prescribed oath. After this, my bandage was taken off, and I saw that I was surrounded by a fence of daggers – while old Andrea Garavini, who directed the meeting, said in a loud voice: "All these daggers will be for your defence in every encounter, if you hold your oath sacred, but they will be turned to your damage and destruction if you fail. The traitor's penalty is death."'[20]

Byron would scarcely have gone to meetings such as these; but he did attend some more important ones – both in the pine forest and in Ravenna, and at Filetto. There he met not only the other conspirators of Ravenna – decent working men of Republican principles like old Andrea Garavini the blacksmith, the jovial inn-keeper Bucina, Giacomo Batuzzi, who later on followed the Gambas in exile to Pisa, and that adventurous merchant, Vincenzo Gallina, who eventually made his way to Greece — but also the representatives of the neighbouring cities, Vincenzo Fattiboni from Cesena, Laderchi and Ginnasi from Faenza, Orselli from Forlì and Hercolani from Bologna. And besides these genuine patriots of all classes, there were a number of hot-headed, irresponsible boys, a few adventurers and criminals – and, inevitably, some spies and informers.

It was a strange mixture of human beings, and very alien must Byron have seemed among them all: the great English Mylord – so proud, so eccentric, and yet so anxious to do his share – so friendly when he chose – so generous. But he was irascible, according to Teresa, at the meetings; he would call for less talk and quicker action, for a concerted plan. Now, as later on with his Greek allies, he felt for his fellow-conspirators a mixture of sympathy and exasperation. But, in Italy as in Greece, he *identified* himself with them. His occasional abuse, as Mr. Nicolson has pointed out, 'was not the superficial contempt of the healthy English wayfarer, but the determined incitation of an angered, intelligent, but sympathetic friend'.[21]

For some weeks nothing further happened, and Byron's letters to Teresa again refer only to personal matters.

BYRON TO CONTESSA GUICCIOLI*

Ravenna   *August 3rd*, 1820

My Love +++ My daughter is ill. I have sent away the old woman – Lega has taken into the house a certain Clara of whom I know nothing. – Lega will answer for his own sins – I can only answer for mine – and hardly for those. –

I have looked and am looking for a country house, but it cannot yet be found.

Guiccioli has no right to sham *blindness* – after your last year's letter of which he sent a copy to Count Pietro – If he did not notice anything then, – he should never have done so – That was the moment to say, 'Make your choice' – and not eight months later – it seems to me that your feelings were already evident.

Papa will make you laugh about the break between Lieutenant Elisei and me – the buffoon has at last done what I hoped for often enough (but did not know how to accomplish) – he has taken upon himself to be offended because I would not buy a *writing-desk* from an artist protected by him. – Poor fool – he wanted to run my house and found he couldn't.

I am writing in a hurry, and am always yours +++++++

P.S. My respects to Count P.

The daughter of Rasponi's coachman has been taken into my house to look after the child.

Ravenna   *August 3rd*, 1820

Allegrina's illness can be confirmed by Dr. Rasi and by Count Ruggero. – She is very ill. – As to the child's maid, Lega will answer you. All that I have to answer for – is that I have never been *below stairs* and that I am not in the habit of going there. – – –

---

* On the upper left-hand corner of the page is written: '... [torn] like you in the Convent'. The missing word must be 'rabbioso', in a rage. See letter of August 7th.

Yesterday a letter from Hobhouse told me that all the Peers who are absent from the Queen's trial* will be condemned to a *fine* or to the Tower (a State prison) – in spite of which I do not think of going – but I do not think I should be rewarded for the trouble I am facing for someone else's sake, by the reproofs of the very person who is causing it.

The child's maid says (I forgot to tell you) that she would not take service in Guiccioli's house – because a poor opinion is held of the Cavaliere everywhere and by everyone. – I cannot go into all the reasons – leaving such things to the steward.

My law-suit is going forward.

Villa Spreti is already taken – and we are thinking of moving in next week.

I am always yours

August 5th, 1820

My Love: I have received the flowers – and the book – and thank you for everything – Yesterday I wrote to you in reply to yours.

If Luigi does not suit you – take another man – only I cannot receive him into my household – we are already too many – and if he remains without employment you know what the probable consequences will be – since that man knows about all our affairs. Lega has gone today to Villa Spreti – the child has a fever and rather high.

I saw Papa yesterday – I am always

Byron's next letter – after laughing at one of Teresa's frequent attacks of jealousy – refers to an agreement suggested by mutual friends. It appears that there had been some trouble over the objects which Teresa – interpreting somewhat freely the Pope's phrase about 'such things as appertain to the decent ornament of a married lady' – had taken away with her from Palazzo Guiccioli; and it was now proposed that an amicable agreement should be reached, by which nothing more would be said about these things, but Teresa's allowance would be reduced from 100 to 60 scudi a month. On August 17th, indeed, this agreement was signed – and in a letter to the Cardinal, Count Gamba hinted at

* Hobhouse was greatly disappointed by Byron's refusal to attend the trial. 'You should really if you can come over', he had written in July, 'to do an act of justice for this "Mobled Queen". It would be a great thing if a person like you who has lived so long in Italy would lend your powerful assistance against this most odious persecution". JOYCE, *My Friend H.*, p. 154.

o

the considerations which had influenced him. 'This conciliatory agreement', he said, 'may perhaps in future bring about a complete reunion – although it could not at present be prudently recommended, in view of everybody's state of mind.'²²

BYRON TO CONTESSA GUICCIOLI

Ravenna   *August 7th,* 1820

My Love+++'Forget what has happened', you say – a fine forgetfulness – but what then did happen? The woman is as ugly as an ogre – a thing of Lega's – not very young – not of bad reputation – not adorned with the slightest quality that might arouse a caprice. But you have condescended to be jealous – which I shall not so easily forget, as you so *generously* forgive yourself. It is a very naughty O: I feel it.

Allegrina has already spoiled your present – breaking one of the little carriages. Her fever is a little better. I shall not go to my fair country of NO – unless you are jealous of filthy maids – in which case I shall.

I think you should neither accept nor refuse Guiccioli's proposal without thinking it over. Perhaps one could do this – reply that he should *assign you* 2000 *scudi* after his death, and in return you would be prepared to give up 400 of the 1200 decreed by the most just of all Popes. Freedom would be a great thing, no doubt – with that head of yours – but 400 scudi is a respectable sum in this country – and not to be given up without any compensation. For the rest – you can trust me – I will make you independent of everyone – at least during my lifetime. But you are made angry by the mere idea – and want to be independent on your own and to write '*Cantate*' in lengthy epistles in the style of Santa Chiara – the convent where you were said to be always in a rage.*

I am reading the second volume of the proposal of that classical cuckold Perticari.† It may be well-written – in a style worthy of Santa Chiara and the *trecento* – but it would be more à propos if the Count, instead of proving that *Dante* was the greatest of men

---

* Byron wrote 'rabbiosa' (in a rage), which Teresa has attempted to change into 'studiosa' (studious).

† Count Giulio Perticari (1790-1822) the son-in-law of the poet Vincenzo Monti, whose wife was notoriously unfaithful to him, was one of the defenders of the classicists, against the new-fangled romantics. The work referred to is *Dell'amor patrio di Dante* (1820).

(which no one at present wishes to deny, as he is now all the fashion) could prove to his contemporaries that his father-in-law Monti* is not the most vile and infamous of men, and such a dishonour to talent itself, that a man of ability ought to blush to belong to the same century as that Judas of Parnassus.

This seems to have become a *cantata*, or at least would be in English, but my thoughts fail me when I must express myself in the effeminate words of the language of musicians. I am in a rage this evening – as you were in the convent. – I kiss and embrace you 100000000 – – – – times. Love me.

P.S. There is a certain O – I feel it in the note itself – and very much – yes. Greet both the G[amba]s – I value their good graces. That blessed villa is being got ready – as quickly as possible on account of the two little girls – Allegra – and *you*.

August 8th, 1820

My Love + + + Your note has not come until now, too late to permit me to go out to the country today – – – I have already given orders to Lega to retain this blessed Villa – but until I have settled my household there – it is not my intention to go to Filetto– as I do not wish, in these circumstances, to give an advantage to the Cavaliere, who would at once run to the Cardinal with a thousand lies and some *truths* – – – – – – –

He has set spies upon me – and yesterday I nearly came to blows with a man in the pine-forest – who had begun to follow me everywhere – stopping when I stopped – and always standing nearby – until I lost patience and made him understand that if he did not go on his way – it would be the worse for him – at that he disappeared.

As to the rest, my love + I wrote to you yesterday, the letter must be already at Papa's. Greet the first-born of the Gambas for me – the Quiroga[23] of Ravenna – and believe me always your most faithful.

P.S. Allegrina is better.

* The reference is to Monti's political unreliability. He was also, like his son-in-law, unfortunate in his matrimonial relations, a fact on which Byron commented in his *Prophecy of Dante*, in lines omitted in the earlier editions of Byron's Poems, but quoted by Moore:

> The prostitution of his Muse and wife,
> Both beautiful, and both by him debased,
> Shall salt his bread and give him means of life.

Byron was right in fearing Count Guiccioli's manœuvres. All through the summer he kept spies assiduously watching the lovers, so as to collect fresh evidence, which might make it possible for him to cease paying his wife's alimony. It is clear from these letters that Byron's first visit to Filetto – in spite of Teresa's urgings, continued to be postponed, owing to Count Gamba's wishes and to the danger of gossip in Ravenna. But Guiccioli's spies reported at least four secret meetings. The first they declared to have taken place in Ravenna, after dark, on August 14th, when two women, both dressed as servants, were seen passing by the door to the stairs which led up to Lord Byron's apartment in Palazzo Guiccioli. One of these women, according to the witnesses (who were standing on the other side of the street) was the Countess Teresa, and the two Gamba brothers were standing on each side of the porch, as the women entered. (This it is quite impossible to believe.)

On the second occasion, August 16th, Lord Byron was said to have driven first to the Villa Bacinetti, which he had taken for the summer for Allegra, and then to have gone on to the Villa Gamba, where he spent the night. This visit, according to the witnesses, he repeated 'on several other occasions'.

Finally, at two o'clock in the morning of October 1st, a servant of Count Guiccioli's heard a great ringing of bells in Byron's room in Ravenna. He got up, hid behind one of the pillars of the hall, and saw Byron's ex-servant Luigi (who was now in Teresa's service) let Teresa in, dressed in black. He also saw her leave again, in the same manner, later on. [24]

How much credence may be attached to the stories of Teresa's visits to Palazzo Guiccioli, it is difficult to say. The visits to Filetto certainly did take place, but openly, after August 16th; and always, Teresa affirms, when her father and brothers were also at home.

BYRON TO CONTESSA GUICCIOLI

Ravenna   *August 12th*, 1820

My love + + + Sunday can't be managed. – the child is going to the country that day and there are a thousand things to be done and undone, you know the members of my household. Pray have a little patience – in two or three days we shall see each other again.

Before receiving the formal notice of the Peers' intentions about the *Gazette*'s announcement [25] – I don't know what answer to

give – when I get it I will find an excuse in the child's illness and
the distance. I don't know if this call includes people who are
out of the country – or only the Lords still in England. It seems
to me a fairly despotic act – and if I really am included in the
number, it will not be without the strongest of protests. – I kiss
you 100000 times and shall be +++++

At last, after so many delays and postponements, Teresa and
Byron saw each other again. On August 16th, Byron – in his
great travelling-coach, and attended by two postillions – set forth
on the fifteen-mile drive to Filetto. He had originally meant to
return to Ravenna on the same day, but a 'magnificent thunder-
storm, and lightning and hail' came to the lovers' aid, rendering
his departure impossible. He accordingly stayed the night, and on
the following morning, 'his friend was able to take him to visit her
Father's rich and beautiful lands'. Byron, she says, was struck by
the air of cleanliness and prosperity of the farms, 'comparing them
most favourably with cottages in Ireland and even in some parts
of England'.[26]

Byron's visits to Filetto now became fairly frequent. Allegra
was settled at the Villa Bacinetti, and he would go and see her
there and then drive on to Filetto – where he rode and hunted
with Teresa's father and brother, took part in an occasional conspiratorial meeting or sat on the banks of the river with Teresa,
reading aloud and talking in a pleasant, desultory fashion. The
more he saw of the Gamba family, the more he became attached
to them. They were all so easy-going and warm-hearted – and
they were so glad to see him – and they admired him so much!
Besides, Byron had always felt the charm of family life – except
when it was his own – and he took an especial pride in the fact
that he knew Italian life from *within*, not as a mere traveller. 'I
have lived in the heart of their houses, in parts of Italy freshest
and least influenced by strangers – have seen and become (*pars
magna fui*) a portion of their hopes, and fears and passions.'[27]

Byron's next letter, addressed to Conte Guiccioli five weeks
after he had taken his wife away from him – is odd in at least two
respects. The first, considering that the letter about which it
complains is Guiccioli's account to Pietro Gamba of his matrimonial grievances, is that it should have been written at all. The
second is that it is written in much better, and more formal,
Italian than any of Byron's other letters.

He seems to have been in a particularly touchy mood about his age, for in the same week he was writing in a similar vein to Moore, who had congratulated him on reaching what Dante calls the *mezzo del cammin di nostra vita*, the age of thirty-three. 'D——n your *mezzo cammin* – you should say "the prime of life" – a much more consolatory phrase. Besides, it is not correct. I was born in 1788, and consequently am but thirty-two.'[28]

BYRON TO CONTE ALESSANDRO GUICCIOLI[29]

Ravenna   *August* 21st, 1820

Sir: I have been informed that in a letter written by you to Rome, dated June 24th, you stated me to have been a man of 35 in 1819, which would now make me 36. This surprises me greatly, since I cannot conceive how, in consulting the *Biography of Living Men* for other information regarding my person, for your own purposes, you should have overlooked only the passage which refers to my birth as having taken place in the year *1788*, which makes me at most *thirty-two*.

I thank you for the 'lustrum' with which you have generously presented me, but not finding myself disposed to accept it, I cannot but tell you so; and I am sure that a man to whom correctness in everything is important, as it is to you, will receive my information in good part, so as to rectify an error which may some day be observed in your archives. If I, in drawing up a memorandum of *your history*, were to make you out a man of *seventy*, adding one seventh to your age, you would not assuredly be pleased, and I will certainly not bear this injustice – not a small one, since it affects the truth. You well know that it is as much in human nature to ask for additional years from *God*, as it is to refuse them from *Men*.

I have the honour to be Your most humble and devoted servant
BYRON

There is no record of Count Guiccioli's feelings on receiving this epistle, nor of any reply.

Byron's next letter to Teresa is wholly occupied with a new source of irritation: an impending visit from Fanny Silvestrini. This was a prospect which he was really unable to face with equanimity – as his remarks to Teresa show.

BYRON TO CONTESSA GUICCIOLI

Ravenna   *August 24th,* 1820

My Love + + + Swoon, indeed! Fanny in theory is bad enough –
Fanny in person would be Death – not to say Hell, in this weather.
Imagine Signora Silvestrini and the heat together! No – no –
no. Write, – send – stop her – deliver me – otherwise I don't
know what will become of me – I said it – I foresaw it – she is
coming. If she really comes – I shall turn monk at once, and the
Church will gain . . . what she has lost in losing Lega, the . . .

I shall be with you on Monday; – Meanwhile I send you a little
book, *Adolphe* – written by an old friend of de Staël – about whom
I heard de Staël say horrible things at Coppet in 1816, with
regard to his feelings and his behaviour to her. – But the book is
well-written and only too true. Love me – remember me and
above all – deliver me from Fanny or I shall swoon! + + + + + + +

The gift of *Adolphe* – that 'well-written book, only too true' –
which accompanied the preceding letter, is a singularly striking
instance of Byron's ferocious egotism.* 'The truest picture of the
misery unhallowed liaisons produce', he told Lady Blessington
later on, 'is in the *Adolphe* of Benjamin Constant. I told Madame
de Staël that there was more morale in that book than in all she
ever wrote, and that it ought always to be given to every young
woman who had read *Corinne*, as an antidote!'[30] It did not, however, occur to him that this summer – a time when Teresa was
lonely, uncertain of her future, and possessed of unlimited leisure
for unhappy broodings – was perhaps not the best moment to ad-
minister such an antidote, and it is probable that the intense
distress which it awakened in her seemed to him both incomprehensible and exasperating.

Her letter – although clothed in the rhetorical diction of S.
Chiara – reveals a most justifiable sadness, and a perfectly clear
realization both of the character of her lover, and of her own
situation.

* This trait was one which particularly distressed Lady Blessington, who said that
from 'a too intense attention' to his own feelings, Byron was capable of 'grievously
wounding' his friends, 'perfectly unconsciously; and of course of even afterwards
neglecting to pour oil and wine into the wound, not through ill nature, but from sheer
ignorance of its existence'. LADY BLESSINGTON, *The Idler in Italy*, I, p. 328.

CONTESSA GUICCIOLI TO BYRON

From the Villa of Filetto   *August 26th,* 1820

My only Love – for Ever!!!

Adolphe! Byron – how much this book has hurt me! You cannot imagine! From the beginning, alas, I foresaw the end – but I read it with the greatest speed – thinking I might thus, at least in part, avoid the too violent impression it made on me. But his words, his expressions, are written in fire. The rapidity with which he glides over things does not defend them from his darts. So my mind, my heart, are deeply wounded. Byron – why did you send me this book? This was not the moment – *indeed perhaps the moment will never come again for me! –* To be able to endure and enjoy that story one must be more remote from the condition of Eleonore *than I am –* and to give it to one's mistress to read, one must be *either very near to* the state of Adolphe, or very far away from it! Either you, my Byron, did not know this book (terrifying mirror of the truth) or you are not yet acquainted with your friend's heart – or you are aware in yourself of a greater or lesser strength than I think you have. How much harm, I repeat, reading this book has done to me! How much! For pity's sake, Byron, if you have other books like it, don't send them to me! This ingenious analysis of the human heart (so miserable) is a medicine fit to prevent trouble, not to cure it, when it is already far advanced. And my suffering may become more bitter – it will never be healed.

On Monday I shall see you. This hope, and every other that concerns you, makes me feel still capable of pleasure . . . Otherwise I should have lost all thought of it, for the memory of having once enjoyed it could now be nothing but a torment. I will give back your book to you – if only I could also get rid of the recollection of it!

Farewell, my Byron! I have already copied the letter from Alessandro to Pierino – of which I learned today that *he has made a circular – and has sent it to all my and his relatives – and to all the principal families of Ravenna.* Who knows whether he will not succeed in getting everyone on his side?*

Farewell, my Byron. Your true friend and lover for Ever

TERESA GUICCIOLI G.

P.S. The Priests of the Suffragio have written, thanking me for my part in the subscription that you have sent me.

* This was a copy of Guiccioli's letter of June 24th to Pietro Gamba, telling his side of the story.

BYRON TO CONTESSA GUICCIOLI

Ravenna   *August 26th*, 1820

My Love +++ The circumstances of Adolphe are very different. Ellenore was not married, she was many years older than Adolphe.– she was not amiable – etc., etc. – Don't think any more about things so dissimilar in every way. –

As to Alessandro's letter you must begin an answer in my name, which I shall sign – telling the truth about his conduct to me – with the various *tricks* used by him in his own interest. Do not forget also the *age*, because it shows, from the beginning, a deliberate determination to conceal the truth. Papa has all the documents necessary for the statement which he has already made to the Cardinal. From the first moment that I knew A[lessandro], he began to make strange proposals to me – wanting me to marry Attilia* – and to buy the *Casa Raisi*[31] here in Ravenna. As to the Bologna affair and the rest, you already know about it.† – See to this. – On Monday we shall see each other again.

Love me – my only love +++ and believe me always your +

Ravenna   *August 27th*, 1820

My Love +++ Papa will write you the chief reasons why I am not coming today as we had arranged, and Lega will tell you another reason. Pray do not add to these troubles your reproaches – because it is not my fault – I have given way only to Papa's arguments – who begged me strongly not to come now – until the Cardinal has calmed down. –

I have no news of you today – So I shall not say any more, except that I am and always shall be your most +++

Allegra was now convalescing from her fever at the Villa Bacinetti, which was not far from Filetto – and Teresa sometimes went over there to see the child, although she emphasizes in the 'Vie', that she never met Byron there. On one of these occasions she sent Byron a lively account of Allegra's high spirits, 'describing the intelligence and grace with which she sang popular songs and mimicked the absurdities of an old servant', and eliciting a disapproving and very paternal comment.

---

* Guiccioli's daughter, who afterwards married Count Antonio Carranti of Ímola, and who was then twelve years old.

† The 'Bologna affair' was the loan which Guiccioli asked of Byron.

My Love + + + I hope to be with you on the day after tomorrow.
You have done very well to scold Papa – instead of me – firstly
because it was not my fault – and then – because a long letter
would have made me *swoon*. What you say about the child com-
forts me very much – except for that tendency to mockery, which
may become a habit very agreeable for others, but which sooner
or later brings trouble to those who practice it.

I will wait to tell you by word of mouth what I think of R. – for
many reasons. Be careful what you write on this subject. I will
tell you why.

My respects to Papa – love me always as your most sincere and
very friendly + + +

P.S. I am sending you a French book in which you will find a lot
about Rousseau and his relations with Mme Epinay. That man
was mad – and not well treated by his friends.

Let us hope we may see each other again the day after tomorrow
– there is a big o– – – – – – – – – – + I feel it – – – + – – – –

The absurd and charming scene described in Teresa's next
letter appears to have taken place immediately after a visit of
Byron's to Filetto. The occasion, according to Teresa, was an
eclipse of the sun, for which she had given an *al fresco* party.

'Byron arrived at the moment when the Countess and the whole
company, armed with optical instruments and smoked glasses,
were observing the heavenly bodies, whose meeting was already
beginning to cast a shadow over the earth. Lord Byron seated
himself in their midst, not wishing to disturb with his arrival the
solemn silence in which they were contemplating the movements
of the Heavens.'

While Byron looked through the telescope, Teresa contemplated
him, allowing her imagination full rein:

'Perhaps he was not only seeing the strange phenomenon that
was being accomplished in our terrestrial orbit, but was following
with the eyes of his soul the incomprehensible and indescribable
beauties of the Infinite Universe! . . . But Man is so near to earth
that as soon as his thoughts have risen to great heights, they
descend again – and as soon as the sun's globe again began to

shine, speech returned to the company, and Lord Byron, too, joined them in a pleasant game of Bowls.'[32]

From the bowling-green the company passed to a trial of marksmanship – a sport, Teresa added, in which Byron excelled, but in which he refused to take part whenever the target was a living bird ('a weakness, but the weakness of a great heart!') – and finally to the banks of the river. Here, in consequence of the eclipse, the water had risen to an unprecedented height, bringing with it a greater quantity of fish than had ever before been seen in that stream. The guests accordingly were hurriedly provided with fishing-nets – but before then, Byron had had enough of it, and had gone back to Ravenna.

CONTESSA GUICCIOLI TO BYRON

Filetto   *September 7th,* 1820

My only Love – for Ever!!! What a fine amusement fishing is, my Love! I am fascinated by it – and envy a fisherman's life – without thinking whether my envy is reasonable or not. – Today I feel like this – Yes, my Love, I should like to be a fisherwoman! – Always, however, on condition that you would be a fisherman – or at least that you would not disdain to love and live with your fisherwoman.

I must have cried out a hundred times on the river bank: Oh, if only Byron (or rather I said my naughty Ducky O ×) were here, how much more I should be enjoying myself – how much he would enjoy it, too! But my cry could not reach you – you had already gone half an hour before – and my pleasure could not become more perfect still. – Ah! if you had been there! But I have not told you anything yet – I have just only noticed it – for the habit of understanding each other without explanation – that wisdom of the heart – takes away my common sense. Well then, my Love.

Half an hour after you left, the tide came up our river, bringing it to a height of a man and a half of water – and a prodigious quantity of fish. Which made us all want to go fishing. – So there were all my astronomers abandoning their smoked glasses and the marksmen their guns – and from the higher regions they descended to the watery ones. You can imagine that our Savage [Pietro] gave himself up with ardour to the new exercise. – Yes, my Love – he stood for more than two hours in the water – trying by his skill to overcome the imperfections of his nets – and I stood meanwhile on the bank catching the fish that he threw to me – which in the end weighed over five pounds. Papa, the servants, and some peasants in other groups did the same. Oh, if you had been there, you would have enjoyed yourself! –

On Sunday I shall perhaps go to see Allegrina – and on Monday!!! I shall see my very naughty Ducky O+. On Saturday you will see Pierino – By whom I send you a written kiss – *as short as I can* – as this one is – isn't it, my Love? I kiss you with all my soul. Your true loving friend   TERESA

P.S. I have read further in the Epinay's Memoirs – that Lady has begun to disgust me, and Grimm a great deal, by their behaviour.

BYRON TO CONTESSA GUICCIOLI

Ravenna   *September 9th,* 1820

My Love + + + Fishing and the Fisherwoman! Always something new . . . Do you know that the Milanese *Gazette* says that I have *arrived* in London about the Queen's Business!! The veracity of Gazettes! The London papers report this – and my friends believe it, saying that for the present I want to be *incognito*. – One friend writes to me that many of them have been to see him – and went away again still not believing that I had not returned – among them the *Lamb* – without delay. She went away incredulous. – All this I found in yesterday's post.*

Nothing from the filthy parents-in-law[23] – Ferdinando is better. . . .

On Monday we shall see each other again . . . . I am charged *with Sentiment*, but don't know how to express it – or spread it over four pages of words – but I swear that I love you in a way that all the letters of Cicero could not express – even if the *self-love* of that celebrated *Egoist* were converted into love of his neighbour – and expressed with all the eloquence of his profession. . . . Love me – my p.o.c.

P.S. – Fishing – – what *Fish*? *B*?

* The news of Byron's return to England had appeared in the *Whig Chronicle* of August 18th. 'We rejoice to learn that Lord Byron yesterday arrived in town from Italy.' Byron at once wrote to Murray: 'Pray do not let the papers paragraph me back to England; they may say what they please, any loathsome abuse but that.' And a few days later: 'My Sister tells me that you sent to her to enquire where I was, believing in my arrival, *"driving a curricle"*, etc., into Palace Yard: do you think me a coxcomb or a madman, to be capable of such an exhibition?' (*L.J.*, V, pp. 72 and 77.)

Ravenna *September 14th,* 1820

My Love: I can't come before Monday – I have so many letters to write and a lot of other things – so on Monday we shall see each other. So you will have time to go to Russi³ ⁴ etc. which in any case I don't feel like doing . . . I would have written yesterday – but have not seen any of your relations. . . .

Ferdinando is still very ill* – Allegra came here yesterday, but still with some fever. –

I am writing in a hurry, and am always +++ Love me ++++++++

Ferdinando must have died that night, for on the following day Teresa was writing to her husband a long letter of condolence – which the author of the Guiccioli Memoirs (who never misses an opportunity of being disagreeable about her) ascribes only to her fear of scandal, and a wish to keep on speaking terms with her husband, in case he could still be of use to her. But it is probable that Teresa, who, like Augusta Leigh, could not really believe that there was any other sin than unkindness, was actuated in this case by much more instinctive motives.

Her whole relationship with her husband had always been odd – and it did not cease to be so, with their separation. Deeply as she had cause both to dislike and fear him – for his injuries to her, and no less for the injuries she had done to him – a curious bond of conjugal solidarity, having little to do with likes or dislikes, still tugged at her from time to time. Even now, she could not wholly keep out of his life; she must send him her condolences, and even her conjugal advice. For the real point of this curious letter appears to be in the last paragraph. It was at this moment that the revolutionary movement in the Romagna was flaring up again. Count Guiccioli, who had at times played the part of a Liberal, had, not unnaturally, withdrawn himself from any open support of the movement, since it was led by the Gamba family and Byron. But it is very probable that in the talk of the conspirators at Filetto, Teresa had heard some threat against him, or at least something that rendered his going to Milan undesirable; for the last sentences of her letter contain an unmistakable warning.

And may there not be another explanation too? Teresa could not resist a chance – any chance – of writing an eloquent letter!

* Count Guiccioli's eldest son. This letter has a postscript in the hand of Lega Zambelli, who says: 'Ferdinando, if not dead, is drawing his last breath.' He adds, 'Poor boy, he has been sacrificed, owing to his family's lack of care.' Teresa only says that he died of sunstroke.

CONTESSA GUICCIOLI TO CONTE ALESSANDRO
GUICCIOLI

Villa di Filetto   *September 15th,* 1820[25]

My Dear Alessandro: If you think that I am only moderately grieved by your loss, you are mistaken, as you are mistaken in thinking that there is any one in the world more anxious than I am, to see you tranquil. A messenger sent me by Lega has brought the sad news, and I cannot tell you how much I have felt it. I had no cause to love your son; perhaps, indeed, some to hate him. But I was neither strong nor weak enough to keep up both of these feelings towards him. So I merely regarded him as your comfort, and that was enough to make his life dear to me, and now that he is dead, this makes me lament his death.

But as the fact is now irrevocable, I feel certain (and this is of some slight consolation) that since you will wish to draw upon your own inner resources to console yourself, you will the more readily be able in future to render great services to your Country, because being freed from more personal claims to turn your mental energies to more glorious thoughts, and assisted by your good fortune, you will come to fill that place in Society which you now do not fill, and of which you could render yourself most worthy!

I do not know whether you will be fully convinced of the sincerity of my feelings, for I do not feel certain, after what has passed between us, how fair your opinion of me may be. But whatever it is, my conscience will be at ease, my witness and my recompense.

However, it is certain, I vow and I shall always do all I can to prove it, that I wish with all my heart to see you happy. In the past, when I could have some direct part in this, I tried to do so, but I did not succeed, because you did not understand me. Owing to this lack of understanding, everything is now over between us, and in a way that is irreparable. But indirectly, may I not still do you some good? *Now I hear you are thinking of going to Milan: how much I should prefer you to give up this journey!* I will not enter into arguments that might hurt us both, and which might perhaps be unnecessary, for I think you have very well understood my intention. Farewell, my Alessandro, keep well. Your most affectionate wife   TERESA GUICCIOLI *née* GAMBA

That Teresa should have written to her husband annoyed Byron so much – even though he presumably did not see the letter – that for a fortnight he neither wrote to her nor visited her. But he seems to have sent her an angry message through Pierino, to which she replied with a letter of apology, and a placatory gift of roses.

BYRON TO CONTESSA GUICCIOLI*

Ravenna   *September 28th*, 1820

My Love+Don G.† is impatient to return, so I have only a moment in which to answer you. – You cannot need my letters so long as you are (or were) in correspondence with your husband – nor can you be in any hurry for my presence – since you have been to Ravenna without telling me to come and see you.

Pierino may perhaps have exaggerated what I said in a moment of ill-humour about *the letter* – or at least I may have exaggerated my feelings, for the same reason. This season kills me with sadness every year. You know my last year's melancholy – and when I have that disease of the Spirit – it is better for others that I should keep away. However – it is only the weather that keeps me here – at the first opportunity we shall see each other again.

Believe me always your most

P.S. Thank you from my heart for the roses. Love me. My soul is like the leaves that fall in autumn – all yellow.‡ – A *cantata*!

Ravenna   *September 29th*, 1820

My Love +++ Your imagination carries you too far. Don Giovanni is a buffoon with his mysteries – Yesterday two filthy ladies were here, one uglier than the other – to try to enter my service. – I saw them in Lega's presence for just a minute – and then did not engage them – because they did not seem to me suitable for waiting on Allegrina. – When I thought it necessary to change the Housekeeper, I sent Lega to the Vicari instead of going in person, – so as not to annoy you. What did you want me to do? I don't know any other Lady but your friend, whom I could trust for advice of this kind.

---

* This letter is headed by Teresa 'Sur sa melancolie'.
† Don Giovanni was the family priest at Filetto.
‡ My days are in the yellow leaf;
  The flowers and fruits of Love are gone.
  On this day I complete my thirty-sixth year, verse II.

As soon as the roads are practicable, I will come to you – then your suspicions will disappear. My letter will have explained to you why I did not write – I had no other reason.

As to my *sadness* – you know that it is in my character – particularly in certain seasons. It is truly a temperamental illness – which sometimes makes me fear the approach of madness – and for this reason, and at these times, I keep away from everyone – not wanting to make others unhappy. – Is this true or not? Is this the first time that you have seen me in this condition?

Love me and believe that we shall see each other soon again, and will love each other more than ever. +

Ravenna   *October 1st,* 1820

My Love +++ I will answer your letter myself when I see you on Wednesday – I do not complain about circumstances or Fortune. My melancholy is something temperamental, inherited from my mother's family – particularly from my *grandfather* – and it is not constant – as you know – but – I don't want to bore you with these trifles. Pray forgive me if I do not write in greater detail – your messenger wants to leave, and I have two letters to write for England.

Love me and believe me +++

Byron's melancholy – on this occasion as on many others – was three parts boredom, and was dispelled by a flare-up of political excitement. At the end of August the Austrians were on the Po, and the whole of the Romagna was in a ferment.

'We are going to fight a little, next month, if the Huns don't cross the Po, and probably if they do: I can't say more now . . . Depend upon it, there will be savage work, if once they begin here. The French courage proceeds from vanity, the German from phlegm, the Turkish from fanaticism and opium, the Spanish from pride, the English from coolness, the Dutch from obstinacy, the Russian from insensibility, but the *Italian* from *anger*; so you'll see that they will spare nothing!'[36]

The uprising to which Byron was referring had been planned at a meeting of the Carbonari in Cesena, at which Vincenzo Gallina of Ravenna was the leading spirit. The rising was to take place on September 3rd or 4th, and Gallina, whose name was always accompanied by the adjectives 'restless', 'impatient', or 'fanatical' in contemporary narratives, expressed the conviction that by then every town in the Romagna would be ready to rise.

That all these plans, and Byron's participation in them, were no secret to the Government, is shown by a police report, on September 2nd:

'It is said that in Ravenna there are some ill-intentioned people who are assisted by the English Lord who has been settled for some time in Cavalier Guiccioli's house, and it is said that they have a secret agreement with the other cities of Romagna and with Bologna, that the Fair at Lugo will be the signal for a general revolution, and that it is their plan to attempt an uprising in Ravenna.'[37]

At the same time Cardinal Rusconi was writing to Cardinal Spina, the Legate at Bologna, a letter which plainly reveals his agitation and irresolution. The 'revolution', he wrote, had been planned for the beginning of September, because at that time the fourth instalment of the taxes would have been paid in, and the insurgents hoped to break into the Government banks at that favourable moment. He added that the chief centre of 'this wicked seditiousness' was Bologna, but that in Ravenna also 'many young men have been presented with little cards bearing the emblem of Liberty, which they keep hidden under their hats'. Yet it would not, he wrote, be prudent to arrest them, in case nothing compromising was found after all. Moreover, he pathetically added, he could only count upon 20 carabinieri (of whom three were ill) instead of 36, and on 150 troops, 'of whom some must be considered suspect. . . .'

'It is also suspected,' he continued, 'that the famous Lord Byron, who for some time has been living in that city, is an accomplice of this dangerous plot. I give this information to His Eminence the Cardinal Secretary of State, but no measure has been taken with regard to him.'[38]

Shortly afterwards, however, the Cardinal's fears were relieved. Bologna, chiefly owing to the influence of Hercolani, dropped out of the league, and Faenza began to waver. Further meetings of conspirators took place – one of them at Filetto – in which Pietro Gamba, speaking on behalf of Gallina, declared that it was now too late to retreat – even for their own sakes. The Government was now aware of their plans and of many of their names, and some of them would certainly be arrested. But the opinion of the company was against him, and although, in another heated meeting, with representatives of the towns of Forlì, Cesena, Faenza and Ravenna, Gallina again urged violent action, declaring himself certain of his own Ravennati, all the more prudent conspirators (including Count Ruggero Gamba) were against him; the defection of Bologna was considered final, and the whole plan was given up for the time being.³⁹

'My last letters', wrote Byron to Murray, 'will have taught you to expect an explosion here: it was primed and loaded, but they hesitated to fire the train. One of the Cities [Bologna] shirked from the league . . . Our *puir hill folk* [Byron is seeing himself as a Jacobite – but his Americani came from the flattest of plains] offered to strike and to raise the first banner. But Bologna paused – and now 't is Autumn, and the season half over. "Oh Jerusalem! Jerusalem!" The Huns are on the Po, but if once they pass it on their march to Naples, all Italy will rise behind them: the Dogs, – the Wolves – may they perish like the Host of Sennacherib!'⁴⁰

Never was there a situation more confused, nor one in which concerted action seemed more difficult. 'One thing only was certain,' says Masi, 'the constant, pitiless tyranny, unheard-of persecution of all those who were thought to be Liberals, and bullying by the Sanfedisti, followed by bloody reprisals.'⁴¹ All the leaders of the recent plots, including the Gambas, had good reason to be anxious – since none of them was certain how much the Government knew of their plans, or who might be arrested the next day.

'Here we all are', wrote Byron, 'in great confusion, some in arrest, some for flying to the hills, and for making a guerrilla fight for it, others for waiting for better times, and both sides watching each other like hunting leopards . . . My *voice* was, like that of Sempronius, somewhat warlike, but the autumnal rains have damped a deal of military ardour.'⁴²

BYRON TO CONTESSA DOMENICA GASPARA
GUICCIOLI*

Ravenna   *October 7th*, 1820

Dearest Gaspara + I shall think about the suggested week – and as you can imagine, very gladly. – Yesterday I received news from

* Byron used this form of address as a joke – one of Teresa's names (according to the Romagna custom of giving the Christian name of one of the Magi to each of their children) being Gaspara. But it was not kind of him to add to the address 'née F°.-18-1799' – a date which Teresa subsequently tried to alter to 1803.

London – Which makes me prefer to stay here and limit my
patriotic services to the Northern part of the 'bel paese' – rather
than go and warm myself on Vesuvius – and then it is not necessary, since your flame-coloured hair is here and the head under
it, hotter than lava. Besides, I feel a certain remorse at the idea
of leaving you – (even if it were only for a few months) which
gives me a poor notion of the pleasures of separation.

Papa is here with me – the Factor is leaving – so my dearest
Gaspara + +

It is not known what news Byron had received from England
about affairs in Naples — but it is certain that the situation there
was not encouraging. On October 1st the first Neapolitan
Parliament – consisting chiefly of priests, lawyers and small
landowners, all members of the Carboneria – had been opened,
with great public rejoicings and many eloquent speeches. Its
meetings were held in a church, and were given up, not to the
much-needed reform of the laws, but to the discussion, adorned
by many classical quotations, of such matters as whether the
name of Naples should be changed to that of Parthenope, and
whether the inhabitants of the Provinces should resume their old
classical titles of Lucans, Samnites, etc. The Parliament was the
slave of the Carbonari, and there was no sign of the numerous
reforms that had been promised. The more timid members of the
aristocracy fled abroad or to their country estates; the people
became increasingly discontented, and the king could think of no
better way to re-establish law and order than to appeal for help
to the rulers of Austria, Germany and Russia, who were meeting
at Troppau – and who immediately decided to send an Austrian
army to Naples.

The Neapolitan government, under the influence of General
Pepe, who asserted his army of forty thousand men to be invincible
– promptly declared war on Austria. And Byron no less promptly
composed a letter to the Neapolitan people, in which, 'having
understood that the Neapolitans permit even foreigners to contribute to the good cause', he not only offered the handsome
sum of two thousand Louis, from 'an Englishman, a friend to
liberty', but also his own services. 'As a member of the English
House of Peers, he would be a traitor to the principles which
placed the reigning family of England on the throne, if he were
not grateful for the noble lesson so lately given both to peoples and
to kings.' The letter continued:

P

'His distance from the frontier, and the feeling of his personal incapacity to contribute efficaciously to the service of the nation, prevented him from proposing himself as worthy of the lowest commission, for which experience and talent might be requisite. But if, as a mere volunteer, his presence were not a burden to whomsoever he might serve under, he would repair to whatever place the Neapolitan Government might point out, there to obey the orders and participate in the dangers of his commanding officer, without any other motive than that of sharing the destiny of a brave nation defending itself against the self-called Holy Alliance, which but combines the vice of hypocrisy with despotism.'[43]

This 'noble letter' gave great pleasure to Teresa.

'What generosity,' she commented, 'what modesty, what greatness of soul! One can only feel compassion for anyone who could remain indifferent after reading it, for God would have deprived him both of intelligence and heart!'[44]

She adds, however, that the letter (of which a draft, in Byron's hand, remained with her) never reached its destination, for it was entrusted to a Neapolitan called Giuseppe Gigante, who declared himself an emissary of General Pepe's, but who had arrived in Ravenna, having been arrested by the Austrian police on the way, without any documents and 'almost naked'. Byron provided him with some clothes, and money and in spite of warnings that he might be a spy, gave him his letter for the Neapolitan government. As might have been expected, Gigante was again arrested on his way back, at Pesaro, and, Teresa affirms, swallowed some of the papers that had been entrusted to him – but whether or no these included Byron's letter, we do not know.

Throughout the autumn, expectations in the Romagna rose high and Byron himself took the prospects of trouble so seriously that he wrote to Kinnaird to sell out some of his investments.

'My motives are the almost immediate explosion which must take place in Italy in the impending event of the passage of the Po by the barbarians, ... and the further fall of the English funds in consequence; as your Tory scoundrels will, right or wrong, take part in any foreign war.'

And in a postscript he added:

'To give you a hint of the doings *here*. Since I began this letter, the news has arrived from Forlì (the next and nearest city) that last night the Liberals blew up, by means of a mine, the house of a *Brigand* (so they call here the Satellites of the tyrants) . . . People were arrested [words torn off] released them and shot a black-guard, or one of the Carabineers. They have also intimated gently to His Eminence of Forlì,* that if he continues to arm *assassins* (here they war in private in this way, there are bands in every town at so much a head, for those who like such expenses) they will throw him out of his palace windows, which are rather lofty. If these things don't prelude 'sword and gun fighting', you can judge for yourself.'[45]

Whether or not Byron really believed in his own danger, it is difficult to say – but he certainly very much enjoyed hinting at it.

'There will be the devil to pay,' he told Moore, 'and there is no saying who will or will not be set down in his bill. If "honour should come unlooked for" to any of your acquaintance, make a Melody of it . . . In case you should not think him worth it, here is a Chant for you instead –

> When a man hath no freedom to fight for at home,
> Let him combat for that of his neighbours;
> Let him think of the glories of Greece and of Rome
> And get knock'd on the head for his labours.'[46]

To Teresa he hardly ever wrote about his conspiratorial activities, and his next letter refers merely to a practical joke played upon one of his servants, and to the French translation of his works which he was sending her. His comment on the translation to Murray was: 'The French translation of us . . . Oimé! Oimé!'[47] – and to Moore: 'Only think of being *traduced* into a foreign language in such an abominable travesty.'[48]

But he appears to have been completely unaware of the effect which his poems – and in particular his *Farewell* verses to his wife and his *Sketch from Private Life*, would be likely to have on Teresa. Her comments – which suggest that she had seen Byron, for the first time, in an unfavourable light – show considerable perceptiveness and moral courage – and a great dis-

* The Legate of Forlì, Cardinal Sanseverino, was especially hated for his conservatorism and for his crafty, obstinate opposition to any kind of reform. He did not hesitate, as Byron suggests, to provide arms for his satellites. Later on, in 1821, he was the first to issue the orders which sent many of the best citizens of the Romagna into exile.

tress. It is, indeed, a tribute to their relationship that she was able to speak so frankly. But it is not surprising that she was bewildered: the motives that prompted Byron's *Farewell* verses have puzzled many other people, both at the time and since. Tears, according to Byron's own account, fell all over the paper as he wrote – and Moore confirmed this: 'It is blotted all over with the marks of tears.' Both these verses and the *Sketch* (which was written twelve days later) were given to Murray for private distribution only; but someone was indiscreet, and shortly before he left England they were published by *The Champion*. 'The turmoil they created was frantic . . . it was made into a party matter, while the Noel side, though scornfully silent, was outraged equally by "the degrading tribute to the world's opinion", in the *Farewell*, and the abuse, "blackguardly beyond belief" of Mrs. Clermont.'[49] But what Byron himself really thought about it all is not known. To his wife he wrote, on the same day that the *Farewell* was printed: 'More last words – not many – and such as you will attend to . . . I have just parted from Augusta – almost the last being you have left me to part with – and the only unshattered tie of my existence. Wherever I may go – and I am going far – you and I can never meet again, in this world – or in the next. Let this content or atone.'[50]

BYRON TO CONTESSA DOMENICA GASPARA GUICCIOLI

> It will have to be in a few days as I want to come on horse-back and the roads won't be practicable after all that rain.

Ravenna   *October* 11*th*, 1820*

Dearest Gasparina + – It must have been a stroke of lightning 'to turn a lacquey to ashes' as Don Magnifico says[51] – – – Nothing has happened – it was a joke of the servants against Luigi to frighten his Lady, the fair dame of your chamber.

Pray do not have such a massacre of geese – as I cannot come for several days. You will always be warned the day before – My love – don't be angry.

Send me the prints – as I want to have some frames made. I

---

* Either this letter or Teresa's answer, acknowledging the receipt of Byron's poems, is obviously misdated.

send you a very bad translation in French of the book you asked
for some time ago. [52] You will find in it (full of foolishness and lies
however) a very different account from that of my Pierinesque
friends in Rome – about the cause of my *separation* from my wife.
It is in the first volume – – – – If you can favour me with the
other volumes of the *biography of famous men*, I shall be grateful.
Always + + +

P.S. The books have come. Thank you.

CONTESSA GUICCIOLI TO BYRON

Filetto   *October 10th*, 1820

My only Love for ever!!! + + + I was infinitely glad to get your
works – I have read one or two of them – *but how astounded I am!*
One must know them to know you. The experience of a year and a
half did not tell me as much about you as reading *two of your pages*.
I must however confess to you that this increase of light on the
subject is to your disadvantage; I do not mean as to your genius,
for that must be adored in silence, but as to *morals*, of which it is
permissible even for a simple mind like mine to speak, and must
indeed be spoken of without reserve between Friends.

Here then, briefly, are my reflections. – I believed you to be
sincere; now I shall not be able to affirm it with such assurance. –
I believed you to be sensitive to misfortune, but *never* affected by
it; this opinion I still have and must have, in order to esteem and
love you; but you have written one thing that, in my opinion,
might give the impression that in some moments of your life you
showed a certain weakness of character. It is your *Farewell*,
and the *Sketch from Private Life* that make me think so. In these
there is more than talent, tenderness and Love; more than was
proper towards a woman who had offended you; and besides it
is completely in contradiction with all that you have told me
about your feelings for your wife. – I do not blame you for having
felt such a tenderness, it only hurts me that you should have
concealed the truth from me; or if indeed you did not feel it, that
you should so have deceived the World. Believe me, Byron, your
Farewell in particular does not give any idea of your independent
character. It gives the impression of a guilty man *asking for pity*;
or at least, too proud to ask for it openly, but hoping that his

prayer for it will be understood; and this is a situation which never should be yours! I assure you that I can hardly persuade myself that this *Farewell* is Byron's. But if it is, and the sentiment expressed in it is sincere, I cannot understand how the proudest, the coldest, of Englishwomen could refrain from coming to throw herself into your arms and beg for mutual forgiveness. – Oh, I no longer understand anything – knowledge of the human heart is very difficult, and perhaps will always be unattainable by me. I will rest on this conviction; asking you meanwhile to forgive my frankness, which however I shall never give up as long as I shall be your friend – that is to say as long as I live. I will say no more to you about this subject.

Come whenever you like – I cannot and do not wish to force your inclinations. – I am sorry, because I had a great deal to say to you.

Your true Friend and Lover for Ever   TERESA G.G.

BYRON TO CONTESSA GUICCIOLI

Ravenna   *October 12th, 1820*[53]

My Love + Perhaps you are right – we will talk about it when we are together – for the present I will only tell you that in the year 1816, when these verses were printed, a French woman then in London, said, more or less in your words, – that 'she could not understand how the proudest woman', etc. etc., 'could restrain herself', etc. etc., and 'As for me,' said she, 'whatever had been the guilt of my lover or husband, I could not have restrained myself a moment from flinging myself in his arms.' This opinion was printed in the daily gazettes – I did not know the person – beyond that it was a Frenchwoman.* – It is singular that a Frenchwoman and an Italian agree in this feeling.

The defence of the blessed *Mathematician*† was – 'that I was not sincere – that all this was *Machiavellism* on my part – to make her seem in the wrong – because *in fact* I wished for a separation', etc. etc. You can judge for yourself – if I am so politic.

We shall see each other in a few days – Love me + my Gaspara + always

---

* The French lady is Madame de Staël.
† Lady Byron.

Byron's next note refers to another letter from Fanny Silvestrini to Teresa – in which it would seem that the lady had been attempting a little blackmail. This is positively her last appearance.

Ravenna   *October 25th*, 1820

My Love + Fanny's letter is a portrait of 'the procuress who wrote it'.* False, sly, arrogant, corrupt, pedantic, toadying and a liar. 'Frank to Ravenna' – frank to Hell – let the devil pay the journey! The only thing I should like for a moment would be to see her effect on Pierino – I am sure he would throw her out of the window the second day.

[torn] . . . . . with her forced compliments about me . . . . the bitch – but I am [torn]. . . . . .

I have no time to say more for the . . . . . courier is impatient. Greet Papa and Pierino and love me always. +++

P.S. I don't know if Lega has an understanding with Signora F. but *I* have reached an understanding with *him* on the subject.

The reference to 'bigoted relatives' in the following letter is to some members of Teresa's family (probably her grand-parents – since we know that her grandfather Count Paolo Gamba was a Sanfedista), who, 'since they considered that friendship with a heretic entailed eternal damnation', had written to her father the Ravenna gossip about Byron's visits. This letter Teresa had forwarded to Byron.

There was, however, more serious trouble than this in Ravenna. The oppression of the Clerical government had now become almost unendurable: it had imposed new and exorbitant taxes, of which the proceeds went to religious bodies; the tribunal showed gross favouritism and injustice; the law-courts were crowded, and the prisons overflowing.

'Here', wrote Byron, 'all is suspicion and terrorism, bullying, arming and disarming; the priests scared, the people gloomy, and the merchants *buying* up corn to *supply the armies*. I am so pleased with the last piece of Italic patriotism, that I have underlined it for your remark; it is just as if our Hampshire farmers should prepare magazines for any two continental scoundrels who could land and fight it out in New Forest.'[54]

* Galeotto fu il libro e chi lo scrisse.' (The reference is to DANTE, *Inf.*, V, v. 137.) Some of this letter appears to have been expressed in such crude terms, that Teresa thought it best to tear off part of the page.

In such circumstances it is hardly surprising that the Papal government would have preferred Lord Byron to be elsewhere. But still no one liked to ask him to go. The local police received orders from the Vatican to arrest those of his servants who – in a city where no one was allowed to carry arms without a special permit – were walking about armed to the teeth, but even this mild step seemed to them too perilous. 'The operation is difficult,' they reported to Cardinal Consalvi, 'because they do not generally carry arms except when their master is with them.' And, since they were in the service of a foreigner – were they to be considered as foreigners themselves, or as Italians? It was all very difficult. – 'Pray send some more precise instructions about Lord.' The Cardinal replied somewhat tartly that he did not see what difficulty there could be in finding out whether Byron's servants were foreigners or Italians, and in arresting those who were Italians – but, after several weeks of correspondence on the subject, the boldest step that the police felt able to take was 'confidentially to warn Lord Byron that it did not look well for his servants to accompany him fully armed'. And there the matter ended.[55]

'He gives orders right and left', says another police report, 'on the strength of the money that he freely distributes to the bad characters who form his society. He has never had any dealings with wise and honest people . . . He is the protector of the Cacciatori Americani and the first revolutionary in Ravenna.'[56]

His very generosity, which had never discriminated between one party and another in cases of need, and which had recently shown itself in a gift for the repairs of a church organ, was now considered suspect; he must be trying, the priests decided, to curry favour with the people. He had flown the tricolour flag of the Carbonari from his balcony they said, and had himself stood at the door of the Palazzo Guiccioli, distributing money, 'in order to create a following'.[57]
Of all this Byron was not unaware, for in November he wrote to Kinnaird:

'They have taken it into their heads that I am popular . . . and are trying by all kinds of petty vexations to disgust and make me retire. This I should hardly believe, it seems so absurd, if some of their priests did not avow it. They try to fix squabbles upon my servants, to involve me in scrapes (no difficult matter), and

lastly they (the governing party) menace to shut Madame Guiccioli up in a *Convent*. The last piece of policy springs from two
motives; the one because her family are suspected of liberal
principles, and the second because mine are known . . . She is, as
women are apt to be by opposition, sufficiently heroic and
obstinate . . . I have seen the correspondence of half a dozen
bigots on the subject, and perceive that they have set about it,
merely as an indirect way of attacking part of her relations, and
myself.'[58]

It was to these attacks that he referred in his next letter to
Teresa:

Ravenna   *October 30th,* 1820

My Love – I can well believe anything of those bigoted relatives
(of yours) – and of the Government, which now suspects everyone
and would do anything – to send away or frighten those it fears –
It will not, however, be directed only at *me* – but also at *your*
family – (Pierino, for example) for being suspect in these recent
patriotic matters. – But it is unjust to attack a woman for a man's
misdoing – – – I had hoped, foreseeing all this, that my conduct
after your separation from your husband had been sufficiently
reserved *(in appearance)* to remove any pretext for taking fresh
measures, particularly after the agreement between Guiccioli and
your family – to give up a part of the allowance.

The bigots' envy naturally always makes them persecute others
for the pleasures of which they have deprived themselves. For my
part I don't see or understand anything – except that – by any
trivial means – they are attempting to rid themselves of my
presence in the Papal States – and were it not for certain *hopes*
and *sentiments* (including, *above all*, my love for you) I should very
quickly *take myself off*.

Greet Papa and Pierino.

Elisei has come back and settled in Faenza – here is his letter
to me. I don't know the circumstances well enough to give Papa
advice. He should know about the character of his relations and
of what the government is or is not capable. Of my love you have
proofs and shall have more.

I am and shall be + + +

Ravenna   *November 8th,* 1820

My Love – I did not write to you – because there was nothing
new to say. 'Out of *Nothing* Nothing can arise', the Lady Mathematician said – which, however, is not true, for I have often seen
a letter of six pages come out of *Nothing.* You know my great
talent for *Silence* – and should forgive me when I do not write on
every slightest occasion. The weather does not seem to be very
favourable for your plan – but I will think about it.

Greet Papa and Pierino – – and love me entirely +

P.S. *Write* if it suits you – otherwise I believe you could not live –
so *write,* great Santa Chiara!

Ravenna   *November* 10*th,* 1820

Thank you a thousand times for your present, my love – a fine
cantata in your note

With this weather it seems to me that your riding plans won't
be very successful in the country round Filetto. I have not come
to you, but I keep the hope of seeing you soon.

Greet Pierino and Papa – keep well and always love me.
I kiss you + + + +

P.S. They are speaking here of a revolution started in England
but I do not believe it, for yesterday I had some recent letters and
some Gazettes from Paris. These did not speak of any riot. The
Queen's trial is going ahead with its usual indecency – it should
have been decided by now.

November 18*th,* 1820

My Love + + Pray forgive me if I don't come to Filetto at this
moment. All that we have to say – can well be said at Ravenna –
so it isn't so very important.

Hoping to see you soon – I am always yours +

November 22*nd,* 1820

My Love, + But what then can be done? Haven't you heard what
Papa and Pierino say? who are your nearest relatives and I hope
also *friends of mine,* as I have behaved in good faith towards them.
. . . These others, the *buffoons* – either in the government or (forgive me) in your family, want to sacrifice you; what is now needed

is common sense and patience. If I did not love you – if I *wished to get rid of you without blame* – and also with the best excuse for myself – the most certain way would be to *visit you* – and to commit such imprudences in the face of the world and of the priests – who make up the *world here*. – I shall always be your

The preceding note – the last of this year – must have been written in answer to one of Teresa's impatient outbursts; she could not, would not, understand, that it was unwise for Byron to go to Filetto. Finally, at the end of the month, she could bear the separation no longer – and moved back to Ravenna herself, to 'a noble and comfortable apartment' in her father's palazzo.

6: FAREWELL TO RAVENNA

Women are much more *attached* than men.
Byron to Lady Melbourne

THE winter months of 1820-21 were spent by Teresa in her
father's house in Ravenna – and by Byron in the Palazzo
Guiccioli, visiting her every day. It was a very different
winter from the previous one. Then the love-affair was in its most
stormy phase: although living in the same house, their meetings
had been uncertain and perilous, their love-making frustrated by
quarrels and mutual reproaches, and their future was still completely uncertain. In public they had maintained the semi-
formal relationship of a lady and her 'Cavalier Servente', driving
together in Teresa's coach-and-six, and attending the theatre and
the carnival balls.

This winter they were never to be seen at the Ravenna parties,
and had settled down to a semi-conjugal domestic routine,
unbroken by emotional storms. In all this period, indeed, from
November 1820 to July 1821, we have only one letter from Byron
to Teresa – the one of January 18th about 'Marino Faliero'. It
is possible, of course, that some others may have been lost; but it
seems more probable that, seeing his *dama* in ease and privacy
every day, – for although living under her father's roof, she had
her own private apartment – Byron felt no need to exchange
frequent love-letters. Teresa writes of this period as having been a
singularly happy one – and she kept to the day of her death,
among her 'Byron relics', a small piece of the wall-hangings of
the room where Byron spent his evenings with her.[1]

'He now saw his friends,' she says, 'released at last from a
dangerous and unbearable position and living under her father's
protection, in a dwelling even more noble and comfortable than
the one she had left in Palazzo Guiccioli; he saw her happy and
cherished by her whole family; and his happiness was increased
by finding himself also the object of the regard and liking of the
whole town.'

Even Teresa's paternal grandparents – 'so highly esteemed and
respected for their domestic and religious virtues' – overcame
their prejudices, and 'could not object to a liaison which confined
itself to the outward tokens of the purest friendship'.[2]
Their indulgence, says Teresa, was partly to be attributed to
the indignation which Guiccioli's conduct had awakened in

them – and partly to the fact that Byron – although an English-man and a Protestant – had shown himself favourable to Catholic-ism to the extent of sending his child – then just four years old – to the convent-school of Bagnacavallo, where the old Count and Countess went to visit her. So poor little Allegra, too, played her part in the story.

Teresa says that his chief reason for reaching this decision was not only that the child was becoming increasingly wilful and uncontrollable, but that he suspected one of the maids of teaching her to tell lies.³ She appears to have gone off to the school happily enough, for on the day of her arrival the brother of one of the Nuns was writing to Byron.

'I think it my duty to send you a report at once about your child Allegrina – a well-chosen name which suits her happy nature. As soon as she arrived she went off to play with several other little girls. Last night she slept quietly, and this morning I have found her more cheerful and lively than ever. She has already chosen her favourite playmate, among the many who are here, and with her she is enjoying herself – always, however, under the eyes of the Mother Superior and of my Sister.'⁴

Teresa has supplied every detail about the strict routine of Byron's life at this time, 'as the best reply to his enemies, who described his life in Italy as one of pleasure and vice'.⁵ Since he worked all night at his studies, he seldom went to bed before dawn, and consequently got up very late – breakfasting on a cup of sugarless tea and the yolk of a raw egg, without bread. He then read or wrote letters until his afternoon ride, which took place regularly two hours before sunset, and almost invariably in the company of Pietro Gamba. The two young men rode in the Pineta and indulged in pistol-practice – frequently followed by a handful of ragamuffins and beggars, who picked up the silver coins the gentlemen threw up into the air to shoot at. At sundown Byron went home again and dined frugally – 'like a Pythagorean philosopher' – while reading, or talking to his dogs; he rested for half an hour, and then went to spend the rest of the evening until 11 o'clock in Teresa's drawing-room, in conversation, with a little music on the pianoforte or the harp. With regard to music, Teresa says that Byron was not hard to please. 'He liked what pleased him, because it had pleased him before'⁶ – a sign of the completely unmusical, but which Teresa preferred to attribute to the innate constancy of his character. Over and over again he would ask her to play to him the same 'simple popular airs' –

which often moved him to tears; but if she attempted 'some variations of the Italian school', he instantly asked her to return to the original melody.

As to conversation, it ranged over a fairly wide field. 'Talked of Italy,' says Byron, 'patriotism, Alfieri, Madame Albany and other branches of learning. Also Sallust's *Conspiracy of Catiline* and the *War of Jugurtha*',[7] until at nine Teresa's father and brother joined them and the conversation turned to farming, fencing and politics. Teresa, though a silly woman, was far from being a stupid one – and there is no doubt that Byron enjoyed talking to her. She almost precisely, indeed, fulfilled his description to Lady Blessington of his *beau idéal*: 'A woman with talent enough to be able to understand and value mine, but not sufficient to be able to shine herself. All men with pretentions,' he added, 'desire this, though few, if any, have the courage to avow it.'[8]

Teresa corrected his proofs,[9] she answered his Italian letters, she even proffered her opinions.

'What do you think a very pretty Italian lady said to me the other day? I said that I suspected it [*Don Juan*] would live longer than *Childe Harold*. "Ah, but (said she) I would rather have the fame of Childe Harold for three years than an *immortality* of Don Juan!" The truth is that it is *too true*, and the women hate every thing which strips off the tinsel of *Sentiment*; and they are right, as it would rob them of their weapons.'[10]

Nor did Teresa content herself with this admission; she extracted a promise – which was kept – that Byron would stop writing *Don Juan* until she herself authorized him to continue it. Her own explanation of her behaviour is that, although she had only read the first two cantos of *Don Juan* (in a French translation) she had been deeply distressed by an article in the Milan *Gazzetta*, quoting the attacks on Byron's morals in the English papers.

'In vain did Lord Byron attempt to calm her by telling her that for his English enemies to be shocked by a burlesque satire was a piece of pure affectation and cant – that the greater part of the Classical literature which was put in the hands of youth was far more licentious – that poetry is never dangerous to morals, because it is not based on argument or reason, and has not the false optimism of a Rousseau's Saint Preux or a de Staël's Corinne ... which do far more damage to women's hearts than all the poems of the present or the past. In vain did he tell her that the last three cantos, written under a *gentler* influence, were irreproachable.'[11]

Teresa would have none of it. 'She only knew that *he* was being attacked, tormented, calumniated' – and she begged him to stop writing a poem which could not fail to bring further attacks upon him. For a long time, she tells us, Byron merely laughed at her, but at last he gave way. 'Very well, I promise you not to write any more of *Don Juan* until you yourself authorize it.'[12] He then wrote to tell Murray of his decision: 'You will therefore look upon these three cantos as the last of the poem'[13] and enclosed Teresa's note of thanks.

'Do not forget, my Byron, the promise you have made me. Never shall I be able to express to you the satisfaction I feel, so great is the sentiment of joy and trust with which this sacrifice you have made has inspired me.' A postscript adds: 'I am only sorry that Don Juan was not left in the infernal regions.'[14]

Hobhouse's comments on Byron's decision, of which he wholeheartedly approved, are amusing:

'Take Doctor's advice: let your readers get up from you with an appetite. This is right with the best works, and of course more right when there is any doubt as to the nature of the performance. La Signora, to be sure, knows her sex and resembles her sex. The comedy of love is not to their or her taste; how should it be? – – – Your Don is too much of a joker to be a real favourite, although the ladies like to be thought able to appreciate his merits, as they do those of substantial vice, for fear of being taken for cold and passionless.'*

A few months later, when Byron was writing *Sardanapalus*, Teresa offered her advice about this work also, deploring the absence of any 'love-interest' in its first draft. She told him 'that in all civilizations alike, men cannot suppress their feelings'; she insisted that 'even without attributing to the Assyrians the hearts of knights errant, his genius would succeed in depicting a noble passion'; she added that a tragedy without love in it could not fail to be tedious.

* Unpublished letter belonging to Sir John Murray. August 12th, 1821. Augusta shared Teresa's feelings about *Don Juan*. 'This new Poem, if persisted in, will be the ruin of him, for what I can learn.' Letter to Mr. Hodgson, April 17th, 1819. *L.J.*, IV, p. 276.

'Lord Byron, who had begun to laugh as he listened to this tirade, became serious and said: "Perhaps you are right. The eloquence of Santa Chiara will reform me. I will think it over." '¹⁵

That evening he wrote in his Journal:

'Having the advantage of her native language, and natural female eloquence, she overcame my fewer arguments. I believe she was right. I must put more love into *Sardanapalus* than I intended.'¹⁶

'The sublime love of Myrrha', proudly asserts Teresa, 'was conceived that evening.'

It was at this time, too, that Byron was telling Teresa of his annoyances about the London performances of *Marino Faliero*. This tragedy which, as has been seen, had been written under great stress, – ('I have', he told Moore, 'too many passions of my own on hand to do justice to those of the dead'¹⁷) was a piece of work which Byron took extremely seriously. 'I have "put my Soul into thistragedy" ', he told Murray,¹⁸ and in some of the Doge's speeches there is more than a touch of self-identification. Perhaps precisely for this reason, he awaited the verdict on this work with unusual anxiety, and reported with satisfaction such varying comments as Foscolo's remark that 'the characters are right Venetian', and Gifford's 'English – *genuine*, sterling English'. But he had no illusions as to the tragedy's fitness for the stage – and was extremely annoyed to receive from Teresa a copy of the Milan *Gazzetta*, stating that it was about to be performed, without his consent, at Drury Lane.

'I have just read in an *Italian paper*', he wrote to Murray on January 20th, ' "that Ld. B. has a tragedy coming out", etc. etc. ... Now I do reiterate and desire that everything may be done to prevent it from coming out on *any theatre* – for *which* it never was designed and on which ... it could never succeed.'¹⁹

In spite, however, of these protests, the play was performed on April 30th and again for five nights in May, coldly received and a loss to the 'speculating buffoons'. The following letter was written when he returned the Milan *Gazzetta* to Teresa.²⁰

BYRON TO CONTESSA GUICCIOLI

January 18*th*, 1821

My Love: Here is the truth of what I said to you a few days ago about how I am being misinterpreted in every way – without knowing *why* or *how*.

The tragedy they are talking about – is not (and never was) either written for or adapted to the theatre – but the form is not romantic – it is rather regular – certainly regular as to the unity of time – and failing but slightly in that of place. You well know whether I ever intended to have it acted – for it was written by your side – and in moments certainly more tragic for me as a *man* than as a writer – for *you* were in distress and danger. In the meantime I hear from your Gazette that a 'Cabala' has been formed – a party – and a devil of a *row* and without my having taken the slightest part in it. – They say that *the author read it aloud*!!! – *here perhaps* – in *Ravenna*! and to whom? perhaps to Fletcher!!! that illustrious man of letters!

This is portentous fooling – I do not feel well – my head aches and my heart a little. –*

I kiss you a 1000 times. Always all yours

But Byron's mind soon turned to other matters than literary quarrels. During the winter and early spring of 1821 Casa Gamba was the centre of the political plots of the Romagna, and Byron was as deeply involved as the rest of the family in the ups and downs of the conspirators' hopes and fears. It is difficult to give an adequate picture of the atmosphere of Ravenna during this time of intense expectation. Here was a little country town, no larger than Guildford or Nottingham (as it was then), but wholly given up to political dissension and strife. Day after day, the narrow streets were the scene of meetings between men of opposing parties, sometimes under the cloak of temporary fraternization, sometimes in open conflict. One evening the Papal guards would be drinking in a tavern with a group of friends – guards and Carbonari together waking the echoes with their songs:

* This letter is quoted by Moore (omitting the last sentence) and is printed in the *Letters and Journals* (V, p. 294) without a date. Byron himself has made a mistake in the year, dating it January 18th, 1820 (before *Marino Faliero* was written) whereas it is clearly of January 1821, two days before his letter to John Murray on the same subject.

Uniti e concordi
Scacciam lo straniero,
Ognun sia guerriero,
Sia pronto a pugnar;
Dall 'Alpi scoscese
All 'Etna infocato
Siam tutti uno Stato
Un popolo sol.[21]

But the next night there would be a shot in the dark, a sudden cry – and one of the soldiers was murdered. Then would come reprisal: the sudden arrest or assassination of a Liberal, to pay for the previous night's treachery. Two strangers met in the street. 'Two or three?' one would ask the other, referring to the *two* colours of the Austrian flag or the *three* of the Carboneria and would know by the answer whether he had met an enemy or a friend.*

On Sunday mornings the Cardinal's procession crossed the Cathedral Square – the old Cardinal, whom the people called *Coccardino*, glaring suspiciously about him – the long train of minor priests and guards following, the devout kneeling for his blessing. Frequently the sermon took the form of a violent diatribe against the new ideas; and during it some of the Liberals went out. But it was chiefly after nightfall that the little city came to life. Then, behind the façades of those gloomy palaces, there were whispering voices: voices of fear in the Cardinal's palace, planning measures of repression and self-defence; voices of conspirators in the houses of Liberal nobles, in the shops, in the taverns, forming childish, impracticable schemes, repeating wild rumours, dreaming yet wilder dreams of freedom and unity. Armed guards entered the houses of those the Government considered suspect, turning the whole place upside down, in their search for arms and compromising papers. If anything suspicious was found, immediate arrest followed; the victims were taken off to one of the state fortresses, where interminable interrogatories awaited them, often followed by exile or execution.

The post-bags were searched and their contents duly reported to Rome and Vienna by the Government spies.

'I wonder if they can read them', wrote Byron, 'when they have opened them! If so, they may see, in my most legible hand, that I think them damned scoundrels and barbarians, their emperor a fool, and themselves more fools than he; all which they may send

* The three colours of the Carboneria (black, red and blue) had a symbolic meaning: the black (coal) stood for faith, the blue (smoke) for hope and the red (fire) for charity.

to Vienna, for anything I care. They have got themselves masters of the Papal police and are bullying away; but some day or other they will pay for it all.'[22]

For already the Carbonari were beginning to risk occasional acts of reprisal. On the evening of December 8th, 1820, as Byron was putting on his greatcoat to go and call on Teresa, he heard a shot, and, running out into the street, found a dying man lying there, wounded in five places. It was an officer of the Cardinal's guard.

'There were about him Diego, his Adjutant, crying like a child; a priest howling; a Surgeon who dared not touch him; two or three confused and frightened soldiers . . . and the street dark as pitch, with the people flying in all directions.' Byron had the man carried into his house, 'but it was too late, he was gone . . . He only said "*O Dio!* and *Gesù!*" two or three times, and appeared to have suffered very little'.*

The officer who had been murdered was a Captain Luigi Dal Pinto, who for two years had been in command of the Papal troops at Ravenna – 'a brave officer,' says Byron, 'but an un-popular man'. The police attempted to find the murderer, but failed to do so – whereupon the Cardinal issued a proclamation offering a reward of 1000 scudi to any informer who would reveal his identity, or to any of his accomplices who would give himself up. The informers were promised secrecy, and the accomplices impunity.[23]

As the winter wore on, snow and mud blocked the roads entirely, and the town suffered the isolation – and, for Byron, the tedium – of a veritable siege. Even the post from England was delayed.

'The snow of last week melting to the scirocco of today, so that there were two damned things at once. Could not even get to ride on horseback in the forest. Stayed at home all the morning – looked at the fire – wondered when the post would come.'[24]

Now and again, in a spell of better weather, a messenger would arrive from Faenza or Forlì, bringing news of what was happening

---

* *L.J.*, V, p. 136. Lieutenant Elisei, with whom Byron used to ride in the Pineta, wrote from Forlì a few days later, to say how much Byron's humane behaviour had been appreciated. 'Many people have asked me about it; I have told the story as it is and everyone said that it did you great honour.' December 30th, 1820. Unpublished letter belonging to Sir John Murray.

in the rest of the Romagna. On January 7th, at a Conversazione, Pietro Gamba took Byron aside and told him that the Patriots had received notice from Forlì that the Cardinal had given orders for several arrests. The Ravenna conspirators were consequently arming themselves, and were prepared – if any arrests were attempted – to start a fight. Byron promptly offered to take into his own house any who feared arrest, and to fight for them, if the house were attacked. He then went home and spent the rest of the night in some exhilaration, awaiting the turn of events.

'Expect to hear the drum and the musquetry momently (for they swear to resist, and are right) – but I hear nothing, as yet, save the plash of the rain and the gusts of the wind . . . Mended the fire – have got the arms – and a book or two, which I shall turn over. I know little of their numbers, but think the Carbonari strong enough to beat the troops, even here. With twenty men this house might be defended for twenty-four hours against any force to be brought against it.'[25]

The next morning, however, there was an anticlimax. Pietro Gamba called to tell him that none of last night's rumours were true. No arrests had yet taken place, but an attack by the San-fedisti was still expected at Forlì. The Sanfedisti – the bitterest opponents of the Carbonari – were members of an association originally founded by law-abiding Jesuits, at the time of the suppression of the Company, to defend the Catholic faith, the institutions of the Church, and the temporal dominion of the Pope, but which had gradually come to include all that was most reactionary in the country: 'ribald clerics, overbearing nobles, trouble-makers, impostors, spies – all standing on guard, like the dragon of the Hesperides, before the altar and the throne'.[26] The solemn oath of fidelity taken by the members of this order was the following:

'In the presence of God the Omnipotent, Father, Son and Holy Ghost, and of Mary the ever Immaculate Virgin, of the whole Celestial Court, and of thee, Honoured Father, I vow to have my hand cut and my throat slit, to perish of hunger or die in cruel martyrdom, to suffer the cruel tortures of Hell, rather than betray or deceive one of the honoured fathers or brothers of this Catholic Apostolic Society, or fail in the duties I have taken on. I swear to sustain with the whole strength of my heart and arm the holy cause to which I have consecrated myself, and show myself unforgiving to any man belonging to the infamous rabble of the Liberals, without any distinction of kinship, rank, sex or age. I swear immortal hatred against all the enemies of our only true and holy Religion, Catholic and Roman.'[27]

Later on, in the risings of 1831 and 1848, the members of this organization rivalled the most extreme revolutionaries in their deeds of violence; and already they were beginning to be feared.

On this occasion Byron listened to Pietro Gamba's story, furnished him with some more arms for his men, and, after repeating that in case of trouble, the conspirators might assemble in his house, offered some very sensible advice.

'I advised them to attack in detail, and in different parties, in different *places* (though at the *same* time) so as to divide the attention of the troops, who, though few, yet, being disciplined, would beat any body of people (not trained) in a regular fight.'[28]

That evening the Gambas came back with more news, which had been given them by Count Alborghetti. This suave and agreeable nobleman, who, in early days, had taken great pleasure in introducing Byron to Ravenna society, had for some time been sending him such political news as, in his capacity of Secretary General of the Province, often reached him, before becoming known by the general public. Thus in November he had been the first to tell Byron of Queen Caroline's acquittal.

'You could not have sent me better news,' Byron replied,[29] 'better for England, for it will prevent a revolution – though it may *hasten* a *reform* – or better for Italy, for if (as is probable) the Ministry is changed – we shall have a pacific administration, who may perhaps interfere to prevent the "bel paese" from becoming the prey alike of factious citizens or of foreign armies. The News are also personally agreeable to me – for I have obligations to the Queen for her kindness to me when she kept her residence at Kensington Palace. My friends in England have reproached me severely for not being present to do my duty on Her Majesty's trial, but it is a satisfaction for me to see by the result that my humble vote and voice were not necessary.

I beg my respects and thanks to His Eminence for the communication, and I request your acceptance of my acknowledgments; you write English so well that I need hardly tell you that you were right in *both* your terms – for if London had not been "illuminated" it is probable that the people would have "fired" it and then it would have been "illuminated" with a vengeance.'

Ten days later, on December 3rd, Alborghetti was asking Byron for more details on the subject.

'Since our publick papers speak with darkness and ambiguity about the Queen's trial and her deliverance, be so kind as to tell me something more clear and precise on purpose. What signifies the adjournment of Parliament for six months? According to your Laws, is the bill to be put on the carpet another time? Is the triumph of the Queen entire or incomplete?'[30]

Byron sent an immediate reply:

'I answer you without hesitation – the Bill is *thrown out entirely* and *completely*: the expression of "read again this day six months" is little more than a form used on the rejection of all Parliamentary Bills whatsoever, and which cannot be dispensed with: it is like saying "the King *never dies*" which is another form of the B. Constitution. The great struggle now will be to throw out the *Ministers* – how this may end we cannot yet know – England at present will *not go to war* – – – France and Prussia are against it – and if the Ministers are beaten – there will perhaps be no foreign war at ·all; but this is problematical. – Whether the Ministers in their agony will try some censure or other in a *different shape* against the Queen – is not certain, but if they do they will be beaten probably.'[31]

On December 11th Alborghetti wrote again about a change of Ministry in England – which, he hopefully considered, 'may change the State of Europe'. And now the news he transmitted began to be more closely related to Italian affairs. At the beginning of December he had told Byron that the Pope, the King of Piedmont and the Grand Duke of Tuscany had been invited to the Congress of Leybach, but that neither the Pope nor Cardinal Consalvi would attend.[32] And, a few days later, he added that the King of Naples had also been invited. 'If', he wrote, 'the [Neapolitan] Nation hinders the king from going, this will afford a proof of his want of liberty, and will be considered as a declaration of war.' The king, according to Alborghetti, had appealed to his Parliament for permission to do so, promising upon *his Royal word* that at his return he would give a Liberal

Constitution, the most apt to the wants of his subjects and entirely grounded on liberal principles'.[33]

At the meeting, indeed, of the Neapolitan Parliament on December 8th, to which Alborghetti referred, the most violent feeling had been shown against the king's going to Leybach. Many of the deputies, including General Pepe, had appeared with daggers in their hands, wearing the colours of the Carboneria, and crying 'The Spanish Constitution or Death!' The streets around the Parliament were filled with a threatening crowd. The Carbonari wished for open war with Austria, and referred to the Abruzzi, somewhat prematurely, as the Neapolitan Thermopylae; but the army itself and the people were all for peace and quiet.[34]

By the end of the month, however, Alborghetti was writing to Byron.

'There is, to my advice, no hope of accommodation between the sovereign and the people of Naples, because it seems decided not to bear the constitution of Spain in Italy. They write from Milan that the Austrian Army shall go to Naples in any case, either as a friend or an enemy.'[35]

Alborghetti's letters requested Byron to maintain the greatest secrecy about his information, and not to give away the name of his informant. Byron, however, did not take either the Count or his news very seriously.

'He is a *trimmer*,' he wrote in his Journal on January 8th, after noting Alborghetti's news from Forlì, 'and deals, at present, his cards with both hands. If he don't mind, they'll be full. He pretends (*I* doubt him – *they* don't – we shall see) that there is no such order (of arrest), and seems staggered by the immense exertions of the Neapolitans and the fierce spirit of the Liberals here. The truth is that [he] cares for little but his place (which is a good one) and wishes to play pretty with both parties. He has changed his mind thirty times these last three moons, to my knowledge, for he corresponds with me. But he is not a bloody fellow – only an avaricious one.'*

* *L.J.*, V, pp. 159-60. Alborghetti's name is replaced by an asterisk, but there can be no doubt about his identity. Teresa gives a similar account of him in the 'Vie', calling him 'a witty and timid man, concerned only with his own interests, who – as he did not know yet who would win – kept a foot in both stirrups. He often went to see Lord Byron, and *pretended* to keep him informed about events. Lord Byron found his company amusing, but knew what to think of him, and was always very careful.' 'Vie', pp. 571-2.

The police, too, kept an eye on Alborghetti. Later on, one of their spies in Ravenna was solemnly reproved by the head of the police for going to the Count's house, because 'he is considered double-faced and greedy'. The spy hastened to justify himself, saying that:

'In that company there is nothing secret, and the conversation is of a kind not to injure either the Government or private individuals. What Alborghetti's views on politics are I would not like to say, for in speaking to me he has certainly been fair and reasonable; as to his being greedy, one has unfortunately only got to have a post, to be subject to this accusation.'³⁶

On this occasion Alborghetti's information to Byron appears to have been exact, and the conspirators realized that, after all, nothing was going to happen for the present.

'It seems that just at this moment (as Lydia Languish says) "there will be no elopement after all". I wish that I had known as much last night . . . And yet I ought not to complain, for, though it is a sirocco, and heavy rain, I have not *yawned* for these two days.'³⁷

The next morning, however, a fresh rumour came from Bologna: the Austrian troops had been placed on war pay and were about to march. The usual conspirators assembled in the evening.

'They mean to *insurrect* here, and are to honour me with a call thereupon. I shall not fall back, though I don't think them in force or heart sufficient to make much of it. But *onward*! – it is now the time to act, and what signifies *self*, if a single spark of that which would be worthy of the past can be bequeathed unquenchedly to the future?'³⁸

And, four days later:

'News come – the *Powers* mean to war with the peoples. The intelligence seems positive . . . The king-times are fast finishing. There will be blood shed like water, and tears like mist; but the peoples will conquer in the end. I shall not live to see it, but I foresee it.'³⁹

But, again, the excitement subsided – and, again, kept indoors by the rain and mud, boredom and melancholy overcame him. January 22nd was his birthday.

' "Tis the middle of the night by the castle-clock," and I am
now thirty-three!

> Through life's road, so dim and dirty,
> I have dragged to three-and-thirty.
> What have these years left to me?
> Nothing – except thirty-three.'

'I go to my bed', he added, 'with a heaviness of heart at having
lived so long, and to so little purpose.'[40]

The thaw was now approaching, and with it the date when,
according to plan, the Neapolitan revolutionary troops were to
march northward and, after joining the insurgents of the
Romagna, to liberate the Papal States. But as the time for action
drew nearer, Byron was appalled by the frivolity and irrespon-
sibility of his fellow-conspirators. Carnival was now again in full
swing – and the revolutionaries were engaged in displaying their
masques on the Corse.

'*Vive la bagatelle!* The Germans are on the Po, the Barbarians at
the gate, and their masters in council at Leybach . . . and lo! they
dance and sing and make merry!'[41]

As for his own friends, they had all gone off on a shooting-party:

'They don't return till Sunday – that is to say, they have been
out for five days, buffooning, while the interests of a whole country
are at stake, and even they themselves compromised. It is a
difficult part to play amongst such a set of assassins and block-
heads, – but, when the scum is skimmed off, or has boiled over,
good may come of it. If this country could but be freed, what
would be too great for the accomplishment of that desire? for the
extinction of that Sigh of Ages? Let us hope. They have hoped
these thousand years.'[42]

The best of the lot, he maintained, were the peasants – 'a fine,
savage race of two-legged leopards,' – and his spirits rose when,
the weather having cleared, he was able to ride out into the forest,
and there met a company of the *Americani* 'all armed and singing
with all their might, "Sem tutti soldat' per la libertà" ("We are all
soldiers for liberty"). They cheered me as I passed. — I returned
their salute, and rode on.'[43]

The date of the rising was fixed at last; it was to be on February 15th, to coincide with the day when the Austrian passage of the Po was expected. But now, again, there was a pitiable piece of mismanagement. The Austrians, having perhaps had word of the plan, put forward the date of their advance, and before the cities of the Romagna had succeeded in uniting their scattered volunteers, 40,000 Austrian troops were across the Po. The Carboneria headquarters in Bologna ordered that they were 'to be allowed to pass, and only to be attacked on all sides on their return'.* And indeed, when they arrived, it was found that some of their officers were themselves Carbonari, so that they were most cordially received and 'even some of those citizens who had been most noted for their predilection for the new ideas, feasted with them'.⁴⁴ The Austrian army thus proceeded southwards without any interference and another opportunity was lost.

The Papal Government at once redoubled its severities. Private houses were searched, there were fresh arrests, and the Cardinal issued a Proclamation – of which a copy was sent beforehand to Byron by Alborghetti – declaring that anyone found in the possession of arms was liable to arrest. Pietro Gamba accordingly decided that the only safe place in Ravenna for the arms of his volunteers, most of which had been purchased with Byron's money, was Byron's cellar, and hastily dumped them there, when he was out, without even consulting him.

'They throw back upon my hands, and into my house, these very arms . . . with which I had furnished them at their own request, and at my own peril and expense . . .' But the next day he added: 'It is no great matter, supposing that Italy could be liberated, who or what is sacrificed. Only think – a free Italy! Why, there has been nothing like it since the days of Augustus.'⁴⁵

For a few days longer hope persisted – a faint hope, since it rested upon the Neapolitans.

'Let the Neapolitans have but the pluck of the Dutch of old, or the Spaniards of now, or of the German Protestants, the Scotch Presbyterians, the Swiss under Tell, or the Greeks under Themistocles . . . and there is yet a resurrection for Italy, and a hope for the world.'⁴⁶

---

* UCCELLINI, op. cit., p. 9. 'But who', he pathetically added, 'could do so, when at last they did come back from their enterprise, triumphant and with branches of myrtle in their helmets?'

On February 24th the Pope issued a decree, warning all good Catholics to abstain from taking part in the forthcoming rising – and Alborghetti confidentially sent a copy of the document, before its publication, to Byron – 'a sign', the latter commented, 'that he does not know what to think. When he wants to be well with the patriots, he sends me some civil message or other'. Byron's own optimism was still unshaken: 'For my own part, it seems to me, that nothing but the most decided success of the Barbarians can prevent a general and immediate rise of the whole nation!'[47]

And then the bad news came.

'The secret intelligence arrived this morning from the frontier to the C[arbonari] is as bad as possible. The *plan* has missed – the Chiefs are betrayed, military as well as civil – and the Neapolitans not only have *not* moved, but have declared to the P[apal] Government and to the Barbarians, that they know nothing of the matter!!! Thus the world goes; and thus the Italians are always lost, for lack of union among themselves.'[48]

The story of the defeat of the Neapolitan army is, indeed, – when we remember how it was formed and what Government it defended – hardly surprising. It was composed of 74,000 men – to confront the Austrian 43,000. But of the Neapolitans, 42,000 were raw recruits, and the rest were the unamalgamated mob of disgruntled veterans and dilettante civilians which we have already described. Moreover, too many members of the Carboneria, who had been responsible beforehand for the most warlike speeches, now found excellent reasons for staying at home, while those who went with the army openly stated their lack of faith in its victory. One person alone remained incorrigibly hopeful: General Pepe, who caused the Naples *Gazette* solemnly to announce the precise date – March 7th – on which his troops would be victorious!

On that day, indeed, his ill-armed, ill-led, undisciplined rabble found themselves face to face, in the plain of Rieti, with the Austrian army – and fled, almost before a shot was fired. In Naples, the greater part of the deputies showed an equal haste to desert the Parliament, and by March 23rd the Austrian troops had occupied Naples. The constitutional regime was over.

Once again it is in Rangone that we find the most vivid account of what happened, in a lampoon of the day:

IL LAMENTO DI PULCINELLA

> Pulcinella malcontento
> Di servir nel reggimento
> Scrive a Mamma a Benevento
> Della patria il triste evento:
> 'Movimento, Parlamento,
> Giuramento, sgiuramento
> Gran fermento e poco argento
> Armamento, e nel cimento
> Siam fuggiti come il vento.
> Me ne pento, me ne pento
> Mamma cara, Mamma bella,
> Prega Dio per Pulcinella.'⁴⁹

It may well be imagined with what consternation the news was received in the Romagna. Not only had the Neapolitan forces been scattered, but their leaders had denied that any plan of union with the Romagna had ever existed.

'The real Italians', wrote Byron, 'are *not* to blame – merely the scoundrels at the *Heel of the Boot* – – – The Neapolitans have betrayed themselves and all the World, and those who would have given their blood for Italy can now only give her their tears.'⁵⁰

Byron now advised his fellow-conspirators to rise at once, rather than wait to be arrested. He again offered 'whatever I can do by money, means or person' – starting with the practical gift of 2500 scudi. But the Carbonari were now deeply disheartened, messages had to be sent to the other cities of the Romagna before any decision could be reached and it soon became evident that nothing would be done. Byron took his disappointment to Teresa, as she sat at her harpsichord:

' "Alas," she said with the tears in her eyes, "the Italians must now return to making operas." "I fear", Byron commented, "*that* and maccaroni are their forte, and 'motley their only wear'. However, there are some high spirits among them still." '⁵¹

And it was precisely these few 'high spirits' who were now in danger. The Papal Government, thanks to its ubiquitous spies, was well informed by now of the names of its enemies.

'I have risked myself with the others *here*, and how far I may or may not be compromised is a problem at this moment; some of them, like "Craigengelt", would "tell all and more than all, to save themselves".'[52]

Others, at the same time, were retorting to the Government's policy of intimidation, with acts of violence. At Faenza a Canon of the Cathedral, Monsignor Montevecchi, well known for his diatribes from the pulpit against the Carbonari, was shot at in the Corso, and a few weeks later was murdered.[53] At Forlì and in Ravenna several other agents of the police were also assassinated.

'A German spy (*boasting* himself such) was stabbed last week, but *not* mortally. The moment I heard that he went about bullying and boasting, it was easy for me, or anyone else, to foretell what would occur to him.'[54]

For a few weeks the Government remained inactive – completing its plans and its lists. Then, quite suddenly, it acted. At Forlì, many scores of arrests were made; a new batch of Liberals was exiled or imprisoned. And now some fresh attempts were made to find a pretext for getting rid of Byron.

First Cardinal Rusconi decided to look into the case of Gigante – the man to whom Byron had entrusted his imprudent address to the Neapolitan insurgents. On behalf of the Secretary of State, Cardinal Rusconi wrote to Byron, to inquire whether it was true:

(*a*) That Gigante, had called upon Lega Zambelli and had presented to Byron a request for money, saying that he had been arrested and robbed;

(*b*) That his request had been granted, and

(*c*) That he had called upon Byron to express his gratitude.[55]

Over Byron's letter a veil of silence was drawn.

Alborghetti forwarded the Cardinal's letter to Byron, with a memorandum for a suitable reply, trusting that 'the transaction will bring no harm to the poor devil who is the object of it'.[56] Byron at once replied:

BYRON TO CONTE GIUSEPPE ALBORGHETTI[57]

Ravenna   *May 25th*, 1821

Dear Sir: I enclose you the copy for one or two slight alterations and also the *petition* of this Signor Giant. The Document itself confirms what I have said . . .

If you would have the goodness to have copied out on the enclosed sheet of paper the *answer* to the Cardinal, I will sign it with pleasure. Yours ever truly   B.

Apparently, however, the Cardinal thought the matter too trivial a one to enable him to get rid of Byron – and only a few weeks later, another expedient was tried. An officer of the Cardinal's guard, in plain clothes, picked a quarrel with Tita, Byron's servant, who, having drawn his stiletto, was imprisoned and threatened with banishment. Byron at once sent off an indignant letter of protest to Alborghetti.

BYRON TO CONTE GIUSEPPE ALBORGHETTI[58]

June 28th, 1821

Dear Sir: It appears to me that there must be some *clerical* intrigue of the low priests about the Cardinal, to render all this nonsense necessary about a squabble in the street of *words only*, between a soldier and a servant. If it is directed against *me*, it shan't succeed – for I desire no better than a fair examination of my conduct, as far as connected with the place or the inhabitants.

If against *the poor* Valet, it is an odious oppression; I desire no more than a process, for then they would see the *falsehood* of all the *trash* about this man, who has *no more to do with political matters than the Man in the Moon.*

If you can get this business settled either *here* (which would be better and shorter) or at Rome, you will not find me less obliged or more ungrateful than you have hitherto found me. Why can't they decide the matter by an investigation, an arrest or a reproof? There never was any objection on my part to his having a punishment proportioned to the offence – but not a chastisement the consequences of which might affect the man's prospects through life. I wish to know what is to be gained by it? If they think to get *rid* of *me* they shan't – for as I am conscious of no fault, I will yield to no oppression, but will go at my own good time, when it suits my inclination and affairs.

That they may disgust me is not difficult – and in that case it may so happen that more than myself may be disgusted in the end. I wrote to the Cardinal in the only style that it became me to use. I am not conscious of being wanting in respect to his age and station – in other points I used the freedom of statement due to my own rank, and the circumstances of the business. Believe me, yours ever and truly   BYRON

Alborghetti seems at this time to have felt himself under some obligation to Byron, for, on June 17th, he had written to him in terms of the most impassioned gratitude:

'What must I say of your kindness and generosity? Or how can I say enough? You are like the Lord, whose rewards are of a hundred for one. The duties of society and friendship prescribed the little service that I made you, and I am confounded in seeing at what a high rate you have put it. I then devote myself to your service for ever, and I sign this protestation with my name without hesitation. I never blushed to make the world acquainted, that I know gratefulness.'⁵⁹

But in spite of all these highflown phrases, Alborghetti did not now compromise himself by calling on Byron, but merely sent him his lawyer:

'Forget for a moment the liberty and the greatness of your country, and pity the necessity which obliges us to every sort of circumspection . . . In the meantime I pray you to calm your heat, and be assured that the Government, *till now*, do not aim at all your respectable Person.'⁶⁰

Alborghetti, however, did not attempt to plead with the Cardinal, but was only able to report that the prelate,

'after many praises of your love of justice and impartiality, insists upon the removal of the same servant, the more so as he has been represented to him as a very bad subject.'

But Alborghetti persevered, and at last wrote to Byron that 'the great business of your servant is over and in the best and in the most satisfactory manner: everyone has dealt with him as with a Knight.' The servant 'did not utter a single word of excuse'; the Cardinal yielded about the banishment and let him out of prison; and Alborghetti could confirm that 'at four o'clock he will be ready to serve you as usual'.⁶¹

The general situation in Ravenna, however, had not improved. The arrests of prominent Liberals continued, and it now seemed inevitable that the Gambas should be included in their number. At last, after some weeks of painful suspense, the blow fell. On

R

the evening of July 10th, as he was coming home from the theatre, Pietro Gamba was arrested and was escorted to the frontier of the State. The next morning his rooms were searched, but Teresa had been warned in time, and was able to destroy any compromising papers. It was believed that Count Ruggero Gamba would be spared – in view of his position as the head of a family, and also of the fact that, although he had made no secret of where his sympathies lay, he was not actually an active member of the Carboneria. But since the principal object of the measures against the Gamba family was to provoke the departure of Byron – whom no one dared to molest directly – Count Ruggero, too, was added to the list of exiles, and ordered to leave the State within twenty-four hours. Since Teresa was now living under her father's protection, it was presumed that she would go with him, and that Byron's departure would therefore also be ensured.

But at this point Teresa seems to have broken down completely. How, she asked, was it possible for her to leave Byron in Ravenna, where she knew his life was threatened 'by sectarian fanatics like the Sanfedisti and Austrian hirelings'? She wrote herself that her courage failed her, and that, 'accablée', she let her father go off alone in the early morning to Filetto, where he was to put his affairs in order, before leaving the State on the next day. From here, still expecting Teresa to join him, he sent her the following letter:

CONTE RUGGERO GAMBA TO CONTESSA GUICCIOLI

July 11*th*, 1821

My Teresa: Your agitation is in my mind all the time and causes me ever greater pain. I had hoped to find comfort in you, and to give some to you in return, but now your weakness frightens me. Take courage, for your own good and for ours, and try to calm your imagination, which can depict nothing but tragedies. As for me, I assure you that this free air makes my spirit feel free too – and that I felt *prouder*, once I stood outside those walls, which now enclose no one but slaves. Try to strengthen your spirit with such thoughts and to be of some support to mine. Remember that Pietro is waiting for us – and not with eyes flooded with tears. Embrace your brothers for me, and most of all my little Faustina* – let your tenderness be the outward expression of mine. Tell

* Faustina was Teresa's youngest sister, born in 1819. Her mother died at her birth.

Lord Byron that I hope to see him again soon. Tomorrow at about four o'clock I think we should do well to start. I will wait for you at the race-track. Think of a happy future – conquer your imagination thus. If you have any important news to send me, give it to the coachman, who alone has my orders. Your affectionate father.

Teresa at once sent on this letter to Byron, together with a note, 'containing the expression of a sorrow which could only increase Byron's own'.

July 11*th*, 1821

My dear Byron: You will not refuse to become the keeper of my troubles – you who are their only cause – you who alone can understand me and give me peace – you who are the only tie that still holds me to life. I cannot describe my state to you – it is a continual agony. What a night! Every hour that passed seemed to me a century of suffering, and yet only a minute, when I thought that so few more were left, before I must leave you. My dear Byron, do you think that I shall be strong enough? I am feeling very unwell – I do not seem to be able to collect my ideas – as perhaps you will see from this letter – my head is all upset – am I losing my mind? Ah, it would be better! I should suffer no more. This is the first moment I have felt alive since last night, because I am talking to you – but when I am certain that you do not hear me any more, when my laments will be lost in space, my God, my God – I feel as if I should not be able to go on living. My Byron, give me strength, make me able to fulfil my duties as a daughter.

Why do you want to take your little girl out of the convent? Would it not be better to leave her in the safe place where she is? This is just a thought that crosses my mind, which I did not express last night because my ideas were so confused, but I do believe that it would be the best thing for her.

My dear Byron, forgive me if I trouble you with my letters – but it relieves me to write to you – and your generosity will bear with me. [62]

'This anguish', Teresa herself comments, 'may seem exaggerated and puerile to anyone who has not known the state of the

R

country at that time.' Byron, she tells us, at once hurried to her side. To a certain extent, he shared her anxiety. He thought it improbable that the exiles would be allowed to remain in Tuscany, and he therefore wished Teresa's departure to be put off, until her father was more certain of his own future. He accordingly sent the following letter to Count Ruggero.

BYRON TO CONTE RUGGERO GAMBA

July 12th, 1821

My dear Ruggero: You are Teresa's master by right – and mine by duty and friendship. But in view of the circumstances I should think it better, also for prudence's sake, for her not to leave for a few days. If you insist, she will give way and so will I – who have not and should not have a voice in the matter. But the passports are equivocal – her presence will not be of any use to prevent them if they want to molest you, or to console you – for you would not want to see a woman left alone in such a situation.

If things go well we shall join you; if ill – even then we shall join you, in any circumstances whatever – and I shall consider it my duty to find you, even if you are in prison. –

But I beg you not to precipitate matters for the present, and particularly to think of all that might happen to Teresa, deprived of you and of Pierino – and in enemy country, – – –

For my part I have no more to say except that I hope to see you and Pierino very soon – which I will do in one place or another. – Keep well and believe me always, Your most affectionate friend   BYRON

P.S. I am returning today's packet – which Teresa made you return to me. Make use freely not only of that, but of everything of mine. –

You will do as you wish – but in any case remember – that if any separation occurs between Teresa and me – it will not be my fault.

Count Gamba, on receiving this letter, at once sent his daughter his consent to her remaining in Ravenna.

'I breathe again,' Teresa wrote to Byron. 'My father is willing for me to remain – read the enclosed letter. Now I am only left with the pain of uncertainty about my father's and my brother's fate – Pierino's especially. But what a compensation to be able to stay here – where you are! This evening we shall see each other again.'[63]

Letters came from the exiles, from Bologna and Florence, and for a few days it seemed possible that Count Ruggero might be allowed to return, as had happened in a few other cases. For Pietro, no such permission was likely, and indeed he wrote that he would not accept it if it came.

'As for me, I neither ask nor wish to return,' he wrote to his sister. 'No power could make me come back to places which, in their present condition, I despise and hate.'[64]

Count Ruggero wrote in a calmer tone.

'Here in Florence', he wrote, 'my spirit is at rest. Those who tried to triumph over us only deserve our contempt and will be sufficiently punished by the opinion of all good and sensible men – and time will avenge us.
The Tuscan Government has welcomed us cordially, and had I no children or business to call me back, I would go so far as to say that this is one of the best moments of my life. Meanwhile public opinion and bewilderment is so clearly on our side, that it somewhat recompenses us for the injustice we have endured. But I belong entirely to my family, and on their account, I should prefer my return to Ravenna to any other satisfaction on earth.'[65]

Moved by these letters, by Teresa's tears and by his own desire to remain in Ravenna, Byron was determined to leave nothing undone to obtain the exiles' return. Elizabeth Duchess of Devonshire, – an old friend of Lady Melbourne's and one of the most charming women of her time – was then living in Rome and enjoyed a considerable influence in Papal circles. Might she not be persuaded to use it on behalf of the Gambas? So Byron took up his pen and sent the Duchess a most pressing letter.

'Among the list of exiles on account of the late *suspicions* and the intrigues of the Austrian Government (the most infamous in history) – there are many of my acquaintances in Romagna and some of my friends; of these more particularly are the two Counts Gamba (father and son) of a noble and respected family in this city. In common with thirty or more of all ranks they have been hurried from their home without process – without hearing – without accusation. The father is universally respected and liked; his family is numerous and mostly young – and these are now left without protection; the son is a very fine young man, with very little of the vices of his age or climate . . . Could your Grace, or would you, ask the repeal of both, or at least of one of these, from those in power in the Holy City? I can assure your Grace and the very pious Government in question, that there can be no danger in this act of *clemency*, shall I call it? It would be but justice with us – but here! – let them call it what they will.'[66]

The Cardinal's chief object in exiling the Gambas having been to get rid of Byron, it can be imagined that he was not too pleased to see Teresa still in Ravenna, with Mylord by her side. The next step, clearly, must be to expedite Teresa's departure. For this purpose Count Alborghetti sent for a family friend and connection of the Gambas, Count Rampi of Faenza – 'a wise, prudent and influential man' – and told him that Guiccioli had once again appealed to Rome – asking that Teresa should be obliged to return to him – or, failing that, be shut up in a convent. Teresa, in her version, implies that in actual fact Guiccioli never *did* make this appeal – though it would very probably have been granted if he had – and that the whole thing was a fabrication of Alborghetti's. In any case, Count Rampi believed it and, in all good faith, hurried to Teresa to warn her of the danger.[67] She at once sent off to Byron the following unhappy letter:[68]

'Only this was lacking to drive me to despair. I am in a terrible state – without you I shall never be able to make up my mind, shall never be able to reach a reasonable decision. Rampi has just left me, having been sent by Alborghetti to tell me that I must leave Ravenna before Tuesday, because Guiccioli has had recourse to Rome to demand that I shall either return to him, or be shut up in a convent. He says that the answer will come in a few days, that I must talk about it to no one – but leave at night – for if my plan were known, they might stop it, and take away my passport, which the goodness of Heaven has enabled me to obtain. Byron! I am in despair . . . If I have to leave you here without knowing when I shall see you again, I am resolved to stay. – But I hardly know what I am saying, I am in such a terrible state – and why? – not certainly on account of my own danger, but only – I call Heaven to witness – only on account of yours . . . Rampi and Alborghetti will call on you at about three o'clock to tell you all this. Your unhappy friend.

On hearing this news, Byron – 'irritated and agitated by all these intrigues' – firmly advised Teresa to leave at once – a piece of advice with which her uncle, Marchese Cavalli, warmly agreed. The latter also very sensibly advised her to take with her all the papers relating to her separation, in case Guiccioli, who had considerable influence in Tuscany, should attempt to make trouble for her at the Court of the Grand Duke. So at last, in floods of tears, Teresa agreed to go – but in a truly feminine manner begged at the last moment for just twenty-four hours' respite. 'Do not oppose this determination, my friend,' she wrote to Byron. 'One more day in the same place as you, is worth a century to me.'[69] She wished, she said, to drive out with him once again, and to see the new – and, as she believed – safer route that he had promised her to follow in future on his rides.

'How great is my gratitude', she added, 'for this new proof of your kindness – and of how great a weight it has relieved my heart – although it is still one of the most tormented on earth!'

The next morning, before leaving, she begged him, in equally high-flown language, for yet another favour – 'like the last boon granted to condemned criminals'. This was, that – since she would not demand of him long letters in a foreign language, 'which might fatigue him' – he would always add at the bottom of Lega's letters by every post, the words 'I am well and we shall see each other again'.[70]

Byron, who by now would doubtless have promised anything to get her off, agreed – and meanwhile wrote to Prof. Costa in Bologna – Teresa's old teacher and a family friend – asking him to look after her there, and if necessary to take her on to Florence. The coach arrived – the postillions were mounted – and at last poor Teresa, 'more dead than alive', set forth. At the first halt, while the horses were being changed, she sent back the following note:

Faenza   *July 25th*, 1821

I am writing here, in the presence of the Sisters* – where I am stopping while the Horses are being changed. My Love – I am utterly desolate – I do not know what will become of me before night! By the love you have felt for me – by all that you hold dearest on earth, swear to me to keep your vow – *never, never to go riding in the Forest*!!! With this hope I can breathe again – other-

* The Sisters of the Convent of Santa Chiara, where Teresa was educated.

wise I should have died at parting from you. What an effort it cost me – several times I thought I should have to give way – but I was sustained by the thought that it would have displeased you – and by the fear of losing you forever! In a few minutes I am leaving for Bologna – for pity's sake, my dearest, write at once to Florence – and if there is anything special to say, send a courier. The Postilion wants to start. Oh God! What a torment! Keep your promise – if not you will be cruel!!! I kiss you a thousand times.

Your friend and lover for ever.

When shall we see each other again, my dearest?   T.G.G.

Send for my letters at the post office. The postmaster has been notified, but send him the enclosed.

At Bologna, Teresa found the Costa family awaiting her and ready to take her at once to Florence. But once again, she confesses, her courage failed her entirely: 'She had not enough strength either of body or of mind to continue the journey.'[1] So, although she knew that, by staying in the Papal States she was still exposed to the same dangers that had caused her to leave Ravenna, she wrote to implore Byron to let her return to Ravenna – or at least to meet her once again half way, at Bagnacavallo. But now Byron was firm. This was the kind of feminine hysteria which jangled his nerves unbearably – and his answer is rather that of an exasperated husband than of a lover.

Teresa herself, later on, described her behaviour at this time as caused by 'a state of exaltation which must have seemed ridiculous', but excuses herself by saying that her apprehensions for Byron's safety were so strong, her sense that some terrible threat was menacing him, so persistent and, she frankly admits, so disproportionate to the actual circumstances, that she completely lost her head. She was suffering, she says, 'from feelings too deeply stirred and from an imagination which had become diseased'.[2]

The following is Byron's reply – and was followed, three days later, by another, even more exasperated letter, which at last succeeded in getting Teresa to start.

BYRON TO CONTESSA GUICCIOLI[3]

Ravenna   *July 26th*, 1821

My Teresa: Pray calm yourself and continue your journey, in the certainty that we shall see each other again soon. If not in Ravenna, then we shall arrange about Switzerland, as soon as I get an answer from Geneva. – Yesterday I saw Uncle C[avalli] who gives some hope . . . Tonino* *is* in Rome, that is certain. Meanwhile don't give way to such unreasonable grief – but think of consoling your father and your brother.

I am sorry about the Duchess's absence† – I had hoped much from her kindness – but perhaps we may do as well without her. – Your plan of coming back here to see each other for a moment would be real folly – such a proposal really makes me think that you wish to be put in a *convent* – as was threatened.

I love you and shall love you as I have always loved you – but I cannot encourage such fatal madness as your return here would be, the day after your departure. –

Lega will write to you enclosing two letters of today's post which I have received for you – as you asked. –

A thousand messages to Ruggero and Pierino. – Write often and quickly. Greet signor Costa and his wife, to whom I am very grateful for their friendship to your family.

'My daughter, be comforted, dry your tears' – and believe me (crede B. you know is my family motto) ever and entirely your friend and lover   B.

P.S. Little gossip – get into a good humour – things will go better than you think . . . Thank you for the flower, which has kept much of its scent . . . Everything here is as it was at your departure.

July 29th, 1821

My Teresa: You left with the intention of joining your family in Florence – that was the only respectable and reasonable excuse for you in the present circumstances. What is detaining you in Bologna? I do not know, and if I knew – I could not approve. – – Once again I *urge* you to continue your journey, for every reason. With your father you are safe – and besides – you are doing your duty as a daughter. Where you are, I can only see a woman without support, and not very kind,[14] who leaves her father in exile without taking an 18 hours' journey to console him. – If you believe that you are safe from the attempts already made (and

---

* Marchese Antonio Cavalli, a leading Carbonaro and a cousin of Teresa.

† The Duchess of Devonshire, whom Byron's July letter had missed in Rome. He sent the letter on to her at Spa with a second note asking her to 'write a few lines to any of your Roman acquaintances in power'. – *L.J.*, V, p. 238.

that would be made again) to put you away in a convent so long
as you remain in the *Papal States – you are mistaken.*

I am always your friend and lover   B.

P.S. I hope to hear that you have left for Florence – then I will
write to you in detail.

At last, on the 2nd of August, Teresa gathered her courage
together and crossed the Apennines, still hoping, however, that a
decree from Rome might allow her father to return to Ravenna,
and herself with him. But instead she found him and her brother
making their preparations for an immediate departure for
Switzerland. Count Ruggero had already sent a power of attorney
to his uncle in Ravenna, Marchese Cavalli, and the plan was to
sail from Pisa to Marseilles (to avoid passing through the States
under Austrian rule) and to proceed from there to Switzerland.
Pietro, especially, was fired with the idea, since he saw in Switzerland, according to Teresa, 'the only country left in Europe where
we could still breathe the air of independence'.

At first Byron too had been inclined to favour the plan.

'This country being in a state of proscription', he had
written to Hoppner on July 23rd, 'and all my friends exiled
or arrested . . . I have determined to remove to Switzerland,
and they also ... I have written by this post to Mr. Hentsch
junior, the banker of Geneva, to provide (if possible) a house for
me, and another for Gamba's family ... on the *Jura* side of the
Lake of Geneva, furnished with stabling (for *me* at least) for
eight horses. I shall bring Allegra with me ... We care nothing
about society, and are only anxious for a temporary and tranquil
asylum and individual freedom.'[75]

But Hentsch's answer was delayed; life in Ravenna, in spite of
the clerical persecution, was still very pleasant; Shelley was
expected; and so Byron took up his pen and wrote to both Teresa
and Pietro – in the evident hope that his letters might keep them
both quiet for a little longer.

BYRON TO PIETRO GAMBA

August 4th, 1821

My dear Pietro: A thousand thanks for your very welcome letter. –
I cannot answer all that I should say, or would wish to, – Her
Excellency ought to have arrived . . . . [line erased by Teresa]

She has written me a thousand insults from Bologna – because, in agreement with every sensible person and with all her friends and relations, I advised her to go to Florence, to join you and her father. – The thing was absolutely necessary – if she did not want to be put in a convent. – Ask anyone.

I am seeing no one – my widower's rides are very tedious; I put holes in *two new shoes* of that poor devil with my pistol the day before yesterday – which cost me *twelve pauls*. One day I saw Tuda on the road – who looked like a lost lamb – squinting a little – and very sentimental about your desertion – She confessed that she had been with you several times, etc. etc. – but who knows if it is true. – Her beauty was however not such as to awaken envy in even the most jealous of women, Her Excellency.[76]

The Martini has disappeared from her usual window – in consequence of the exile of her beloved. Instead of her – I saw Mrs. Santino Fabbri there – of whom I was made aware by more senses than that of sight. – For the rest, all your numerous widows are inconsolable – one hears nothing but sighs – which makes a little breeze – a pleasant thing in this weather.

Lega will have written to Papa all my news and hopes and the steps we propose to take. Meanwhile I am and always shall be your affectionate and obliged friend.

P.S. 1000 messages to Papa. Be happy. [Here eight lines have been completely erased by Teresa, which began: 'They write me from Paris that' . . . .] This was written before the arrival of yours. I am awaiting an answer from Switzerland where I wrote before Teresa's departure. Meanwhile let us wait a bit and see – Haste can but do harm to your family and to all of us. Lega has been told to write more in detail. –

BYRON TO CONTESSA GUICCIOLI

Ravenna   *August 4th*, 1821*

My Teresa: I hope that you are happy in Florence – and safe with your relations. Lega, in the letter he is writing to Papa by this post, will explain in detail the reasons which rendered urgent your departure from Bologna. – It is enough to say that Costa,

* This letter is inscribed by Teresa: '1821. First letter to Florence after the exile of the Gambas.'

Cavalli, and all your friends were persuaded that it was the only decision possible in your very delicate situation. For my part, I have nothing to reproach myself with, as to this advice – nor to reply to the insults with which it has pleased you to honour me in your recent letters.

I have received a noble and comforting letter from Pierino; it appears that he is preserving his friendship for me, which will always be 1eciprocated by me.

Here we are doing all we can for the return of Count Ruggero. I have sent off the letter to the D[uchess] of D[evonshire] who is now at Spa near Liège – but who could write from there to Rome. I have had no answer as yet to my letters from Geneva. I am awaiting your news with impatience.

As for me – I am neither well nor ill; my hopes are naturally turned towards you all. – I don't see anyone – I live with my books and my horses.

Without translating so many pages of *Corinne*, or forcing so great a semblance of romance, I assure you that I love you as I always have loved you; time will show, which of us will be the most untiring in our love. But in eloquence I give way to you for two reasons – firstly, I don't know the language – secondly, too many words are always suspect – the great *preachers* of exaggerated sentiment limit the practice of their maxims to their pulpit; – true love says little.

Please salute Papa and Pierino cordially and beg them to command me in everything – as their (and your) most sincere and affectionate friend.

Yet another letter to Pietro Gamba from Lega, written the next day, added little to what Byron had already said, and was followed by a postscript from Byron."

It will be impossible for me to leave just now – before the arrival of my letters and of a relation of Allegra's* whom I am expecting at any moment from Pisa, to decide about the child's future. Your impatience is perhaps natural – but it doesn't seem to me necessary, under the circumstances, to be in so great a hurry to go one does not know where. In ten days I ought to have an answer from Geneva about the two houses. Always and entirely.

* Shelley.

Pietro, however, must have continued to bombard Byron with letters expressing alike the nobility of his sentiments and the firmness of his determination to leave the country, for four days later Byron was writing again.

BYRON TO PIETRO GAMBA

Ravenna   *August 9th,* 1821

My Dear Pietro: Your sentiments do you honour, but nevertheless I keep my own opinion regarding Count R. – your father – and Teresa. It is enough for me, however, to have expressed my reasons. If you are determined to go – go – and I will come, – I should have been much better pleased, and it would have been much better for everyone, if you had had the patience to wait for an answer from Geneva. Then you would have known precisely where to go – to a house – instead of finding yourself in a miserable inn full of travellers. As for myself – the idea of returning to Switzerland is most unpleasant – for many reasons – which you will become well aware of when we are there and it will be too late. – Teresa should certainly go with her father and her brother – but in spite of that protection – I am afraid that she will find herself in a very painful situation – on account of the gossip of all the good citizens of Geneva – and of the English travellers – for both of whom it is enough that people should enjoy *my acquaintance* for them to be exposed to the most infamous calumny. I hoped – and am still convinced – that with a little time and courage – your father will be able to return to R[avenna] and Teresa too, without trouble for either of them.

Teresa writes to me like a lunatic – as if I wished to give her up, etc. etc. If I had had that intention – why did I beg her to leave R[avenna]? and B[ologna]? In a few days – she would have been shut up in a convent – and the affair finished – without its being in the least my fault – in the eyes of the world. Assuredly I would not have taken so much trouble for a woman from whom I was planning a separation.

So far no answer has come – and my banker's drafts have not arrived, which certainly it would not be desirable to leave trailing around the country after my departure. They ought to have come three posts ago, and the delay surprises and annoys me. For me they are not necessary at present – for I have enough. But meanwhile I don't much like not knowing what has happened to a sum of several thousand scudi – which in the ordinary course of events should have arrived twenty days ago. It matters the more to me because Switzerland is perhaps the dearest country in Europe for foreigners, its people being the most canny and rascally in the world about all that has to do with money – and deceitfulness – and avarice. I only suggested a stay in that country because there seemed to be an absolute necessity for leaving Italy – and only because it is the nearest country. This *necessity* to leave no longer exists. The government of Tuscany is very mild – far, far milder than the present government of Geneva – which is now under the yoke of the anti-liberals.

A friend of mine here* is writing, at my request, to Teresa – some forcible reasons why it would be better to stay in Italy.

Believe me with the most complete esteem and friendship always your friend and servant

BYRON TO CONTESSA GUICCIOLI

Ravenna   *August 10th*, 1821

My Love: Pray do not render our unhappiness greater by un-merited reproaches. I have always been faithful and loyal to you and to all your family. My friend's letter, written at my request, will be a very veracious statement of the numerous reasons for not exposing ourselves to residing in the states of Switzerland. I have never thought of separating myself from you – but leave me a little time and freedom to think [what is best] for us – and above all for you. My letter to Pierino contains what I have to say on this subject. I will not say any more.

Love me as I love you, Entirely yours.

All this, however, was much too vague to satisfy Teresa – and at once a special messenger was sent by her across the Apennines, carrying a letter in which she implored Byron to keep his promises, and join her, not some day, but *at once*.

August 11th, 1821
'If your promises remain vague and uncertain, if the future holds nothing but anguish for me, shall I be able to bear it? I am in a beautiful great city full of people, with my father and my

* Shelley.

brother – but I feel as if I were in a desert, and alone, quite alone ... The two hours before sunset are two hours of agony for me.* The saddest thoughts, the most horrible visions, fill my imagination and torment me: the sight of a funeral, the cry of a night-bird – if you only knew what an effect they have on me! The night that follows such an inward struggle is consequently feverish. How shall the body not succumb to such a deep depression of soul? – I shall not leave Florence unless I am certain of seeing you again within a few days. I hate travelling, I hate everything that does not lead to the only object of my thoughts.'[78]

Her father and brother, she told Byron, had gone off to the races; but she had refused to go with them, she only wanted to write to him.

'My Byron, what are you doing? What are you thinking and feeling? What do you mean to do for your friend? Papa will not return to Ravenna, he says he will let all his property and take the family to a free country. Even if he were called back, he would not go home, because he does not believe in the promises of the priests. Pierino says the same – but I? I wish for nothing but to see my friend again – to live where he lives; I fear nothing but to lose him.'[79]

To all this Byron replied with extreme firmness.

Ravenna   *August* 13th, 1821

Dearest: The letters from Geneva are not favourable to our departure. The State is full of English people – and every house is occupied – and so it will be for over fifty days more – until October.

Besides, Geneva and all its surroundings are full of English people, even in the winter. You know whether I could live in the same air as that race ... Pray therefore abandon that plan – and persuade Ruggero and Pietro to do the same. We can establish ourselves in Tuscany; it will be much better from every point of view. . . .

My friend's letter[80] by the last messenger will have explained to you my situation in that country, Switzerland, in 1816. If you wish to renew my persecution, which would now be directed with

* This was the time of Byron's daily rides, which she feared would end in his assassination.

equal fury against you, you have only to go to Switzerland. I still
hope that with a little time and patience your father may be
allowed to return to his own country – and that you will be able
to go with him. If Pierino is determined to travel – I do not
oppose it. Certainly he would be much better off in his travels
without so many ties – and without cutting the sorry figure that
he would cut, if we were in his company . . . At any rate – if
Papa is not allowed to return, we can establish ourselves in
Tuscany.

At this point your letter has come, by the hand of one of the
returned exiles. By now you will have had my answer. Your
father is looking for a *free* country – where will he find it? Certainly
not in Switzerland – where they exile once more those who have
already been exiled.

My first choice would be for him to return to Ravenna. The
second (but even that unwillingly), that he should establish himself in Tuscany – Switzerland does not seem to be at all suitable
and I only thought of that country as preferable to San Leo.*
Now that there is no more danger for him – to go to Switzerland
would be – but – I have already expressed all this in my preceding
letters. Always and ever yours

P.S. I have had a letter from the Benzoni, who greets you – so
does her Beppe.† Greet Pierino and Papa for me.

The friend on whom Byron depended to influence Teresa and
Pietro, was Shelley. He had arrived on August 6th to stay with
Byron, after a most exhausting journey – travelling from Florence
to Bologna 'all night, at the rate of two miles and a half an hour,
in a little open carriage' – and thence proceeding at once to
Ravenna, where he arrived at ten o'clock at night, and sat up
talking with Byron until five the next morning. His impressions
of Byron were wholly favourable. 'He has . . . completely
recovered his health, and lives a life totally the reverse of that
which he led at Venice.' Byron, as well as showing Shelley some
of Teresa's letters, depicted her as a victim both of marital and
clerical tyranny. 'She was compelled to escape from the Papal
territory in great haste, as measures had already been taken to
place her in a convent, where she would have been unrelentingly
confined for life.' Shelley's sympathy was instantly awakened –

* A fortress near Rimini, used for political prisoners.
† Conte Giuseppe Rangone, the Contessa Benzoni's Cavalier Servente.

and his thoughts turned to Emilia Viviani, in *her* convent. 'The oppression of the marriage contract, as existing in the laws and opinions of Italy . . . is far severer than that of England. I tremble to think of what poor Emilia is destined to.'[81]

As to Byron's liaison, it was entirely in harmony with Shelley's own views – which, indeed, in this case, were nearer to the facts than those of Byron's other friends. 'This attachment', he told Mary, 'has reclaimed him from the excesses into which he threw himself from carelessness and pride, rather than taste.' And in a subsequent letter: 'L. B. is greatly improved in every respect. In genius, in temper, in moral views, in health, in happiness. The connection with *La Guiccioli* has been an inestimable benefit to him.'[82] Moreover, Shelley was naive enough to accept at its face value Byron's boasting about the riches and noble rank of his mistress's husband, the splendour of his own establishment. 'Lord B. has here splendid apartments in the palace of his mistress's husband, who is one of the richest men in Romagna.' Even the servants were seen in a romantic light. 'Tita the Venetian is here and operating as my valet; a fine fellow, with a prodigious black beard, and who has stabbed two or three people, and is the most good-natured looking fellow I ever saw.'

Only one unpleasant incident appears to have occurred: on August 15th Shelley, who wished to visit the Duomo, was refused admittance – and Byron at once sent off an indignant letter of protest to Alborghetti.[83]

August 15th, 1821

Dear Sir: An English gentleman and friend of mine has this day been refused admittance into the Duomo by the *Campanaro* in the most insolent manner. As I have not the honour of personal acquaintance with the Archbishop I should thank you to represent this to him. Whatever his feelings may be towards me – I presume that he does not encourage his people's insults to strangers, especially as I never encourage or protect mine in such things.

The readiness of your authorities to inculpate my servants on all occasions will not permit me to pass over this – If the Archbishop chastises his insolent dependent it is well, if *not*, I will find means to punish him at any cost. . . .

Excuse my troubling you, but as I do not know the Prelate personally and you do – I thought my application would come better thus than by a direct address. If he or others suppose that political circumstances have at all diminished my power to make

S

myself properly respected – they will discover the difference.
Believe me very truly yours, dear Sir

We have not got Alborghetti's answer – and Shelley's letters do
not refer to the incident. He merely tells us that he and Byron
spent the hours between two and six, every day, in conversation,
rode together from six to eight – and then, after dining, talked
again 'until six in the morning'. If some of their subjects were
unpleasant and painful – the slander about the Shelleys spread by
the Hoppners, the reproaches of Claire, and the fate of poor little
Allegra – there was also much talk of politics and poetry; and
finally, Byron succeeded in enlisting Shelley's aid in the solution of
his own immediate problem: how to persuade Teresa and her
young brother not to go to Switzerland. 'The gossip and the
cabals of those anglicized coteries would torment him, as they did
before, and might exasperate him to a relapse of libertinism, which
he says he plunged into, not from taste but despair.' So Shelley
was set to write, as he says,

'a long letter to her [Teresa] to engage her to remain – an odd
thing enough for an utter stranger to write on subjects of the
utmost delicacy to his friend's mistress . . . I have set down, in
lame Italian, the strongest reasons I can think of against the Swiss
emigration – to tell you truth I should be very glad to accept,
as my fee, his establishment in Tuscany. Ravenna is a miserable
place; the people are barbarous and wild, and their language the
most infernal patois that you can imagine. He would be, in every
respect, better among the Tuscans.'[84]

Teresa has printed Shelley's letter in an appendix to her book,
'Lord Byron jugé par les témoins de sa vie',[85] – but she has unfortunately translated it from the Italian in which it was written into
her own very peculiar French. Some passages, however, are worth
quoting for their content.

'Allow me, Madam, to lay before you the reasons for which I
feel that Geneva would be an undesirable retreat. Your circumstances present some analogy with those in which my family and
Lord Byron found themselves, in the summer of 1816. Our houses
were close together and, not seeking any other society, our mode
of life was retired and tranquil; one could not imagine a simpler
life than ours, or one less calculated to attract the calumnies that
were aimed at us.
These calumnies were monstrous, and really too infamous to
leave us, their victims, even the refuge of contempt. The natives

of Geneva and the English people who were living there did not
hesitate to affirm that we were leading a life of the most unbridled
libertinism. They said that we had formed a pact to outrage all
that is regarded as most sacred in human society. Allow me,
Madam, to spare you the details. I will only tell you that atheism,
incest, and many other things – sometimes ridiculous and sometimes terrible – were imputed to us. The English papers did not
delay to spread the scandal, and the people believed it.

Hardly any affliction was spared us. The inhabitants on the
banks of the lake opposite Lord Byron's house used telescopes to
spy upon his movements. One English lady fainted from horror
(or pretended to!) on seeing him enter a drawing-room.* The
most outrageous caricatures of him and his friends were daily
spread about; and all this took place in the short space of three
months.

The effect of all this on Lord Byron's spirits was very unfortunate. His natural gaiety had almost entirely left him. A man
must be more or less than a Stoic to bear with such insults
patiently.

Do not delude yourself, Madame, with the idea that the
English people – accepting Lord Byron as the greatest poet of our
time – would on that account abstain from troubling him and
from persecuting him in so far as they were able. Their admiration
for his works is involuntary and they slander him in consequence
of their immoderate prejudices, as much as they read him, for
their pleasure.

You cannot, Madame, conceive the excessive violence with
which a certain class of the English detest those whose conduct and
opinions are not precisely modelled on their own. The systems
of those ideas forms a superstition, which constantly demands and
constantly finds fresh victims. Strong as theological hatred may
be, it always yields to social hatred. This state of mind is, in
Geneva, the order of the day, and was awakened in order to
torment Lord Byron and his friends. I very much fear that similar
causes would not fail to produce the same consequences, if the
journey you are planning should take place. Accustomed as you
are, Madame, to the gentle manners of Italy, you can hardly
conceive what an intensity this social hatred has reached in less
happy climes. I have had to experience this, I have seen all who
were dearest to me inextricably entangled in these calumnies. My
position had some analogy with that of your brother,† and this is

* This lady was the novelist Mrs. Hervey.
† The reference is to Claire, Allegra's mother, who was then living with the Shelleys.
The whole letter, however, should be taken with caution.

S

why I am eager to write you all this, to spare you all the evils
which I have so fatally experienced.'

By August 15th Teresa's answer had reached Ravenna. She
thanked Shelley for his advice, and decided to take it.

'My representations,' wrote Shelley to Mary, 'seem to have
reconciled them to the unfitness of that step. At the conclusion of
a letter, full of all the fine things she says she has heard of me, is
the request which I transcribe: "Signore, la vostra bontà mi fa
ardita di chiedervi un favore – me lo accorderete voi? Non partite
da Ravenna senza Mylord!" '*

All Shelley's chivalry, 'this chivalric submission of mine to the
great general laws of antique courtesy, against which I never
rebel, and which is my religion', was at once awakened.

'I shall reply, of course, that the *boon* is granted, and that if her
lover is reluctant to leave Ravenna after I have made arrangements for receiving him at Pisa, I am bound to place myself in
the same situation as now, to assail him with importunities to
rejoin her.'

Byron, moreover – perhaps sincerely, so long as Shelley's charm
was still influencing him – declared himself not only willing
but anxious to start at once. 'Such is his impatience, that he has
desired me to write to you to inquire for the best unfurnished
palace in Pisa, and to enter upon treating for it.'**
Teresa had realized by now that Byron's mind was made up –
and she accordingly gave way with a fairly good grace, even
promising to go to Prato to look for a house there. She was, however, unable to resist the pleasure of indulging in 'hurt feelings'
over the tone of his letters, writing to him:

'What have I ever wished for, except to live beside you? Why
have you thought so many arguments necessary to convince me to
remain in Italy, if you prefer to stay there? Before I knew you I
had a will of my own – some preferences, some wishes – since I
have known you they have all disappeared, to give place 'to one
single feeling – and my will, wishes, pleasures, sorrows, – have
for me one source only – and that source is you. This being so,
you should not have thought it necessary to convince me, and I

---

* SHELLEY, op. cit., Letter LXXXI, August 18th, 1821. 'Sir – your kindness makes
me dare to ask you a favour – will you grant it? Do not leave Ravenna without
Mylord.'

should be offended if I did not realize that you had done so only
in order to convince my relations.'

Her father, she added, was also willing to give way to Byron's
wishes and to settle in Prato, but her brother had still set his heart
on going to Switzerland.

'He is determined to leave Italy and every other slave-country
– because a free and persecuted man cannot endure the sight of
chains, even of gold. But he is much attached to his family and
friends, and says that he must unfailingly see you again, and will
not go away until my future is settled and I do not need him any
more.

My dear Byron, I am a little more tranquil because I hope to
see you in a few days – and also because I trust that your excellent
friend Mr. Shelley will grant me the favour I shall venture to ask
him, which will add one more cause for the gratitude and affection
that, as your friend, I feel towards him.'[87]

The next day Teresa and her father went to Prato, but their
house-hunting seems to have been unsuccessful, for she told Byron
it was a 'miserable, inhospitable town, without any house that was
at all suitable'.

This letter was enclosed in one to Lega Zambelli, giving further
particulars about Prato, 'an unbearable place, in which it is impossible to find a decent lodging . . . Who ever suggested the idea
of living there?' – and ending with a postscript that is not without
pathos:

'Lega, write me the truth. Is Mylord pretending? Or does he
really mean to leave Ravenna? Tell me, Lega, I beseech you. This
uncertainty is an unbearable torment for me.'[88]

But meanwhile Shelley had succeeded in persuading Byron to
settle in Pisa, and on August 17th he was leaving Ravenna, taking
Teresa and Pietro the following letters.

BYRON TO CONTESSA GUICCIOLI

Ravenna   *August* [16*th*,] 1821

My Love: My letters have arrived, so there is little to keep me
here. My intention is to take a house in Pisa where there will be
apartments for your family – and for me – separate, but near. If

that does not please you – tell me – and we will take a separate house for each of us. This letter will be taken to you by the Englishman who is here now, and is leaving tomorrow. He will explain to everyone many things difficult and lengthy to set down in writing, which is not my talent in a language *not* barbarous. When all is decided, I will send a part of the household with the heavier effects, furniture, etc., needed for the house – then I will come with the others.

Greet Papa and Pietro. I am always

P.S. If you have found an apartment in Prato – and can find a house for me, it will do as well – but Pisa would be a more agreeable place to stay in – according to what I am told. I am leaving Ravenna so unwillingly – and so persuaded that my departure can only lead from one evil to a greater one – that I have no heart to write any more just now.

BYRON TO PIETRO GAMBA

[August 17th, 1821]

Dear Pietro: Here is the result of the most reasonable ideas that I can form under the present circumstances. I shall, however, leave Ravenna most unwillingly – being convinced that my departure can do nothing but injure Teresa in every way.

The embarrassment (as always happens where the fair sex is concerned) is very great for her and for us – for that reason it would have been a thousand times more respectable and prudent – if she and Count Ruggero could have returned here. But the will of God – or of the devil – or of the most sainted Lucrezia of Imola – and the most sainted grandparents – be done! A curse on all grandparents – on Lucrezia of Imola* and of any where else in the world!

A thousand greetings to Papa.

This letter was followed three days later, in answer to more complaints from Teresa about his silence, by an exàsperated note, saying that he had written by every post.

'We have not sent any other couriers, so as not to expose those poor devils to the infamous oppression which the last one met with

* Count Ruggero's sister, Lucrezia, married to a Count Ginnasi of Imola.

on the road . . . If the letters have not arrived – blame the post and not us.'

Teresa – although she herself had written to tell Byron that one of the couriers had been arrested and flung into jail for two days – has enclosed this note in a folder on which she has pencilled the words 'Bad temper!'

At last, on August 21st, Shelley arrived in Florence, and at once called upon Contessa Guiccioli, attempting to reassure her about Byron's safety, by telling her that he had given way to her wishes about giving up his rides in the lonelier parts of the pine-forest.

'Your letter,' Teresa wrote to Byron, 'your promises, your friend's visit, the assurance he has given me that I shall soon see you again, and that he on his part will at once take an apartment in Pisa for you, have given back to me a partial tranquillity – but complete tranquillity will only return to me on the day I see you again. My Byron, I am aware how great a sacrifice this move will be to you. How shall I be able to show you my gratitude? I have only affection to give to you, and that cannot be increased. I am very sorry to see that you are so reluctant to leave Ravenna, and have such forebodings for the future – but what else can be done?

'I vow that if it were allowed me I would fly to Ravenna, with the firm resolution of never leaving again, for my whole life, provided you too were willing to remain there. Since I have known you, I have had no other desire than to be where you are — and in your heart. But reason clearly shows that Papa will not be recalled for the present.

Your friend has told me that he rode with you every day and has added a *detail* (*you will understand me*) which would increase my love for you, if it could be increased. I hardly hoped, I admit, to obtain this favour from you, which costs you a sacrifice. I thank you, my Byron!'[89]

Before her next letter she had seen Shelley again, and sent Byron an account of him.

'Your friend pleases me very much,' she told him. 'His countenance is full of goodness and talent. He came to see me twice, and I can assure you that he has been of a great comfort to me. But his health seems to be very poor. When first I saw him, I thought he was having an attack of fever, and yet he assured me that on the contrary, journeys were very good for him, and that he felt very well. But how, dear friend, how is it possible to be so thin, so worn out?'**

Teresa must have expressed to Shelley her intense longing for Byron's arrival, for, as soon as he had arrived in Pisa, he wrote to her – in fairly correct Italian – the following letter:

SHELLEY TO CONTESSA GUICCIOLI

Pisa   *August 22nd, 1821*

I have only a moment in which to answer your letter, and I feel quite incapable of expressing to you my feelings about the confidence with which you have wished to honour me. I hope that you will find me worthy of it. Be assured that I shall omit no measure that may hurry the departure of Mylord, for I am certain that his happiness, no less than yours, depends on the nearness of her who has been his good Angel, of her who has led him from darkness to light, and who deserves not only his gratitude, but that of everyone who loves him.

I have almost settled on your house, and hope to be in time to announce the signing of the contract, before the post goes. Forgive the rough phrases of a sincere heart and do not doubt the profound interest you have awakened in me, and that I am and always shall be, with the greatest devotion

Your servant and friend   PERCY B. SHELLEY

Pray give my friendly greetings to your esteemed brother.**

Shelley succeeded in securing the house for Byron – the Palazzo Lanfranchi on the Lungarno – and soon after the whole Gamba family moved to Pisa. But two months more passed before Byron joined them, and his letters in the interval show a most unlover-like tendency to delay.

BYRON TO CONTESSA GUICCIOLI

                                            August 24th, 1821

My Teresa: Lega will have told Pierino and Papa about the preparations for our journey to Pisa.** I have nothing more to add. When everything is arranged in Pisa and the furniture has arrived, etc., then we shall start.

You know that my letters are hardly ever long – and will not expect very much from this one – knowing that I have a great deal to think about. I do not deny that I am leaving very unwillingly – foreseeing very serious evils for you all – and *especially for you.* I will not say more – you will see. I am

Greet Pietro and Papa.

Ravenna *August 26th,* 1821

My Teresa: We are getting ready – If there is any delay it will be that blessed Lega's – whom I abandon to your reproaches. Pray be in a good humour. I will come to you the moment I can. Hoping to see you equally . . . .⁹³ and less p.* . . . . I am always your friend and lover for ever

P.S. A thousand greetings to the two male Excellencies – that is Papa and Pierino. I am writing to Shelley, to settle on the house.

September 4th, 1821

Dear P . . .† That man Lega has not gone on with the preparations – so scold him well. For my part I am only waiting to see the business of the furniture, etc., finished. What happened to Papa and Pierino? Are they in Pisa? Your letter does not speak of them. . . .

Love me and believe me

P.S. Today I took Lega to the beach to teach him to swim – you can imagine that priest in the sea.

LEGA ZAMBELLI TO CONTE RUGGERO GAMBA

September 5th, 1821

Most Honoured Count: The noble Lord has heard that Count Guiccioli *might* take steps with the present Government against the *Contessina.* Whether this news be true or false, it is useful to know it in order to be careful and forestall any possible attack. The same noble Lord orders me to warn her for all ends and purposes by means of a special Messenger.

* p. stands for 'pettegola' – gossip. This letter was received by Teresa in Pisa.
† Erased. The word was pettegola – gossip.

This morning I posted a double letter to the Contessina, in the contents of which she will note the temporary delay in sending off the furniture.

Also today I have sent a message to your major-domo to send me the trunk, the guns and the box with the hunting equipment, but have received nothing up to now. Tomorrow I shall go myself to the said major-domo, and to Barezzi, and will do anything possible to obtain the things, which should have been handed over some days ago. Now Tita has come back, whom I sent to the major-domo, and says that I shall have everything by tomorrow morning.

With most respectful regards I have the honour to be your most obliged and devoted servant   LEGA ZAMBELLI

[in Byron's writing] il P[torn] F. to*

There is a postscript from Byron:

I did not say 'he might' – I said he was doing it – according to what I am told.

That buffoon Lega tells things in his own way. Besides Mr. Lega does all this – so that he may (or can) delay my departure. I am writing this, so that you may know that the only reason that is keeping me here now is Lega's slowness. I am always your affectionate friend. 10000 greetings to Teresa.

BYRON TO CONTESSA GUICCIOLI

Ravenna   *September 9th*, 1821

Excellency P . . . .: The Duchess of Devonshire has written the enclosed, which Mr. S[helley] will translate, if it interests you. Pray return it to me after reading. As for teachers of the *English language*, it would be better for the present to avoid giving any occasion for gossip. You do not know the state of the factions in England – and the horrible things that are said about Shelley and me – and if you are not careful the English in Florence and Pisa will say that, *being tired of you*, I handed you on to him. I say this frankly and openly, in so many words. So, having been warned – it depends on you to behave as you think best.

* Possibly 'Porco f——to', which might be mildly translated 'bloody swine'.

We are making preparations to leave Ravenna – which may well be quite useless – and has in many cases been entirely *contrary* to my ideas. A little patience would have put everything right, as you will see from the enclosed letter (of the lady).

We must also think of two things – the first is – that if Papa is recalled from exile *I shall return that instant* to Ravenna – and the second is – that if he is recalled *before my departure* – I shall not leave. As to the cost of the new house, etc., I would pay them willingly 1000 times so as not to have the trouble of moving for nothing. About that there will be no difficulty.

I am always
Greet Papa and Pierino.

The Duchess of Devonshire's answer, to which Byron refers, had been sent from Spa, Byron's letter having missed her in Rome. She promised to write to the Vatican. 'Believe me also that there is a character of justice, goodness and benevolence in the present Government of Rome, which, if they are convinced of the just claims of the Comtes de Gamba, will make them grant their request.'[14] But the Duchess's faith in the Vatican proved to be excessive.

As to the English lessons, Teresa says that she had written to tell Byron of Shelley's offer to teach her himself English, but that, as soon as she received his reply, she gave up the plan. She had then no idea of Shelley's reputation in England – 'a reputation monstrously unjust, but nevertheless partly explainable'.[15]

And now comes a whole series of apologetic, explanatory letters to Teresa from the wretched Lega, describing his troubles over the packing, his bargaining with the carriers, his quarrels with the other servants, his applications for permits, which had to be renewed when their dates expired, his patience in bearing with the ill-humour of Mylord – in short all the turmoil that preceded so complicated and momentous a move. They are the letters of a prolix, inefficient, stupid, but faithful bungler, who cannot see the point of all this hurry to leave a place where both he and his master would prefer to remain, and who seizes thankfully upon any pretext for delay. But it is possible to suspect that some of the excuses were Byron's, and that the master found it very convenient to put all the blame on the servant. Byron's own contribution to the correspondence is an occasional brief and hurried postscript.

In the first of Lega's letters, early in September, he announced that the packing of the furniture could not be completed until the end of the week – although an extra man was being employed as an upholsterer, and another was doing nothing but pack the books. Finally he told Teresa that her maid, who had previously promised to go to Pisa, had now gone back on her promise. Byron added a postscript:

'My Teresa: I am surprised that you should have condescended to write about a maid who had already refused to go to you – and who is little else than a public wh . . . I have no time to say more now. Write to me – love me.'

Lega's next three letters continue on the same lines. The first, on September 8th, announced a fresh cause of delay: the carriers of Ravenna had proved so exorbitant that Byron had asked Shelley to engage some from Pisa, to fetch all the luggage. 'I am poisoned', wrote Lega, 'by this further delay – but what is one to do, when one will not throw money away for nothing?' Mylord, he added, was well, and bathing every other day – but had, apparently, no time to write.

On September 15th Lega wrote that the permit for the convoy to enter Tuscany had expired; it was necessary to renew it before the travellers could start. Byron added a postscript:

'Gossip Excellency! You have done well to scold the buffoon – and will do better still to scold him some more. He is not in good faith – meanwhile we are only waiting for the carriers to get the things off. I will write more by the first post. I am always your friend and lover for ever.

P.S. Greet the two manly Excellencies; and tell Pierino that I have some things to tell him which would make him laugh if it were not Friday, as it is today, so I shall wait to see him – or to write on some other occasion. I kiss you [words cut out by Teresa] 100 times.'

On the 17th Lega wrote that the carriers had arrived: 'Tomorrow, if God wills, we shall begin to load.' But they had brought only three big carts and a smaller one, and it might be necessary to hire another. He begged that whoever put up the bed of Mylord on its arrival at Pisa, would see to it that the paint was touched up with good varnish, as it had been slightly damaged. This must be the same bed of which Lady Blessington gives such a fascinating description:

'I saw his bed in Genoa, when I passed through in 1826, and it certainly was the most gaudily vulgar thing I ever saw; the curtains in the worst taste and the cornice having his family motto of "Crede Byron", surmounted by baronial coronets. His carriage and his liveries were in the same bad taste, having an affectation of finery, but *mesquin* in the details, and tawdry in the *ensemble*: and it was evident that he piqued himself on them, by the complacency with which they were referred to . . . He has even asked us if they were not rich and handsome, and then remarked that no wonder they were so, as they cost him a great deal of money.'**

To Lega's note of the 17th, Byron added:
Gossip Ex[cellency]: We are all preparing – packing – sweating – swearing – and other *-ings*.

It has cost me two hours to put in order the archives of your Excellency's letters – being at least five hundred; a full translation of *Corinne* – i.e. *The Gossip*, the romance of Her Excellency Our Lady Countess Gaspara Domenica Teresa Guiccioli, born Gamba Ghiselli and Respected Gossip.

Love me. Always and entirely yours.

P.S. 1000 messages to Papa and the fraternal Excellency. Go on scolding Lega – who deserves it more every day.

At the same time Byron was writing to Moore: 'I am in all the sweat, dust and blasphemy of a universal packing of all my things, furniture, etc., for Pisa, whither I go for the Winter.' Teresa, he said, had been obliged to follow her father,

'because the Pope's decree of separation required her to reside in *casa paterna*, or else, for decorum's sake, in a convent. As I could not say with Hamlet "Get thee to a nunnery", I am preparing to follow them. It is awful work, this love, and prevents all a man's projects of good or glory. I wanted to go to Greece lately (as everything seems up here) with her brother, who is a very fine, brave fellow (I have seen him put to the proof) and wild about liberty. But the tears of a woman who has left her husband for a man, and the weakness of one's own heart, are paramount to these projects, and I can hardly indulge them.'**

On the 23rd, the four carts got off, carrying furniture, books, saddles, Pierino's dogs, and even Teresa's 'nerve lotion'. 'Mylord's house', writes Lega sadly, 'now seems a desert. I am sleeping on bare straw, with every comfort lacking.'

Byron adds:

Goss. Excellency –
'The wood is desolate,' etc. etc. – there's no comfort left for a cat. . . .
Lega will leave in a few days, I towards the first of next month. I want to leave in time for the convoy to arrive and the various animals of my Natural History – of, not Buffon, but Buffoon. I greet Your Gossip tenderly. I am, with the usual bows to the other two Excellencies,
Your most humble, devoted, obliged, etc. Servant

P.S. I cannot understand your hatred for a town where you have never been persecuted and where you were born. If *I* do not love *my* country – there is more than one reason, as your Excellency well knows. As to the rest, I am leaving because *you* wish me to – but I warn you that it is very improbable that I shall not return here – at the first opportunity – and before long.

But still Mylord managed to delay. On the 28th Lega wrote that he was getting off at last – together with 'the carriage and saddle-horses, the landau and the green wagonette' – and that he would travel over the Apennines by Covigliaio, Pistoia and the Via Pisana, without touching Florence. But on October 5th he was still in Ravenna, and a hurried P.S. from Byron provided a new excuse:

October 5th, 1821

My Love: We should have left this week, had it not been for the uncertainty caused by the rumour, which has now become general, about a new exile of the Romagnoli in Tuscany, which was told me by Uncle Cavalli.
Tell me the truth – and what I shall do (if it is true) so that we may meet. Believe me always – all yours –

The rumours of fresh severities against the Liberals were well founded. On September 13th the Pope had issued an Encyclical

against the Carbonari, menacing with Excommunic
those who still persisted in remaining within their ranks.
Society', the Encyclical said, 'while pretending singular resp
for the Catholic religion and for the person and tradition o
Jesus Christ', and 'exacting from its followers the practice of
charity and every kind of virtue', was nevertheless to be condemned for its false doctrines, and in particular for teaching its
followers to rise against their rulers and to punish with death
those who betrayed their secrets.'[98]

The effect of the Pope's words was great and immediate.
Throughout Italy large numbers of good Catholics, who until
then had believed that they could reconcile their religion and
their political ideals, sacrificed the latter, and not only confessed
all their own misdeeds, but very frequently gave away their
fellow conspirators as well.

'One cannot imagine', says a report in the *Diario di Roma* of
October 5th, 'the impression produced by the Papal Bull against
the Carbonari. We have had a very large number of people
saying aloud, in accents of the greatest distress, that they abjured
their association, that they had been deceived, that they had been
told that the Society was approved by the Pope.'[99]

Teresa too describes the dismay produced by the Encyclical –
and the sudden change of heart that it effected in many of the
Catholic Liberals. Moreover, it was believed that their defection
would result in a more violent persecution of the remainder, and
that the Vatican would try to influence the Tuscan 'Buon
Governo' to expel such men from Tuscany, too.

At the same time, a certain number of exiles, owing to the
petitions of their families, had been allowed to return to Ravenna,
but Teresa said that this permission had been obtained only by
those exiles who were prepared to bribe the Curia and to accept
any condition imposed upon them by the Church.

'Pierino', she wrote, 'has assured me that Papa will never do
anything so dishonourable as to *buy* the venal Roman Curia, and
that he would prefer never to go home, than to return there
ashamed and dishonoured!'[100]

All these uncertainties and hopes, however, had given Byron
a fresh excuse to delay, and now increased his unwillingness to
start. Teresa, in one of her sudden movements of perceptiveness,
remarks that Ravenna had become for him a *harbour* – the only

safe.[101] Only by proclaiming that he would
re, and soon, could he bear to go away at all.
pe as if to counteract the unreasonable weight
now oppressed him. And yet, try as he would,
y shake it off. 'I am convinced that my leaving
lead from one evil to greater ones.'

ill, too: he had caught an 'intermittent fever',
of malaria, which was prevalent at Ravenna at
that time – and had occasional attacks which left him feeling 'as
if one had got rid of one's body for good and all'.[102] He was so
low that, even though, one evening, 'under the thin crescent of a
very young moon', he walked 'in an avenue with a Signora for
an hour', he felt so unromantic ('and yet it was a *new* woman –
that is, new to me – and of course expecting to be made love to')
that he 'merely made a few commonplace speeches'. 'I feel, as
your poor friend Curran said, before his death, "a mountain of
lead upon my heart", which I believe to be constitutional, and
that nothing will remove it but the same remedy.'[103]

Teresa was gone – the Gambas were gone – his horses and
'menagerie' were on the road to Pisa – his Carbonari cronies were
scattered – his revolutionary adventure had come to an end. In
the great, bare rooms of Palazzo Guiccioli – barer than ever now,
with the books packed and even most of the furniture removed –
Byron spent his evenings alone, looking back, thinking of the
past. This was for him one of those rare interludes when, before
a new act begins, there is a breathing space in which to remember,
measure and appraise. What was left, at the last, of all that the
years had brought?

'My master, the Padre Pasquale Aucher . . . assured me that
"the terrestial Paradise had been certainly in Armenia". I went
seeking it – God knows where – did I find it? Umph! Now and
then, for a minute or two.'[104]

In that 'minute or two' lies the key, I think, to much of Byron's
life – and certainly to all the 'debauchery', about which so much
too much fuss has been made – by others, and most of all by
himself.
'No man would live his life over again, is an old and true saying,
which all can resolve for themselves. At the same time there are
probably *moments* in most men's lives, which they would live over
the rest of life to *regain*. Else why do we live at all? Because Hope
recurs to Memory, both false; but – but – but – and this *but* drags
on till – What? I do not know, and who does?'[105]

Life at Ravenna, what had it given him? Popularity, certainly, with the poor. A fresh petition (the second) had been sent by them to the Cardinal, imploring him not to let the kind, the unfailingly generous Mylord go. A certain companionship with the Carbonari – a fraternal, slightly condescending affection for Pietro Gamba. But no *equal* friendships, none to compare with those of his youth. Certainly no intellectual bond. Except for one reference to Giordani and one to Mezzofanti the linguist, there is in all the pages of the Ravenna Journal no mention of any Italian friend. Memories of Harrow and Cambridge – a long list of the men he had been compared to – London friends – Lewis, Rogers, Curran, Grattan, Clare, Sheridan, – his London clubs – again Harrow and Cambridge – these, in the evenings at Palazzo Guiccioli, filled Byron's thoughts. Of his whole life in Italy there is only one other mention – and that is an Englishman's comment.

'Lewis said. to me: "Why do you talk *Venetian* (such as I could talk, not very fine, to be sure) to the Venetians, and not the usual Italian?" I answered, partly from habit, and partly to be understood, if possible. "It may be so," said Lewis, "but it sounds to me like talking with a *brogue* to an *Irishman*." '[106]

What then was left? Teresa? Well, yes, Teresa.

'I can say that, without being so furiously in love as at first, I am more attached to her than I thought it possible to be to any woman after three years (except *one* – and who was she – can *you* guess?) and have not the least wish or prospect of separation from her.'[107]

To whom is he writing? To Augusta, of course – as once before in a very similar mood in Venice – to Augusta, to whom, sooner or later, the truth must out. But this letter – which tells the whole story of his liaison, from the time of his second return to Ravenna to his present plan of joining her in Pisa – strikes a new note: one of absolute finality:

'This is a finisher; for you know when a woman is separated from her husband for her *Amant*, he is bound both by honour (and inclination, at least I am) to live with her all his days . . . So you see that I have closed as Papa *began*, and *you* will probably never see me again as long as you live . . . It is nearly three years that this *liaison* has lasted. I was dreadfully in love, and she

T

blindly so – for she has sacrificed everything to this headlong passion. That comes of being romantic.'[108]

Yes, 'this is a finisher'. And again he turns to his Journal.

'I have written my memoirs, but omitted *all* the really *consequential* and *important* parts . . . I sometimes think that I should have written the *whole* as a *lesson*, but it might have proved a *lesson* to be *learnt* rather than avoided: for passion is a whirlpool, which is not to be viewed nearly without attraction from its Vortex.'[109]

And, a few pages later:

'Man is born *passionate* of body, but with an innate though secret tendency to the love of Good in his Mainspring of Mind. But God help us all! It is at present a sad jar of atoms.'[110]

Heigho – perhaps, after all, it was best to take the road to Pisa and Teresa. But if only she would not go on being so romantic!

BYRON TO CONTESSA GUICCIOLI

Ravenna   *October 12th, 1821*

My Love: Now that you are certain that I am coming – a few days more or less can make no difference – nor should they upset you. It is necessary that I should wait for another post (only on the 18th) to have the answer to a packet sent to England last month. I expected it yesterday, but since it has not come, I must wait this week. If it does not arrive on Thursday I will start all the same, without delaying further. For five days we have had nothing but pouring rain – Otherwise I would have sent off my horses this morning. With all this the roads are in an awful condition for the Dutch horses which the coachman naturally wishes to preserve in good health [torn] . . . . man servant who was your coachman (and now I don't know what) I never made any promise to take him into my service and now I cannot do so – without turning out one of my own – which would be an injustice, unless first they had failed in their duties. If this man is ill I will do everything possible to come to his aid and then he shall be paid, for the time he has stayed with the furniture and for his work – but I can neither do nor promise anything more. Greet Papa and Pierino in all cordiality and friendship.

Keep well. And do not exaggerate with that turgid epistolar imagination of Santa Chiara – (blessed be the Convent) the most simple and necessary things into evils and wrongs, etc. etc., which do not exist except in your romanesque or rather *romantic* head. For it upsets all the rules of thought in order to behave *à la De Staël*. Forgive this sermon. In the hope of seeing you again soon, I am, as I have always been, your Friend and Lover for Ever.

P.S. I leave Lega to your very just indignation and deserved punishment. We will do with him what you will on my arrival. He will start two or three days before me – I believe on the 20th, that is Saturday. But it will depend a little on the weather on account of the more delicate horses. I am thinking of leaving Ravenna on Monday week – the 22nd of this month.

October 19th, 1821

My Love: Lega leaves tomorrow, definitely. — He will be accompanied by all the grooms, etc. etc.; with the horses and two carriages.

I shall leave within the week – towards Thursday, probably. I assure you that the slowness and confusion of Lega is something astounding, surpassing my not slight opinion of his *qualities*.

You have added to the various troubles that I have had to encounter recently with your complaints, etc., about my *non*-departure. I left the moment it was possible. Pray spare me more complaints – which are neither just nor reasonable.

Hoping to embrace you soon – I am with all my heart your friend and lover for ever

P.S. Pray scold and even *beat* (with those) Lega. Beat him well he deserves it – if it were not for my *insistence* he would not have started even now.

By now Teresa must have almost despaired of Byron's coming. Two days later Shelley was writing: 'When may we expect you? The Countess is very patient, though sometimes she seems apprehensive that you will *never* leave Ravenna.'

But on the 23rd Lega was off at last – and Byron on the point of following him – although still with greater concern for the Dutch horses, than for his mistress's impatience.

T

BYRON TO CONTESSA GUICCIOLI

October 23rd, 1821

My Love: Lega left on Saturday – my departure is settled for
next Saturday – that is in four days . . . I hope you will be pleased.
Lega should be in Pisa before this note – but supposing that the
rapidity of that man's journey corresponds to his other movements – this note may arrive before the fool.

I have preferred to give him a week to do the journey – If I
had started first he would never have got to Pisa. He has already
committed one crime in paying too much to a coachman for
two horses to Lugo. But I shall.not pay him, when we come to the
travelling accounts. The help of these horses was necessary, to
save from too much fatigue the two Dutch horses, the coachman's
favourites. . . .

Greet Papa and Pierino for me, and I embrace you *à la Corinne.*
Love me – my love – I am always yours   F.a.L.f.E.

P.S. I am sorry about the servant's illness. See that nothing
necessary for his health is lacking. Being still young, we can hope
for him.

October 26th, 1821

My Love: The day after tomorrow I shall start. The weather is
not very favourable, but that does not matter much – it mattered
more for the Dutch horses, which must already be in Pisa.

So let us hope to see each other before long – be reassured and
believe me yours   F.a.L.f.E.

P.S. Vittoria is marrying a man from Imola (I am told). Tuda
is making love with the new Vice Legate (another bit of gossip
perhaps) – all Pierino's loves are already provided for therefore;
old and young; the grandparents are in the country still – Giulia
is here. Grandfather continues to have that inconvenient facility
for . . . but otherwise is well. The two boys were in town but
have already returned to the Villa. Greet the other two Excellencies.

This is Byron's last letter from Ravenna. He left behind him –
in the charge of Pellegrino Ghigi, his banker at Ravenna – those
animals of his menagerie which even he thought too unattractive
to take with him all the way to Pisa: 'a Goat with a broken leg,

an ugly peasant's Dog, a Bird which would only eat fish [the Egyptian crane?], a Badger on a chain, and two ugly old Monkeys.'[111] On October 29th, at last, he left the Palazzo Guiccioli and set off in his great travelling coach on the road to Pisa. 'There are probably moments', he had written only two weeks before, 'in most mens' lives which they would live over the rest of their life to regain.' And now, on this most reluctant journey, he encountered one of these moments. His coach and that of another English traveller met; they both got out – and suddenly recognized one another. It was the friend of his boyhood – the man of whom he had written, a fortnight before, that he could never hear his name mentioned 'without a beating of the heart' – Lord Clare. The meeting only lasted a few minutes, on the road, but it 'annihilated for a moment all the years between the present time and the days of *Harrow*. It was a new and inexplicable feeling, like rising from the grave'.[112]

Three or four days later – after a short pause in Bologna and Florence – Byron was in Pisa with Teresa. He brought with him some verses written between Florence and Pisa – which, whether out of kindness or because it was really so, he allowed Teresa to believe were inspired by her. She would have been less than a woman, had she not then forgiven the long months of waiting.

Oh FAME! If I e'er took delight in thy praises,
   'Twas less for the sake of thy high-sounding phrases,
Than to see the bright eyes of the dear One discover,
   She thought that I was not unworthy to love her.

There chiefly I sought thee, there only I found thee;
   Her glance was the best of the rays that surround thee,
When it sparkled o'er ought that was bright in my story,
   I knew it was Love, and I felt it was Glory.

7 : PISA–MONTENERO

A heroine by the side of a poet

LEIGH HUNT

'AT that time the rumour spread in Pisa that an extraordinary
man had arrived there, of whom people told a hundred
different tales, all contradictory and many absurd. They
said that he was of royal blood, of very great wealth, of sanguine
temperament, of fierce habits, masterly in knightly exercises,
possessing an evil genius, but a more than human intellect. He
was said to wander through the world like Job's Satan ... It
was George Byron. I wished to see him; he appeared to me like
the Vatican Apollo.'[1]

This passage, written by Francesco Domenico Guerrazzi, who
was then a student at Pisa University – gives an impression of the
legendary aspect which Byron took on for Italians during the
latter part of his stay in Italy, and which was one of the fruits of
his isolation. In Venice, at least at first, he had moved freely in
Venetian society; in Ravenna he had shared in Italian family life
and taken part in local politics. In both places, although always
considered a *stravagante*, he had become, at least for a few inti-
mates, a *real* person, a human being of flesh and blood. But in
Pisa, and later on in Genoa, he never made friends with any
Italians of his own station at all. Like so many other Englishmen
abroad, he lived in a narrow – and highly eccentric – circle of
his own fellow-countrymen, regarding the country in which he
was living merely as a stage-setting, with shifting scenery, on
which to enact his own dramas.

It was in this that Byron's contemporaries differed from the
travellers of the preceding century. The young man of the
eighteenth century, on his 'grand tour', frequented as a matter of
course the society of the lands he visited. Travel was then the
prerogative of a single class; the aristocratic salons of Europe did
not recognize national barriers. But in the nineteenth century
another kind of traveller appeared, the middle-class intellectual.
These 'romantics' sought the beauties of nature rather than the
pleasures of society; they carried their own world with them, and,
with few exceptions, felt little need for any human contacts with
the inhabitants of the countries they visited – except for their
servants, their coachmen, or an occasional mistress. This attitude,
which has not made the British race beloved abroad, has also
given prominence to the eccentricities from which few of its

distinguished travellers have been free. They have always remained behind the footlights, and it is hardly surprising that their foreign audience – never coming close enough to them to see the man beneath the make-up – judged them exclusively by their very curious appearance and behaviour.

The little group of English people in Pisa whom Byron now joined was certainly, to all outward appearances, very odd. There was that tall, thin, bony young man, Mr. Shelley, ('il Capitano Scellyny, sedicente Ateo', as he appeared on one of the official reports of his death), who wandered about the city in a short school-boy's jacket reading an encyclopaedia, who left his meagre dinner of bread and water untasted on the mantelpiece, who disappeared into the forest for hours together, and who lay motionless at the bottom of a pool in the Arno, when a friend tried to teach him to swim. There was old Mr. Dolby, who went about singing at the top of his voice, his pocket bulging with books, and young Mr. Taaffe – stout, pompous and amiable – interminably holding forth about his Commentary and his translation of Dante, but wholly unable to control his horse, which seemed to take a pleasure in depositing him in the gutter. There was Walter Savage Landor, who refused to speak to any other Englishman; and, later on, the Leigh Hunts, who could hardly be prevailed upon to speak to an Italian. There was an elderly clergyman, Dr. Nott, who held religious services every Sunday for a dozen or so of his fellow-countrymen – and took the opportunity to attack, in the most violent terms, the atheism of the husband of one of his small congregation.* And, strangest of all, there was that great hawk-like sailor, as dark as an Arab, with flashing eyes and teeth, loquacious and violent – a Pirate out of a school-boy's picture-book, Trelawny. As for Byron, even Trelawny, who 'saw no peculiarity' in the costume (a braided tartan jacket, loose nankeen trousers and blue velvet cap) in which the poet rode abroad, yet observed that 'his long absence had not effaced the mark John Bull brands his children with; the instant he loomed above the horizon, on foot or on horseback you saw at a glance he was a Britisher'.[2]

The family relationships of these people, too, were somewhat confusing. The real name of the brawny, middle-aged lady, 'as stiff as a grenadier', 'with gigantic naked arms' and a mild, beaming countenance, who had lived in Pisa in complete domestic seclusion for the past eight years with a young Irishman and their two little girls, was apparently Lady Mountcashell, and *his* name

---

* Dr. Nott, said Byron, had revised one of the Ten Commandments to read: 'Thou shalt, Nott, bear false witness against thy neighbour.'

was Mr. Tighe. But they called themselves simply Mr. and Mrs. Mason. Then there were Ned and Jane Williams – a charming young couple with two small children, and deeply in love. But Jane was not really Mrs. Williams, she was the wife of a brother-officer of Ned's. Yet apparently both the Masons and the Williams were accepted by their friends as respectable married couples.

The position of Contessa Guiccioli was far easier to assess. She was simply Byron's mistress, and there was no question of her going about in the society of Pisa. She lived quietly with her father and brother in a small house on the Lungarno, Casa Parra, while waiting, with such patience as she could muster, for Byron's arrival.

Too much has already been written about Byron's and Shelley's circle in Pisa, to repeat the same stories here. The Gamba papers contain no new letter of Byron's during this time, and only a few short notes of Teresa's. But the 'Vie', which at this point becomes more detailed and prolix than ever, does throw some amusing sidelights on Byron and his friends, as seen through Teresa's anxious, critical, and often bewildered eyes. From the only society she had known until then – that of the Convent-school of S. Chiara, of the provincial drawing-rooms of Ravenna, and of the formal 'conversazioni' of Venice, – she was suddenly plunged into this strange foreign world. It is hardly surprising that she did not quite know what to make of it.

In the time before Byron's arrival, she saw no one but the Shelleys and the Williams. They were sorry for her, and kind. Shelley offered to teach her English; Mary, and sometimes Jane, went out driving with her. But none of them had a very clear idea of what she was really like. To Mary she seemed 'a nice pretty girl without pretentions, good-hearted and amiable'; to Shelley, 'a very pretty, sentimental, innocent, superficial Italian, who has sacrificed an immense fortune for the sake of Lord Byron; and who, if I know anything of my friend, of her, and of human nature, will hereafter have plenty of leisure and opportunity to repent her rashness'.³ As for Teresa, she thought Jane Williams charming, 'gentle and sweet', and her life with Williams 'a true idyll'. Besides, she admired Ned Williams for his simple masculinity, as 'un officier qui a chassé le Tigre et le Lion et dont la conversation honnête et animée portait sur ces sujets'.⁴ Mary, on the other hand, with her bookishness and her cold, prim manner, was a little intimidating. She refers to her frequently as 'une femme supérieure', who possessed 'a high intelligence and a noble heart', but it is evident that she was never wholly at ease with her, and she takes some pleasure in stating that 'Byron did not feel much liking for her'.⁵ For Shelley alone – in all the group of alien human beings among whom she now found herself – Teresa had nothing but admiration and praise.

'Lord Byron', she writes, 'had often spoken to her about Shelley, and she was prepared to see a remarkable man, but the reality surpassed her expectations. Shelley was really not a man like any other, he was an unequalled combination of contrasts and harmonies, both physical and moral . . . It was said that in his adolescence he was beautiful – but at this time he was so no longer. His features were delicate, but irregular – except for the mouth, which, however, was ugly in laughter and was a little spoilt by his teeth . . . His skin, which one could see must have been fine, had been marred – either through exposure to the weather or through poor health – by freckles. His hair, which crowned a very small head, was chestnut-coloured and abundant, but not well cared-for, and had already got some premature threads of silver. He was very tall, but so bent that he seemed of ordinary height, and although his figure was so fragile, his bones and joints stood out too much, even grossly. And yet all these details, themselves unbeautiful, still formed an extremely sympathetic being – and really one must use the word being, for truly Shelley seemed rather Spirit than man. He was also extraordinary in his dress, for he generally wore a schoolboy's jacket, never any gloves, and unpolished shoes – and yet, among a thousand gentlemen, he would always have seemed the most accomplished. His voice was high-pitched – even strident – but nevertheless took on inflections, to suit his thoughts, of a grace, a softness and a delicacy which went straight to the heart.'⁶

Yet Shelley, too, sometimes, behaved in a manner that must have seemed to Teresa more than a little odd. On returning home, for instance, one day in Carnival, after he had been obliged to thread his way among the merrymakers thronging the Lungarno, he flung himself half-fainting in a chair, 'overpowered by the atmosphere of evil passions in that sensual and unintellectual crowd'.⁷ In the midst of a philosophical argument with Byron, he flung up his arms and cried, 'I do believe, Mary, he is little better than a Christian!' And, having heard a rumour that a man who had stolen a chalice from an altar was to be burned alive in Lucca for sacrilege, he came rushing to Byron to suggest that they should at once form a company to ride to Lucca and rescue the victim by force!⁸ Such hysterical behaviour was not likely to appeal to any sane Latin woman. As for Shelley's cham-

pionship of Emilia Viviani, Teresa thought it remarkably silly.
To be in a convent, while waiting for her wedding-day – even
with a man she did not like – seemed to her a very natural fate
for any young woman. Emilia's sufferings, she concluded, had
been greatly exaggerated by her admirer. So highly developed
an imagination, and so intense a sensibility as his, 'si parfois elles
produisent le sublime, plus souvent produisent le bizarre, l'incom-
préhensible, et même le ridicule'.⁹ She declared herself thankful
that Byron's genius did not take this form, 'if by imagination one
means that poetic exaltation which stretches to the last boundaries
of human reason, and sometimes oversteps them'.¹⁰

Yet Byron's imagination, too, sometimes ran away with him.
The Palazzo Lanfranchi on the Lungarno, which Shelley had
taken for him, was a fine Renaissance palace, whose foundations
descend to the edge of the river. Byron, however, – recognizing
the name Lanfranchi as that of one of the tormentors of Conte
Ugolino in Dante's *Inferno* – preferred to refer to his new abode as

'a famous old feudal palazzo, large enough for a garrison, with
dungeons below and cells in the walls . . . There is one place where
people were evidently *walled up*; for there is but one possible
passage, *broken* through the wall, and then meant to be closed
again upon the inmate.'¹¹

From this it was an easy step to imagine the presence of ghosts.

'Fletcher', said Shelley to Medwin, 'is as superstitious as his
master, and says the house is haunted, so that he cannot sleep
from rumbling noises overhead, which he compares to the rolling
of bowls. No wonder; old Lanfranchi's ghost is unquiet and walks
at night'.¹²

In sober fact, however, the houses on this part of the Lungarno
did not exist at the time of Conte Ugolino, and the underground
dungeons were merely the storehouses of the silk-merchants of
Pisa, from which they used to load their wares on to the Arno
barges.¹³

The palazzo, – haunted or not – was an admirable setting for
Byron's present mode of life. According to Teresa he was, after
his long period of seclusion in Ravenna, in a most sociable mood.
As at Ravenna, he worked during the greater part of the night,
rose late, and breakfasted only on a cup of bitter green tea – and,
after dinner, spent most of his evenings with Teresa. But the
greater part of the afternoon was spent in long rides with Shelley,

Williams, Trelawny, Taaffe, Medwin, and any other visitor who
turned up – and on every Wednesday he gave a men's dinner-
party, at which he entertained his guests 'with a grace, a generosity, an affability which has never been surpassed'. 'Never', said
Shelley, 'did Byron display himself to more advantage than on
these occasions; being at once polite and cordial, full of social
hilarity and the most perfect good humour; never diverging into
ungraceful merriment, and yet keeping up the spirit of liveliness
throughout the evening.'[14]

These evenings, according to Teresa, often prolonged themselves far into the night, and she comments somewhat acidly that:
'Mr. Medwin was always the last to leave the hospitable board.'
It was on these occasions, she adds, 'unfavourable to exactitude',
that Medwin collected the material for the *Conversations with L^d.
Byron*, which he published so soon after his host's death, and which
Teresa describes as 'an exploitation of the honour of an acquaintance that so many people desired in vain'.* The adjectives which
she applies to this book are 'light, exaggerated, indelicate – partly
indiscreet and partly untrue'. And she proceeds to enumerate nine
inaccurate statements in it – including 'the confiscation of the
property of Count Gamba', 'the return of Byron from the East on
account of his mother's death', 'Byron's plans for his daughter
Allegra', 'The black hair of Mme la Contesse Guiccioli', and 'the
peacocks of Byron's menagerie'.

Byron, she says, found Medwin's company pleasant enough,
but had so poor an opinion of his character that when, one
evening, Teresa's carriage was late and she accepted Medwin's
arm to go home, Byron afterwards scolded her severely, 'saying
that he was not a man with whom a young woman could allow
herself to be seen in public'.[15]

It was ungrateful of Teresa to be so superior about Medwin,
for, of all Byron's biographers, he is, with the exception of Moore,
the one who has been kindest to her. It was he who granted her
'eyes large, dark and languishing (and) shaded by the longest
eyelashes in the world', and 'the most beautiful mouth and teeth
imaginable'.

'It is impossible', he added, 'to see without admiring, to hear
the Guiccioli speak without being fascinated. Her amiability and
gentleness show themselves in every intonation of her voice, which,
and her perfect Italian, give a peculiar charm to everything she
utters. Grace and elegance seem component parts of her nature.'[16]

* 'Vie', pp. 900-1. Byron himself, however, was fully aware of what his guest was
about.

Moreover, he was tactful enough to attribute her occasional melancholy, not – like Trelawny or the odious Leigh Hunt – to any deficiency of Byron's, but to such a highly respectable cause as 'the exile and poverty of her aged father'.* But on the other hand, while admitting that Byron was 'very much attached to her', he added the words, 'without actually being in love'.[17] Perhaps it was this that Teresa could not forgive.

But it was Trelawny who, of all the strange creatures whom Teresa now encountered, seemed to her the strangest and most incomprehensible. It is probable that, left to herself, she would have found his extreme masculinity, his resounding voice and his tall stories, attractive; she would have taken him at his own valuation. Certainly the Shelleys, in early days, did so. They and the Williams spent part of the spring in planning a romantic drama to be founded upon his singular adventures, – the tale of 'a Pirate, a man of savage but noble nature', of which Shelley actually wrote the first 250 lines.[18] But Byron, from the first, was on his guard.

'I have met today the personification of my Corsair,' he told Teresa after Trelawny's first call upon him. 'He sleeps with the poem under his pillow, and all his past adventures and present manners aim at this personification.' – 'I feel curious to see him,' said Teresa. 'You will not like him,' Byron firmly replied.[19]

And indeed when, the next day, Teresa met him in the street, as he was riding home with Byron, she declared herself terrified by his *étrange regard*, and begged Byron to give up the acquaintance. Byron, however, only laughed at her, and continued to see Trelawny every day. Soon he began to plan the building of the *Bolivar*, of which Trelawny was to be the captain. Teresa says – but this is rather difficult to believe – that it was Byron's first intention to call the boat *The Countess Guiccioli*, and that only the fear of compromising her and of annoying her father, caused the name to be altered.[20]

It was, according to Trelawny, at about this time that a modest request from a tenor called Sinclair, of the Pisa opera-house, that Byron and Shelley should each write a song for him, set both poets good-naturedly to work, putting words to an Indian air which Jane Williams had often played to them. The Hindustani words of the air, Trelawny affirms, which begin 'Allah Malla punca' [*sic*] 'are as hackneyed in Bengal as Malbrouk or Cherry-ripe in Covent Garden'.[21] The result of these poetic efforts were,

* The Count was then fifty-four.

he states, Shelley's exquisite lyric, 'I arise from dreams of thee',[22] and perhaps one of the worst, as well as the most absurd, of Byron's many bad poems, a lyric of which it is perhaps sufficient to quote the first verse:

Oh my lonely – lonely – lonely pillow!
Where is my lover, where is my lover?
Is it his bark which my dreary dreams discover?
Far far away! and alone among the billow.[23]

Trelawny adds that poor Teresa, when she attempted

'to marry the long verses of the English song to the allegro air – found it was impossible – notwithstanding which Byron maintained that the words corresponded excellently. The Contessa, when her patience and ingenuity (which were great) became exhausted, declared it was she who spoiled both the beautiful words (from not understanding them) and the music. The songs were not given to Sinclair – and Byron confessed his songs in general were not good and that he had great difficulty in composing them – yet, he added, you must all allow, the one I wrote to the Indian air is very good!'[24]

Poor Teresa! She tried very hard to play up to the mysterious new standards of the company in which she now found herself! Mary, she discovered, was having Greek lessons every day – and this appeared to constitute a further bond between her and Shelley. Perhaps, she thought, Byron would be pleased if she, too, showed an equal studiousness.

'I will leave you now,' she wrote to him half playfully and half in earnest, 'so as not to bore you – and to lose time, *which should be given up entirely to the history of Hannibal*. But will you love me more when I know by heart the names of the river Trebbia, of Lake Trasimene, and of Cannae? If you will, my memory will accomplish miracles, and I will even accept the principles of T[aaff]e who says in a didactic tone "that a philosopher is superficial, if there is in his works a single mistake in date!" But let this remain between us, my treasure. Love me, for I adore you and forgive you.'[25]

It was at this time, too, that Teresa – perhaps influenced by Shelley's intense admiration for *Don Juan* – began to feel that she had been foolish about this poem and removed her ban on its completion, saying that 'she had only asked this sacrifice of him, to spare him further attacks, like those on the two earlier cantos, written *pendant les mauvais jours de Venice*'.[26]

'I obtained a permission from my Dictatress to continue it,' wrote Byron on July 8th, '*provided* always it was to be more guarded and decorous and sentimental in the continuation than in the commencement . . . The embargo was only taken off upon these stipulations.'[27]

On the following day, said Teresa, the sixth canto of *Don Juan* was begun. It was in this canto that Byron made use of the stories that Teresa had told him of her life at S. Chiara, where, during the Carnival, some of the girls dressed up in their brothers' clothes. 'The others followed them everywhere, and would dance only with them, which awakened great alarm among the nuns, so that this form of dressing-up was forbidden.'*

While Byron was working on these cantos, according to Teresa,

'His pen moved so rapidly over the page that one day I said to him, "One would almost believe that someone was dictating to you!" "Yes," he replied, "a mischievous spirit who sometimes even makes me write what I am not thinking. There now, for instance – I have just been writing something against love!" "Why don't you erase it, then?" I asked. "It's written," he replied, smiling, "the stanza would be spoiled." And the stanza remained.'[28]

Trelawny was equally struck with Byron's facility, and commented besides that in all the manuscripts he had seen in Pisa (*Don Juan, Cain, Mazeppa* and the tragedies) there was 'scarcely a single correction or alteration'.

* This story, according to Teresa, suggested to Byron the idea of introducing Don Juan into the seraglio, and inspired the description of the other maidens' feelings towards the newcomer:

> But certain 'tis they all felt for this new
>   Companion something newer still, as 'twere
> A sentimental friendship through and through,
>   Extremely pure, which made them all concur
> In wishing her their sister, save a few
>   Who wished they had a brother just like her. . . .
>   *Don Juan*, VI, xxxix.

Later on she told Lord Malmesbury that Byron 'wrote all the last cantos on playbills or on any odd piece of paper at hand and with repeated glasses of gin-punch by his side. He then used to rush out of his room to read her what he had written, making many alterations and laughing immoderately'. MALMESBURY, *Memoirs of an Ex-Minister*, I, p. 27.

'The reason was that he had an extraordinarily retentive memory – he composed in his brain, during his morning walks and rides, and at night hastily wrote what he had composed during the day. I have often heard him muttering over and over his rhymes, and sometimes he repeated a stanza or two of Don Juan, which I have afterwards seen him set down on paper.'[29]

He had not, however, much patience with Trelawny's long stories.

'He one day suddenly interrupted the description of a hurricane I was narrating, and said abruptly, putting his hand on my horse's mane – "T., have you ever written a Book?" I answered, no! "I am glad of that," he replied, "for then it is possible we may be friends!" – I told him a friend of mine wished his opinion of a MSS. – "He wants me to praise it!" he replied. "Tell him I have praised it. – But I won't peruse it – When they give me their MSS. I know what they want – praise – and they have it. I used to be fool enough to read them – I am wiser now." '[30]

All these activities of the little British colony in Pisa seem innocent enough. But to the Italian police, who from the first had kept an anxious and vigilant eye upon them, they bore a very different aspect. Like specialists in other fields, they saw the whole of life in terms of their own preoccupation, and having once firmly ticketed Byron and the Gambas as subversive Liberals, imagined them never to be engaged in any other pursuit! This naive and sincere conviction, underlying all the police reports sent off from Pisa, gives them the same curious twist that distorted the similar reports about Byron in Bologna; to read them is like reading about busy termites, not about human beings.

When first the Gambas arrived in Pisa, as exiles from the Papal States, the Government of Tuscany granted them a permit to reside there for two months (which later on was extended, with some difficulty, to four) but at the same time ordered the local police to keep them under constant supervision. At first they reported that the Gamba family 'was behaving in a very reserved manner. The lady, who is very attractive, has only gone out a few times with her father'.[31] But a little later on they observed that Count Gamba's house was becoming a regular meeting-place for exiled Ravennati, whose ostensible position in the Count's household was only a cloak for their political activities.[32] The opening of the Pisa University, they feared, would also bring there

some subversive students who had been exiled from Turin, and
moreover the arrival was now expected of a certain Lord Byron,
who had asked for a permit to bring all his furniture from Ravenna
to Pisa, without paying the customary duties. So now a letter
went off to the Buongoverno from the head of the Financial
Department of Pisa:

'We are aware of certain rumours about the political attitude
of this Englishman, who combines with high birth, literary celebrity, and a considerable fortune, a great determination to favour
all political novelties.' The writer, therefore, 'in view of the opening
of the University', and a fear that Byron might become 'the Protector and Centre of all those young fanatics', suggested that 'the
most careful and secret instructions should be sent for the supervision of the aforesaid foreigner.' [33]

For this purpose an admirable tool was available, in the person
of the Cavaliere Luigi Torelli – an arch-informer who had achieved
such eminence in his profession that he corresponded directly
with Metternich, and was known by the title of 'the spy of spies'. [34]
A true fanatic in the cause of despotic government – to which he
always referred as 'the good cause' – he kept a voluminous diary
entitled 'Arcana politicae anticarbonariae', of which many pages,
from the time when Byron's arrival was expected, were given up
to the English Mylord. 'This famous poet, if he were not considered a madman, would deserve the supervision of the police
of the whole Europe.' But, he added, Mylord's coming was still
far from certain. He had taken the Palazzo Lanfranchi for a
yearly rent of 200 zecchini and had paid six months in advance,
'but some people still wager that *questo stravagante* will change his
mind and will not come'. [35] Byron, however, did arrive, with
his whole great menagerie – and now once again, as at Bologna,
the police were confronted with the problem of how to spy on
him at once effectively and unobtrusively.

'The police of Pisa', says the report of 'the spy of spies', 'not
knowing how to enter into contact with so noble a personage,
limits itself to observing the Palazzo, to see who is entering it.' [36]

They stood about at the street corners – no doubt as conspicuous and unmistakable as plain-clothes policemen everywhere
else – they chattered to Byron's servants, they opened, once again,
his letters – and, since there was nothing to learn, they learned
remarkably little. His works, however, were more easily accessible

than his person, and, curiously enough, a translation of his *Prophecy of Dante* had got as far as Volterra, to fall into the hands of the Commissioner of that small city. Its contents struck him as extremely dangerous:

'It is most decidedly not written in the spirit of our government, nor of any of the Italian governments. To me, indeed, it seems designed to augment popular agitation, which is already sufficiently aroused. Lord Byron makes Dante foresee democracy and independence, as the true *goods* of this country. . . .'[37]

It was ideas like these, the Commissioner stated, and even more those expressed 'by that Lady, whom her own English papers describe as a Fury' [Lady Morgan] which 'cause weak heads to become heated' and do all the more harm in the provinces, 'because of the ignorance of those in whose hands they fall'.[38]

To all this the Florentine Government replied in some perplexity that it would like to see a copy of this dangerous work (of which the circulation was meanwhile prohibited) – and within ten days the Commissioner forwarded it, quoting the far from complimentary comments of the translator:

'A thousand have said these things before Byron, but the present times make me consider them dangerous . . . The translator confesses that he found the poem difficult to digest, and adds that it was hard work to divest certain images of their prosaic garb. "The style of the greater part of living English poets is, in truth, so turgid and extravagant as to deform their ideas, even when they are magniloquent or acute." Why then take so much trouble to translate a bad poet? Probably because everything is good that serves a party purpose.'[39]

All this was absurd enough. But the suspicions of the Buongoverno were by now thoroughly awakened, and when Byron sent a message to the Governor of Pisa – Marchese Niccolo' Viviani, the father of Shelley's Emilia – to ask whether he might indulge in pistol-practice in his own garden (it being forbidden to carry arms) the Governor felt bound to reply that he could permit nothing of the kind. The young Englishmen – it should perhaps be remembered that, of all this company, Byron alone was over thirty – were thus obliged to ride out for their shooting to a farm outside the town, and would return home at sunset, laughing and shouting, their horses clattering down the narrow streets. And soon Torelli had a real piece of news to report:

'At last', he wrote triumphantly, 'Lord Byron and his company of assassins have given us a taste of the temper they have already shown elsewhere, as the Government has been expecting ever since their arrival in Pisa.'⁴⁰

The incident to which he referred was what is known as the 'Masi affray' – trivial and absurd in itself, but far-reaching in its consequences. Briefly, on the evening of March 24th, Byron and his rowdy party in fancy-dress were riding home as usual, just outside the town, followed by Mary Shelley and Teresa in a carriage. A sergeant-major of the Italian Dragoons, called Masi, who was in a hurry to enter the city, came galloping up and, since the road was almost completely obstructed by the English party, pushed his way through somewhat roughly, causing the horse of that uncertain rider, Mr. Taaffe, to shy violently, while Taaffe, in fear and annoyance, called out to Byron, 'Did you ever see such a thing!' They caught Masi up, and, with their whips raised, accused him of insulting one of their friends; Masi replied with considerable heat; a crowd gathered; and finally Byron, under the erroneous impression that Masi was an officer, threw his visiting-card to him.* On reaching the city gates Masi, with the help of two old soldiers, attempted to arrest the Englishmen; they pushed past him; Pietro Gamba slashed at him with his whip, Masi drew his sword, Shelley got hit on the head and Captain Hay received a cut on the nose. After they had all taken refuge, with the two ladies, in the Palazzo Lanfranchi, Byron galloped back and resumed the altercation. As, however, a few minutes later, Masi rode past the palazzo, one of Byron's servants rushed out with a pitchfork (or possibly only with a large toasting-fork – Teresa calls the instrument 'une petite fourche') severely wounded him in the abdomen, and rushed back into the palazzo, says Teresa, 'before he could be recognized'.⁴¹

'I saw Masi', wrote an eye-witness, 'tottering in the saddle, ride as far as Don Beppe's café, where, no longer able to sit his horse, his helmet fell off; his hair was standing on end, his face was as white as a sheet and he fell down exclaiming "I am killed!".'⁴²

His wound was fortunately not fatal, but the story spread through the city, and lost nothing in the telling. The mad Englishmen, it

* 'It is proper to add', wrote Byron to Mr. Dawkins, the British Minister in Florence, 'that I conceived the man to have been an officer, as he was well dressed, with scaled epaulettes, and not ill-mounted, and *not* a serjeant-major (the son of a washerwoman, it is said), as he turns out to be.' Masi was a veteran of the Napoleonic wars, who had served in Spain and Germany.

was said, had placed themselves at the head of a peasant insurrection; Trelawny had been killed, and Byron seriously wounded. No, said another version, Taaffe had killed the dragoon and was now lying concealed in Palazzo Lanfranchi, guarded by Byron's bulldog.

'I am told', wrote Torelli, 'that Lord Byron has mounted two small pieces of field-artillery at the door of his room, and keeps a quantity of guns, pistols and daggers on the table. So that a hunchback carrier, who was sent from the Maremma with a small wild boar and a letter to Byron, was so alarmed at this warlike show, that he threw down the boar, gave the letter to a servant, and fled from Palazzo Lanfranchi without even waiting to be paid.'[43]

Feeling in the town ran high and when, on the day after the incident and in spite of Teresa's protests, Byron went out riding as usual, the Pisans murmured, 'Have those assassins been arrested, or are they still walking about the town?'[44] At the height of the trouble, the young student Guerrazzi saw a little scene that made upon him an indelible impression.

'I saw', he wrote, 'all the Englishmen who were then living in Pisa, whether they were friends of Byron's or not, going off with their arms to his palazzo, to defend their great national poet. And then I thought if he had been an Italian, the Italians would have united to stone him. And so I began to understand why the English are a great people.'[45]

Teresa, however, was frankly terrified.

'My Byron,' she wrote, 'is it indeed necessary for you to go out again today, too? Others will tell you that the city is quiet; but what a difference there is between their friendship for you and the feelings that fills *my* whole heart! No one else will tell you that the most precious of all these lives is the one that is in the greatest danger: yours, my Byron.'[46]

Byron continued to go for his daily rides, but he did send a careful account of the whole incident to the British Minister in Florence, Mr. Dawkins, – first consulting Trelawny as to the correct way to address the letter, and asking 'if Dawkins was an Hon,ble'.

U

'I said, "A Monsieur, Monsieur Dawkins, Secretary of Legation." "No, no," said Byron, "that won't do. Dress and address
is everything." He then concluded his letter with, "honour to
yr very humble obedient servant" and addressed it to His Excellency the Hon.ble etc. and smiling observed, "With as little a
net as this will I ensnare as great a fly as Cassio." '[47]

Byron's letter to Dawkins stated that 'several British subjects
have been insulted and some wounded', and stated that he had
no wish 'to prevent or evade the fullest investigation of the business'.[48] And indeed, three days after the brawl, a police Commissioner arrived from Florence, depositions were taken, and
Byron made use of the privilege of his rank to be examined, with
Teresa, in his own house. Torelli says that the examining magis-
trate, Lapini, prepared himself for the formidable interview by
reading the article on Byron in the French Biography of Famous
Men, from which he learned that 'the poet descended from the
Scottish kings, had murdered one of his mistresses, and habitually
used her skull as a drinking-cup'. After this, 'he was quite astonished by the courteous and high-bred manner in which he was
received by this enemy of the human race'.[49]

All his servants, too, were examined, but only two – a servant
of the Gambas, Antonio Maluchielli, and Byron's *barbuto
servo*, Tita Falcieri (who arrived in court for his examination
armed with two pistols and a dagger), were kept in prison for
trial. According to Teresa, the culprit was undoubtedly one of
Byron's coachmen, who had actually confessed his misdeed to his
master. Byron had then held a council of war with his friends as
to whether to help the man to escape to Lucca, and tell the police
the truth. But in the end they decided to keep silence, and 'leave
everything to the course of justice'. Teresa was much upset by
all this, fearing that – as indeed occurred – suspicion would fall
on the Gamba servants, and they would all be involved in the
consequences.

'I can no longer keep silence,' she wrote to Byron, after a disagreement on the subject. 'Won't you at least take a decision
about the coachman? Papa assures me that this uncertainty will
be very dangerous for our family.'[50]

Papa was right. Tita Falcieri was acquitted and sent home –
'which all proves', Torelli commented acidly, 'that guineas are
common currency in all countries' – but Maluchielli was kept in
prison for many months, and the whole incident was used as a

pretext by the government for requesting the Gamba family to leave Pisa. Moreover, at much the same time as these events, fresh forces were being marshalled against them from another direction. At the beginning of the year Count Guiccioli, after having paid to his wife for six months the allowance ordered by the Pope, had sent her a most disquieting letter, in which he actually asked her to return to him. Teresa's answer was very clear, if not precisely tactful.

Pisa   *February 25th, 1822*

I am grateful to you for your proposals, for I attribute them to the interest you still feel for me. Be assured that what I feel for you is not less; and the only reason that could induce me even to listen to such proposals would be my desire to contribute to your happiness – for as to my own, I think I have already attained it, and am enjoying it in my present situation. But is it indeed probable that our reunion would add to your welfare and not lessen mine? I, for my part, doubt it very much. On the contrary I am persuaded that no interview or agreement would ever be sufficient to obtain for us an assurance of future mutual tranquillity. I must repeat to you that I am perfectly happy in my present situation and I think that no other would ever again suit me. When one has attained the tranquillity I now enjoy, at the cost of so many sacrifices and so much suffering, it is not easy to renounce it.

Keep yourself as well and happy as I from my heart desire.
Your Wife   TERESA GAMBA GUICCIOLI[51]

On receiving this unequivocal reply, Count Guiccioli decided to resort to action. Why, he thought, should he continue to pay a regular allowance to a woman who not only had no intention of returning to him, but who manifestly had not kept her side of the bargain? He at once took counsel with his advocate in Rome, Vincenzo Taglioni, who replied that he considered the Count's case 'difficult – but I will not say, desperate'.

'I have diligently examined your letter and taken advice of it and I say frankly that you are in the right. But all depends on proving to others that you are as right as I believe you to be.'

For this purpose, the advocate continued, it would first be necessary to prove that the Gambas, father and son, had been banished to Pisa, and that Teresa had gone there with them, that Byron was also living there; and that 'there was proof from public report of amorous intercourse'.

'With such proofs as these I am of opinion that we can be very hopeful . . . With all sincerity, however, I cannot conceal that the person whom I have consulted, before entering into details, has mentioned the great expense you will incur. You will know how to manage the business, as you are a man of the world.'⁵²

Apparently, however, the Count considered that the expense (in other words, a bribe) was worth incurring, for very soon afterwards he sent to the Pope a long petition. In this he pointed out that His Holiness's rescript

'permitted the Contessa Teresa Gamba to be separated from her husband and live with her father, Conte Ruggero Gamba, *ut ea laudabile ratione vivat, quae honestam nobilem mulierem a viro seniunctam decet* (that she may live the worthy life which becomes an honest and noble wife separated from her husband).'⁵³

But, said the Count, Teresa's first step on leaving her husband's house

'was not to go to her father's house and stay there, but she went instead to a country-house near which also lived an English gentleman who was fond of the company of the said Teresa, and had her waited upon and served by his own servants.'

Moreover, he added, Teresa's father and brother were now living in Pisa,

'and in common with them live the aforesaid Contessa Teresa and the English gentleman. What sort of life the Contessa is leading in Pisa, and what the public opinion about her is, Your Holiness may easily learn at Your leisure, by asking the Archbishop of that city. . . .'

'On such evidence,' the Count concluded, 'it does not seem just that the petitioner should pay to such a wife the allowance promised to her in accordance with the provisional Rescript . . . But merely out of leniency towards her, the most that should be accorded to her, would be the interest on 3000 silver scudi, which is the portion of her dowry which I received, and still retain . . . It is repugnant not only to the Rescript but to every law, that a wife separated from her husband should be supported by him however and wherever her fancy and luck may take her.'[54]

Soon after this petition the Count, who had got a spy among Byron's servants,* from whom he received regular reports, was able to send the further news that, the Gamba family having been told to leave Pisa, Teresa was now actually living under the same roof with Byron, in a villa at Montenero, near Leghorn. And at last Guiccioli was successful: on July 11th the Pope, 'in order to dissuade the imprudent young woman from a life which, she boasted, made her happy', revoked his earlier Rescript and suspended Teresa's allowance.

The 'villeggiatura' at Montenero, where Byron and Teresa stayed from the end of May to the beginning of July, was not wholly agreeable. The Villa Dupuy – a large, square, 'flimsy-built villa' of a deep salmon colour, – 'the hottest-looking house', in Leigh Hunt's opinion, that he had ever seen, – stood at the end of a long, dusty road in the suburbs of Leghorn. It had a fine garden, which Teresa described as containing simultaneously, in full bloom, roses and jasmin, heliotrope and tuberoses – and a great terrace from which Byron could see 'the islands of Elba and Corsica – and my old friend the Mediterranean rolling blue at my feet'.[55] Here Byron and Teresa spent their evenings, playing draughts (but Byron cheated) and watching the little fishing-boats in the bay – and, on June 17th, saw across the harbour, the flickering lights of the Pisa 'Luminara' in the distance.†

The summer, unfortunately, was an unusually hot one – another token, in Teresa's eyes, of 'the evil fate conspiring against our peace' – and though they tried to counteract the glare in their hot rooms ('ten times hotter', wrote Trelawny, 'than the old solid palazzo he had left') by hanging damp green boughs against the window, and to refresh themselves by eating a succession of water-ices, the heat told heavily upon their health and spirits. Moreover in June the water-supply gave out, so that every drop, 'even for the most common domestic uses',[56] had to be fetched on muleback from a spring in the hills, over a mile away. This gave rise to a long and tedious law suit between Byron and the owner of the villa, Francesco Dupuy, in the course of which Byron characteristically refused to pay to his lawyers the security for costs required of

---

* Elliot Papers. The spy was Gaetano Forestieri, Byron's cook. Two of his letters were forwarded by Guiccioli to Taglioni.

† The Pisa 'Luminara', which took place every year on the feast of S. Ranieri, consisted in an illumination, by little oil lamps, of all the chief churches and houses.

all foreigners, but eventually allowed a Maltese shopkeeper of Leghorn to pay it for him. He also instructed Lega Zambelli to complain in writing that his opponent's advocate had referred to him as 'Signore' instead of using his proper title of 'Lord'. 'If the rank of my master', Zambelli wrote, 'is not stated in future documents, he intends to make a diplomatic protest, through his Minister.'[57]

As if these annoyances were not enough, Count Gamba, who had gone to Florence for the Masi trial, to try and free his servant Maluchielli, was constantly writing long, querulous letters about the tyranny of the Tuscan Government. As the trial dragged on, Gamba received an increasingly strong impression that the delays were deliberate, while the Government was looking for some pretext to aim, through his friends and their servants, at Byron himself. No further permits were granted to the Gambas, but they were told that they might go to Montenero 'provisionally, without any papers'.[58]

All this left Teresa in a state of constant apprehension, while Byron was both exasperated and bored. Moreover it is clear from Teresa's account that he was at this time sunk in one of his dark moods of melancholy. Only a month earlier, on April 22nd, the news had reached him of the sudden death of Allegra – and although now he never spoke of the child, he went on brooding over her loss – and, in spite of his asseverations to the contrary, not without some qualms of conscience.*

Teresa's account of the child's death in the 'Vie' adds little to what she told to Moore, but a number of letters to Lega Zambelli and Fletcher from Pellegrino Ghigi – Byron's banker at Ravenna, who had been left in charge of Allegra's expenses – show that several reports of her illness were sent to Pisa.[59] On April 13th, after she had already had several attacks of 'little slow fevers', Dr. Rasi – believing her to be suffering from a consumptive attack – ordered her to be bled three times. On the 15th she was considered to be out of danger, but, wrote Ghigi, 'I assure you that she has been very ill, of a dangerous illness'. He went to see her and found her 'in her little bed in a fine room', surrounded by three doctors and by all the nuns, asking for 'some tender cheese'. 'If there is any fault, it is of too much care.'

Byron, according to Teresa, was 'very much agitated' by this account and at once sent off a courier to Bagnacavallo, asking for

---

* L.J., VI, p. 54. April 23rd, 1822. 'I do not know that I have anything to reproach in my conduct,' he told Shelley, 'and certainly nothing in my feelings and intentions towards the dead. But it is a moment when we are apt to think that, if this or that had been done, such event might have been prevented.'

more details and telling the nuns to call in Professor Tommasini of Bologna, if necessary. But it plainly never occurred, either to him or to Teresa, to go to the child themselves – and on the 20th Ghigi was sending Lega Zambelli the news of her death, – 'after a convulsive catarrhal attack'. 'I am so upset', he added, 'by this misfortune that I wish I had never met the Noble Lord.'

At Bagnacavallo, where the nuns had made much of 'Allegrina', the strange, pretty child who had come to them from the great world of fashion and sin, a tradition lingered that on August 10th – four months too late – Byron had come to visit the convent under an assumed name.

'I remember', said an old woman who had lived nearby as a child, 'that one day we heard loud cries from the convent, and people said it was Mylord lamenting the child's death and reproaching the Sisters, because they had not told him of her illness. I myself saw the poor gentleman. I thought him a good-looking man, with curly hair and blue eyes. I noticed that he could not walk very well.'[60]

This story appears to be completely apocryphal. Far from going to Bagnacavallo himself, Byron even refused to receive the two messengers (one of them a priest) who had brought poor little Allegra's embalmed body to Leghorn, and who had made the journey in order to be able to give him a full account of her illness. They returned to Bagnacavallo 'greatly mortified, and I too', wrote Ghigi, 'blush to think that one day (for now it is being concealed) it will be known that they were refused admittance. I am prepared to believe that Mylord is very sensitive and deeply grieved, but I also recognize that every man has his own self-respect . . . and sorrow must not make one forget one's manners towards others'.[61]

The good nuns of Bagnacavallo – one of whom took to her bed with grief after Allegra's death – made a little statue of her, 'to preserve the memory of a most lovable child', and dressed it in her own clothes – 'a chemise, a silken dress, a little fur tippit and a chain of gold round her neck'.[62] She had died, they said, because she was 'too intelligent to live'; never had they had so gifted and promising a pupil. A fragment of Byron's Peer's robe, sent by him to the convent to be made up into a frock for his daughter, was afterwards used as a cope for one of the Canons. And Allegra's little waxen statue of the Madonna – dressed in puce-coloured silk, with gold braid and a golden crown – was given by the nuns to another of their little pupils, called Elettra Malagola, who treasured it until her death and bequeathed it to her daughter.⁶³ By her, in 1943 it was saved from the ruins of their bombed house during the war, and is now in my possession – probably the last tangible link with Allegrina.

It is, of course, possible to make a sweeping condemnation of Byron's attitude to Allegra – to accuse him of heartlessness and indifference. But perhaps the truth was not so simple. The references to the child in his letters and Teresa's, and especially the frequent ones in the 'Vie', as well as Byron's correspondence about her with Scott and Hoppner, show a complete masculine unawareness of a small child's character or needs – but not deliberate neglect, still less indifference. In this, as in many other human relationships, his cynicism and indifference were a form of bravado; he felt, as Moore had perceived, 'more naturally than he will allow'.⁶⁴ He was a man capable of both cruelty and real kindness; he was cruel in cold blood, or if stirred to the self-defensive sadism which hysterical appeals from women awoke in him; but more often, – and this is a trait as to which, in particular, all his Italian observers have agreed – he could be kind, with a quick, warm generosity. With Allegra, as with everyone else, he was an egotist; but many an egotist has loved his children dearly, as projections of himself. The trouble was that Allegra was a most disconcerting little mirror. If sometimes she pleased him by seeming 'a true Byron', she had also all the traits which Byron most disliked in himself: the tendency to mockery and malice, the violent temper, the wilfulness. 'Obstinate as a mule and ravenous as a vulture, who thinks herself handsome, and will do as she pleases.'⁶⁵ A spoiled man and a spoiled child – or rather a man and a child who had been both over and under indulged – could hardly be expected to live happily in the same house. Byron petted the child as long as she was amiable; sent her to scream and kick upstairs with the maids, as soon as she was not – or, above all, as soon as she reminded him of Claire⁶⁶ – and, in the end, packed her off to her convent-school, in a genuine belief that she would receive a wiser upbringing there than under the erratic care of the Shelleys, or exposed to the hysterical affection of her mother.

Moreover, in the queer mixture of his feelings for Allegra – bravado, affection, impatience, guilt – there was also a feeling of resentment (unjust, but not wholly unnatural), on behalf of that other child of his, whom he could never see. Allegra, the little bastard, drove in his carriage and sat on his knee, but it was Ada's birthday that he noted in his journal; Ada's miniature that stood on his writing-desk; Ada's education, her disposition and her future, that were always on his lips. It needed Allegra's death for her to find a place in the world of his imagination, so much more real to him than the actual one; only then did she acquire for him – for a short time – the reality that she had lacked when she was alive. This, I fancy, is what Byron meant when he said to Lady Blessington that his imagination, like that of all poets, was warmer than his heart.

'We are always so much more occupied by the ideal than the present, that we forget all that is actual . . . But', he added, 'let the object of affection be snatched away by death, and how is all the pain ever inflicted on them avenged! The same imagination that led us to slight or overlook their sufferings, now that they are forever lost to us, magnifies their estimable qualities . . . How did I feel this when my daughter, Allegra, died! While she lived, her existence never seemed necessary to my happiness; but no sooner did I lose her, than it appeared to me as if I could not live without her.'⁶⁷

He shut himself away from Teresa, brooding on all this, and letting his thoughts drift back from Allegra's unhappy childhood to his own, and to his days at Harrow. He wrote to Murray to tell him that he had had the child's body embalmed, and was sending it ('in what ship I know not' – but Teresa was seeing to the details) to be buried under the large elm tree 'where I used to sit for hours and hours when a boy'.⁶⁸ And then his thoughts went back again to Teresa, – sitting downstairs at that moment, in the darkened drawing-room in the heat, waiting for him. What would he feel, he wondered, if *she* died?

'How much more severely would the death of Teresa afflict me with the dreadful consciousness that while I had been soaring into the fields of romance and fancy, I had left her to weep over my coldness or infidelities of imagination! . . . It is a dreadful proof', he added sententiously, 'of the weakness of our natures, that we cannot control ourselves sufficiently to form the happiness of those we love, or to bear their loss without agony.'⁶⁹

But still he did not go downstairs, to join her.
It was during this unhappy time that he received a short visit from 'his earliest and best friend', Lord Clare. 'As I have always loved him better than any (*male*) thing in the world, I need hardly say what a melancholy pleasure it was to see him for a *day* only.'⁷⁰

Of all the men who called themselves Byron's friends, Clare was the only one whose friendship he himself never denied.

'As to friendship, it is a propensity in which my genius is very limited. I do not know the *male* human being, except Lord Clare . . . for whom I feel anything that deserves the name. All my others are men-of-the-world friendships. I did not even feel it for Shelley, however much I admired and esteemed him . . . I have had, and may have still, a thousand friends, as they are called, in *life*, who are like one's partners in the waltz of this world – not much remembered when the ball is over.'⁷¹

On this occasion, according to Teresa, his parting with Clare was clouded not only by sadness, but by a heavy sense of foreboding.

' "I have a presentiment that I shall not see him again," he said, and his eyes filled with tears. I saw the same melancholy come over him during the first weeks after Lord Clare's departure, whenever the conversation turned upon his friend.'⁷²

His melancholy was temporarily dispelled by a flattering incident, at a party given for him by the officers of the American Squadron, which had just arrived in Leghorn.

'As I was going away, an American Lady took a rose from me (which had been given to me by a very pretty Italian lady that very morning) because, she said, "she was determined to take something which I had about me, to America" . . . I would rather', he added, 'have a nod from an American, than a snuff-box from an emperor.'⁷³

At Montenero, too, an occasional American tribute came to break the monotony of the long, hot days. A young scholar, Mr. Bancroft, came to call and was presented with a copy of *Don Juan*; and for several days Byron and Teresa sat for their portraits to an American artist, Edward West. On the first day Byron was silent, 'assuming a countenance as though he were thinking of a frontispiece for *Childe Harold*', but later on, giving way to the 'incontinence of speech' which Lady Blessington considered his besetting sin, he regaled his visitor with 'the whole history of his connection with the Countess, and said he hoped it would last for ever'. West, plainly an impressionable young man, was greatly struck by his first glimpse of Teresa.

'While I was painting, I heard a voice exclaim "E' troppo bello!" I turned, and discovered a beautiful female stooping down to look in. Her long golden hair hung about her face and shoulders; her complexion was exquisite, and her smile completed one of the most romantic-looking heads I had ever beheld.'

Before leaving, however, West told Byron that, in his opinion, he was not a happy man.

'He inquired earnestly what reason I had for thinking so; and I asked him if he had never observed in little children, after a paroxysm of grief, that they had at intervals a convulsive or tremulous manner of drawing in a long breath. Wherever I had observed this in persons of whatever age, I had always found that it came from sorrow.'[74]

But the American fleet sailed away, and Mr. West packed up his easel – and Byron and Teresa (except for an occasional brief visit from Pietro Gamba) were once again thrown upon their own resources. To Lady Blessington, only a few weeks later, he expressed the theory that such a *tête-à-tête* was the happiest of all forms of existence.

'We are all better in solitude . . . I do not mean the solitude of country neighbourhoods; where people pass their time *à dire, redire et médire*. No! I mean a regular retirement with a woman that one loves, and interrupted only by a correspondence with a man that one esteems.'[75]

But when, in actual fact, he found himself leading such an existence, his spirits sank extremely low. It was not only that he was sometimes bored by Teresa – and certainly not that he had ceased to feel affection for her. On the contrary, all the evidence points to his having shown her – except in waves of moodiness or exasperation – a more simple kindliness than ever before. Medwin has described them sitting together (a few weeks later), in the shade of the orange trees of Palazzo Lanfranchi, while he called her his *piccinina*[76] – and even Hunt, the least well-disposed of all their observers, was forced to admit that he had seen Teresa 'both smile very sweetly, and look very intelligently, when Lord Byron had said something kind to her'.[77] Now, as in the early days at La Mira, her chief charm for him was her warm-hearted naturalness. 'I feel with an Italian woman as if she was a full-grown child, possessing the buoyancy and playfulness of infancy with the deep feelings of womanhood.'[78]

But a full-grown child, with the feelings of a woman, is an exacting companion; and Byron was now, very often, too tired to respond.

'The truth is, my habits are not those requisite to form the happiness of any woman. I am worn out in feelings, for, though thirty-six, I feel sixty in mind, and am less capable than ever of those nameless attentions that all women, but, above all, Italian women, require.'[79]

He could not, simply could not, keep up the eternal stream of tenderness, of endearments, of little kindnesses which, Teresa said, 'made the world a Paradise for me'. He was 'distrait and gloomy' at meals; he forgot to bring her any flowers; he shut himself up for longer and longer hours in his study – and came out, to find her in tears.

'We witness, without the power of alleviating, the anxiety and dissatisfaction our conduct occasions. We are not so totally unfeeling as not to be grieved at the unhappiness we cause, but this same power of imagination transports our thoughts to other scenes.'[80]

The scene to which they were now transported was, once again, South America. He sent a letter to Edward Ellice, asking for information about the opportunities there ('is it true that for a few thousand dollars a large tract of land may be obtained?'),[81] and with the members of his household he discussed the subject so freely that Guiccioli wrote to his lawyer to inform him that Byron was sailing to America in the *Bolivar*.[82]

Teresa, who loyally ascribed this new plan to 'a profound disgust in Byron's loyal and noble soul' at the lack of freedom in Europe, took it for granted that she and her brother would both go with him. 'Neither of them would have hesitated to cross the Atlantic.'[83] But nothing in Byron's letters suggests that he had any such intention.

'I had, and still have, thoughts of South America,' he wrote some weeks later to Moore, 'but am fluctuating between it and Greece. I should have gone, long ago, to one of them, but for my liaison with Countess G.i. *She* would be delighted to go too, but I do not choose to expose her to a long voyage, and a residence in an unsettled country.'[84]

Yet it was becoming increasingly evident that the Gamba family, at least, would have to go somewhere – since they would not be allowed to stay on in Tuscany. By the end of June Count Ruggero and Pietro had also arrived at Montenero, after an unsatisfactory conclusion of the Masi trial and the banishment, in spite of his innocence, of their servant Maluchielli. But they still had no permit to reside at Montenero. Their servants quarrelled unceasingly with Byron's, and the cook, Gaetano Forestieri, who was in Guiccioli's pay, wrote to him to complain that 'Count Pietro and his sister made themselves so much the masters in the house of Mylord, that there is no living there ... Every day', he added, 'something new happens.'[85]

The most recent incident – one which Torelli refers to as 'a scene of the sort that Byron has stirred up in every place where he has been'[86] – was started by a Romagnole servant of Byron's, Papi, who, having been sent to fetch water from the spring, suddenly refused to do so, and 'began declaiming', says Teresa, 'against the rich and the aristocracy, and speaking of equality and fraternity'.[87] The other servants crowded round, crying and shouting; Pietro came out to see what all the noise was about, and gave some peremptory orders; Papi drew his knife and appears to have grazed Pietro's arm; he pulled out his pistol; Byron, from the balcony, threatened to fire upon the whole pack – and at last the police was sent for, to re-establish order. Long before their arrival, however, the scene was over. The chief culprit, according to Teresa, 'was walking up and down by the front door, alternatively sobbing and swearing', – and it was precisely at this moment that a new and malicious British observer arrived upon the scene. Leigh Hunt, after long delays and a most trying journey, already disposed to consider every Italian a scoundrel and to wonder whether he was wise to have brought his Marianne and their brood to such a country, observed with a startled eye the reconciliation scene: Teresa 'flushed, her eyes lit up and her hair streaming as if in disorder' – Pietro with his arm in a sling – the culprit (of 'a most sinister aspect, and meagre – a proper caitiff') imploring Byron's forgiveness and receiving his hand to kiss – and finally, later on, Shelley presenting the man with some money 'out of his very disgust; for he thought nobody would help such a fellow if he did not'.[88]

The whole absurd incident gave the Government the pretext they had been waiting for. Byron's courier and Gamba's valet were immediately exiled, and the Gambas were warned that unless they left the country within three days, a final sentence of banishment would be passed on them. Whereupon Byron at once

wrote to the Governor of Leghorn that he preferred to leave the
State himself, in their company. 'I will not remain any longer in
a place where my friends are persecuted, and a refuge is denied to
the unfortunate.'⁸⁹ He asked, however, for a short delay, so that
he might first settle his affairs – and meanwhile the whole party
returned to Pisa.

————

Here tragedy awaited them. At midnight on July 13th Teresa,
who was standing on her balcony in Palazzo Lanfranchi with her
maid, looking out at the moonlight on the Lungarno, saw a carriage come hurrying up to the door. The maid called: 'Who is it?'
– 'Me – Mary Shelley – pray open at once.' Teresa hurried down:
Mary, 'as white as marble', stood in the doorway. 'Where is he?
'Sapete alcuna cosa di Shelley?' But they knew nothing – and poor
Mary and Jane Williams got into their carriage again, and drove
on through the night to Leghorn. It was only after another five
days of torturing uncertainty, when the two bodies were at last
washed up upon the shore, that they were certain of the truth.*
The rest of the tragedy, up to the final burning of the bodies on
the Tuscan shore, is too well known, and too indirectly connected
with this story, to be repeated here. But certainly Shelley's death,
which so deeply changed the lives of all the members of that little
community, affected Byron and Teresa no less than the rest. 'The
fine spirit that had animated and held them together, was gone.'
The rest of Byron's stay in Pisa – nearly three months, until on
September 28th they set off for Genoa – was a time of waiting and
indecision. The Gambas, father and son, had been obliged to
leave Pisa at once, and were staying in Lucca, where Byron and
Teresa intended to join them. But Pietro, who had made a trip
to Lucca earlier in the spring, to find out whether their presence
would be welcome there, had then reported that the official he had
seen had been 'prodigal of courtesies and politenesses as of the
Holy Water of the Madonna – but nothing more', and that 'Byron
was much feared, as a gentleman of great merit, but too *warm*'.⁹⁰
Byron therefore now requested the British Minister, Dawkins,
to find out whether the Government of Lucca would allow the
Gambas to reside there permanently, and Byron as well – since
'Lord Byron is determined not to abandon a family to whom he
has been attached for a long period'.⁹¹

* 'Do you know anything about poor Shelley', wrote Pietro Gamba to Teresa from
Lucca on July 17th. 'I cannot think of him without horror – and have almost lost
hope. But who is looking after those poor women? I am afraid of their doing something desperate, and hope they are not being left alone.'

The Minister for Foreign Affairs of Lucca, Marchese Mansi, passed on the request to Queen Marie Louise with the comment:

'I have no intelligence as to the motives which have led the governments of Rome and Florence to exile the Count Gamba. All I know is that Lord Byron pays his court to Countess Guiccioli, daughter of Count Gamba, and that the said Lord is as much renowned for his poetic talents and literary culture as for his pernicious principles.'[92]

A further report sent to Marie Louise, a few days later, respectfully submitted that 'even if it should be decided to tolerate the presence of the Counts Gamba, the same would not be possible in the case of Baylon' [sic] owing to 'the fiery nature, great talents and financial resources' of the latter, and suggested that if it was desired to promote Mylord's departure, the simplest method would be 'to order the aforesaid Countess to seek a residence in another State'.[93]

For meanwhile Teresa – her father and brother having left – had moved into Palazzo Lanfranchi, a step which caused her relations some anxiety.

'I told you yesterday', wrote Pietro from Lucca, 'that your stay in casa Lanfranchi may be used as a weapon by the "guileful patrician"* [Guiccioli] and I still think so, especially if you were to remain there for some time without us. Take Mylord's advice . . . and decide something, but quickly.'[94]

At the same time Torelli's diary was irritably deploring that 'owing to the imbecility of the Governor . . . Madame Guiccioli still remains in Pisa, and Byron, too, shows no sign of leaving. On the contrary, he is expecting a certain Smith, another English Poet, who has arranged to write with him and with that other Englishman who likes to call himself an Atheist on his passport, [Shelley] a paper about the Italian Governments, which will be printed in England, in order to make his fortune.'[95]

The 'certain Smith' – whose arrival had indeed already taken place on that inauspicious day at Montenero – was Leigh Hunt, who, with his Marianne and their brood of six, was now firmly established on the ground floor of Palazzo Lanfranchi. They did not like it; they did not like Teresa; and Teresa did not like them. It was, indeed, hardly to have been expected. Mrs. Hunt – one

* The reference is to Monti's 'Mascheroniana' in which he calls Guiccioli 'quel sottile ravegnan patrizio – si di frodi perito. . . .'

of the most uncompromisingly British matrons who has ever set foot upon the Continent – was as intransigent in her middle-class independence as in her moral outlook. Everything about the life in Palazzo Lanfranchi was to her not only unfamiliar, but distasteful – and she did not hesitate to show it. Perhaps, indeed, if Teresa had been extremely cordial to her, if she had petted and praised the Hunt's dirty, ill-mannered and precocious children, Marianne might have been mollified. But Teresa and Byron did nothing of the kind. Teresa, who still knew very little English (while Marianne 'knew nothing of Italian, and did not care to learn it')⁹⁶ saw no reason for cultivating the acquaintance of this prolific, dowdy, middle-class Englishwoman, who pinched her lips in disapproval whenever they met. After a first formal introduction, she never set foot in the Hunt's apartment. And Byron's welcome, too, can hardly be described as cordial. 'Lord B.'s reception of Mrs. H. was – as S[helley] tells me – most shameful. She came into his house sick and exhausted, and he scarcely deigned to notice her, was silent, and scarcely bowed.'⁹⁷ Later on he did, apparently, make some attempts at friendly intercourse, but the tartness of Marianne's retorts (which her husband took for wit) 'reduced him to silence', while the eldest boy's glib self-reassurance pleased him as little as the second one's untimely frankness.⁹⁸ They were all, he complained, 'dirtier and more mischievous than Yahoos. What they can't destroy with their filth they will with their fingers'.⁹⁹ The Hunts' attitude to such matters was less fussy.

'Can anything be more absurd,' wrote Marianne in her Diary, 'than a peer of the realm and a *poet* making such a fuss about three or four children disfiguring the walls of a few rooms. The very children would blush for him – fye, Lord B. – fye!'¹⁰⁰

'Hunt's theory and practice', wrote Trelawny, 'were that children should be unrestrained until they were of an age to be reasoned with' – and consequently their shouts and yells, as well as the litter of their toys, took complete possession of the hall and marble staircase of the palazzo. But at that point their kingdom ended, for Byron trained his bulldog Moretto to stand growling at the top of the stairs. 'Don't let any Cockneys pass this way!'¹⁰¹

Before Hunt's arrival Byron had observed to Trelawny. 'You will find Leigh Hunt a gentleman in dress and address; at least he was so when I last saw him in England, with a taint of Cockneyism.'¹⁰² But perhaps in Italy the Cockneyism became more marked, for it was not long before Byron was writing to Murray:

'As to any community of feeling, thought or opinion between Leigh Hunt and me, there is little or none . . . I do not know what world he has lived in, but I have lived in three or four; and none of them like his Keats and Kangaroo *terra incognita*. Alas! Poor Shelley! how we would have laughed had he lived, and how we used to laugh now and then, at various things, which are grave in the Suburbs.'[103]

Nevertheless, so long as they were all together at Palazzo Lanfranchi, Byron did sometimes try to be friendly. In the mornings he would come down into the garden singing, and would call 'Leontius' at the window of Hunt's study. Teresa, 'with her sleek tresses', would sit with them under the orange trees, and smile good-naturedly at Hunt's literary Italian. (But in the 'Vie' she wrote that it was hardly intelligible, and that she had the greatest difficulty in not laughing in his face.) Byron would imitate Dr. Johnson ' "Why, sir," ' in a high mouthing way; there was always some joking going forward. And yet, says Hunt, 'it was not pleasant, it was not cordial. There was a sense of mistake on both sides'.[104]

The truth was that neither Hunt nor Byron were able for a moment to forget that the poorer poet – since Shelley's death – was wholly dependent upon the richer one. Hunt had come to Italy, at Shelley's bidding, to edit the new joint periodical, *The Liberal*, full of the highest hopes. 'We will divide the world between us, like the Triumvirate.' But Shelley died, *The Liberal*,[105] from the first number, was a failure – and there, in Pisa, were the Leigh Hunts, completely on Byron's hands.

'I was thrown, after Shelley's death, *per force*, on Lord Byron for his assistance; he even offered it; and bitter indeed, for the first time in my life, was the taste I then had of obligation.'[106]

Both Hunt and Marianne attempted to save their pride by the simple method of disavowing any gratitude. They did not feel grateful, they pointed out, for the apartment which Byron had put at their disposal, because the ground floor was the servants' floor, and, in any case, he himself did not make use of it;[107] they were not grateful for the furniture (which had been chosen by Shelley) because it was cheap.[108] Both of them were constantly on the lookout for any slight, real or imaginary. 'In England [Byron] never ventured upon a raillery. In Italy he soon began to treat me with it, and I was obliged, for both our sakes, to tell him I did not like it.'[109] If Byron was silent Hunt accused him of

X

ill-temper; if loquacious, he commented acidly that 'everybody was not prepared, like the Captain [Medwin] to be thankful for stories of the noble Lord and all his acquaintances'. [110]

'If Lord Byron appeared to be in good spirits', wrote Teresa in the 'Vie', 'Hunt called him heartless; if he took a bath, a sybarite. If he tried to joke with him, he was guilty of the insufferable liberties that a great nobleman will allow himself with a poor man. If he presented Hunt with numerous copyrights, with the sole intention of helping him, it could only be because he lacked an editor. If he was charitable, it was out of ostentation. If he was adored by the lady who regarded him as superior to the rest of humanity, it was because she had the soul of a slave and a mediocre intelligence. And finally, when he sacrificed all that he cared for, to serve the Greek cause, it was because he was tired of the sentimentality of Mme Guiccioli.' [111]

Any last hope of friendly relations between the two families was destroyed when Hunt discovered in what a tone Byron had been writing about him and his family, to friends in England.

'I had scarcely put up under the same roof with his lordship, than our "host", if he can be so called, commenced his claims upon our delicacy by writing disagreeable letters about us to his friends.'

The nature of Byron's comments was revealed by Theodore Hook in his review of the first number of *The Liberal*: ' "Hunt is a bore, he is," says his Lordship, "a proser; Mrs. Hunt is no great things; and their six children perfectly intractable." ' [112] To all this Hunt – when the time came — did not fail to retaliate. Lord Byron's mistress, he said, was nothing but 'a kind of buxom parlour-boarder, compressing herself artificially into dignity and elegance, and fancying she walked, in the eyes of the whole world, a heroine by the side of a poet', [113] and her feelings for Byron were alloyed by 'a good deal of the self-love natural to a flattered beauty'. [114] Moreover he described at length not only the light and coarse way in which he [Byron] would speak about her, but Teresa's own querulous jealousy and complaints. '"There was no real love', he concluded, 'on either side.' [115]

Teresa, for her part, described Hunt in the 'Vie', as 'cette sombre figure de l'ingrat et du calomniateur', – and added that after looking at 'his low forehead, his sinister expression and the vulgarity of his whole person', she remarked to Byron that she was now inclined to believe in the 'humiliating theory' of our descent from animals.[116] As to her alleged complaints, she observed with some verisimilitude that if she had ever wished to indulge in any, she would hardly have chosen Hunt as her confidant – and that in any case they had no more than a few words of any language in common. 'Tout cela', she sums up in the fly-leaf of her copy of Hunt's book, 'est un chef d'œuvre de méchanceté, qui n'a d'égal que dans l'énormité du mensonge.'

For nearly three months this inharmonious party lived together at Palazzo Lanfranchi, with all their tempers growing thinner. During the first weeks Byron went on hoping that the Gambas might be allowed to return to Pisa, or even to Ravenna; then, as that hope failed, and it became evident that their prolonged residence in Lucca – which, besides, was full of English people – would be equally unwelcome, he took the advice of Mr. Hill, the British Minister in Genoa, and decided to go there.

Byron's last visitor in Pisa – his *alter ego*, Hobhouse – arrived shortly before their departure. His arrival was, for Byron, the happiest event for many months.

'We were sitting one evening in the garden of Palazzo Lanfranchi,' records Teresa. 'A soft melancholy was spread over his [Byron's] countenance; he recalled to mind the events of his life, and compared them with his present situation, and with that which it might have been if his affection for me had not caused him to remain in Italy, saying things which would have made this earth a paradise for me, if I had not already been tormented by the possibility of losing so much happiness. At that moment a servant announced Mr. Hobhouse. The slight shade of melancholy on Lord Byron's face gave instant place to the liveliest joy; but it was so great, that it almost deprived him of his strength. A fearful paleness came over his cheeks, and his eyes were filled with tears, as he embraced his friend. His emotion was so great that he was forced to sit down.'[117]

Hobhouse's own account is considerably dryer. He observed that Byron was 'much changed – his face fatter, and the expression of it injured',[118] and remarked that they were both at first 'a little formal'. Moreover, he maintained an attitude of supercilious detachment and disapproval towards every aspect of Byron's life in Italy. The Ravenna insurrection, in his record, appears as little more than one of the caprices that kept Byron busy and amused, although in an unworthy cause. 'The Romagnoles are a testy and shabby people.'[119] And his relationship with Teresa was treated with little more respect. 'It seems Madame Guiccioli and her father and brother lived together in a house apart until the Gambas went to prepare Lord Byron's house at Genoa. This is Italian morality.'[120] Byron retorted by repeating to Hobhouse a remark of Tom Moore's: 'Hobhouse is praised by everybody, but he is a companion I would sooner praise than live with.'[121]

Nevertheless, when the moment for parting came, both friends were moved. 'Hobhouse', said Byron, 'you should never have come, or you should never go.' Teresa gave Hobhouse some letters of introduction in Florence and, after his departure, sent him another to her aunt, Marchesa Sacrati, in Rome, with a letter which shows how anxious she was to be on good terms with him.

'Mylord, after having suffered from his rheumatism for two days, is now much relieved by a cure suggested by Vaccà',* to whom he has subjected himself with a docility so unlike him on similar occasions, that I do not know to what to attribute it, except to your wise advice. And this effect is so great a comfort to me, that I shall not be able to help wishing for your presence, to keep him in such a good frame of mind, like a good genius – even if I were not already moved to wish it by your unusual qualities, and by the pleasure of seeing Byron happier.'[122]

A few days later, on September 28th, the whole Pisa party – Byron and Teresa by land, and Trelawny with the Hunts by sea – set off for Genoa. For the last time, Byron's name is recorded in Torelli's diary.

'Mylord has at length decided to leave for Genoa. It is said that he is already tired of his new favourite, the Guiccioli. He has expressed his intention of not remaining in Genoa, but of going on to Athens to purchase adoration from the Greeks.'[123]

---

* Andrea Vaccà' Berlinghieri (1772-1826), a very famous doctor and surgeon of Pisa. A great friend of the Gambas, he also attended Byron and – after her arrival in Pisa – Mrs. Hunt, whom he declared to be dangerously ill and consumptive (she survived him, however, by thirty-six years). Hunt, in spite of his invincible prejudice against all Italians, was obliged to admit that he had 'a pleasing intelligent face, and was the most gentlemanlike Italian I ever saw'. (*Autobiography*, III, pp. 12-13.)

Regain'd my freedom with a sigh.
The Prisoner of Chillon.

THE journey to Genoa was not a pleasant one. It might have been expected, after so much friction at Pisa, that Byron, and still more Teresa, would have been only too glad to leave the Hunts behind them. But Byron was still committed to *The Liberal*; the Hunts had no other means of support; and so he wryly made the best of taking the whole 'kraal' with him. 'The death of Shelley left them totally aground; and I could not see them in such a state without using the common feelings of humanity, and what means were in my power, to set them afloat again.'¹

The preparations for the journey took place in the poet's usual manner. 'If the Palazzo Lanfranchi had been on fire at midnight', wrote Trelawny, 'it could not have been worse.'²

'Not only did Byron wish to travel patriarchally,' explained Teresa, 'without leaving his menagerie behind, but he also wished to provide generously for the furnishing of the second house he had taken at Albaro, for the Hunts. The arrangements for the transportation of all these effects across rivers and mountains, over bad roads, and with all the complicated customs regulations then in force, required a great deal of time and patience.'³

Byron's menagerie, moreover, on this occasion included three large geese – since he feared he would not be able to procure any on his travels, and insisted on eating one on Michaelmas day, 'otherwise the year would be fatal'. They swung in a cage behind his carriage, punctuating the journey with their cackling. But when the time came to wring their necks, he would not give the order, and decided instead to keep them, 'to test the theory of their longevity'. 'On arriving in Genoa, they at once became the guardians and mistresses of the yard, as sacred as those of the Capitol', and waddled about in the garden and the lower floor of the house, accompanying Byron wherever he went. 'Plus d'une fois il est entré chez Madame Guiccioli, précédé par ces reconnaissants volatiles.'⁴

The 'caravan', geese and all, halted for a few days at Lucca, where Ruggero and Pietro Gamba were awaiting them, and Byron and Teresa were both invited to a gala evening at the theatre. This Byron declined, presumably from his usual morbid dread of encountering English acquaintances, and Teresa followed his example. 'She had lost', she comments rather sadly, 'all the tastes of her youth and of her country.'⁵

The road over the Apennines was so bad that it was decided to go to Lerici for one night and to proceed from there by sea to Sestri. At Lerici they were joined again by all the Hunts and Trelawny, who had come by sea in the *Bolivar*, and Byron was unfortunately moved to try a swimming-match with the Pirate. 'We were to swim to the Yacht, dine in the sea alongside of her, treading water the while, and then return to the shore.'⁶ The programme was carried out – the dinner including a bottle of ale – and was not unnaturally followed, for Byron, by a violent chill and bilious attack, which kept him in bed for four days 'in the worst inn's worst room', dosing himself out of Thomas's *Domestic Medicine*. 'How do you feel?' inquired Trelawny. 'Feel! why, just as that damned obstreperous fellow felt chained to a rock, the vultures gnawing my midriff, and my vitals, too.'⁷

At last, however, the whole party was able to proceed – by sea, as far as Sestri, and in three boats – one for Byron and Teresa, one for Trelawny, and a third for Hunt and his family. 'It was pretty', wrote Hunt, 'to see the boats with their white sails, gliding by the rocks over that blue sea' – and Byron, in one of his sudden gusts of high spirits, 'ate the Sailor's cold fish and drank a Gallon of country wine'.⁸ But poor Mrs. Hunt, who, after her voyage from England, had hoped 'never to see the sea again as long as I live', was not so happy, and was overcome with terror when, on landing at Sestri, 'a dozen odiously dirty men with beards unshaven and long shaggy hair, up to the middle in water, began fighting for me and Mr. H. to carry us through the water. What lovely sea-nymphs!'⁹

Late that same night, Byron and Teresa arrived in Genoa. The villa that Pietro had taken for them was at Albaro, on a hill outside the town, and had a fine view of the harbour. It was large enough to contain two entirely separate apartments – as Teresa is again careful to emphasize – one for the Gamba family, and one for Byron himself, while the Villa Negrotto, which the Hunts were to share with Mary Shelley, was some little distance down the hill.

Any pleasure that Teresa might have felt over her new abode was destroyed, she says, by the sense that it was only provisional, and also by the imminent arrival of the Hunts. He, 'with his six little blackguards', was still crossing the Apennines, which he described as 'great doughy billows, like so much pudding or petrified mud', while Marianne performed most of the journey with her eyes shut, 'as the carriage went within a yard or not so much of some frightful precipice'.¹⁰ On their arrival, they were not entirely pleased with their new residence; for although Hunt enjoyed writing about 'the marble steps to the staircase and a marble terrace over the portico', and observed that 'it would be fit for a nobleman in England', Marianne considered that 'the number and size of the doors and windows made it look anything but *snug*'.¹¹ She was feeling very ill, poor woman, for the journey had brought on again the bad cough from which she suffered. One great – and surprising – consolation, however, was soon afforded her: 'To my comfort I have found an English washer-woman!'¹² And with this the diary closes.

According to Teresa, the routine of daily life at Casa Saluzzo was very much like life in Pisa – except that, mercifully, the Hunts were now more than a mile away. They were sharing the Casa Negrotto with Mary Shelley – who, lonely as she had been before their arrival, found their company at such close quarters more than a little trying. As winter approached the weather became very cold and the house held only one fireplace. 'So I am obliged to pass the greater part of my time in the Hunts' sitting-room, which is, as you may guess, the annihilation of study, and even of pleasure to a great degree. For, after all, Hunt does not like me; it is both our faults and I do not blame him, but so it is.'¹³

There was little association between the two houses. Very occasionally Hunt rode to Casa Saluzzo, prefacing his visits with letters of an embarrassing facetiousness, to show that he was quite at his ease. Teresa, whose dislike for him had become almost an obsession, hastily retreated into her own rooms, and the two men walked in the garden, 'endeavouring to joke away the conscious-ness of our position'. One evening, indeed, Hunt invited himself to dinner, and over their wine Byron paid his guest 'the com-pliment of being excited to his véry best feelings'; he even, when Hunt rose to go, held him back, saying 'Not yet!' But the next morning 'the happy moment had gone, and nothing remained but to despair and joke'.¹⁴ To this grim little story Teresa, in the margin of her copy of Hunt's book, has added the melancholy comment: 'C'est comme tout le monde!'

About once a month Teresa (but never Byron) went to the Casa Negrotto to call on Mary, and sometimes Mary – who was also doing some copying for Byron – came to Casa Saluzzo. But the two women had little in common, and each, besides, was shut away in the self-absorption of her own feelings – 'Mary entirely given up to her grief, and the Contessa to her exclusive affection.'¹⁵ Byron tried to be kind, but was irritated by the tinge of self-pity in Mary's unhappiness, and also by a certain prosaic, prim quality in her character. 'It contained', wrote Teresa, 'no spark of Utopism; she was "un esprit pratique".'[16] She wrote Byron long, priggish, self-righteous letters, reminding him that Hunt was 'after all, a very good man' – and at the same time she confided to her Journal that Byron's mere voice and presence evoked such painful memories that she could hardly bear to be with him. 'I do not think', she wrote after one of her visits, 'that any person's voice has the same power of awakening melancholy in me as Albé's. I have been accustomed, when hearing it, to listen and to speak little; another voice, not mine, ever replied – a voice whose strings are broken.'[17]

There is a moment in most men's lives when they become aware that the horizon, instead of stretching out indefinitely before them, as it does in youth, is closing in; when there is no longer a constant stream of new acquaintances to take the place of the friends removed by death, separation or attrition; when old ideas and affections have become stale, and new ones are too much trouble. At such times it is natural to seek, if not a new passion, at least a new game to play. Byron, who had never lacked 'an exceeding respect for the smallest current coin of any realm', now found – or at least sought – relief from tedium in 'the noble feeling of cupidity'.[18] From Pisa, early in 1822, he had written to Moore: 'They say that Knowledge is Power. I used to think so; but now I know that they meant money.' And by the time he had settled at Albaro, the 'due care of the needful' had come to absorb a large portion of his thoughts.

'You will perhaps wonder,' he told Kinnaird, 'at this recent and furious fit of accumulation and retrenchment, but it is not so unnatural . . . I always looked to about thirty as the barrier of any rich or fierce delight in the passions, and determined to work them out in the younger ore and better veins of the mine . . . And now the *dross* is coming, and I *loves lucre*. For we must love something . . . At any rate, then, I have a passion the more, and thus a feeling.'[19]

'I loves lucre.' Byron, in the way which unfailingly bewildered poor Teresa, was parodying himself. But for all that, he meant what he said. Among all the contradictions of his character, none is more curious than the mixture of prodigality and cheese-paring that governed his attitude towards money. And, as he grew older, – and much richer, for the death of Lady Milbanke, in 1822, brought him a share in the fortune of Annabella's uncle, the rich Lord Wentworth – the cheese-paring decidedly prevailed.

> So, for a good old gentlemanly vice
> I think I shall take up with avarice.[20]

Hunt, with the shrewdness that was sharpened by his spite, remarked that this couplet was intended for the public *not* to believe. 'They were to regard it only as a pleasantry, issuing from a generous mouth.'[21] Nevertheless, there was in it more than a little truth. The 'noble feeling of cupidity' had turned into a habit.

One day, when Trelawny came to call, he looked in at the open window of Byron's study and found him sitting 'with his papers before him, with a painfully puzzled expression and heated brow'. He was poring over Lega Zambelli's accounts. 'My tottle don't square with Lega's. In the time thus lost I might have written half a canto of *Don Juan* – and the amount of the bill is only 143 lire.'[22] He sent an exasperated little note to Teresa, to complain that someone had swindled him, saying that he was beginning to think the Italians quite as dishonest as the English: 'Some Italian, worthy of being an Englishman, has stolen 50 louis from me.'[23] He made a futile attempt to get back at least the interest on a loan of a thousand pounds, made ten years before, to his old acquaintance, Sir James Wedderburn Webster;* he argued with Trelawny about the upkeep of the *Bolivar* ('on the strength of what you will realize', wrote Trelawny, [from *The Liberal*] 'you can afford to keep us afloat'.[24] – and finally he quarrelled about money with both Mary Shelley and Hunt. Both of them ended by accusing him of meanness; but in the case of Hunt, this was certainly unfair. Byron advanced him (through Shelley) £150 before he ever left England, he gave him £250 in 1822 and another £300 within the next six months. Moreover he surrendered to him and his brother the copyrights of the *Vision of Judgement*, of *The Age of Bronze*, and of eight whole cantos of *Don Juan*. But the money, Hunt complained, was given to him 'in driblets', through Lega Zambelli – who may well have been unpleasant about it. 'What a pity it is', wrote Marianne, 'that the good actions of *noblemen* are not done in a *noble manner*! Aye, princely I would have them be!'[25] On the other hand Hunt himself admitted that 'the common rules of arithmetic were, by a singular chance, omitted in my education',[26] and his attempts to save his self-respect took the unfortunate form of couching his requests in the most arrogant of tones. 'I will trouble you for another "cool hundred" of your crowns.'[27] It is not surprising that Byron, who was not a patient

* The husband of Lady Frances Webster, whom Byron was in love with in 1813. Sir James had then taken the opportunity to borrow £1000 from Byron.

man, was soon exasperated to the point of frenzy. He had started
by asking Moore, 'You would not have had me leave him in the
street with his family, would you?'²⁸ and had refused, against the
united advice of Hobhouse, Murray and Moore, to dissociate
himself from *The Liberal*, because 'it would *humiliate* him – that
his writings should be supposed to be dead weight'!²⁹ But from
Albaro he was writing to Murray: 'I cannot describe to you the
despairing sensation of trying to do something for a man who seems
incapable or unwilling of doing anything for himself . . . It is like
pulling a man out of a river who directly throws himself in again.'³⁰

It was at this stage of their relations that Hunt, with the same
tactlessness that he had shown about his own affairs, attacked his
patron on Mary Shelley's behalf, threatening that, if Byron did
not immediately come to her aid, she would turn to Trelawny
instead. He could hardly have chosen a more unfortunate
argument. Byron, who had at first been fully disposed to be
generous, refusing the legacy that Shelley had left him and making
Mary 'frequent offers of money',³¹ now replied to Hunt with a
sharp and peevish refusal – which Hunt promptly showed to Mary,
while at the same time quoting some of Byron's unpleasant
remarks. According to Teresa, 'he told Mary that Byron had
often spoken of the insufferable tediousness of her visits, and had
said that he did not mind supplying her with money, but wished
he need never see her again'.³² Teresa, who genuinely disliked all
unpleasantness, was much distressed.

'*Dio buono!*' she wrote to Mary, 'I don't know what to say to you,
my dear, for I can't do anything. I feel that I can be of little use,
that L. B. will not take advice, that he is very much irritated. But
I also feel so much friendship for you, and so much gratitude –
for I shall never in my life forget the goodness you showed me
during a very trying time for me – and I venture to offer, if I can
do so in any way, to be of help to you. If only my usefulness and
my circumstances were as strong as my good will!'³³

Mary's reply is quoted in full in the 'Vie'.

MRS. SHELLEY TO CONTESSA GUICCIOLI³⁴

Dear Contessina, your letter has given me great pleasure. A
feeling of unfriendliness is so painful that it is a great relief to
me to find that the poison has not reached you, too.

I thank you warmly for your offer, but if I am to understand that you wish to be a peace-maker between me and Lord Byron, you will not succeed. I felt no repugnance at the idea of receiving obligations and kindnesses from a friend – and I imagined, or rather I flattered myself, that Lord B. would be glad to hold me not only by the ties of friendship, but by those of gratitude. But now all that is over – a man who does not esteem me cannot be my benefactor. Lord Byron having said that it would be disagreeable to him to see me, I cannot have the pleasure of calling on you, but I shall be delighted to see you here.

Again Teresa attempted to pour oil upon the waters, but in vain:

'To tell you the truth,' Mary answered, 'my awkward position weighs less heavily upon my heart than Lord Byron's expressions about me, and still more about Shelley. *From a friend* I would accept anything, and if he will show me the least sign of friendship and will again be *glad* to help me, I will feel a renewed obligation to him and be grateful.' [35]

But by now Byron was thoroughly exasperated. Mary turned for help to Trelawny instead – and when, a few months later, the *Hercules* sailed for Greece, she did not even see Byron to say good-bye. 'His unconquerable avarice prevented his supplying me with money, and a remnant of shame caused him to avoid me.' [36] To Teresa, however, shortly before Byron's departure, she wrote in a more cordial strain:

MRS. SHELLEY TO CONTESSA GUICCIOLI*

Dear Contessina: I truly feel the full value of your friendly feelings under these circumstances and am grateful to you . . . . It seems to me that you are almost more distressed by this bad business than I am myself. I have suffered so much that I have lost the capacity to be agitated by matters that only concern money. I am too poor to lose my friends as well – and if the friendship of Lord Byron has failed me, the rest is not worth much and could not be accepted by me. If Lord Byron will forget anything painful that he may have endured from me and on

* 'Vie', pp. 1372-3. Undated. Teresa implies that, after all, Byron did supply Mary with funds for her journey home, but this was not the case.

account of me, if he will recognize what Shelley deserves, it will
be with real pleasure that I shall wish him by word of mouth
what I now wish him by letter – a good voyage and all the success
that I feel sure his plans will have in Greece. Your cordial offers
have given me great pleasure and I am most sincerely your
affectionate friend   MARY SHELLEY

Meanwhile the long winter dragged on. Once or twice Byron
drove in to Genoa to dine with Mr. Hill [37] the British Minister, who
found him 'most delightful but most vindictive when he takes
dislikes'. Trelawny looked in fairly frequently – an unsettling
visitor, who showed only too clearly that he despised all Byron's
mode of life in Italy, which he considered was rendering him
'peevish, sickly and indifferent, and discontented with everything',
and who continually teased him with new plans. [38] Now and again
Mr. Barry – the worthy, punctilious English banker at Genoa [39] –
came to call and went away fascinated. (For it was the good, the
careful and the steady who could never resist Byron's charm.) He
wrote to Byron later on that he was under a great obligation to him,

'and so I shall always consider myself, in having been noticed by
you in the way I was, when hundreds and thousands would have
gladly done all I could do for you, merely for the pleasure of
saying that they had known Lord Byron. Don't take this my Lord
as flattery, for I hate and despise a flatterer. I would that you
knew how much I wish you well.' [40]

Early in the spring an old acquaintance, Sir James Wedderburn
Webster, turned up and delighted his host – whose own grey locks
were growing distinctly scanty – by being obliged to wear a curly
black wig and by looking considerably older than his age. Hunt's
eldest son, after this visit, broke into unmannerly guffaws, so often
did Byron introduce the word 'wig' into the conversation. Byron,
with Trelawny, returned the call at the Croce di Malta hotel in
Genoa – and looked up Webster's name in the visitors' book.
'Damn the fellow's presumption – look here – he is booked
Baronet and aged 32 – Why, he is much older than I am!' He
then took a pen and wrote *Knight* – aged 40 – and said, "Does he
think to hum – us with his black wig?" ' [41]
But none of these visitors really relieved Byron's tedium. The
winter, according to Teresa, was an unusually severe one – as cold
as the previous summer had been hot – and the great draughty
summer villa, with its stone floors and high ceilings, was, like Casa

Negrotto, 'far from snug'. December brought a series of floods, and on the 9th there was a violent thunder-storm, which Byron insisted on watching, with Teresa beside him, at an open window. 'Appuyée à son bras, elle puisait dans cet appui le courage de ne pas se montrer effrayée,'⁴² when the lightning actually fell on the lightning-conductor, immediately outside their window, half blinding and stunning them both. 'Madame Guiccioli was frightened, as you may suppose,' wrote Byron to Murray, adding that doubtless, if they had been killed, 'your bigots would have "saddled me with a judgment" '.⁴³

The two households were entirely separate, even for meals – since Byron greatly preferred reading to Teresa's chatter or to the prosy, if amiable, conversation of her father – and there seems to have been some tacit agreement by which Teresa did not even go into Byron's rooms without an invitation, but waited for him to call on her or join her in the garden.

Sometimes – but not very often – he would ask her to come and help him to entertain some traveller who had turned up with an introduction to him. On one such occasion the visitor – a friend of John Galt's – observed to Byron that he was much struck by 'the harshness of the Italian language'. Byron at once got up and went to fetch Teresa. 'I shall make her speak each of the principal dialects,' he said to his guest – and when Teresa had finished he inquired, 'Now what do you think?' But the listener's opinion remained unaltered, and in the letter in which he related the incident to Galt, he added his opinion of Teresa: 'In my eyes her graces did not rank above mediocrity. They were youth, plumpness and good nature.'⁴⁴

Sometimes, however, Byron and Teresa would not meet all day – and then they would exchange little domestic notes, from one part of the house to the other. He would tell her, one evening when he had been dining out, that he had 'got home safely, without delays or difficulties, don't be anxious',⁴⁵ or when he had caught a cold, that 'the doctor says the ailment may last some time, but will pass; the swelling under the eye is better'.* On another occasion he asked Teresa if she knew where he had put 'the little American edition of the *Prophecy of Dante*, with the translation by Da Prato'.⁴⁶

One day Teresa sent him a letter from her very devout aunt, Lucrezia Gamba, who had sent her a Life of Santa Teresa, with the comment that that was the true road to happiness.

* V. p. 476, letter No. 135, February 15th, 1823. Byron was subject this winter to attacks of inflammation of the face, and had a similar one in March, after dining out with the British Minister.

'By God,' Byron replied, 'your aunt is right – and I too would like to lead the life of Saint Catherine – and make the acquaintance of the "loving Jesuits". She [the devotee of St. Catherine] has found Happiness. She says so – and I believe her – and what else are we all seeking?'⁴⁷

In the mornings, if Byron was feeling sociable, he would take a short stroll with Teresa in the garden or down a steep cliff to the sea – or, if the weather was bad, they would inspect the menagerie. After dinner and a short siesta, Byron would go for his ride, spend another hour or two with Teresa in the evening, and then work for the greater part of the night. Such an existence – so Teresa repeats with an emphasis that suggests a lack of inner conviction – was the one, above all others, that suited Byron's *real* nature.

'He loved simple pleasures – sometimes solitude – always retreat. He was never tired today of what he had enjoyed yesterday . . . He felt no desire for movement nor activity, except for great purposes – then indeed he seemed lifted above the earth by mysterious wings of glory and virtue.'⁴⁸

Nevertheless, an old Italian friend of Teresa's, Giuliani, who came from Florence to stay with them during the winter, received the impression that they were all extremely bored. 'He was amazed that a man like Byron – so young – so handsome – so rich – could lead a life so monotonous and severe'⁴⁹ – and he hurried back, as soon as he decently could, to the more amusing life of the Florentine Carnival, and wrote Teresa a long account of the fancy-dress ball given by the British Colony, where Lady Londonderry had appeared as Cleopatra, covered with diamonds. 'Lord Byron', Teresa comments, 'had definitely given up all such futile pleasures,' – but there is a certain wistfulness in her tone.

She was, after all, even now only twenty-three – and she had always enjoyed gay parties. Surely sometimes her thoughts must have gone back to the Ravenna Carnival – to her coach-and-six on the Corso, and the cheerful, cosy Conversazioni, where every guest was a relation or an old acquaintance, and she herself the prettiest, gayest young bride of the party. Yet – for she was an amiable young woman after all, and really did not need much to be happy – she would have been contented enough, if all three of her companions had not been so restless. Count Ruggero, after nearly three years of exile, could think and talk of nothing but his return to the Romagna, to his children and his estates. His father,

Count Paolo, had appealed to the Pope on his behalf; many other exiles had already been allowed to return; and every day he hoped for the repeal of his banishment. In February, moreover, tragic news reached them from Ravenna: the sudden death of Teresa's younger sister Carolina, the prettiest and sweetest of all Count Ruggero's daughters. Byron should, of course, have hurried to Teresa to comfort her. But he did not like tears – and Teresa, in her sentimental, blundering way, was sure to talk, between her sobs, of Allegra. It was easier to send over an unconvincing, conventional little note of condolence – Teresa would probably take it at its face value.

'I cannot express to you my sorrow over your sister's death – but She is happy – it is the living who deserve compassion and sympathy – I have not come to you because I know – by sad experience – that in the first moments sorrow shrinks alike from comfort – from society – and even from friendship itself. And words – what are they? I pity you in silence – and recommend you to Heaven and to Time. Entirely yours*

Meanwhile this news increased Count Ruggero's anxiety to get home – and to take Teresa with him. He had surely been, he told her, the most tolerant of fathers; he had stood by her until now. But now it was time for her to help him, to come home and look after the younger sisters. It was only her duty – and it was also her interest, for how could she ask the Pope to restore her allowance, while still living under Byron's roof?

Pietro's restlessness was of a different kind. His bitter disappointment over the failure of the Romagna insurrection had left him disgusted with all Italian politics – but still, with his incurable hopefulness, he believed that the freedom and justice that he had failed to find at home, were to be met with elsewhere. 'His heart', says Teresa, 'had not yet awakened to any great affection'; there was nothing to keep him in Italy, everything to attract him abroad. First he had dreamed of Switzerland, then of America; then he had wanted to go to Spain as a volunteer; and now all his ardent hopes were centred upon Greece.

For already – although Teresa did not yet know it – Greece loomed upon the horizon.

The events which turned Byron's thoughts to Greece, and the fluctuations of his feelings, the strange mixture of motives, which

* This signature – 'tutto tuo' – was sometimes used by Byron at this time, instead of the old 'a.a. in e.' The note is undated.

Y

moved him at this time, have been admirably described else-where.[50] Here we are only concerned with them, in so far as they relate to the present story. Throughout the winter, Teresa says, she became increasingly and unhappily aware that for Byron Albaro was only a temporary halting-place, an inn upon the road. He told Captain Roberts that he was 'tired of this place, the shore, and all the people on it'.[51]

'I once', wrote Pietro Gamba, 'saw him nearly on the point of departure [for America]. He often felt the want of some other occupation than that of writing, and frequently said that the public must be tired of his compositions and that he was certainly more so.'[52] But where he should go next, he had still no idea. He played for a while with a plan of settling in the South of France; he thought of 'taking a run down to Naples (*solus*, or at most *cum sola*)'*, to gather material for two or more cantos of *Childe Harold*. 'He exhausted himself', says Trelawny, 'in planning, projecting, beginning, wishing, intending, postponing, regretting and doing nothing.'[53] Trelawny, who considered even the most foolish action better than inaction, lost patience, and went off for a riding-tour in the Maremma. But meanwhile – without Teresa's knowledge – Byron was already in correspondence with the Committee which had been formed in London, and had offered them his services, and in March he received a note from one of its members, Edward Blaquière, stating that he proposed to call on Byron, together with the Greek representative in London, Andreas Luriottis, on their way to Greece. Byron replied that he would be delighted to see them, 'and the sooner the better'.[54] But now the problem of Teresa had become urgent: something must be said to prepare her, before these gentlemen arrived. 'To this project', he wrote to Sir John Bowring, the secretary of the Greek Committee, in a letter in which he offered 'to go up into the Levant in person', 'the only objection is of a domestic nature, and I shall try to get over it; if I fail in this I must do what I can where I am, but it will always be a source of regret to me.'[55]

But, as Mary Shelley shrewdly remarked, Byron was always 'far more able to take a decided than a petty step in contradiction to the wishes of those about him . . . He does not seem disposed', she added, 'to make a mountain of her [Teresa's] resistance.'[56] And she, of course, had already begun to guess that something was in the wind.

* *L.J.*, VI, p. 157. 'I was glad', wrote Hobhouse, who had always disapproved of Teresa, 'to hear you thought of Nice, because a removal would be a means of entering upon a new course of life.' For he considered that Byron's health would never be good 'as long as you have daily demands of a certain nature upon your health and spirits'. March 2nd, 1823. Unpublished letter belonging to Sir John Murray.

'He had opened his heart', Teresa wrote, 'to the young Count
Gamba, asking him however not to say anything yet to his sister,
since, the letter being confidential, the decision was not yet
irrevocable. But the eyes of the heart penetrate most mysteries,
and she saw so unusual a preoccupation, and sometimes so great
a sadness, on his face, that she was very anxious. To quieten
and reassure herself she tried to imagine all sorts of possible
causes: the temporary nature of their stay in Genoa, the possible
necessity of her return to the Romagna to assert her rights, the
annoyance caused to him by Hunt and the disapproval that all
his friends felt of that unhappy collaboration, etc. etc.'[57]

But in her heart she knew well enough that none of these were
the real causes.

'One day when he was sitting beside her on the terrace which
looked out over the bay, he said, looking at her sadly: "I have
not even got a portrait of you which is like you. A miniaturist
has been recommended to me; will you sit to him for me?" She
could only answer him with her tears. On another day, seeing
him go down into the garden, she hurried to follow him, as she
often did, but this time he told her to leave him alone. She was
going away, when he was afraid of having been rough, and came
back again to join her. "How worried you look," she said, "what
is the matter?" He was on the point of telling her everything – but
then his courage failed him.'[58]

Characteristically, he told Pietro that he must break the news
to his sister, as best he could.

'He asked her brother to prepare her gradually, by degrees.
The young Count did all he could to soften the blow. He was
made eloquent by his kind heart, by his friendship for Lord
Byron, by his enthusiasm for the cause. But it was all in vain. To
her a death-sentence would have seemed less terrible. She even,
in the first moments of her anguish, became unjust towards Lord
Byron. She poured out her misery in a letter, in which she
accused him of sacrificing everything to his reputation, and
added, "I know that we shall never see each other again".'[59]

The scenes of despair succeeded one another. When she was
with Byron, she wept and pleaded; and at night, 'unable to find
rest, she took up her pen and wrote to him'. Often, she says, she

Y

tore up those letters before sending them – 'for she wanted to be worthy of him' – but one day, 'coming into her sitting-room when she was not there, he found a fragment addressed to him and read it'.

Even a less irritable man than Byron might well have felt some exasperation, and it must have been in the mood induced by a succession of such incidents that he relieved his feelings to Kinnaird:

'I am doing all I can to get away, but I have all kinds of obstacles thrown in my way by "the absurd womankind", who seems determined on sacrificing herself in every way, and preventing me from doing any good . . . She wants to go up to Greece too! forsooth, a precious place to go to at present. Of course the idea is ridiculous, as everything must there be sacrificed to seeing her out of harm's way. It is a case, too, in which interest does not enter, and therefore hard to deal with; for I have no kind of control in that way, and if she makes a scene (and she has a turn that way) we shall have another romance, and tale of ill-usage and abandonment, and Lady Carolining and Lady Byroning and Glenarvoning, all cut and dry. There never was a man who gave up so much to women, and all I have gained by it has been the character of treating them harshly . . . If I left a woman for another woman, she might have cause to complain, but really when a man merely wishes to go on a great duty, for a good cause, this selfishness on the part of the "feminie" is rather too much.'[60]

Such letters – for there were two similar ones to Hobhouse* – were outbursts of spleen, such as Byron had always been subject to. 'However, I *will* go ("d—n my eye, I *will* go ashore").'[61] But it is probable that to Teresa herself – since he was both weak, and, in the *presence* of suffering, kind – he presented a decent appearance of tenderness and regret. And his depression – which she naturally put down wholly to his sorrow at leaving her – did not need to be assumed. For now that he had definitely committed himself to heroism and glory, he was seized by one of his customary revulsions of feeling.

'It is not pleasant', he remarked to Lady Blessington, 'that my eyes should never open to the folly of the undertakings passion

* On April 7th and April 19th. 'She [Teresa] . . . stands out upon sentiment, and so forth, against the will of half the families in the Romagna, with the Pope at their head.' *Correspondence*, II, p. 258.

prompts me to engage in, until I am so far embarked that retreat (at least with honour) is impossible . . . It is all an uphill affair with me afterwards; I cannot for my life "échauffer" my imagination again; and my position excites such ludicrous images and thoughts in my mind, that the whole subject, which, seen through the veil of passion, looked fit for a sublime epic, and I one of the heroes, examined now through reason's glass, appears fit only for a travestie, and my poor self a Major Sturgeon, marching and counter-marching, not from Acton to Ealing, and from Ealing to Acton, but from Corinth to Athens, and from Athens to Corinth.'[62]

Moreover, his forthcoming expedition seemed to him not only ridiculous and futile; he felt an unconquerable premonition that it would also be fatal. One day he said to Teresa: ' "*You* will write my life in Italy. – Write it", he added laughing, "in your fine style of S. Chiara!" – "What can you mean?" she cried. "One does not write the life of a living man!" Lord Byron began to say something, then he cut his sentence short.'[63] But with Lady Blessington he could be more explicit. 'He said that he had a conviction that he should never return from Greece. He had dreamt more than once, he assured me, of dying there.'[64]

With such thoughts haunting him, it was more than a little irritating to have to deal, besides, with Teresa's heroics. He almost preferred the moments when she clung weeping round his neck to those when – 'trying to be worthy of him' – she would make a hero of him perforce, and talk about nobility and self-sacrifice.

And when at last she went away, he was joined by her brother – dear, candid, enthusiastic Pierino, the 'thorough Liberty boy',[65] who was now completely happy, busying himself with preparations for the journey. He hurried down to the port, to report on the various vessels that Barry was examining; he went to the tailor's, to take him Byron's design for their uniforms; he entertained two young German volunteers, who had tramped from Ancona to Genoa, after the defeat and dispersal of the European camp in Greece, and drank in their stories of hardship and adventure. He wrote to Dr. Vaccà in Pisa to ask him if he knew of a clever young doctor, who would be prepared to sail with them; he would receive a salary of one hundred pounds, and would be treated 'as a companion and a gentleman'. Dr. Vaccà replied with regret that he knew of no one suitable among his pupils; if he had not had a family and so many ties, he would have been only too glad to go himself. And in the end a young

Dr. Francesco Bruno, recommended by the English doctor of Genoa, was engaged instead.*

Old Count Ruggero was happier, too, – for at last he had been recalled from his exile. Soon he would be back in his own familiar world – riding in the cool early morning along the banks of the green canals, looking at his crops – talking to his peasants – playing with his little Faustina – discussing local politics with his old friends. Only one proviso had been attached to his return: he must take Teresa with him. And now, owing to Byron's departure, that problem, too, was solved. She would go home with him and take her mother's place, and surely – when once the parting was over, and Byron was away in Greece – common sense would return to her. She might even consider her husband's insistent proposals, and go back to him; or at any rate, once she was living respectably at home, the Pope would restore her allowance.

Yes, thought poor Teresa, as Papa prosed on, and Pierino came back from Genoa with three new Homeric helmets (but Trelawny said they were ridiculous, and, after all, they were put away), yes, they were all against her. Every consideration, with men, came before sentiment: it was always the woman who was sacrificed.

And now a new trial – more trivial, but perhaps no less galling – was put upon her. 'In the midst of these grave thoughts', she wrote, 'there came into Byron's life a social interlude – but one which played a far more superficial part than the vanity of the other actors has wished the public to believe.'⁶⁶ The interlude was created by Lady Blessington.

On the first day after his arrival in Genoa, Lord Blessington – to whom Teresa always refers as 'son collègue dans la Pairie' – came to call; on the second, Lady Blessington herself sat outside the door in an open carriage. It was, declares Teresa, 'une sorte de ruse', for it was a heavy, thundery day, with a storm threatening. And indeed, while Lord Blessington was indoors with Byron, the storm did burst and his guest confessed that his wife and sister-in-law were sitting outside. 'Could Byron do less than go downstairs and ask them in? The Lady's plot had succeeded!'⁶⁷ Teresa may have been watching from a window, but neither on this, nor on any subsequent occasion, did she consent to be introduced to Lady Blessington.

* GAMBA, op. cit., p. 6. For Byron's own letter to Vaccà, L.J., VI, pp. 222-3. Trelawny greatly resented anyone being asked to see to this but himself. 'If he had left it to me I could have induced a clever gentlemanly fellow to have gone with us, an Englishman ... [but] Vaccà will most likely engage some hungry mercenary Italian.' (Letters, p. 64.)

'*La mia dama*', wrote Byron, 'Mme la Comtesse G., was seized
with a furious fit of Italian jealousy and was as unreasonable and
perverse as can well be imagined. God He knows she paid me the
greatest compliment . . . I have long come to years of discretion
and would much rather fall into the sea than in love, any day of
the week.'[68]

Byron was speaking the truth. For all her charm, wit and
beauty, he did not fall in love with Lady Blessington. He only,
for the whole ten weeks of her time in Genoa, rode with her, took
tea with her, laughed and gossiped with her – and talked and
talked about himself, as he had laughed and talked with no woman
since Lady Melbourne. If indeed he did not always say precisely
what Lady Blessington afterwards put down, Teresa's acid
remark that her book should be called 'Imaginary Conversations'[69]
is certainly unjustified. In vain did she try to fight the newcomer
with the primitive weapons at her disposal. 'Madame G. (who
never saw her) won't allow her to be pretty and *will* allow her to
be not young. I dared not form a judgment on the subject
before one who argues with all the insolence of four and twenty.'[70]
But Teresa was much too shrewd not to realize that Lady
Blessington's real attraction for Byron was of a very different
nature. After three years of exile, she brought to him the very
breath of the London drawing-rooms of which he spoke with
such contempt – and had never been able to forget. She had all
the qualities that Teresa lacked: quickness, irony, *usage du monde*,
lightness of touch. She knew, unfailingly, what he was talking
about; she could tell him the latest gossip about everyone he had
ever met. And when – very soon – he began to talk about himself, how unfeigned was her interest, how perceptive her comments!
If there was a faint touch of malice, too, that was a quality that
Byron had always found attractive. It was only poor Teresa,
many years later, who was to resent it on his behalf.
But meanwhile it was to Lady Blessington that he could take
his confidences. It was to her that he could ruefully remark, after
one of Teresa's scenes, that 'liaisons that are not cemented by
marriage must produce unhappiness, when there is refinement of
mind, and that honourable *fierté* which accompanies it. The
humiliations and vexations a woman, under such circumstances,
is exposed to, cannot fail to have a certain effect on her temper and
spirits, which robs her of the charms that won affection'.[71] And
then, in a sudden outburst of candour, he would confess that,
though he was not happy, it was his own fault. 'Contessa Guiccioli, the only object of his love, has all the qualities to render a

CASA SALUZZO3421823

reasonable being happy.' Lady Blessington dryly remarked that, from what she had heard, she feared that the Countess Guiccioli, too, 'had little reason to be satisfied with her lot'.[72]

But the next day, in a different mood, Byron would hold forth, instead, on Teresa's virtues: her disinterestedness, her unselfishness, her sweetness – and her noble birth! 'He said that he had been passionately in love with her, and that she had sacrificed everything for him; that the whole of her conduct towards him had been admirable, and that not only did he feel the strongest personal attachment to her, but the highest sentiment of esteem . . . I am persuaded', concluded Lady Blessington, 'this is his last attachment.'[73]

I have before me Teresa's copy of Lady Blessington's *Conversations of Lord Byron*, in which the above remarks are written.[74] It is very informative. Teresa, who was always prodigal of marginal notes in her books, has in this case also interlarded the pages with little slips of paper, on which she has written her longer comments.

'Evidently', says the first of these, 'Lady Blessington has written this book to make Lord Byron express her own personal opinions. She has put into his mouth a great many of her poor opinions of England, so that the blame might fall on him – and then she has taken on for herself the pose of an apologist of England, in order to gain the good graces of high society – a thing in which she has failed. She has also tried to suggest that Lord Byron conceived a great liking for her. Nothing could be more untrue. She did all she could to seduce his mind (at least) but Lord Byron was aware of the trick and said so to me, adding, "I am studying her character for Don Juan's Adeline".'

Almost every page has an underscoring or an annotation – occasionally approving, but more often a simple 'Non', 'Nonsense', 'Mensonge', or even 'Pah!' The simple remark 'Byron's was a fine nature', receives the comment 'Oh! True!' And so does the passage in which Lady Blessington remarks that 'all the malice of his nature has lodged itself in his lips and the fingers of his right hand – for there is none, I am persuaded, to be found in his heart'. In the margin of the passage describing 'the bad and vulgar taste predominating in all Byron's equipments, whether in dress or in furniture', and his complacent delight in them, Teresa indignantly scribbled, 'Mais ce sont des mensonges, pour plaire à d'Orset!' [*sic*] Finally there is a passage in which Lady Blessington, with her usual acuteness, has remarked that Byron's 'incontinence of speech' was often accompanied by 'a sort of mental reserve', which caused him 'to disclaim any sentiment of friendship for those he so trusted . . . It was as though he said "I think aloud, and you hear my thoughts; but I have no feeling of friendship towards you" '.* 'C'était précisément son idée', cries Teresa triumphantly, 'en parlant à Lady Blessington. Il ne voulait pas qu'elle se fît illusion sur ses sentiments.' The last page of the book contains Teresa's summing-up: 'Fortunately this homage to hypocrisy and cant has done no good to the author: it has not produced the consequences that she hoped for, from her insinuations and exaggerations. Mme de Boissy.'

At last, after ten weeks of rides and talks and calls (although beside Lady Blessington's reference to 'a nearly *daily* intercourse of ten weeks', Teresa has written, 'Non!') the Blessington's stay in Genoa came to an end. Before they left, Byron, who had already had a somewhat dubious transaction with Lady Blessington over the purchase of her horse, Mameluke, succeeded in selling the *Bolivar* to Lord Blessington, and was about to remove its guns, when Barry quietly suggested that it was hardly possible to do so, since the purchaser had already seen them.[75]

On the evening of June 2nd, 'Lord Byron accepta encore un dîner d'adieu'. But now, once again, Teresa's version differs considerably from Lady Blessington's own. Teresa affirms that she knows precisely what occurred because, very early in the Blessingtons' stay, she had extracted a promise from Byron never to visit them without taking her brother with him – and so Pietro, too, was at the farewell party. Both he and Byron himself, on their return, gave the same account of the evening: it was not Byron, but Lady Blessington, who had 'une véritable crise de nerfs', and burst into tears! ' "I felt", said Byron, "that emotion might soon overcome me, too, and got up to cut short the scene, which Pietro and d'Orsay (whose nerves were probably solider) were watching with some curiosity." '† To this version we should perhaps add, in fairness to Teresa, Hobhouse's comment on the passage in

* LADY BLESSINGTON, op. cit., p. 265. 'His heart was upon his lips,' wrote Moore, 'and it depended wholly upon themselves [his acquaintances] whether they might not at once become the depositories of every secret, if it might be so called, of his whole life.' MOORE, II, p. 796.

† 'Vie', pp. 1497-8. Lady Blessington's own account was the following: 'Byron seemed to have a conviction that we met for the last time, and yielding to the melancholy caused by this presentiment, made scarcely an effort to check the tears that flowed plentifully down his cheeks . . . Again he reproached me for not remaining at Genoa until he sailed for Greece, and the recollection brought back a portion of the pique he had formerly felt at our refusing to stay, for he dried his eyes and, apparently ashamed of his emotion, made some sarcastic observation as to his nervousness, although his voice was inarticulate, and his lips quivered when uttering it.' LADY BLESSINGTON, *The Idler in Italy*, I, p. 358.

Moore's *Life*, where Moore has described Byron's emotion at parting with the Blessingtons. Hobhouse dryly remarked: 'Very unlike him.'⁷⁶

And now, with the Blessingtons gone, there was nothing left to fill the days, but the preparations for departure.

'I want your aid,' wrote Byron to Trelawny in Rome, 'and am exceedingly anxious to see you. Pray come, for I am at last determined to go to Greece; it is the only place I was ever contented in. I am serious, and did not write before, as I might have given you a journey for nothing; they all say I can be of use in Greece. I do not know how, nor do they, but at all events let us go.'⁷⁷

A ship – 'a collier-built tub of 120 tons' – had already been chartered – the choice being made not so much on its own merits, as in consequence of Byron's 'insuperable objection to the flag of this country'.⁷⁸ Dr. Francesco Bruno, – in a state of 'perpetual terror', since he had been told that for the slightest fault Byron was capable of having him torn to pieces by his dogs⁷⁹ – had agreed to accompany them. Trelawny, complaining of every arrangement that had not been made by himself, arrived. Two dogs and five horses were also to go to Greece; the geese were to remain with Mr. Barry.⁸⁰

Wearily, with no flicker of enthusiasm, Byron settled down to the last dreary arrangements: packing and winding up accounts, and sorting all his manuscripts.

'One day', says the 'Vie', 'he came into Madame Guiccioli's room with a great bundle of manuscripts. "Here are some of my scribblings", he said, "as they came out of my head – Murray has sent them back to me." "I will keep them for you until you come back," she replied. "Do what you like with them," said he, "unless you think they had better be burned. But perhaps", he added, "some day they may be prized!" '⁸¹

On the following day Byron tried to speak to Teresa about his Will – only to rouse her to one of her most ill-timed exhibitions of sensibility.

'After having begged her to listen to him calmly, and having pointed out that this was only considered an act of ordinary prudence in his own country, he told her that he had arranged with Mr. Barry to make his Will. "But", says Teresa, "the mere idea of an act which presupposed the possibility of so terrible a misfortune caused her to break into such cries of pain, such supplications to give up the idea, that he promised to do so." '[82]

Byron's chief motive in drawing up the Will had been the very natural one of making some provision for Teresa before his departure. He intended to add a Codicil, leaving her the £5000 which he had originally bequeathed to Allegra. But Teresa would have none of it.

'She declined in the most positive, and indeed, displeased terms, declaring that she should consider such a bequest as not only an injustice to my daughter by Lady B. and to my sister's family, but as a posthumous insult to herself. It is true', he characteristically added, 'Madame G. has her separate allowance (by the Pope's decree) from her husband, and will have a considerable jointure at his demise, but it is not unhandsome conduct nevertheless.'[83]

Byron indeed, in all the four years of their liaison, seems never to have been able fully to accustom himself to the idea that in Teresa he had met a woman who was completely disinterested.

'I can assure you,' he wrote in amazement to Kinnaird, during the first autumn at La Mira, 'that *She* has never cost me, directly or indirectly, a sixpence . . . I never offered her but one present – a brooch of brilliants – and she sent it back to me with her *own hair* in it . . . and a note to say that she was not in the habit of receiving presents of that value, but hoped that I would not consider her sending it back as an affront, nor the value diminished by the enclosure.'[84]

In the following year, after Teresa had left her husband, he was no less astonished by the disinterestedness of her family. 'I offered any settlement,' he told Moore, 'but they refused to accept it.'[85] To Teresa herself he had written: 'You can trust me – I will make you independent of everyone – at least during my lifetime,' – but he added that he knew she would not accept his offer. 'You are made angry by the mere idea, and want to be independent on your own!'[86] And now this independence was showing its inconvenient side. 'A case in which interest does not enter', he was discovering, was harder to deal with than those he had known before.

Teresa, according to her own account, was still obstinately refusing to return to the Romagna, saying that she would greatly prefer to await Byron's return in Genoa, living 'with a respectable old lady, the Comtesse d'Yson'[87] – or else to retire to the Convent of the Visitation in Nice. Byron, she says, even wrote to the Mother Superior of the Convent, Mère Schlegel, asking whether she could go there.[88] But the reply was unsatisfactory: the Convent was prepared to receive the Contessa, but since it was a cloistered order, it would not be possible for her to go down to the beach every day to bathe, as she wished to do. The old lady in Genoa, too, declined the honour – and so 'Madame Guiccioli was obliged to give way to necessity and duty and prepare herself to follow her father to the Romagna'.[89]

And indeed, as the date of Byron's departure approached, she no longer cared what happened to her. Again and again she made him repeat the same promise: he would send for her, if he could – and if not, he would come back soon – and never leave her again. He promised – and she pretended to believe him. But, she says, it was not easy to be brave when he himself looked so unhappy – and so very ill. Since his illness at Lerici he had become very thin; the curls which she had always so much admired, were wispy and streaked with grey; and he hardly attempted to conceal his depression and indecision. 'Every person', she wrote in the account she gave to Moore, 'who was near him at that time, can bear witness to the struggle his heart underwent (however much he endeavoured to hide it) as the period fixed for his departure approached.'[90] What seemed to her strangest, most ominous of all, was the date that he had chosen: he who had never made any secret of his superstitious feelings, who had never been willing to do anything of the slightest importance on the thirteenth of the month, deliberately chose to sail upon this day.

Three days before it, in a sudden need for feminine understanding and comfort, Teresa went to call upon Mary Shelley, but found her out.

'Perhaps it was better for you, my dear,' she wrote when she got home, 'my company was never worth much, and now must be unbearable. My feelings are such as cannot be described, and at best can only arouse compassion.'

While she was writing, Byron came into the room, and, on finding out to whom the letter was addressed, gave her a note of his to enclose, adding that 'it had to do with business which was no concern of his'. He also sent a message to Hunt, to say that 'he had left detailed orders about his affairs with . . . ' – Teresa had helpfully forgotten with whom, but she *thought* it was Mr. Barry! – 'that he sent him cordial greetings, believing that he would excuse him from saying goodbye', and that he also greeted Mary, saying 'he had no feeling of enmity for her'.

When he had gone out of the room again, poor Teresa sat miserably turning over the letter.

'I fear that the letter I enclose may distress you – I dare not open it. But Ld. Byron's tone as he gave it me, made me anxious. – And yet I *must* send it . . .' 'Now,' she added, 'he has gone back to his own room – and he, too, is very sad. What a world, my God!'[91]

So the last days passed. On July 12th Byron spent the whole day receiving callers and settling his affairs, and did not even go near Teresa, who remained alone upon her sofa. 'I have not seen L. B. at all today,' she wrote to Mary Shelley, 'but from Lega I have just heard that perhaps he will not get off tomorrow. Only a few hours more! – and yet, since that moment, I have breathed a little more freely.'[92]

But when the next morning came, the departure *did* take place.

'The fatal day', says the 'Vie', 'arrived at last. In order to sleep on board, he was to leave Albaro at 5 o'clock. From 3 to 5 he stayed with Madame Guiccioli – and he asked Mrs. Shelley to come and stay with her at 5, so that she should not be alone after he had gone.'[93]

From the garden terrace the two women – from both of whom the sea had taken all that they loved best – watched the ungainly little brig which still lay becalmed in the bay. The next morning Teresa, – half dazed with sorrow – set off with her father for the Romagna.

Half way across the pass, at midday, she felt so faint that her father told the coachman to stop. They got out and, sitting on a stone, she scribbled a few incoherent, heart-broken sentences.

'I have promised more than I can perform, and you have asked of me what is beyond my strength . . . I feel as if I were dying, Byron, have pity on me.' The next day she added: 'With every step that brings me nearer to Bologna, I feel my grief increasing. My God, help me! Come and fetch me, Byron, if you still want to see me alive, or let me run away and join you, at any cost.'

Teresa must have meant to send this note to Barry to forward, for she added a few words to him: 'Mr. Barry je vous prie redisez à Lord Byron que je ne puis plus supporter cette main de fer qui m'opprime? Qu'il retourne ou que je meure.'⁹⁴

But the letter was never sent. And while Teresa was still travelling northwards, Byron's departure had been marked by a series of anticlimaxes. On the 14th, with his ship still becalmed in the harbour, he landed again, and spent a queer, ghost-like day with Gamba, Barry and Trelawny in the gardens of Villa Lomellina.

For there had been yet another delay. On the morning of the 15th the *Hercules*, – by the kind offices of the American fleet – had been towed out of port. But that night a strong wind at last began to blow, and the absurd old tub, 'built on the lines of a baby's cradle', began to 'play at pitch and toss' so violently that the horses, in terror, kicked down their partitions, Pietro Gamba was 'half-dead with seasickness' – and the next morning, with Byron cheerfully remarking that 'he considered a bad beginning a good omen', they were all back in the harbour again. It was then that Byron, with Pietro, paid a last visit to the empty Casa Saluzzo. 'His conversation was somewhat melancholy on our way to Albaro: he spoke much of his past life and of the uncertainty of the future. "Where", said he, "shall we be in a year?" '⁹⁵ He sent Pietro away, and for several hours sat alone at the writing-table in his study. When, a few days later, Mr. Barry opened its drawers he found there a singular object: a long tress of Teresa's hair.

Before finally sailing from Genoa, Pietro sent Teresa a kind but hurried fraternal note – 'written', he wrote, 'with matches dipped in water, so that you may not accuse me of negligence'.

'Byron', he added, 'is well in health, but tired by the activities of the night and day, and by a hot bath – he begs you to excuse him from writing. . . .

Keep up your spirits, find comfort in your hopes, wait for our letters – try to find in your friendship some consolation for your present sufferings, though I fully imagine how great they are.'

To these consolations Byron added no word. There was nothing left to say.

From Leghorn, on July 22nd, Pietro wrote again to tell his sister that Byron – 'very much occupied, and happy in his occupations'– had told him to write on his behalf. They had landed in Leghorn at 4 p.m. on the preceding day, and hoped to sail for Zante the following afternoon, 'where we shall find news from Blaquière, and then decide what to do'. He would write again from Messina 'and from wherever I can, be sure of it. Meanwhile keep up your spirits and bear this passing trouble with the fortitude you have shown on other occasions.'

'And you, my Teresa,' he added, 'what are you doing? How were you received? In which house? In what a situation? What was the journey like? How is your health standing so much distress? How is it with Papa? Tell me everything, everything.

Among these Livornese Greeks there has been some intriguing which does not promise well. The news is always the same – fortunately we have started in so unenthusiastic a spirit, that nothing can surprise us – and in sight of the world we are not committed to anything more than going there to see how things are, and be of use if we can, but nothing more.'

Finally, in a postscript, there was a little news of Byron.

'Byron is still very well – and all of us too. Our doctor pursues us with pills and other medicines, but luckily we are obliged to send him away, as no one needs them yet. Mylord leads a more active life, both as to bodily exercise and conversation, than anyone on board – but I think he has entirely abandoned his pen.'

And then poor Pietro (for he was the best of brothers), must have imagined Teresa opening this letter, like his preceding one, and looking for a single word from Byron, in vain. 'Mio caro Bairon', he must have exclaimed, with his quick flush flooding his cheeks, 'you really *must* add one line!' And so, at the top of the page, we have three scribbled lines in English, in Byron's hand – his last words to Teresa from Italy.

BYRON TO CONTESSA GUICCIOLI

Livorno   *July 22nd*, 1823

My dearest Teresa: I have but a few moments to say that we are all well – and thus far on our way to the Levant. Believe that I always *love* you and that a thousand words could only express the same idea.

Ever dearest yours   N.B.

And with that meagre farewell, on July 23rd, 1823, Byron was off to Greece.

If thou regret'st thy youth, *why live?*

FOR the first few months after her return to the Romagna, very little is known about Teresa. The 'Vie' ends with Byron's departure for Greece, and her letters, both to Byron and to her brother, have unfortunately been lost.¹

It is not difficult to surmise that she was unhappy. Not only was she lonely and humiliated – a woman, in the eyes of all her little world, who had been 'planted' by her lover – but she was also, since the Pope had suspended her allowance from Guiccioli, and she had firmly refused to accept anything from Byron, completely penniless. Moreover, she had now no home. According to a letter that she wrote to Mary Shelley in November,² her father – in spite of having a permit from the Consul of the Papal States in Genoa – was stopped at the frontier of the Romagna by the police and was sent off to Ferrara – where he remained 'in Purgatory', in the company of several other exiles, for many months. Teresa herself was allowed to proceed to Bologna – and there was taken in by her old friend and teacher Paolo Costa³ – and it was to his house – 'in a retired situation by the city walls' – that all Byron's and Pietro's letters were addressed. 'I owe to my friends', she told Mary, 'any strength that has supported me up till now.' Her days were spent in waiting – for Byron to summon her, for Byron's return to her – and for Byron's letters.

Very long must the intervals between them have seemed – and very meagre the comfort to be derived from them, when at last they did arrive. Both her lover and her brother were now very far away, caught up in an incomprehensible, impersonal masculine world, in which there was no place for her. Moreover it was evident that they were both enjoying themselves. In a general comment on Byron's letters, half a lifetime later, Teresa loyally refused to admit any disappointment. 'His epistolary style,' she wrote, 'even in the most passionate circumstances, was always simple.' He was 'too sincere to use the flowery phrases of other lovers', but his letters – 'so natural, so kind – without exclamation marks – without any form of affectation – show him as he really was'.⁴

But this, unfortunately, is precisely what his letters from Greece fail to do. Even in the early days, when his letters to Teresa were still passionate, they were not intimate; he never wrote to her with the wit and ease of his correspondence with Lady Melbourne or his men friends, and it plainly did not occur to him to confide in her when he was troubled. And certainly none of his earlier letters had been so short and flat as those which now came from Greece. Not only did they contain little news and no clue to his state of mind, but they showed very little interest in hers. There were no inquiries about her welfare, no references to shared recollections; the dry little notes, with their mechanical endearments, suggest that, like the first one, they were all scribbled off in a hurry – with Pietro, apologetic but pressing, standing over the writer with a pen. The best that one can say for them – and it is not much – is that they were fairly frequent, and that their flatness was a conjugal flatness – a tacit acceptance of the fact that, if he did come back, it would be to her. For after all – he wrote it to Barry, even if these letters show few signs of it – 'I left my heart in Italy.' [5]

For all this there is, I think, an explanation. Nearly two years before leaving for Greece, Byron had written to Augusta about his liaison with Teresa, 'This is a finisher.' He meant, as is clear from the context, an end to his casual love-affairs – and most of all to his relationship with Augusta herself. 'You will probably never see me again as long as you live.' [6] But in a wider sense the phrase is equally applicable: when he sailed for Greece he was already, in emotional capacity, 'un uomo finito'; he had come to an end.

When, in 1819, he had told Hoppner, 'I can hope no more to inspire attachment, and trust never again to feel it', – as when he assured Teresa herself that she would be his 'last Passion' – he was not merely making a vow of fidelity. Already then, though not yet thirty-one, Byron was conscious of a physical decay far in advance of his years – and of a corresponding, overwhelming weariness. 'At thirty', he told Webster, 'there is no more to look forward to.' Three years later both Henry Fox and Lady Blessington noted, with faint amusement, that he spoke of himself as an old man; they both thought that this, too, was one of his poses. [7] But it was Byron who was right. When the autopsy of his body was made at Missolonghi, the doctors found, not only an acute condition of inflammation of the brain, but 'the skull like that of an octogenarian', [8] with the sutures fused together, as in extreme old age.

The best proof of the degree to which Teresa had been both a vitalizing and a stabilizing influence in his life, is the sheer amount of work he got through, during their liaison. But when, in 1823, he turned his back on 'poeshie', he had come to an end, at the same time, of the stuff of which a large part of poetry is made: human tenderness, passion, attachment.

Z

He had had enough. Not, in particular, enough of Teresa. He recognized her affection, her disinterestedness, her loyalty; if he came back to anyone, he would come back to her. But he had had enough of all women – all scenes – all emotional demands – which perhaps is merely another way of saying, that he had had enough of life. This is, I believe, what gives their peculiar flatness and unconvincingness to his meagre little notes to Teresa from Greece. He could not very well write to the poor woman: 'I neither believe I will come back, nor wish to; and if I did, the only person I care to see, is a little girl in England.' And so he wrote instead: 'Perhaps in the spring you can come out to join us', 'We are not forgetting your Excellency and her sentimental projects', 'all will go well by and by'. But it is all quite unconvincing; these are the letters of a ghost.

Pietro's letters, on the other hand, are those of a most affectionate and considerate brother, who can still find time to be sorry for Teresa. Even in his excitement over his own adventures, he never fails to inquire, with Latin warmth and correctness of family feeling, about his sister's and father's concerns. Although his letters add very little that is unknown to us about the Greek adventure, they provide a straightforward record of it, as seen through his candid and hopeful, but by no means stupid, eyes, – a picture so sympathetic, and, within its limitations, so unmistakably truthful, that even at the risk of repeating what has already been told elsewhere, it has seemed desirable to quote most of his letters. As, in the earlier part of this book, Byron has been revealed in the descriptions of Teresa and of his Italian friends – so now he appears, in Greece, through Pietro's eyes. It must, however, be remembered that, in writing to his sister, Pietro was anxious to omit anything that would stir up what he called her 'diseased imagination', and might even, perhaps, bring her rushing across to Greece to join them.

His letters, which he sometimes sent by way of Ancona and sometimes to Genoa, to be forwarded by Barry, seem to have taken five or six weeks;[10] and often there was a longer interval, in which Teresa received no letter at all. She had hoped for news from Messina or Zante, but – after many long weary weeks of waiting – the first was from Argostoli, in the Island of Cephalonia. It was dated August 4th and told her that they had arrived that same morning.

'You will have been surprised not to receive any letters from Messina or from Zante. When we sailed past Messina the wind was so favourable and we were so well provided with water, that we thought it unnecessary, indeed undesirable, to stop. Another reason which determined us to go to Cephalonia, rather than Zante, was that our travelling-companion, Mr. Hamilton-Browne* is a particular friend of the Governor of the island, from whom we can therefore expect every kindness. Indeed, I hope we have not made a mistake – I say hope, because we have not found him in the island, but are expecting him tomorrow.

No reliable news from Greece, so that we shall stay here a while before taking any steps – indeed, I think we shall not move until we have had further news, and have fully weighed the state of matters here. However, go on addressing our letters to Zante, because wherever we may be, they will certainly reach us from there – and we are in touch every day.

My lord is in excellent health – and good humour. If only you could be, too!'

At the bottom of the page there was a postscript from Byron, in English:†

My dearest Teresa: I cannot write long letters as you know – but you also know or ought to know how much and entirely I ever am your A.A. in E.‡   N.B.

Then there were three more lines from Pietro:

'At Messina, by the pilot-boat, I sent a message on a piece of wood, to a Banker, to tell you we had passed by. I couldn't write on paper, without landing.'

Pietro also wrote an account of the journey to his father, adding: 'The news that we have been able to collect here is that the Turkish fleet has imposed a strict blockade on all the coast of Morea, and the Greek one has not yet appeared – it is believed – for lack of money to pay the crews – but is expected any day. On land the Turks are said to be marching against the Morea in three bodies, but the Greeks are awaiting them without moving – indeed there is a rumour of a passage of arms favourable to the Greeks at Thermopylae.'

* A young Scotsman, of strong philhellenic sympathies, who had come aboard at Livorno.
† Byron's letters to Teresa from Greece are all in English, since before he left, Teresa, who could speak the language a little, had stated her intention of mastering it before his return.
‡ Amico Amante in Eterno = Friend and Lover for Ever.

z

During the nine days of the voyage Byron's spirits had gradually revived. Trelawny – in what Mr. Nicolson calls 'his particularly vivid and untruthful manner' – has described the fluctuations of his moods, 'cold fits alternating with hot ones', and uproarious high spirits, expressed in schoolboyish practical jokes, followed by dark forebodings. 'Lord Byron and myself', boasted Trelawny to the builder of the *Bolivar*, Captain Roberts, 'are extraordinary thick, we are inseparable, but mind, this does not flatter me. He has known me long enough to see the sacrifices I make in devoting myself to serve him.'[11]

One of Trelawny's notes, jotted down at this time, differs slightly from the version he polished up later on, for the *Records*:

' "I can assure you, Mr. Trelawny, you will find there is nothing in Greece but robbers, rocks and vermin," said Byron's yeoman bold (Fletcher) as we lay becalmed in the Ionian sea on board the brig *Hercules*. I was going up the companion ladder, and Fletcher was what he called making himself comfortable – with bottled ale – gin – biscuits and a Cheshire cheese. "My Lord can't deny what I say. Lord Sir, my Lord's linen was covered with them!"

I found Byron seated, as usual, on deck. He had heard Fletcher's discourse and answered "No, I do not deny it, – it's very true – for those who take a hog's eye view of things!"

After a considerable pause he continued: "I was happier in Greece than I have ever been before or since – and if I have ever written [well?] (as the world says I have, but which they will pardon my doubting) it was in Greece – or of Greece – or if I have ever acted wisely – it was leaving that cursed Italy.

Till I went to Italy – I knew nothing – and now am I – if a man should speak truly – little better than one of the wicked – I will leave off – sack – and live cleanly, as a nobleman should do.'[12]

Pietro's next letter on August 10th, from Argostoli, showed that they had still reached no decision about their plans.

'We are not yet decided where we shall go, or when, or if – but you can be assured of one thing, that we shall take every care of our health and safety. You will hear a great many stories of every kind about Greek affairs – and perhaps about us – but pray, if your imagination allows it, keep them in quarantine. The news that we have received from Greece is not yet such as to enable us to take a decision. I cannot tell you how much kindness Mylord has received from the Governor,[13] from the officers of the garrison,[14] and from all his compatriots in this district. His health is excellent and his good spirits also continue constant. It is not possible that we may be able to settle down honourably and conveniently in these islands – but until we have taken some decision pray do not let yourself be tempted to any foolish action.'

Then followed a few lines in Byron's writing:

My dearest T.ª We are here all very well and extremely well used by all the English here. Of Greece and of the Greeks – I can say little – for everything is as yet very uncertain on that point. I pray you to remain tranquil and not to believe any nonsense that you may hear; for the present we remain in this island – till we have better intelligence. Tomorrow we are going to make a tour in the island – for a day or two – ever your most affectly A.A. in e.

N.B.

On the following day Byron was sending another letter by way of Ancona.

BYRON TO CONTESSA GUICCIOLI

St. Euphemia—Cephalonia   *Ag.° 11.° 1823*

My dearest Teresa: – All Well! and doing well. We are on the point of embarking for Ithaca – after a warm ride in the Sun from Argostoli. Pietro your brother will have told you the rest. Do not be alarmed as our present voyage is merely for pleasure in the Islands. Ever and entirely A.A. in e+++   N.B.

P.S. We have received great kindness and hospitality from the English here, both military and civil.

Pietro added:

We have this morning begun our journey to Ithaca, and after 9 hours of travel on muleback have reached the port, from which we shall soon embark for the home of Ulysses and Penelope. Here in the Vice-Governor's house we have received every possible kindness – the fruit of the many which we received in Argostoli from the Governor and from the officers of his garrison. Our trip will last several days, and then we shall return on board – waiting for news. For the present we propose to wait and form a mature opinion, and Byron will certainly not change this resolution. Do not take any step without hearing from me.   PIETRO G.

Pietro's and Byron's next letter was written on August 19th, after their return from Ithaca.

'We got back two days ago,' wrote Pietro. 'Our voyage was fortunate. It lasted seven days, of which we spent three visiting the interior of the Island. We enjoyed our cavalcade very much. The island is really enchanting, and although it is full of classical memories, or at least of places where the imagination can create them, we have enjoyed ourselves more in looking at the beautiful views and tasting the exquisite grapes, than in wearing out our brains over some crumbling ruins.[15] Mylord was pleased, in good health and excellent spirits – he led a very tiring life in this hot weather, and what is more, in the hottest hours of the day – on muleback and on foot he climbed up mountains which by God were not mild, – and is none the worse.

From all the British officials in the island we received, as we have here, a thousand kindnesses. We dined three times with the Governor,[16] and once with the Greek Regent or Gonfaloniere of the Island – an excellent man. The memory of this little journey will always be delightful.

No letter, not a word from Italy since our departure. I am beginning to be a little anxious, for it is already 39 days since we left you, and in a month letters should come – but the sea will not obey our laws – so we are waiting. You, too, try to be calm if our letters should be delayed – for that would be the only cause, not my negligence – you see that I am missing no opportunity.'

Byron's letter followed.

Cephalonia   *Ag°* 20° 1823

My dearest Teresa: Pietro will have satisfied you with the account of our health and safety. We have been travelling in this Island and in Ithaca and have visited the places to which the remembrances of Ulysses and his family are attached. – Of political news we can say but little as little is actually known – and even that is partly contradictory. – – – – – Let me hope that you keep up your spirits and that you will continue to do so. – –

I write in English as you desired, and I suppose that you are as well acquainted with that language as at Genoa. – – We have already written three or four times, and will continue to do so by every good opportunity. – I am just going to take a ride on shore with Colonel D[uffie] and take advantage of the fresco for that purpose.

Ever dearest T. a.a. in e. + + + +   N.B.

Pietro's account of Byron's constant good health and spirits was only partly accurate. He entirely failed to mention, for instance, a most curious and frightening paroxysm of rage – terminating in a convulsive fit – by which Byron was seized on the night of their return to Cephalonia, during a formal reception given for him by the monks of the monastery on the hill of Samos. In the midst of the ceremonies, when the Abbot, – who with his monks, had received him with the highest honours – was intoning a long eulogy, Byron 'suddenly burst into a paroxysm of rage,' and 'turning to us with flashing eyes, vehemently exclaimed "Will no one release me from the presence of these pestilential idiots? They drive me mad!" Seizing a lamp, he left the room. The amazed Abbot, in a low, tremulous voice said, significantly putting his finger to his forehead – "Ecco, è matto, poveretto!" '[17] Byron was then seized with violent spasms in the stomach and liver, 'stamped and swore at the others like a maniac' – and it was only after several vain attempts on the part of the terrified Dr. Bruno and of the rest of the party that he was at last persuaded to take a soothing pill. By the next day it was all over – and in the evening Byron was happily singing Tom Moore's songs, as they rode back over the mountains to the *Hercules*.[18]

Pietro's next letter to Teresa was written from Argostoli on August 23rd; it contained no fresh news, and Byron's brief postscript was equally flat and uninformative.

My dearest T.ª I have opened Pietro's letter just to add a few words – not having [at] present time for more as the Post goes this evening. – We are all well – and I am ever as usual yours a.a. in e.

N.B.

P.S. I feel sure that you will rather be glad to hear from us briefly but frequently – than at length but rarely.

The scarcity of news in both these letters was partly due to the genuine uncertainty of the writers. On Byron's return from Ithaca he had received a flattering letter from England, appointing him as the principal agent in Greece of the Greek Committee; but the news from Greece itself was not so satisfactory. The Eastern part of the country, he heard, was under the control of the military chieftain Odysseus; the Western acknowledged the rule of Prince Mavrocordato,* who, however, was a refugee in the island of

* This was the same Mavrocordato whose Greek lessons Mary Shelley had so much enjoyed, during his exile in Pisa in 1821. 'Do you not envy my luck', she wrote to Mrs. Gisborne, 'that an amiable, young, agreeable and learned Greek Prince comes every morning to give me a lesson?' Shelley, however, never cared much for 'our turban'd friend', and Trelawny wrote later on to Mary: 'I hope ere long to see his head removed

Hydra. Emissaries of each of the contending parties hurried to Cephalonia – since the news of Byron's arrival had now become known, – to secure the help of the rich English Lord. 'To nobody', says Finlay, 'did the Greeks ever unmask their selfishness and self-deceit so candidly.'[19] After listening to them all, Byron was forced to comment that 'there never was such an incapacity for veracity shown, since Eve lived in Paradise'.[20]

Nevertheless, in the third week of August, he did intend – in much the same spirit 'as Mrs. Fry went to Newgate'[21] – to sail across to the Morea. But the captain of the *Hercules* had no wish to have his ship captured by the Turks. 'No, my Lord,' he cried, when Byron proposed that they should sail upon a Sunday, 'there shall be no heathenish and outlandish doings upon my ship on a Sunday.'[22] When however, the date of sailing was shifted to a weekday, the captain was no less reluctant. Finally yet another piece of bad news arrived from Greece: the patriot Marco Botzaris – the most estimable of the Greek chieftains, with whom Byron had been in correspondence – had been shot in the head by a Turkish bullet.

It was at this point that Byron decided to pay off the *Hercules* and to disembark in Cephalonia, to await the turn of events. In order not to embarrass Colonel Napier by his presence, he did not settle at Argostoli, but took a small house in the village of Metaxata, four miles away. Here, in the company of Pietro Gamba and Dr. Bruno – and attended, in addition to Lega Zambelli, Fletcher and Tita, by an unruly bodyguard of forty Suliots, who soon had to be shipped to Missolonghi – he spent a monotonous, and very agreeable, four months. His health was excellent: the climate delightful. Trelawny had taken off his heroic attitudes to the Morea, from where he subsequently sent accounts of the 'potent leaders of the Greek military factions ... each and all intent on their own immediate interests'.[23] In the evenings Colonel Napier and the other officers of the garrison rode out to dine, and on Sunday mornings Dr. Kennedy, that worthy Scottish Methodist, would hold Gospel meetings, one of which Byron actually attended, and listened (although with 'signs of impatience') for no less than four hours. 'I would have no Hell at all,' said Dr. Kennedy at one point of the subsequent discussion, 'but would pardon all, purify all. ...'

' "I would save", cried his Lordship, "my sister and my daughter, and some of my friends – and a few others, and let the rest shift

from his worthless and heartless body. He is a mere shuffling soldier, an aristocratic brute.' (But this was after Byron's death, when Trelawny wanted Mavrocordato's stores for Odysseus.)

for themselves." "And your wife also?" I exclaimed. "No," he said. "But your wife, surely you would save your wife?" "Well," he said, "I would save her too, if you like." '²⁴

In these discussions Dr. Kennedy found himself considerably hampered by the fact that none of his listeners – although Byron fetched a Bible from his bedroom and said that it was given to him by his sister, and he read it very often – were even familiar with the meaning of his words. Thus Byron asked him what he meant by the word 'grace'. 'I the more readily closed the book,' said Dr. Kennedy, 'as I perceived they had no distinct conception of many of the words I used.'²⁵ Finally Byron inquired, 'What more do you wish of me in order to consider me a good Christian?' 'To kneel down and pray God.' 'This', he exclaimed, 'is too much, my dear doctor.'²⁶

In one of the more tedious chapters of her published book about Byron, the one about his religious views, Teresa has referred at great length to those conversations – in which she liked to find a confirmation of Byron's essentially religious attitude to life. Once, she said, when Byron was riding with Pietro Gamba at Ravenna, he cried out, at the end of a long religious argument: 'Vous confondez vos idées religieuses avec vos antipathies politiques. Je considère l'athéisme comme une folie.'²⁷

On another occasion, at La Mira, when a religious procession was passing and one of Byron's grooms failed to dismount and fall on his knees, he reproved him severely. The man excused himself, saying that he was no Catholic, whereupon Byron firmly replied: 'Nor am I a Catholic, but a Christian.'²⁸

Finally one evening, in Pisa, when the whole company was laughing at the tale of a miracle that had taken place in Lucca, Byron alone took the story seriously. 'Mockery,' he said, 'is perhaps a faculty which God has given us to make up for our lack of faith – as one gives toys to sick children.'²⁹

Teresa – herself a *pratiquante* rather than a *croyante* – did not observe that all these remarks, which she quotes as proofs of faith, are rather evidences of a profound respect for conformity.

Religion, however, was not the only subject that was discussed in the little house at Metaxata. Often it was filled with emissaries from the various Greek parties, who would crowd into Byron's room, vehemently pointing out that their faction, and theirs alone, deserved the support – and the dollars – of the English Mylord. Their dissensions provided the best possible excuse for Byron's present inaction. 'It must be the cause,' he told Hobhouse, 'and not individuals or parties, that I endeavour to benefit.'³⁰ Thus he was enabled to attribute to prudence and impartiality delays which had perhaps a deeper source in an acute, torturing lack of self-confidence, an overwhelming desire to postpone the time when he would have to turn from deliberation to action.*

And Pietro, dear Pietro – although very much bored at Metaxata – took it all at its face value. Of all the services he rendered to Byron, this – an unswerving loyalty and acceptance, not only of his orders, but of his motives – was perhaps the greatest. Every picture of himself that Byron most wished to present, was mirrored in Pietro's candid eyes. And is it not possible – since we all, in a measure, resemble the image that our friends form of us – that Byron, when with Pietro, indeed became not unlike the single-minded, generous, heroic figure that Pietro saw?

In spite, however, of all his loyalty, Pietro was finding the prolonged delays at Metaxata more than a little trying.

'Four days ago we left Argostoli and returned to this village, 9 miles from the town. It is placed on a pretty hill – on the left one sees the Mount Revitos, or Black Mountain, which is considered the first of all Greece after the Pindo – and on the right a fine plain, the sea, Zante opposite, and far off the Morea. You can see a fine picture, but by God, there is nothing but a picture. Imagine our adventures in this exile. Every morning I go out and shoot snipe and by bad luck the best place for them is near the house of a damned old woman, who swears at me every morning, in Greek and Venetian, because she is afraid that with my shooting I will set fire to her house. We have not made the acquaintance of any Christians, male or female, in this country.

In view of the very uncertain condition of things in the Morea, M[ylord] has decided to stay here for a while, until he can reach a mature decision, for one can learn the truth here only with the greatest difficulty – perhaps no better than in Italy[31] – and this is not surprising, for we have learned from frequent experience that one often discovers things less well and more slowly from nearby, than from far away. The opinion of the Greek Nation that we have heard in Italy is not mistaken, if what we have gathered until now is true. Whatever gossip you may hear about us, do not be anxious – our conduct should reassure you. Trelawny with Mr. Browne, one of our companions, has gone to Tripolitza to learn more details about the state of things. We are waiting for their reports soon.

* NICOLSON, op. cit., p. 155. 'At Metaxata he could be generous, be acute, be prudent; at Missolonghi he would have to *control*.'

Poor Papa! what a lot of trouble – all falling on him!* If the affection of his children can be of some comfort to him in his persecution, pray do not neglect anything to give him further proofs of it. I am glad about grandfather's behaviour – a fanatical Christian but an excellent man; and his nature has shown itself on this occasion.† God grant him a long life. . . .

Byron is very well indeed and always has been. I look after him as well as I know how, both for his health and everything that concerns him – and he is well, and everything goes well. In all that we have met with so far, he is much more pleased with his own compatriots than with the Greek patriots, and by God he is right. We shall see in future.

Take heart, and bear stoutly your anxiety and your troubles. I am glad to see you resigned and tranquil. That is the way to conquer and change one's fortune, my Teresa, be sure of it!'

BYRON TO CONTESSA GUICCIOLI[32]

September 11th, 1823

My dearest T.: We have received y[r] letters safely, and I am rejoiced to hear so good an account of y[r] health. [We are still in Cephalonia waiting for news of a more accurate description, for all is contradiction and division in the reports of the state of the Greeks etc. – – – – I shall fulfil the object of my mission from the committee – and then (probably) return into Italy for it does not seem likely that as an individual I can be of use to them. At least no one other foreigner has yet appeared to be so – nor does it seem likely that any will be at present. (Pietro will have said more perhaps on this subject.)

Pray be as cheerful and tranquil as you can – and be assured that there is nothing here that can excite anything but a wish to be with you again – though we are very kindly treated by the English here of all descriptions. Of the Greeks I can't say much good hitherto and I do not like to speak ill of them though they do so of one another.]‡ We are here in a very pretty village –

* Count Ruggero was still living in half-banishment at Ferrara.
† Count Paolo Gamba, Count Ruggero's father, was a *Sanfedista*, and could not but disapprove of his son's and grandson's activities; but on this occasion family seems to have been stronger than politics.
‡ See notes 32, 36 and 39 on page 516.

with fine scenery of every description – and we have kept our
health very well. Pray remember me to Costa and his wife – and
to Papa and all our acquaintances and allies. $+++$

When we meet again (if it please God) I hope to tell you several
things that will make you smile. I kiss your Eyes (*occhi*) and am
most affectly a.a. in e. $++++$ N.B.

It was now some months since Byron had sailed, and it must
have begun to be clear to Teresa, in spite of his reassuring sentences, that he was hardly likely to return before the winter. She
appears still to have been staying with Paolo Costa, for a letter
from Pietro to him thanks him for 'helping Papa to obtain justice',
and for 'alleviating poor Teresa's situation by your Friendship.'[33]
Moreover, Teresa seems now to have made a valiant attempt,
under the influence of her old teacher, to conquer her fears and
occupy her mind by undertaking a course of philosophical studies
– a decision to which Pietro refers with whole-hearted, and Byron
with somewhat ironic, approval. She felt, perhaps, that she was
likely to need any philosophy she could acquire, and it was,
indeed, nearly another month before any more news from Pietro
reached her.

'Here we are still in Metaxata – that is in Cephalonia – and I
don't see how we shall find a way out. – I imagine you are in
Bologna, and Papa in Ferrara; everything therefore in *statu quo*.
How many tales have you heard? What spectres have been called
up by your diseased imagination? I do not know better remedies
than Paolo's philosophic-philological dissertations, Giuditta's[*]
affectionate care – and the task that you have set yourself, or that
Paolo has given you. I believe that he, as a moral adviser, has
considered it the best remedy for your imaginary ills; and the
work will deserve great praise and will have made a good
beginning if it has a good effect on you. From your letters I will
judge what it achieves.

You ask me why we are here and perhaps shall stay on here. I
will answer you briefly (for a whole book would not be enough for
a detailed description) that the Greek situation has not yet given
us any opportunity in which one could believe B[yron]'s help to be
truly efficacious and useful, because there are as many parties in
this happy land as there are people who can have some hope of
acquiring power or plunder – because the best have already been
exiled or are disgusted – and because the general interests of

* Paolo Costa's wife.

Greece are understood by few Greeks, and desired by even fewer. We cannot feel much surprised, and the reasons are well known. But meanwhile what can a foreigner do, in the midst of these rascals (I am speaking of the chiefs), but wait for a better opportunity? Byron has confirmed his original opinion of these people, but has not therefore changed his intentions. And this certainly deserves all the greater praise. You will not be of my opinion.

Greek affairs in general are not in a bad way, and will proceed – chiefly following the law of inertia in physics, which ordains that bodies in motion shall advance, and motionless ones remain still. The Greeks obey the first law, and the Turks the second – they are the most indolent and bestial race ever seen under the Moon. Let them proceed. For my part I wish with all my heart that Greece should be free – and would like to co-operate, if it is in my power – then, good night. With all possible freedom and every desirable advantage, nothing could keep me long among the Greeks. They are the vainest and most insincere race on earth, a chemical aggregate of all the vices of their ancestors, plus many taken from the Turks, and a good dose of the Jewish – diluted and mixed in the melting-pot of slavery. If Heaven helps them to freedom, they will cast them off [the vices] – but it will not be for us, or for our sons, to see them cleansed. My opinion may be – I hope it is – too severe! the fruit perhaps of the bitterness that has come over me at the constant sight of the cowardice and intrigues of these damned Ionians. The others I only know about by hearsay. But – but – we started in such a tranquil state of mind, and so prepared for the worst, that I am almost ashamed to find myself so heated.

Everyone, from all sides, is besieging Byron to extract his *duros* [dollars], but after having prodigally scattered about a thousand – he has now again become so much attached to them, that I very much doubt whether they will find a blacksmith capable of making a key to his purse. And he is right, if he does not know why or to whom.

Oh, if I tried to count up all the victories, and defeats and marvellous captures that are rumoured every day! It appears, however, to be an incontestable fact that during the last few days eighteen thousand Turks have been besieging Missolonghi – in which there are five or seven thousand Greeks. Marco Botzari, a true hero, and the Chief of the Suliotes, was killed a month and a half ago: and Mavrocordato wrote to us recently from Hydra, where he had fled from the threats and persecutions of his fellow-countrymen. The usual Greek recompense to talents and virtue.

To come back to us. We are well. Byron has returned to his

hermit's life, and is satisfied with it. We have a fine view, good air – and sometimes we are given a fine dance, which is not too agreeable. One day we felt 7 earthquakes. At the first and strongest we were obliged to run away. There is a staircase down into the court. Byron ran down it *fast enough*, I jumped down half of it – and there is a great argument between us as to who deserves the prize for running fastest. His argument is, that I touched the ground first, mine, that I went out of the house behind him. You judge.³⁴

What is happening? Has a new Pope been elected? It should surely bring about some change, and for us it could hardly be for the worse. Do not be too inactive, for perhaps this is a good moment to reacquire your rights.'³⁵

BYRON TO CONTESSA GUICCIOLI

8ᵇʳᵉ 7ᵐᵒ 1823

My dearest T.:³⁶ [Pietro has told you all the gossip of the island – our earthquakes – our politics – and present abode in a pretty village. (But he has not told you the result of one of his gallantries – which I leave to himself to describe.)

As his opinions and mine on the Greeks are nearly similar – I need say little on that subject. I was a fool to come here but being here I must see what is to be done.]

If we were not at such a distance, I could tell you many things that would make you smile – but I hope to do so at no very long period. Pray keep well and love me as you are beloved by yours ever a.a.+++in e.   N.B.

Pietro's next letter, written on October 14th, brought little fresh news.

'Our situation is unchanged – nor is there any reason why a change should come. Nothing from Greece since my last letter. Missolonghi besieged by land and blockaded by sea, but in the Turkish manner, that is not strictly. It is well ammunitioned, well furnished, sufficiently provisioned, and here they are raising collections to send off more stores. Byron is becoming very uneasy about his *duros*, and will hardly escape having to give up some of them.

Poor Byron! He has been much saddened by the news that reached him a fortnight ago about an illness in the head of his dear Ada.³⁷ You can imagine how his imagination raised up a thousand melancholy phantoms and added to them the fear that some months might pass before he received any more news, the suspicion that the information was sent to him on purpose to torment him, and the dread that it might be an hereditary disease. However another bulletin has arrived, saying that she is much better and out of danger, but is having trouble with her eyes. His sadness is much decreased, but not over.

You must add another remarkable reason [for his depression]. He ate a goose on the 29th, a solemn feast as you know [Michaelmas day]. He wanted another for the 10th, which is also a feastday.[88] The servants deceived him and gave it him on the 11th. You can imagine the uproar!

Byron is impatient to go out riding. I cannot write any more.'

Byron's postscript reflects his hurry:

My dearest T. – We have not heard from you for some time. Why do not you write? We have sent several letters – ever and entirely yours a.a. in e.+ N.B.

A few days later, on October 21st, Pietro sent another letter by hand, by means of 'a German baron', on his way back to Italy. He told his sister to 'thank Paolo on my behalf for the trouble he is taking to straighten out your ideas', implored her 'to temper your heated and sometimes feverish imagination', and enclosed a postscript from Byron.

BYRON TO CONTESSA GUICCIOLI

[*October 21st*, 1823]

My dearest T. – I shall merely add two words to Pietro's letter – to scold you for not having written. – We are all tolerably well and tranquil – and except an earthquake or two daily – (one of which broke the Lambico for filtering the water – last night) which rock us to and fro a little – things are much as when we wrote before.

I hear you are turned moral philosopher – and are meditating various works for the occupation of your old age – all which is very proper. – ever yours a+a+in e+ N.B.

Another letter followed before the end of the month.

BYRON TO CONTESSA GUICCIOLI[39]

8bre 29th, 1823

My dearest T.: Enclosed is a letter from Pietro written upon a scurvy scrap of paper – but containing, I believe, all that is to the purpose relative to our present situation. – We are tolerably well and so forth – but the weather is cool – and *mi-me ne* etc. etc. etc. *Capite Eccellenza?* – – – – –* I received yr letter of the date of 7bre and we have written by every opportunity. – – –

Under Costa's tuition I presume that you have made a great progress in Metaphysics; – I have written nothing but letters or dispatches lately. A connection of mine – Lord Sydney Osborne, came from Corfu yesterday to see me – and Pietro and I dine this afternoon with the English Resident to meet him. –[40]

I hope that your philosophical studies will furnish you with a little patience – and all will go well by and bye. – [You may be sure that the moment I can join you again will be as welcome to me as at any period of our recollection. – There is nothing very attractive here to divide my attention – but I must attend to the Greek Cause both from honour and inclination.

Messrs. Browne and Trelawny are in the Morea – where they have been very well received – and both of them write in good spirits and hopes. I am anxious to hear how the Spanish Cause will be arranged – as I think that it may have an influence on the Greek Contest. – – I wish that both were fairly and favourably settled – that I might return quietly to Italy – and talk over with you *our*, or rather Pietro's adventures – some of which are very amusing – as also some of the incidents of our voyages and travels. – But I reserve them in the hope that we may laugh over them together at no very remote period.] – We must now get on horse-back to ride over to Argostoli.–

Ever my dearest T. il tuo A.A. in E. + + +   N.B.

This letter was followed by a note from Pietro, evidently written in answer to an anxious and unhappy letter from Teresa, and once more exhorting her to overcome her 'imaginary sufferings' by diligence in her philosophical studies, 'for leisure will be your worst enemy'. 'No danger', he added, 'attacks us or will attack us. Have confidence in our prudence.'

---

* The nearest equivalent to this sentence is the French 'je m'en f . . . s'.

'Byron', the letter went on, 'is in excellent health, and whatever
people say, I have noticed that he is much better when enduring
hardships. Not that I would advise them, but I should like to
convince you that he is not the worse for them, as you fear. . . .

You cannot imagine how much the European Gazettes make us
laugh – the English and French ones, which sometimes arrive here,
and talk about victories, battles, heroism. Oh, my Teresa, this
is a veritable school of disillusion.'

As to Teresa herself, he surmised that she must have her hands
full 'with G., the guileful Patrician, and with the priests. It is
said here that Cardinal Della Genga has been elected Pope'.

The news was true – and, since the new Pope's views were supposed to be more liberal than those of his predecessor, Teresa had
realized that this was the most likely moment for her to obtain
redress. On October 15th she had addressed to the new Pope,
Leo XII, a petition for the restoration of her allowance, pointing
out that her husband had succeeded in obtaining its suspension
from his predecessor 'by unknown means, but doubtless through
calumnies and intrigues'. It was now, she added, more thañ a
year since she had received a penny from her husband, so that
'she had added to all her other misfortunes, that of being wholly
dependent upon her family', and she pleaded for an allowance
'suitable to her noble birth and proportionate to the great riches
of her husband'.[41] The slow, careful machinery of the Vatican was
then set in motion. On January 6th, 1824, Cardinal Rusconi's
secretary wrote to tell her that her husband had been interrogated
about her allowance,* and at the beginning of March – presumably
in an attempt to intimidate the old Count – Teresa's younger
brother Ippolito, a boy of seventeen, forced his way into Palazzo
Guiccioli. 'You promised an allowance to my sister, and as a man
of honour you should keep your promise,' he shouted, as soon as
he entered the courtyard – but the Count, taking him by the arm,
led him politely into a sitting-room, and at the same time, 'being
rather alarmed by his manner', told one of his servants to keep
within earshot. 'My dear young Count,' he then said to his fiery
young brother-in-law, 'don't you see that for me to grant her an
allowance is to go against a reunion which would be advantageous
to us all!' 'A reunion!' said the boy rudely – 'with a man who has
calumniated her! No, never! I did not come to treat with you,
but –' Whereupon the Count, on the pretext of ringing for a glass
of water, left the room, locked himself up in his study, and told his

---

* Gamba Papers. Letter dated January 6th, 1824, from Gioacchino Tridenti
to Contessa Guiccioli.

AA

servants to inform Ippolito, 'as he seems to be mad', that he had left the house.[42]

Ippolito then went away, but not without a parting shot: 'I came to tell him that a new Rescript in favour of my sister has already been signed by the Court of Rome, and is expected here.'

Guiccioli at once sent off a most characteristic letter to his lawyer in Rome, Vincenzo Taglioni.

'I think it best to inform you that her father and brother Ippolito are strongly opposed to a reconciliation, under the pretext that I have calumniated her. I, however, think it likely that their opposition really comes from a wish to make money out of her. It is certain that up till now they have been receiving support from Lord Byron, and that also they have at present the advantage of having placed another brother, Pietro, with him in Greece. Thus the family is relieved from all care and expenditure on his account, and perhaps they hope and expect as much for another brother, and still more besides, from Lord Byron. If to all that they can add a large allowance from me, they may be satisfied with their bargain.'[43]

The Count then proceeded to suggest that his lawyer should 'make these ideas the subject of consideration' in the Vatican. But meanwhile Cardinal Rusconi had already written to Teresa, stating her husband's accusations against her – and she had sent a long self-justificatory reply. Guiccioli's chief grounds for demanding the revocation of the allowance appear to have been Byron's visits to Filetto in 1820 – his life with Teresa in Pisa – and Teresa's refusal to return to her husband, when he asked her to do so in 1822.

In reply to the first accusation, Teresa once again denied that she had ever seen Byron at Filetto, except in the presence of her father and brothers. And as to his coming to call – 'What', she cried, 'could possibly have made her interpret the Pope's general clause about "honest behaviour" as forbidding the visits of one special individual? – and the one to whom, above all others, she owed the deepest obligations?' Lord Byron, she repeated, had saved her life by sending for Prof. Aglietti when her husband's avarice had refused to call in any consultant; he had undertaken all the expenses of Aglietti's visit, and later on of her convalescence at La Mira. Was it not natural, she pleaded, that, 'at a time when I needed comfort and friendship more than ever, owing to my sad situation, this generous man should come to see me?'

As to Byron's residence in Pisa, Teresa stoutly affirmed that he only came there to be near some of his compatriots and that she only saw him 'two or three times a week, for an hour, in the time which everyone gives to the conversazione'.

And finally, as to her letter to her husband from Pisa, her refusal to return to him was entirely due to the stories she had heard about the immoral life he was leading in her absence, and her knowledge of the incompatibility of their characters. 'How could I think that he would give so malicious and false an interpretation to my letter?' [44]

What the Cardinal thought on reading these disingenuous remarks, is not recorded. But the final decision of the Vatican was in Teresa's favour, for on April 6th – only a few days before Byron's death – Cardinal Rusconi himself informed her that her petition was granted: her allowance would be renewed, and the arrears paid. [45]

She had now, at least, regained a measure of independence. But, as the long months passed and Byron's letters became rarer and more meagre, her sense of hopelessness increased. To Lord Malmesbury, some years later, she said that at this time she was convinced that Byron had forgotten her. [46] For almost a month there was no further news – and when at last a letter came, the greater part of it, once again, was written by Pietro.

'You are right to be angry with us,' he began, 'for we have not written for at least 20 days – but also we have had no letters for over a month. I don't know how much longer we shall stay in this Island, for we are completely the slaves of circumstance. When we left Genoa we had no intention of landing here – when we landed we did not intend to stay more than a few days – now we have been here for four months – nor do I know when we shall get away. Don't complain about the post – or at least complain of Fortune – for I see that she is the ruler of our destinies. Let no rumour nor gossip distress you. You have nothing to dread but your own fancies. For the rest, put your trust in our prudence.' [47]

A postscript, written three days later, acknowledged the arrival of letters from Teresa, 'after almost two months of silence', and added

'We have been here in Metaxata for almost 3 months. You know that Byron puts down roots easily wherever he is, but by God, the circumstances here have so far been such that his immobility has been put down to the most profound *policy* – and rightly – for it would not be possible to act more prudently – nor to attain better results. Although the discussions that had been suspended in Greece, owing to his influence, have now begun again, our hopes for the Greeks are stronger than ever. However, they are and always will remain the scum I have described to you. I believe that their master – the Turk – will no longer do for them – because he is no longer capable of keeping any servants, but should perhaps turn into one himself – but by God I wonder whether they will not need another master.* If they remain independent, it will be because nobody wants them – and those who might want them, will not be allowed to, by their friends.

We can't make any further plans yet, but be sure that when the opportunity offers we shall do all we can *so that your torments may have an end* – in so far as they lie in us, and not in your own brain.'

Byron's postscript brought little comfort:

9*bre* 29*th*, 1823

My dearest T.: What Pietro says is very reasonable, but we are at present so busy – that I have little time to write much in addition to his letter.

Here are arrived – English – Germans – Greeks – all kinds of people, in short – proceeding to or coming from Greece – and all with something to say to me – so that every day – I have to receive them here, or visit them in Argostoli.

The Greek affairs go on better – they have taken Corinth – and their fleet has had a victory near the Islands – but not in *these* waters. I still hope to see you in Spring – and in the mean time entreat you to quiet your apprehensions and believe me ever yr. a.a. in e+++   N.B.

P.S. I regret to see in the English papers that Colonel Fitz Gibbon brother to my particular friend *Lord Clare* has eloped from Ireland with the wife of a friend; the affair makes much noise. The woman had four children and carried two with her.

Among the English people on their way to Greece, to whom Byron's letter refers, was Colonel Leicester Stanhope,⁴⁸ who had

---

* Here Pietro is echoing the opinion that Byron had expressed in a letter to Prince Mavrocordato: 'Greece is at present placed between three measures: either to reconquer her liberty, to become a dependence of the sovereigns of Europe, or to return to a Turkish province. She has the choice only of these three . . . If she is desirous of the fate of Walachia and the Crimea, she may obtain it tomorrow; if of that of Italy, the day after; but if she wishes to become truly Greece, free and independent, she must resolve today.' GAMBA, op. cit., pp. 61-2.

been sent out to Greece by the Greek Committee. An ardent Benthamite, he arrived at Argostoli full of enthusiastic plans, which totally disregarded the existent chaotic conditions, for the immediate establishment of a Greek Republic. Byron, from the first, did not care for his 'Nabob airs', and had too much sense of reality to embrace his opinions. ' "The typographical Colonel", as Lord Byron sarcastically termed him, seemed to think that newspapers would be more effectual in driving back the Ottomans than well-drilled troops and military tactics.'⁴⁹ After a few conversations with Byron and Colonel Napier, who strove to dispel in him some of the 'high-flown notions of the sixth form at Eton',⁵⁰ he crossed, early in December, to Missolonghi, taking with him letters from Byron to Mavrocordato and the Greek Government. These contained the warning that 'unless union and order are established, all the assistance which the Greeks could expect from abroad . . . will be suspended or destroyed'.

'Allow me to add once for all – I desire the well-being of Greece and nothing else; I will do all I can to secure it; but I cannot consent, I never will consent, that the English public, or English individuals, should be deceived as to the real state of Greek affairs. The rest, Gentlemen, depends on you.'⁵¹

A copy of this letter was sent by Pietro, on the same day, to Teresa, with the comment she was to make any use of it she liked. Byron 'wishes this letter of his to be known, so that, in the question of the loan, no unfair responsibilities should fall upon his shoulders, as usual.'

For another three weeks silence fell – and when Pietro wrote again, on December 14th, it was to complain that they had not heard from Teresa since the end of October. 'The winter', he added, 'has come upon us without our being aware of it. I hope you have resigned yourself [to wait] until the spring.' As for themselves, he was at some pains to impress her with the patience they had been showing. 'For four months hermits upon these rocks! Can you believe in the *monkish virtues* of Byron? They are above all praise.'

Teresa may well have smiled wryly at this – and the best comment is provided by a letter from Byron himself to Barry.

'If these gentlemen . . . [the members of the Greek factions] discover my weak side, viz. a propensity to be governed, and were to set a pretty woman, or a clever woman, about me, with a turn for political or any other sort of intrigue, – why, they

would make a fool of me, no very difficult matter probably, even
without such an intervention. But if I can keep passion, at least
that passion, out of the question (which may be the more easy, as
I left my heart in Italy) they will not weather me with quite so
much facility.'[52]

Byron's next letter to Teresa, however, must have slightly
raised her spirits, since for the first time he referred to the possibility of her joining them.

BYRON TO CONTESSA GUICCIOLI

December 14th, 1823

Carissima Pettegola:* But I forgot that I must write to you in
English by your own request, – well! – here we are still – but how
long we may be so I cannot say. The Greek affairs go on rather
better – but I won't bore you with politics.

Perhaps in the Spring we shall be able to invite you to Zante to
stay with the Grassettis'† and then I could come over and see
you from the Morea or elsewhere. Or Pietro or I could run down
to Ancona to convoy you hither. So you see – we think of your
Excellency – and of your sentimental projects.

The Climate, up to this day, has been quite beautiful. Tuscany
is Lapland in comparison – but today we have a high wind – and
rain – but it is still as *warm* as your Primavera.

Pietro and I are occupied all day and every day with Greek
business – and our correspondence already amounts to more
volumes than that of Santa Chiara – even when your Eccellenza
was in the course of your education.

Pietro is full of magnificent projects – and the Greeks also –
most of which *commence*, and will, I presume, *end* (those of the
Greeks I mean, for Pietro is more sparing than I of our Soldi)
in asking me for some money.

There is a rumour that the Legislative Govt. of the Morea –
have named me jointly with Mavrocordato in some commission
or other – but *which* or *what* I do not yet know, – and perhaps it is
only a rumour.

* 'Dearest gossip', but Teresa has tried to erase the word.
† Dr. Gaetano Grassetti was a doctor of Ravenna who had been obliged to fly
from the Romagna in 1815, owing to having taken sides with the French. He was at
that time living in Patras.

For my part 'me-me ne etc. etc.' and leave them to project as they please – being neither ambitious nor enthusiastic on such points as you know – but always very much dearest T. your a.a. in E.+   N.B.

P.S.[53] Greet Olimpia* from me as much and when you can and also Giulia and Laurina, not forgetting Papa and your two brothers. My respects to Costa and a thousand compliments to his good lady [*siora*, in Venetian dialect].

Yesterday I was caught in the rain and I *ache* . . . But it is only temporary. Pietro has been ill (I will let *him* tell you of *what ailment*) but thanks to the attentions of our little doctor Bruno, who has been christened Brunetto Latini,[54] being rather pedantic, he is quite well again.

The preceding letter is mainly remarkable for the complete omission of the subject that was filling the writer's mind: his imminent departure for the Greek mainland. For Byron – whatever his inner misgivings – had realized that the moment for action had come. The Western Greeks (Mavrocordato's party) had at last succeeded in scoring some successes against the Turks; the Greek fleet, such as it was, had arrived in the waters of Missolonghi; the London Committee had sent a letter-press, some medical stores, some mechanical instruments and several trumpets ('but till we have an engineer and a trumpeter [they are] mere pearls to swine')[55] – and now both Mavrocordato and Colonel Stanhope urged him to join them as soon as possible. 'Your counsels', wrote Mavrocordato, 'will be listened to like oracles.' 'A great deal is expected of you', wrote Stanhope, 'both in the way of counsel and money.'[56] It was plain that the time had come to start.

'You had better write to the Countess Guic.i', wrote Byron to Barry, 'to state that her brother and I are going (or gone) to Missolonghi, and that everything is *quite pacific*, as well as the *business* we are upon. This perhaps is not the exact or entire truth, but it is as much as needs to be stated to one who will naturally be anxious about her brother, etc. etc. etc.'[57]

So at last, on December 28th, in two ships – Byron in a small light 'mystico', and Pietro in a larger ship with the baggage -- the party set sail for Missolonghi.

* Olimpia, Giulia and Laurina were sisters of Teresa's.

'The wind favourable, a clear sky, the air fresh but not sharp. Our sailors sang alternately patriotic songs . . . and we took part in them. We were all, but Lord Byron particularly, in excellent spirits. The Mystico sailed the fastest. When the waves divided us and our voices could no longer reach each other, we made signals by firing pistols and carabines. Tomorrow we meet at Missolonghi – tomorrow.'[58]

As usual, however, Pietro's hopes were too high. The two boats lost sight of each other; and in the Gulf of Patras Byron's mystico having sighted a Turkish frigate, was obliged to take refuge for three days at Dragomestri, until the arrival of a Greek escort. Meanwhile Pietro, in the other boat, had succeeded in getting himself captured, – together with Tita, Lega Zambelli, the horses, the stores, and Byron's dollars – by another Turkish frigate, and only owing his life to the singularly fortunate circumstance that the commander of the frigate, Zacharia Bey, had once had his life saved from shipwreck by the Greek captain of Gamba's ship. So Zacharia Bey accepted Pietro's improbable story that he was merely a traveller proceeding to the island of Kalimnos, in the service of an English Lord, and towed him into Patras – where he visited the Pasha's divan, shot his woodcock – and reached Missolonghi in time to take part, on the morning of January 5th, in Byron's welcome at Missolonghi.

Three days later, in spite of difficulties calculated to damp any nature less optimistic than his own – he was sending his sister the following cheerful but uninformative letter.

'Here is the prospectus of the first Greek Gazette – in Greek[59] – but it will be published in Italian, too, as soon as we have Italian compositors capable of printing it – we have already sent for them. The price is 6 dollars a month.

I hope we shall find subscriptions in Bologna too. Recommend it. I hope there will be no obstacles from the Italian Government, or indeed from any Government, for the Greek cause cannot be unpopular with any Christian Power, and also because we have made it a principle not to deal with any subject that would in any way offend the policy of the European Cabinets, or of the Supreme Pontiff. The Greeks feel a special gratitude for the benefits received from Him, when others were still cold to the point of hostility.

Lord Byron has been received like a delivering Angel. Affairs are going better and better towards the establishment of order –

there is no fear of the Turks – and the Greeks all turn to Byron for the composition of their discussions, which are now completely resolved. I will write soon at length.

Pietro's next letter, dated January 14th, was only a brief note to reassure her as to 'our health – our good hopes – and the complete lack of danger – unless your fancy creates it'.

'Keep well,' he added, 'be calm – be happy – if you can. Byron would not mind your going occasionally to some conversazioni, like those of Hortensia Buonaparte. I hope that in the spring we shall see each other again, that is, if you will see us – for it will be easier for you to take a journey with someone – your brother or Giuliani – to the Islands – than for us to return to Italy, for the present. But we will talk about it.'

A postscript added: 'Byron has never enjoyed such vigorous health.' This letter suggests that Byron was genuinely intending, as he had told Teresa in his last letter, to let her come to join him in the Greek Islands in the spring. But in his next note, enclosed in one of Pietro's, Byron makes no reference to the plan.

[*January 27th, 1824*]

My dearest Teresa: We have been here since 10bre 31°, or rather since G°. 8° for that was the day on which we arrived. – You will have heard of our adventures from other quarters. – We are well and all here is well – I will write soon at greater length – in the interim Love me – and be assured that you are the most Beloved of yours+++ N.B.ⁿ

On February 11th another note from Pietro contained no news of any interest, and was followed by a few lines from Byron.

My dearest T. – All well. – I will write shortly at greater length. – – I have found a very pretty Turkish female infant of ten years old – whom I mean to send to you by and bye – she is beautiful as the Sun – and very lively – you can educate her –. yours ever N.B.ⁿ

This little girl, whose name was Hato or Hatadje, was one of the Turkish inhabitants of Missolonghi, who, when the town proclaimed itself part of Western Greece, were either massacred or cast into slavery. Byron sent twenty-four women and children to safety in Prevesa, and proposed – disregarding the fact that the child's father, Husein Aga, was still alive in Patras – to take charge of the child, who had taken a great fancy to him, and send her back for Teresa to bring up. A few days later, however, he had another happy idea:

'If I thought', he wrote to Augusta, 'that Lady B[yron] would let her come to England as a Companion to Ada (they are about the same age) and we could easily provide for her; if not I can send her to Italy for her education. She is very lively and quick, and with great black Oriental eyes, and Asiatic features . . . You can mention this matter if you think it worth while. I merely wish her to be respectably educated and treated, and, if my years and all things be considered, I presume it would be difficult to conceive me to have any other views.'*

Meanwhile he dressed up the child 'in fine clothes, in the fashion of the country', and made much of her – rather as he would have petted a promising puppy – until she became 'pert and forward', when he decided to hand her over temporarily to Dr. Kennedy and his wife, in Cephalonia. 'Your future convert', he wrote to Kennedy, 'appears to me lively, and intelligent and promising, and possesses an interesting countenance.'⁶⁰ Dr. Kennedy, in reply, wrote to Pietro:

'that he was very glad to take Mylord's little protégée, that these good works did him greater honour than all his writings, but that he would not advise Byron to send her to Italy, where she cannot receive a good religious and moral education, but rather to England. This', commented Pietro in some amusement to Teresa, 'will serve to keep alive your angry defence of Santa Chiara!'⁶¹

But Hato did not become either a good little Methodist, or Ada's playmate. Before she could be shipped off to Cephalonia, Byron's death once again changed her destiny. She now implored, after all, to be sent back with her mother to her own father in Patras. 'I thought you slaves', said Husein Aga when they arrived, 'and lo! you return to me decked like brides!'⁶²

* L.J., VI, pp. 331-2. February 23rd, 1824. This absurd suggestion, however, never reached Lady Byron, since the letter was found on Byron's writing-desk after death.

Pietro's next letter (February 24th) referred to his capture by the Turkish frigate, which he had concealed from Teresa until then, and would appear only to have mentioned now in the hope of distracting her from the graver news contained in the rest of his letter.

'If you have heard of our, or rather my, capture by the Turks – and who knows how much exaggerated – Oh God! What terrors! what swooning! what convulsions! And perhaps not without some reason this time. But luckily everything ended happily – and to have escaped an impending danger, can be considered a good omen. I sent an exact account of all that happened to Papa; I think it best to tell you first about the bad, rather than the good, events, otherwise the news will reach you in a distorted and vague form and will distress you doubly. Here is another, which has also ended well.

Less than eight days ago, when Mylord was laughing and sitting on a sofa with a glass in his hand in the company of other Englishmen* (I was out of the house) he tried to get up from the sofa and was suddenly assailed by a strong convulsion, which prevented him from moving. He was lifted up, placed on his bed, the doctor came running, etc. He was unable to speak – although not unconscious – for a few seconds. You can imagine the general dismay.

He soon recovered his senses, was carried to bed, cured with purgatives and other medicines. The next day he got out of bed, his head was very heavy. Eight leeches were then applied to his temples. It is now six days since his complete recovery.

I hope that this misfortune will have one excellent effect. For some time Byron had been forming the habit of a very bad way of life. He was eating very little, only strong cheese and salad, he was drinking a great deal, strong wine and liquor, especially a damned grog and brandy – that is a sort of English aquavitae, which is their passion.

Through the damned example of an excellent rough Englishman who has been sent here by the Committee, Mr. Parry,† who makes Congreve rockets and is an immoderate drinker, Mylord drank seven very strong punches on the day before his accident, and five on the same day.** Add to this constant anxiety about

* This attack took place in Stanhope's rooms.

† Mr. William Parry, who subsequently styled himself 'Major Parry of Lord Byron's Brigade, Commanding Officer of Artillery and Engineer in the service of the Greeks', had been sent to Byron by the Greek Committee, with a recommendation as a 'very intelligent fire-master'. He subsequently – by his hero-worship and a certain bluntness which Byron took for sincerity – acquired a considerable influence over Byron, and wrote one of the most vivid accounts of Byron's last days.

business, and his being unable to ride on the bad roads in wet weather.

This attack has brought him to his senses and the good it has done has been to make him change his way of life entirely. He eats enough, chicken and wholesome food, he drinks moderately, and takes exercise when possible. To tell you the truth, I have never seen him in better health than in the midst of the greatest hardships. Riding eight hours a day under a broiling sun in August, he was perfectly well. Sleeping for eight nights without undressing, on board a miserable brig in the rawest December, and bathing in the sea in that season (all folly) he could not have been better. You see that the follies of idleness are most to be feared for him. I trust that I will not have to torment you with any more misfortunes. Mylord received your letter through Barry. So his fame is always increasing in Italy – as it is here and in England. With the last Cantos of *Don Juan* he has made more than 16.000 dollars and his friends write to him that when he returns home he will be received with enthusiasm. This journey has also been very favourable to him in English opinion. So he will be encouraged, esteemed; I am delighted about it. Pray therefore observe that my advice and prophecies were not mistaken and that this temporary separation, although it caused you great suffering, will in the end produce an excellent result for everyone, and most of all for [him]. . . .

A postscript followed from Byron:

$F.°\ 24°,\ 1824$

My dearest T.: Pietro will have told you all the news – but I have not read the whole of his letter. We are all very well *now* – and everything appears to wear a hopeful aspect. – Of course you may suppose that a country like this is not exactly the place to pass the Carnival in; but it is nevertheless better than could be expected all things considered. I am going out on horseback and Pietro has hardly left me room enough on this paper to add more at present – but I hope to see you this Spring and to talk over these and all other matters – so be of good cheer and love ever yours most a.a. in e+++   N.B.[n]

At the bottom of the page were a few more words from Pietro: 'Byron complains that I have been too severe in imputing all the fault for his ailment to *punch* – – – –'

It is perhaps indicative of Byron's lack of intimacy with Teresa – although it may also partly have sprung from a wish to spare her anxiety – that the preceding note has no reference whatever to his severe attack. But in truth he had been deeply perturbed by it. In his Journal he wrote down a detailed account of what had occurred; he made Dr. Bruno draw up a memorandum for him, analysing the symptoms and causes of epilepsy; and to Augusta he wrote: 'It is also fit, though unpleasant, that I should mention that my recent attack, and a very severe one, had a strong appearance of *epilepsy*.'⁶⁴ To his friends in Greece he attempted to make light of it, but they all noted his deep depression – which only lifted in moments when some activity was required of him, or in sudden gusts of immoderate, almost hysterical, high spirits. These, according to Parry, found a vent in a series of practical jokes – which were often far from agreeable for their victims. Thus one day, soon after his fit, he succeeded in terrifying all his companions, who had recently experienced a severe earthquake, by another simulated one – caused by the violent trampling of his Souliot brigands overhead, 'so as to shake the house'. Parry was so much annoyed that he 'threatened to quit his Lordship's service if such jokes were repeated'.⁶⁵ On several other occasions he amused himself by firing with his pistols at 'the little turrets' of a neighbouring 'house built in the Turkish fashion . . . and inhabited chiefly by women', – until the turrets were destroyed. The women, Parry relates, would come out on the housetop, chattering and screaming, 'and Byron said he liked so much to hear and see them, that he would not be without the sport for a considerable sum'.⁶⁶ Gamba's book maintains a discreet silence about such incidents, but in a letter to his sister he does describe the last of them.

'The other day', he wrote on March 17th, 'we had cause for several days' laughter with our Mameluke Fletcher.⁶⁷ He always complained he could find no woman. Mylord thought of dressing up a boy as a young girl and having him offered to Fletcher. The matter was carried through admirably by a Greek, the owner of the house. The virgin – for he was assured that she was so – came, they gave her three dollars and promised three more after the event. Then he took her into the attic of our house. While he was using every possible endearment in the Greek tongue, to conquer her virginal reluctance, a great row was heard on the stairs. It was the brother of the seduced girl, who was asking for his betrayed sister and swearing and threatening. You can imagine Fletcher's terror. The virgin with her threatening brother

were taken before Byron who with all the severity of an offended
master and the gravity of a judge, called his household before him
to examine them and discover the culprit. Fletcher denied everything and tried to put the fault on this man or that, and on the
doctor or me. You can imagine the fine scene . . . A letter was
written in Prince Mavrocordato's name, demanding justice for
the insult to public morals, committed by some members of
Mylord's family. Fletcher drew out some more dollars to quieten
the aggrieved brother. Another letter from the Police had been
prepared to discover the culprit, but on the next day some
busybody gave the joke away to the poor fool. Then he lost his
temper, quarrelled with the household, and ended by being
thrashed by Tita and dismissed by Mylord. But the poor devil
had suffered enough; the affair was patched up.'

'No boy cornet', wrote Trelawny, 'enjoyed a practical joke more
than Byron.' But this appears to have been the last occasion when
his spirits were high enough to indulge in such pranks. The
colourless and uninteresting note that follows Pietro's letter
contains his last words to Teresa.

BYRON TO CONTESSA GUICCIOLI

[*March* 17*th*, 1824]

My dearest T. – The Spring is come – I have seen a Swallow today
– and it was time – for we have had but a wet winter hitherto –
even in Greece. – We are all very well, which will I hope – keep
up your hopes and Spirits. I do not write to you letters about
politics – which would only be tiresome, and yet we have little
else to write about – except some private anecdotes which I
reserve for 'viva voce' when we meet – to divert you at the
expense of Pietro and some others. – – The Carnival here is
curious – though not quite so elegant as those of Italy. – – –
We are a good many foreigners here of all Nations – and a
curious mixture they compose. – – – I write to you in English
without apologies – as you say you have become a great proficient
in that language of birds. – – – To the English and Greeks – I
generally write in Italian – from a Spirit of contradiction, I
suppose – and to show that I am Italianized by my long stay in
your Climate. – – – Salute Costa and his lady – and Papa and
Olimpia and Giulia and Laurina – and believe me – dearest T.
t.A.A. – in E. + + +   N.B.ⁿ

The 'famous general' to whom Pietro's next letter refers, was Odysseus Andritzinos, an unscrupulous but able mountain chief, who had taken command of the forces in Eastern Greece, and had established his headquarters in Athens. Here he had been joined by Trelawny, who conceived for him a passionate admiration ('a glorious being,' he wrote, 'brave, clever and noble',) and who wrote in Odysseus's name to Byron on the latter's arrival at Missolonghi, 'to welcome you to Greece' and 'to enlist your aid for this important part of it'. Trelawny, after having purchased a harem of ten or twelve Greek ladies (whom Pietro later described as *brutti mostri*) – then further allied himself to the great chieftain by 'marrying his infant half-sister'. Odysseus also succeeded in gaining the confidence of the impressionable Colonel Stanhope, who wrote in the most pressing terms to ask Byron and Mavrocordato to attend a conference which Odysseus was holding at Salona, for the ostensible purpose of 'uniting the interests of Eastern and Western Greece', and the real one of getting hold of some of Byron's money. 'I implore your Lordship and the Prince,' wrote Stanhope, 'as you love Greece and her sacred cause, to attend at Salona.' Byron himself shared none of these illusions, but nevertheless decided to accept the invitation.

'Fifteen days ago', wrote Pietro, 'we promised to go to Salona to meet the famous general Ulysses, but the unfavourable weather and the impossible roads have kept us here until now. We shall perhaps leave in a few days; in two weeks we shall be back in Missolonghi again. We shall not leave this region until the first payments of the loan have arrived. You will already have learned from the newspapers how it was made, and on excellent terms.

Now we trust that with time and a little patience our fine hopes will be fulfilled. Arm yourself, too, with patience and sacrifice your sufferings to this unhappy Greece and to Byron's glory, which is now spreading more and more to the most remote districts.

I seem to foresee that fatigue and glory will be followed by happy and prosperous days and that we shall enjoy them all together in peace. The influence of Mylord is necessary in Greece every day, and he seems to have a great role to play there. The confidence in him of his fellow-countrymen, has also increased in consequence. He has already received a naturalization paper from the Greek government and has been awarded the citizenship of the town of Missolonghi.

We have organized here, as best we could, a corps of artillery and infantry, which Mylord pays for, and is also the C.O. I am his Lieutenant Colonel. The government has sent us regular commissions.

You will already have received the *Greek Telegraph*.* I do the greater part of its editing. I hope you will find us subscribers in Italy.

Tell Loreta[68] to join me quickly and to bring with him all the young men who he thinks could render successful services to Greece, – not limp young men, not hot-heads, and not adventurers. See to it that our brothers improve themselves intellectually and physically, that they do not neglect military exercises, and if that career pleases them, I shall soon be able to offer them a suitable rank and fine prospects. The fortunes of war, and especially of this one, are always uncertain, but if we succeed as well as we dare to hope, we shall all form a new country for ourselves.'

The buoyant spirits revealed by Pietro's letter – the last that he wrote to Teresa from Greece – are a testimony to his incorrigible hopefulness. The brigade in which he offered his brothers 'a suitable rank and fine prospects' consisted of a handful of undisciplined and dissatisfied polyglots, at odds with each other. The *Greek Telegraph* which he took such pains in editing, had only been subsidized by Byron 'to get rid of Stanhope's importunities, and it may be, to keep Gamba out of mischief'.[69] As to the hopes for Greek unity which Pietro was cherishing, in view of the forthcoming journey to Salona, they were to be rudely dispelled on the very day that his letter was written. That day a Souliot leader, together with the men of a new Greek chieftain, Kariaskaki, who had come to an understanding with the Turks, seized a small fort at the entrance of the lagoon, while, on the following morning, the Turkish fleet appeared. Missolonghi had been betrayed. The plot – largely owing to Byron's energy and common sense – failed: other Souliot leaders came marching to the relief of Missolonghi, Kariaskaki was captured and the Turkish fleet sailed away again. But Byron had now lost his last illusions – and, unlike Pietro, all his hopes. The 'confidence of his fellow-countrymen, had so far shown itself only in a disquieting silence – for an encouraging letter from Hobhouse arrived, by a tragic delay, only when Byron was already unconscious. As to his 'increasing influence' in Greece – he had been betrayed by the unruly Souliots, abandoned by Trelawny and Stanhope; he had failed to reconcile the Greek parties; his funds were running short.[70] Above all – with no friend with whom he could share these perplexities or to whom

* A polyglot weekly, of which Pietro Gamba was the sub-editor.

he could even speak openly – he was utterly alone. 'He felt himself', wrote Parry, 'deceived and abandoned – I had almost said betrayed.'[71] Finally, he was a very sick man. Within a fortnight of Pietro's prophecy of 'happy and prosperous days all together in peace', Byron was already dead.

To Lady Blessington, before sailing for Greece, Byron had said that he hoped he might die in action, for 'I have a horror of death-bed scenes'. 'But', he added, 'as I have not been famous for my luck in life, most probably I shall not have more in the manner of my death.'[72] To Trelawny, too, he had expressed a similar fear: 'I shall have that cursed fever again – and perhaps – for I am not a strong man, die – well, I do not mind that – I can die very heroically – but I cannot bear pain.'[73]

His hopes were not fulfilled. He died in feverish pain, with a prolonged 'death-bed scene' ('Che bella Scena!' he exclaimed with a half-smile to the weeping Tita and Fletcher). Moreover, in spite of all the agitated figures that crowded round his bed, he died in utter loneliness. The well-meaning, panic-stricken Dr. Bruno, the sinuous, officious Dr. Millingen, could bring as little relief to his body, as the coarse-grained Parry to his mind. Pierino was in such floods of tears, that he could not stay in the room; even the faithful, stupid Fletcher, bending over him, could not understand what he tried, so painfully, to say. 'Can it be possible you have not understood me?' he repeated – and then 'It is now too late'.

Did he think of Teresa and wish for her feminine tenderness, in those last hours? It does not seem very probable. 'My wife – my child – my sister' were the only women's names that he mentioned. Afterwards, each of the witnesses told his own version of the story – the doctors, not unnaturally, in the form that would cast the least reflection on their professional skill – and each of the others, so as to make it appear that *he* was the one who enjoyed the greatest degree of intimacy with Byron. Of all the accounts, Pietro Gamba's is the most simple, straightforward and moving. 'Io lascio qualche cosa di caro al mondo'* – that well-known sentence is in his version only. Was it indeed a last, veiled message to Teresa? And if so, was it inspired merely by kindness, or by love?

These are questions which the biographer should hesitate to answer. We cannot, alas, share the unquestioning certainties of

---

* This phrase is translated inaccurately by Hobhouse: 'I leave those that I love behind me' – and the end of the sentence, too, is incorrect. Pietro wrote 'Per il resto son contento di morire' ('as to the rest, I am *glad* to die') which Hobhouse renders 'I am *willing* to die'.

Pierino. 'Those who are acquainted only with his writings', he wrote to Augusta, 'will lament the loss of so great a genius. But *I* knew his heart.'

How the tragic news reached Teresa, we do not know. Pietro had not the courage to send it, but wrote instead to his father. Costa, too, heard the news from the British Consul at Ancona, and at once wrote to Guiccioli, expressing his hopes that 'this evil may produce the good that every honest person must desire', but also his fear that 'the Countess may be driven by grief to commit some act which would cause grave concern to all her relatives'.

'I feel it my duty, Signor Conte, to inform you of what has occurred, and of what I have done to avoid such evil consequences. Know then that I have used the greatest influence with Cardinal Spina,[74] so that he may allow Count Ruggero Gamba to return to Bologna to break the sad news to his daughter.'[75]

It is not known what Guiccioli replied. According to his grandson's Memoirs, he sent his son Ignazio – a schoolboy of eighteen, who was being coached by Paolo Costa – to tell Teresa of her loss. 'It was in the morning and she was still in bed. She turned away for a moment – was silent a little – and that was all.'[76]

It was hardly likely, indeed, that it would be to her young stepson that Teresa would pour out her grief. But it is probable that the news had already reached her, for Rangone says that Conte Ruggero did receive permission to go to Bologna, and a letter written by Costa on the following day speaks of Teresa bearing her loss 'with grief, but dignity . . . If', Costa added, 'Madonna Laura, who loved a Canon of the Church, has received the compassion of posterity, I trust that this lady, too – who today is not forgiven for having loved a man of letters and a philosopher – may in some future time cease to be insulted and mocked. We certainly are not ashamed of pitying her, even now.'[77]

10: LIVING AFTER

But you were living before that
And also you were living after.
BROWNING

I. THE FIRST YEARS

THE weeks after Byron's death were spent by Pietro Gamba in a series of most unenviable tasks. To him, as to every other member of the Greek expedition, Byron's death brought the end of all his hopes. Gone were the 'suitable rank and fine prospects' which he had promised to his brothers in Byron's brigade; gone the dreams of a new free country! Gone, above all, was the friend and leader whom he had served with uncritical, disinterested, unfailing devotion.

Sitting in the bare, dingy little room by the lagoon on the day after Byron's death, with the rain beating down so heavily that the funeral had to be postponed, he began a series of heartbroken letters to Byron's friends.

'The blow that has been dealt us', he told Hobhouse, 'is terrible, is irreparable. I hardly have words to express it: – Lord Byron is dead. Your friend, my friend and father, the light of the century, the pride of your country, the saviour of Greece, is dead.'[1]

While the four doctors in the next room, having completed their grisly autopsy, drew up their report and embalmed the body, while outside all the shops of the little town were closed and the streets hushed, while the mountain tribesmen came down from the hills to be present at the hero's funeral, poor Pietro, with tears running down his cheeks wrote on: to Kinnaird, to Barff in Zante, to Sidney Osborne, to Barry. 'It is no use speaking of our sorrow. You can judge it from your own.'[2] Then, mastering his grief, he turned to work.

'Owing to the long, entire confidence', he told Hobhouse, 'that Lord Byron reposed in me and that I shall eternally be proud of having enjoyed, I have thought it my duty to take into my charge everything concerning him here.'[3]

He docketed and sealed all Byron's papers; he wound up the tangled accounts and sent them off to Hobhouse; he extracted a receipt from Mavrocordato for the £4000 that he had received from the Greek Committee, and another receipt from the Magistrates of the City of Missolonghi for the 'rispettabili viscere del sullodato nobile e benemerito Lord Byron'. 'If all these affairs are intricate', he wrote to Hobhouse, 'it is not my fault.'[4] He attempted to meet, in so far as was possible, the innumerable rapacious requests that immediately assailed him. The officers of Byron's brigade sent a petition demanding that the corps should be maintained for at least another three months on full pay.[5] The magistrates of the city of Missolonghi required to be reimbursed for the large sums which they said that the city had paid out to Byron's 500 Souliots.[6] A Candiote Greek, who, on the strength of Byron's name, had hoped to raise a loan in Zante of 20,000 dollars, now wrote to complain that, as soon as Byron's death was known, the credit was denied him. Other volunteers for the Greek cause, who had come out with well-filled purses as far as Corfu, heard of Byron's death and changed their minds: 'the pilgrim of eternity having departed, they turned back'.[7] Trelawny spared no effort and wasted no scruples, in attempting to secure for Odysseus all that remained of Byron's organization: stores, arms and men. 'Do, my dear Sir,' he wrote at once to Colonel Stanhope, 'take some prompt and decisive steps. You know the wants of Eastern Greece. Could you not consign some portion of these stores to that part?'[8]

To all these troubles were added the distressing arguments about the disposal of Byron's remains. Trelawny and Stanhope wished him to be buried in Athens, if possible on the Acropolis; the city of Missolonghi claimed the honour for itself. Each of Byron's companions maintained that to him, and him alone, had the poet expressed his true wishes. To Dr. Millingen he had said that he wished to be buried where he died, 'in the first corner, without pomp or nonsense'. To Parry and to Fletcher he had said that he wished his body to be sent to England.* Torn by these conflicting reports, poor Pietro – with the Latin sense of the claims, in such matters, of a relation, however distant, – wrote to Lord Sidney Osborne for his views, and he replied that the body should be shipped to England.[9] Accordingly, – in a black packing-case, deposited in a large barrel full of spirits – the remains (except for the organs presented to the City of Missolonghi) were placed on board the brig *Florida*. 'Conceive a man going one way', Byron had once written to Moore, 'and his intestines another, and his immortal soul a third! Was there ever such a distribution?'[10]

Colonel Stanhope was in charge on the voyage, and Dr. Bruno,

* ' "Fletcher, if I die in Greece, what will you do with me?" "My Lord," replied Fletcher, "what should we do but take you home?" "Why," said Byron, "it is not worth while to take such a body as this home." But a little afterwards he added, "Perhaps on the whole, it would be better so." ' LORD BROUGHTON, op. cit., III, p. 60.

Fletcher, Lega Zambelli and Tita were all on board. Only Pietro was not there. 'Many considerations of a delicate nature', he wrote to Hobhouse, 'have dissuaded me from accompanying him, as was my wish and duty.'[11] To his father he was more explicit.

'I have resolved to put the convoy in the charge of Colonel Stanhope, because I know it is feared that my accompanying it openly might produce gossip and bitterness in Byron's family, on account of his well-known relations with T . . . a.

From London I will write my decisions. I cannot take any definite ones until then, but I believe that I shall return to Greece next winter – by way of Italy, if the Government allows it.'[12]

Pietro did not return to Italy. The ferocious sentence of Cardinal Rivarola on August 31st, 1825, which exiled or imprisoned more than 500 of the Liberals of the Romagna and condemned his father to imprisonment for twenty years, ordered him to return to Italy for trial, where he would assuredly have received no less severe a sentence. He therefore some months later set forth again for Greece, where he became a Colonel in the Greek Army. In 1827, having contracted typhoid, he died on the isthmus of Metana and was buried in the fortress of Diamantopoulos. The fortress was destroyed, and no trace remains of his grave. There is not even, in the Gamba family's possession, a portrait or a drawing of him.[13] Nothing remains but his little book about the Greek expedition, his letters, – and the tradition of his courage, his fidelity and his high hopes.

His father, Count Ruggero Gamba, spent nearly six years in exile and imprisonment in Ferrara. During the first part of his time in exile, he was allowed a considerable measure of freedom, and employed some of his time in writing verses – among them, curiously enough, an ode *In praise of Lord Byron*! But in August 1825 the Rivarola sentence flung him into the Ferrara fortress and it was not until 1831 that he was able to return home again. He then took command of the National Guard of Ravenna, and fought at its head against the Austrians at Rimini. He suffered the further grief of the death of his son Vincenzo and of his youngest daughter, Faustina,* and spent the last years of his life on his estate at Filetto, where he died in 1846.

* She died of consumption, at the age of fourteen, in 1833, and Vincenzo in 1835.

As to the minor characters in the story: – Fletcher and Lega Zambelli, who had so often been jealous of each other in Byron's lifetime, were apparently united by his death, for they set up a macaroni factory in England together. Teresa saw them in England in 1832, and in the following year John Murray forwarded to her a letter from Fletcher, asking her to be kind enough to forward through a banker some money owed to 'Mr. Lega' in Ravenna.[14] But the money, if it ever reached them, did not do them much good; for in 1835 Fletcher was writing to Hobhouse to tell him that Mr. Thompson had 'taken the duty off the foreign macaroni', and 'after that dreadful blow we are completely ruined'. He reminded Hobhouse that by the terms of Byron's first will: 'I was mentioned for fifty pounds per annum, . . . and I have had many escapes by sea and land since then.'[15] Neither Hobhouse nor Mrs. Leigh, however, seem to have felt the obligation.

Tita Falcieri served both James Clay and Disraeli in Greece, married Mrs. Isaac D'Israeli's maid, and became, for many years, a Home Service messenger in the India Office.[16]

Dr. Bruno, whom Byron had quizzed and abused and liked, and in the end had called 'the most sincere Italian I ever met',[17] attended Byron's funeral at Hucknell Torkard – and then, without having taken a penny from the executors for his services, sadly returned to Italy.

––––––

This book does not propose to describe in detail the rest of Teresa's long life: it is the story of Byron and Teresa, and thus only concerned with what relates to them both. But her brief and disastrous return to her husband in 1826, which ended in their second and definite separation, does throw some light not only upon the character of Count Guiccioli, but upon earlier events – in particular upon that strange, uneasy winter of 1820, when Teresa and her husband and Byron were all still living together in Ravenna. It certainly suggests that the indignation of Teresa's family at that time, which caused them to take sides with her and Byron against Guiccioli, was not without some foundation – and that there may, after all, have been some truth in her persistent assertion that, although it was her passion for Byron which brought matters to a head, she would in any case have been obliged to leave her husband.

It is possible, in face of this assertion, to ask why she ever agreed to a second experiment; but the explanation is not really hard to find. For over five years Guiccioli – for reasons best known to himself – had been urging her to return; the life of a woman alone, in a dubious position – and without much money, had not proved easy; her father who, according to Teresa, did not approve of the experiment, was still in exile at Ferrara; the rest of her family urged her to return to respectability; her husband was lavish of promises. 'So at last', she wrote, 'I allowed myself to be persuaded by his protestations, hoping that time and experience might have produced some change in his character, and I went to join him in Venice, hoping to find a situation that would at least be bearable.'[18]

In case, however, it should not prove to be so, both she and her husband – with a cold-blooded foresight which throws a curious light upon their attitude to each other – signed before a notary an agreement, stipulating that 'in case this reunion should not prove to be to our mutual satisfaction', their previous contract would, on their separating once more, again become valid.[19] Only after signing this document – early in July 1826 – did Teresa return to her husband.

It was not long before she decided that her situation in his house was not endurable. The events that led her to this conclusion form a story too long and too unpleasant to be related here.* Not only did Guiccioli ostentatiously continue his relations with the Venetian prostitute on whose account the Cardinal of Ravenna had requested him to leave Ravenna, but the 'eccentricities' of his character manifested themselves in a series of violent and peculiar scenes – culminating in various proposals which – if Teresa is to be believed – can only be ascribed to a cold-blooded determination to place his wife in a hopelessly compromising situation, or else to force her to leave him – in either case freeing himself from any future obligation towards her.[20]

Teresa, however, met his machinations with an equal shrewdness. Backed up by her stepson and her eldest stepdaughter Attilia, who at that time (no doubt partly owing to their own dislike and fear of their father) were wholly upon her side, she avoided falling into any of his traps, and endured, for several months longer, his provocations – while she sent a statement of her case to the Vatican, and to the Patriarch of Venice. The latter made inquiries (which included the testimony of Teresa's stepdaughter and the servants) and finally the Pope's answer came:

* The details are given in the long and curious letter from Teresa to her Parish priest, already quoted, of which there is a draft among her papers; and some of them are repeated in later statements to her lawyers. They are, she affirms, 'of so strange and evil a nature, that they can only be confessed to one's priest or lawyer, but should not be made known to the public'.

a new Rescript, permitting Teresa to leave her husband once again, and increasing her allowance to 150 scudi a month.* And so, on a winter's night, five months after her return, Teresa – fearing her husband's violence as soon as he heard the news – stole out of his house and hurried to her father at Ferrara.

'The hours that followed your departure', wrote her stepson Ignazio, 'were very stormy: he hurried to the Police, to the Patriarch . . . He was prodigiously discomposed not by your desertion, but by the allowance. Now he spends his whole time shouting and fantasticating about the illegality of the Patriarch's behaviour. . . .'[21]

Shortly afterwards, in a series of vain attempts to obtain a repeal of the Pope's decree, Guiccioli instructed his lawyer to summon Teresa for slander, on the grounds of her having stated that 'he treated his wife with violence and persecuted her, to the irreparable damage of her health,' that he 'threatened to carry his persecutions so far that she would be obliged, in despair, to leave him,' and that 'he was guilty towards her of the darkest perfidiousness, and a kind of immorality peculiar to himself'.[22]

What indeed the real truth of all this may have been, it is difficult to say. Such a peculiar list of accusations, 'specified by the accused, not the accuser – is hardly likely to have arisen without some foundation. And there is, on the same side, the testimony of Teresa's stepchildren, Guiccioli's oldest daughter Attilia, who during that autumn married Count Carranti of Imola, wrote to her stepmother to inquire

'Since my departure, what trials and domestic tyrannies have you endured? Does that Fury [Guiccioli's mistress] continue to rule my father and to fan the fire of discord? Has it been necessary for you to place yourself under the protection of the Parish Priest or the Government?'[23]

And, after Teresa had gone away, her stepson Ignazio wrote her the following letter:

'My father's treatment of me has reached that ultimate point, beyond which I cannot be hurt any more. Now I see why he quarrelled with his Mother, why he quarrelled with his brothers, why he came to destroy three wives, of whom only my unhappy

* The Pope's Rescript justified this increase as 'proportioned to her husband's income, which was then estimated at 6000 scudi a year'.

mother [Angelica] could put up with him, and wore herself out
in vain tears; I see why my sister weeps, why now he is tormenting
me, why his lawyers, his accountants and his secretaries have
turned against him, why no Friend has ever clasped his hand, why
the Government is against him, why everybody hates him.'[24]

It is so complete a condemnation that Teresa herself, in quoting
it to her lawyer after Guiccioli's death, remarks that 'its language
must seem unsuitable to every modest and calm person'.* But
Teresa, with all her faults, was incapable of bearing malice. By
then, after fifteen years of independence, all her resentment had
died down, and her final estimate of her husband is unexpectedly
indulgent.

'After many years Count Guiccioli's disposition seemed to have
been favourably affected by thinking things over, or perhaps by
the decrease of his physical strength. He wrote to me, asking for
several small services, and I answered him kindly, without any
sign of resentment, which did not exist at all in my heart. For I
always attributed his behaviour to me to an intense and invincible
eccentricity, rather than to perfidiousness.'[25]

Among Teresa's papers there are various letters to her from
oculists abroad, whom she had consulted on Guiccioli's behalf.† –
For, as he grew older, he suffered from cataract and was unable
to walk about the city without an attendant. His avarice and
his domineering temper, however, appear to have remained
unaltered, for his grandson's Memoirs relate that, on his nightly
visits to the theatre, he peremptorily refused to pay for his
attendant's ticket, and, rather than give way, preferred to buy up,
at vast expense, all the bills of exchange of the unfortunate
impresario of the theatre, thus gaining a hold over him and
forcing him to concede a free ticket.[26] In spite of his half-blind-
ness, his passion for the theatre persisted, 'almost to the point of

* Autobiographical statement, in Teresa's hand, addressed to Avvocato Armellini
in Rome, 1841. It should also in fairness be added that after Guiccioli's death – when
his heirs were quarrelling with Teresa about the inheritance of his estate, both Attilia
and Ignazio went back upon these letters, Attilia saying that Teresa had 'deceived
an inexperienced girl' as to her character and the real nature of the circumstances,
and Ignazio saying that Teresa had blackmailed him, by threatening to make use of
this letter, written in his youth. Secret Archives of the Vatican. Summarium
additionale 8988-9410.
† She communicated the results of these consultations to her husband in long letters
'of a most amiable tone, writing volumes about her consultations on his behalf with
celebrated doctors, oculists, quacks and other people whose eyes were affected'.
I Guiccioli, I, p. 54. The author concludes that Teresa's only motive can have been
to profit under her husband's will.

mania', and every night his tall, rigid figure was to be seen hurrying to the playhouse – or, if no play was being given, standing in the Venetian squares ('hiding his medal of St. Stephen under his overcoat') to watch the outdoor performances of the marionettes.

His quarrels with his children continued, and the scenes of 'bizarre violence' (the expression is his grandson's) became so frequent that at last Ignazio helped his sisters to run away to their married sister Attilia; but 'after a few days the girls had to come back and submit themselves'.[27] He died on April 21st, 1840, at the age of 79.*

After her second separation from her husband, Teresa was free to lead – within the limits of her allowance – the life that she preferred, and for several years she spent a part of every winter in Rome.

Here, once again – it was one of the things that her husband had complained about – she saw practically none but English people. Perhaps she could hardly herself have said why. She was not wholly at ease with them – her knowledge of the English language was still imperfect – she thought their manners stiff and formal, and their jokes often incomprehensible. And yet, and yet – when she was with them there was (though young Lord Fitzharris, with all the assurance of twenty-two, might decide that she had 'forgotten her poet'[28]) a part of herself that came to life again. Perhaps the unkindest of all Byron's legacies to her was to have rendered her unsuited to the society to which she was born, without fitting her for any other. Half the 'affectations' which have been so much ridiculed sprang from that source: she was always trying to fit into an alien world. At Pisa – exiled from her own society, bewildered by the queer people among whom she found herself – she had begun to see herself as 'a heroine by the side of a poet'; in later years, in London, she continued the pose; and in Paris, in her old age, she was described as 'trying to resemble a great English lady who had married a Frenchman'.[29] But she never wholly left behind either the good-hearted warmth of

* Lady Blessington sent Teresa an effusive letter of condolence: '... I have not ceased to think of you and of the influence it may have on your happiness. Rest assured that the confidence you reposed in me will never be violated, and that I know too well what is due to your delicacy to breathe even a hint to *any one*. I trust in Heaven that Ct. Guiccioli, before he left this world, has as far as fortune could do, made amends for the misery inflicted in your early youth.' Lady Blessington's wish was not fulfilled. Guiccioli, perhaps not unnaturally, felt no obligation towards the wife who had left him more than twenty years before, and a long lawsuit ensued between Teresa and his heirs. In the end, a compromise was reached.

manner, or the slight harshness of accent, of her native Romagna; in the end, as at the beginning, she remained a provincial lady of Ravenna.

During her Roman winters she had a considerable success with the British tourists who arrived for the winter in their great coaches, to sight-see and picnic and hunt in the Campagna and entertain each other, and who considered Byron's mistress as not the least interesting of the sights of Rome. Already in the winter of 1825, before her return to her husband, she had spent some months there, staying with her great-aunt Marchesa Sacrati,[20] and seeing a great deal of fashionable English society. She had met Lady Bute and dined with Lady Davy, the hospitable wife of her old acquaintance Sir Humphry. She had visited Shelley's grave and expressed her feelings in some highly romantic and sentimental verses.[21] She had talked about Shelley and Byron to Jefferson Hogg, who, having come to see her with an introduction from Jane Williams, 'found her well-informed, clever, amiable, and I think handsome'.[22] He added, however, that he had been annoyed at being 'shown about as the Englishman who was going to marry Mrs. W.', and protested to Teresa about it, saying that it was 'hardly fair to a shy and reserved Englishman'.[23]

And then, at a ball on New Year's Eve, 1827, in casa Torlonia, Teresa had met another poet: the author of *Le Dernier Chant du Pélerinage d'Harold*, the tall, handsome, supercilious Alphonse de Lamartine. A murmur of disapproval and dislike (but she thought it was of admiration) greeted his entry. His recent poem had contained not only a disparaging reference to Teresa as a 'Venetian Aspasia' but some most contemptuous remarks about the modern Italians.* It had, however, contained a highly romantic portrait of Byron – and for this Teresa could forgive all the rest.

In the days that followed he often went to see her; they walked together in the long alleys of the Doria-Pamphili gardens; and always he made her talk about Byron – about their first meeting, their rides in the Pine Forest, and his wonderful devotion. But certain passages of the story were slurred over; she skated rapidly over the days at La Mira: 'pour les âmes vulgaires ce vrai-là ne serait peut-être pas vraisemblable.'[24] Their love, she said, had always been 'pure'; if he ever told the story, it must be in that light. He listened – and promised. Thirty years later she was to regret that she had talked so freely.

Early in 1825, however, another important figure had entered

---

* Je vais chercher ailleurs (pardonne, ombre romaine!)
Des hommes, et non pas de la poussière humaine.
Dernier Chant du Pélerinage d'Harold, XIII

Teresa's life. At dinner at Lady Davy's she had met a fastidious, handsome, faintly malicious young Englishman – with a soft voice and a slight limp, 'a halting angel'.* He had known Byron, he told her, as a boy, and had felt a real adoration for him, when – remembering his own boyhood – the poet had protected him against the harsh taunts of his mother, Lady Holland. In Genoa, too, in 1823, Byron had received him with the greatest kindness, and had described his guest as having 'the softest and most amiable expression of countenance I ever saw, and manners correspondent'.† His name was Henry Edward Fox.

The details of Teresa's tempestuous liaison with him, which began in Naples in the following summer, have no place in this book. But it must be admitted that the later story is, in several ways, reminiscent of the earlier one – and Fox's remarks about Teresa are only too painfully like Byron's. It was Teresa's misfortune to fall in love only with beautiful and charming cads; it was her good fortune that she never discovered them to be so. Moreover, if her lovers started by speaking of her contemptuously they ended by changing their tone. At first Fox – like Byron in Venice – was considerably disconcerted by her passionate temperament, he wrote of her crudely and coarsely: he considered 'her manners bad and her sentiments affected'; – he commented that 'she is an instance of those who live with clever people, thinking it their duty to be clever too'.³⁵ After one of their quarrels, he declared that she was 'jealous and exigent and troublesome. Poor Ld. Byron! I do not wonder at his going to Greece!'³⁶

But as he got to know her better, his opinion began to change.

'Her frankness and sincerity', he wrote three years after meeting her, 'are unparalleled among all the women I have ever known, and her affectation (for affected she is, and perhaps the only Italian that is so) arises from trying to assume manners that sit well on others, but to obtain which she has never had the opportunities, or during her connection with Lord B. the least desire. She is clever and has read more than I could have believed.'³⁷

'Her heart is good,' he added, 'and her talents very superior to what I first supposed them to be.' And finally, after their liaison had been broken off, he wrote: 'We took a tender leave. I shall

---

* 'He appears a halting angel', wrote Byron to Moore, 'who has tripped against a star; whilst I am *Le Diable Boiteux*.' *L.J.*, VI, p. 179.

† *L.J.*, VI, p. 178, April 2nd, 1823. Fox, on the same occasion, returned the compliment by observing of Byron that 'the tones of his voice are as beautiful as ever, and I am not surprised at any woman falling in love with him'. Fox, *Journal*, p. 160.

always feel excessive interest and regard for T. G., and I think she has shown much generosity and nobleness of character on many occasions. Certainly her conduct to me has always been most admirable.'[38]

Poor Teresa! Fox's remarks have a *post mortem* touch singularly reminiscent of Byron's eulogies to Lady Blessington. Apparently her lovers could only find praise when they had ceased to love her.

Fox, however, was not Teresa's only English friend in Rome. Among the travellers in the spring of 1828 came the 'Blessington Circus' – and this time, at last, at a ball at the French Embassy, Teresa met her old rival, Lady Blessington – who needed material for her chatty Social Journal, and chose to be generous in her description.

'She [Teresa] is much admired and liked, and merits to be so, for her appearance is highly prepossessing, her manners remarkably distinguished, and her conversation *spirituelle* and interesting. Her face is decidedly handsome, the features regular and well proportioned, her complexion delicately fair, her teeth very fine and her hair of that rich golden tint which is peculiar to the female pictures by Titian and Georgioni [*sic*] ... The Countess Guiccioli is well educated and highly accomplished, she speaks her native language with remarkable purity, French with great fluency, and understands English perfectly. Her reading has been extensive, her memory retentive. ...'[39]

However, after these agreeable remarks, Lady Blessington was unable to resist the temptation of making trouble between Teresa and Fox, by telling Teresa that Fox was repeating to everyone Byron's remark 'that one of his reasons for going to Greece was to get rid of her and her family'. 'Of course', Fox commented, 'I denied it, but it is true.'[40]
But by now Teresa's liaison with Fox – 'le bel Ecossais' – was coming to an end – and apparently without having caused any open scandal, for at this time E. Patterson-Bonaparte was writing to her from Florence, 'Croyez-vous qu'il soit amoureux? Ce n'est pas possible. L'Apollon du Belvedere deviendrait sensible aussi vite que lui.' And Mrs. Patterson added some good worldly advice about the necessity of 'éviter les esclandres, et avec d'autres que les Anglais il y a toujours à craindre que les Amants ne jasent. Je déteste les jaseurs, et en Angleterre on est mal vu lorsqu'on se vante'.[41]

This tribute, as applied to Byron and Fox, may scarcely seem appropriate – but certainly Teresa's liaison with Fox was not widely known, for in 1830, at a dinner in Queen Hortense's house, where Teresa was present, Prince Louis Napoleon whispered to another guest that 'her illustrious lover had not yet been replaced by her'.[42]

Another friend whom Teresa made in Rome in 1828 was young Lord Fitzharris, whom she met at the Austrian Ambassador's ball. He was only twenty-two and very much admired her 'brilliant complexion and blue eyes', and her face 'full of animation, showing splendid teeth when she laughed, which she was doing heartily when I remarked her'.* He was told that ' "this was the Countess Guiccioli of Byronic memory", and also that she was fond of the English and courted their acquaintance'. A few months later, having been forbidden by the Papal police to return to the Romagna, she persuaded Fitzharris to bring his carriage to meet her outside the gates of the city, and took him off with her to Filetto, where he shot partridge with her father and brothers, pronounced them 'all sportsmen', and presented Teresa's younger brother Vincenzo with his 'double-barrelled Purdy'. Teresa talked to him constantly about 'her poet'.

'She was very proud and fond of him, but described him as having a very capricious temper, and with nothing of the passion which pervades his poetry and which he was in the habit of ridiculing – in fact, with a cold temperament.'[43]

Are we to conclude from these stories that Teresa did not really love Byron – or at least that she very soon forgot him? I do not think that this is the right conclusion. Even Mary Shelley – an observer not over-kind – felt no doubts about the genuineness of her grief. 'I sincerely pity her,' she wrote, 'for she truly loved him.'[44] But Teresa was not, and refused to be turned into, a tragic or an austere figure. She was a sentimentalist, a romantic, a warm-hearted, amoral, unstable creature. And she was also a woman of extremely strong passions – played upon in early youth by her experienced and unscrupulous husband, further developed during her years with Byron – who suddenly, at the age of twenty-four,

---

* MALMESBURY, op. cit., I, p. 26. Another traveller, in the following year, was less favourably impressed. Chateaubriand saw her driving by in her carriage: 'A ses cheveux blonds, au galbe mal ébauché de sa taille, à l'inélégance de sa beauté, je l'ai prise pour une grasse et blanche étrangère de Westphalie: c'était Mme Guiccioli.' *Mémoires d'Outre-Tombe*, V, p. 150.

found herself alone, neither wife nor widow, – avoided by the conventional and made much of by those whose chief feeling for her was curiosity about 'Byron's mistress'. A woman of stronger character or of more rigid principles, could have risen above such a situation; a more experienced woman of the world would have handled it more discreetly. But Teresa was neither the one nor the other. She behaved wrongly, foolishly, indiscreetly; she made people disapprove of her and laugh at her; she made other women jealous;* she never failed to puzzle her friends by her disconcerting mixture of intelligence and folly, of shrewdness and simplicity, of sincerity and affectation.

But she did not cease, for the whole remaining forty-nine years of her life, to remember Byron. 'There are moments in most men's lives', he himself had written, 'which they would live over the rest of their life to regain.' She had had those moments; she had recognized them; and all her pitiful subsequent strivings for romance were, I believe, only attempts to regain their shadow. Finally, if we must admit that she was not wholly faithful to Byron, we can hardly deny that she showed him a fierce and unfailing loyalty. She lived long enough to read all that was said against him by the people who had called themselves his friends. She must have heard, when she went about in the society of London and Paris, all the tales in his disfavour. Worst of all, she read, in Moore, the flippant and unkind remarks that he himself had made about their love. But none of it affected her. Of all the women who had loved him, including Augusta, she alone stood up for him to the end.

II. ENGLAND AND LADY BLESSINGTON

Ever since Byron's death, Teresa's dearest wish had been to go to England. She wished to 'make a pilgrimage' to Newstead Abbey; she hoped to renew her acquaintance with some of Byron's old friends and to make that of several others; and – though this she kept to herself – she intended to dispose of some of Byron's manuscripts. And so at last, in the spring of 1832 – eight years after Byron's death – she set off, accompanied by her brother Vincenzo, on her first visit to England.

* A malicious school friend, M. sa Florenzi, the mistress of Louis of Bavaria, who had always disliked her, wrote in 1831: 'Lord Byron was held by the woman for a moment, but afterwards, being unfaithful, he ill-treated her and beat her, as is told in the towns where they lived together . . . She, to my mind, was not in love, but was flattered in her vanity, and therefore bore this without knowing how to break so disgraceful a chain. After his death she wore mourning for him, which everyone laughed at, and began to preach her love for Byron with such romanticism and exaggeration as to turn it into a comedy.' ZUCCONI, *Lodovico Innamorato*, p. 199.

　　Some of the English friends she had made in Italy appeared, on her arrival, to have forgotten the warmth of their previous invitations. But two people were outstandingly kind: John Murray and Lady Blessington. Mr. Murray asked her to little family dinner-parties, sent her books and theatre tickets, took her to Regent's Park, and provided her with introductions to Augusta Leigh and to Dr. Drury at Harrow, to Colonel Wildman and the Pigots. Moreover, he helped her to dispose of her Byron manuscripts, and replied with scrupulous politeness and patience to her effusive, almost daily letters.

　　But the first door to be opened to her in London was, somewhat surprisingly, Lady Blessington's. Both ladies, indeed, had favours to exchange. Lady Blessington – now fully launched, in the exquisite décor of Seamore Place, upon her conquest of London – must have thought that Lord Byron's mistress, still young, pretty and high-spirited, would constitute an attractive novelty in her salon. And on her side Teresa, a stranger in England, could not but be glad to attend Lady Blessington's parties, where she met, if not the great ladies of London, at least all its most agreeable men, where Byron's name still awakened interest, and where she herself was made much of and flattered – and laughed at a little (but this she seldom became aware of) behind her back. Almost every day Lady Blessington's famous green chariot would be at the door of Teresa's lodgings in Piccadilly,* and Teresa and Vincenzo would be taken to dine in the mirror-lined dining-room in Seamore Place or to spend the evening in the great red-and-gold drawing-room looking out over Hyde Park. Sometimes, on a fine summer evening, they would set off to a party at Greenwich, first visiting 'some of the pretty places in the neighbourhood'[45] – or else Lady Blessington would send them tickets for 'fashionable bazaars, which are worth seeing', or would call to take Teresa to see the London shops. She sent her tickets, too, for the opening of the House of Lords, warning her that she must wear full dress.

　　'Full dress means your hair dressed with feathers, or else an evening Hat or Bonnet with feathers. The rose-coloured one you wore last time I had the pleasure of seeing you, would be just the thing to wear. Any gown you like, that is low at the breast, and short sleeves.'[46]

_____

　　* During this visit Teresa first lived in lodgings at 35 Piccadilly, but was unable to get used to 'the dreadful noise of Piccadilly and to the English songs'. Lady Blessington gave her the address of some lodgings in Half Moon Street, at 3 guineas a week, but she preferred to move to Sablonier's Hotel in Leicester Square.

She even constituted herself Teresa's Mentor on more delicate points of conduct:

'I received a letter this morning from Mr. Walewsky soliciting me to ask you to dine with him on Thursday next . . . I do not know whether you have any objections to accept the Invitation of a Bachelor . . . I see no impropriety in your being the guest of Mr. Walewsky in the presence of myself and Mr. A. Mr. W. is a gentleman and a man of information. You, however, with your penetration, must have perceived that he has a great taste for display and a great deal of vanity. He fancies himself a great deal like the late Lord Byron, and has often amused me by trying to imitate him, but oh! ye Gods! look at the difference between their respective Brows and chin and the Mouth . . . Men are strange animals, God bless them.'[47]

The correspondence – which began at this time and continued for over sixteen years (since Teresa kept not only all Lady Blessington's notes, but the drafts of many of her own) is a very curious one.[48] Both ladies were inordinately prodigal of compliments, of little attentions, of endearments; they condoled with each other in times of sorrow; they exchanged confidences (or, at least, half-confidences). And they kept it all up for over sixteen years! And yet, as Dr. Madden (who saw them together) shrewdly observed, it is more than doubtful whether 'a sincere, ardent and disinterested attachment existed between them'.[49] The letters suggest that there was familiarity, but no intimacy, cordiality but little kindness. They did not really either like or interest each other. Moreover, there was in all their references to Byron a constant struggle for position. Teresa had been his mistress, indeed – but it was Lady Blessington's book about him that was being read, Lady Blessington's opinions of him that were being quoted, by the whole of London. Lady Blessington verbally deferred to Teresa's closer intimacy: 'You saw him in his best light, that of the Lover and the Friend.' Teresa awarded recognition to Lady Blessington's *ideés si justes et si bien exprimées*. She sent Lady Blessington a lock of Byron's hair; Lady Blessington later on, presented her with an engraving of D'Orsay's portrait of the poet. But each lady thought – and wished others to think – that she alone knew *the real Byron*.

One of the main purposes of Teresa's visit to England had been to make the acquaintance of Augusta Leigh. From the first she had felt an intense curiosity about this sister of Byron's – the only woman about whom he had never said an unkind word. Like

cc

LIVING AFTER

several of Byron's other mistresses, Teresa could not see why Byron would not let her write to this charming sister of his, and make friends with her.

'It is a very odd fancy that they all take to her', Byron had written to Murray. 'It was only six months ago that I had some difficulty in preventing the Countess G. from invading her with an Italian letter. I should like to have seen Augusta's face, with an Etruscan Epistle, and all its Meridional style of *issimas*, and other superlatives, before her.'[50]

Teresa's feelings for Augusta, in the past, had not been unmixed with jealousy. 'How often', she said later on, 'I was irritated by Byron's tender affection for his sister! Augusta! C'était un refrain perpétuel!'[51] But after Byron's death Augusta had sent her kind messages, and had returned the locket and chain of her hair – and she was, after all, the only one of Byron's relatives whom Teresa could hope to see. So at last Mr. Murray conveyed messages to Augusta from her, and Mrs. Leigh called – and at last Teresa spent three hours with her in St. James's Palace, 'always speaking of him'.[52] What indeed was said in that interview? What did the two women, so alike in some ways, so very different in others – now brought together by so strange and uncomfortable a bond – make of each other? 'All my loves . . . make a point of calling on her,' Byron had written, 'which puts her in a flutter (no difficult matter)'[53] – and surely this must have been the most distressing interview of all. But whether a sincere word was spoken at it, whether for a moment either of the two ladies dropped her guard, has never been revealed. The only two comments recorded are not informative. 'I hope you were as much satisfied with the interview yesterday', wrote Murray discreetly to Teresa, 'as a certain person has expressed herself to have been.'[54] And Teresa, on getting home that evening, told Lady Blessington that: 'Mrs. Leigh is the most good-natured, amiable person in the world; and besides poor Lord Byron was so fond of her, that she is a very interesting person for me.'[55] And that was all; they never saw each other again.

Such effusiveness as was to be displayed on the occasion, was reserved to Lady Blessington; the adjectives she chooses for Augusta are interesting, as applied to the woman whom Annabella described as 'a moral half-idiot'.

'I must write a line to say how gratified I am that you have seen the *nearest* and *dearest* relative of *him* for whom you sacrificed *all*, and who would, had Providence spared his life, have consoled you for all. Mrs. Leigh is considered to be the most excellent, the most kind, the most faultless woman in England, but were she even less perfect, I well know how your affectionate heart would turn towards her, as the sister of *him* you so truly loved. The interview must have been a melancholy pleasure for both of you, and I shall always value Mrs. Leigh for cherishing *one* whom her Brother so highly esteemed, as *I* well know he did you.

All who valued Lord Byron ought to love you, as the last and *only* true object of his affection. I never see you without this feeling, and I want the whole world to know, as *I do*, the high esteem and respect *he* entertained for your principles, delicacy and noble conduct towards him, all of which he often told me and my dear lost Husband. I often want to talk to you on this interesting subject, but I fear to give you pain.'

All this was very fine – and in a style well suited to Teresa's taste. But with the mention of Byron's name, a more guarded note was heard: the two ladies ceased their curtsying and drew out their foils. It was in this spring that the first instalment of Lady Blessington's *Conversations of Lord Byron* appeared and, soon after Teresa's arrival, Lady Blessington herself sent her the first two instalments. Teresa's first comments were both polite and guarded.

'Je trouve des idées si *justes* et si bien *exprimées* dans les extraits de votre Journal, que je n'aurais pas désiré mieux. Seulement les passages relatifs à cette dame [Lady Byron] et vos reflexions sur elle, peuvent inspirer une sympathie pour elle qu'elle ne mérite pas, vu qu'elle a été la cause, volontaire et obstinée, de tous les malheurs de Lord Byron.

Je trouve aussi que quelques unes de vos reflexions sur le genre de vie que B. menait à Venise sont un peu trop sévères et exagèrent la vérité. Comme il aimait à se calomnier, il était bien lui la cause principale des fausses opinions qu'on entretenait de lui.'[56]

Even so mild a criticism put Lady Blessington on the defensive.

LADY BLESSINGTON TO CONTESSA GUICCIOLI[57]

My Dear Contessa: I can well enter into your feelings, and excuse your criticism on the parts of my Journal that pain you. I wrote down my reflections at the moment they occurred. If they were

CC

erroneous, and we are all liable to error in judging others, they have not been wilfully so, and were formed, I assure you, from Lord Byron's own confessions, made both to my dear Lost Husband and myself, confessions that his own letters from Venice, to Messrs. Moore and Murray, describing the mode of life there, bear out. – My Journal was written with as much freedom from prejudice, and with as much charity towards failings that sully even the best natures, as I could write. How many imprudent confessions of Lord Byron touching himself and others have I not suppressed, but you will allow that each individual who writes, must give his or her own impression, and that such impressions are little calculated to satisfy a sensitiveness like yours, towards the object of your fond and devoted attachment. You had better opportunities of knowing and judging Lord Byron than anyone else, you saw him in his best light, that of the Lover and the Friend, and I can understand how dissatisfied you must be with the less favourable views taken of him by others. I am sure that if *you* wrote your impressions of him, they will do honour to his memory and to yourself, and cannot fail to be received by the public, with that interest that anything coming from the pen of one who had the best and longest opportunities of judging him, must invite.

Recollect that I only saw Lord Byron for the first time at Genoa, and that our acquaintance was of but 10 weeks' duration; he was always misrepresenting himself and his motives to our circle, as well as to his other acquaintances and correspondents. If you read his letters in Moore's Life, though, you will find that he represents himself in much harder colours than I could do, and that consequently my work is more calculated to palliate than darken his errors. There is no betrayal of confidences, because I have good reason to know, Lord Byron looked on my Husband and self as acquaintances only, and not as friends, and the confidence reposed in us, he reposed in all who approached him, or to whom he wrote.

I have entered into this explanation because I really feel a sincere affection for you, founded on admiration of your noble and truly disinterested conduct, and that it would grieve me to give you pain. Let who will write of Byron (except yourself) you cannot be satisfied, for no one saw him under such favourable circumstances for forming a good opinion as yourself, and each must write his own impressions from what he saw of the person, liable as all impressions are, and ever must be, to error.

You may always, my dear Contessa, count on the sincerity and affection of your attached friend   M. BLESSINGTON

Teresa, however, would not let herself be mollified.

'Yes, you are right, my dear Lady Blessington,' she replied, 'when you say that, on account of my sensitiveness towards Lord Byron (which has its sources not only in my exalted sense of his perfections, but in all the results of my experience of the world) I cannot be satisfied with any of his biographers. But if I ever shall give my own impressions of him to the public (which I look upon as a duty it remains for me to perform towards his memory one day or other) I fear, my dear Lady Blessington, that instead of being received by the public with the interest you say, they would find I have seen Lord Byron through a medium of affection, and would laugh, perhaps, at what I feel so deeply in my heart. . . .'[58]

The truth was that Teresa was now thoroughly upon her guard. It was all very well to be lionized – but she did not intend to be exploited. Above all, she had a most lively sense of the value of Byron's manuscripts and letters, and was not inclined to yield to even the most specious arguments for giving any of them up. It was not long, indeed, before Lady Blessington made the attempt.

'The more I reflect, my dearest Friend, on the extreme delicacy of your feelings and position, the more I am convinced that it would be for your honour, and that of poor dear Lord Byron, that the world should know how devoted and attached he continued to be to you, from the first commencement of your liaison up to his death. I therefore wish you to furnish me with any extract on this subject, from his letters from Greece, and it will give me sincerely pleasure, not less from my respect for his memory than my affection for, and esteem for you, to be able to publish *a refutation* of all the vile reports circulated as to his having ceased to feel the same attachment as at the commencement. *To me* he invariably expressed himself as being fondly and truly devoted to you, and spoke of you in the *highest, warmest* terms imaginable. *I*, therefore, can have no *doubt*, but I wish the World to judge as I do, and *you* alone can furnish satisfactory proof on this point.

Anything you wish to be inserted in my book, shall find a place, for I might state *many things* relative to you and Lord B. that you would not like to state yourself – and yet that would be creditable to both of you to have known. You may depend on my affection, and tact, to do you justice, but I wish you to specify all that you wish to be said on the subject. The more generally it is known, that Byron truly and dearly loved you, the more honourable it will be to you both.'"

This letter placed Teresa in an extremely difficult position. She was shrewd enough to realize that Lady Blessington had set her heart upon getting hold of Byron's letters from Greece to enrich her book, and she also was aware that she could not afford to quarrel with her. But those letters – alas, how well she knew it! – were not of a kind to furnish the proof that was required. There was nothing for it but to take refuge in high-mindedness.

You ask me for some documents, for some extracts of Lord Byron's letters to me from Greece, to prove how his attachment for me continued to be the same till his death. My dear Lady Blessington, what shall I answer you? Perhaps you will blame me – but I cannot conceal from you that I have the greatest dislike to publish any of Lord Byron's letters to me. One day or other they will be published, that is to say after my death, not now. And if I was to give you the extracts and names, don't you think that the malicious could suspect that you were influenced by your friendship towards me, and also by my entreaties, to speak in honourable terms of Lord B.'s affection for me? I am so persuaded of this, that the world would give you much more credit for everything you could uphold, had your pen published it before you had any acquaintance or friendship for me. But upon all that, I will speak about with you, the first time I shall have the pleasure to see you.

Good evening, my dear Lady Blessington, and many thanks for all your kindness towards me. Believe me always Your friend

T. GUICCIOLI[60]

Lady Blessington seems to have accepted these excuses at their face value, and shortly afterwards Teresa was sending her two of Byron's portraits to examine.

'Here are the portraits of L. B. I mentioned to you; the little one is in my opinion *the most striking likeness* I ever saw of him – the other is worse – though of the same author: who is a man without a spark of genius, but only considered a good painter for likeness.

As pictures they are very bad – and with a total want of the expression which formed one of the peculiar beauties of Lord
Byron's countenance. But after all they are like, and particularly
the smallest, and for that account I prize them very much – being
so rare if not impossible to find any other picture of him which is
not a caricature, having been abused by his painters almost as
much as his biographers.'[61]

Lady Blessington, however, did not care much for the likenesses.

'I return you the portraits of Lord Byron, which I agree with
you [in] thinking do not render justice to the original. As I never
saw him until at Genoa, where he was so remarkably thin, I cannot judge if either of the portraits could have been like, but it
appears to me that he looked handsomer when thin, than fat,
which both the portraits represent him.'[62]

And now the correspondence records a less agreeable incident.
A review in the *Morning Herald* of September 11th of the *Conversations* referred to both Teresa and Byron in such crude terms
that Teresa sent Lady Blessington a letter of protest. She replied
in great distress:[63]

'I have rarely felt more pain than on reading the cruel and disgusting paragraph in the *Morning Herald*, I am so accustomed to
seeing people attacked, that I in general pay little attention to
the newspapers, and as far as regards myself, I never notice them,
knowing that in two days they are forgotten and that any attempt
to correct their mis-statements only draws more attention to what
would otherwise be forgotten . . : But to see you, a stranger, and
for whom I feel a warm and sincere regard, exposed to such
insolence, was really too provoking, and I immediately wrote to
Mr. Galt, the only person I know who has any knowledge of the
Editor of the *Herald*, to request him to have something done. I
send you his answer, and one or two other clever people whom I
have consulted, all advise that no notice should be taken of the
scurrilous paragraph.'

Nevertheless, on the surface, the most cordial relations were
maintained. In addition to the constant stream of letters and
invitations, Lady Blessington's footman would appear in Piccadilly with a series of more tangible proofs of her good will: a
'small paté with some Bologna sausage',[64] to make Teresa feel

less homesick, or some Sicilian wine – or some boots, 'to keep your feet warm during your travels'. Teresa responded with 'une plume travaillée en Italie. Je suis sure que votre amitié pour moi et la mienne pour vous élèveront cette plume à l'honneur qu'elle ne mérite pas, d'être quelquefois l'interprète de vos idées et de vos sentences et d'être touchée par vos jolies mains'.[65]

'I accept with pleasure', Lady Blessington replied, 'the token of friendship you have given, which I shall always prize and preserve as a proof of your affection – though, be assured, I need no such gift to remind me of you. – I do not lightly profess friendship, but when I do, the sentiment is real and profound. This feeling exists for you, and it will always give me pleasure to prove, by any or every means in my power, its sincerity.

I hope you do not forget that you have promised me a lock of your hair, and if you could spare me ever so small a lock of Lord Byron's I should esteem it a favour . . . Let the lock of hair be folded in a paper with a little inscription in your own writing and signed by you, and ages hence, when our dust shall have mingled with their native earth, the worshippers of Genius, Beauty and Love will look on these precious relics with veneration.'[66]

The circle of Teresa's English acquaintances was now widening. She had met Moore and Henry Bulwer at Lady Blessington's, as well as Thomas Campbell, the poet, who sent her a flattering poem about her fan, and invited her to visit a school in Hampstead, in which he was interested.[67] He also introduced her to Lady Morgan, who was on a visit to London. The two ladies exchanged courtesies; Teresa was once again prodigal of locks of hair; and before Lady Morgan returned to Ireland, she sent Teresa a cordial invitation.

'Lady Morgan cannot sufficiently express her sense of the Countess Guiccioli's kindness nor of the high value she places upon relics so rare and precious . . . Should she [Contessa Guiccioli] be *tempted* to *visit* Ireland, Lady Morgan will be in Dublin in August ready to *receive her*, and to do the honours by one destined to live in literary history, with the *Laura* of *Petrarch* and the *Beatrice* of *Dante*!'

Teresa, however, did not go to Ireland. She went, instead, to Harrow, where she 'enjoyed many melancholy pleasures', and spent a whole day with the family of the Rev. Dr. Drury, Byron's tutor, 'from one o'clock in the morning to ten in the evening . . . a

fatiguing, melancholy, but very interesting day'.⁶⁸ She stayed for
a few weeks at Brighton, 'living quite an English life, a quiet,
serious life, speaking all day the language of the English people' –
although she confessed that she felt 'that this kind of life is a little
too formal, too cold, there is too much restraint in it on the feelings
and makes me feel a kind of oppression on my breast'.⁶⁹ Then, on
returning to London, she tasted the peculiarities of a London fog.
'What a weather, dear Lady Blessington! When I saw for the first
time in my life the mixture of yellow and red tint of the sky, it
seemed to me as to have been transported in some other planet.'⁷⁰
But on the whole she had enjoyed herself in England.

And now, before her time there came to an end, she made the
expedition to which she had looked forward with a mixture of
romantic anticipation and dread: her 'pilgrimage' to Newstead.
She set out armed with letters to the owner of the Abbey, Colonel
Wildman,* from both Lady Blessington and Mr. Murray. The
latter assured her that he had written in terms 'calculated to
obtain for you the kindest attentions', and these she appears to
have received.

'I cannot express to you', she wrote to Murray on her return,
'how much gratified I have been with Colonel Wildman's reception, and with all the kind attentions he has bestowed upon me.
He is a very amiable and gallant man – and I cannot express how
extremely glad I have been to see this interesting spot in the hands
of a person who is so very sincerely attached to the memory of Ld.
Byron. In all the improvements he has done and is doing to the
building (which are considerable and of a very refined taste) he
seems rather to consult the intentions of the last possessor of the
Abbey than his own. The *arms* of Ld. Byron, his *likenesses*, his *very
name* engraved on a beech tree – together with that of his sister –
are shown by the Colonel to the visitors to the Abbey with a kind
of religious feeling, which you may imagine what sincere though
melancholy pleasure has given to me!'⁷¹

Before leaving the Abbey, Teresa gathered some souvenirs: a
rose, an acorn, a branch from one of the beech trees on which
Byron's and Augusta's names were carved, and a piece of the
silk of Byron's bed curtains. These, when she got back to Italy,
she placed in the mahogany casket which contained his portraits
and her 'relics' – and there they still lie.

* Colonel Thomas Wildman, a schoolfellow of Byron's at Harrow, had purchased
Newstead in 1817 for £94,500. Byron wrote to Hoppner: 'I recollect him as my old
schoolfellow and a man of honour, and would rather, as far as my personal feelings are
concerned, that he should be the purchaser than another.' *L.J.*, IV, p. 187.

On the day after her visit to Newstead, Teresa received a call from another of Byron's oldest friends, Dr. John Pigot[72] and her charms seemed to have surpassed his most romantic expectations.

'. . . I trust', he wrote on the day after their meeting, 'you will give me credit for the serenity of expression I lay claim to, when I assure you that the high, *very high* ideas which I had formed of the mental and bodily perfections of the Countess Guiccioli have been most fully realized. Beauty of structure *would* attract my late beloved friend, but I am convinced that it would be only a superior mind, with suitable accomplishments and cultivation, which could permanently retain the affections of his high-wrought spirit. I should be indeed insensible to everything lovely in form, to everything perfect in mind, manners, tact and conversation, did I not feel and acknowledge the charms of the Countess Guiccioli. I should have felt mortified and disappointed, had I found you otherwise, it would have been an impeachment of the taste and the judgment of my lamented friend, which I should have been most reluctant to be *forced* to admit.'[73]

To all this, however, Teresa did not even reply. And at the beginning of January, 1833, after sending 'one kiss more' to Lady Blessington,[74] she returned to Italy. 'What she found to please her in this dingy land', wrote Mary Shelley, 'I cannot guess. Still, she did like it and was sorry to go.'[75]

This was, however, far from being the end of Teresa's connection with England. As soon as she got back to Ravenna, she was writing to John Murray Jr., who had asked for some drawings to illustrate Byron's works,[76] sending him a view of the Camposanto of Bologna, but regretting that she could not add one of the garden of Palazzo Savioli, 'because the garden has been so much changed, altered and neglected since we left'.[77] Mr. Murray, on his part, wrote to tell her about Ada's presentation at Court on April 18th, – 'and the next day is the anniversary of her Father's death',[78] and Teresa replied begging for more details

'Pray write to me of her début into the world, does she resemble her father? Does she see her good aunt Mrs. Leigh? . . . Thank you dear, very dear Mr. Murray for all the news you have given to me of England; nothing can be indifferent to me which has reference to a country I am so very fond of.'[79]

By the summer of 1834 she was back in England again, enjoying the acquaintance of a new friend – that versatile and talkative Irishman, Dionysius Lardner'[80] and in May 1835 Teresa was making a tour of Southern England – sometimes travelling under her brother's name, for Dr. Lardner wrote that, in his opinion, 'in general in travelling in England, you would find it convenient to use another name – Madame Gamba would do very well'.[81] She dined with Trelawny and saw Mary Shelley several times – although, apparently, without much satisfaction on either side, and on Mary's – since her conventionality increased with the years – with some reluctance.* For Teresa was still only received, in England, by those who were not afraid of seeming unconventional. 'You know we are not fastidious about the morals of our lady friends' – wrote one spinster lady who entertained her – 'from the example of Countess Guiccioli.'[82]

She stayed with Lady Blessington at Anglesey, and gradually the two ladies seem to have dropped their guard and to have formed a warmer and more genuine – if still extremely *complimentoso* – friendship. When Teresa returned to Paris, Lady Blessington wrote to her with much indignation about 'the trial of our Prince and la belle Norton'.

'The evidence, though enough to convict the lady of imprudence, did not satisfy the judge of any actual guilt, but the proceedings were of a nature to inflict great pain on a delicate-minded woman's feelings and to furnish a handle to the censorious for further attacks. I pity her very much, for though many will receive her as before the disgusting trial, still all the privacy and decorum of her domestic life are violated, and her pride must be grievously wounded and her modesty outraged.'[83]

This comment is characteristic of the woman who said of herself: 'There are so few before whom one could condescend to appear otherwise than happy.'

It was in this year that Lady Blessington had moved into her new and delightful house in Kensington, Gore House, and when, in the following summer, Teresa paid yet another visit to England, it was natural that she should stay there. She was now no longer a novelty in London, and at Lady Blessington's fashionable parties she seems to have cut a somewhat dowdy figure.[84] Captain Gronow, who saw her at about this time, considered that she had 'nothing in physical appearance or intellectual gifts to account for her having inspired a romantic passion'.[85] And when William Archer Shee met her in the spring of 1837, he saw in her 'neither youth, striking beauty or grace,' and found it difficult

---

* 'I have such a dread', wrote Mary, 'of her coming to see me here – imagine the talk.' To Mrs. Gisborne, June 14th, 1835.

to believe that she *ever* could have been the great poet's ideal. 'She is not tall and is thickset, devoid of air or style, and whatever she may have been, is no longer attractive ... She sang several Italian airs to her own accompaniment in a very pretentious manner, and her voice is loud and somewhat harsh.'[86]

It would appear that Teresa, – grown no less sentimental with the years, but stouter, plainer and more affected – had become something of a figure of fun in London society – but on the whole, of good-humoured and affectionate fun.

'Any little peculiarities of the Italian lady', says Dr. Madden, 'were seized hold of eagerly and made the most of ... The Guiccioli could not understand anything like a joke, [and] Lady Blessington, who delighted in certain kinds of mystification, used sometimes to take advantage of Madame Guiccioli's simplicity and amusing peculiarities, her exaggerated ideas of Italian superiority in all matters of refinement, her invariable persuasion that Italians excelled all other Europeans in genius, virtue and patriotism.'[87]

Lady Blessington, with her gentle, malicious smile, would lead Teresa on, the men would pay her extravagant compliments, which she would take at their face value, with a coy tap of her fan. And then she would shake her long auburn ringlets (already out of fashion) and seating herself at the harpsichord with a great sigh, would burst, after a few arpeggios, into somewhat metallic song. 'Oh my lonely, lonely, *lonely* Pillow!' On one such occasion, Archer Shee relates, when she was asked to sing in one of the great London houses:

'After preluding with much pretension, and when all round her were on the tiptoe of expectation, she suddenly stopped, put her hands behind her with a convulsive effort to loosen some unseen but apparently not unfelt pressure in the region of her waist, and exclaimed with a laugh "Dio Buono, ho mangiato troppo!*" '

A faint echo of her audience's laughter still lingers in the 'Anglo-Gallic' poem which James Smith wrote for her at that time.†

* Molloy, op. cit., II, p. 226. 'Good heavens, I've eaten too much!'

† James Smith (1775-1859) was, with his brother Horace, the author of the parodies entitled 'Rejected Addresses', greatly admired at that time. Byron, who was the subject of one of these addresses, wrote: 'Tell him I forgive him, were he twenty times over our satirist.' The poem to Teresa was entitled 'Babel, an Anglo-Gallic Epistle', and was sent to her on September 13th, 1837, under cover to Lady Blessington with the comment 'The enclosed is *Anglo-Gallic* that the Countess may at least comprehend half'. Morrison, op. cit., p. 220.

Teresa, belle Italian Countess
Je write, dependent sur vos Bounties,
Sur papier bleu, with pen metallic,
Cette longue Epistle Anglo-Gallic
To Kensington – en Espérance
Que vous will carry it to France.
To Honoré's très distant Rue
To show how much moi honour You.

. . . . . .

Vos auburn Locks et Corkscrew Curls
Entangle, dangeureusement, Earls.
Corkscrews we use, pour wet our Throttles,
To séparer les corks from Bottles,
Mais ces belles corkscrews wave above
Not pull *out* wine, mais put *in* Love;
So, malheureusement, they affect us
Par Cupidon et non par Bacchus.

On getting back to Paris – after having had some of her English purchases confiscated by the French customs – Teresa wrote to Lady Blessington that she had become 'so much accustomed to your company and to the delightful existence of Gore House', that she would never be able to settle down again. 'On se fait si vite au bonheur.'[88] It was another two years, however, before Teresa returned to England. But the correspondence continued and in August 1839 she was telling Lady Blessington that the *Idler in Italy* was 'délicieux'.

'La modestie du titre de ce charmant ouvrage doit confondre tous ceux qui, se faisant une préoccupation d'écrire leŭrs impressions de voyage, ne savent y mettre une centième partie de la finesse, de la grace, de la profondeur d'observation que vous, grande dame ... [four words illegible] vous avez su y mettre.'[89]

And in 1839 Teresa was back in London again, making a great impression on a new admirer, Henry Reeve.* 'I have been a good deal at Gore House lately,' he wrote in his Journal on October 15th, 'attracted and amused by Madame de Guiccioli, who is staying with my lady.' Unlike Gronow and Shee, he considered Teresa 'still exceedingly beautiful. She has sunbeams of hair, a fine person, and a milky complexion'.[90]

* Henry Reeve (1813-93) became a considerable social and literary figure in Paris as well as London, knew most of the celebrated people of his time in both cities and edited for forty years the *Edinburgh Review*.

Mr. Reeve, who was a very cosmopolitan young man, talked beautiful French to Teresa; he wrote verses in her honour,* and he maintained that she was as clever as she was attractive.

'Her spirits are wonderful and her conversation brilliant even in the most witty houses in London ... Besides a fine taste ... she has a good share of literary attainments, which, as her beauty fails, will smooth a track from coquetry to pedantry, from the courted beauty to the courted blue.'[91]

Like many other guests at Gore House – Prince Louis Napoleon, Henry Bulwer,† James Smith, who remained Teresa's friends in later years – he was disarmed by the unfailing good humour with which she took alike their compliments and their quizzing. 'One can't help loving the Guiccioli for her bonhomie,' wrote Henry Reeve, when the time came for her to return to France, 'and though we have all been hoaxing her for six weeks, I am sure she likes us all the better for it.' And a few days later, not perhaps without a smile, he was writing to Teresa herself, to describe the void she had left behind her.

'Si vous pouvez vous figurer, ma belle et bonne Comtesse, votre Gore House un peu triste, un peu démontée, je vous dirai que cela s'est vu le jour suivant votre départ. On y est allé pour savoir de vos nouvelles, qui n'arrivaient pas – enfin vous nous annoncez les ennuis qui ont accompagné votre voyage, puis les souffrances qui attendent votre retour. Oh! Mer! Oh! Paris! Que de mal nous avons dit de vous: enfin ce qui nous a remis tout à fait c'est votre charmante lettre, qui a été lue et relue et que le Comte emporte avec lui tous les soirs pour lui donner de beaux rêves, quand il la met sous ses coussins de lit.'[92]

Can even Teresa have believed the last sentence? If indeed D'Orsay, that heartless dandy, ever placed any woman's letter under his pillow, it certainly was not hers!

Teresa did not return to England again until 1859. But she

---

*   Th'Italian Muse from whose delicious eyes
         Great England's Poet drew his melodies,
         Sat floating captive in a sunny calm,
         Her shallop lulled by some Magician's charm.
         One hand festooned her amber-scented tress –
         The loosened scarf of Love in idleness.

And so on, at a considerable length.

† William Henry Lytton, Earl Bulwer (1801-71). Diplomat and man of letters. In 1824 was sent with Hamilton Browne by the Greek Committee to the Morea, to hand over to Mavrocordato £80,000 of the Greek Loan. In later years he often visited Teresa in Paris and Florence (where he was Minister from 1852 to 1855) and kept up a correspondence with her, of which ten letters are among Teresa's papers.

assiduously kept up her correspondence with her English friends. In 1845 Lady Blessington sent her an engraving of D'Orsay's picture of Byron, 'pronounced by Sir John Cam Hobhouse, and all who remember Lord Byron to be the best likeness of him ever painted. Who', she asked, 'could so well judge of the resemblance as you?'[93] But by now Teresa had become so prudish that she put a piece of blank paper over the sentence, writing over it the word 'supprimé'.

And in 1848, after Teresa had become Marquise de Boissy, her friendship with Lady Blessington had a strange epilogue. Lady Blessington – with her fortune gambled away by D'Orsay, her beautiful house and fine possessions sold by auction, and her heart broken – came to live in Paris. Now, after so many years, the situation was reversed; it was Teresa who was able to condescend to Lady Blessington. It was she, now, who paid little attentions, who sent invitations to evening parties, who offered to lend her carriage.[94] But Lady Blessington had had enough – of social life, and of any life. Her later letters to Teresa are flat and sad – but they have a note of affectionate sincerity lacking in all her earlier effusions. One of them tells Teresa of her sister's death – 'She lived to judge me rightly . . . [and] died in my arms, blessing me . . . Alas! dearest friend, who would wish to live to grow old?'[95]

III. POOR DEAR LORD BYRON

Of the last, and most prosperous, twenty-five years of Teresa's life, there is not much to say that is relevant to this story. In 1847, while living quietly with her brother Ippolito, after her father's death, at Filetto, she received the visit of Hilaire Etienne Victor Rouillé, Marquis de Boissy – an eccentric, generous and witty middle-aged peer, and one of the richest men in France – who had already been courting her for several years. Even now she was in no hurry to accept his hand. 'She thinks', the Marquis wrote in his Journal, 'that liberty has some value, that the ties of marriage are not always gentle or light chains. She is a woman who has her own ideas, who thinks for herself, who believes she is capable of managing her own life.'[96] But her elderly lover liked to be held off. 'Cette femme qui paraît effrayée est charmante.' He followed her to Florence, and then to Rome. 'J'aime à suivre comme un caniche.'[97] And on December 15th, 1847, with great pomp, they were married in the chapel of the Luxembourg – the bride being then forty-seven and the bridegroom forty-nine.*

* 'I sincerely share', wrote Lamartine to Teresa on this occasion, 'in the happiness which renders you French, as you render us Italian by the admiration we feel for you.' February 12th [1848].

They settled at 95 Rue St. Lazare, in a luxurious hotel which the Marquis de Boissy – who never for a moment forgot that he was a 'pair de France' – provided with a deep red carpet covered with legs (the Gamba crest) and hands (the de Boissy crest). The rooms, which were generally kept in a dim romantic light, were also adorned by several little fountains, whose gentle trickle provided an accompaniment to the conversation, and a series of steps, leading from one room to the other, had the purpose – according to the host – of breaking the monotony and thus preventing his guests from ever being bored.⁹⁸ This purpose, however, was only partially achieved – since the hostess had lost the infectious good humour of her youth. 'I found the bonhomie of the Italian', wrote Lord Malmesbury after being entertained at 'a great banquet' there, 'altered for the artificial manner of a *grande dame*, and not to its advantage, although she retained the kindly instincts of her nature.'⁹⁹

She continued to entertain a stream of English visitors – drove about the town in a green carriage lined with white satin, modelled on Lady Blessington's – dressed in the fashion of the 'forties – and scented herself with nothing but lavender water. 'Her aspiration, in short,' says her stepson, 'was to seem a great English lady of the forties.'¹⁰⁰

For now she was again upon friendly terms with Ignazio Guiccioli – who, on visiting Paris in 1856, took his whole family to see her – thus enabling his son, who was then a little boy, to draw for us a somewhat malicious portrait.

'An oval face, fine, regular, noble features, a lovely nose, a pretty mouth, but when she was speaking, and even when she was silent, she seemed to be careful to make it seem even smaller than it was; I even suspect that some enamel or paint prevented her from moving it freely. Magnificently shaped eyes, large, blue and serene, eyebrows admirably drawn by the hand of God and also by that of man, a rosy complexion, still fresh, but which evidently had been helped by art. Hair rather of a cendré colour than red, dressed with *boucles à l'Anglaise*, which with the progress of the years, came further and further forward over her face, so that, towards the end of her life, little more than the eyes and nose were left uncovered. Shoulders, breast and arms very fine, and much fresher than is usual at her age. In short, on the whole, still a fine woman, who might still easily find someone to pay court to her.'*

---

* *I Guiccioli*, II, p. 88. Teresa's reconciliation with Ignazio Guiccioli is ascribed by his son solely to her wish to consolidate her recent respectability in French society by proving that she was 'loved and respected even by the family of her first husband'. Ibid., p. 86.

As to the manners of the Marquise, he says they were 'kindly but very affected. She wished to seem a very kind, very sweet woman, whose position obliged her to lead a social life, but who would have preferred to live in the country, in the midst of flowers, birds, lapdogs, trickling fountains, moonlight and sincere affections'. The writer's opinion, however, was that her kindness did not amount to anything more than a preference for seeing contented faces rather than discontented ones – and that at heart she cared for nothing but money and her own beauty.

Her cult of Byron, as the years passed, became increasingly tinged with absurdity. A full-length portrait of him hung over the mantelpiece, and she would stand before it murmuring: 'Qu'il était beau! Mon Dieu, qu'il était beau!'[101] Her husband, no less than herself, showed himself proud of the connection, and it was said by the malicious that when the Duc Pasquier, the doyen of the House of Peers, asked him a little guardedly whether the lady to whom he had become engaged were any relation of the Countess Guiccioli whose name had been connected with Lord Byron's: 'Comment donc,' Boissy replied with a radiant smile, 'mais c'est elle-même, c'est elle!'[102]

After making the acquaintance of Daniel Home, the spiritualist, she took to automatic writing, and was, she said, in frequent communication with Byron's spirit. 'His answers', according to a lady who attended one of the séances, a Miss Darby Smith of Philadelphia, 'came like magic and were written down with the utmost rapidity and facility, in a large square book with a crimson cover.' Teresa told Miss Smith 'that when writing about him in the book she has since published, if she was in doubt about a matter or a date, she would appeal to him from the Spirit land, and he satisfactorily answered'. She also told this lady 'that Byron from the spirit world had advised her not to allow their correspondence to be published until fifty years after her death'. When the Marquis de Boissy died, in 1866, she established a similar correspondence with him, too. 'They are together now,' she affirmed, 'and are the best of friends.'[103]

Now, in her old age, she had repeated the legend of their platonic love so often that it would almost seem that – looking down the years in a golden haze – she herself had come to believe it. To Miss Smith, too, she repeated the details of the legend – 'The young victim of an ill-assorted marriage and the unhappy Childe could not marry, though they loved. Yet, I reiterate, she was always under the protection of her father and her brother, and because they could not marry Lord Byron went to Greece.'[104]

This is not merely the silliness of Miss Smith of Philadelphia.

DD

In *Lord Byron jugé par les témoins de sa vie*, as in all her later comments on Byron's biographers, Teresa herself repeated the same refrain. 'In all their writings', she declared, 'they have romanticized my person, and converted into love and passion a sentiment which no one has the right to see in any other light than that of a warm and enthusiastic friendship!'[105] Self-delusion, surely, can go no further.

The alterations which had been made at her request[106] in the second edition of Moore – 'that great *Magazine*', as she called it, 'where a quantity of useless, harmful and good things are lying together' – no longer satisfied her. In every place where the words 'love' or 'lover' still remained, she altered them to 'devotion' or 'friend'. And she filled the margins with her agitated (but still plainly legible) comments and emendations.

'He [Byron] wished me *older*, and sometimes he persuaded himself that I *was* so! I wish *that was known* by the public – because the responsibility of an unhappy marriage cannot fall upon a girl of sixteen as upon a young lady of eighteen – two years at that period of a woman's life makes an immense difference.'

And, after reading Moore's reference to Count Guiccioli's having written to his wife at La Mira, '*not* to express any censure of her conduct, but to extract a further loan from Byron', she indignantly scrawled: 'Indeed, there was no censure to express on her conduct, as she was at La Mira only on account of her health and with the consentment of her husband!'

'What was lacking in Moore,' she wrote to John Murray Jr., 'was a social position equal to his tastes – a more independent position, and perhaps also a more generous character, to enable him to say frankly and courageously what he really thought – and to express himself so as to bring conviction to his readers. I also imagine that the part he had taken (whether active or passive) in the destruction of Lord Byron's Memoirs, must have weighed upon his conscience, for he owed a duty to the world as to this charge. But the subject is too painful for me to dwell on it.'[107]

Her final comment is scribbled on the last page of Moore. 'It was a *duty* in his friends to employ *delicacy in the task*. In what manner they have satisfied it, this work shows sufficiently. Poor dear Lord Byron!'

And then one more occasion arose, when she felt she must take up the cudgels in 'her poet's' defence. In 1858, ten years after her marriage to the Marquis de Boissy, she read Leigh Hunt's *Lord*

Byron and his Contemporaries.[108] On the margins she expressed her first indignant comments: 'Faux! Faux! Menteur! Hypocrite!' And then, taking up her fluent pen, she poured forth her feelings – for *her* Mr. Murray was dead – to John Murray Junior.[109]

'. . . No words are capable of expressing the disgust that he [Hunt] has aroused in me. Remembering what Lord Byron said to me about Mr. Hunt, and having been a witness of all the kind and generous things he did for Mr. Hunt and his family in Pisa and Genoa – without being influenced by any personal liking or duty, and on the contrary aware that he was acting against the advice of his best friends, and only from simple and generous humanity – I regard such a book as the ultimate expression of human perversity, and its author as more guilty than the wretch who demands "your money or your life" from men who can still defend themselves . . . Everything in this book breathes hostility, calumny, falsehood.'

Every statement, she declares, was falsified or distorted. Even Byron's portrait, on the frontispiece, made him 'like a fool instead of a being sublime for beauty and genius'; the facsimile of his writing was chosen 'to give a false impression that he composed laboriously,'[110] and the confidences which she herself was supposed to have made to Hunt were 'completely impossible and imaginary'.

Teresa's only consolation, she declared, was that the book had been received in England 'as it deserved'.

'But if this has occurred in England (with some exceptions, for calumny never fails to leave some trace) the contrary has happened abroad, and especially in France, where the greater part of the biographies and analyses of Ld. Byron's character, owing to superficiality and insufficient knowledge, have found their inspiration in these inimical books, and it is thus that public opinion of him has been formed. . . .'[111]

Moreover, Teresa remarked that this estimate of Byron was accepted largely owing to 'the too complete silence of Lord Byron's friends, and in particular of Lord Broughton'.

'Since the last word on Lord Byron (not as a poet, but as a moral and social being) is far from having been said, I have always hoped and still hope, that it will be said one day by Lord Broughton. No one has lived for so long and as intimately with Lord Byron as he . . . Who then better than Lord Broughton, for whom he felt so deep a friendship, could show the world the *true* Byron, with so few faults and so many virtues? Lord Broughton, I feel sure, will not repudiate this sacred duty; he will not forget that posterity requires this of him as a debt of honour – and reserves as much glory to Lord Byron's friend, as to the illustrious writer and statesman. As for what it is in my power to do for this purpose, within the limits of my capacity, I hope that, – as you may imagine – it will be done, after my death. Whatever the consequences may be to my reputation is unimportant, so long as none of the documents and letters are lost, which can reveal in its true light the great and kind heart of Lord Byron.'

This is, surely, a very remarkable letter. It must be remembered that when it was written – 34 years after Byron's death – Teresa had already read in Moore Byron's own flippant and selfish letters. She had read Medwin, and Parry, and Lady Blessington – and now the spiteful distortions of Mr. Hunt. But her loyalty and self-assurance was proof against it all. She was certain that *she* knew the truth.

She was, indeed, mistaken in thinking that Hobhouse would be the best biographer for her purpose.[112] It was true that he had known Byron for longer – and in some ways better – than any of his other friends, but his attitude to him had always been tinged with condescension, perhaps with jealousy. Even the Greek venture had seemed to him, at least at first, little more than a new toy, to keep Byron quiet. And he had always disapproved of Teresa. And now, – respectable, self-absorbed, very much the correct English statesman – he was the last man to take Byron's fame seriously, to consolidate, as Teresa wished, the Byronic legend.

But all this Teresa could not know. And, unfortunately, two years earlier, she had already placed some of the material for Byron's biography in other, and less scrupulous, hands. Early in 1856 Lamartine – remembering those early indiscreet talks with Teresa in Rome thirty years before – had written to ask her for any further information she could give him, or any papers she would allow him to peruse.

'I have', he wrote, 'a literary favour to ask of you. I am going to write, in the *Vie des grands hommes*, the story of the great poet of modern England. Would you be able to enrich me with some recollections, or some unpublished documents, which I should use *with your permission* and under your control, to consecrate still further the cult of his genius?'[113]

A scribbled draft among Teresa's papers gives us a part of her reply.

'... I shall be glad to put my recollections at your disposal, even the most intimate, those which I keep, like holy relics, at the bottom of my heart. For one is always certain of being fairly judged by a great heart, worthy of a great genius.

'Once again, make free use of my time and of everything that is in my power to do for you – for no one, pray believe it, has a more sincere devotion for you, and a more unlimited admiration.'

She sent Lamartine an account of her life with Byron: 'J'ai voulu me confesser à vous, car ... vous êtes vous. Mais je ne pense pas qu'il soit nécessaire de tout dire au monde indiscret ou indifférent ... Vous serez le juge suprème.'[114] She even sent him some of Byron's letters – 'ces feuilles pour moi sacrées' – but asked for 'une séance pour vous les lire moi-même et vous expliquer une foule de petites choses'.[115]

Lamartine, however, did not think much of the letters. He noted that they only revealed 'la stérilité de l'imagination, lorsqu'elle est absorbée par le cœur'. And in the following year, in the sixteenth Entretien of his *Cours familier de Littérature*, he printed a jibe against Byron which Teresa was never able to forgive: if Byron had not been lame, he said, he would never have written *Don Juan* – 'cette vengeance d'un esprit perverti par l'orgueil souffrant contre ceux qui marchent droit'. Teresa ceased to collaborate with Lamartine, but nevertheless, in 1865, the French poet's *Vie de Byron* began to appear as a feuilleton in *Le Constitutionnel*.[116] In this serial the whole story of Teresa and Byron was told – with numerous indiscretions and with some very unfavourable reflections on Byron's character – in the first person, as if narrated by Teresa herself. In vain did she send a despairing letter to Lamartine, appealing to his 'loyalty and delicacy' and asking him to substitute 'elle' for 'je'. He promised to do so, when the work would appear in book form – but meanwhile the feuilleton continued to appear. Teresa commented that 'although the world had expected this work to be conceived in a spirit of hostility, it has surpassed, in this respect, all expectations. The sentiments which it awakens are astonishment and regret.'[117]

But Lamartine's behaviour spurred on Teresa to produce her own account – a book eventually published anonymously in 1868, and entitled *Lord Byron jugé par les témoins de sa vie*. While she was preparing it, her unfortunate French publisher told Mr. Jerningham that the Marquise 'ne me laisse pas un instant tranquille avec son Byron. Au fait je n'ai jamais réalisé jusqu'à ce jour combien Lord Byron peut être ennuyeux.'[118]

The remark was justified. Teresa's book is a remarkably tedious one – but it is chiefly tedious because there is nothing in it that is not second-hand. Had Teresa written a straightforward account of her life with Byron, or her own opinion of him, the book might have been diffuse, disingenuous, and sometimes silly – but it could hardly have failed to hold some interest. But she felt that she could not publish such a book during her lifetime. She did indeed write it, and in her published book she referred to it several times;[119] but then she put it away, with Byron's letters, at Settimello. It was the 'Vie de Lord Byron en Italie' on which part of this story is based; its seventeen hundred pages have never been perused until now.

The book that appeared in 1868 was a hotch-potch of other people's opinions, of quotations from Moore, Parry, Galt, Medwin, Lady Blessington and Byron himself, of attacks on the poet's detractors, and of her own fulsome eulogies. Why, the Emperor Louis Napoleon asked Hubert Jerningham when the translation of the book was brought to him some years later, why had the Marquise written this book? 'To prove that Lord Byron was perfect, Sir,' said Mr. Jerningham. 'But here', said the Emperor, 'I see the word "irritability".' – 'No doubt, Sire, to refute an accusation.' Mr. Jerningham then proceeded to tell Louis Napoleon that Mme de Boissy was planning to write a book about her husband. The Emperor replied that 'the book about her lover should be called *Mes Folies*, that about her husband *Mes Regrets*'.[120]

The last seven years of Teresa's life, after her husband's death, were mostly spent at the villa he had bought for her at Settimello, near Florence. The pleasant, spacious villa, with its orangery and its little chapel, stands on a slight rise above the Pistoiese plain, shaded by a few great trees. The salon is still adorned by somewhat pretentious frescoes of the grand châteaux of the Marquis de Boissy. The chapel contains Teresa's tomb.

In this villa – until, in the last war, they were moved elsewhere for safe-keeping – remained Teresa's box of relics and all her papers – bequeathed by her, with the villa and all that it contained, to her two and a half year old great nephew, Count Carlo Gamba. The bookshelves, to this day, still hold her books – her annotated copies of Moore, Medwin, Lady Blessington, Leigh Hunt, and Byron's complete works. But except for these, there are surprisingly few books of her own time; the rest are elegant sets of standard works, or bound volumes of French reviews, and political pamphlets, belonging to de Boissy. One is forced to conclude that Teresa's love of literature, like many another woman's, was a second-hand product: she only 'learned by heart the names of Trasimene and Cannae', so long as that would make Byron 'love her more'.

Here it was that she finished the 'Vie de Lord Byron' which she had begun many years before; and here, an old lady now, at last, but still proud of her long ringlets à l'anglaise and her plump little white hands – she would draw out her letters and 'relics', and go back into the past. There they all lay – Byron's letters to her, her own letters to him – Pierino's letters from Greece – and, in the great mahogany box, Byron's miniatures, his handkerchief, the little acorn from Newstead . . . So much passion and ecstasy and pain. What now was left of it all? What should she destroy and what preserve?

Her decisions were marked by a most characteristic inconsistency. She must have destroyed – for no trace of them remains – the box of letters to Byron from other women, about which she told Lord Malmesbury.[121] She may have destroyed some of her own. She put a little blank sheet of paper with the word 'supprimé' over some perfectly harmless sentences in Lady Blessington's letters. And then she turned to Byron's. On some of them – those, presumably, that she had chosen to show to Moore and Lamartine – she wrote the word 'ostensible'; she erased in them a few words that seemed to her coarse, or compromising, and she even sometimes substituted Byron's favourite nickname for her, 'pettegola', by the more tender 'piccinina'. But she fortunately did all this so badly that it is possible to decipher what was written in the first place. And then she came to Byron's angry, passionate letters – to his outbursts of jealousy and suspiciousness in those tormented months at Palazzo Guiccioli. What should she do with them? About these, too, she could never make up her mind. Some of them she clearly meant to destroy, for among the papers there is a folder on which she has written, 'Letters of unreasonable and unjust jealousy – destroyed'. But parts of the letters, after all, are still there – with some offending passages cut out with her embroidery scissors. On another occasion, she threw a compromising letter into the fire – and then, as she saw the paper curling up and the beloved familiar writing standing out among the flames, she hurriedly pulled it out again with the tongs – and left the fragments, still partly decipherable, for us to read. And yet other letters, at least as compromising, she either forgot about, or believed to be unintelligible to anyone else; in any case, she kept them – a complete and final refutation of all her own asseverations.

What was her real opinion of the past, as she sat there by the fire, alone, looking back down the years? Did she ever realize how much destruction her connection with Byron had brought, not only on herself, but on her family? Byron undoubtedly did a great deal of harm to the Gambas, who had felt themselves so honoured by his friendship. Although Pierino would certainly, in any case, have been an ardent Carbonaro and might well have been exiled, it is hardly probable that, without Byron, he would have gone to meet his death in Greece. And Count Ruggero would have suffered neither exile nor imprisonment.[122] As for Teresa – in unequal relationships it is always the less complex, less brilliant partner who suffers in the end. Had Teresa fallen in love with an Italian of her own world, she would undoubtedly have conducted her liaison within the convenient framework permitted by the social customs of her time. She would not have been uprooted; she would have lost neither her home nor her fortune. But Byron dazzled her. Perhaps, indeed, of all his friends or mistresses, Pietro and Teresa Gamba were the only two who took him entirely seriously – who doggedly, whole-heartedly, and against all evidence, *believed* in him. They believed not only in his noble aspirations and his poetic genius, but in his romantic attitudes, his kindness, his heroism. Pietro died, while continuing to support the cause which Byron had inspired. Teresa went on 'living after' – sometimes disingenuous, frequently absurd – but always fiercely loyal. And in the end, her silliness and vanity fell from her. She said that *all* her papers, 'whatever the effect upon my reputation', were to be published, for the sake of showing 'Lord Byron's good and kind heart'. Is not this, after all, fidelity?

When Teresa was a woman of nearly seventy, in Paris, an old Marquis de Flamarens, who had known her all her life, told Hubert Jerningham that as he saw her that evening, so she had always been.

'In what way?' the Englishman inquired.

'Attachante,' he replied. 'Attachante et attachée.'

BYRON'S LETTERS IN ITALIAN

BYRON'S LETTERS IN ITALIAN

THE following pages contain the complete text of Byron's Italian letters in the Gamba Papers – even of those only quoted in part, or omitted (owing to their lack of interest, or the difficulty of establishing their precise date) in the body of the book. The letters thus omitted are marked thus ***. They are in chronological order – the letters of which it has been possible to determine the year, but not the precise date, being grouped together at the end of the year to which they belong.

Byron was very proud of his fluent knowledge of Italian. 'Now Italian I *can* speak with some fluency, and write sufficiently for my purposes,' he told Rogers in 1818,* and in the following year he wrote to Moore, 'I mean to write my best work in *Italian*', adding, however, that it would take him 'nine years more thoroughly to master the language'.† He was fully conscious of his own inaccuracies, for in 1821 he wrote to Murray about 'some hundreds of Italian notes of mine, scribbled with a noble contempt of the grammar and dictionary, in very English Etruscan; for I *speak* Italian very fluently, but write it carelessly and incorrectly to a degree'.‡

This is true. But it must also be added that Byron's Italian letters, if they have not always got grammar, have style. They show a feeling for the essential harmony of the language; and their mistakes are not of a kind either to obscure the clarity of his thought or to impair the strength of his emotion. His mistakes – most of which it has seemed best to leave unaltered – are of various kinds. Among the more noticeable grammatical ones are his very odd verbs – his occasional use of *mi* and *ti* instead of *me* and *te*§ – and frequent mistakes in gender. He also constantly made use of apostrophes, even where they were not needed – since he apparently believed that in Italian an apostrophe was required not only to mark the actual elision of one vowel before another (*l'anima, all'amore, un'ottima*) but also when any shortened form was used (*un' dolor, cavalier'servente*‖ and even *al'mio*). He even occasionally placed an apostrophe at the beginning of a word, where he thought a letter should be ('*storia* for *istoria*). On the other hand, he was apparently not aware that before words beginning with vowels one should write *dell'* (for *dello, della,* and *all'* for *allo, alla*) and thus he would write *del'anima*.

All these mistakes – none of which are consistent – have been left unaltered. The only ones which have been corrected are such as are plainly due to carelessness, and some elementary mistakes in spelling, accentuation and punctuation.

1. *Spelling:* the use of double consonants in place of single – sometimes arising from his odd formation of the letter *s* – (*cossa* for *cosa, forsse* for *forse* and *sse* for *se*) – and sometimes, but more rarely, vice versa (*abandonato* for *abbandonato*). This is not consistent, and in the later letters it becomes far less frequent. No other mistakes in spelling have been corrected, and some forms which the modern reader may think mistakes, were current spelling at the time (*pigneta* for *pineta,* etc.).

---

* *L.J.,* IV, p. 209. March 3rd, 1818.   † *L.J.,* IV, p. 284. April 6th, 1819.
‡ *L.J.,* V, p. 381. September 8th, 1821.
§ This may have partly been caused by the Venetian popular use of *mi* for *io.* Cf. Margarita Cogni '*Se Ella è dama, mi (io) son' Veneziana.*' *L.J.,* IV, p. 337.
‖ See letter to Murray, April 17th, 1818. *L.J.,* IV, p. 226.

2. *Accentuation.* Omission of accents on the last syllable (*pero* for *però*, *saro* for *sarò*, *cioe* for *cioè*, etc.). This has been rectified.

3. *Punctuation.* The constant use (as in his English letters) of dashes. These have generally been replaced – except when the text seems to call for that kind of pause – by comma, semi-colon, full stop, etc. – and sometimes, when the dashes have merely been used to fill up a line, by the beginning of a new paragraph.

[1]
A Madame
Madame La Comtesse Guiccioli
Ravenna

Venezia

22 Ap.le 1819

Carissimo il mio Bene: La tua carissima arrivata oggi m'ha fatta provare il primo momento di piacere dopo la tua partenza. Il sentimento espresso nella tua lettera è pur troppo corrisposto da parte mia, ma sarà ben difficile per me rispondere nella tua bella lingua alle espressioni dolcissime che meritano una risposta piuttosto di fatti che di parole: mi lusingo però che il tuo Cuor saprà soggerire *cosa* e *quanto* il mio vorrebbe dirti. Forse se ti amassi meno non mi costarebbe tanto a spiegare i pensieri miei, poichè adesso ho di superare la doppia difficoltà di esprimere un 'dolor' insopportabile in una lingua per me straniera. Perdona ai miei spropositi, il più barbaro che sarà lo Stile mio più rassomiglierà al' mio Destin' lontano da te. Tu che sei il mio unico ed ultimo Amor, tu che sei il mio solo diletto, la delizia di mia vita – tu che fosti la mia sola Speranza, tu che fosti – almeno per un momento – tutta mia, tu sei partita – ed io resto isolato nella desolazione. Ecco in poche parole la 'storia nostra! è un caso comune il quale abbiamo di soffrire con tanti altri poichè l'Amor non è mai felice, ma noi altri l'abbiamo di soffrire di più perchè le tue circostanze e le mie sono egualmente fuori dell'ordinario – ma di queste non voglio pensare, amiamo

'. . . amiamo or quando
Esser si puote riamato amando.'*

Quando l'Amor non è *Sovrano* del' Cuore, quando tutto non cede a lui, quando tutto non viene sacrificato per lui, allora è Amicizia – Stima – quel' che vuoi – ma non più *Amor*. Tu mi giurasti la tua costanza – ed io non ti giuro nulla, vedremo chi di noi due sarà più fedele. Ricordati quando arriva il momento che tu non sentirai più per me non avrai da ricevere rimproveri; è vero che soffrirò, ma in silenzio. Conosco pur troppo il cuor dell'uomo, e forse anche un poco quello della donna. Conosco che il Sentimento non dipende da noi – ma che è la cosa più bella e fragile della nostra esistenza; dunque – quando tu senti per un altro quel' che hai sentita per me – dimmi sinceramente – non cercarò annojarti – non ti vedrò più – porterò invidia alla felicità di mio rivale, ma non ti darò più disturbo. Questo ti prometto però – tu mi dici qualche volta che sono stato il tuo *primo* Amor vero, ed io t'assicuro che tu sarai l'ultima mia Passione. Posso ben sperare di non innamorarmi più, adesso tutto è divenuto indifferente per me; prima di conoscerti – molte m'interessarono ma giammai una sola, ora amo a te, e per me non v'ha altra donna in terra.

Tu parli di pianti, e della tua infelicità; il mio dolor è interno, io non verso lacrime. Tu hai attaccata al' tuo braccio un'immagine – che non merita tanto; ma la tua è nel' mio cuor, è divenuta una parte di mia vita, della mia anima, e se vi fosse una vita dopo questa anche colà saresti mia: senza di te dove sarebbe il Paradiso? Piuttosto che il Cielo privo di te preferirei l'Inferno di quel' Grande sepolto in tua Città, basta che tu fosti meco come Francesca col' suo Amante.

Ben' mio dolcissimo – io tremo scrivendoti, siccome tremai nel' vederti – ma non più – con quei soavi palpiti. Ho mille cose a dirti, e non so come

* Tasso, *Gerusalemme Liberata*, Canto XVI, stanza xv.

dirle, mille baci a mandarti – ed' Oimè! quanti Sospiri! Amami – non come *io* ti amo; perchè questo sarebbe renderti troppo infelice. Amami – non come io merito perchè questo sarebbe troppo poco, ma come il tuo Cuor ti dirigerà. Non dubitare di me – sono e sarò sempre il tuo più tenero Amante.

BYRON

P.S.   Quanto più beato di me sarà questo foglio! che tra pochi giorni sarà nelle tue mani – e forse anche potrà essere portato vicino alle tue labbra: con tale lusinga lo bacio prima che 'l parti. Addio – Anima mia.

Ap.le 23, 4 ore.

In questo momento ricevo due altre lettere; l'irregolarità della posta è stata la causa di dispiaceri a tutti due, ma ti prego – Amor mio – di non sospettarmi. Quando non ricevi delle nuove mie, credi che sono morto piuttosto che infedele o ingrato. Risponderò presto alle tue carissime. Adesso la posta parti.
Ti bacio 10000 volte.

On the superscription is added, beneath the address and in Byron's hand: Scritto 22 aple 1819 – Aprile 28, 1820. L'ho riletto a Ravenna dopo un anno di avventure singolarissime.

[2]

Venezia   *addì 25 aprile 1819*

Amor Mio: Spero che avrai ricevuta la mia in data li 22 ed indirizzata alla persona in Ravenna già indicata da te prima di partire da Venezia. Tu mi fai rimproveri per non averti scritta in campagna – ma come? Ben mio dolcissimo tu non m'hai data altro indirizzo che quello di Ravenna. Se tu sapessi quanto e quale è l'Amor che mi anima non mi crederesti capace di dimenticarti per un solo istante; impara a conoscermi meglio – saprai forse un giorno che quantunque non ti merito – pur troppo ti amo.

Vorresti sapere chi sia la persona che vedo con maggior piacere dopo la tua partenza? Chi mi fa tremare e sentire – non quello che tu sola puoi creare nella mia anima – ma qualche cosa che lo rassomiglia? Ebbene – ti dirò – è il *vecchio facchino* mandato dalla Fanni coi tuoi biglietti quando tu fosti in Venezia – e adesso il latore delle tue lettere sempre care, ma non care come quelle che mi lusingarono colla speranza di vederti lo stesso giorno alla solita ora. Teresa mia dove sei? tutto costì mi fa ricordare di te – tutto è lo stesso, ma tu non ci sei ed io ci sono. Nei distacchi chi parte soffre meno di chi resta. La distrazione del' viaggio, il cangiar' del' sito, la Campagna, il Moto, forse anche la lontananza dissipa il pensier' ed alleggerisce il cuore. Ma Chi resta si trova circondato dalle medesime cose, domani è come jeri – mancando solamente quella che faceva dimenticare che domani potrebbe arrivare.

Quando vado alla Conversazione, mi abbandono alla noja, troppo felice ad annojarmi piuttosto che soffrire. Vedo le medesime fisonomie – sento le medesime voci – ma non oso guardare quel' Sofà dove non *ti* vedrei più – ma in vece qualche vecchiarda chi parirebbe essere la Maldicenza in persona. Sento senza la minima emozione aprirsi quella porta che io guardava con tanta ansietà quando mi ci trovai prima di te – sperando vederti entrare. Non ti parlerò *dei siti più cari assai*, perchè *là*, finchè tu torni, non vado; io non ho altro piacere che pensare a te, ma non so come – vedendo i luoghi dove siamo stati insieme – massimamente quelli più consecrati al' amor nostro – mi farebbero morire di dolor.

La Fanni è adesso a Treviso – e Dio sa quando avrò ancora delle tue lettere – ma intanto ho ricevuto tre; tu sarai arrivata a Ravenna – bramo di sentire di quel tuo arrivo; il mio destin' dipende dalla tua decisione. La Fanni tornerà in qualchi giorni – ma domani la mando un biglietto per man' di un mio amico, di pregarla di non dimenticare a mandarmi delle tue nuove, in caso che riceve delle lettere prima di tornare a Venezia.

Ben Mio – la mia Vita è divenuta la più monotona e trista – nè libri – nè la musica – nè *cavalli* – (cosa rara a Venezia – ma tu sai che gli miei sono sul' lido) – nè cani mi danno piacer; la Società di donne non più mi alletta; non parlo della Società dei uomini; perchè gli ho sempre sprezzato.

Sono alcuni anni ch'io cercava per Sistema di evitare le passioni forti avendo sofferto troppo della tirannia d'Amor. Il *non* ammirare – ed' il divertirmi senza metter troppa importanza nel divertimento stesso – l'Indifferenza per l'affari humani – il disprezzo per molti, ma l'odio per nessuno, era la base della mia filosofia. Non volevo più amar – nè sperava di esser' più riamato. Tu hai messa in fuga tutte le mie risoluzioni, adesso son tutto a te, e divenirò quel' che tu vuoi – forse felice nel' amor tuo – ma mai più tranquillo. Tu hai fatto male nel' risvegliare il mio cuore – poichè – (almeno in mio paese) l'amor mio è stato fatale a coloro che amai – ed a me stesso. Ma questi riflessi vengano troppo tardi, tu sei stata mia – e qualunque sia l'esito – io sono e sarò eternamente tutto tuo.

Ti bacio mille e mille volte – ma –

> 'Che giova a te, cor mio, l'esser amato?
> Che giova a me l'aver si cara amante?
> Perchè, crudo destino –
> Ne disunisci tu, s'Amor ne stringe?'*

Amami – come sempre il tuo più tenero e fedele.   B

[3]
All'Ornatissima Signora Silvestrini
San Vidal N° 2449
Calle Vetturi

Venezia   *3° M° 1819*
or ora di casa.

La lettera di Teresa non mi dice niente della ricevuta delle *mie due lettere* – ed io sono nel' maggior turbamento. Che sarà di queste lettere? Ti prego di scriverla ed assicurarla che io non ò mancato alla mia promessa – nè ai miei doveri – e che l'amo assai – assai più della mia vita. Forse le vostre saranno più fortunate – intanto ecco la mia *terza* – che potete mandare al' indirizzo solito. Fatemi la somma grazia di venire da me *alle quattro ore* per un' momento. Non so cosa dire, o pensare – la lettera di T. è del' dato *26*.

Perdonatemi questo e tanti altri disturbi. Sempre vostro.

[4]
Alla Contessa Guiccioli
Ravenna

Venezia   *3 Maggio 1819*
Anima Mia: Questa volta l'amicizia ti preme più del' amor, e la Fanni è stata più fortunata di me nel' veder' i tuoi caratteri. La tua carissima da Ravenna mi dava però sommo dispiacere nel' dirmi che fosti ammalata, colla

* G.B. GUARINI, *Il Pastor Fido* – tragicommedia pastorale, Act III°, scene IV.

lusinga nonostante che non porterà ad altre conseguenze; e con questa speranza scrivo di pregarti delle informazioni più precise sul' stato della tua Salute. Avrei attribuito la tua malattia al' andar' a cavallo – ma tu mi scrivi come se fosse qualche *altra causa*, e non mi dici la vera cagione; ti prego mettermi a giorno del' *mistero* che non hai voluto dir' ai medici.

La Fanni è già ritornata da Treviso. Io attendo il tuo riscontro per sapere quando entraprendere il viaggio – e come condurmi al' mio arrivo. Ricordati che non avrò altro oggetto nel' fare questo viaggio che quello di vederti – e di amarti. Io non cerco nè voglio divertimenti – presentazioni – Società cose per me piene di noja. Mi anderebbe più a genio essere con te in un deserto che di esser senza di te nel' paradiso di Maometto, il quale vale qualche cosa più del' nostro.

Te – Te sola cercharò, se potrò vederti per alcuni momenti ogni giorno, saprò passare le altre ore colla tua immagine; se vi potrebbe esser' un' istante, in cui io non pensassi a te, mi parirebbe una infedeltà. L'Amor nostro – ed i miei pensieri – saranno i miei soli compagni, i libri e i cavalli la mia unica distrazione, fuorchè il viaggetto a *Rimini*, per non mancare alla promessa fatta ad un mio amico in Inghilterra – tre anni sono – in caso mai che io vedessi quella città gli mandarai qualunque tradizione più di quella che si trova in Dante (se tale esistesse) sulla storia di Francesca. Quella storia di amor funesto, che sempre m'interessava, adesso m'interessa doppiamente, dopo che Ravenna rinchiude il mio cuore.

Sospiro di abbracciarti e lascio il resto al' destino, che non sarà crudele finchè mi conserva l'amor tuo. Ti bacio con tutta l'anima – mille e mille volte – e sono eternamente il tuo amante.

P.S. Questa è la mia *terza* lettera – al' *indirizzo indicato* – spero in Dio che nessuna avrà mancata.

[5]

Venice

My. 14th. 1819*

(recto)

Io ti aveva scritto una	I had written you a . . . .
. . . ho mandato per	. . . send by . . . . . .
. . . perchè la tu	. . . . because your . . . . .
. . . . . . giorno era	. . . . day was . . . . . .

(verso)

. . . . incontro colà sarebbe	. . . . . meeting there would be, . . .
. . . . non soltanto per	. . . . . not only for . . . . .
. . . anche per la	. . . . . also for . . . . . .
. . . . amente saresti la . . .	. . . . tainly you would there be
. . . icerie, che	. . . . . ossip, than

* This letter consists of two fragments, scorched and evidently snatched from the fire into which Teresa had thrown the whole letter. The fragments are wrapped, together with a piece of two other half-destroyed letters, in a folder on which Teresa has written: 'Unkind letters – to be destroyed'.

The curious thing about this is that six days later, on May 20th, Byron wrote to Teresa a letter, the one given in chapter 1, p. 57, which contains *all* the sentences still legibly in the fragments of the above letter.

(recto)

. . tu dici tante belle cose! ! . .	. . . you say so many nice things! . . .
. . . anima mia . se ella	. . . my Soul – if she . . . . . .
. . . dici – bisognerebbe che io	. . . say . it would be necessary for me
facessi	to . . .
. . . lei – si o no; se lo fo	. . . her – yes or no? if I do . . . .
. . . . avrà certi dir	. . . will have a certain ri . . . .
. . . . pia . e se no	. . . py . and if not . . . . .

(verso)

. . . . . . di lei senza spiegarmene	. . . about her without explaining to me
il m	the rea .
. . . . Amor mio . ti bacio co	. . . . my Love . I kiss you wi . . . .
. . . ensa di me come eterna	. . . . ink of me as, eternal . . . .
. . . . . tenero e fedele.	. . . . tender and faithful.

B.

B.

[6]

Venezia   *20 Mag° 1819.*

Amor Mio: Io ti aveva scritto una lettera per l'ordinario passato che non ho
mandato perchè la tua arrivatami nello stesso giorno era in fatto una risposta
alle ricerche fatte da me – sul' viaggio concertato. Spero che la Fanni ti
avrà scritta come la pregai di fare. La tua malattia mi inquieta moltissimo, e
mi pare che tu non ti sii ben decisa se il mio arrivo in questo momento sarebbe
convenevole; intanto attendo ancora delle tue nuove per sapere s'io deggio
ora partire o no. Mi ricordo che tu dicesti, che nel mese di Giugno faresti un
viaggio a Bologna, e pensando forse di tutte le tue circostanze il nostro incontro
colà sarebbe più conveniente non soltanto per i riguardi – ma anche per la
nostra felicità. Sicuramente saresti là meno esposta alle dicerie che nel' tuo
paese.

Ti scrivo in gran fretta e con molta inquietudine – ma ti prego di credere che
sono sempre lo stesso verso di te; ti amo – non trovo parole per esprimere a
qual' grado – ma il tempo proverà e tu stessa troverai, che tu sei divenuta
l'unico oggetto per cui respiro, e pel quale spirerei.

Le tue istruzioni, mio Bene, sono un poco intortigliate; nostro primo incontro
non dovrebbe aver luogo '*in teatro*'; e 'la Padrona' del' Albergo della quale tu
dici tante belle cose! ! Senti Anima Mia – se Ella è come dici – bisognerebbe
ch'io fecessi all'amore* con lei – *si o no;* se lo fo, Ella avrà certi diritti di fare la
Spia – e se *no*, la farà per dispetto, poichè una donna di tal Sorte non perdona
mai al disprezzo.

Io non intendo nulla delle tue allusioni alla Signora Z. la quale non ho
avuto l'onor di conoscere senonchè di vista nel Carnevale – dunque come mai
può quella donna entrare nelle nostre interese? io non la conosco – Ella non
mi conosce – come può o potrebbe essere nel poter di colei di affliggerti?
Eppure tu mi dici che tu sei afflitta per cagione di lei senza spiegarmine il
motivo.

Amor mio ti bacio con tutta l'anima – pensa di me come eternamente il
tuo più tenero e fedele.

---

* Teresa has substituted *la corte* for *all'amore* but Byron's words are plainly legible.

[7]

(Postcript to a letter from Fanny Silvestrini to Contessa Guiccioli.)
Venezia   *Addi 24 maggio 1819*
Io sarei già partito Mercoledi se avessi avuto tue lettere. Essendone privo
sono di pessimo umore e non altro desidero che di averne per potermi deter-
minar alla partenza – Io ti prego di scrivermi, ma in ogni modo partirò
Sabbato – ti bacio mille volte di Cuore e sono eternamente il tuo più tenero e
fedele Amante.

[8]

[Venezia]   *[28 Maggio 1819]*
(Interpolated in a letter from Fanny Silvestrini to Contessa Guiccioli.)
Amor mio: Sento con massimo dispiacere il tuo male e tanto più quanto
credeva coll'ordinario d'oggi, di sentire il tuo perfetto ristabilimento. Ad ogni
modo malgrado quello che tu mi scrivi io partirò da di qui Sabbato 29 cor.
Andrò a Bologna e colà aspetterò la lettera che tu mi dici di scrivermi, e che
la Fanny non mancherà di subito inoltrarmi. Eguale al' tuo è il mio desiderio
di vederti, di abbracciarti – e di dirti mille volte ch'io ti amo. Ti bacio con
tutta l'anima e sono sempre tutto tuo.

[9]

                Ost.ble Son premier billet en arrivant à Ravenna
Giugno 10. 1819
Ben mio: Eccomi giunto a Ravenna. Se puoi combinare a vedermi sarò
felice – se no, in ogni modo – non ho mancato alla mia parola – e spero
almeno sentire che tu stai meglio di salute. Sempre.

[10]

                2ᵈ billet id. Ost.ᵇˡᵉ
A Madame
Madame La Comtesse Guiccioli
P.O.   *Giugno 10. 1819*
Amor mio: Sono stato al teatro senza trovarti, e sentiva colla più viva dispiacen-
za che tu sei ancora in un stato di debolezza. Il tuo marito è venuto a trovarmi
in palco e ha risposto cortesemente alle poche ricerche che osava fare in quel'
momento. – Il Conte Z. è poi capitato e mi sollecitava tanto di andare in
palco suo – che non avrei potuto evitare quella visita senza scortesia – ed in
fatto sono stato là per un momento.
    Anima mia dolcissima – credi che vivo per te sola – e non dubitare di me.
Mi tratterrò qui finchè so più precisamente il tuo desiderio; e anche se tu
non puoi combinare a vedermi, non mi allontanarò. Ti imploro disporre di
me come tutto ed eternamente tuo. Sagrificarei tutta la mia speranza in
questo mondo – e tutto che si crede trovare nel' altro – vederti felice.
    Non posso pensare del' stato di tua Salute senza cordoglio e lagrime. Ahi
mio Bene ! Quanto abbiamo passati – e quanto abbiamo a passare! e tu così
giovane – così bella – così buona – tu hai avuta di soffrire per causa mia
– qual' pensier!
    Ti bacio mille – mille – mille volte con tutta l'anima.
P.S.   Ti mandai questa sera un' viglietto per mezzo di P. ma il latore non lo
trovava prima di mezza notte.
    Ti scrivo adesso dopo il teatro prima di andar in letto – spero che tu
riceverai ambedue.

[11]

3me Billet Ost^{ble}

Giugno 11. 1819

Amor mio: Ti prego di istruirmi come debbo condurmi in queste circostanze. Io non sono a giorno di ciò che si convenerebbe fare. Penso di fermarmi quì finchè tù parti – ed allora trovare la maniera di riunirsi a Bologna, e poi a Ferrara. Ma tutti questi progetti dipendono della tua volontà. Io non vivo più senonchè per te. La mia pace è perduta in ogni modo, ma preferirei la morte a questa incertezza. Ti prego perdonarmi e compatirmi. Ricordati che sono quì perchè tu mi comandasti – e che ogni momento in cui non . . . ma è inutile che scrivo – io sento un' dolor' inesprimibile, ti vedo – ma in qual' maniera? e in qual' stato?

Cercai a distrarmi con quella farsa del' antichità – per mi una noja la più insopportabile – ma in questo momento tutto il resto è egualmente disgustoso. Il poco che mi interesserebbe, il sepolcro di Dante – e alcune cose nella biblioteca – ho già guardato con un' indifferenza perdonabile al' stato di mio cuore.

Tu vedi che non vado in società – e che cerco solamente i mezzi di avvicinarti – ma come mai? – tu sei così circondata: io son' forestiere in Italia – e ancora più forestiere in Ravenna – e naturalmente poco praticato nel' uso del paese – temo di comprometterti, per mi stesso non c'è più a temere: il mio destino è già deciso. E impossibile per mi vivere per lungo tempo in questa agitazione – ti scrivo colle lagrime – ed io non son' uomo a piangere facilmente – quando piango le mie lagrime, vengono dal' cuor' e sono di sangue.

In questo punto – (mezzanotte) ricevo le tue lettere – e il fazzoletto – e son' un poco calmato. Studierò a fare tutto ciò che tu comandi.

Continuo questo viglietto senza cambiare una parola – per mostrarti cosa era lo stato di quel' inferno che portai in petto dopo il mio arrivo. Se tu sapessi quanto mi costò a reggermi in tua presenza – ma non dirò di più; speriamo che il tempo m'insegnerà l'ipocrisia. Tu parli di 'Sacrifizii miei ecc.' – non dire di più – il mio cuor è già sacrificato – e dopo quella vittima non può essere più sacrifizio. Basta un' tuo cenno a condurmi o mandarmi – non solamente a Bologna ma alla tomba.

Non dubitare di me – io non dubito di te – ma delle difficoltà di nostre circostanze – vorrei sperare – ma – ma – sempre un *Ma*. Intanto *tu* speri – e ciò basta.

Ti ringrazio – ti abbraccio – ti bacio mille – mille volte.

P.S.   Perchè vuoi rimandarmi il *mio* fazzoletto? – vedo dal' ciffro che è quello che ti detti la sera prima di tua partenza – io non ti darei *un' filo* di tuo (che tengo sempre presso a me) per ottenere un' impero. . . .

[12]

Ost^{ble}!
4me billet id

Giugno 14. 1819

Sbaglio forse – mio Bene – ma questa villeggiatura improvvisa del' tuo Zio con P. mi da dei sospetti che siamo traditi – e che P. sia portato in campagna per troncare la corrispondenza. La Passione mi fa temer' tutto e tutti. Se ti perdo cosa sarà di me? Era questo viaggio premeditato prima del' mìo venire – o no? Se *no*, sentirò dei grandi dubbi.

In ogni caso come faremo adesso per ricevere le nostre lettere? come potrò consegnarti anche questa senza rischio di una scoperta trista per te – e per

EE

me fatale. Nel perdermi tu perdi poco – ma io difficilmente sopravviverei a un' distacco da te. Finora la frutta di mio viaggio è piuttosto amara – ma se tu sei contenta – non mi chiamerò pentito di ciò che soffro – poichè soffro per causa tua.

L'Amor ha i suoi martiri come la Religione – con questa differenza – che le vittime del' Amor perdono il Paradiso in questo mondo, senza ricuperarlo nel' altro, mentre i devoti del' altro culto guadagnano dal' cambiamento.

Intanto – Amor mio – insegnami cosa debbo fare? stare qui? o tornare a B.? Se nascono dei contrasti – c'è una sola rimedia efficace – cioè di andar' via insieme – e per questo bisogna del' gran Amor – e qualche coraggio – l'hai abbastanza?

Posso già anticipare la tua risposta: sarà lunga e scritta divinamente – ma terminerà col' negativo.

Ti bacio di Cuor 10000000 volte.

[13]

5me billet id

Giugno 15. 1819

Tu hai ragione – ma quando si *ragiona* assai non c'è un' Amor capace dei grandi 'sacrifizi. La risposta è quella che aspettai – non mi sorprende e ciò basta. Ricordati che la proposizione non era fatta per *questo momento* – io soltanto domandai *in caso dell'alternativa cosa faresti?* Tu hai risposto bene – e adesso so che partito debbo prendere.

I pensieri sono giustissimi – solamente sono venuti un poco troppo tardi – poichè il più gran' torto a . . . era già fatto in Venezia. Il andare via sarebbe una somma imprudenza – ed una cosa che si farebbe soltanto in caso d'una scoperta – e nell'alternativa di esser' obbligata ad abbandonare *uno* dei due. Ma perdonami se ti dico che (adesso che parliamo della moralità) il più gran *torto* è l'inganno – e non l'abbandonamento – di un' uomo già nelle circostanze della maggior parte dei mariti.

Per altro lo stimo moltissimo – e farei amicizia con lui ben volentieri – ad ogni costo.

Tornando all'*alternativa* – posso dirti che *io anche* perderei molto – ma preferendoti ad ogni interesse – amandoti – ma non parlerò più d'amor – adesso tu non puoi dubitare del' *mio*, vedendo a qual' grado io son' stato capace a sacrificare tutto per te.

Intanto tu non hai risposta alla mia demanda – cioè se sarà più convenevole alle tue brame il fermarmi qui, o il partire per B.

Ti bacio e sono sempre.

[14]

Ost^{ble}
6me billet id

Giugno 15, 1819

Anima mia: Io parlo d'*Amor* e tu mi rispondi del '*Tasso*' – scrivo di *te* e tu mi domandi di '*Eleanora*'. Se vuoi farmi divenire più pazzo di lui – ti assicuro che sei nel' caso di riuscire. In fatto mia Cara la tua ricerca mi pare superflua, tu conosci almeno in parte la mia storia – e puoi anche senza questa immaginarti che per dipingere le passioni forti bisogna averle provate. Uno di questi giorni – (se *mai mai* più occorrono ciò che dubito pur troppo) quando ci troviamo soli – ti dirò a voce se tua conghiettura sopra l'originale del' *ritratto* è fondata o no sulla verità.

Se tu sai cosa è Amore – se tu ami – se tu senti – come puoi in questi momenti – vedendo lo stato in cui ci troviamo, pensare o parlare di cose ideali? non abbiamo pur' troppo la *realtà*? Ti giuro che questi ultimi giorni sono stati dei più infelici della mia vita – l'amor – il dubbio – l'incertezza – il timore di comprometterti quando ti vedo in presenza dei altri – l'impossibilità di vederti sola – l'idea di perderti per sempre – combinano a distruggere la poca speranza che finora mi animò.

La Società m'inquieta – la Solitudine mi spaventa. La mia unica consolazione è il vederti rimessa in salute.

Attendo colla maggior '*impazienza*' tua risposta alle mie due lettere, cosa debbo fare?

Mi pare che il tuo Padre ti guarda con qualche sospetto – e che naturalmente non è troppo ben' disposto vedermi così vicino – e questo viaggio del' Zio – con *P.* – e l'improvvisa partenza del' *amica* non sono dei presagi più felici per noi – – –

Intanto il mio venire a R., come previdi – invece di accrescere la nostra corrispondenza – l'ha diminuito. Oh Venezia! – Venezia! *là* siamo stati uniti almeno per alcune ore.

P.S. Perdona se t'ho risposto troppo *Inglesamente* nelle prime parole di questo viglietto – ma io non son' venuto in Italia per parlare di me stesso e dei fatti miei – ma piuttosto a dimenticare la mia vita *oltramontana* – e sopra tutto, per amarti – *te*, – la mia unica ed ultima delizia. –

Ecco la ragione per quale m'impazientai nel' risponder' alla tua domanda se l'*E.* fosse la ecc. ecc.

[15]

Ost^ble
7me billet id

Giugno 16. 1819

Amor mio: Non ci parliamo più adesso sopra quel' argomento. Basti che tu non puoi dubitare di me, vedendo di quanto sarei capace per causa tua. In ogni modo e in tutte le circostanze la tua felicità sarà il mio unico pensier. Se arriva il tempo dei contrasti e dei affanni per causa del' amor nostro allora tu deciderai secondo il' sentimento tuo. Io non cercarò a persuaderti, o ad influire la tua scelta. *I miei 'doveri'*, Carissima Teresa – sono sempre i stessi – e mi pare che io dimostro tutta la premura possibile per adempirli.

Tutto dipende da te – la mia vita – il mio onor – il mio amor. Amami dunque – il mio sentimento per te merita di esser corrisposto. Io soffro tanto nel' amare – che cercai ad evitare le passioni forti – per i ultimi tre anni – ma invano come *ora* tu vedi. Il amarti è per me il *passaggio* del *Rubicone* e già ha deciso il mio destino.

Non mancarò ad osservare tutto ciò che tu dici . . .

Ti bacio 100000 volte.

[16]

Ost^ble
8me billet id

Giugno 17. 1819

Sì – Amor mio – sono '*ben indifferente*'. Ho fatto il viaggio da Venezia – sono stato così felice dopo il mio arrivo – i miei divertimenti sono frequentissimi – me ne trovo così allegro . . . sì – tu hai ragione in questo come in tutto – non v'è dubbio della *mia indifferenza*.

Pensa un poco – Ben mio – e poi sfidarò qualunque che sia a trovare nella mia condotta dopo che ti ho conosciuto, la minima cosa che merita un' tale rimprovero. Ti amai pur' troppo – ma in *Amor* il *troppo* non *basta*. Ciò mi sento anche io – poichè credo che tu non mi ami al' grado che sospiro; e intanto sono sicurissimo che il mio cuore è più impegnato del' tuo – ma ciò dovrebbe essere – perchè tu *meriti* un'amor il quale io non potrei nè sperare nè inspirare. Tal' amor io ti porto – vuoi delle prove?

Tu mi dici – ch'io '*e non il cavalcare*' vi hanno cagionato tanto 'male'.* Questo vuol' dire che la causa del' male è stata qualche colpa mia. Questa è la prima volta che tu mi lo dici – ed essendo un' accusa piuttosto seria – e fatta seriamente – bramerei avere qualche spiegazione. Se tu sapessi, ma è inutile – ciò che scrivo – ciò che dico.

Amor mio – noi avremmo abbastanza del' infelicità senza perderci nei sospetti mal' fondati – e nei tormenti cagionati dal' amor proprio offeso forse senza ragione. Un' schiavo non è più umile in presenza del' suo Padrone che io sono nella tua, ma non abusare del' potere, perchè tu sei troppo potente. Pensa soltanto se veramente merito i rimproveri di tuo ultimo biglietto – e poi perdona . . . *te stessa* – se tu puoi.

Credimi eternamente il tuo più immutabile ed amante.   B

[17]

Ost^{ble}
10me billet id

Giugno. 20; 1819

'*E voi potreste*' . . . cosa è che non '*potreste*,' Amor mio, se 'l vuoi?

Non può essere cosa più lusinghiera per me della speranza di fare 'il viaggio insieme.'

Il tuo biglietto termina – o piuttosto *non* termina, – quando mi dirai il resto?

Come ti dissi tante volte – il mio destino è nelle mani tue; dove tu sei, sarà la mia patria – e ciò che tu dici è la mia legge. Intanto sospiro l'ora di rivederti – e ti bacio con tutta l'anima instancabilmente.

[18]

11me billet id†

. . . .
Vado in letto e sarebbe meglio per me che il sonno mio (se pure sarà possibile che dormo) divenisse eterno.   ‒
. . . .
la maniera di farlo scordare a venire da voi. Forse questo è solamente un prologo – e finirete . . .
. . . .
ma vi amai – e dopo esser stato un uomo riconosciuto per l'indipendenza e la forza dello suo animo.
. . . .
Disgraziatamente per me ha perdute le sue ale. Forse le ritroverà – almeno lo spero. Addio.

* Byron seems to have written *abortire* (miscarry) but the word *male* (illness) has been written over it.
† This letter consists of two fragments.

[19]
12me billet id

'I miei pensieri in me dormir' non ponno'. Ebbi dunque ragione – cosa fa quel' uomo ogni Sera e tante ore al' vostro fianco in palco? *'Dunque siamo intesi'* – belle parole! – *'Siete intesi'* a ciò che mi pare. Ho veduto che ogni momento in quale io voltai la testa verso il palco scenico voi voltaste gli occhi a guardare quella persona – e ciò dopo tutto che è passato oggi! . . . Ma non temete, dimane sera lo lascierò il campo libero.

Io non ho forza a sostenere ogni giorno un' tormento nuovo – m'avete fatto divenire spregevole nei miei proprii occhi – e fra poco forse anche in quelli dei altri. Non avete veduto i martiri miei? non l'avete compatita? vi perdono ciò che mi fate soffrire – ma non posso mai perdonare a me stesso la debolezza di cuore la quale m'impedisce finora a prendere il solo partito onorevole in tali circostanze – ciò – di dirvi Addio – in eterno.

Mezza notte . . .
Ora di riposo per me prima di conoscervi.

Lasciami partire – è meglio morire del' dolore della lontananza – piuttosto che del' tradimento. La mia vita adesso è un'agonia sempiterna – ho goduto della felicità unica ed ultima nelle tue braccia – ma – Oh Dio! – quanto mi costano quei momenti! – e *questi, questo*! ora che ti scrivo – solo – solissimo. Io non ebbi che te nel' mondo – e adesso non avendoti più (senza il cuore cosa è il resto?) la solitudine è divenuta noiosa come la società – poichè quel' immagine che io figurava così pura, così cara – non è più che un' ombra perfida e minacciante, – e pure – sempre la *tua*.

[20]
13me billet id

Amor mio: Perchè non dopo pranzo? Cosa m'importa della 'passeggiata' e delle 'prescrizioni'? tu sai bene *cosa* mi 'piace' – . . . ogni giorno in quale non ci *amiamo* in atto come in cuore è (per me almeno) la perdita più irreparabile, una felicità di meno. Dimmi il *quando* – sempre e tutto *tua*.

[21]
15me billet id

Ravenna   *Ag.° 4° 1819*

Mio Bene: Ricordati del' ritratto tuo, e del' cuor mio. – Addio. Qual' momento! Addio! –   BYRON

[22]
16me billet id

Ravenna   *4° Ag.° 1819*

Mio Bene: Tu mi rimproveri ingiustamente. Alessandro e il tuo papà essendo presenti – non potendo io più allora stringerti al' mio cuore – ti baciava la mano e m'affrettava andare via per non dimostrare un dolore il quale pur troppo avrebbe manifestato tutta, tutta la verità!

Io ti giuro che ti amo mille volte più, che quando ti conobbi a V. Tu lo sai, Tu lo sai, tu lo senti. *Pensa*, Amor mio – di *quei* momenti – deliziosi – pericolosi – ma *felici* in tutti i sensi – non solamente per il piacere più di estatico – che mi diedero, ma pel pericolo (a cui tu eri esposta) fortunatamente evitato. Quella sala! quelle camere! le porte aperte! la servitù così curiosa e vicina – Ferdinando! le visite! Quanti ostacoli! ma tutti vinti – è stato il vero trionfo del' Amor – cento volte Vincitore! Addio – mio solo Bene – mia unica Speranza. Addio – ti bacio instancabilmente di cuore, e sono sempre il tuo.

P.S. Mandami il biglietto *della tomba di Dante* col tuo nome sopra. L'ho veduto sopra la tua tavolina jeri l'altro. Amami come ti amo. Per l'indirizzo tutto va bene come istabilito – in caso che io non arrivo a B. sul giorno proposto.

Cosa vuol dire l' *a. a. a.* in quel' tuo carissimo libretto? Non dimenticare mandare da *Imsom* avvisarli consegnare le mie lettere solamente nelle mani della persona che viene da te. In questo punto ricevo il tuo. Ti giuro di non baciare altro che *quella* memoria di te finchè ti rivedo. Addio! –

[23]
17me billet id

Ravenna   *Addi. 7. Agosto. 1819*

Mio Bene: Ho scritto una risposta in Inglese ad *A.* Mi rincresce infinitamente il non rivederti a Forlì, ma ben presto (Lunedì o Martedì) spero esser' giunto a Bologna. Ti scrivo con qualche timore del' esito di questo biglietto – poichè bisogna che lo fido al mio Corriere. Spero pure che la Fortuna non ci abandonerà due amanti in tal' punto.

Dunque tu hai perduto *l'anello* – senza dirmi una sola parola! Questo è una diffidenza che mi sorprende e mi duole, *io* non ho mai avuto dei misteri con *te.* Non posso dirti più adesso.

Ti amo + + + + + + +m'intendi? Per noi – si debbono essere poche croci più sante che queste.

Tu non puoi immaginarti quanto la tua lontananza m'affligge; sospiro il rivederti, ma tremo credendomi sempre sul' punto di perderti – e ne dubito – poichè quella tua testa è un' enigma, e *cuore tu non hai.* Mi pare vederti nel' atto di leggere queste ultime parole – 'Oh *Rabbia*'! come dice il tiranno di nostra comica compagnia – Oimè! *non più comica* dopo la tua partenza. Il teatro è divenuto un' deserto – non oso guardare il tuo palco. Non pensare dunque che dico seriamente che tu non hai del' cuore. Tu l'hai (per gli abiti?) – *Questo* fu solamente una gentilezza Inglese! un' scherzo tramontano! *è la mia vendetta* – non – per *la perdita* – del' *anello* ma per avermi trattato con poca confidenza tacendo sul' fatto.

Addio, carissimo il mio *Male* – Addio, mio tormento – Addio, mio *tutto* – (ma *non tutto* mio!). Ti bacio più volte che t'ho mai baciato – e questo (se la Memoria non m'inganna) dovrebbe essere un' bel' numero, contato dal' principio. Intanto tu puoi star' sicura di me – del' amor mio – e del' poter' tuo. 'Imploro pace' . . .

Amami – non come ti amo – ciò sarebbe troppo pel' tuo Cuor' gentile – ma come tu ami il tuo *Elmò.* Addio.

Ti bacio 1000000 volte di cuore, insaziabilmente.

[24]*₊*
A Madame
Madame La Comtesse *Guiccioli*

[*Bologna*]   [*Settembre*]

Ti prego non lasciarlo fuori delle mani tue. Come tu non saprai aprirlo – ho messo il *padre* e il *figlio dentro* la scatola – la mamma è dove era prima.

Ti lo mando perchè tu lo commandi – ma mal volentieri; io non mi fido niente – a cui non conosco – ed assai poco a loro già conosciuti. Ecco la frutta dell'esperienza. Addio.*

[25]
     Postscript to a letter from Fanny Silvestrini to Contessa Guiccioli.

[*Venezia*]   [*6 Dicembre 1819*]

Amor mio: In questo momento – è impossibile per me scriverti in dettaglio – ma col tempo tu riconoscerai che sono e sarò sempre tuo.

* The above letter is undated, and is headed by Teresa 'Eighteenth note – from Bologna'. She says in the 'Vie' (pp. 1436-9) that it was a magnificent snuff-box, bearing on its lid the portrait of the Empress Marie Louise, and having inside it a hidden spring which, when released, revealed two other miniatures: one of Napoleon (then at St. Helena) and one of the little King of Rome.

[26]
Nobil' Donna
La Contessa Guiccioli
S.R.M.

*Gen.*ᵃⁱᵒ *3. 1820*

Amica: Farai ciò che ti pare meglio. Io non ho dettato ciò che debbi fare; ho risposto quando tu mi rimproverasti di aver fatto visita alla Vicari – 'che era meno disonorante per me visitare la tua amica più riconosciuta – che per te avere in casa una persona come la Teresa, mantenuta da tanti anni – allora per *un' oggetto* – e adesso – secondo a tutte le apparenze – per un' *altro'*.

Se non avevi cominciato rimproverarmi per una cosa la più innocente, ti avrei lasciato senza dire una parola sopra quel' articolo – con tutto ciò – che ora credo come che ho sempre creduto – dagl'indicii esterni – da ciò che ho opinato – e da ciò che ho sentito – che quella donna – e il suo antico drudo – hanno imbrogliato per loro servizio.

Le familiarità di quel' uomo possono esser' innocenti – ma *decenti* non sono – anche questa sera – quando tu credevi che io leggeva – quel' mano-scritto che A. mi metteva nelle mani – io osservava (presso al' fuoco) certe cose che non mi convengono, e che tu saprai ben intendere – senza che ti dico di più.

Avresti fatto assai meglio nel' lasciarmi partire prima di venire qui; dopo la mia venuta – ho provato dei piaceri che tu sola puoi darmi – ma dell'altra parte – ho sofferto moltissimo nel' vederti al' mio parere o disonorata o debole. V'è del mistero, delle cose che io non posso intendere: un' morale senza principii – un'amor senza fede – e un'amicizia senza stima o confidenza – sono pur troppo manifestati ultimamente in un' grado che è stato impossibile per me cavare una parola di verità, della parte di una persona per quale io ho abbandonato tutto. Se voi potete reconciliare i vostri principii come una donna ben nata colla vostra difesa della sopradetta persona ora in vostro servizio; se potete reconciliare il amor vostro per me colle libertà che avete permesso a un' altro in mia presenza; – la vostra amicizia più sincera – (*o piu finta*) per la Vicari colla maniera in cui avete parlato di lei questa sera – vi riconoscerò per una dama di grandissimo talento – ma non più per mia amica.

Il vostro A. questa sera mi accusò di indecisione. *Egli mi accusò* – va bene *Egli*, dopo tutte le scene di Venezia – tutti i suoi progetti di viaggi a Vienna, a Firenze, di cangiar' paese – di mandar i suoi figli in Collegio, poi in Inghil-terra – di rompere la vostra relazione ecc. ecc., veramente questo è bello! Cosa voleva Costui? che io – straniero – lontano dalla patria, e degli costumi, morale – e maniera di pensare, e di agire di miei connazionali – che io *decidessi* pei *indecisi* di un' altro paese. Dopo averti conosciuto, ho vissuto *per te* – e *con te* – questa è forse indecisione; se vedo la mia patria in pericolo di perdersi – gli miei amici, alcuni in arresto, e gli altri sul' punto di esser' precipitati in una guerra civile – la mia famiglia senza il mio appoggio – molti dei miei beni non troppo ben' assicurati – nelle circostanze attuali del' governo vacillante – se in un' tal' momento pare a voi, o ai altri, che sono turbato – merita questo il nome di indecisione? Poichè debbo pensare che ho lasciato tutto in un' tal' stato – per una donna che non solamente non mi ama – ma non* . . . .

* A whole line h as been cut out – and other words have been torn away.

amato. – Io non posso negarvi il talento e la bellezza; scrivete dei biglietti eloquenti . . . nelle vostre qualità fisiche – siete . . . che non si può desiderare del' meglio – – – – –

[27]

G.° 4° 1820

In risposta alla vostra di questa mattina non posso dire altro – senonchè – non ci intendiamo bene. Se voi non m'avete rimproverato per esser stato per un' momento far'una visita la più insignificante – ad una vostra amica, carissima sei mesi fa, e come io credeva, cara anche *adesso* – non mi sarebbe mai venuto il pensiero di dirvi ciò che mi pareva poco per onor vostro – in una casa ben ordinata. Per il resto io non posso esser' il latore delle vostre comunicazioni per il Sr. C. R. nè per bene nè per male – e non voglio in nessuna maniera entrare nei affari di quei due personaggi. Per il ricevere delle persone in casa – perchè *non tutto il mondo?* – allora sarebbe niente.

Intanto – mi importarebbe poco chi veniva o andava – se voi eravate di quella sincerità che disgraziatamente non può esistere nelle vostre circostanze – secondo lo stato attuale del' morale Italiano. Solamente vorrei dire che quando fate un'accoglienza così graziosa e gentile alla vostra amica – è ben difficile per me indovinare che in quel' momento l'odiate più. Io non ho più dire sopra questo argomento non troppo aggradevole. Mi dispiace moltissimo sentire che non state troppo bene questa sera, e spero che domani vi troverete meglio.

Sono stato con Lega al' quartiere Bacinetti – che non trovo conveniente per il locale – il sito mi piace – ma in quel' apartamento sarebbe impossibile – per mi abitare colla mia famiglia – senza quasi rifabbricando la casa.

Vi prego di credermi ciò che son sempre stato per voi – e non attribuirmi dei motivi indegni – come sarebbe 'il *provarvi* io dico ciò che sento. Non sono venuto qui – per oggetti così triviali. Io non metto gran' fede nel' bel' stile – nè nel' eloquenza del' biglietto – che nessuno possiede più di voi – ma nelle azioni oneste – nella sincerità – colle amiche come coi amici – e in una condotta non equivoca nè anche nelle apparenze.

Sono ecc. ecc.

[28]

A Madame
Madame La Comtesse Guiccioli

Chez Elle

6 ore

Ti scrissi la lettera acchiusa – prima di ricevere la tua – Lega non essendo tornato dal porto, che in questo momento. Ciò mostrerà il mio sentimento e la mia risoluzione – che era ed è inalterabile. Del resto la T. non perderà molto (fuori della tua Grazia – che sarebbe assai più per mi perdere che per lei). In rapporto delle interesse io farò tutto che si può fare finchè essa può collocarsi – e l'avrei fatto senza nessuno sforzo – io non cerco nè *vendetta* – nè vedere le persone *soffrire* – ma solamente che quella donna non sia vicina a te non solamente per causa [tua] e mia – ma per tante altre persone che tu conosci – io ho dato ordini a Lega – provve [derà] in tutto . . .

[29]

Tu dici che A. ti ha detto che io non 't'amai . . .!' io non so cosa quell'uomo vuol' dire – ma io so di aver detto in faccia sua – che anche se egli non voleva, io ti voleva *bene* e *per sempre.* Si può dire di più ad un marito? Pel resto – tu sai se ti *amai* – e come – e quanto – anche nei ultimi dispiaceri più forti – ed *oppresso colla febbre* – sono stato il tuo amante – come sarò sul, letto della morte – fin' almeno che mi resta la medesima forza.

[On the back of the page]: Questo era il poscritto della ultima lettera – ma non la mandai.

[30]
Verrò. Mi pare che ho fatto giustizia a quelle qualità le quali sono veramente vostre – e pei difetti che vi ho detto (con troppa onestà forse) gli avete in comune con una nazione entiera – e con un' morale di società fatale per uno straniero che ama un' Italiana.

[31]
G.° *10. 1820*
Mio Bene: Ti prego spiegare ciò che A. ha detto questa sera – dell'associazione per le feste – l'Intendo pochissimo – la cosa può essere una Gentilezza Romagnola, o una malagrazia. Io per sicuro non avrei esibito associarmi se la presenza di A. e di Cristino R. non mi avrebbero guarantito quando lo feci. In ogni modo mi stimo essere almeno al pari dei Socii per *nascita* – che non dipende da noi, e per tutto il resto che può dipenderne da noi stessi. Ti prego istruirmi per norma mia – poichè non voglio avvilirmi – nè anche per causa tua, ma in tutto ciò che tu desideri (credendomi sicuro che tu non puoi desiderare ciò che mortificarebbe il tuo amico) sono e sarò sempre tuo (come tu dici) '*in eterno*'.

P.S. Ti giuro che mi piacerebbe assai più il non andare in queste feste – e che solamente perchè tu lo desideri pensava andare.

[32]
Scusate questa Charta *della locanda.*
Amor Mio: Mi dispiace che non posso accompagnarti – ma sto poco bene questa sera – e poi il cambiare di casa domanda la mia cura particolare – ciò tu intenderai bene conoscendo il carattere di mia gente. Penso venire da te in pochi momenti – ma pure non voglio che tu te privi della conversazione della C.C. per causa mia – sono

[33]
G.° *17. 1820*
Mio Bene: Elisei mi confirmò ciò che tu dicesti sulla '*prima donna*' per conto mio – ma era già persuaso che non era vero – ed io l'ho pregato di bel nuovo – caldamente di contraddire quella ciarla dappertutto; ed Egli m'ha promesso, anche con premura.
Non ho veduto Giulio Rasponi – quando lo vedo – dirò la medesima cosa anche a lui. Non sono venuto da te – perchè tu sei andata far visita, e poi A. non ritrovò la chiave del palco; dunque, come fare. Vuoi che vengo alle 6 o no, e come debbo regolarmi in riguardo tuo alla festa?
A. mi pareva di mal umore.
Credi, che io sono in *fatto* ciò che tu sei in *detto* – il tuo '*amante in`eterno*'.

[34]
[Fragment of a letter.]
Sì – e *se no* – pagarò il viaggio qui – e di ritorno a F. – con qualche cosa di
più per il disturbo – ma voglio riservare a me stesso il diritto di rifiutare in
caso che il landau non corrisponde alla descrizione. A. è un buffone – che
non sa cosa volere o dire quando è imbestialito di mal' umore. – ditelo.

[35]*.*
Alla Nobil Donna
La Contessa Guiccioli
S.R.M.

Ravenna   *G.° 29. 1820*

Ben Mio: Tu hai sbagliato. Io non mi ricordo niente, e ti prego non fare delle
cose simili senza ragione. Tu non hai debiti con me se non del' *Amor* per cui
'resto in credito a tutto il presente giorno R.i 1000000000.'

P.S.   Ti rimando i tuoi quattrini. Cosa so io – sei pazza?

[36]
                                                             31 st. 1820*
Voi avete sentito il vostro Genitore parlare di quella donna – e se non volete
sentire nè lui nè il vostro amico – basta sentire il paese. Essa ha portato dei
dispiaceri in tutte le famiglie dove è stata. Io pregava Ferdinando dirvi *in
orecchio;* – forse egli m'avrà mal' inteso.
\ L'altra sera vi diedi la mia parola d'*onor* di non intrare più in casa dove
stava quella donna – e in mia patria, questa diviene più d'un giuramento.
Per il resto – ognuno è padrone di Casa sua – e nessuno più di A. Egli farà
ciò che lo piace – e farà bene. Io ho parlato *con* voi – ed anche in presenza del
Conte Ruggiero – credete che c'è una differenza d'opinione sopra la vostra
protezione di questa donna? Domandate.
   Io non cerco l'avvilimento di nessuno – ma nè il vostro onore – nè il mio mi
permetterà tacere quando vedo delle cose alle quali non voglio dare loro *vero*
nome per non dirvi delle parole che potrebbero offendervi. L'imprudenza di
Ferdinando è stata Colpa mia in parte, ma io non aveva altra maniera in
quel' momento comunicare con voi – e credeva ch'egli vi direbbe in un
momento più opportuno – ciò che era solamente la replica della mia risoluzione già presa, e spiegata da molto tempo. La mia intenzione non era di
offendere nè A. nè nessuno – ma non sono pentito di avere ad ogni rischio
fatto il possibile per impedire il progresso di un'imprudenza che andava per
finire in un disonore.
   Bisogna fare ciò che se debbe – e non quello che può piacere solamente –
così ho fatto io.
   Sono e sarò il vostro umil. Serv. ed amico.

[37]
                                                                   7 Ore
Amor mio: E' difficile prevedere come questo affare abbia a terminare. In
ogni caso tu puoi essere sempre certo dell'amor il più sincero, il più sviscerato.
                          * Page torn.

Tu sei in caso di sapere più di me l'idee di A. Io ho mandato Lega a dirlo che nè Papà, nè la Rasponi m'aveva parlato – nè fatto parlare – di questa cosa come è il fatto.

Della donna – ritengo la mia opinione e la mia risoluzione – adesso le ragioni si raddoppiano ad ogni momento perchè io non potrei intrare nessuna casa dove abita questa bella Elena della nuova guerra di Troja. Tu sai che il nome di *Paride* nel Greco è *Alessandro* – come tu avrai veduto nella traduzione di Omero da Monti.

Cosa sarà di te – io non so – cosa sarà di me – ora e sempre – dipende quasi tutto di te – e del' grado e costanza del' bene che tu mi vuoi. Io non sono venuto a R. per abbandonarti – ma le circonstanze – la fortuna e la *morte* – sono i Sovrani dei uomini; vedremo col' tempo, lo sviluppo di nostro destino.

Ti bacio 100000 volte – carissima.

[38]

Febbraio 1. 1820

Attendo con impazienza – mio Bene – la tua lettera – che debbe decidere molto – forse tutto per me. – Io sono così persuaso di aver ragione nella risoluzione mia – che anche se mi costasse la mia felicità, mi ritengo fermo. La nuova predilezione di A. in favore di quella persona di cui si tratta – io non posso ben capire; a Venezia egli aveva un'opinione tutta opposta – e se tu ti ricordi – la diceva anche in parole molto grosse.

Le mie ragioni ho già spiegato – ho delle altre – ma non torno a ripeterle. Io non ho diritto di dire nè a lui nè a te più di ciò che ho detto – ma sono anche io padrone di me stesso di venire o non venire in una casa dove habita una persona che io conosco per essere cattiva in ogni rapporto; particolarmente quando si tratta – (come recentemente si trattò) del mio occupare una parte della casa. Ti prego dirmi una volta la decisione; sè dopo tutto quello che ho passato debba essere sacrificato mi dispiace che non sia per una migliore ragione – e per un soggetto un poco più degno che questa mantenuta, ma ciò che sarà sarà.

Ricordati che sono venuto due volte a Ravenna – per compiacerti – *che ti amai con tutto il mio cuore* – e che partirò non per capriccio mio – nè per stanchezza – nè per mancanza della minima parte di quel' amor che t'ho sempre portato e *che sempre ti portarò* – ma perchè vedo che il restar in un paese dove non ti vedrò più che di ben' rado, sarebbe peggiore della lontananza – per tutti due.

Fammi sapere ti prego, e subito – se puoi – poichè – ho delle ordini di dare a Lega – e ti raccomando spiegare a Papà e al tuo fratello che la nostra relazione finiva per nessuna leggerezza della parte mia.

[39]

6 ore

Ben Mio: Jersera ho detto 'forse' – e con tutto ciò che per più ragioni fuori anche dell'amor che sento per tè – vorrei vederti in casa tua – non posso risolvere in' un' momento prendere un passo che mi sembra una viltà e di cui sono sicuro che, dopo i primi momenti che *fanno dimenticare tutto*, io non perdonerei a mi stesso di aver' fatto – riflettendo sopra tutte le circonstanze che sono le cause e compagni di questa discordia.

Io lascio alla bella Elena tutto il vantaggio di suo degno trionfo. Ho promesso ed in ogni modo tenerò parola – di non cercare più farla sortire diretta-mente nè indirettamente – e questo è in fatto il solo partito – perchè A. ha il vero diritto di licenziarla.

Io ho pensato tutta la notte – ma con tutto l'amor che ti porto – non posso in un momento reconciliarmi a tornare dove questa abita. Forse – col' tempo sarà possibile – ma in questo punto – sarebbe comprare troppo caramente anche il piacere di rivenire nelle tue braccia.

Ci vedremo alla festa, spero – io vado alle 7 precisamente. A. voleva che io facessi una risposta a lui questa mattina – ma sono troppo combattuto per darla finora, potrei darla facilmente – il mio Cuor la dittarebbe pur troppo – ma *dopo*? Intanto ci vedremo alla festa – credimi sempre e tutto tuo.

[40]

A Madame
Madame la Comtesse Guiccioli

Chez Elle

7 Febbr. 1820

Amor Mio: La rivoluzione Guiccioli è la conseguenza della rivoluzione in Spagna ed il buon' umore di Alessandro dopo aver letto il supplemento alla Gazzetta di Lugano. Gran cosa ch'è la politica in questo mondo! Basta che le buone nuove non siano contradette la domenica ventura – allora avrei paura che il despotismo di Ferdinando il settimo, e di Teresa la seconda si rinascerebbe ensieme – per altro – la Cameriera ha più talento di Sua Maestà Catholica – ed è altrotanto più pericolosa. . . .

Siccome tu lo desideri – la Signorina Biron sarà alle tue ordini – ma – ma – non importa.

Io vengo da te quando tu vuoi – andare alla festa senza te non sarebbe nè convenienza nè piacere – almeno per me. Io non penso di farti veruno dispiacere ma se tu lo temi è assai facile restare ensieme in casa. La festa stessa è la cosa più indifferente ed anche noiosa. Io sono stato alle passate perchè tu volevi, e non per altra ragione.

Vieni, se tu vuoi, per la bambina – è già vestita.

Credimi – con tutta l'anima sempre e tutto tuo aman. in e.°

[41]

Pessimo O. Bramerei sapere cosa era quella charta che tu leggesti al ritorno dalla Conversazione in questo momento – e che poi non hai voluto mostrarmi. Aveva tutta l'aria d'un' contrabbando. Pensate subito di un' ripiego e mandatemi la bugia più probabile che potete inventare.

[42]

Adesso la tua testina è riscaldata con quel maledetto romanzo di quale l'autore è sempre, in ogni paese ed in ogni tempo, stato il mio Genio maligno. Del resto, vi giuro, che non so cosa vi ho fatto – non v'era la Tuda – della Zinnantina tu non puoi dubitare – la Zinnani tu conosci – dunque cosa è? – Io non vado a Cavallo oggi – dunque quando tu puoi – o vuoi – sono qui e sempre – e tutto tuo.

[43]

Il biglietto è copiato da qualche libro Francese. Le Sentenze sono attaccate come cavalli di diverso colore – e fanno una muta piuttosto singolare. *'Besoin'* non ha bisogno di un' *e* per terminarlo. Dieu *sait* e non *'sais'* (come tu scrivi) che tu sei una pessima piccinina – e un' pessimo O. La vostra fedeltà è come il vostro progresso nella nuova lingua, difficile . . .*.
Bon Soir.
Bon repos.

Bonne nuit non è F.

[44]

A. M. in E.: Ci vedremo. Io non ho le lettere di Maintenon – la quale era una p—— divota – e non allegra come la Clemilda – dunque non posso nemmeno capire cosa la detta Clemilda può volere col' tal libro. Se l'avessi – per certo ti avrei mandato. Ho letto le vostre 'due righe di biglietto' con tutta la dovuta attenzione – sono scritte colla solita eloquenza che non ti manca mai – finchè non ti manca – non Cuore ma Corinna.

[45]

Marzo. 3.° 1820

'Egli creditore a me?' come? – e si fosse vero, avendo pagato due cento scudi – non v'è una ragione di più per darmi una ricevuta? Egli non dovrebbe aver' sottoscritto veruna obbligazione – ma queste sono inezie. Veniamo al' fatto. La Somma che io dovrei pagare al' Comune – o ai Signori deputati – è di 400 Scudi – l'*ho esibito* – e lo *faccio ben volentieri* e con tutto il *piacere* possibile. Di questo è già pagata la Somma di due Cento Scudi – pei quali Egli mi rifiuta *una ricevuta* – per delle ragioni – ch'io non m'intendo, e non voglio intendere. Io sono prontissimo pagare la somma totale dimane – e fra le altre ragioni – per non aver' il Signor C. G. esposto alle obbligazioni pel' conto mio – ma pagandolo – torno a domandare una ricevuta – il primo dovere di lui *chi riceve,* se fosse di un' suo Contadino.

[46]

M°. 4. 1820

La tua Immaginazione è troppo forte. Il mandarti un libro che tu da qualche tempo desiderasti vedere non ha niente nè di sorprendente, nè di riflesso.
'Tu non mi vedrai più' – Perchè? Cosa t'ho fatto? E' vero che non sono stato al tuo fianco per giocare alle Charte questa sera in Casa C., perchè tu sei messa in un' cantone dove non si trovava luogo per il tuo amico – per delle ragioni forse più conosciute da te, che da me. Ma questa non mi pare una ragione sufficiente per disfare un'amicizia di qualche tempo e di molte prove. Se sono reo di torti contro te, tu puoi informarti. In un piccolo paese – si può trovare la verità quando si vuole e dir' male, o sentirlo.
Se tu sei *seria* nella tua risoluzione – Io non sono l'uomo per importunarti – ma voglio che *in sangue freddo – tu ripeti in iscritto* questa risoluzione – ed allora io prenderò il mio partito. Ricordati solamente che *tu* vuoi così, ed io no.

* Here the page is torn and some words are missing.

[47]

Marzo. 5. 1820

Vi ho mandato due volte per la risposta vostra alla *mia* di jersera. Almeno qualunque che sia la vostra decisione mi pare che per la mia giustificazione dovreste indicarmi più precisamente per norma mia, la vostra risoluzione – e la ragione. Io ho un' dovere col' vostro padre – con cui prima di prendere le misure che (in caso che tu sei veramente decisa in questa stranissima risoluzione) bisognerà che prendo – voglio parlare per un momento.

Ricordati sempre che *tu* sei quella che vuole terminare la relazione – e non io – e che io non vi ho mai fatto torto in detto in fatto nè in pensiere.

. . . caso che sei attualmente risoluta . . . perchè – non vi importunerò più – e partirò sul momento.

Sono nonostante sempre il vostro amico ed amante.

[48]

Sarebbe meglio dirmelo questa sera – tutto è meglio del' incertezza.

Io sono partito perchè la serata minacciava divenire ben lunga – e vedeva Papà – che non ebbe l'aria di partire presto. Vi prego dirmi adesso ciò ch' avete a dire invece di dimane – perchè io ho anche le mie ragioni per voler' sapere, e ho delle cose a decidere prima di Sabbato.

P.S.   Luigi è tornato dicendo che siete andata a letto. Direte ciò che vi comoda – ma vi prego dirlo presto – perchè io non voglio essere più esposto ai capricci nè di mariti – nè di amiche che sono compiaciute nel fare tutte le malagrazie possibili.

[49]

Amor mio: . . .* Voi contate sopra il potere che finora avete avuto sopra me e le mie azioni – i miei pensieri – il mio cuore – per farmi creder' ciò – e tutto ciò che volete – e che vi comoda più: per ora e per sempre. Non dirò che ora non riuscirete, perchè avete già riuscita troppo spesso; ma vi prevengo che un momento verrà quando le vostre [arti] saranno in vano.

[50]

E' meglio che non ci vediamo più questa sera – dimane parleremo forse con più tranquillità. Io sono disposto creder ciò che tu dici – ma anche io ho dei miei sospetti qualche volta e tu che sei almeno egualmente sospettosa dovresti piuttosto compatire che condannarmi. Ti prego di non venire da me adesso – perchè il vederci in questo momento non può fare altro se nonchè accrescere il mio dolore.

Dimane ti vedrò e parleremo.

[51]

Avant

A.M. + '*La Contro-chiave*': ecco perchè voleva le mie lettere in mani mie *per ora* – e nonostante tu mi dicesti tutte le ingiurie – per quella richiesta.

* Here the page is torn and some words are missing.

Ti prego guardare bene tutte quelle lettere che sono chiuse in tua Scrivame (colla musica che era alla Mira) poichè si potrebbe trovare se non del' *mio* – almeno qualche cosa che non ti piacerebbe.

La mia opinione è sempre l'istessa – ma se non v'è rimedio – io per certo farò il mio dovere. – Del'amor mio tu non puoi dubitare – e forse la prova più grande è stata – che io preferiva sagrificare mi stesso – piuttosto di te. Credimi sempre e tutto.

P.S.   La malattia tua non mi pare che *cutanea* – quando ci vedremo – dimane? . . .

Ricorda – non *sottoscrivere* niente per quel' *Scelerato per eccellenza*.

[52]

Avant

A.M.: Io non lo stimo e non lo temo. – Egli farà ciò che vuole. Per me, io ho del' amor e dei doveri, con te – ma non voglio influire in nessun modo sopra la tua decisione. Dopo aver' fatto ciò ch' Egli ha fatto – nessuna viltà – nessuna nefandità – dalla parte sua sorprenderebbe nè a me – nè a nessuno. Parla coi tuoi amici e parenti e come tu decidi – deciderà anche il tuo.

[53]

Avant

A.M. + 'Donne! Donne! chi v'arriva ecc.' Cosa vuoi che ne faccia? tu non sai – egli mai fa niente senza un' perchè – e questo e solamente il principio. Io torno a dirti che non c'è e non sarà mai altro rimedio ch'il mio partire.

Del amor mio sei certa – ma io non capisco come può essere un' amor *vero* il quale sagrifica l'amato oggetto – *con me* sareste infelice – e sagrificata nei occhi del' mondo – con' lo marito sareste se non felice almeno sempre rispettabile e rispettata. Come che non vedo alternativo se non una disunione che tosto o tardi dovrebbe accadere.

Io voglio salvarti – anche al' prezzo del' odio tuo – ingiusto – ma che al' tempo darà luogo a un sentimento di riconoscenza.

Di cosa puoi accusarmi? Son' venuto, son' partito – son' tornato, sono stato – v'è più d'un' anno che non ho fatto altro ch'ubbidirti in tutto – finchè poteva conciliare il tuo ben essere col' tuo desiderio* ed ora chi vedo che questo non si può fare di più – prenderò il solo partito che può essere o ragionevole o nobile. – Verrò da te questa sera – e parleremo.

Credimi sempre e tutto il tuo vero am.° ed am. te!

[54]

Avant

A.M. + Verrò, ma quando e come? Se non temi per te stessa, si debba pensare di tua famiglia – perchè è in fatto contra di loro che queste cose sono dirette. Contra me stesso (finchè di ciò che sento per te) non possono far niente – ma non sarebbe gran' Eroisma in me comprometervi tutti quanti senza participare nel' pericolo. Dunque voglio prima essere istruito come debbo condurmi – e per quel' oggetto vorrei parlare con' Papà.

* Byron had first written *colla nostra rispettabilità*.

[55]

In fatto è meglio per te in ogni modo esser con A. In sei mesi tu anche penserai così, e sarai persuasa che io sono stato il tuo amico *vero* – e sacrificato. . . . Tu m'accusi – io non lo merito – e tu lo sai. Il tempo di decidere è stato prima di partire da V., in quale infelice paese tu ricorderai quanto e come ti pregava non sforzarmi ritornare. Ecco le conseguenze.*

[56]

Avant

A.M.: Cosa vuoi che ne rispondo? Egli ha saputo, o debbe aver saputo, tutte queste cose per molti mesi – v'è del mistero che non capisco e che non preme capire. E' solamente *adesso* che Egli sa della tua *infedeltà*?† Cosa avrà creduto – che siamo di stucco? o che io sono *piu* o *meno* d'un' uomo? Io non conosco che un' sol rimedio – ciò che ho già suggerito. *Il mio partire* sarebbe un *sagrifizio grande*, ma piuttosto che incontrare ogni giorno di cose simili deviene necessario – quasi un' dovere in me – il non rimanere più in queste parti.

Egli dice ch'è impossibile per lui più soffrire questa relazione – io rispondo che non *dovrebbe* averlo mai sofferto – e che per certo non è lo stato più felice nè anche per me esser' esposto alle sue 'stravaganze ormai troppo tarde. Ma farò ciò che un' galant'uomo dovrebbe fare, cioè non portare dei disturbi nelle famiglie.

Tutto questo sarebbe stato già finito – se quel' uomo m'avesse permesso di partire in 10ᵇʳᵉ del' anno scorso. Egli non solamente *voleva* che *venissi* – ma mi diceva colla sua propria bocca che non *dovrei* partire – 'essendo un' rimedio troppo lontano'. In queste circostanze non ci vedremo questa sera.

Sempre e *tutto tuo*!

[57]

Avant

A.M. + Nelle circostanze attuali è meglio *non* venire – in questo momento – per prudenza. Se Egli è serio – farà il possibile (secondo sua indole – e per vendetta) di non lasciarti pretendere nessun' *mantenimento* – in ciò bisogna non *cedere* – non tanto per la cosa in se stessa – ma per la tua reputazione.

Qualche fine egli ha per certo – è un uomo – in cui non si può fidare un momento.

Me pare che la sua intenzione era sempre di far la cosa finire *così* – e che mi fece venire la *seconda volta* apposto.

Parla con papà – e poi (o prima) ci parleremo. Vuoi che ti conduco al teatro o no! Fammi sapere.

Se l'affare va finire nel' disunirti da lui – (ciò ch'io non desidero – ma che per l'altra parte non mi sorprenderebbe) noi prenderemo il nostro partito, ed io farò tutto che si debba fare in tali circostanze.

Mi dispiace solamente per te – ed appunto perchè *ti amo;* mi dispiace anche per la tua famiglia – per me non può importare – se posso contribuire a renderti meno infelice.

Adesso sento doppiamente il peso di non essere in libertà per renderti giustizia nei occhi del' mondo, e per assicurarti dell'indipendenza dopo il

* Two fragments cut out of a longer letter.
† Teresa has tried to change this sentence to '*Sospetta la tua fedeltà*'.

mio mancare – in caso che (come spero) tu mi sopravivi. Ma farò in qualche
maniera – per superare quella difficoltà.
Verrò da te dopo il vestirmi al mio ritorno dalla Pigneta.
Credimi sempre e tutto tuo am.° ed am.°.

[58]

Avant

A.M. + Io non vado in messun luogo di divertimento – sinchè questo affare
non viene terminato in una maniera o l'altra. Anderò a cavallo perchè
quello è un esercizio – in un sito solitario – e non per farsi vedere.
Se A. vuole parlare con me – è padrone – ma per certo io avrò ben poco a
risponderlo. Se dopo l'insulto di esser divisa da letto – per la pazzia di un
maniaco – tu torni a cedere alle sue falsissime lusinghe e tenerezze di vecchio
rimbambito – il torto si rigetterà sopra di te, e il tuo carattere per debolezza
sarà più che mai confirmato. Farai ciò però che ti comoda – basta che io lo so
per norma mia.
Sono.

[59]

E' appunto perchè ti amo tanto – che non posso avere pazienza quando
s'entra del'*interesso* – particolarmente con *lui*. Farei qualunque sagrifizio per
te – ma in tal' caso ti voglio a me – entieramente adesso – tutte quelle cose
m'avviliscono nella mia opinione.
A lui non posso cedere. Egli mi tratta con tutta l'insolenza d'un suo dipen-
dente, e nol soffrirò più delle cose simili. Mi assoggetterò alla decisione di
qualunque Signore, che in questo affare Egli ha mancato egualmente in
gentilezza ed in buona fede. Ma basta. Addio ti bacio.

[60]

Avant

Amor Mio + Si voleva anche questo per compire la nostra infelicità. Non mi
sorprende però. E in queste circostanze non sarà accordato che vengo trovarti.
Ma più di tutto mi affliggono le ultime parole di tuo biglietto, sono ingiuste
sempre, e più che mai adesso. Io t'ebbi consigliato sempre per il tuo bene – e
vedendo ch'era inutile, finalmente cedeva al' tuo desiderio – e per ciò tu mi
rimproveri. Mal grado questo sono e sarò eternamente il tuo più sincero ed
amantissimo amico.

[61]

Après l'abboccamento.

A.M. + + + Le solite cose inconcludenti – ed *inconcludibili* – se sia una tale
parola.
Egli propone o che io *parto* (dicendo che questa è l'opinione e il *desiderio
publico* – e che il suo amico Marini se meraviglia che io ne resto per portare dei
dispiaceri nelle famiglie) o che mi servo della mia ascendenza sopra di te – per
persuaderti di distaccarti da *me* ed *amare lui* – ed anche per *attaccarmi* il più
presto che posso ad *un'altra*.

Per la separazione dice – che egli non la vuole – non essendo disposto 'perdere la donna – disgustare i suoi parenti – e sopra tutto *pagare* un assegnamento. Non vuole fare la figura di 'b—— contento' – (dice) e m'incarica di persuaderti che il vero amore e quello dei *conjugi*. Mi servo delle sue proprie parole. Dice che l'amor mio non essendo una prima passione – come la tua – io dovrei agíre così ecc. ecc. ecc. *Non vuole* – *non vuole* – e non sa cosa vuole – ma intanto non vuole che ci vogliamo bene – ciò però che io farò sempre.

[62]

· · · · · · · · · Io non ebbi il minimo sospetto – ma la tua premura – la tua *violenza* mi rendeva *non il sospetto* – ma la *certezza*. Il motivo debbe essere ben forte – per spargere del sangue nella difesa di una cosa generalmente indifferente, ed esposta a tutto il mondo. Credi tu che io sono come. . . . a vanità – e indegn. . . . . fa arrossire ciò che ho sofferto – ciò tu m'hai veduto soffrire per te – . . . . Italia sempre perfida . . . . sata nascondere · · · · · · · · ·
Ebbi la debolezza di amarti; trovarò la forza per superare un' amor del' quale tutti anticipavano le conseguenze . . . – Non son sorpreso ma ben avvilito . . . [five words erased] . . . Addio – un giorno tu saprai cosa era quello che tu sacrificasti.

[On the other side of the page.]

Questo era scritto jer sera – lo mando per mostrarvi a qual stato mi avete ridotto – se non eravate accorta prima; anche in presenza di A. – io non poteva più reggere.*

[63]
Aprés
Promesse!! d'être mon Epoux!!

Amor Mio + La mia condotta sincera e gli miei consigli furono *tali*, perchè non volevo *precipitarti* – e metterti in una situazione dove bisognerebbe reciprocamente dei più grandi sagrifizi. Si vuole in una donna del molto carattere, della più vera amicizia, del amore più sviscerato ed' *instancabile*, e spesso e lungamente provato, per decidere per un partito così asvantaggioso in tutti gli sensi – ed *irrevocabile* per tutto il rimanente della vita. Ma se in detto ed in fatto quel uomo ti perseguita per dei torti ai quali nessun ha *contribuito* – nessuno ha dato la *protezione* più di lui – allora io non posso esitare di più – egli può abbandonarti – *ma io mai*. Io ho degli *anni* più di te – in età – ed altritanti *secoli* nella trista esperienza, prevedo dei dispiaceri e dei sagrifizi per te – ma saranno *participati;* il mio amore – il mio dovere – il mio onore – tutto e tutti mi renderebbero in eterno ciò che sono *adesso*, il tuo amante amico (e quando le circostanze permettessene) *marito!*

P.S. Non *precipitare* niente per *delle ragioni* – che in parte ti ho spiegato a *voce*, ma se egli va avante – *io* non ti mancarò.
Parla a papà prima.

* This letter consists of three fragments contained in a folder on which Teresa has written: '*Lettere ingiuste e da distruggere*'.

[64]
                               Aprés
Amor Mio + Si – spero vederti questa sera – e risanata ben presto. Calmati
e credi che ciò che ho sempre detto – era un vero sagrificio per me – ma che
nonostante era il mio dovere di farti vedere le conseguenze della tua risoluzione.
Ho avuto due lettere, una da Parigi, l'altra da Bologna. L'indirizzo della
lettera francese ti farà ridere. Eccole. Sempre e tutto, il tuo amantiss.o amico.

[65]
                          Aprés la decision
A.M. + + + Ti ho sempre detto – che io non voleva precipitar niente – ma che
la cosa una volta decisa – *tu potevi disporre di me*. Ora che siamo in questo
punto, vedrai che io non temo nè vacillo, e non ho mai esitato se non principal-
mente per *causa tua*. P. ti avrà raccontato ciò che io ho detto sui tuoi affari.
Io non vado al' Corso – quest'oggi – perchè non voglio prendere nessun
divertimento quando la mia amica ha il più piccolo disturbo. – A rivederti
quando tu vuoi – credimi – sempre tutto – tuo.

[66]
A.M. + In *20 minuti* sarò in libertà – e tu puoi fare ciò che ti pare meglio.
Io non so cosa dirti – tu non vuoi sentire la ragione, e voi precipitarti per
sempre.
Ma ——— sono.

[67]
R[avenna]   *Luglio – 15. 1820*
Amor Mio + Appena partita tutta la Città ha saputa la tua partenza. Io
sono stato fare la solita trottata e al' mio ritorno son informato che il P[orco]*
di San Stefano (tu sai che Sant'Antonio ebbe un' altro simile ma beato e
più pulito del' animale† di cui si tratta) è sortito con un' muso rispettabilmente
burbero ed offuscato – il quale credo non sarà molto cambiato in allegria
dimane quando saprà le conseguenze *quatrinesche*. Egli è adesso al' teatro,
il suo sollievo e diletto. Ti mando Valeriano, pregandoti per ora ritenerlo con
te – per *soddisfazione mia* assieme con Luigi – finchè sappiamo qualche cosa.
Non disturbarti per rispondere ma non mortificarmi con rimandare V. in
cui fido molto. Aspetto le tue nuove ed *ordini superiori*. Io farò ciò che tu
vuoi – ma spero che in fine *saremo felici*. Dell'amor mio tu non puoi dubitare
– continua il tuo; mi raccomando al Sr C. G. il tuo Genitore e sono sempre il
tuo più.

P.S. Si dice che A. fa una cattiva figura. Scrivimi nel più bel Stile di Santa
Chiara. Pessimo O. + + + + + + + Guardati bene!!!

[68]
Ravenna   *Luglio 17. 1820*
Amor mio, + + + La tua carissima m'è stata consegnata da P. jeri sera.
Egli partirà quasi subito; dunque non ho che pochi momenti per risponderti,
ma tu mi perdonerai.

* Teresa has tried to erase the word *porco*.
† Teresa has replaced the word *animale* by *N.N.* but the original word is still legible.

Cosa si pensa, cosa si dice, sarebbe difficile per me indovinare poichè non sorto – nè sortirò mai (se non alle mie solite trottate a Cavallo) finchè noi due non siamo in uno stato di essere insieme nella Società. Ho rifiutato di andare al' teatro – come feci quando tu eri qui ancora. Papà ti saprà dire le nuove del' mondo private e politiche, delle ultime, non sappiamo più niente. La Gazzetta di Lugano dice che la nostra Regina avendo rigettato ogni proposizione di pace – la camera dei Lord ha già cominciato il processo. Non ti avrei seccato così tanto se tu non avesti domandato delle *nuove 'politiche.'* P. ti dirà cosa Egli pensa sopra le *visite* per ora – ma se tu non sei persuasa ti ubbidirò, come debbo fare.

Ti scrivo in grandissima fretta. Tieni Val. senza rimorso. Ho trovato un Vice-Coco provvisorio il quale riesce a meraviglia – in tartufoli – *anitre* (senza cipolle però, tu lo dici credo per ridere) ed anche in bocca di dama★ dunque non faccio magro. Ho compito la tragedia – adesso viene il lavoro delle correzioni – e non ho copista.

Intanto mi occupo – e colla speranza di ritrovarti con un amor ancora non molto inferiore al' mio, sarò sempre il tuo + + +

P.S. *Sandri* dice che il decreto '*è un decreto bestiale*' ecco le conseguenze di non aver' accordato a quel' Sciagurato – gli 60 Scudi di sua domanda. Così sono gli uomini – se non si fa del' bene a loro – vi odiano – e se lo fate vi odiano di più per aver avuto il potere e la facoltà. Luigi 14° di Francia diceva bene che quando egli accordava qualche favore – 'fece cento malcontenti – ed *un'* ingrato'. Per Sandri però troverò una maniera di castigarlo.

C'è un certo . . .? no? – mi pare di sentirlo – 'ricordati di me che son'la Pia' . . .

Lega ti saluta umilmente – egli viene strapazzato discretamente secondo il solito del' amabile Padrone, – Elisei gira i palchi senza esser più vicino al' disiato nido; si fa qualche festa per Donzelli ma non come si fece per la Morandi e la Cortesi. Ho mandato la medicina al' Cardinale, la quale se egli la prende come si deve lo gioverà – credo. Ma l'ho detto di far' venire il Chirurgo Rima prima di prenderla. Jeri è stato amazzato un Prete di Faenza – e un fattore di Alessandro. Domani termina il teatro – ma tu lo sapevi prima di partire. Addio. + + +

[69]

Ravenna   *Luglio. 18. 1820*

Amor Mio + In verità io non so niente; vedendo solamente Elisei nelle solite cavalcate, ed Egli adesso è troppo occupato di una sua disgrazia di jeri per pensare di noi o del' paese. Nel fare un salto con me nei campi egli è caduto insieme col suo cavallo – e s'è fatto male in un occhio – non gran male – ma abbastanza per farlo sfigurare nel' bel' mondo per alcuni giorni. Il peggio è che essendo egli gran' Cavallarizzo in sua propria opinione (e con ragione poichè cavalca bene) erano [pure] presenti per asardo molti spettatori in carrozza ecc. di questa sua avventura – e per conseguenza l'amor proprio è stato non men ferito del' occhio. La sua berretta – il vestito – e tutta la montatura fin alli . . . *speroni* – sono anche mezzo rovinati nella caduta ch'era piuttosto forte . . . Fortunatamente per lui v'era dell'erba – e nessun sasso.

La tua lettera è stata la mia prima informazione del' colloquio di A. col Cardinale e coll'Alborghetti. Da questo tu saprai che io non so niente di tutto ciò che tu dici e domandi. Luigi e Valeriano furono tuoi servitori prima di

★ A delicious, rich cake, made of eggs, sugar and almonds.

essere i miei – e queste sono ciarle che non dureranno più di qualchi giorni.
Sarebbe bello che non puoi avere un' domestico perchè egli m'ha servito
prima di servirti!

Guiccioli ha detto a Lega questa mattina che egli non vuole portare avanti
la lite *per la casa* – io ho risposto che resta con lui farla cessare.

Per la lontananza non so cosa dirti – tu sai cosa voglio – ma resta con te
e coi tuoi parenti decidere. Per me (se vuoi) staremo insieme e manderemo A.
e il suo assegnamento *a farsi* s . . .*.

Io non sono stato molto bene jeri del gran caldo – ma oggi sto meglio.
Ti ringrazio cordialmente delle tue rose che erano fresche ancora – l'ho
baciate e messe in acqua fresca subito.

Tu temi per me – io non so perchè – ma cosa vuoi che ne faccio? ciò che
sarà sarà – e un sito non è più sicuro di un altro. Pensa guardarti bene, – ciò
mi preme assai più di me e tutto ciò che può accadere a mia persona . . .
Papà ti informerà delle dic[erie] (se lo sono) ma ricordati che finiscono
sempre in un' mese – se siano buone o cattive. Questa sera è la Serata di
Donzelli, ma io non son' andato.

Ti prego amarmi e credermi il tuo più sincero ed amantissimo. + + + + +
+ + + +

[70]

Ravenna   *Luglio 23. 1820*

Amor mio + + + Mi pare non troppo ben fatto l'aver mandato Luigi nelle
circostanze attuali – ma però non serve molto; Io lo faccio partire questa sera.
Non dovreste aver' paura di violenza contra di me – *tu stesso* hai assai più di
temere da tuo marito, questo lo *so* – e perciò ti raccomando di tenere i vostri
servitori sempre vicini a tua persona, quando tu sorti. Per le nuove Luigi
ti porterà tutte, domestiche e politiche. Io non so niente. Un Carabiniere
è stato ferito – una commedia è venuta – ecco tutto che ho imparato in questi
giorni.

Ti scrivo in gran'fretta – per non far' aspettare il servitore. Elisei è guarito
di sua ferita ma non del' suo amor proprio. Non saprei cosa dirti di più se
non chè *ti amo* – e *ti amero sempre* – ma quando ci rivedremo non resta con me a
decidere. Con un' *raggiratore* come il Cavaliere non si può sapere niente –
nè calculare niente. Egli gira come un buffone e coll'istesso effetto.

Io sto' bene – fuorchè un piccolo dolor in una mano – per aver sparato una
pistola troppo caricata l'altro jeri in Pigneta.

Ti mando dei altri libri – e sono sempre il tuo più sincero ed amantissimo.

[71]

Ravenna   *Luglio. 24. 1820*

Amor Mio + + + Non temere – ti assicuro che fosse solamente per divertimento che scaricai le pistole mie in Pigneta e non per difesa contro un' assas-
sino. I miei servitori l'avevano troppo caricati e ho sofferto un poco di dolore
in una mano – il quale è già passato.

Io licenziai tre servitori perchè in vece di far' loro dovere si trovono all'osteria
– poco prima di mezza notte – una cosa insopportabile – lasciare a quell'ora
8 cavalli, finimenti, tre carrozze ec. senza nessuno per custodirli. Ma se
vuoi – bisogna che li perdono.

* Word illegible – page torn.

Tu non sei obbligata, amor mio + leggere tutti quei libri – io creddi che tu fosti come me. Mi piace leggere ora un' libro ora l'altro, poche pagine alla volta – e cambiare spesso – *cio* vuol dire cangiare *i libri* – ma nessun' altra cosa fuori della *biancheria*, essendo io l'estratto della fedeltà.

Ti scrissi jeri in mal'umore; il non vederti – e mille altre cose me disturbavano – piccole ma noiose, cose di casa – il caldo ecc. ecc.

Non ho nuove particolari dall'Inghilterra. Le Gazzette sono piene della benedetta Regina – gran cosa in questo mondo che non si può farsi *amare* in pace – senza tutto questo chiasso. La sua Maestà ha messo il morale del' mio moralissimo paese in gran periglio e scandalo. Mi pare già deteriorato perchè leggo nelle gazzette di una dama Irlandese di 37 anni che è scappata con un' giovane Inglese di 24, piantando un' marito di 50 – e una figlia di 16.

Ti bacio 100000 volte – e mi consolo coll'idea che in ogni caso ci rivedremo.

Amami – sono sempre il tuo..

[72]

Ravenna   *Luglio 26°. 1820*

Amor Mio + + + + + Ho mandato subito a Giulio Rasponi per la villeggiatura – ma egli dice che la Contessa Capra la vuole per se – e che egli non è padrone senza il di lei permesso.

Pessimo O + dunque tu sei divenuta cacciatrice, ma è un' principio piuttosto non buono amazzare i poveri cani. Tu non puoi desiderare a rivolermi quanto ti voglio io – l'amor mi punge moltissimo (senza contare . . .) speriamo però che fra poco tempo si può combinare tutto. Il Cavaliere fa spargere delle voci – che tu sei venuta qui per trovarmi, (ma guai!) che egli ha trovato delle mie lettere le quali ha fatto *bollare* ecc. che vuole far' causa – *e mille altri sogni*. Una cosa è certa: Egli cerca (e trova in alcuni) delle testimonianze di non averti in apparenza *mal trattato*. Ma chi può mai sapere ciò? nè il publico nè gli amici – poiche sono cose di casa e di famiglia.

V'è qui la Commedia – ma non son' stato. Faccio delle trottate – e scarico delle pistole – leggo e scrivo – ecco tutto!

La lontananza m'incommoda molto – m'intendi . . .

Lega mi dice che la Fanni l'ha fatto un' altro bastardo – un' maschio – del' quale credo si farà regalo allo 'spedale di Venezia. Io lo consigliai di mandare anche *l'Aspasia*, sarebbe una brutta C . . . di meno in quella sua non troppo bella famiglia.

Le altre *cadreghe* (questa non è parola di Santa Chiara ma di un San' Marco) sono venute da Forlì – con dell'altra roba – bella – ma vogliono troppi *quatrini*, e Lega ha avuto di soffrire delle strapazzate furiose . . .

Ti prego perdonarmi tutte queste sciocczze e credermi il tuo + più fedele + + +

P.S. Si, Cocchina – ti ho inteso – con tutti i tuoi + + + povera piccinina! – spero che caveremo tutti questi nostri desiderii ben presto, ancora un poco di pazienza.

[73]

Ravenna   *Luglio 29°. 1820*

Amor Mio + + + Il tuo fratellino mi piace molto – egli mostra del' carattere e del' talento – grandi sopraciglie! e una statura di quale egli (mi pare) s'è arrichito a spese tua, almeno di quelle – m'intendi? La sua testa è un poco troppo riscaldato per le rivoluzioni – basta – che non si precipita.

Se A. vuole far' pace – spero che prima ti darà *una costituzione* – essendo la moda adesso dei tiranni.

Ti mando una lettera da Monaco – di una certa Baronessa Miltitz – che vuole la mia corrispondenza – sarà qualche pazza letterata – vuoi che ne risponda?

V'è qualche speranza per la villa Colombani – io farò il possibile come tu ben sai per averla. Ti scrivo nella più gran fretta – poichè Papa parte a momenti. Lega è qui – lo faccio agire come un dizionario – quando mi bisogna una parola – la domando di lui.

Ti prego continuare il tuo amor per me – e credermi sempre il tuo più sincero ed amantissimo. + + + + +

[74]

Ravenna   *Ago°. 2°. 1820*

(La figlia del' Cocchiere Rasponi è stata già ricevuta in casa mia per servizio della bimba.)

Amor mio + + +La mia figlia è ammalata. Ho licenziato la vecchia. Lega ha preso in casa questa Clara di quale io non so niente. Lega risponderà pei suoi proprii peccati – io posso rispondere solamente pei miei – ed appena per quei. Ho cercato e cerco per un' casino, sinora non si trova.

Guiccioli non ebbe diritto di fare il *cieco* – dopo la tua lettera del' anno scorso – di quale egli mandò la copia al Conte Pietro. Se egli non era accorto allora – non dovrebbe esserlo mai più. Quello era il momento di dire, 'fate la vostra scelta' – e non otto mesi dopo – mi pare che il tuo sentimento fu già spiegato.

Papà ti farà ridere della rottura fra il *tenente Elisei* – e me. – Quel buffone ha fatto finalmente ciò che io ho desiderato abbastanza (ma non seppi come compilrlo). Egli ha preso sopra di lui di essere offeso perchè io non voleva comprare *una scrivania* da un' artista protetto di lui. Povero Sciocco – che voleva fare il maestro di casa – e non fù capace.

Ti scrivo in fretta e sono sempre il tuo. + + + + + + +

P.S.   I miei rispetti al' Conte P. . . . Perdona il mal umor in cui ho scritto, la malattia della bimba mi ha disturbato assai.

[75]

'[rabbiosa] come in Convento . . .'

Ravenna   *Agosto 3. 1820*

La malattia dell'Allegrina – si può verificare dal medico Rasi – o dal Conte Ruggiero. Sta male molto. Per la Cameriera della bimba – Lega dovrebbe rispondere; tutto che tocca a me rispondere – è che io *non sono mai stato abasso* e che non è mio costume.

Jeri una lettera del Signor Hobhouse mi prevenga che tutti i pari che si allontanano dal' processo della Regina – saranno condannati ad una *multa* – o alla *Torre* (una prigione di Stato) con tutto ciò io non pensai andare – ma non credeva di ricevere per il premio dei disgusti che vado soffrendo per causa di altrui + delle rimprovere della persona stessà che gli cagiona.

La serva della bambina dice (ti dimenticai dirlo) che non voleva servire in casa *Guiccioli* – perchè il Signor Cavaliere gode poca opinione in *tutto* – e *dappertutto*. – In queste ragioni io non posso entrare – lasciando cose simili al' mastro di casa.

La mia Lite va in appello. La Villa Spreti è già presa – e si pensa andare la settimana ventura. Sono sempre il.

[76]

Agosto 5°. 1820

A.M.: Ho ricevuto i fiori – ed il libro vi ringrazio per tutto. Jeri vi scriveva in risposta alla vostra.

Se Luigi non vi conviene – prendete un' altro – solamente io non posso adesso riceverlo in mia famiglia – siamo già troppi – e se egli resta affatto senza impiego – voi conoscete cosa saranno le probabili conseguenze – essendo quell'uomo a giorno dei fatti nostri.

Lega è andato quest'oggi – alla villa Spreti. La bambina ha la febbre, e piuttosto gagliarda. Ho veduto papà jeri sera. – Sono sempre.

[77]

Da Ravenna

Agosto 7°. 1820

Amor mio + + +'*Si dimentichi cio che è fatto*' tu dici – la bella dimenticanza! cosa dunque era mai *fatto*? la donna è brutta come l'Orco – una roba di Lega – non giovanissima, non di cattiva condotta – non ornata con la minima qualità per eccitare un' capriccio – e tu sei degnata essere gelosa – ciò che io non dimentico così facilmente come tu lo perdoni *generosamente* a te stessa. V'è un'*pessimo O.;* lo sento.

Allegrina si è già abusata di tuo regalo – rompendo una delle carozzine. La sua febbre è un' poco cessata.

Io non anderò in mio 'bel paese' *di No* – se tu non sei gelosa delle Cameriere lercie – altrimenti si.

La proposizione di G. – mi pare non da accettare nè da rifiutare senza aver' prima ben pensata sopra. Forse se potrebbe far' così – rispondendo – che egli *dopo la sua morte* dovrebbe assicurarti *due mila scudi di assegnamento* – ed allora tu sarai disposta ceder 400 delle 1200 decretate da quel' più giusto di tutti i papi. La libertà sarebbe una gran' cosa non v'è dubbio – con quella tua testa – ma 400 scudi sono una somma rispettabile in questi paesi, e non essere abbandonati senza qualche compensa. Per il resto – se vuoi fidare in me – io ti renderò indipendente di tutti – almeno per la mia vita. Ma tu vai in collera sull'idea – volendo esser indipendente da te e di scrivere delle '*cantate*' nelle lunghissime epistole alla moda di Santa Chiara, – il convento dove si dice che tu eri sempre rabbiosa.★

Sto leggendo il secondo volume della proposta di quel becco classico Perticari. Sarà ben scritto – nello stile degno di Santa Chiara e del' trecento – – ma sarebbe più *apropos* se il Signor Conte in vece di provare che *Dante* fosse il più grande degli uomini (ciò che nessuno vuole per ora disdire, essendo la moda del tempo presente) potrebbe assicurare i suoi contemporanei che il Suocero *Monti non* è il più vile ed infame, e un' disonore tale al' talento stesso che un' uomo di ingegno debbe arrossire appartenere al 'istesso secolo con quel' Giuda di Parnaso.

★ Teresa has tried to change *rabbiosa* into *studiosa*.

Mi pare che questa è una 'cantata' o almeno la sarebbe in Inglese – ma i miei pensieri cadono sotto l'effeminate parole della lingua dei musici. Sono rabbioso – come tu eri 'in convento'* – questa sera . . . Ti bacio ed abbraccio 1000000 + + + + volte. – Amami.

P.S.   C'è un certo o lo sento nel' biglietto stesso – e molto, si – si . . . Saluta i Signori G. ambedue – mi preme di essere in loro bone grazie. Si sta preparando questa benedetta villa – il più presto che sia possibile – per causa delle due bambine – Allegra – e *tu.*

[78]

Ravenna   *Agosto 8° 1820*

Amor mio + + + Il tuo biglietto non è venuto che in questo punto – troppo tardi per permettere ch'io vado in campagna oggidì.   Io ho già dato l'ordine a Lega fermare questa benedetta villa – ma finchè mando la mia famiglia là – non sono stato nell'intenzione di venire a Filetto – non volendo nelle circostanze attuali dare nessun' vantaggio al' Signor Cavaliere, il quale correrebbe subito dal' Cardinale con mila bugie e con qualche *verità.*

Egli tiene delle spie sopra di me – e jeri mancava poco che io non bastonassi un' uomo in Pigneta – che si metteva seguirmi dappertutto – fermarsi dove mi fermai – e sempre tenersi vicino – finchè io perdetti la pazienza e lo feci intendere che se egli non seguitava la sua strada – sarebbe peggio per lui. Allora egli è scomparso.

Per il resto – amor mio – ti ho scritto jeri – la lettera sarà già da papà. Salutami il primogenito di casa Gamba – il *Quiroga* di Ravenna – e credimi sempre il tuo più fed + + + + +

P.S.   L'Allegrina sta meglio.

[79]*₊*

Ravenna   *Agosto 11° 1820*

Amor Mio + + + + Ti mando Lega, che ti dirà tutto che pensiamo fare per il casino ecc.   Io verrò il più presto che si può combinare.   Io sono disposto di pensare in rapporto ai accomodamenti con A. come la tua famiglia ne pensa per il tuo vantaggio.

Sono nella più gran' fretta il tuo più

P.S.   Scrivimi tutto che tu hai da dire contra E. – si debbe dire.

[80]*₊*

Ravenna   *Agosto 12°. 1820*

Amor Mio + Bisogna che tu mi dica la tua *autorità* – per ciò che tu hai contato di E. – Non potrebbe venire ne' dal' tuo padre ne' dal' tuo fratello – perchè non ha confidenza con loro – dunque tu hai avuto delle visite – di quali non parli.   Ti prego di dirmi il nome del' narratore altrimenti io *non* verrò in campagna.   Se tu mi rispondi subito, io verrò la Settimana ventura – senza dubbio – ma per la domenica prossima, non posso promettere.

Son sempre e tutto tuo. Dimmi il nome di quello che dice che E. ha detto così.   + + +

P.S.   Delle altre cose che tu domandi ti risponderò a voce. . . .

* Teresa has altered *in convento* to *un momento.*

[81]

Ravenna *Agosto 12° 1820*

Amor Mio + + + Per la domenica non si può combinare, la bambina va in campagna quel' giorno – e vi sono mille cose di fare e disfare, tu conosci il numero di mia famiglia – ec. Ti prego avere un' poco di pazienza – in due o tre giorni ci rivedremo.

Prima di avere l'avviso formale del' intenzione dei Pari sopra ciò che la Gazzetta annunzia, io non so che risposta dare; quando l' avrò trovarò una difesa nella malattia della bambina, e nella distanza. Io non so se la richiamata comprende anche quei via dal' paese – o solamente i lords ancora in Inghilterra. Mi pare un' atto discretamente dispotico, e se veramente tocca a me di essere compreso in questo numero, non sarà senza una protesta delle più forti.

Ti bacio 10000 volte e sarò + + + + +

[82]

Ravenna *Agosto 24° 1820*

Amor Mio + + + Altro che deliquio! – la Fanni in idea basta – la Fanni in persona sarebbe la Morte – per non dire l'inferno – in questa stagione. Immagina pure la Signora Silvestrini e il caldo insieme! no – no – no. Scrivi, manda, fermala, liberami – altramente non so cosa sarà di me. Lo diceva – lo prevedeva viene; se veramente arriva, mi faccio frate subito, e la Chiesa guadagnerà . . . che ha perduto, perdendo Lega il . . .

Sarò da te Lunedì, intanto ti mando un' certo libretto – Adolphe – scritto da un' antico amico della De Stael, di cui ho sentito la detta de Stael in 1816 dire delle orrori a Coppet del' suo cuore e di sua condotta verso di lei. Ma il libretto è ben scritto e pur troppo vero.

Amami, ricordami e – sopratutto – risparmiami la Fanni o vado in deliquio. + + + + + +

[83]

Ravenna *Agosto 26° 1820*

Amor Mio + + + Le circostanze di 'Adolphe' furono assai differenti. Ellenore non era mai *maritata*, ebbe molti anni più del' *Adolphe*, non era amabile, ecc. ecc. Non pensare più sopra cose così dissimili in tutte le forme.

Per la lettera di A. bisogna cominciare una risposta in nome *mio* il quale io sottoscriverò – facendo conoscere la verità della sua condotta con *me* – coi varj raggiri usati da lui per le interesse. Non dimenticare anche l'*età* – perchè mostra dal' principio una sofistica determinazione di nascondere la verità. Papà ha tutti i documenti necessarj – nella representazione già fatta da lui al' Cardinale.

Dal' momento che io conobbi A. egli fece delle proposizioni strane, volendo ch'io sposassi l'Attilia, e che comprassi la *Casa Raisi* qui a Ravenna. Per l'affare di Bologna e del resto siete già informati. Pensa a questo.

Lunedì ci rivedremo, amami – mio solo amore + + + e credimi sempre tutto tuo +

[84]

R.a. *A.° 27° 1820*

Amor Mio + + + Papà ti spiegherà la ragione più forte perchè non vengo da te oggi come si era combinato, e Lega ti dirà un'altra ragione. Ti prego, a questi dispiaceri non aggiungere delle tue rimprovere, poichè io non ho colpa. Ho ceduto solamente alle ragioni di papà – il quale mi pregò fortamente non andare adesso . . . finchè il Cardinale sia chetato.

Non ho avuto delle tue nuove oggi. Dunque non dirò più senonchè sono e sempre sarò il tuo più + + +

[85]

Ravenna   *Agosto 30 1820*

Amor Mio + + +Post dimani spero di essere con te. Tu hai fatto benissimo nel strapazzare Papà in vece di me; prima perchè non era colpa mia, e poi perchè una lettera lunga avrebbe fatto venire un forte *deliquio*.

Ciò che tu dici della bambina mi consola molto – fuori di quella disposizione di *canzonare* la quale può divenire un costume molto piacevole pei altri, ma che tosto o tardi porta del' danno a chi lo pratica.

Mi riservo per dirti a voce ciò che penso della R. – per tante ragioni.– Guarda cosa tu scrivi sopra quel' proposito. Ti dirò perchè . . . I miei rispetti a Papà – amami sempre come il tuo – più sincero e amicissimo + + +

P.S. Ti mando un libro francese dove troverai molto sopra Rousseau e le sue relazioni con l' Epinay. – Quell'uomo era pazzo – e non ben trattato dai suoi amici.

Post dimani speriamo a rivederci; vi è un gran' o . . . + lo sento. . . .

[86]

Ravenna   *Sett. 9.° 1820*

A.M. + + +La Pesca e la Pescatrice!! Sempre qualche cosa di nuovo.

Sai che la Gazzetta di Milano dice che sono *arrivato* in Londra pei affari della Regina!! – La gran' verità delle Gazzette! Quelle di Londra ripetono questa verità! – e gli miei amici là, la credeno, dicendo che voglio essere per ora *incognito*. Un' mio amico mi scrive che molti sono venuti da lui – e andati via senza credere che non sono tornato, tra altri la *Lamb* – subito. Ella è partita incredula. Tutto questo – ho trovato jeri per la posta.

Nulla dei Suoceri – lercj! Ferdinando sta meglio.

Lunedì ci rivedremo – sono *carico di Sentimento* ma non so come esprimerlo – o istenderlo in quattro pagine di parole – ma ti giuro che ti amo in una maniera che tutte le epistole di Cicerone non potrebbero spiegare mai, se anche l'*amor proprio* di quel' celebre Egoista fosse convertito in amore di altrui – e espresso con quell'eloquenza che fu il suo mestiere.

Amami – mio *p. o. c.* + + +

P.S. La Pesca – che Pesce? в.?

[87]

Ravenna   *S.e 14° 1820*

Amor Mio + + +Prima di Lunedì non posso venire – ho tante lettere da scrivere e molte altre cose – dunque Lunedì ci rivedremo. Così avrai tempo di andare a Russi ecc. cosa che io non mi sento in caso di fare. Avrei scritto jeri – ma non ho veduto alcuno di tuoi parenti.

Ferdinando è ancora molto ammalato – l'Allegra è venuta qui jeri – sempre colla febbre però. Ti scrivo in fretta e sono sempre + + +

Amami + + + + + + +

[88]

R   7bre 28° 1820

Amor Mio + Don G. è impaziente per ritornare, dunque non ho che un solo
momento per risponderti. Delle mie lettere non puoi aver' bisogno finchè
che sei (o eri) in corrispondenza col'tuo marito – e della mia presenza nessuna
premura – poichè sei stata in R. senza dire che ti venga trovare.

Pierino avrà forse esagerato ciò che io dissi in un' momento di mal' umore
sopra *le lettere* – o almeno io avrei esagerato ciò che sentiva per l'istessa
ragione. Questa stagione m'uccide di tristezza in tutti gli anni, maggiormente
in questo. Tu sai la mia malinconia del' anno scorso – e quando ho quella
malattia del' Spirito – è meglio per gli altri che mi tengo. lontano. Però
– il tempo solo mi ha trattenuto qui – per la prima occasione ci rivedremo.
      Credimi sempre il tuo più

P.S. Ti ringrazio di cuore per le rose – amami. La mia anima è come le
foglie che cadono nell'autunno: *tutta gialla.* – Una Cantata!!!

[89]

R   7bre 29° 1820

Amor Mio + + +La tua Immaginazione ti porta troppo lontano. Don
Giovanni è un buffone coi suoi misteri. Vi erano qui jeri due *lercje,* una più
brutta dell'altra – per concorrere al servizio – l'ho vedute in presenza di
Lega per un solo momento – e poi non le ricevo – perchè non mi paiono
adattate a servire l'Allegrina. Quando mi pareva necessaria cangiare la
Governante – io mandai Lega dalla Vicari – in vece di andare in persona – per
non darti ombra. Cosa vuoi che ne faccio? io non conobbi altra Signora
fuorchè della tua amica – in cui potrei fidarmi per una tale raccomandazione.

Il momento che le strade saranno praticabili verrò da te – e allora non
saranno più questi sospetti. La mia lettera ti avrà spiegata la ragione perchè
non scrissi; io non ebbi altra ragione.

Per la mia *tristezza* – tu sai se non è nel' mio carattere – particolarmente
in certe stagioni. E' una vera malattia di temperamento – che mì fà delle
volte temere anche un' principio di pazzia – e per questa causa – mi tengo in
quei momenti lontano da tutti – non volendo rendere infelici gli altri. E'
questo vero o no? O è la prima volta che tu m'hai veduto in quel' stato? . . .
Amami – e credi che ci rivedremo e ameremo più che mai. +

[90]

R   8bre. 1. 1820

Amor Mio + + +Ti risponderò a voce alla tua lettera *mercoledi* venturo. Io
non mi lagno delle circostanze – nè della fortuna. La mia malinconia è una
cosa di temperamento ereditata dalla famiglia di mia madre – particolarmente
dal' *Nonno* – e poi non è costante – come tu sai – ma – non voglio seccarti con
queste inezie.

Ti prego perdonarmi se non scrivo più in dettaglio – il tuo espresso vuol
partire – ed io ho delle lettere da scrivere per Inghilterra.
      Amami – e credimi + + +

[91]
Alla Nobil Donna
La Contessa Domenica Gaspara Guiccioli
nata (F.° 18° 1799) Gamba Ghiselli
S.R.M.

R   8bre 7° 1820

Carissima Gaspara + Penserò per la Settimana proposta – e tu puoi immaginare ben volentieri. Jeri ho ricevuto delle nuove da Londra – le quali mi faranno preferire il rimanere qui – e limitare i miei servizj *patriottici* piuttosto alla parte Settentrionale del' *'bel' paese'* – che andare a scaldarmi a Monte Vesuvio – e dappiù non è necessario, poichè vi sono i *tuoi capelli* – color di fiamma – e la testa di sotto più calda della lava. Poi sento certi rimorsi nel' idea di lasciarti – (se anche fosse per pochi mesi) i quali mi danno una cattiva idea dei piaceri della lontananza.

Papà è qui con me – il Fattore parte – dunque Mia Carissima Gaspara
+ + +

[92]
Alla Nobil' Donna
La Contessa Gaspara Guiccioli
S.R.M.
Si vuole qualche giorno ancora perchè penso
di venire a *cavallo* – e le strade saranno
poco praticabili dopo la gran' pioggia.

Ravenna   8bre 11° 1820

Carissima Gasparina, + Sarà stato un fulmine per 'incenerire il Cameriere' come dice Don Magnifico. Non v'è caduto niente – fù una buffonata dei servitori contra Luigi per spaventare la sua bella, la degna dama di tua camera.

Ti prego non fare tanto macello delle .oche, perchè non posso venire per qualchi giorni ancora. Sarai prevenuta sempre un' giorno prima.

Amor mio non andare in collera. Mandami le stampe – perchè voglio far fare delle cornici.

Ti mando una pessima traduzione in francese di quel'. libro che tu domandasti tempo fa. Troverai nella notizia (piena di Sciocczze e menzogne però) un' racconto ben diverso di quello dei amici Pierineschi – a Roma – della causa della *divisione* colla moglie. Vi è nel primo tomo.

Se puoi favorirmi coi altri volumi della *biografia* – des hommes . . .* sarò riconoscente. Sempre + + +

P.S. I libri sono venuti. – Grazie.

[93]
Alla Nobil' Donna
La Contessa G. Guiccioli
S.R.M.
R.a   8bre. 12° 1820

Amor mio + Forse tu hai ragione – di ciò discorreremo quando siamo insieme. Per ora mi limiterò a dirti che nell'anno 1816 quando quei versi erano stampati

* Word erased.

– una *Signora Francese* allora in Londra diceva appresso poco nelle tue parole – che 'non poteva comprendere come la più orgogliosa donna ecc. ecc. poteva resistere' ecc. ecc. e per me diceva – 'qualunque che fosse stato il torto di mio amante o di mio marito – non sarei ritenuto un momento dal gittarmi fra le sue braccia ecc. ecc.'

Questa opinione fu stampata nelle gazzette del giorno – io non conobbi mai la persona – oltrechè fosse una dama Francese. E' singolare che una Francese ed una Italiana se uniscono in quel' sentimento. La difesa della beata *Matematica* era – 'che non fui sincero – ma che tutto questo fosse un' *Machiavelismo* mio – per metterla lei in apparente torto – perchè in *fatto* io desiderava di separarmi ecc. ecc.' Tu puoi giudicare per te stessa – se io sono così politico. Ci rivedremo in pochi giorni amami × mia Gaspara. – sempre

[94]
Alla Nobil' Donna
La Contessa Gaspara Domenica
Ro.a Pett.° Guiccioli
S.R.M.

   Ravenna 8ᵇʳᵉ 25. *1820*
Amor Mio + La lettera della Fanni è un' ritratto del carattere di quella 'Galeotta che la scrisse', Falsa – furba – arrogante – venale – pedantesca – adulante – e bugiarda. '*Franca* a Ravenna!' – franca al' inferno – che il diavolo paga il viaggio! La sola cosa che mi piacerebbe un' istante sarebbe il vedere *l'effetto sopra Pierino* – no ccert oe per la gittarebbe per la finestra – il secondo giorno.
·. . . . . coi suoi sforzati complimenti sul' riguardo . . . . . la lercia! – ma io sono di . . . . di lei. . . . Non ho tempo a dirti di più – poichè il . . . . corriere è impaziente – saluta Papa e Pierino ed amami sempre + + +*

P.S. Non so se Lega sarà inteso colla Signora F. ma io mi sono *inteso* con lui sopra quel' argomento.

[95]
   Ravenna 8ᵇʳᵉ 30° *1820*
Amor Mio + – Posso ben credere qualunque cosa dei bigotti parenti – o del' governo che adesso sospetta di tutti e farebbe del tutto per allontanare o spaventare quelli che teme. Non sarà però solamente diretta a *me*, ma anche a *tua* famiglia (Pierino per esempio) per essere stati sospettati in queste ultime cose patriotiche. Ma c'è un'ingiustizia nel' far la guerra a una donna per le colpe di un' uomo.

Io aveva sperato (prevedendo queste cose) che la mia condotta dopo la tua separazione dal' marito fù stata abbastantemente riservata (*in apparenza*) per allontanare ogni pretesta di prendere delle nuove misure, particolarmente dopo i patti con Guiccioli e la tua famiglia, per rilasciare tanto del' assegno. L'invidia dei bigotti naturalmente gli fa sempre perseguitare gli altri per piaceri dei quali si privono loro stessi. Per me, io non vedo nè capisco nulla – senonchè per ogni piccolo mezzo cercano di disfarsi della mia presenza nei stati pontifizj – e se non fosse per *certe speranze* – e *sentimento* – (compreso *sopra tutto* l'amore per te) io ben presto gli leverei il disturbo.

* Several words in this letter have been torn away by Teresa.

Saluta papà e Pierino.

Elisei è tornato e collocato a Faenza – ecco la sua lettere a me. - - - Io non conosco abbastantamente le circostanze per dare dei consigli a *papà* – egli dovrebbe essere a giorno del' indole de' suoi parenti – e di quanto il governo sarà o non sarà capace. Del' amor mio tu hai avuto delle prove ed avrai – sono e sarò + + +

[96]

Alla Nobil' Donna
La Contessa Gaspara R.ª P.ª
Guiccioli
S.R.M.

Ravenna   9ᵇʳᵉ. 8°. *1820*

Amor Mio + Non ti scrissi, perchè non fu nulla di nuovo a dirti. 'Da *Nulla Nulla* può venire', dice la Matematica – ciò che non è vero però, poichè ho veduto delle volte da *Nulla* sortire una lettera di sei pagine. Ma io non ho l'eloquenza di Santa Chi.ʳᵃ, nemmeno della *Fanni*. Tu sai il mio gran' *talento* per il *Silenzio* – e dovresti perdonarmi quando non scrivo per ogni piccola occasione.

Il tempo non mi pare molto favorevole per il tuo progetto – ma ne pensarò. Salutami Papà e Pierino; ed amami – tutto +

P.S. *Scrivi* se ti commoda – altramente credo che non vivresti più – dunque *Scrivi* – gran Santa C.ª

[97]

Ravenna   9ᵇʳᵉ 10° *1820*

Ti ringrazio 1000 volte per il regalo, amor mio × gran *cantata* in quel' biglietto tuo!! Con questo tempo mi pare che i tuoi progetti di andare a cavallo non riuscirebbero troppo bene nei contorni di Filetto. Non sono venuto ma ritengo la speranza di vederti presto.

Saluta Pierino e Papà – conservati bene ed amami sempre. Ti bacio + + + +

P.S. Si parla qui di una rivoluzione nata in Inghilterra – ma non credo nulla – poichè jeri ho ricevuto delle lettere di data fresca ed altrettante Gazette da Parigi. Queste non parlano di nessun' tumulto. – Il processo della Regina va avante colla solita indecenza; dovrebbe essere ormai deciso . . .

[98]

                                                  9ᵇʳᵉ. 18°. *1820*

Amor Mio + Ti prego perdonarmi che non posso in questo momento andare a Filetto. Tutto ciò che abbiamo a dire si può ben dire a Ravenna, – dunque non è una cosa di tanta importanza. Nella lusinga di vederti così presto sono sempre il tuo

[99]

9bre 22 1820

A.M. + Ma cosa dunque si può fare? Non hai sentito Papà e Pierino? che sono i tuoi prossimi parenti, spero anche amici *miei* poichè mi sono condotto con buona fede verso loro. Quei *altri* – i buffoni – o del' governo – o (perdonami) di tua famiglia, vogliono sacrificarti; si vuole adesso del giudizio e della pazienza. Se non ti amava – se voleva *disfarmi di te senza biasimo* – ed anche coi ripieghi più bei in favor mio – il modo più certo sarebbe di *venire da te* – e di fare altre simili imprudenze in faccia del' mondo e dei preti – che formano il *mondo qui.* Sarò sempre il tuo

[100]*₊*

[*1820*]

Perdonatemi il non essere venuto questa sera, ma veramente sto poco bene – cagione forse del tempo – e del' non esser stato a Cavallo; forse delle gentilezze vostre di jeri sera – e di quest'oggi.
Colla speranza di rivederci dimane sono e sarò sempre

[101]*₊*

[*1820*]

Io credeva che il tuo venire qui ti piaceva più - per causa della maggiore confidenza. In tanto vengo da voi – per me è eguale.

[102]*₊*

[*1820*]

A.M. + – Scusi – che ho da scrivere 5 *lettere* tutte sopra affari questa sera. Ecco la causa di così corta e poco cortese risposta. Credimi sempre per tutto – il tuo

P.S. Anche temo di scrivere *più* chiaramente in circostanze tue. Ti bacio 10000 volte. Ti ringrazio per la bellissima *rosa.*

[103]*₊*

[*1820*]

A. M. in E.: Come faranno i altri? o come faremo per sapere? – Non sarà gran' gusto andare alla Sala del' Comune per non trovare senonchè della canaglia. Io farò ciò che tu vuoi – decidi.

[104]*₊*

[*1820*]

A.M. + Si può appena leggere qualche parola – l'aqua ha resa il resto poco intelligibile. Domane parleremo più in dettaglio. Io non son venuto in palco, *prima* – perchè non voleva ricevere delle Sgarberie dal' S.° A. e poi, perchè son venute delle persone – le quali per convenienza come padrone del palco non potrei lasciare. Sempre e tutto

GG

[105]*⁎*

[*1820*]

Tita non m'ha inteso. – Io lo diceva pregarvi dispensarmi da venire questa sera – per sentire Legniani . . .*

In questo momento capita il vostro biglietto – verrò dunque – perchè voi lo desiderate – basta che Luigi m'indica quando viene Legniani.

[106]*⁎*

[*1820*]

A.M. + Ho letto – ma intendo poco. Chi è 'Alessandro' di cui parla – è il tuo Marito? Per il resto c'intendiamo qualche cosa dalle procedure antecedenti – spiegami cosa è Sⁿ. Domenico e 'i rescritti' e cosa può o *non* può fare il Cardinale.

Mi spiace che Papà non è qui. Non sono venuo per le ragioni già dette, perchè tu stavi male jersera.

* Luigi Legnani was a famous tenor.

[107]
Alla Nobil' Donna
La Contessa Gamba Guiccioli
ec. ec. ec.
S.R.M.

R.ª   G.° 18° – [1821]

Amor Mio +Ecco la verità di ciò che io ti dissi pochi giorni fa come vengo
sagrificato in tutte le maniere – senza sapere il *perchè* o il *come*.

La tragedia di sui si parla – non è (e non era mai) nè scritta nè adattata al
teatro – ma non è però romantico il disegno – è piuttosto regolare – regola-
rissimo per l'unità del tempo – e mancando poco a quella del' sito. Tu sai
bene se io poteva avere intenzione di farla rappresentare – poichè fosse
scritta al' tuo fianco – e nei momenti per certo più *tragici* per me come *uomo*
– che come autore – perchè *tu* fosti in affanno ed in pericolo.

In tanto – sento dalla tua Gazzetta che sia nata una cabala – 'un partito –'
ed una diavolezza – e senza che io ho preso la minima parte. Se dice che
'*l'autore ne fece la lettura*!!!!! *qui forse – a Ravenna!* – ed a Chi? forse a Fletcher!!!
quel' illustre letterato! Ecco delle buffonate solenni. Non istò bene – mi
duole la testa – ed un poco il cuore.

Ti bacio 1000 volte, sempre tutto tuo +

[108]
Al Sigʳ. Conte Ruggero Gamba.

                                          Luglio 12°. 1821

Mio Caro Ruggiero: Tu sei padrone della Teresa per diritto – e di me per
dovere ed amicizia. Ma viste le circostanze, io crederei bene per *prudenza*
anche – che Ella non partisse per alcuni giorni. Se tu insisti ella cederà – come
io – che non ho, nè debbo avere, che una voce in questo affare. Ma i passa-
porti sono equivoci – la presenza di lei non può giovare nulla – per impedirli,
se loro vogliono molestarti – nè per consolarti – poichè non vorresti vedere
una donna isolata in tale situazione.

Se accade del bene noi ti raggiungeremo, se del male – anche ti raggiungeremo, in qualunque circostanza – ed io mi farei un dovere trovarti anche se
fosse in fortezza.

Ma ti prego non precipitare la cosa per ora, – e particolarmente pensare di
tutto ciò che potrebbe accadere alla Teresa priva di te e di Pierino – in un
paese inimico.

Per me io non ho altro a dire senochè desiderare vederti e Pierino ben'
presto – ciò che farò o in un paese o l'altro. – Sta sano e credimi sempre il,
tuo aff.ᵐᵒ amico   BRYON

P.S. Ti rimando il pacco di *quest'oggi* – che la Teresa ti ebbe fatto rimandarmi. – Serviti liberamente non solamente di quello – ma di tutto il mio.

Tu farai come tu vuoi – ma in ogni modo ricordati – che se arriva del
distacco tra la Teresa e me, che non era colpa mia.

[109]

Alla Nobil' Donna
La Contessa Gamba Guiccioli.
Bologna
S.R.M.

R.a   *Luglio 26°. 1821*

Mia Teresa: Ti prego calmarti, ed andare avante colla certezza che dovressimo
rivederci tra poco. Se non in Ravenna, combineremo per la Svizzera quando
mi viene la eisposta da Ginevra. Ieri ò veduto il *zio* C., che da delle speranze.
Tonino *è a Roma – ciò è certo*. Intanto non cedere a un' dolore così irragionevole
– ma pensa di consolare il tuo padre e fratello.

Mi rincresce della lontananza della Duchessa – della bontà di quale sperava
molto – ma forse se può fare egualmente senza di lei. Il tuo progetto di
tornare qui solo per rivederci un' istante sarebbe una vera pazzia. Mi pare
che con una tale proposizione tu – hai desiderio di farti mettere in *convento* –
come venne minacciato.

Ti amo e ti amerò – come ti ho sempre amato – ma non posso incoraggire
un' delirio così fatale come sarebbe il tuo ritorno il giorno dopo la tua partenza.

Lega ti scriverà accludendo due lettere della posta di oggidì – che io ho
ricevuto per te – come tu dicesti.

Mille cose a Ruggiero e Pierino, scrivi spesso e presto. – Saluta il Sr. Costa
e la sua consorte – ai quali sono gratissimo della loro amicizia per la tua
famiglia.

'Figlia consolati – stergi le lacrime' – e credimi ('crede B.' – tu sai – è la
parola di mia famiglia) sempre e tutto il tuo amico amte.   B.

P.S. Pet . . . mettiti in buon' umore – le cose anderanno meglio che tu
pensi . . . Ti ringrazio per il fiore accluso – che ebbe conservato molto il suo
odorino. Tutto qui è come era al' tuo partire.

[110]

                                                      L.° 29 1821

Mia Teresa: Voi siete partita coll'intenzione di ritrovare la vostra famiglia
in Firenze. Questo fu il solo partito rispettabile o ragionevole per voi nelle
circostanze attuali. Cosa vi fa trattenervi in Bologna? Io non so, e se lo
sapessi, non lo potrei approvare.

Vi *raccomando* dunque di bel nuovo di *proseguire* il viaggio per tutte le ragioni.
Col vostro padre siete salva – e dappiù, fate il vostro dovere come figlia.
Dove siete, io non vedo che una donna senza appoggio – e non d'un molto
buon cuore che lascia stare il suo padre nel' esilio senza fare un viaggio di 18
ore per consolarlo. Se credete di essere sicura dalle tentative già fatte (e per
fare ancora) per mettervi in un' ritiro – finchè rimanete nei *stati del Papa*,
Sbagliate. Sono sempre il vostro a.a.   B.

P.S. Spero sentire che siete partita per Firenze – allora vi scriverò in dettaglio.

[111]
Al' Nobil' Uomo
Il Conte Pietro Gamba
S.R.M.

A.° 4. *1821*

Mio Caro Pietro: Mille grazie per la vostra lettera gratissima. Non posso rispondere tutto ciò che debbo e vorrei dire. La Sua Eccellenza sarà avvisata. Mi ha scritto 1000 ingiurie da Bologna* – perchè io d'accordo con tutti i savj – e tutti i suoi amici e Parenti – la consigliava di giungere a Firenze, per ritrovare voi e il suo Padre. La cosa era assolutamente necessaria – se ella non voleva essere messa in Convento. Domandate di tutti.

Non vedo nessuno – le mie passeggiate vedove sono *ben' seccanti;* ho colpito colla pistola – due *scarpe nuove* del' poveretto l'altro jeri, ciò che mi costò dodici paoli! Ho visto per la strada un' giorno la Tuda – che pareva una pecorella smarrita – un' poco losca – e molto sentimentale per causa di vostro abbandono – mi confessò di essere varie volte da voi ec. ec. ma chi sa se questo è vero. La sua bellezza non fu però tale da dare del' invidia nè anche a quella più gelosa delle donne – la sua Eccellenza.

La Martini è sparita dalla finestra solita – in conseguenza del' esilio del' amato bene – in vece di lei – ho veduto *Santino Fabbri* – la – ciò che mi veniva indicato di più sensi che quella della *vista.* Intanto tutte le vostre numerose vedove sono inconsolabili – non si sente che dei sospiri – ciò che fa un' poco d'aria – cosa piacevole in questa stagione. Lega avrà scritta a Papà tutte le nuove e le speranze – ed i passi che pensiamo fare. Io intanto sono e sarò sempre il vostro affe. ed obbl. amico

P.S. 1000 cose a Papà. Vivete felici.

[8 lines erased. They began: 'Mi scrivono da Parigi che . . . .'

Questo fu scritto prima del' arrivo del' vostro preg.mo. Io aspetto una risposta da Svizzera dove scrissi prima della partenza della Teresa – intanto stiamo a vedere un' poco – la precipitazione non può se non pregiudicare alla vostra famiglia e a tutti quanti. Lega ha ordine di scrivere più in dettaglio.

[112]
Alla Nobil' Donna –
La Contessa Guiccioli Gamba
Firenze

Agosto 4° 1821

Teresa Mia: Spero che tu ti trovi bene a Firenze – e salva coi tuoi parenti. Lega nella lettera che scrive a Papà per questo ordinario – spiegherà in dettaglio le ragioni le quali rendevano urgente la tua partenza da Bologna. Basta dire – che Costa, Cavalli, e tutti quanti i tuoi amici erano persuasissimi che fosse il solo partito nelle tue delicatissime circostanze. Per me, io non ho niente di rimproverarmi in questi consigli – nè da rispondere alle ingiurie con quali ti ha piaciuta onorarmi nelle ultime tue lettere.

Ho ricevuto una lettera nobile e consolante da Pierino; pare che egli mi conserva la sua amicizia – che sarà sempre reciproca dalla parte mia.

Qui facciamo tutto che possiamo per il ritorno del Conte Ruggiero; io ho spedito la lettera alla D. di D. che ora si trova a Spa presso Liège – ma che potrebbe scrivere di là a Roma.

* Line completely erased.

Non ho risposta finora alle mie lettere di Ginevra; aspetto le tue nuove con impazienza.

Per me, io non istò nè bene nè male; la mia speranza naturalmente è voltata a voi altri; non vedo nessuno – vivo coi miei libri e coi cavalli.

Senza tradurre tante pagine di 'Corinna', nè sforzare tanta apparenza del romancesco, ti assicuro che ti amo come t'ho sempre amato; si vedrà col' tempo chi sarà il più instancabile nel' amarci; ma in eloquenza ti cedo per due ragioni, – 1°, non conosco la lingua – 2°, troppe parole danno sempre da sospettare, ed i grandi *predicatori* del' sentimento esaggerato limitano la pratica di loro massime alla Cattedra; l'amor vero dice poco.

Ti prego di salutare cordialmente Papà e Pierino e pregarli comandarmi in tutto – come loro (e il tuo) amico più sincero, ed affmo.

[113]
Postcript to a letter from Lega Zambelli to Conte Pietro Gamba

[*Ravenna*]   *5 agosto 1821*

Mio caro Pietro: Sarebbe impossibile per me partire in questo momento, prima dell'arrivo delle mie lettere, e d'un' parente del' Allegra – che aspetto momentaneamente da Pisa – per decidere sopra il destino della bambina. La vostra impazienza è forse naturale, ma non me pare necessaria nelle circostanze questa gran' fretta andare non si sa dove. In 10 giorni devo avere una risposta da Ginevra per le due case. Sempre e tutto

[114]
Al' Nobil' Uomo Il Conte P. Gamba
S.P.M.

Ra   *A°. 9°. 1821*

Mio caro Pietro: I vostri sentimenti vi fanno onore, ma nonostante io ritengo la mia opinione sul' riguardo del conte R., il vostro padre, e la Teresa. Mi basta però di avere esposto le mie ragioni. Se siete decisi partire, partite – io verrò. M'avrebbe più piaciuto, sarebbe stato anche assai meglio per tutti quanti se avreste avuto la pazienza aspettare la risposta da Ginevra. Allora avreste saputo dove andare precisamente – in una casa – invece di trovarvi in una miserabile locanda piena di viaggiatori.

Per mi stesso – l'idea di ritornare in Svizzera è disgustosissima – per tante ragioni, delle quali sarete ben accorto quando siamo là – e sarà troppo tardi. Teresa dovrebbe senza altro accompagnare il suo padre e fratello – ma nonostante quella protezione, io credo che ella si troverà in una situazione assai penosa – per le dicerie dei buoni Ginevrini – ed i viaggiatori Inglesi - per tutti i due dei quali basta per delle persone essere della *mia conoscenza*, per essere esposte alla più infame calonnia. Io sperai – e anche sono persuasi – che con un poco di tempo e coraggio – il vostro padre potrebbe tornare a R. e la Teresa anche, senza disturbi per uno o l'altra.

La Teresa scrive a me delle vere pazzie – come se io volessi abbandonare ec. ec. Se ebbi quell'intenzione, perchè la pregava di partire da R., da B.? In pochi giorni Ella sarebbe rinchiusa in un' ritiro e l'affare finito, senza che io ebbi la minima colpa nei occhi del' mondo. Sicuramente non mi sarei dato tante premure per una donna con cui meditava una separazione.

Finora non è venuta risposta – non sono venuti i miei cambiali – i quali per certo non sarebbe bene lasciare girando il paese dopo la mia partenza. Sono tre ordinarie che dovrebbe essere arrivate, e la tardanza mi sorprende e disgusta. Non sono necessarie per me adesso – perchè n'ho abbastanza – ma intanto non piace troppo di non sapere niente di una somma di qualche migliaia di Scudi – la quale nel' corso ordinario dei affari – dovrebbe essere già arrivata 20 giorni fa.

Mi preme di più perchè la Svizzera è forse il paese più caro in Europa pei stranieri – il popolo essendo il più furbo e birbante sulla terra, in tutto ciò che risguarda il denaro, e l'inganno, e l'avarizia. Io non suggeriva un' soggiorno in quel' paese se non colla idea di un'assoluta necessità di lasciare l'Italia – e solamente perchè v'è il paese più vicino. Questa *necessità* di partenza non esiste più. Il Governo della Toscana è assai mite, assai assai più del' governo attuale di Ginevra – che adesso è sotto il giogo dei anti-liberali. Un' mio amico qui scrive alla mia richiesta a Teresa delle ragioni forti pei quali sarebbe meglio di rimanere in Italia.

Credetemi con pienissima stima ed amicizia sempre il vostro, a. e s.

[115]
Alla Nobil' Donna
La Contessa Guiccioli Gamba

*R*ª.   *A.° 10° 1821*

Amore Mio: Ti prego di non rendere la nostra infelicità più grande colle rimprovere non meritate. Io sono sempre stato fedele e leale a te e a tutta la tua famiglia. La lettera del' mio amico scritta alla mia richiesta sarà un'esposizione veracissima delle tantissime ragioni per non esporci ad una residenza nei stati della Svizzera.

Non ho mai pensato di dividermi da te – ma lasciami un' poco di tempo e di libertà di pensare per noi – e sopra tutto per te. La mia lettera a Pierino contiene ciò che ho da dire sopra quei argomenti. Non dico altro. Amami come ti amo. tutto tuo.

[116]
R.a.   *A°. 13°. 1821*

Carissima: Le lettere da Ginevra non sono favorevoli a nostra partenza. Lo Stato è pieno di Inglesi – e ogni casa occupata – e così sarà per più di cinquanta giorni ancora, fin' al' 8ᵇʳᵉ. – Dappiù, Ginevra e tutti i contorni suoi sono pieni di Inglesi anche per tutto l'inverno. Tu conosci se io poteva vivere nella stessa atmosfera con quella razza. Ti prego dunque abbandonare quell'idea – e persuadere R. e P. di fare altro tanto. Si può stabilirsi in Toscana – ed assai meglio per ogni rapporto.

La lettera di mio amico – per l'ultimo espresso – ti avrà spiegata la mia situazione in quel paese di Svizzera – nell'anno 1816. Se vuoi rinnovare quelle persecuzioni che sarebbero dirette con eguale furia contro di te – non hai che andare in Svizzera.

Io conservo ancora la speranza che con un poco di tempo e di pazienza il tuo padre potrebbe essere richiamato in sua patria – ed allora tu puoi accompagnarlo. Se Pierino è deciso di viaggiare – non mi oppongo – per certo egli sarebbe assai più contento viaggiando senza tanti impegni – e senza fare la cattiva figura che farebbe – se *noi* due eravamo della sua compagnia. In ogni modo – se papà non può tornare – possiamo stabilirsi in Toscana.

In questo punto ricevo la tua lettera per mezzo di uno dei *richiamati:* Già avrete la mia risposta. Il tuo padre cerca un paese *libero;* dove lo troverà? Per certo non in Svizzera – dove esigliano di nuovo i già *esigliati!*

Il mio primo desiderio sarebbe che egli tornava a Ravenna – il secondo (ma anche quello assai mal volentieri) che si stabiliva in Toscana – la Svizzera non mi pare niente adattata, ed io pensai solamente di quel paese come preferibile a *San Leo*. Adesso che non v'è più pericolo di quello per lui, l'andare in Svizzera sarebbe – ma ... ho già esposto tutto nelle lettere passate. – Sempre e tutto tuo

P.S.   M'è venuta una lettera della Benzona chi ti saluta, anche il suo Beppe; saluta Pierino e Papà della parte mia.

[117]
*R.*ª   *Ag.to [16] 1821*

A.M.: Le mie lettere sono arrivate.   Dunque v'è poco trattenermi qui.   La mia intenzione è di prendere una casa in Pisa dove sarà dei quartieri per la famiglia tua, e la mia – separati, ma vicini.   Se ciò non ti piace – dimmi – e si prenderà una casa separata per tutti i dui.   Questa lettera sarà portata dal' Inglese che adesso sta qui – il quale partirà domane.   Egli spiegerà a tutti quanti – molte cose difficili e lunghe nel' scrivere – che non è il mio talento nelle lingue *non* barbare. . . . Quando tutto è deciso – spedirò una parte della servitù coi effetti più pesanti, *mobili* ec. necessarj per la casa.   Poi verrò coi altri.

Saluta Papà e Pietro – sono sempre

P.S.   Se avete preso un' quartiere in Prato – e si trova la casa per me, è l'istesso; ma Pisa sarebbe il miglior soggiorno, secondo a ciò che mi dicono. Io lascio Ravenna così mal-volentieri – e così persuaso che la mia partenza non può che condurre da un' male a un' altro più grande, che non ho cuore di scriver' altro in questo punto.

[118]
       Postcript to a letter from Lega Zambelli to Conte Pietro Gamba.

[*Ravenna*]   [*17 agosto 1821*]

Caro Pietro: Ecco il risultato dei pensieri più ragionevoli che io posso formare nelle circostanze attuali.   Io partirò però molto mal' volentieri da Ravenna – persuaso che la mia partenza non può fare altro che male alla Teresa in ogni maniera.

L'imbarazzo – (come sempre accade dove entra il bel' sesso) – è sommo – per lei e per noi per quella ragione.   Sarebbe stato 1000 volte più rispettabile e prudente – se Ella e il Conte Ruggiero potrebbero tornare qui.   Ma la volontà di Dio – o del diavolo – e della santissima Lucrezia di Imola e dei santissimi Nonni sia fatta!   Maledetti siano tutti i Nonni, e Lucrezia di Imola e d'altra che mai furono nel' Mondo!

Mille cose a Papà.

[119]
Alla Nobil' Donna –
La Contessa Guiccioli Gamba
S.R.M.

                                                        A.° 20 1821

Mia Cara T: Io ho scritto per ogni ordinario.   Non abbiamo spedito dei altri esspressi, per non esporre quei poveri diavoli alla infame oppressione che l'ultimo incontrava per la sua strada.

Il Signor S. dovrebbe essere già a Firenze – e avrà spiegato le mie intenzioni. Se le lettere non sono capitate – biasimate la posta e non noi altri. Lega scriverà a Papà e Pierino pei affari.
Salutate tutti i dui e credetemi sempre

P.S. Qui non sono nuove senonchè quel' buffo di Coccardino* ha rimandato i due richiamati. – La colpa di Ranuzzi fù di essere *rivale* di un' frate – questo si sa – il 'bel paese'!!

[120]

A°. 24°. 1821

Mia Teresa: Lega avrà informato Pierino e Papà dei nostri preparativi per partire per Pisa. Io non posso aggiungere altro. Quando tutto è accomodato [a] Pisa, ed i mobili son arrivati ec. ec; allora partiremo.
Tu sai che le mie lettere non sono lunghe quasi mai – e non aspetterai molto da questa – sapendo che io ho tante cose da pensare. Io non niego che parto molto mal volentieri, prevedendo dei mali assai grandi per voi altri – e *massima per te*. – Altro non dico – lo vedrai.
Sono

P.S. Saluta P. e Papà.

[121]
Alla Nobil' Donna –
La Sua Eccellenza R.P.
La Contessa G.G. Guiccioli
S.R.M.
Pisa o Firenze.
*R.*ª

A.° 26° 1821

Teresa Mia: Stiamo preparando. Si v'è della lentezza sarà di quel' benedetto Lega – il quale abbandono alle tue rimprovere. Ti prego di stare in buon' umore – verrò il momento che posso. Sperando rivederti egualmente [erased] e meno pic . . .†
Sono sempre il tuo a – a in e

P.S. 1000 saluti alle altre due Eccellenze maschie – cioè a Papà e Pierino. Scrivo a Sh. per firmare la casa. . . .

[122]
A Sua Eccellenza
La Eccellenza R. P. –
La Contessa Gaspara ecc.

S°. 4° 1821

Cara P . . .:‡ Quel'Lega non ha fatto nessun' progresso nei preparativi – dunque gridatelo bene. Per me io non aspetto che per vedere terminata questo affare

* A nickname for the Cardinal.
† Byron had written *pettegola*, but Teresa erased it, and wrote *pic* . . . the first letters of the word *piccinina*.
‡ Byron had written *Pettegola*, but Teresa erased all but the P.

dei mobili ec. Cosa è divenuto di Papà e Pierino? Sono a Pisa? La tua lettera non parla di loro.

Amami – e credimi +

P.S. Oggi ho portato Lega alla Marina per insegnarlo a nuotare – puoi imaginare quel' prete nel' mare. . . .

[123]
  Postscript to a letter from Lega Zambelli to Conte Ruggero Gamba.

[*Ravenna*]   [5 7bre *1821*]

Amico Preg.mo: *Io* non ho detto che '*possa*' – ho detto che lo *fa* – secondo a ciò che mi riferiscono.

Quel' buffo di Lega conta le cose in sua maniera. Dappiù il Signor Lega fa tutto ciò che egli '*possa*' (o *può*) – per *ritardare* la mia partenza. Ciò scrivo – perchè sapete la sola ragione che mi trattenga qui per ora, è la lentezza di Lega. Sono sempre il Vostro amico affmo.

1000 saluti alla Teresina.

[124]
Alla Nobile P . . .
La Contessa Gaspara G.a
S.R.M.

 Ra.   *Sett. 9. 1821*

Eccellenza Pic . . .*: La Duchessa di Devonshire – ha scritto l'acchiusa – che sarà tradotta da Sr. S., se quella ti preme. La prego di mandarmila in dietro, dopo averla letta.

Pei maestri della *lingua Inglese* – sarebbe meglio per ora evitare l'occasione di dar' luogo alle dicerie. Tu non conosci lo stato dei partiti in Inghilterra – e le orrori che dicono di Shelley e di me – e se non hai un' poco di riguardo I Inglesi di Pisa e di Firenze diranno che *essendo stanco io*, ti ho consegnato a lui. Ti dico questo schietto e netto – in tante parole – per farti conoscere a cosa può condurre la minima imprudenza. Dunque essendo avvisato – dipende da te di condurti come vuoi.

Noi andiamo facendo dei preparativi per lasciare Ravenna – ciò che forse sarà ben' inutile – ed in ogni modo è stato sempre *contrarissimo* a miei pensieri. Un poco di pazienza avrebbe ristabilito tutto, come vedrai della lettera (della dama) acchiusa.

Bisogna anche pensare di due cose – la prima è, che se papà è richiamato – io *torno in*' *quel*' *istante* a R., e la seconda è, che se egli viene richiamato *prima di mia partenza*, io non parto. Per le spese della casa nuòva – ec. io li pagarei 1000 volte volentieri per non avere il disturbo di traslocarmi per delle inezie. Per quello non sarà difficoltà. Sono sempre

 Saluti Papà e Pierino.

[125]
  Postscript to a letter from Lega Zambelli to Contessa Guiccioli.

[*Ravenna*]   [*undated but September 1821*]

Teresa Mia: Mi maraviglio che siete degnata scrivere per una cameriera che già rifiutava di venire da te – e che è poco meno di una p— pubblica.

Non ho tempo dirti altro per ora. Scrivimi – amami ecc. ecc.

 * Here, too, the word *pettegola* has been erased and substituted by *Pic* (for *piccinina*).

[126]

Postscript to a letter from Lega Zambelli to Contessa Guiccioli.

Ravenna   *15 7bre 1821*

Eccellenza Pettegola: Tu hai fatta bene gridare questo buffone – e farai meglio ancora rimproverarlo dappiù. Egli non è di buona fede. Intanto non aspettiamo che l'arrivo dei vetturali per spedire la roba. Per il primo ordinario ti scriverò più. Sono sempre il tuo – a – a. in e. –

P.S. Saluti alle due Eccellenze virili; e di a Pierino che ho delle cose di dirlo che lo farebbero ridere se non fosse un' Venerdi – come lo è quest'oggi – dunque mi trattengo per rivederlo – o per scriverlo per un'altra occasione.

Ti bacio [paper torn] 1100 volte.

[127]

Postscript to a letter from Lega Zambelli to Contessa Guiccioli.

[Ravenna]   *[17 7bre 1821]*

Eccellenza Pettegola:* Siamo tutti preparando – imballando – sudando – bestemmiando – *ec.ando*.

Mi ha costato due ore di mettere in ordine i archivi delle lettere di vostra Eccellenza – essendo almeno cinque cento; una piena traduzione di Corinna – ossia – la Pettegola, romanzo di S.E. la N.D. C.ª G.D.T.G. nata G.G. e R.P.

Amami sempre tuo e tutto

P.S. 1000 cose a Papà, e l'Eccellenza fraterna. Continua a gridare Lega – che lo merita più ogni giorno.

[128]

Postscript to a letter from Lega Zambelli to Contessa Guiccioli.

[Ravenna]   *[26 settembre 1821]*

Eccellenza P.: 'E' deserto il bosco ec. ec.'. – non v'è più comodo per il gatto.

Lega partirà in alcuni giorni – io verso il 1° del mese venturo. Voglio dare del tempo per l'arrivo del convoglio e le varie bestie – della mia storia Naturale di (non Buffon ma) Buffoni.

Saluto teneramente la tua P . . . lezza e sono colle solite riverenze alle altre due Eccellenze dell'Eccellenza vostra

umilissimo
divotissimo
oblig.mo
ecc. terissimo
Servitore

P.S. Capisco poco dell'odio vostro per una Città dove non siete mai stata perseguitata – e dove foste nata. Se *io* non amo il *mio* paese – v'è più di una ragione, come la vostra Ec. sa bene. Per il resto io parto perchè lo volete – ma vi prevengo che sarà ben' difficile che io non torno qui – colla prima occasione, e dopo poco tempo.

* Here, too, *Pettegola* has been erased, leaving only the P.

[129]
        Postcript to a letter from Lega Zambelli to Contessa Guiccioli
[*Ravenna*]   [*5 ottobre 1821*]
A.ʳ Mio: Saressimo partiti in questa settimana se non fosse per l'incertezza
cagionata da questa voce adesso generale del' nuovo esiglio dei Romagnoli in
Toscana che mi veniva anche detto dal Zio Cavalli.

Fammi sapere la verità – e come debbo regolarmi (si è vero) per trovarci
insieme. Credimi sempre, tutto tuo

[130]
A Sua Eccellenza
La Sigra Contessa Teresa P. Guiccioli
ferma in Posta   PISA

                                                           12. 8ᵇʳᵉ 1821

A. M°.:Ora che sei certa che vengo – la differenza di alcuni giorni più o meno
non può importare – nè dovrebbe inquietarti nulla. E' necessario che io
aspetto un' altro ordinario (il *18* solamente) per avere la risposta ad un' pacco
spedito in Inghilterra nel' mese scorso. Io l'aspettava jeri – ma non essendo
capitato – bisogna che l'attendo questa settimana. Se non arriva Giovedì –
partirò l'istesso senza aspettare oltre.

Per cinque giorni non abbiamo avuto che una dirotta pioggia – altrimenti
spedirei i miei cavalli la mattina – con tutto ciò che le strade sono in un' stato
pesante pei cavalli Olandesi – i quali naturalmente il Cocchiere vuole con-
servare in buona salute . . . Servitore già Cocchiere tuo (ed ora non so che) io
[non p]rendeva mai impegno di riceverlo nel' servizio [mio] nè posso farlo
senza cacciare dei miei – ciò che sarebbe un' ingiustizia – se prima non
mancono ai doveri loro. Se questo uomo è ammalato io farò il possibile per
soccorrerlo – e poi egli sarà pagato per il tempo che restò coi mobili – e per
sue fatiche – ma non posso nè fare nè promettere altro.

Saluta Papà e Pierino con tutta la cordialità ed amicizia.

Sta Sana – e non esaggerare con quell'*ampollosa epistolare* immaginazione
di Santa Chiara (benedetto sia il Convento) le cose più semplici e necessarie
in mali e torti ec. ec. che non esistono se non in tua testa romancesca o piuttosto
romantica – poichè rovescia tutte le regole del' pensare – per agire alla *De
Stael.*

Perdonami questa predica; nella speranza rivederti presto *sono, come son'
sempre stato,* il tuo   a – a – in E.

P.S. Abbandono Lega a tutta la tua degnissima indignazione e castighi
meritati. Faremo di lui ciò che vuoi al' mio arrivo. Egli partirà due o tre
giorni prima di me – credo il *20.*ᵐᵒ, cioè Sabbato – ma dipenderà un' poco
del' tempo per causa dei cavalli più fini. Io penso di lasciare R.ᵃ Lunedì
otto, il 22° del' corrente.

[131]
                                                  8ᵇʳᵉ. 19°. 1821

Amore Mio + Lega parte domattina, senza altro. – Sarà accompagnato di
tutti i Servitori della Scuderia – ec. coi cavalli e due legni.

Io partirò dentro la settimana – verso Giovedì probabilmente. Ti assicuro
che la lentezza e la confusione di Lega è una cosa sorprendente – oltra passando
le mie idee non piccole di sue *qualità.*

Tu hai aggiunta ai varii dispiaceri che ho dovuto incontrare da qualche tempo, colle tue lagnanze ecc. per la mia *non* partenza. Io sono partito il momento che fosse possibile. Ti prego di risparmiarmi tali lagnanze che non sono nè giuste nè ragionevoli. Sperando abbracciarti presto sono di tutto cuore il tuo   a – a – in e.

P.S.   Ti prego rimpro [verare] ed anche *darne* (con quelle) a Lega – *Bastonalo bene* – lo merita – se non fosse per la *mia insistenza* non sarebbe partito nè anche adesso.

[132]
A Sua Eccellenza
La Contessa G. Guiccioli
S.R.M.

8bre. 23° 1821

Amore Mio: Lega partì Sabbato. La mia partenza è fissata per il Sabbato venturo, cioè in quattro giorni. Spero che sarai contenta.

Lega debbe essere in Pisa prima di questa letterina – ma supponendo che la rapidità di suoi viaggi corresponda coi altri movimenti di quell'uomo – potrebbe essere che il biglietto arriva prima del balordo.

Ho voluto darlo una settimana di tempo per fare il viaggio – se io fossi partito il primo *egli* non sarebbe mai a Pisa Egli ha già commesso un' delitto, nel' accordare troppo ad un' vetturino per due cavalli fin' a Lugo. Ma non lo pagherò, quando veniamo ai conti della strada. L'aiuto di questi cavalli era necessario per risparmiare troppa fatica ai due Olandesi, prediletti del' Cocchiere.

Saluto Papà e Pierino e ti abbraccio alla *Corinna*.

Amami – Amor mio – sono sempre il tuo   A.A. in E.

P.S.   Mi dispiace la malattia del domestico – Guarda che non manca niente di necessario per il suo stato. Essendo di fresca eta si può sperare per lui.

[133]

8bre 26° 1821

A.M.: Post dimani me metterò in viaggio. Il tempo non è molto favorevole ma ciò importa poco; importava più pei cavalli Olandesi, che già debbono essere a Pisa. Dunque speriamo rivederci fra poco – sta tranquilla, e credami il tuo   a. a. in e.

P.S.   La Vittoria – si sposa con uno di Imola – (mi vién' detto) la Tuda si *fa*-al' amore col' nuovo Vice-legato (un'altra diceria forse). Tutte le amorose di Pierino sono già provedute – vecchie e giovani, dunque; i nonni sono in campagna ancora – la Giulia qui. Il Signor Nonno continua avere quella facilità inconveniente pei . . . ma in tutto il resto sta bene. I due ragazzi furono in città ma sono già tornati alla villa. Saluta le due altre Eccellenze.

[134]*₊*
A Madame
La Comtesse Guiccioli
ec. ec. ec.

[*1822 or 1823*]

A.M.: Molto volentieri ma vieni *accompagnata* da Pierino o Papà. – tutto tuo

N.B.

P.S.   Ritirate il Cocchiere tuo – almeno per ora.*

[135]

F. 15° 1823

A.M.: Il Medico mi dice che potrebbe durare qualche tempo il mio incomodo, ma che passerà; la gonfiezza sotto l'occhio è diminuito. Ti rispondo sopra questo perchè tu lo desideri.

Io non posso esprimerti il dolore che mi cagiona la mancanza di tua sorella, ma Ella è felice. Sono i viventi che meritano la compassione e la simpatia. Non sono venuto da te – perchè so, dalla trista esperienza, che nei primi momenti il dolore aborrisce egualmente la consolazione – la società – ed anche l'amicizia stessa – e le parole! cosa sono? Ti compiango in silenzio, e ti raccomando al Cielo ed al Tempo. t. t.†

N.B.

[136]

F°. 20. 1823

A.M.: Per dio! – ne ha ragione la zia – e voglio anche io avere la vita di S. Catarina – e la conoscenza dei '*amorosi Gesuiti*'. – Ella – (la divota di S. Catarina) ha trovato la Felicità. Lo dice – e la credo – e cosa è dunque che noi cerchiamo?

N.B.

Alle dieci spero di vederti.

[137]

F°. 21. 1823

A.M.: Ti rimando la tua lettera di Giuliani insieme colla sua indirizzata a me. Spero che il Sʳ. Ugolini‡ si mostrerà galantuomo . . . se no, sarà una birbanteria ed ingratitude di più – che mi farà credere li Italiani anche peggiori degli Inglesi. Un' degno della nazione Britannica mi ha già rubato l'altro jeri 50 Luigi – e mi sarebbe incommodo che un bravo Romagnolo prendesse esempio di un tal' soggetto. S. t.

N.B.

* The reference may be to the Gamba's coachman in Pisa, who had been accused of taking part in the Masi affray.
† *t.t.* stands for *tutto tuo* – a signature which Byron sometimes used in this time, instead of the previous *a.a. in e.*
‡ Paolo Ugolini was a Carbonaro of Ravenna. Giuliani was an old friend of the Gamba's who lived in Florence and visited Byron at Casa Saluzzo in January 1823.

[138]

[*1823*]

A. M.: Sai tu ove è quella piccola edizione Americana colla traduzione di Da Prato della P[rofezia] di Dante? t. t. in e.*   N.B.

[139]

[*1823*]

Amor Mio: Sono arrivato senza ritardo o disturbo. Sta tranquilla e credimi sempre il tuo A. A. in e.   N.B.

* '*Tutto tuo in eterno.*'

APPENDICES

UNPUBLISHED DOCUMENTS AND BIBLIOGRAPHY

The unpublished documents upon which this book is based are the following:

I.   THE GAMBA PAPERS

II.   THE ELLIOT MANUSCRIPT

III. THE RANGONE PAPERS

IV. DOCUMENTS IN THE SECRET ARCHIVES OF THE VATICAN

V.   DOCUMENTS IN THE STATE ARCHIVES OF THE VATICAN, VENICE, BOLOGNA, RAVENNA, FLORENCE, PISA, LUCCA, AND IN THE PUBLIC LIBRARY OF FORLI.

VI. DOCUMENTS IN THE KEATS-SHELLEY MEMORIAL LIBRARY IN ROME

VII. LETTERS IN THE PIERPONT MORGAN LIBRARY, NEW YORK

VIII. LETTERS IN THE POSSESSION OF SIR JOHN MURRAY IN LONDON

I. THE GAMBA PAPERS

A. LETTERS WRITTEN DURING BYRON'S LIFETIME

149 Letters from Byron to Contessa Guiccioli
2   „   „   „   „ Conte Ruggero Gamba
4   „   „   „   „ Conte Pietro Gamba
1 Letter „   „   „ Fanny Silvestrini
4 Letters „ Contessa Guiccioli to Byron
1 Letter   „ Conte Alessandro Guiccioli to Byron
24 Letters „ Conte Pietro Gamba to Contessa Guiccioli
1 Letter   „   „   „   „   „ Conte Ruggero Gamba
1   „   „   „   „   „   „ Professor Paolo Costa
1   „   „   „   „   „   „ Charles Barry
2 Letters „ Fanny Silvestrini to Byron
6   „   „   „   „   „ Contessa Guiccioli
6   „   „ Antonio Lega Zambelli to Contessa Guiccioli
1 Letter „   „   „   „   „ Conte Ruggero Gamba
2 Letters „   „   „   „   „ Conte Pietro Gamba

These letters have all been carefully kept by Contessa Guiccioli; many are enclosed in folders, with annotations in her handwriting. They are all in Italian, except for 17 letters from Byron to Contessa Guiccioli from Greece, in 1823 and 1824, which are in English. The original text, in Italian, of all Byron's letters, has been given on pp. 425–77; all the other Italian letters are only printed in the English version.

B. LA VIE DE LORD BYRON EN ITALIE*

This prolix and woolly, but informative account, in French, of Byron's life in Italy, appears to be Contessa Guiccioli's *third version* of the story.

The first was the account she gave to Moore, of which he wrote to Mary Shelley, 'I should like to print it entire, but suppose I must not'.†

* About 1700 pages of manuscript.   † Boscombe Papers.

The second was the account she wrote for Lamartine in 1856, of which he published, she maintained, a garbled and distorted version in a series of articles in 'Le Constitutionnel' from September-December 1865. See chapter x. The third version is this manuscript. By far the most detailed of her accounts, it goes up to Byron's departure for Greece, but is unfinished. Unlike 'Lord Byron jugé par les témoins de sa vie', it is a first-hand account of Byron's and Teresa's life together, as she wished it to be transmitted to posterity. The picture, for this purpose, has been romanticized and idealized. We are made aware, to quote Hunt's malicious phrase, that 'she fancied she walked, in the eyes of the whole world, a heroine by the side of a poet'. Certain important facts, too, are either omitted or slurred over; but her omissions are nearly as informative as her statements.

Contessa Guiccioli quotes (although not always either completely or accurately) most of Byron's letters to her, as well as many others, most of which she has unfortunately translated into very bad French. These are:

19 letters from Contessa Guiccioli to Byron
3 ,, ,, Pietro Gamba to Contessa Guiccioli
2 ,, ,, Ruggero Gamba to Contessa Guiccioli
8 ,, ,, Mary Shelley to Contessa Guiccioli
1 letter ,, Shelley to Contessa Guiccioli
1 ,, ,, Charles Barry to Contessa Guiccioli

C. LETTERS TO CONTESSA GUICCIOLI AFTER BYRON'S DEATH

This interesting collection includes eighty letters from Lady Blessington, twenty-eight from John Murray and two from Sir John Murray Jr., eleven from Napoleon III, six from Lamartine, ten from Henry Bulwer, and others from Charles Babbage, Contessa Marina Benzoni, Principessa di Belgioioso, Thomas Campbell, Philarète Chasles, Louise Colet, Lady Davy, Henry Fox, T. J. Hogg, Dionysius Lardner, R. R. Madden, Lord Malmesbury, Lady Morgan, Thomas Moore, Alfred D'Orsay, Carlo Pepoli, John Pigot, Henry Reeve, James Smith, Colonel Wildman, etc. etc.

Those which are relevant to the story of Byron and Teresa have been quoted or referred to in chapter x. There are also drafts of some of Contessa Guiccioli's answers.

D. PAPERS RELATING TO THE SEPARATION BETWEEN CONTE AND CONTESSA GUICCIOLI

These are legal documents, or drafts of legal documents, referring either to Teresa's second separation from her husband in 1826 (after Byron's death) or to the law-suit between Teresa and her step-children after Count Guiccioli's death in 1840, about the settlement of his estate. These documents include the detailed accounts given by Teresa to her lawyers about the earlier events which led to her first separation from her husband in 1820, and clear up many points which until now had remained obscure. There are also copies of various petitions to the Vatican (by both Teresa and her husband) about the vexed question of her allowance, and copies of letters to Teresa from various ecclesiastics and lawyers.

II. THE ELLIOT MANUSCRIPT

This manuscript has a curious history. In the 'nineties Mrs. Minto Elliot, wife of the Dean of Bristol and author of a number of books (including An Idle Woman in Italy, An Idle Woman in Spain, etc. etc.), whose daughter married

Marchese Bonaventura Chigi Zondadari of Siena, decided to go to Ravenna to see what she could find out about Lord Byron. There she met Giovanni Sabbatini, an old man who had been in the service of Count Alessandro Guiccioli, and who subsequently passed into that of Count Pier Desiderio Pasolini dall'Onda of Ravenna. Sabbatini, who remembered Byron, not only gave Mrs. Elliot a great deal of information, but allowed her to copy some papers in the Guiccioli family archives – papers which have not since then been accessible, although some of them were included in the Memoirs of Marchese Alessandro Guiccioli, the grandson of Teresa's husband, 'I Guiccioli – Memorie di una famiglia patrizia'. These documents – some of them of great interest, – Mrs. Elliot then incorporated in a novel, which she never finished, but of which three copies still exist: one belonging to the Chigi Zondadari family in Siena, one to Conte Guido Pasolini dall'Onda, and one in the Keats-Shelley Memorial Library in Rome. Unfortunately, in copying the Guiccioli documents, Mrs. Elliot frequently omitted their date – and in some cases she only copied her translation, not the original. Nevertheless, on comparing her translation with such of these papers as are to be found in the Secret Archives of the Vatican, or have been published in the Guiccioli Memoirs, they prove to be so exact that there seems no reason to deny an equal authenticity to the other documents she has quoted.

III. THE RANGONE PAPERS

The 'Rangone Papers', in the Biblioteca dell'Archiginnasio in Bologna, consist of the Chronicle of Count Francesco Rangone, a man of letters of Ferrara, and letters written to him by his friends. These papers contain several amusing stories about Byron, and an account of him entitled 'Peep at a very culti-vated and rich, but strange Mylord'. Numerous quotations from these papers are to be found in Cantoni (see bibliography).

IV. DOCUMENTS IN THE
SECRET ARCHIVES OF THE VATICAN

These include the papers relating to a law-suit, after Count Guiccioli's death, in 1842-43, before the Tribunal of the Sacra Rota, between Teresa Guiccioli and her step-daughter Livia Saracco Riminaldi (Guiccioli's youngest daughter) about Count Guiccioli's estate – and the documents (letters, testimony of witnesses, etc.), presented as evidence on both sides. Many of these papers refer to Teresa and Byron.

V. STATE ARCHIVES AND LIBRARIES

The State Archives of the Vatican, Venice, Bologna, Ravenna, Florence, Pisa and Lucca contain: (1) Numerous Police Reports about Byron, the Gamba family, and Count Guiccioli. (2) A correspondence between the Legation of Ravenna and the Vatican about Teresa's separation from her husband in 1820. (3) Police Reports about the activities of the Carbonari, sent to the Papal, Austrian and Tuscan governments.

The Public Library of Forlì (Piancastelli collection) contains an original unpublished letter from Byron to Count Giuseppe Alborghetti and copies of six other unpublished letters from Byron to Alborghetti, and also holograph copies of many letters to Lega Zambelli from Pellegrino Ghigi, Byron's banker in Ravenna, about Allegra's illness, death and funeral.

VI. DOCUMENTS IN THE
KEATS-SHELLEY MEMORIAL LIBRARY IN ROME

In addition to a fine collection of Byron's works and portraits, and of books about the period (many of them difficult to obtain elsewhere) this library contains some unpublished papers:

(1) *Three letters to Contessa Guiccioli from Fanny Silvestrini*, 1819, and *one letter to Byron from Fanny Silvestrini*, 1820.

These letters, which were presented to the Library by Lord Rennell, with a letter stating that he did not remember how they came into his possession, would appear to come from the Guiccioli Archives, since two are reproduced by Mrs. Elliot in her book.

(2). *Three large boxes of unpublished and uncatalogued papers* about Byron, left to the Library by *Mr. H. Nelson Gay*, who intended to write a Life of Byron.

These boxes contain a varied collection of papers, including:

(a) *Copies* of a vast amount of material from the Archives of the Vatican and from the State Archives of Bologna, Florence, Pisa, Lucca, Livorno, etc. These copies appear to be reliable.

(b) A *copy* of the *Elliot Manuscript* (see p. 480) which is referred to as the 'Chigi-Guiccioli Documents' (presumably owing to Mrs. Elliot's connection with the Chigi family).

(c) Various classified information (under the names of persons or places) about Byron, from published, but often not easily accessible material such as Italian contemporary Memoirs, periodicals, etc.

VII. LETTERS IN THE
PIERPONT MORGAN LIBRARY, NEW YORK

Those which I have quoted from, wholly or in part, are:

7 Letters from Byron to Alexander Scott in 1819
1 Letter   ,,   Byron to Augusta Leigh, July 26th, 1819
1   ,,   ,,   Hoppner to Byron, July 9th, 1819
1   ,,   ,,   Contessa Guiccioli to Alexander Scott, July 23rd, 1819
1 Sonnet by Contessa Teresa Guiccioli
1 Letter from Byron to Conte Giuseppe Alborghetti

VIII. LETTERS BELONGING
TO SIR JOHN MURRAY

Those which I have been generously allowed to consult, are too numerous to be listed here. Those quoted, wholly or in part, are the following:

6 Letters from Byron to   Douglas Kinnaird
4 ,, to ,, from Contessa Guiccioli
6 ,, ,, ,, ,, John Cam Hobhouse
4 ,, ,, ,, ,, Fanny Silvestrini
2 ,, ,, ,, ,, Contessa Marina Querini Benzoni
7 ,, ,, ,, ,, Conte Giuseppe Alborghetti
4 ,, ,, ,, ,, Alexander Scott
2 ,, ,, ,, ,, Trelawny and some unpublished notes about Byron by Trelawny

9 Letters to Byron from Richard Hoppner
2 ,, ,, ,, ,, Charles F. Barry

and single letters to Byron from Cardinal Rusconi, Dr. Aglietti, Don Gaspare Perelli, Lieutenant Elisei, Felice Tellarini.

14 Letters from Contessa Guiccioli to John Murray and 2 to John Murray Jr.
1 Letter ,, ,, ,, ,, Lega Zambelli
1 ,, ,, ,, ,, ,, Charles F. Barry
1 ,, ,, ,, ,, ,, John Cam Hobhouse

and various letters from Pietro Gamba to Hobhouse, Barry, Barff, Lord Sydney Osborne and Lord Guilford.

BIBLIOGRAPHY

I. BYRON'S WORKS

Letters and Journals, 6 vols, edited by R. E. Prothero (Lord Ernle), Murray, 1898-1904.
Lord Byron's Correspondence, 2 vols, Murray, 1822.
The Works, 7 vols, edited by E. H. Coleridge, Murray, 1898-1904.

II. BIOGRAPHIES OF BYRON AND WORKS RELATING TO BYRON OR CONTESSA GUICCIOLI

ENGLISH

BLESSINGTON, THE COUNTESS OF, *Conversations of Lord Byron with . . .* London, 1834.
DRINKWATER, JOHN, *The Pilgrim of Eternity,* London, 1925.
GALT, JOHN, *The Life of Lord Byron,* London, 1830.
GAMBA, PIETRO, *A narrative of Lord Pyron's last journey to Greece,* Paris, 1825.
GRAY, AUSTIN K., *Teresa, the story of Byron's last mistress,* Harrap, 1948.
HUNT, LEIGH, *Lord Byron and some of his contemporaries,* 2 vols, London, 1828.
JEAFFRESON, JOHN CORDY, *The real Lord Byron,* 2 vols, 1883.
KENNEDY, JAMES, *Conversations on Religion with Lord Byron,* London, 1830.
MAYNE, ETHEL COLBURN, *Byron,* London, 1924.
MAYNE, ETHEL COLBURN, *The Life and Letters of Anne Isabel – Lady Noel Byron,* London, 1929.
MEDWIN, THOMAS, *Journal of the Conversations with Lord Byron,* Paris, 1824.
MILBANKE, RALPH (Lord Lovelace), *Astarte,* privately printed, London, 1921.
MILLINGEN, JULIUS, *Memoirs of the Affairs of Greece . . . with various Anecdotes relating to Lord Byron . . . his last Illness and Death,* 1831.
MOORE, THOMAS, *Life, Letters and Journals of Lord Byron,* London, 1830.
NICOLSON, HAROLD, *Byron, the Last Journey,* Constable, 1924.
PARRY, WILLIAM, *The Last Days of Lord Byron: with His Lordship's opinions on various subjects,* London, 1825.
QUENNELL, PETER, *Byron in Italy,* London, 1941.
ROSS, JANET, *Byron in Pisa,* 'Nineteenth Century', 1891.
SMITH DARBY, MARY R., *My reminiscences of Madame la Marquise de Boissy,* 'The Victorian Magazine', 1873.
TRELAWNY, E. J., *Records of Shelley, Byron and the Author,* 2 vols, London, 1878.
VARÉ, DANIELE, *Byron and the Guiccioli,* 'Quarterly Review', 1934.
VULLIAMY, C. E., *Byron,* London, 1948.

ITALIAN AND FRENCH

BARETTA ANNA, *Byron e i romantici attraverso le relazioni di un emissario segreto del Governo Toscano,* 'Rassegna Nazionale', Firenze, 1911.
CANTONI, FULVIO, *Byron e la Guiccioli a Bologna,* Bologna, 1927.
CANTONI, FULVIO, *La prima dimora di Lord Byron a Bologna,* 1926.
FOA', GIOVANNA, *Lord Byron poeta e carbonaro,* Firenze, 1935.
GUICCIOLI, TERESA (Marquise de Boissy), *Lord Byron jugé par les témoins de sa vie,* Paris, 1868 – Translated 1869.
GUILLAUMIN, HENRY, *Lamartine, Byron et Madame Guiccioli,* 'Revue de Littérature Comparée', Paris, 1939; No. 3.
LAMARTINE, ALPHONSE DE, *Vie de Byron,* 'Le Constitutionnel', September 26th-December 6th, 1863, Paris.

MAUROIS, ANDRÉ, *Byron*, 2 vols, Paris, Grasset, 1930.
MAZZINI, GIUSEPPE, *Byron e Goethe*, Scritti editi ed inediti, vol. XXI, Imola, 1915.
MENEGHETTI, NAZZARENO, *Byron a Venezia*, Fabris, Venezia, 1918.
MORDANI, FILIPPO, *Elogio di Giorgio Byron*, in *Prose*, Bologna, 1847.
MUONI, GUIDO, *La fama del Byron e il Byronismo in Italia*, Milano, 1904.
NICOLINI, GIUSEPPE, *Vita di Byron*, Truffi, Milano, 1835.
RAVA, LUIGI, *Lord Byron e P. B. Shelley a Ravenna e Teresa Guiccioli Gamba*, Roma, 1929.
TRIBOLATI, FELICE, *Lord Byron a Pisa* and *Processo civile di L. B.*, in *Saggi Critici e biografici*, Pisa, 1891.

III. WORKS ON THE HISTORY OF THE CARBONARI AND THE INSURRECTION IN THE ROMAGNA

BANDINI, GINO, *Giornali e Scritti politici della Carboneria Romagnola*, Soc. Ed. Dante Alighieri, Roma, 1908.
Carte Segrete e Atti Ufficiali della Polizia Austriaca in Italia dal 1814 al 1848, Capolago, Tipografia Elvetica, 1851.
COLLETTA, PIETRO, *Storia del Reame di Napoli*, Firenze, Le Monnier, 1846.
DEL CERRO, EMILIO, *Fra le Quinte della Staria*, Torino, Bocca, 1903.
DEL CERRO, EMILIO, *Misteri di Polizia*, Firenze, Salani, 1890.
DITO, ORESTE, *Massoneria, Carboneria ed altre Società Segrete*, Torino, Roux e Viarengo, 1905.
FABBRI, EDOARDO, *Sei anni e due mesi della mia vita*, Memorie a cura di N. Trovanelli, Bontempelli, Roma, 1915.
FARINI, DOMENICO ANTONIO, *Memoria storica sulla Romagna dal 1796 al 1828*, pubblicata da L. Rava, Roma, 1908.
FARINI, LUIGI CARLO, *Storia dello Stato Romano dal 1815 al 1850*, Firenze, Le Monnier, 1850.
GUALTERIO, F. A., *Gli ultimi rivolgimenti italiani-Memorie storiche*, Firenze, Le Monnier, 1852.
LUZIO, ALESSANDRO, *La Massoneria e il Risorgimento Italiano*, Bologna, Zanichelli, 1925.
MAIOLI GIOVANNI E ZAMA PIETRO, *Patrioti e legittimisti delle Romagne*, Roma, 1935.
MASI, ERNESTO, *Cospiratori in Romagna dal 1815 al 1859*, Bologna, Zanichelli, 1891.
Memoirs of the Secret Societies of the South of Italy, Particularly the Carbonari (translated from an Italian manuscript), London, Murray, 1821.
NITTI, FRANCESCO SAVERIO, *Sui moti di Napoli del 1820*. Firenze, 1898.
PIERANTONI, AUGUSTO, *I Carbonari dello Stato Pontificio*, Soc. Ed. Dante Alighieri, Roma, 1910.
RAVA, LUIGI, *Angelo Frignani, Memorie autobiografiche di un patriota romagnolo*, Bologna, Zanichelli, 1899.
RAVA, LUIGI, *La restaurazione pontificia in Romagna*, Bologna, Zanichelli, 1899.
SCARAMELLA, GINO, *Spirito pubblico, società segrete e polizia a Livorno dal 1815 al 1821*, Roma, 1901.
SPADONI, DOMENICO, *Sette, cospirazioni e cospiratori nello Stato Pontificio*, Torino, 1904.
UCCELLINI, PRIMO, *Memorie di un vecchio Carbonaro ravegnano*, Soc. Ed. Dante Alighieri, Roma, 1898.
VICCHI, LEONE, *Vincenzo Monti, le lettere e la politica in Italia dal 1780 al 1830*, Fusignano, 1887.

486

APPENDIX I

IV. VARIOUS

ENGLISH

BLESSINGTON, THE COUNTESS OF, *The Idler in Italy*, London, 1839.

BLUNDEN, EDMUND, *Life of Leigh Hunt*, London, 1946.

Bulletin and Review of the Keats-Shelley Memorial Library, Rome, 1913.

FINLAY, GEORGE, *History of the Greek Revolution*, 1863.

GRYLLS, GLYN R., *Mary Shelley*, London, 1938.

HOBHOUSE, JOHN CAM (Lord Broughton), *Recollections of a long life*, 6 vols, Murray, 1909.

HUNT, LEIGH, *The Autobiography of . . .* 3 vols, London, 1850.

ILCHESTER, THE EARL OF, *The Journal of the Hon. H. E. Fox*, London, 1923.

JERNINGHAM, HUBERT, *Reminiscences of an Attaché*, 1886.

LAUGHTON, J. K., *Memoirs of the Life and Correspondence of Henry Reeve*, London, 1898.

JOYCE, MICHAEL, *My Friend H.*, John Murray, 1948.

MACKAY, CHARLES, *Medora Leigh*, 1869.

MADDEN, R. R., *The literary life and correspondence of the Countess of Blessington*, 3 vols, London, 1855.

MALMESBURY, LORD, *Memoirs of an ex-Minister*, 1884.

MARSHALL, JULIAN, *Life and Letters of Mary Wollstonecraft Shelley*, 2 vols, London, 1889.

MASSINGHAM, H. I., *The friend of Shelley. A memoir of E. J. Trelawny*, London, 1930.

MEDWIN, THOMAS JR., *Revised Life of Shelley*, London, 1913.

MOLLOY, FITZGERALD J., *The most gorgeous Lady Blessington*, London, 1896.

MORGAN, LADY, *Italy*, 3 vols, London, 1824.

MORRISON, ALFRED, *The Collection of Autograph and historical documents formed by . . . 'The Blessington Papers'.* Printed for private circulation, London, 1895.

ROBINSON, HENRY CRABB, *Diary, Memoirs and Correspondence*, 1872.

ROSSETTI ANGELI, HELEN, *Shelley and his friends in Italy*, 1911.

RUSSELL, BERTRAND, *History of Western Philosophy*.

SADLEIR, MICHAEL, *Blessington-D'Orsay, a Masquerade*, Constable, 1947.

SHELLEY, MARY W., *The Letters of . . .* ed. by F. L. Jones, Oklahoma, 1944.

SHELLEY, P. B., *Works*, ed. by H. B. Forman, 1876-1880.

SMILES, SAMUEL, *Memoirs and correspondence of the late Murray*, 2 vols, 1891.

TRELAWNY, E. J., *Letters of . . .* ed. by H. B. Forman, 1910.

WHITE, NEWMAN IVEY, *Shelley*, 2 vols, Secker and Warburg, 1947.

WILLIS, N. P., *Pencilling by the Way*, 1850.

WILSON, HARRIET, *Memoirs of herself and others*, 1929.

ITALIAN AND FRENCH

ALBICINI, CESARE, *Carlo Pepoli-Saggio Storico*, Bologna, 1888.

BRETON, PAUL, *Mémoires du Marquis de Boissy*, Paris, 1876.

CHIARINI, GIUSEPPE, *Donne e poeti*, Roma, 1885.

FOSCOLO, UGO, *Epistolario*, Firenze, 1850-62.

GIORDANI, PIETRO, *Opere*, Milano, 1854-63.

GIRONI, PRIMO, *Il Teatro Comunale di Ravenna nel secolo XIX*, Bologna, 1934.

GUERRAZZI, F. D., *Memorie*, Livorno, 1848.

GUICCIOLI, ALESSANDRO, *I Guiccioli – Memorie di una famiglia patrizia*, Bologna, 1934.

LAMARTINE, ALPHONSE DE, *Cours familier de littérature*, Paris, 1857.
LEOPARDI, MONALDO, *Autobiografia di . . .* pubblicata da A. Avoli, Recanati, 1891.
MALAMANI, VITTORIO, *Isabella Teotochi Albrizzi, i suoi amici, il suo tempo*, Torino, 1882.
MALAMANI, VITTORIO, *Il Settecento veneziano*, Roma-Torino, 1891.
MISEROCCHI, LORENZO, *Ravenna e i Ravennati nel secolo XIX*, Ravenna, 1927.
MISEROCCHI, LORENZO, *Musica e teatro in Ravenna dal 1800 al 1920*, Ravenna, 1921.
PASOLINI, PIER DESIDERIO, *Ravenna e le sue grandi memorie*, Roma, 1912.
PERA, FRANCESCO, *Curiosita livornesi*, Livorno, 1888.
PRAZ, MARIO, *La Carne, la Morte e il Diavolo*, Milano, 1930.
STENDHAL (Henry Beyle), *Correspondance inédite*, Paris, 1855.
STENDHAL (Henry Beyle), *Rome, Naples et Florence*, Paris, 1854.
UCCELLINI, PRIMO, *Dizionario Storico di Ravenna*, Ravenna, 1855.
VIVIANI DELLA ROBBIA, ENRICA, *Vita di una donna (L'Emilia di Shelley)*, Firenze, 1936.
ZUCCONI, ANGELA, *Ludovico Innamorato*, Milano, 1944.

NOTE. Signora Maria Borgese's *L'Appassionata di Byron* (Milano, Garzanti 1949) containing some of the same material from the Gamba Papers, appeared only when my book was already in proof.

COMPLETE LIST OF BYRON'S HITHERTO UNPUBLISHED LETTERS IN THE GAMBA COLLECTION

NOTES TO THE TEXT

Whenever no reference is given, the letter or document comes from the Gamba Papers.

'Vie' – Teresa Guiccioli, 'Vie de Lord Byron en Italie'.

'Moore' is abbreviation for *Letters and Journals of Lord Byron with Notice of his Life* by Thomas Moore, London, Murray 1830.

'*L.J.*' is abbreviation for *Letters and Journals* edited by Rowland E. Prothero, 6 vols, London, Murray, 1898-1901.

'*Correspondence*' is abbreviation for *Lord Byron's Correspondence* edited by John Murray, London, Murray, 1922.

NOTES

INTRODUCTION

1. September 21st, 1827.
2. Unpublished letter, belonging to Sir John Murray, June 2nd, 1858.
3. Elliot Papers.
4. *Letters and Journals*, V, p. 79. To John Murray, September 23rd, 1820.
5. Ibid., V, p. 70. To Moore, August 31st, 1820.
6. *Correspondence*, II, p. 109. To Douglas Kinnaird.
7. Journal of Lady Byron – quoted by MAUROIS, *Byron*, II, p. 17.
8. LOVELACE, *Astarte*, p. 308. October 5th, 1821.
9. Byron to Augusta Leigh, July 26th, 1819. Pierpont Morgan Library, New York.
10. MAUROIS, *Byron*, I, p. 251.
11. HUNT, *Lord Byron and some of his contemporaries*, I, p. 68.
12. MAYNE, *Byron*, p. 350.
13. *I Guiccioli*, I, p. 18 and II, p. 88.
14. DRINKWATER, *The Pilgrim of Eternity*, p. 293.
15. HUNT, op. cit., I, p. 68.
16. *L.J.*, V, p. 403. Ravenna, May 21st, 1821.
17. MENEGHETTI, *Lord Byron a Venezia*, p. 166. There is no other record of this incident.
18. RUSSELL, *History of Western Philosophy*, p. 776.
19. *L.J.*, V, p. 205.
20. Ravenna Journal, January 11th, 1821. *L.J.*, V, pp. 163-4.
21. RUSSELL, op. cit., p. 780.
22. LADY BLESSINGTON, *Conversations of Lord Byron*, p. 402.
23. *L.J.*, IV, p. 62.
24. Ibid., V, p. 182.

PROLOGUE

1. Secret Archives of the Vatican. Fondo della Sacra Romana Rota. Uditore Bonini, 1843.
2. Guiccioli, who was born in 1761, was 57. As to Teresa's age, it was not – as she subsequently affirmed – 16, but 18. Every effort on the part of the Gamba family to find her birth certificate or a record of her baptism, has failed. But from the dates of birth of her brothers and sisters, she must have been born either in 1799 or at the beginning of 1800.
3. One of these school fellows, Marianna Bacinetti, who in later years became the Marchesa Florenzi of Perugia and the mistress of King Louis of Bavaria, wrote: 'She was with me at S. Chiara, but I am not at all fond of her, because she is so proud, and I think heartless; her feelings are ambition and vanity, and I do not think her capable of loving, but only of saying so.' Nevertheless she granted her beauty, 'plenty of intelligence and knowledge, but affected even in this. Her body is her only reality'. ZUCCONI, *Lodovico innamorato*, p. 199.
4. *I Guiccioli*, I, p. 18.
5. Ibid., I, p. 22.
6. Report of Conte de'Medici Spada, 1827. Museo Civico Correr, Venice. Protocollo Polizia N.4.
7. FARINI, *La Romagna dal 1796 al 1828*.
8. MONALDO LEOPARDI, *Autobiografia*.
9. *I Guiccioli*, I, p. 3.
10. Unpublished passage in a letter from Byron to Hobhouse dated May 17th, 1819. The Vice Legate's report, already quoted, refers to the rumour, but carefully adds that it has no foundation beyond gossip.
11. July 1st, 1812. From unpublished papers of the Archbishop Antonio Codronchi, in the Pasolini family archives.

12. Guiccioli was then living at Forlì.

13. The sentences from Teresa's letters to her husband are taken from *I Guiccioli*, pp. 18-23 and from quotations in a law-suit between Teresa and her stepdaughter Livia Saracco Riminaldi. Secret Archives of the Vatican. Fondo della Sacra Romana Rota, Uditore Bonini, 1843.

14. *I Guiccioli*, I, p. 20.

15. Letter to the parish priest of Santo Stefano, in Venice, in 1826.

16. Statement by Teresa to the Tribunal of the Sacra Rota.

17. *I Guiccioli*, p. 55.

18. 'Vie', p. 299.

19. Statement by Teresa to her advocate Armellini, 1841.

20. RANGONE, Papers in the Biblioteca dell'Archiginnasio, Bologna.

21. 'Vie', p. 610.

22. RANGONE, op. cit.

23. Ibid.

24. The passages from Mengaldo's Diary are quoted from Meneghetti's *Lord Byron a Venezia*. The Diary itself (which is unpublished), was left by Mengaldo at his death to his friend Abate Jacopo Bernardi.

25. STENDHAL, *Correspondance Inédite*, p. 167. December 22nd, 1820.

26. *L.J.*, V, p. 248. Later on, when he had quarrelled with Mengaldo, Byron's comments were even less kind: 'I wish you had heard', he wrote to Scott, 'the account he had left at Ferrara of the swimming-match; *you* were sunk and omitted altogether and he had passed the Rialto and was only beaten by me by some accident. We knew him to be a liar before – but I thought that the complete drossing we both gave him in the swimming-match would have silenced him on that score.' Byron to Scott, July 31st, 1819. Pierpont Morgan Library, New York.

27. Nicolini's *Life of Byron*, vol. II, p. 126, tells us that the Casino was at Santa Maria Zobenigo (Santa Maria del Giglio).

28. *L.J.*, IV, p. 307.

29. MENEGHETTI, op. cit., p. 163. This cross, which was given to Byron by a soldier who had picked it up on the field of Waterloo, inspired Byron to write his 'Ode on the Star of the Legion of Honour' – and Louis XVIII, after reading the poem, sent him a message, granting him the right to wear it. He did so, however, only twice: when entertaining a Greek who had come to ask his help for the cause of his country's independence, and at a ball in Palazzo Mocenigo. It can now be seen in the Museo Correr in Venice.

30. Byron to Alexander Scott, July 31st, 1819. Pierpont Morgan Library, New York.

31. *L.J.*, V, p. 435. *Detached Thoughts*, No. 53.

32. GIORDANI, *Opere*, vol. IV.

33. Of this bust, Byron wrote: [It] 'is without exception, to my mind the most perfectly beautiful of human conceptions, and far beyond my ideas of human execution.'

> In this beloved marble view
>> Above the works and thoughts of Man,
> What nature *could*, but *would not*, do,
>> And beauty and Canova *can*!
> Beyond Imagination's power,
>> Beyond the Bard's defeated art,
> With Immortality her dower,
>> Behold the *Helen* of the *heart*!
>> *L.J.*, IV, p. 15.

34. 'Vie', p. 46.

35. Byron to Alexander Scott, July 24th, 1819. Pierpont Morgan Library, New York. Scott answered: 'The "adoration" was a term made use of by the old Benzoni, when talking of your disgust with said V[enetian]s, which reached her through Mengaldo, I suppose.' Scott to Byron, July 26th, 1819 U published letter belonging to Sir John Murray.

36. *L.J.*, IV, p. 256. To Webster.

CHAPTER I

1. 'Vie', pp. 51-2.
2. Elliot Papers, 'Confession of Countess T. G. G. to Count A. G.' The casino appears to have been the one at S. Maria Zobenigo.
3. 'Vie', p. 64.
4. *Correspondence*, II, p. 107.
5. Rangone Papers, Bologna.
6. April 24th, 1819. Suppressed passage.
7. May 26th, 1819. From the unpublished letters to be published in *Byron, a Self-Portrait*, the new two-volume edition of Byron's Correspondence, Murray, London.
8. 'Vie', pp. 66-7. This story is also told by Rangone as an example of Teresa's lack of decorum.
9. 'Vie', p. 70.
10. Unpublished letter belonging to Sir John Murray.
11. *L.J.*, IV, p. 319.
12. August 18th, 1819. From an unpublished letter belonging to Sir John Murray.
13. TASSO, *Gerusalemme Liberata*, Canto XVI, stanza xv.
14. This letter is written in a clear copy-book hand, very unlike Byron's hurried scrawl when he knew Teresa better. It may be the fair copy of a rough draft.
15. 'Not to admire is all the art I know.' *Don Juan*, Canto IV, stanza CI.
16. 'Vie', p. 81.
17. Byron wrote to Murray later on that Teresa had been 'very unwell after her miscarriage which occurred in May last at Pomposa on her way home from Lombardy [*sic*] . . . I fear that neither the medical remedies – nor some recent attempts of our own to repair at least the miscarriage – have done any great good'. Unpublished passage in letter dated June 29th, 1819.
18. From an unpublished letter, May 15th, 1819, to be published in *Byron, a Self-Portrait*, the new two-volume edition of Byron's Correspondence, Murray, London.
19. From an unpublished letter, May 26th, 1819, to be published in *Byron, a Self-Portrait*, the new two-volume edition of Byron's Correspondence, Murray, London.
20. The friend was Leigh Hunt, and the promise was kept by Byron later on, when he was living in Ravenna, for on July 20th of that year, he wrote to Lady Byron: 'I have tried to discover for Leigh Hunt some traces of Francesca but, except for her father Guido's tomb and the mere notice of the fact in the Latin commentary of Benvenuto d'Imola in MS. in the Library, I could discover nothing for him.' LOVELACE, *Astarte*, p. 292.
21. From the unpublished letter dated May 26th, 1819, to be published in *Byron, a Self-Portrait*, the new two-volume edition of Byron's Correspondence, Murray, London.
22. *Correspondence*, II, p. 109. To Kinnaird, April 24th, 1819.
23. 'Vie', p. 78.
24. April 27th [1819]. Unpublished letter belonging to Sir John Murray.
25. *L.J.*, IV, p. 301. To John Murray, May 18th, 1819.
26. LOVELACE, *Astarte*, p. 82. May 17th, 1819.
27. Ibid., p. 84.
28. *Correspondence*, II, p. 109. To Kinnaird, April 24th, 1819.
29. Byron to Hobhouse, May 17th, 1819. Unpublished passage.
30. *L.J.*, IV, pp. 307-8. June 2nd, 1819.
31. Ibid., IV, p. 313. June 7th, 1819.
32. Ibid., IV, p. 310. June 5th, 1819.

CHAPTER 2

1. It was said to be a copy of Napoleon's, and cost £500.
2. MISEROCCHI, *Ravenna e i ravennati nel secolo XIX*.
3. This version of the story, which Teresa also told to Moore, in somewhat less detail, is from the 'Vie', pp. 121-2.

4. Note 9 has disappeared; in its place there is a sheet of paper bearing the words 'missing'. The folded sheet of paper which had contained this note bears, in Teresa's handwriting, the words '9th Note'. Note 14 was dated January 29th, 1820, and has accordingly been placed among the letters of that year. Note 19 is also missing. In its place there is a sheet on which Teresa has written '19th Note. At B[ologna]. An unreasonable jealousy. *Destroyed*.'

5. Inscribed by Teresa: 'His first note, on arriving in Ravenna. Can be shown.'
6. 'Second note – Can be shown.'
7. 'Third note. – Can be shown.'
8. 'Vie', p. 128.
9. Ibid., p. 133.
10. RANGONE, op. cit.
11. *L.J.*, IV, pp. 318-19.
12. 'Vie', p. 134.
13. 'Fourth Note – Can be shown.'
14. 'Fifth Note.'
15. 'Vie', p. 134. Teresa, who knew very little, if any, English at this time, must have read the poem either in a French translation or in the first Italian translation by Magenta, Leoni and Martelli.
16. 'Sixth Note. Can be shown.' The first two sentences, with their note of exasperation, are omitted in Teresa's quotation of the rest of this letter in the 'Vie'.
17. 'Vie', p. 137.
18. The dedication is dated June 26th, not 16th – but Teresa was always a little hazy about dates. In 1822, when Murray published the 17 vol. edition of Byron's *Works*, he sent Teresa the proofs of his note concerning this dedication, asking for her approval. 'Tis for you to speak and be obeyed.' The note – which Teresa considered 'so very delicate and modest' that she hoped it would be included in all future editions – confined itself to quoting Teresa's own version of the poem's origin. 'On my departure from Venice, Lord Byron had promised to come and see me in Ravenna. Dante's tomb, the classical pine wood, the relics of antiquity which are to be found in that place, afforded a sufficient pretext for me to invite him to come and for him to accept my invitation . . . Being deprived at that time of his books, his horses, and all that occupied him in Venice, I begged him to gratify me by writing something on the subject of Dante, and with his usual facility and rapidity he composed his Prophecy.'
19. 'Not translated, but betrayed.' 'Vie', p. 146.
20. MOORE, II, p. 228.
21. 'Seventh Note. Can be shown.'
22. 'Eighth Note. Can be shown.'
23. Byron to Alexander Scott, June 20th, 1819. Pierpont Morgan Library, New York.
24. Ibid.
25. 'Tenth Note. Can be shown.'
26. 'Eleventh Note.'
27. *Correspondence*, II, p. 118.
28. The words italicized were added later, in a different ink.
29. 'Twelfth Note'.
30. 'Thirteenth Note.'
31. *L.J.*, IV, p. 323.
32. *Correspondence*, II, p. 121.
33. June 8th, 1819.
34. June 15th, 1819.
35. July 6th, 1819. All three are unpublished letters, belonging to Sir John Murray.
36. *L.J.*, IV, pp. 325-6. To Hoppner, July 2nd, 1819.
37. Ibid., IV, p. 321. June 29th, 1819.
38. June 29th, 1819. Pierpont Morgan Library, New York.
39. MALAMANI, op. cit., p. 41.
40. FILIPPO MORDANI, *Prose*.
41. *Don Juan*, Canto III, stanza cv.
42. The Sonnet was written by Teresa for the wedding of her cousin Marchesa

Teresa Cavalli to Count Francesco Sassi, urging the young bride to be as constant as
she had been herself:

> . . . Ed al mio Sposo qui dinnanzi a Dio
> Eternamente mi legai con Fede.
> E' saldo nel suo giuro sì il cor mio,
> Che d'adamante alla forza non cede. . . .

So wrote Teresa, and in the margin Byron commented, '150 volte' [150 times] adding:
'ask Hobhouse to translate this for you – and tell him the reason . . .' July 26th, 1819.
Pierpoint Morgan Library, New York.

43. 'Vie', p. 151
44. MISEROCCHI, op. cit.
45. 'Vie', p. 153.
46. RANGONE, *Cronaca.*
47.

> Of Lord enamoured, all the world now knows,
> The wife her falcon has a Cuckoo made,
> While still in ignorance the old bird goes
> That low he now should hang his horned head.
>
> The very stones start laughing when they hear
> Tales of the Cuckold and his Lady, too –
> Still more about the cures he gets his dear
> From Venice and from London and Perù.

Teresa does not give the verses, but they are quoted in Rangone's *Cronaca.* For their
translation I am indebted to Mr. K. Walter.

48. 'Vie', pp. 268-71.
49. July 1st, 1819. New York Public Library. Berg collection. Copy in the
Public Library of Forlì.
50. From an unpublished letter to be published in *Byron, a Self-Portrait*, the new
two-volume edition of Byron's Correspondence, Murray, London.
51. July 9th, 1819. From an unpublished letter belonging to Sir John Murray.
Alborghetti's letters to Byron are all in English.
52. Unpublished letter in the Public Library at Forlì.
53. 'Vie', pp. 268-71. Undated.
54. June 16th, 1819. From an unpublished letter belonging to Sir John Murray.
55. June 29th, 1819. From an unpublished letter belonging to Sir John Murray.
56. *L.J.*, IV, p. 317. To Hoppner, June 20th, 1819.
57. July 1st, 1819. From an unpublished letter belonging to Sir John Murray.
58. Ibid.
59. Byron to Alexander Scott, July 7th, 1819. Pierpont Morgan Library, New
York.
60. July 9th, 1819. Pierpont Morgan Library.
61. Pierpont Morgan Library.
62. July 31st, 1819. Pierpont Morgan Library.
63. July 24th, 1819. Pierpont Morgan Library.
64. July 23rd, 1819. The letter is unsigned, a somewhat belated precaution.
Pierpont Morgan Library.
65. 'Vie', p. 167.
66. October 22nd, 1819. *L.J.*, IV, p. 361, 'To reason with men in such a situation', Byron added, 'is like reasoning with a drunkard in his cups – the only answer
you will get from him is, that he is sober, and you are drunk'.
67. October 23rd, 1819. Unpublished letter belonging to Sir John Murray.
68. July 31st, 1819. Pierpont Morgan Library, New York.
69. July 5th, 1819. From an unpublished letter, to be published in *Byron, a Self-
Portrait*, the new two-volume edition of Byron's Correspondence, Murray, London.
70. Ibid.
71. July 24th, 1819. Pierpont Morgan Library.
72. July 26th, 1819. Unpublished letter belonging to Sir John Murray.
73. Dated only 'July'. Unpublished letter belonging to Sir John Murray. In
this letter, as in the following one, Contessa Benzoni uses the intimate *tu*. Byron

refers to this letter in a letter to Scott. 'She writes that Madame Dempsen has carried you off to joke at Scaccs' [*sic*].

74. July 27th, 1819. Unpublished letter belonging to Sir John Murray.
75. 'Fifteenth Note.'
76. 'Vie', pp. 189-90.
77. This letter is also published in *I Guiccioli*, p. 26, in English.
78. 'Imploro pace.' At Ferrara, on his way to Bologna, Byron had visited the burial-ground at the Certosa and had read two of the epitaphs on the tombs:

MARTINI LUIGI
IMPLORA PACE

LUCREZIA PISANI
IMPLORA ETERNA QUIETE.

'It appears to me,' he commented, 'that these two and three words comprise and compress all that can be said on the subject. They contain doubt, hope and humility. They have had enough of life – they want nothing but rest – they implore it, and 'eterna quiete'. *L.J.*, IV, p. 310.

CHAPTER 3

1. *L.J.*, IV, p. 338.
2. Even this piece of information was not thought too trivial to be reported to the police. 'I am assured that an old servant of the Contessa Guiccioli has been ordered by her to get certain articles of furniture, and that he has bought some from various second-hand shops, and particularly from Agostino Montanari ... It would seem, moreover, that the aforesaid Lord has paid for the articles.' Archivio di Stato di Bologna, Police Reports, August 22nd, 1819.
3. State Archives, Rome. Miscellanea di Carte politiche Busta 50. Fasc. 17111.
4. Letter to the police in Ravenna from Mons. Tiberio Pacca, the Governor of Rome, referring to the 'political correspondence of Cav. Guiccioli with some members of the neighbouring Tuscan State'. May 1st, 1819. GUALTIERIO, *Gli ultimi rivolgimenti italiani*, I, p. 254.
5. BARETTA, *Byron e i Romantici*, pp. 6-12, and DITO, *Massoneria, Carboneria ed altre società segrete*, p. 304.
6. Vide LUZIO's chapter on *Carboneria e Massoneria*, in *La Massoneria e il Risorgimento Italiano*.
7. LUZIO, op. cit., p. 165.
8. DITO, op. cit., pp. 141-51.
9. *Memoirs of the Secret Societies of the South of Italy, particularly the Carbonari*.
10. DITO, op. cit., p. 302.
11. Archivio di Stato, Bologna.
12. From a report sent to Valtancoli by a correspondent of his in the Masonic Lodge of Milan. State Archives, Florence. The 'Romantici' were the members of the Società Romantica = Roma Antica.
13. Valtancoli report.
14. Archivio di Stato, Bologna.
15. RANGONE, *Cronaca*.
16. *L.J.*, IV, p. 348. August 24th, 1819.
17. Ibid., IV, p. 340. August 12th, 1819.
18. 'Vie', p. 190. 'Already once before', Teresa adds, 'at Ravenna while watching Alfieri's *Filippo*, his nerves were touched and one could perceive tears in his eyes. But this time the impression was certainly strong – for he himself admitted that he still felt its effects fifteen days later.'
19. 'Vie', p. 196.
20. From a letter written by Hoppner to *The Athenaeum*, May 22nd, 1869.
21. Mrs. Hoppner to Mrs. Shelley, Venice, January 6th, 1819. From R. GLYN GRYLLS, *Mary Shelley*. Appendix C, p. 281.
22. Hoppner to Byron, June 29th, 1819. Unpublished letter belonging to Sir John Murray.

23. Byron to Alexander Scott, August 22nd, 1819. Pierpont Morgan Library. Edgecombe was the clerk of the British Consulate in Venice, but was also keeping some of Byron's accounts.

24. Alexander Scott to Byron, July 1st, 1819. Unpublished letter belonging to Sir John Murray.

25. Byron to Scott. August 28th, 1819. Pierpont Morgan Library.

26. LOVELACE, *Astarte*, p. 294.

27. *L.J.*, V, p. 435. Michele Leoni had translated, in addition to the greater part of Shakespeare's tragedies, the 4th Canto of *Childe Harold*. Mons. Mezzofanti, who later became a Cardinal, was the Librarian of the Bologna Library.

28. STENDHAL, *Rome, Naples et Florence*, 1854, p. 117.

29. *L.J.*, IV, p. 349.

30. *Correspondence*, II, pp. 123-4.

31. MOORE, II, p. 240.

32. *L.J.*, IV, p. 350. August 25th, 1819 (quoted from Moore).

33. DE STAEL, *Corinne*, Italian translation published by Guglielmo Piatti, 1808, p. 81.

34. Ibid., p. 81.

35. Ibid., Chap. V, Book 18. This note too is quoted by Moore. Later on Teresa complained that both the letter and the notes in *Corinne* had been shown to Moore not by herself, but by Mary Shelley. 'Mrs. Shelley, having been allowed in Pisa to read what Byron had written in a volume of *Corinne*, copied it all, and gave it, after Byron's death, to Moore, together with other documents. We will not express a judgment on such conduct. Mrs. Shelley was a woman of great merit, and no doubt did not consider that she was committing a double indelicacy.' 'Vie', p. 202.

36. 'Vie', p. 208.

37. Ibid., p. 211.

38. *L.J.*, IV, p. 344. August 12th, 1819.

39. Statement made to the Sacra Rota Tribunal by Teresa in 1841. Secret Archives of the Vatican. Fondo della Sacra Romana Rota, Uditore Bonini, 1842. The contemporary police reports told the story rather differently: 'It is said that Sig. Cavalier Guiccioli intends to place him [Byron] near his wife, in order to persuade him to expend some money and to associate with himself in certain commercial ventures ... Some say that the Cavalier Guiccioli is very jealous of his wife; if that were so, his step in taking the Englishman into his house is incomprehensible, unless the passion for profit be stronger than that of jealousy.' Archivio di Stato, Bologna.

40. 'Vie', p. 215.

41. 'Confession of Countess T. G. G. to Count A. G.'

42. From the account that Teresa gave to Moore, op. cit., II, p. 246. But all the rest of the description of the journey, from the much fuller account of the 'Vie'.

43. 'Vie', pp. 243-8.

44. MOORE, II, p. 259.

45. *Correspondence*, II, p. 126. November 16th, 1819.

46. Secret Archives of the Vatican. Fondo della Sacra Romana, Rota Uditore Bonini, 1842. Summarium No. 3839-8. Teresa's own 'Confession' confirmed the statement: 'Hardly had I arrived in Venice, than Lega turned up to take me there, but I found excuses for postponing, and stayed with Byron.'

47. *I Guiccioli*, I, p. 28. Venice, September 15th, 1819.

48. 'Vie', p. 258.

49. *Don Juan*, Canto III, stanza LXXIV.

50. The originals of three of Fanny's letters to Teresa, and of one later letter from her to Byron (January 21st, 1820) are among the papers given by Sir Rennell Rodd to the Keats-Shelley Memorial Library, Rome. The others are from the Elliot Papers.

51. A petition sent by Guiccioli to the Pope in 1822 refers to this correspondence: '*L'amico Lega* replied to the most affectionate interest of Guiccioli in his wife's health, and informed him of her state of health and of what she required, according to what he heard from the Englishman's cunning doctor.' Elliot Papers.

52. Byron, who had already entered upon his cheese-paring period, followed this boring business with great interest, and wrote about it all to Hoppner, not forgetting the question of the comb! It is not clear at what point Lega, who was still, apparently,

in Guiccioli's service, passed into Byron's but by the next spring we find him firmly established there, and there he faithfully remained, and was still muddling the accounts in Metaxata.

53. *I Guiccioli*, I, p. 29. September 27th, 1819. The cuts in this letter are by the editor of the Memoirs.

54. Ibid., I, p. 30. La Mira, September 30th, 1819.

55. 'Vie', p. 284.

56. From a pencilled note on the back of a letter from Carlo Pepoli to Teresa in London (December 1832). Mrs. Beecher Stowe's attack on Byron in *The Atlantic Monthly* appeared in September 1869.

57. 'Vie', p. 292.

58. Byron to Alexander Scott – La Mira, October 2nd, 1819. Pierpont Morgan Library, New York.

59. *I Guiccioli*, I, p. 31. October 3rd, 1819. Of this letter – which apparently was shown to her – Fanny wrote to Teresa: 'Your letter to the Cavaliere your husband was just what it should be, and no doubt will make a great impression on him, if his indifference has not taken away from him his senses.' Keats-Shelley Memorial Library, Rome.

60. Ibid., I, p. 32.

61. MOORE, II, p. 267.

62. 'Vie', p. 216.

63. Ibid., p. 297.

64. Ibid., p. 300.

65. MOORE, II, p. 274. One sentence is mistranslated by Moore – he translates 'quando ti sei ben sfogato a ridere' as 'whenever you feel *inclined* to laugh'.

66. *L.J.*, IV, pp. 371-2. October 29th, 1819. To Hoppner.

67. *Don Juan*, III, VII.

68. MOORE, I, p. 641.

69. *L.J.*, IV, p. 357. To Hobhouse, October 3rd, 1819.

70. Autobiographical Statement by Teresa for her advocate.

71. 'Vie', p. 318.

72. Secret Archives of the Vatican. Fondo della Sacra Romana Rota, Uditore Bonini, Summarium 3839-9. Teresa does not refer to this letter in the 'Vie', nor is it quoted in *I Guiccioli*.

73. 'Vie', p. 317.

74. *L.J.*, IV, p. 375.

75. 'Vie', p. 318.

76. Ibid., p. 320.

77. *L.J.*, IV, p. 375. To Murray, November 8th, 1819.

78. *Correspondence*, II, pp. 126-7. Letter to Douglas Kinnaird, November 16th, 1819.

79. *I Guiccioli*, I, p. 33.

80. *Correspondence*, II, p. 129. To Hobhouse, November 20th, 1819.

81. Ibid., II, p. 127. To Kinnaird, November 16th, 1819.

82. Ibid., II, p. 130. To Kinnaird, November 21st.

83. Ibid., II, p. 128. To Kinnaird.

84. Ibid., II, p. 127. November 16th, 1819.

85. Ibid., II, p. 130. November 21st, 1819.

86. Unpublished letter belonging to Sir John Murray.

87. Ibid.

88. *Correspondence*, II, p. 130.

89. Moore quotes this letter as the second half of the letter quoted on p. 136.

90. Moore gives the Italian text of this letter, but mistranslates one sentence. It is, Non basta lasciarti per dei motivi dei quali tu eri persuasa (non molto tempo fa)', which he renders as 'It is not enough that I must leave you from motives of which *ere long you will be convinced*'.

91. LADY BLESSINGTON, *Conversations of Lord Byron*, pp. 141-7.

92. Unpublished letter in English belonging to Sir John Murray. Undated, but obviously written after Byron's death.

93. *Correspondence*, II, p. 128.

94. LOVELACE, *Astarte*, p. 297. December 4th, 1819.

95.   Ibid., p. 90.
96.   Ibid., pp. 92-3.
97.   This letter is dated November 6th, but it must be December 6th, for on November 8th the Guicciolis were still in Venice (vide Byron to Murray, November 8th. *L.J.*, IV, p. 375). Moreover it fits with the undated fragment from Fanny on the next page, and with Byron's letter to Murray at this date. On December 4th he was still writing about his departure; on December 10th he had changed his mind, and would not go. (*L.J.*, IV, pp. 383-4.)
98.   It is plain, from the style and content, that the writer is Fanny, but the original letter is missing, and we have only this fragment, quoted both by Teresa in the 'Vie', and by Moore.
99.   *L.J.*, IV, p. 385. Footnote quoting Blackwood's *Edinburgh Magazine* (August 1819).
100.   Ibid., IV. December 10th, 1819.
101.   Ibid., IV, p. 380. This letter, when it got to England, was sent on by Murray to Augusta, and then from Augusta to Annabella.
102.   'Vie', p. 339.
103.   *L.J.*, IV, p. 389. December 23rd, 1819.
104.   Ibid., IV, p. 384. December 10th, 1819.
105.   *Correspondence*, II, p. 132. December 10th, 1819.
106.   *L.J.*, IV, p. 391. This letter is quoted by Teresa in the 'Vie', but the original is not among the Gamba Papers.

CHAPTER 4

1.   *L.J.*, IV, p. 398. January 20th, 1820.
2.   Ibid., IV, p. 393. 'The Marquis is her uncle and naturally considers me as her relation.'
3.   'Vie', p. 348.
4.   Ibid., p. 350.
5.   *I Guiccioli*, I, pp. 40-1.
6.   From a draft in her own writing among Teresa's papers. A later statement of Teresa's to the Vatican Tribunal repeats the same story.
7.   'Vie', p. 352.
8.   RANGONE, op. cit.
9.   See 'Vie', pp. 350-2.
10.   'Vie', pp. 375-6.
11.   Byron to Augusta Leigh, July 26th, 1819. Pierpont Morgan Library, New York.
12.   Undated, but by the note-paper it appears to belong to this set of letters.
13.   The date is G° 10, but the reference to the assemblies, which took place only in the winter months, enables us to fix it as *January*, not June.
14.   This letter also is undated – but was almost certainly written in January 1820, since we know that Byron moved out of the Albergo Imperiale to the Palazzo Guiccioli at the end of the month.
15.   January 21st, 1820. Keats-Shelley Memorial Library.
16.   January 17th, 1820. Unpublished letter belonging to Sir John Murray.
17.   Undated but written at the end of January or early February, since it was then that Byron quarrelled with Guiccioli about a carriage and some furniture which he had ordered from Florence. 'Vie', pp. 368-73.
18.   This letter also is written with the formal *voi*. The month is missing from the date, but from the context of this and the two following letters, all written on the same kind of note-paper, it is presumably January.
19.   Prose fragment – 'An Italian Carnival' – written in February 1823, probably for *The Liberal*. *L.J.*, VI, appendix VIII.
20.   Ibid., IV, pp. 427-8. To Hoppner, March 31st, 1820.

21. Byron to Kinnaird, May 3rd, 1820. From an unpublished letter to be published in *Byron, a Self-Portrait*, the new two-volume edition of Byron's Correspondence, Murray, London.

22. *L.J.*, IV, p. 408. February 21st, 1820. Murray had written asking Byron to send him 'a volume of manners, etc., in Italy' but the poet, with unexpected delicacy of feeling, refused. 'I have lived in their houses and in the heart of their families, sometimes merely as *amico di casa* and sometimes as *Amico di cuore* of the *Dama*, and in neither case do I feel myself authorized in making a book of them.'

23. *Correspondence*, II, p. 136. To Hobhouse, March 3rd, 1820.

24. *L.J.*, IV, p. 408. February 21st, 1820.

25. Ibid., IV, p. 409.

26. This and the following two notes are undated, but all, from their context and their wording, appear to have been written at this time. The 'damned novel' was *Glenarvon*, by Lady Caroline Lamb, which apparently Byron had lent to Teresa. Of this copy Edward Henry Fox's *Journal* said, in 1829: 'I found him [Fitzharris] slightly clothed reading T. G.'s copy of *Glenarvon*, of which the history is droll. Lady C. Lamb gave it to Henry Webster. He gave it to Madame Martinetti. She sent it to Lord Byron. T. G. became possessed of it after his death, and now it has been read by each of her admirers. Edward Henry Fox, *Journal*, p. 339.

27. Undated – but written on the same kind of paper as that of March 5th.

28. *L.J.*, IV, p. 409. February 21st, 1820.

29. Journal of Lady Byron. Quoted by MAUROIS, *Byron*, II, p. 13.

30. Undated – but it appears to be about Teresa's 'decision', referred to in her letters of March 4th and 5th, and is written on the same kind of paper as that of March 5th.

31. Undated, the page is torn. But both this note and the following one seem to refer to the same incident and are written on the same paper as the letter of March 4th. The familiar *tu* was first used, and then replaced by the formal *voi*.

32. Undated – see note to preceding letter.

33. *L.J.*, IV, p. 415.

34. HARRIETTE WILSON, *Memoirs*, p. 612.

35. Byron to Kinnaird, May 3rd, 1820. From an unpublished letter, to be published in *Byron, a Self-Portrait*, the new two-volume edition of Byron's Correspondence, Murray, London.

36. *L.J.*, V, pp. 90-1.

37. FARINI, *La Romagna dal 1796 al 1828*; and UCCELLINI, *Memorie di un vecchio Carbonaro ravegnano*. The extent to which the Church interfered with the private lives of citizens is indicated by the decree by which, only a few years later, Cardinal Rivarola required that all political suspects under police surveillance should report themselves to the police every fortnight, and should offer proof that they had fulfilled their religious duties in Holy Week, under penalty of being thrown into prison for three years.

38. STENDHAL, *Correspondance inédite*, I, p. 141.

39. *L.J.*, V, pp. 19-20. To Murray, April 23rd, 1820.

40. Ibid., V, pp. 42-3. To Moore, June 9th, 1820. 'If there turns up anything,' he wrote to Hobhouse, 'I may, perhaps, "wink and hold out mine iron" with the rest; or at any rate be a well-wishing spectator of a push against those rascally Austrians.' *Correspondence*, II, p. 144.

41. February 5th, 1820. From the unpublished letters of the Archbishop Antonio Codronchi, in the Archives of the Pasolini family at Ravenna.

42. 'Vie', pp. 388-90.

43. Ibid., pp. 404-6.

44. Secret Archives of the Vatican. Fondo della Sacra Romana Rota, Uditore Bonini, 1842.

45. HARRIETTE WILSON, *Memoirs*, p. 614.

46. Secret Archives of the Vatican. Fondo della Sacra Romana Rota, Uditore Bonini, 1842. Summarium No. 3839-11.

47. This was the daily 'carriage parade' in the Corso, where Teresa would appear in her husband's coach-and-six.

48. Elliot Papers. There is no copy of this statement in the Vatican Secret

Archives, while the preceding one – signed by Guiccioli's eighteen servants – is given in full, and dated July 25th, 1820.

49. *L.J.*, V, p. 28. To Murray, May 20th, 1820.
50. Ibid., V, pp. 31-2. To Moore, May 24th, 1820.
51. Ibid., V, p. 32.
52. This letter is quoted by Teresa in the 'Vie'. She adds that she had already sent Byron all her Father's letters and had added to them any 'books' she possessed with Byron's notes in them. 'They contain memories too dear to be exposed to the danger of losing them. I have become suspicious since the experiment of the skeleton-key, about which I can have no doubts. I am afraid of the very air I breathe.' 'Vie' p. 397.
53. *L.J.*, V, p. 35. To Moore, June 1st, 1820.
54. Elliot Papers.
55. RANGONE, *Cronaca.* – Another version merely says: 'The Cavaliere tried to make use of his wife's offices to obtain a new and larger loan' (without specifying the sum), 'but the Lord refused.'
56. Museo Civico Correr, Venice. Protocollo Polizia N.4 (1827).
57. *L.J.*, V, p. 67. August 29th, 1820. Lady Morgan's book on Italy had recently appeared.
58. The authenticity of this letter is indubitable. The second half of it is quoted in one of the Guiccioli-Gamba law-suits, preserved in the Secret Archives of the Vatican.
59. Byron to Kinnaird, July 20th, 1820. From an unpublished letter, to be published in *Byron, a Self-Portrait*, the new two-volume edition of Byron's Correspondence, Murray, London.
60. *I Guiccioli*, I, p. 25. Stendhal, however, also preferred the more picturesque version. 'Le mari', he wrote, 'a cinquante mille livres de rente. Il est très capable d'assassiner le noble lord.' *Correspondance inédite*, p. 167. December 22nd, 1820.
61. *L.J.*, V, p. 49. To Moore, July 13th, 1820.
62. Teresa's annotated copy of Moore, which is still at Settimello, is the 1832 edition. All her marginal notes are in English.
63. Ravenna Archives. Copy in Keats-Shelley Memorial Library.
64. Ibid.
65. Ibid., July 19th, 1820.
66. Secret Archives of the Vatican. Fondo della Sacra Romana Rota, Uditore Bonini, 1842. Summarium No. 3839-10.
67. He extended the same treatment to his daughters 'treating their marriage like any other piece of business, and telling his advocates to procure him sons-in-law, as if he were buying cattle'. *I Guiccioli*, I, p. 55.
68. Secret Archives of the Vatican. Evidence in Summarium No. 3839-11, already quoted.
69. 'Vie', p. 421.

CHAPTER 5

1. MALMESBURY, *Memoirs of an ex-Minister*, I, p. 31.
2. *L.J.*, V, p. 50. To Moore, July 13th, 1820.
3. See letter of September 17th, 1821, p. 283.
4. *Marino Faliero.* To Murray Byron wrote on the same day: 'The tragedy is completed, but now comes the task of copying.' *L.J.*, V, p. 52.
5. The general opinion as to Queen Caroline in Italy is reflected in one of Stendhal's letters: 'Tout ce que je puis vous conter de moins innocent, c'est que la reine Caroline d'Angleterre faisait ici l'amour publiquement avec un palefrénier du général Pino, nommé Bergami, qu'elle a créé baron, et avec lequel elle entrait tous les soirs dans sa chambre à coucher, à dix heures ... Elle est folle d'amour.' STENDHAL, *Correspondance inédite*, I, p. 145. July 12th, 1820.
6. The reference is to the Constitution granted by King Ferdinand I to the Neapolitans.
7. *L.J.*, V, p. 365.

8. 'Vie', p. 643.
9. *L.J.*, V, p. 205.
10. Ibid., V, p. 8. April 16th, 1820.
11. Ibid.
12. MANZONI, *Il proclama di Rimini*. His vision was of an Italy 'Una d'armi, di lingue e d'altare – Di memorie, di sangue e di cor.'
13. DITO, *Massoneria, Carboneria ed altre società segrete*.
14. *L.J.*, V, p. 57. July 22nd, 1820.
15. Ibid.
16. Ibid., V, p. 358. The uniform of the *Cacciatori Americani* was a red cap, red shirt, and white and red striped trousers.
17. Foᴬ', *Lord Byron Poeta e Carbonaro*, p. 182. Later on the Papal government deliberately made no distinction, in the punishments it awarded, between political conspirators and ordinary criminals.
18. MASI, *Cospiratori in Romagna dal 1815 al 1859*.
19. This branch of the Society was also known as '*Cavalieri Guelfi*'.
20. UCCELLINI, *Memorie di un vecchio Carbonaro ravegnano*. Uccellini also took an active part in the uprisings of 1831, 1848 and 1869, and suffered exile and imprisonment – and died at the age of seventy-three with the words: 'I was born a Republican and a Republican I shall die.' Andrea Garavini, a blacksmith, had been the leader of the Carbonari of Ravenna since 1775, and had taken part, with Ruggero Gamba, in the Jacobin movement in 1796. He 'became the idol of the people of Ravenna, who personified in him the democratic tradition of several generations'.
21. NICOLSON, *Byron, The Last Journey*, p. 49.
22. Ravenna Archives.
23. Quiroga was a Spanish general who in 1820 became the head of the Spanish revolutionaries. The word '*Quiroga*' was one of the passwords of the Romagna Carbonari, the reply being 'Guglielmo Tell'.
24. Elliot Papers. Report of Count Guiccioli's spies.
25. See Byron's letter of August 3rd.
26. 'Vie', p. 465.
27. *L.J.*, V, p. 70. To Moore, August 31st, 1820.
28. Ibid.
29. *I Guiccioli*, I, p. 42.
30. LADY BLESSINGTON, *Conversations of Lord Byron*, p. 147.
31. The *palazzo* of Count Pompeo Raisi, a historian of Ravenna who had died in 1818, and whose house was for sale.
32. 'Vie', pp. 469-71.
33. Teresa's grand-parents who were intensely anti-Liberals.
34. A small town not far from Filetto.
35. *I Guiccioli*, I, pp. 43-4.
36. *L.J.*, V, p. 68. To Murray, August 31st, 1820.
37. Vatican Archives, Segreteria di Stato-Sezione Interni.
38. Ravenna, August 18th, 1820. Published by F. A. GUALTIERIO, *Gli ultimi rivolgimenti italiani*, I, p. 264.
39. PIERANTONI, *I Carbonari dello Stato Pontificio*, p. 11. The story of this plot is taken from the interrogation of Count Giacomo Laderchi, by the Austrian police.
40. *L.J.*, V, p. 72. To Murray, September 7th, 1820.
41. MASI, op. cit., p. 236.
42. *Correspondence*, II, p. 156. To Kinnaird, October 1st, 1820.
43. *L.J.*, V, appendix v.
44. 'Vie', p. 578.
45. *Correspondence*, II, pp. 159-60. October 26th, 1820.
46. *L.J.*, V, p. 111. November 5th, 1820.
47. Ibid., V, p. 96. The translation was by R. E. de Chastepollis (Paris 1820) and was preceded by a brief biographical note, which included an account of his separation. 'A league of women was formed against Lord Byron in the name of morality, religion and national honour.'
48. Ibid., V, p. 105.
49. MAYNE, *The Life of Lady Byron*, p. 220.

50. *Astarte*, p. 51.
51.. A character in ROSSINI's *La Cenerentola*, which was being performed that year.
52. A copy of his own works in French. The reference is to the people in Rome who originally told Pietro Gamba scandalous tales about Byron.
53. This letter is enclosed in a folder, on which Teresa has written: 'In this letter he speaks of his separation from Lady Byron. He answers my letter in which, having read *Farewell* I told him the impression it had made on me.'
54. See p. 231 for note 54.
55. Vatican Archives, Segreteria di Stato, Sezione Interni.
56. Museo Civico Correr, Venice. Documenti Polizia Austriaca (1825-33).
57. 'Arcana Politicae Anticarbonariae', Diary of Torelli. See chapter VII, p. 302.
58. *Correspondence*, II, pp. 163-4. To Kinnaird, November 22nd, 1820.

CHAPTER 6

1. The stuff – crimson stripes on a pale ivory ground – is still in the possession of Count Carlo Gamba. It is wrapped in a piece of paper on which Teresa has written: 'Tapisserie et rideau du salon où je recevais Lord Byron, dans la maison de mon père à Ravenna.'
2. 'Vie', pp. 483-4.
3. Ibid., pp. 461-85.
4. Felice Tellarini to Byron, Bagnacavallo, March 11th, 1821. Unpublished letter belonging to Sir John Murray.
5. 'Vie', p. 492.
6. Ibid., p. 529.
7. *L.J.*, V, p. 153. January 5th, 1821.
8. LADY BLESSINGTON, *Conversations of Lord Byron*, p. 183.
9. 'They are corrected by one who passes for the prettiest woman in the Romagna, and even the Marches, as far as Ancona', *L.J.*, V, p. 17.
10. Ibid., V, pp. 96-7. October 12th, 1820.
11. 'Vie', pp. 632-8.
12. Ibid., p. 640.
13. *L.J.*, V, p. 321.
14. This note, of which the original is in the possession of Sir John Murray, is also quoted by Teresa in the 'Vie', p. 641.
15. 'Vie', pp. 524-6.
16. *L.J.*, V, p. 173.
17. Ibid., V, p. 42.
18. Ibid., V, p. 67.
19. Ibid., V, p. 228.
20. 'Vie', p. 613.
21. UCCELLINI, op. cit.
22. *L.J.*, V, p. 129.
23. '*Editto di impunità e premio*' (Edict of impunity and reward) issued by Cardinal Antonio Rusconi, January 22nd, 1821. Keats-Shelley Memorial Library. Nelson Gay Papers.
24. *L.J.*, V, p. 147. Ravenna Journal, January 4th, 1821.
25. Ibid., p. 158. January 7th, 1821.
26. ALBICINI, *Saggio su Carlo Pepoli*.
27. DITO, op. cit., p. 289.
28. *L.J.*, V, p. 159.
29. November 23rd, 1820. A copy of this letter, together with copies of six other letters from Byron to Alborghetti, is in the Public Library of Forlì. This one is quoted in Maggs' Catalogue, No. 266, p. 54.
30. December 3rd, 1820. Unpublished letter belonging to Sir John Murray. All Alborghetti's letters are in English.

KK

31. December 3rd, 1820. Pierpont Morgan Library, New York. Copy in the Public Library at Forlì.

32. From an unpublished letter belonging to Sir John Murray. December 10th, 1820.

33. From an unpublished letter belonging to Sir John Murray. December 13th, 1820.

34. DITO, op. cit., pp. 250-9.

35. Unpublished letter belonging to Sir John Murray. December 28th, 1820.

36. October 14th, 1821. Archivio di Stato di Roma. Copy in Keats-Shelley Memorial Library, Rome.

37. *L.J.*, V, p. 160.

38. Ibid., V, p. 163. January 9th, 1821.

39. Ibid., V, p. 173. January 13th, 1821.

40. Ibid., V, pp. 181-2. January 21st, 1821.

41. Ibid., V, p. 183. January 24th, 1821.

42. Ibid., V, p. 188. January 26th, 1821.

43. The phrase is misquoted (*L.J.*, V, pp. 192-3). It should be, in the Romagnolo dialect, 'A sen tot suldé par la libarté'.

44. FARINI, op. cit., p. 84.

45. *L.J.*, V, pp. 203-5. Journal for February 16th and 18th, 1821.

46. Ibid., V, p. 206. February 19th, 1821.

47. Ibid., V, p. 207. February 21st, 1821.

48. Ibid., V, p. 208. February 24th, 1821.

49. RANGONE, op. cit.

50. Ravenna Journal, May 1st, 1821. *L.J.*, V, p. 403.

51. *L.J.*, V, p. 272. To Moore, April 28th, 1821.

52. Ibid., V, p. 404. Ravenna Journal.

53. FARINI, op. cit., p. 87. This was the same Canon whose sermon against the *filosofi* (the free-thinking Carbonari) was heard by Lady Morgan in Bologna and reported in her *Italy*, II, p. 255.

54. *L.J.*, V, p. 305.

55. From an unpublished letter belonging to Sir John Murray.

56. May 23rd, 1821. Unpublished letter belonging to Sir John Murray.

57. Unpublished letter. Copy in the Public Library of Forlì.

58. From an unpublished letter belonging to Professor Leslie Marchand. Copy in the Public Library, Forlì. The whole story was told by Byron to Murray, *L.J.*, V, p. 326. 'I gave them a remonstrance that had some effect.'

59. June 17th. Unpublished letter belonging to Sir John Murray.

60. June 29th, 1821. Unpublished letter belonging to Sir John Murray.

61. Dated only 'Thursday', but it must be July 19th. Unpublished letter belonging to Sir John Murray.

62. We have not got the original of this letter, nor of Count Gamba's. Teresa has copies of them in the 'Vie', pp. 651-4.

63. Ibid., p. 660.

64. Ibid., p. 662.

65. Ibid., pp. 664-5. Of these three letters also we have only got Teresa's copies in the 'Vie', though she adds in a footnote 'See the originals in the Appendix'.

66. *L.J.*, V, pp. 239-40. This letter is given the date of February 15th, 1821, but it was certainly July 15th since, as we have seen, the Gambas were not exiled until July 10th.

67. 'Vie', pp. 670, 672.

68. This letter is quoted by Moore, II, p. 502, with slight variations, and the omission of names. The version here given is taken from the 'Vie', pp. 672-4.

69. 'Vie', p. 678.

70. Ibid., p. 680.

71. Ibid., p. 686.

72. Ibid., p. 687.

73. On this letter Teresa has written in pencil 'First to Bologna'.

74. Teresa had erased 'not very kind', substituting for it 'who should not leave'.

75. *L.J.*, V, p. 327.

76. The word 'jealous' has been written by Teresa in place of some word which she evidently did not like.

77. August 5th, 1821.

78. 'Vie', p. 714. This letter of Teresa's is quoted in the 'Vie' in the original Italian, instead of, like the others, in French.

79. Ibid., pp. 718-9.

80. Shelley's.

81. SHELLEY, *Prose Works*, ed. Buxton Forman, IV, Letter LXXVI, August 7th, 1821.

82. Ibid., IV, p. 217, Letter LXXVII, August 9th, 1821.

83. A copy of this letter is in the Public Library, Forlì; it has not been possible to trace the original.

84. SHELLEY, op. cit., IV, p. 218, Letter LXXVII.

85. Vol. II, appendix v. Teresa had the original of the letter. In the 'Vie' she intended to include it, but left the pages blank in which it was to have been copied out.

86. SHELLEY, op. cit., IV, p. 228, Letter LXXXI, August 18th, 1821.

87. 'Vie', pp. 737-9.

88. August 11th, 1821. Unpublished letter belonging to Sir John Murray.

89. 'Vie', pp. 773-4.

90. Ibid., p. 775.

91. Ibid., pp. 780-2.

92. These preparations included a request to the Government of the Grand Duchy of Tuscany to be allowed to bring with him his books and numerous other possessions, free of tax. The document is to be seen in the State Archives in Florence. (Keats-Shelley Memorial Library, Nelson Gay Papers.)

93. Erased by Teresa.

94. *L.J.*, V, p. 238.

95. 'Vie', p. 802.

96. LADY BLESSINGTON, *Conversations of Lord Byron*, p. 264. In the margin of her copy Teresa has written: 'Mensonges!'

97. *L.J.*, V, p. 365, September 19th, 1821.

98. LUZIO, *La Massoneria e il Risorgimento Italiano*, p. 174.

99. Ibid., pp. 175-6.

100. 'Vie', p. 725.

101. Ibid., p. 873.

102. *L.J.*, V, p. 385. To Moore, October 1st, 1821.

103. Ibid.

104. *Detached Thoughts*, No. 55; *L.J.*, V, p. 436.

105. Ibid., No. 60; *L.J.*, V, p. 439.

106. Ibid., No. 18; *L.J.*, V, p. 419.

107. LOVELACE, *Astarte*, pp. 307-8. October 5th, 1821.

108. Ibid.

109. *Detached Thoughts*, Nos. 74 and 75; *L.J.*, V, pp. 446-7.

110. Ibid., No. 96; *L.J.*, V, p. 457.

111. An assiduous correspondence between Ghigi and Lega Zambelli – preserved in the Public Library of Forlì – enables us to follow the subsequent fate of these wretched animals, and the trouble they caused to their custodian. The badger died first, in September. 'Tell Mylord, if you think it will not make him angry; otherwise conceal it and tell me, so that I may look for another one.' The monkeys caught cold in the winter and had to be revived with wine and warm blankets, and in summer, suffered no less from the heat. 'If Mylord would make arrangements for them, he would do me a great favour, for I am always afraid of their dying.' The crane pined without a daily supply of fish. Eventually Lega Zambelli omitted to send the money for their food, and after Byron's death Ghigi sent to his executors a demand for payment, declaring that 'he had kept them for fourteen months, during which time they died at various intervals'.

112. *Detached Thoughts*, No. 113. November 5th, 1821; *L.J.*, V, p. 462.

CHAPTER 7

1. GUERRAZZI, *Memorie*.
2. TRELAWNY, *Records of Shelley, Byron and the Author*, I, p. 39.
3. Shelley to John Gisborne, October 22nd, 1821. *Prose Works*, IV, 243.
4. 'Vie', p. 896.
5. Ibid., p. 1353.
6. Ibid., pp. 775-9.
7. MEDWIN, *Revised Life of Shelley*, p. 268.
8. 'Vie', p. 962.
9. Ibid., p. 958.
10. Ibid., p. 957.
11. *L.J.*, V, p. 487.
12. MEDWIN, *Conversations of Lord Byron*, p. 3.
13. TRIBOLATI, *Saggi critici e biografici*, Lord Byron a Pisa.
14. MOORE, II, p. 612.
15. 'Vie', p. 907. As soon as Medwin's book appeared, Teresa, curiously enough, sent a copy of it to Cardinal Rivarola, who dryly replied that he had 'glanced at it superficially', and had seen 'that not much will be lost by postponing a closer study of it'. October 21st, 1824.
16. MEDWIN, op. cit., p. 17. As to Teresa's 'perfect Italian', Medwin was mistaken. She preserved all her life a strong Romagnole accent, whether speaking Italian, French, or in her later years – English.
17. Ibid., op. cit., p. 18.
18. NEWMAN IVEY WHITE, *Shelley*, II, p. 342, quoting Williams' Diary. The phrase about the Pirate is Mary Shelley's.
19. 'Vie', p. 910.
20. Ibid., p. 917.
21. From an unpublished note of Trelawny's belonging to Sir John Murray.
22. As to this, Trelawny must have been mistaken, for Helen Rossetti Angeli's *Shelley and his friends in Italy*, p. 98, quotes the Journal of Sophia Stacey – a young lady with whom Shelley had a sentimental friendship in Florence in November 1818 – as stating that the poem was written then for her.
23. BYRON, *Works*, XIV, 35. There are three other verses, all equally bad. Teresa carefully preserved them all – intending to publish them herself, and was much annoyed when, in 1832, she found them included in the proofs which Murray sent her of the forthcoming edition of Byron's *Works*. 'You knew', she wrote, 'that the *original* work had been given to me by Lord Byron, and I think to have mentioned to you that *it was not my intention to have it published now*. Verses not published of Lord Byron are now such a treasure for everybody – but particularly for me – that you could not be surprised if I did not offer them to you – and now if I cannot conceal from you my disappointment . . . In what manner did you have these verses, dear Mr. Murray. Perhaps from Mrs. Shelley? who can only have copied them from my original, and who not only had no right to make *such a use of them*, but who was *particularly requested by me of that* . . . I hope, dear Mr. Murray, that you will not deprive me of the *dear property* – which is almost the only one that remains to me – having all the other published works been stolen from my hands in the same indelicate manner.' [December 11th, 1832. Unpublished letter belonging to Sir John Murray.]

To all this Murray replied with some firmness: 'Whenever you allow', he said, 'the means for a copy being taken of any of Lord Byron's poems, you incur the *risque* of its being printed – and if it is, there is no help for it – for a mere gift by the author, without a legal assignement, does not constitute property. The Stanzas to the Pillow is almost certain of being published – is it not better, therefore, that it should appear in the author's works? . . .' [G.P., December 12th, 1832.]

Teresa then allowed herself a childish outburst of ill-temper: 'My intention as I told you it was to publish the song together with the music – but it seems that you do not agree with me in this idea – and then make what you like – what your interest advises you to do. For me I shall have in that a new lesson about friendship – which will make me more prudent in future – and now no more about this disagreeable subject.' [December 13th, 1832. Unpublished letter belonging to Sir John Murray.]

But Murray remained both polite and firm, and in the end it was Teresa who had to give way. 'Pray to assure me that you don't believe any longer that I could be unkind towards you – I am quite ignorant about the person who could wish to have the song published – perhaps it has not been any friends of mine – and if you accepted it you were quite right. [December 14th, 1832. Unpublished letter belonging to Sir John Murray.]

24.   Unpublished note, belonging to Sir John Murray.
25.   Unpublished letter belonging to Sir John Murray; Pisa, May 9th. The corner of the letter is torn, but the year must be 1822, since that was the only year in which Teresa was in Pisa in May.
26.   'Vie', p. 1067.
27.   *L.J.*, VI, p. 95.
28.   'Vie', pp. 1071-2.
29.   Trelawny. Unpublished note belonging to Sir John Murray.
30.   Ibid.
31.   State Archives, Florence, file LVIII, Affari 2885. Report of Andrea Bandelloni to the Bargello di Pisa, September 26th, 1821.
32.   Ibid., September 28th. The report mentions the names of Giacomo Batuzzi, who had indeed been one of the leading Carbonari of Ravenna and who now called himself Gamba's factor, of a Sebastiano Foscari, who called himself a doctor, but seemed much too young to be one, and of a certain Tabanelli, the cook, to whom the government had only granted the *biglietto delle 24*, which meant that he might not leave the house after sunset.
33.   Florence State Archives, Letter from Aurelio Puccini, President of the Segreteria di Finanza, October 4th, 1821.
34.   TRIBOLATI, *Saggi critici e biografici*, Lord Byron a Pisa.
35.   TORELLI, 'Arcana Politicae Anticarbonariae'.
36.   Ibid.
37.   Florence State Archives, Comune, XVIII, Affari 723. Letter to the Buongoverno from Cerbone Cerboni, February 1822.
38.   Ibid., February.
39.   Ibid.
40.   TORELLI, op. cit.
41.   'Vie', p. 1115.
42.   TRIBOLATI, op. cit.
43.   TORELLI, op. cit.
44.   TRIBOLATI, op. cit.
45.   Ibid., op. cit., quoting a letter to him from Guerrazzi.
46.   'Vie', p. 1127.
47.   Unpublished note by Trelawny, belonging to Sir John Murray.
48.   *L.J.*, VI, p. 43.
49.   TORELLI, op. cit.
50.   'Vie', p. 1135.
51.   Secret Archives of the Vatican. Fondo della Sacra Romana Rota, Uditore Bonini, 1842. Summarium No. 3839.
52.   Elliot Papers.
53.   Secret Archives of the Vatican. Fondo della Sacra Romana Rota, Uditore Bonini, 1843. Summarium Add.
54.   Secret Archives of the Vatican. Fondo della Sacra Romana Rota, Uditore Bonini, 1843. Summarium Add.
55.   *L.J.*, VI, p. 89.
56.   'Vie', p. 1197.
57.   TRIBOLATI, op. cit., *Un processo civile di Lord Byron*. The law-suit dragged on until July 1823, when it was settled against Byron, who was condemned to pay three months' rent.
58.   'Vie', pp. 1173-9.
59.   All these letters are in the Public Library at Forlì.
60.   BIONDI, *La figlia di Lord Byron*. There is also a record that two Englishmen, calling themselves Giacomo Ovad (Howard) of London and Giuliano Emanuele Desamps of Carson [*sic*] arrived on that day in Bagnacavallo, at the Albergo della Colombina.

61. Pellegrino Ghigi to Lega Zambelli, May 7th, 1822. Public Library, Forlì.

62. From an inventory of Allegra's effects, sent to Byron after her death. These included three coloured cotton frocks, one velvet frock, one of muslin and one of 'velo'; a little cap, four gloves, a string of corals and a silver spoon and fork, besides a sufficiency of underclothes and bed-linen, and her own furniture.

63. After her death, the obituary notice in the Ravenna paper (in 1922) stated that she had been 'educated at the convent of Bagnacavallo, together with the daughter of Lord Byron'.

64. MOORE, *Memoirs*, etc., III, p. 358.

65. *L.J.*, IV, p. 428.

66. 'Each time she [Allegra] came into her father's presence, he used to turn away in disgust and exclaim 'Enlevez-la: elle ressemble trop à sa mère!' HUBERT E. JERNINGHAM, *Reminiscences of an Attaché*, p. 106.

67. LADY BLESSINGTON, *Conversations of Lord Byron*, pp. 71-2.

68. *L.J.*, VI, p. 69. Byron's wishes, owing to the objections of the churchwarden of the parish, were not carried out. The child was buried at the entrance to Harrow church, without any tablet or memorial. It is unpleasant to relate that subsequently Lega Zambelli – on Byron's behalf – haggled with Pellegrino Ghigi about the child funeral expenses in Bagnacavallo, complaining in particular that the apothecary's bill was too high, the amount of spices that was used for her embalmment being what would be required for a grown-up person!

69. LADY BLESSINGTON, op. cit., pp. 72-3.

70. *L.J.*, VI, p. 80.

71. Ibid., VI, p. 175, Lady Blessington, who considered this habit of disclaiming friendship 'very injudicious', wrote that 'Long acquaintance, habitual correspondence and reciprocity of kind action, which are the general bonds of friendship, were not admitted by Byron to be sufficient claims to the title of friends'.

72. MOORE, II, p. 615, quoting Teresa's account.

73. *L.J.*, VI, p. 82.

74. MOORE, II, pp. 602-3, quoting West's account.

75. LADY BLESSINGTON, *Conversations of Lord Byron*, p. 371. In Teresa's copy, this passage is heavily underscored.

76. MEDWIN, op. cit., p. 185.

77. LEIGH HUNT, op. cit., I, p. 67.

78. LADY BLESSINGTON, op. cit., p. 188.

79. Ibid , p. 70.

80. Ibid., p. 71.

81. *L.J.*, VI, p. 91.

82. Elliot Papers. Letters from Guiccioli to Avvocato Vincenzo Taglioni, July 9th, 1822.

83. 'Vie', p. 1183.

84. *L.J.*, VI, p. 111. August 27th, 1822.

85. Elliot Papers. Letter from Gaetano Forestieri to Conte Guiccioli, June 30th, 1822.

86. TORELLI, op. cit.

87. 'Vie', p. 1281.

88. HUNT, *Lord Byron and some of his Contemporaries*, I, p. 18.

89. TRIBOLATI, op. cit. This letter, although written by Byron in English, is quoted in Italian.

90. April 8th, 1822. Unpublished note belonging to Lord Abinger.

91. LUCCA, State Archives, 1822. Fasc. 230; No. 330. W. Dawkins to the Marchese Mansi, July 7th, 1822.

92. Ibid.

93. Ibid. This letter is not quoted by Tribolati.

94. July 17th, 1822. Gamba Papers.

95. TORELLI, op. cit. 'This', he adds, 'will be far worse than Lady Morgan's work.

96. LEIGH HUNT, op. cit., I, p. 44.

97. Letter from Williams to Trelawny, quoted by EDMUND BLUNDEN, *Leigh Hunt*, p. 173.

98. HUNT, op. cit., I, p. 48. 'To the same he said one day, that he must take care how he got notions in his head about truth and sincerity, for they would hinder him getting on in the world'.

99. *L.J.*, VI, p. 119. Byron to Mary Shelley. October 6th, 1822.

100. Mrs. Hunt's Diary, September 23rd, 1822. Published in the Bulletin of the Keats-Shelley Memorial Library. Carlyle's description of Hunt's house twelve years later, is perhaps Byron's best justification. 'In his family room, where are a sickly large wife and a whole shoal of well-conditioned, wild children, you will find half a dozen old rickety chairs, gotten from half a dozen of Hunt's hucksters . . . On these and around them and over the dusty table and ragged carpet lie all kinds of litter – books, papers, egg-shells, scissors, and last night when I was there, the torn heart of a half of a pound loaf.' S. A. FROUDE, *The man Carlyle*, II, p. 439.

101. TRELAWNY, op. cit., p. 174.

102. Ibid., p. 172.

103. *L.J.*, VI, p. 157. December 25th, 1822.

104. HUNT, op. cit., I, pp. 63-4.

105. The first number, published on October 15th, 1822, called by the *Courier* 'a rascally publication' – included Byron's *Vision of Judgment* and *Epigrams on Lord Castlereagh*, Shelley's *May day night* (translated from Faust) and a *Letter from Abroad*, about Pisa, by Leigh Hunt. *The Literary Gazette* commented that 'Lord Byron has contributed impiety, vulgarity, inhumanity and heartlessness; Mr. Shelley, a burlesque upon Goethe; and Mr. Leigh Hunt conceit, trumpery, ignorance and untold verses.' Three other numbers were published, which did not even attract the negative compliment of such violent criticism – and with the fourth number for July 1823 and Byron's departure for Greece, the review came to an end.

106. Letter from Hunt to the Editor of the *Morning Chronicle*, in the *Examiner*, January 27th, 1828, quoted in *Lord Byron*, etc., II, p. 413.

107. Ibid., II, p. 412. 'The nature of the occupation of this floor in his house . . . was very different from being entertained as his guest.'

108. BLUNDEN, op. cit., p. 166.

109. HUNT, *Lord Byron and some of his Contemporaries*, I, p. 141.

110. Ibid., I, p. 169.

111. 'Vie', p. 1532.

112. Review by Theodore Hook in *John Bull*. Quoted by BLUNDEN, op. cit., p. 182.

113. HUNT, preface to *Lord Byron and some of his Contemporaries*, I, p. 68.

114. Ibid., I, p. 41.

115. Ibid., I, p. 39.

116. 'Vie', p. 1328.

117. MOORE, II, p. 614.

118. In a later letter, replying to one of Byron's letters from Geneva, in which he said he had become much thinner, Hobhouse said: 'You were not a bit too fat in the body at Pisa, and if you would but have your hair of a Christian length, or rather shortness, you would not have been too fat in the face.' Unpublished letter belonging to Sir John Murray, March 2nd, 1823.

119. LORD BROUGHTON, *Recollections of a Long Life*, II, p. 4. His visit to Pisa was from September 15th to 21st.

120. Ibid., p. 3.

121. Ibid., p. 8.

122. Pisa, September 23rd, 1822. Keats-Shelley Memorial Library, Rome. Nelson Gay Papers.

123. TORELLI, op. cit.

CHAPTER 8

1. *L.J.*, VI, p. 125.

2. TRELAWNY, *Records*, etc., II, p. 49.

3. 'Vie', p. 1315.

4. Ibid., p. 1397.

5. Ibid., p. 1314.

6. TRELAWNY, op. cit., I, p. 70.
7. Ibid., II, p. 50.
8. *L.J.*, VI, p. 122.
9. Mrs. Hunt's Diary, October 3rd, 1822. Bulletin of the K.S.M. Rome.
10. Ibid., October 5th, 1822.
11. Ibid., October 7th.
12. Ibid., October 14th.
13. MARSHALL, *Life and Letters of Mary Wollstonecraft Shelley*, II, p. 56.
14. HUNT, *Autobiography*, II, pp. 66-7.
15. 'Vie', p. 1367.
16. Ibid., p. 1382.
17. MARSHALL, op. cit., II, p. 45. Mary Shelley, Journal, October 7th, 1822.
18. *Correspondence*, II, p. 217, February 23rd, 1822.
19. *L.J.*, VI, p. 11, February 6th, 1822, and *L.J.*, VI, pp. 163-4, January 18th, 1823.
20. *Don Juan*, I, XVI.
21. HUNT, *Lord Byron and some of his Contemporaries*, I, p. 130.
22. TRELAWNY, op. cit., II, p. 74.
23. Byron to Teresa, February 21st, 1823.
24. Unpublished letter from Trelawny to Byron, belonging to Sir John Murray.
25. Mrs. Hunt's Diary, September 19th, 1822.
26. Hunt's letter to *The Examiner*, July 27th, 1828.
27. Quoted by Harold Nicolson in *Byron, The Last Journey*, p. 29.
28. *L.J.*, VI, p. 167. February 20th, 1823.
29. Ibid.
30. Ibid., VI, p. 182. April 2nd, 1823.
31. MARSHALL, op. cit., p. 64. Mary Shelley to Trelawny, January 30th, 1823.
32. 'Vie', p. 1369.
33. Abinger Papers. The date is illegible, but a postscript says 'Trelawny has written that he will be here in a few days'.
34. 'Vie', p. 1369. Mary's letters were written in Italian, which she wrote quite fluently, though incorrectly.
35. Ibid., p. 1371.
36. MARSHALL, op. cit., p. 82. Mary Shelley to Jane Williams, July 23rd, 1823.
37. William Noel-Hill, who succeeded his brother as third Lord Berwick.
38. Trelawny to Hobhouse from Missolonghi, April 18th, 1824.
39. Charles F. Barry, a partner in the firm of Messrs. Webb & Co., bankers of Genoa and Leghorn.
40. July 19th, 1823. Unpublished letter belonging to Sir John Murray.
41. Unpublished note of Trelawny's, belonging to Sir John Murray.
42. 'Vie', p. 1390.
43. *L.J.*, VI, p. 147.
44. GALT, *Life of Lord Byron*, p. 198.
45. Letter No. 139.
46. Letter No. 138.
47. Letter No. 136, February 20th, 1823 (Italian, p. 476). The curious thing about this letter is that Byron refers to a life of Saint *Catherine* – who never had anything to do with the Jesuits – while what Teresa sent him was a life of *Saint Teresa* by G. Hoyoman, entitled 'The mutual and uninterrupted love of St. Teresa and the Company of Jesus' (translated from the Spanish, 1794). Teresa misquoted the letter in her *Lord Byron jugé*, etc. (Vol. II, p. 412) as a proof of Byron's respect for other people's opinions, gratuitously adding a whole sentence: 'I think all this very estimable, and what is more, enviable.'
48. 'Vie', pp. 1513-15.
49. Ibid, p. 1404.
50. HAROLD NICOLSON, *Byron, the Last Journey*, chapter II.
51. TRELAWNY, op. cit., II, p. 62.
52. PIETRO GAMBA, *Lord Byron's Last Journey to Greece*, p. 3.
53. TRELAWNY, *Records*, etc., II, p. 55.
54. *L.J.*, VI, p. 185, April 5th, 1823.

55. *L.J.*, VI, p. 206. May 12th, 1823.
56. MARSHALL, op. cit., II, p. 75.
57. 'Vie', p. 1574.
58. Ibid., pp. 1576-8. All the part of the 'Vie' describing Byron's preparation for Greece and his departure – about 100 pages of manuscript – is a rough draft written, according to Teresa, 'many years before either my published or unpublished works about Lord Byron' – and has indeed a much greater freshness and directness.
59. Ibid., pp. 1574-5.
60. *Correspondence*, II, pp. 260-1.
61. To Hobhouse, April 19th, 1823. *Correspondence*, II, p. 259.
62. LADY BLESSINGTON, *Conversations*, etc., pp. 318-19.
63. 'Vie', p. 1190.
64. LADY BLESSINGTON, *The Idler in Italy*, I, p. 347.
65. *Correspondence*, II, p. 258.
66. 'Vie', p. 1451.
67. Ibid.
68. To Lady Hardy, *The Cornhill*, LXIV, New Series, 1928.
69. 'Vie', pp. 1491-1500. 'Lady Blessington avait beaucoup d'imagination et une presque nécessité de faire un roman de la plus simple histoire . . . On les a appelées imaginaires et elles le sont en réalité, ces conversations qui trahissent dans l'auteur un secret sentiment de dépit et de malaise'.
70. To Lady Hardy, *The Cornhill*, LXIV, New Series, 1928.
71. LADY BLESSINGTON, *Conversations*, etc., p. 142.
72. Ibid., p. 70.
73. Ibid., p. 69. These lines are underscored in Teresa's own copy.
74. The copy is the 1834 edition. Teresa's comments are mostly in French.
75. Barry to Byron, June 15th, 1823. Unpublished letter belonging to Sir John Murray.
76. HAROLD NICOLSON, op. cit., p. 20.
77. *L.J.*, VI, p. 224. June 15th, 1823. In quoting this letter to Colonel Stanhope, after Byron's death, Trelawny characteristically altered the words 'I want your aid', into 'I cannot do anything without you'. Letters of E. J. Trelawny, ed. J. Buxton Forman, p. 73.
78. Had it not been for this objection, Byron might have chartered 'a Genoese trawl – a very fine and commodious ship, larger than the Genoa packet'. Barry to Byron, June 13th, 1823. Unpublished letter belonging to Sir John Murray.
79. GAMBA, op. cit., p. 285.
80. Before sailing Byron told Barry to take good care of them, 'it being his intention to keep them as long as they lived'. – 'Here', commented Hobhouse, 'is a plain case of mystification, which succeeded with the worthy Mr. Barry.' BROUGHTON, op. cit., III, p. 57. But apparently the poor man was saddled with the geese for good, for in 1827 Teresa was writing 'Pray give me news of them!'
81. 'Vie', pp. 1589-90. Teresa remembered Byron's remarks, and when, in 1832, she paid her first visit to England she took those manuscripts with her. According to the titles on the back of a large leather folder, still in the possession of the Gamba family – but now empty – they were the first drafts of *Manfred*, the *Ode on Venice*, *Werner*, *Marino Faliero*, *Morgante Maggiore*, *Stanzas to the Po*, *Francesca of Rimini*, the *Prophecy of Dante*, *Beppo*, *Mazeppa*, and the first five cantos of *Don Juan* – as well as one or two minor poems. It was not, however, until six months after her arrival, on October 24th, 1832, that she consulted Mr. Murray about them.
  . . . 'Your kindness to me', she wrote then, 'as well as your real attachment and devotion to the memory of Lord Byron, assure me that nobody could advise me better than yourself. It was always my wish and intention to raise some sort of monument to the memory of Ld. Byron in my birth-town, Ravenna, near the *Tomb of Dante* – but I was always prevented to do it by my dependent circumstances – which *may change* from one day to the other, but which *may last* for many and many years more, and perhaps all my life. In the uncertainty I made my will some years ago, *and bequeathed a part of my property, together with the price it was possible to get for the manuscripts of Lord Byron* (which I requested my parents to bring and sell in England) in order to *erect* a *monumento* to Lord Byron in Ravenna.

But after some reflections which passed through my mind some days ago *I asked myself whether it was not better to do all that* (if possible) *during my lifetime than after my death. I felt and feel* inclined to answer myself in the *affirmative* – but if I am wrong or right in thinking so is the answer I ask from your kindness. I feel that England is the only country who has *the right* to possess the original manuscripts of her first modern poet – but being a property of mine I think I have the right too not to depart from such a treasure for me, without asking for what they are worth – and particularly so when their price must be employed soon or later *to honour his Memory*.

But though those manuscripts are so dear and valuable to me, I do not illude myself to think an easy task to find a *purchaser*. They are but a *literary luxury*, and very few persons in the world will employ a large sum of money in such a luxury. However, my intention now is to make an *advertisement* that such and such original MSS. of Lord Byron are now *to be sold* in order to raise a monument to him with the result. Before to do this, I wish to have your advice.'

Murray replied upon the following day: 'As soon as I received your letter I called upon Mr. Evans, Bookseller and Auctioneer, Pall Mall, who is the most eminent in his line for selling great libraries and valuable MSS. by auction. He sold, in this way, the autograph MSS. of the *Waverley Novels* last year, and also the MSS. of Lord Byron's *Curse of Minerva* a few months ago. He told me that he thought the MSS. of Lord Byron in your possession, of which you know I made an inventory, were valuable and might produce a good sum, if sold by auction at the proper season, which will not, however, occur before the meeting of Parliament, which brings everyone to London, in February next – and therefore your best plan would be, to deposit the MSS. in safe custody, if you cannot remain in England until that period. I would try, if you preferred it, to ascertain what some Collector of MSS. would give, to purchase them by private contract.' In spite, however, of all these suggestions, Teresa apparently did not succeed in disposing of her MSS. during her first visit to England, for in 1835 she was writing about them to Mr. Heath, the Consul General for Sardinia in London. 'I should above all have desired to sell the whole collection of MSS. in my possession, as being that which is most worthy of them; but I see that unless they are acquired by some library or public institute, it will be impossible to obtain from a private purchaser the sum I have in mind and which is necessary for my projects, that is £3000 sterling.' She was, however, also prepared to sell the MSS. separately, but had strong – and somewhat peculiar – views on the value to be placed on each of them. 'Thus for example I imagine that everyone would prefer the original MSS. of *Manfred* to that of the *Prophecy of Dante*, so that consequently for an equal volume, one would ask more for the former than the latter. As to the MSS. of *Mazeppa*, I think we may give its value at about £230 ... You tell me, dear Mr. Heath', she concluded, 'to ask little and my prices may appear to you exaggerated. I agree that it is high, since these MSS. have only a value of affection, but it is the same with all prices of affection, and it is only rich people, admirers of Lord Byron's genius, who are able to make these purchases.' When and how Teresa eventually disposed of her MSS. is not known. What is certain is that now only the empty folder remains among her papers.

82. Ibid., p. 1591. Byron made no will in Italy, though he often talked of it. BROUGHTON, III, p. 51.

83. *Correspondence*, II, pp. 284-5. Byron to Kinnaird, October 29th, 1823.

84. Ibid., II, pp. 124-5. Byron to Kinnaird, October 26th, 1819.

85. *L.J.*, V, p. 50. Byron to Moore, July 13th, 1820.

86. Letter of August 7th, 1820, p. 208.

87. 'Vie', p. 1591.

88. Ibid., p. 1544.

89. Ibid., p. 1591.

90. MOORE, II, p. 664.

91. Unpublished letter belonging to Lord Abinger. July 10th, 1823.

92. Unpublished letter belonging to Lord Abinger. Undated.

93. 'Vie', p. 1591.

94. These lines were scribbled in a little green leather note-book of Byron's, previously belonging to the Gamba family and now in the possession of the University of Texas Library. On the paper in which the note-book was wrapped, Teresa wrote: 'Portefeuille de Lord Byron rempli de son écriture et de quelques lignes au crayon de

Mme Guiccioli . . . dans des moments où par l'excès du chagrin elle était presque en délire.' Quoted by Maria Borgese, in *L'Appassionata di Byron*, pp. 293 and 309-10.

95. GAMBA, op. cit.

CHAPTER 9

1. Antonio Morandi, in his *Giornale del 1848-1850*, says that Pietro Gamba, on his deathbed in Metana in 1827, gave him a packet of about forty letters to return to Teresa – but that he lost them, in escaping from the Italian police. He also says that Teresa's letters to Byron were *sometimes* written in red or blue ink between the lines of Byron's own letters. Since, however, Teresa plainly says in the 'Vie' 'Voir mes lettres à Pietro et à Ld. Byron en Grèce', one can only conclude that at least one other packet must have been returned to her, and been lost or destroyed later on.

2. Bologna, November 10th, 1823. Unpublished letter belonging to Lord Abinger.

3. Paolo Costa (1771-1836), a distinguished man of letters and philosopher, was forbidden to teach in the University of Bologna on account of his Liberal opinions, and coached private pupils (among them Guiccioli's son, Ignazio, and the younger Gamba brothers) in his own house. He was exiled in 1831, visited England, where Teresa gave him a letter to Lady Blessington, and spent his last years in Corfu.

4. 'Vie', p. 699.

5. Byron to Barry, October 25th, 1823. *L.J.*, VI, p. 269.

6. LOVELACE, *Astarte*, p. 307. October 5th, 1821.

7. 'A few grey locks . . . are all that announces the approach of that age that has made such an impression on his mind, and of which he speaks so much.' *Journal of Henry Fox*, p. 161.

8. GAMBA, *A Narrative of Lord Byron's last journey to Greece*, p. 266.

9. Byron to Barry, October 25th, 1823. *L.J.*, VI, p. 269. The passages or letters which have been omitted are purely repetitions, where Pietro has given the same news to Teresa and to his father, or Costa.

10. The first, according to a letter from Teresa to Mary Shelley, took 40 days.

11. *Letters of E. J. Trelawny*, ed. H. Buxton Forman, p. 72.

12. Unpublished note belonging to Sir John Murray.

13. Colonel Charles Napier, field officer of the Ionian Islands, had been appointed by Sir Thomas Maitland ('King of Corfu') as Resident of Cephalonia, and had brought to his new post a passionate Philhellenic enthusiasm, as well as remarkable energy and ability. He built roads, quays, warehouses, light-houses and market halls. ('I would rather', he wrote, 'have finished the roads of Cephalonia than have fought at Austerlitz or Waterloo.') He was, in short, a first-rate administrator and a man singularly suited to encourage and support Byron's present purpose.

14. Commanded by Lieut.-Colonel John Duffie. It was on one of these occasions that, according to the Methodist Minister Kennedy, Byron, replying to the toast of the officers of the garrison, said 'that he was afraid that he could not express his sense of the obligation as he ought, having been so long on the practice of speaking a foreign language!' KENNEDY, *Conversations on Religion with Lord Byron*, p. 4.

15. Here Pietro was echoing Byron. 'I detest antiquarian twaddle,' he said peevishly to Trelawny. 'Do people think that I have no lucid intervals, that I come to Greece to scribble more verses? I will show them I can do something better.' TRELAWNY, *Records*, etc., II, p. 110.

16. Captain Knox, who, with his wife, had given Byron a most cordial reception. 'Our Pilgrim,' Trelawny said, 'was received as if he had been a prince.'

17. TRELAWNY, op. cit., II, p. 113.

18. CHARLES MACKAY, *Medora Leigh*. The whole story is told in detail by HAROLD NICOLSON, op. cit., pp. 130-3.

19. NICOLSON, op. cit., p. 136.

20. *L.J.*, VI, p. 247. Journal in Cephalonia.

21. Ibid., VI, p. 246.

22. KENNEDY, op. cit., p. 8.

23. Quoted by NICOLSON, op. cit., p. 152. 'I well knew', wrote Trelawny, 'that

once on shore, Byron would fall back on his old routine of dawdling habits, plotting, planning, shilly-shallying and doing nothing.' *Records*, II, p. 117.

24. KENNEDY, *Conversations on Religion with Lord Byron*, pp. 166-7.

25. Ibid., p. 29.

26. Ibid., p. 260. Appendix. Letter from Pietro Gamba to Dr. Kennedy.

27. *Lord Byron jugé par les temoins de sa vie*, I, p. 156.

28. KENNEDY, op. cit., p. 252. Letter from Fletcher, May 19th, 1824.

29. *Lord Byron jugé*, etc., I, p. 240.

30. *Correspondence*, II, p. 282, October 6th, 1823.

31. 'One of them [the Greeks] found fault the other day with the English language, because it had so few shades of a Negative, whereas a Greek can so modify a "No" to a "Yes", and vice versa, by the slippery qualities of his language, that prevarication may be carried to any extent.' (*L.J.*, VI, p. 247. Journal in Cephalonia.)

32. The passage in brackets is printed in *L.J.*, VI, p. 276, with the exception of the words in round brackets. The letter is misdated (October instead of September 7th).

33. Pietro Gamba to Prof. Paolo Costa, August 11th, 1823.

34. Byron himself said, 'I ran out of the room as fast as my legs would carry me, and left Gamba behind, but when I got down, I saw Gamba before me, for he had jumped over the staircase'. KENNEDY, op. cit., p. 387.

35. October 8th, 1823.

36. The passage in square brackets is published in *L.J.*, VI, p. 275, omitting the sentence in round brackets.

37. Byron was so upset by this news that he stopped writing his Journal. 'My journal', he wrote on Dec. 17th, 'was discontinued abruptly and has not been resumed sooner, because on the day of its former date I received a letter from my sister Augusta, that intimated the illness of my daughter, and I had not then the heart to continue it. Subsequently I heard through the same channel that she was better, and since that she is well; if so, for me all is well.' *L.J.*, VI, p. 249.

38. Ada's birthday. At Casa Saluzzo, in 1822, Byron had celebrated it with 'a mutton chop and a bottle of ale'. Since neither agreed with him, he partook of them 'only on great jubilees'. *L.J.*, VI, p. 147.

39. The part of this letter in square brackets is published in *L.J.*, VI, pp. 276-7, omitting the word 'quietly' and substituting the word 'distant' for the original 'remote'.

40. Lord Sydney Godolphin Osborne, a distant connection and old acquaintance of Byron's. 'He is a merry fellow,' said Byron of him to Dr. Kennedy, 'and has some fine qualities, but I do not know if he is religious. Do you know him?' I answered 'No.' 'Then,' he said, 'you must stay and try to convert him.' KENNEDY, op. cit., p. 149.

41. Secret Archives of the Vatican. Fondo della Sacra Romana Rota, Uditore Bonini, 1843. Summarium Additionale No. 6.

42. This story, according to the Elliot Papers, was written down, with all the details, by Count Guiccioli himself. The interview took place on March 3rd, 1824.

43. Elliot Papers. March 6th, 1824.

44. Secret Archives of the Vatican. Fondo della Sacra Romana Rota, Uditore Bonini, 1842. Summarium Additionale No. 3938-1. Teresa Guiccioli to Cardinal Rivarola, February 24th, 1827.

45. The Cardinal's letter – dated April 6th, 1824 – is among Teresa's papers.

46. MALMESBURY, *Memoirs of an ex-Minister*, I, p. 33.

47. November 26th, 1823.

48. Colonel the Hon. Leicester Stanhope, fourth Earl of Harrington, who had previously been an officer in the Indian Army.

49. FINLAY, *History of the Greek Revolution*, VI, p. 327.

50. *L.J.*, VI, p. 293. To John Bowring, December 26th, 1823.

51. Ibid., VI, p. 278. To the General Government of Greece, November 30th, 1823.

52. Ibid., VI, p. 269. October 25th, 1823.

53. This P.S. is in Italian in the original.

54. A Florentine man of letters of the Trecento, a contemporary of Dante's, who wrote a long didactic work entitled *Il Tesoretto*.

55. *L.J.*, VI, p. 286, to John Bowring, December 13th, 1823. 'The use of the trumpets, too', he added in a latter letter, 'may be doubted, unless Constantinople were Jericho.'

56. GAMBA, op. cit., p. 296.

57. *L.J.*, VI, p. 291, December 23rd, 1823.

58. GAMBA, op. cit., p. 67.

59. This paper – entitled the *Greek Chronicle* – was the fruit of the activities of Colonel Stanhope, who had chosen for it the motto of 'The happiness of the greatest number'. Byron had subscribed to it, but only under protest. 'From the very first', he wrote to Barry, 'I foretold to Col. Stanhope and to P. Mavrocordato that a Greek newspaper (as indeed any other) *in the present state of Greece*, might and probably *would* lead to much mischief and misconstruction.' (*L.J.*, VI, p. 354.) This view of Byron's led to considerable friction with Colonel Stanhope, who accused Byron of 'attacking Mr. Bentham's principles'. 'I said that Bentham had a truly British heart, but that Lord Byron, after professing Liberal principles from his boyhood, had, when called upon to act, proved himself a Turk.' See NICOLSON, op. cit., pp. 207-8.

60. *L.J.*, VI, p. 340.

61. Pietro Gamba to Contessa Guiccioli, March 17th, 1824.

62. MILLINGEN, *Memoirs*, p. 146.

63. In his 'Journal' Byron says of this attack, 'I have also been in an anxious state, and perhaps not uniformly so temperate as I may generally affirm that I was wont to be'. *L.J.*, VI, p. 324. Parry himself was convinced that all that Byron needed was, as to his diet, 'to return to the habits of an English gentleman'. PARRY, *Last Days of Byron*, p. 46.

64. *L.J.*, VI, p. 332. February 23rd, 1824.

65. PARRY, op. cit., p. 154.

66. Ibid., p. 155.

67. The story is also told by Parry, as showing Byron's method of curing Fletcher of 'his unrestrained attachment to women!' Op. cit., p. 152.

68. Loreta was a friend of Pietro's in Ravenna, whom Pietro had asked to collect some more volunteers for Byron's International Brigade. 'We were', he says, 'a sort of Crusade in miniature. The word of command was given in Greek, but French and Italian were the languages in common use.'

69. PARRY, op. cit., p. 191. 'Lord Byron', Parry explained, 'had a curious opinion of this young nobleman; he thought him destined to be unfortunate.'

70. NICOLSON, op. cit., pp. 244, 255.

71. PARRY, op. cit., p. 28.

72. LADY BLESSINGTON, *Conversations*, p. 391.

73. Unpublished note belonging to Sir John Murray. Trelawny characteristically added a sentence which bears the stamp of his own invention: 'You', he said, 'are as hard as granite, and accustomed to savage life – you will be delighted with Greece!' In the *Records*, II, pp. 97-8, he quotes Byron's remarks in a slightly different form.

74. The Legate in Bologna.

75. May 8th, 1824. Elliot Papers.

76. *I Guiccioli*, I, p. 47.

77. From a letter in the Archives of Marchese Aldobrandino Malvezzi de' Medici, quoted by Borgese, op. cit., p. 341.

CHAPTER 10

1. April 20th, 1824. Unpublished letter belonging to Sir John Murray. 'His friend Gamba says to me', wrote Hobhouse in his Journal of one of Pietro's other letters, 'that, though cut off in the flower of his age, in the midst of his hopes, Byron will always be regarded as the saviour of Greece, *always!*' LORD BROUGHTON, op. cit., vol. III, p. 43.

2. May 8th, 1824.

3. April 20th, 1824.

4. August 15th, 1824. Unpublished letter belonging to Sir John Murray.

5. A translation of this petition, in Gamba's hand, is among the papers belonging to Sir John Murray.

6. This petition has also been translated by Gamba. His reply pointed out that (a) The unruly and unreliable Souliots, after having been paid by Byron for several months, had been dismissed by him with a month's pay, and had only stayed on at Missolonghi at their own wish, and (b) that Mylord had lent the city 15,000 dollars, had repaired their fortifications, restored their laboratories, and maintained a Brigade at his expense for their defence.

7. TRELAWNY, *Letters*, p. 80.

8. Ibid., p. 81.

9. Gamba to Colonel Stoven, the Resident of Zante, quoting Sidney Osborne's letter to him. Gamba added that if he had had any doubts about Byron's own wishes, they would have been dispelled by his recollection of the poet's insistence on sending Allegra's body to England.

10. April 11th, 1817. *L.J.*

11. May 14th, 1824. Unpublished letter belonging to Sir John Murray.

12. From an unpublished letter sequestrated by the Austrian Police. Museo Ciria Correr, Venice.

13. The drawing at Chatsworth by d'Orsay, which was thought to be of Pietro, appears to be of d'Orsay himself.

14. Undated but enclosed by John Murray in a letter written in 1833.

15. June 6th, 1835. Quoted by NICOLSON, op. cit., pp. 280-1.

16. Ibid., p. 279.

17. Charles Hancock to Alexander Muir, June 1st, 1824. *L.J.*, VI, p. 429.

18. Letter from Teresa to the Parish Priest of Santo Stefano in Venice, 1826.

19. July 6th, 1826. Secret Archives of the Vatican. Fondo della Sacra Romana Rota, Uditore Bonini, 1843. Summarium Additionale No. 3988-8.

20. Statement prepared by Teresa for her advocate in Rome, Armellini (1841).

21. Letter from Ignazio Guiccioli to Contessa Teresa Guiccioli, June 12th, 1827. Quoted in the lawsuit already mentioned.

22. Appeal of Alessandro Guiccioli against his wife, before the Austrian Tribunal in Venice, November 26th, 1826. Copy in Teresa's hand.

23. Secret Archives of the Vatican. Fondo della Sacra Romana Rota, Uditore Bonini, 1842. Letter from Attilia Guiccioli Carranti to Teresa Guiccioli, November 11th, 1826.

24. Ibid. Ignazio Guiccioli to Contessa Teresa Guiccioli, February 20th, 1827. Ignazio asked Teresa to burn this letter.

25. Secret Archives of the Vatican. Fondo della Romana Rota, Uditore Bonini, 1843.

26. *I Guiccioli*, I, p. 59.

27. Ibid., I, p. 55.

28. MALMESBURY, *Memoirs of an ex-Minister*, p. 26.

29. *I Guiccioli*, II, p. 88.

30. Marchesa Orinzia Sacrati, had held in her youth a celebrated literary salon in Rome. In her old age Leopardi described her as 'a fat little old woman in a yellow wig, who was always to be found spinning silk, never rising from her seat'.

31.
          Io la conobbi l'anima gentile,
          La cui polve è rinchiusa in questo avello,
          Peregrina smarrita in questa terra . . .

The poem – a long one – was first published in *La Ghirlanda* in Bologna in 1843, and reprinted by RAVA, *Lord Byron e P. B. Shelley a Ravenna.*

32. SYLVA NORMAN, *After Shelley*, p. 51. Thomas Jefferson Hogg, Shelley's friend and biographer, was then living with Jane Williams.

33. December 1826.

34. From a letter of Teresa's to Lamartine, at Saint Point, published by Guillemin in the *Revue de Littérature Comparée*, July-September 1939: 'Lamartine, Byron et Mme Guiccioli.'

35. FOX, *Journal*, p. 215.

36. Ibid., p. 216. August 1825.

37. Ibid., p. 268. February 17th, 1828.

38. Ibid., p. 343. June 27th, 1829.

39. LADY BLESSINGTON, *The Idler in Italy*, II, p. 357, May 1828.
40. Fox, *Journal*, p. 298. May 9th, 1828.
41. Unpublished letter from E. Patterson Bonaparte to Contessa Guiccioli, March 1st, 1828. Mrs. Patterson was Jerome Bonaparte's American first wife. 'Her manners are so vulgar', wrote Fox of her, 'and her conversation so malicious, so indecent and so profligate, that even her very pretty features do not make one excuse such want of delicacy or feminine feeling in a woman.' Fox, *Journal*, p. 315. September 4th, 1828.
42. Mémoires de Mlle Valérie Masuyer: *La Reine Hortense et le Prince Louis*, published in the *Revue des Deux Mondes*, August 1914, p. 613.
43. MALMESBURY, op. cit., p. 31.
44. To Miss Curran, January 2nd, 1825. *Letters of Mary W. Shelley*, ed. by F. L. Jones.
45. Lady Blessington to Contessa Guiccioli 1832. Teresa had inquired 'what was precisely this full dress, short or long dress? and if, on entering the bonnet is worn on the head, or a simple morning hat?' MORRISON, *The Blessington Papers*, p. 68.
46. Lady Blessington to Contessa Guiccioli 1832.
47. The same, undated.
48. Teresa's papers contain no less than eighty letters from Lady Blessington – but some are short notes of little interest. Sixteen of them she sent – at his request – in July 1854 to Dr. Madden, saying 'Mme de Boissy a recouvert avec une bande de papier les passages qu'elle veut qui soient supprimés'. MORRISON, op. cit., p. 80.
49. MADDEN, *The Literary Life and Correspondence of the Countess of Blessington*, II, p. 226.
50. *L.J.*, V, p. 371. September 20th, 1821.
51. JERNINGHAM, *Reminiscences of an Attaché*, p. 107.
52. Contessa Guiccioli to Lady Blessington. MADDEN, op. cit., II, p. 250.
53. *L.J.*, V, p. 371. Byron to John Murray, September 20th, 1821.
54. Dated 'Albemarle Street, Friday'.
55. Draft among Teresa's papers. Dated 'Thursday evening'.
56. Draft dated 1832. A part of this letter is in MADDEN, op. cit., pp. 250-1.
57. Undated, but written in August 1832, since Teresa's answer to it is dated August 27th, 1832.
58. Draft among Teresa's papers. Brighton, August 27th, 1832. Also partially printed in MADDEN, op. cit., II, p. 251.
59. Dated only 'Friday evening'.
60. Undated draft, among Teresa's papers. A slightly different version, with the English corrected, is given by MADDEN, op. cit., II, p. 249.
61. Undated draft among Teresa's papers.
62. Dated only 'Monday', but written in November or December 1832, as it refers to Teresa's trip to Nottinghamshire, which took place in December.
63. Dated only 'Monday evening', but written in the summer of 1832, as it is addressed to Teresa in Brighton.
64. May 3rd, 1832.
65. Draft among Teresa's papers – undated.
66. November 11th, 1832. The lock was sent on Teresa's departure from England, and the inscription said: 'T. Guiccioli's hair. To the Countess of Blessington. Friendship's offering.' MORRISON, op. cit., p. 64.
67. June 2nd, 1832. Thomas Campbell (1777-1844) besides being a poet, had been the editor of the *New Monthly Messenger*, in which Lady Blessington published her *Conversations of Lord Byron*, and was an assiduous member of her circle.
68. MADDEN, op. cit., II, p. 249.
69. Ibid., II, p. 251. August 27th, 1832.
70. Draft of letter from Teresa to Lady Blessington, November, 1832.
71. December 11th, 1832. Unpublished letter belonging to Sir John Murray.
72. J. M. B. Pigot was the brother of Elizabeth, Byron's friend in 1804. She then described the poet as 'a fat bashful boy', who used to come in and go out of their house at all hours. Those months remained, for the whole Pigot family, the high romantic peak of their lives – and when, after Byron's death, Moore was taken to call on old Mrs. Pigot, he recounted that 'she kissed my hand most affectionately, and said that,

much as she had admired me as a poet, it was as the friend of Byron that she valued and loved me'. MOORE, *Memoirs*, V, p. 349.

73. Teresa kept this letter in a folder on which she wrote that such a letter, written by 'un homme très respectable et magistrat vertueux' showed 'his devotion to Lord Byron's memory, a devotion which is a testimonial of Lord Byron's qualities'. December 6th, 1832.

74. MORRISON, op. cit., p. 64. January 7th, 1833.

75. To Mrs. Gisborne, January 16th, 1833. *Letters of Mary W. Shelley*, ed. F. J. Jones.

76. He had asked for the Pineta at Ravenna, the Palazzo Guiccioli, the Monument to Gaston de Foix and the Tomb of Dante – besides the garden of the Guiccioli Palazzo in Bologna, and the Camposanto. John Murray Junior to Contessa Guiccioli, October 18th, 1832.

77. May 3rd, 1833. Draft in Teresa's hand of a letter to John Murray.

78. April 12th, 1833.

79. May 3rd, 1833.

80. Dionysius Lardner, whom Thackeray satirized as Dionysius Diddler in the *Miscellanies*, was one of the most successful popularizers of his time. Most of the eminent writers of his time (Scott, Moore, Southey) wrote for his *Cabinet Cyclopedia*. Teresa kept nearly 40 of his letters – most of them of very slight interest.

81. September 11th, 1835.

82. The writer was a Miss Allen, of whom Mme Patterson Bonaparte had written to Teresa, 'Je vous assure qu'elle est moins insipide que la plupart des femmes'.

83. July 21st, 1836. In MADDEN (op. cit., II, pp. 40-1) the last sentence has been omitted. The trial was that of Caroline Norton, who was accused by her husband of adultery with Lord Melbourne, and who was triumphantly acquitted – but nevertheless lost her home, her children, her money and her reputation. Teresa had written to ask 'ce qu'il y à de vrai au sujet de Mrs. Norton'. MORRISON, op. cit., p. 71.

84. 'Our hostess and her sister, Madame St. Marsault, were both radiant and their brilliant toilettes cast into shade the somewhat dowdy costume of the Countess.' MOLLOY, *The Most Gorgeous Lady Blessington*.

85. GRONOW, *Reminiscences and Recollections*, pp. 311-12.

86. MOLLOY, op. cit., II, p. 191.

87. MADDEN, op. cit., II, p. 226.

88. October 16th, 1837. MORRISON, op cit., p. 73.

89. MADDEN, op. cit., II, p. 256. August 7th, 1839.

90. LAUGHTON, *Memoirs of the Life and Correspondence of Henry Reeve*, I, p. 95.

91. Ibid., I, p. 25.

92. December 16th, 1839.

93. January 8th, 1845.

94. Letter from Lady Blessington's maid to Doctor Madden. MORRISON, op. cit., p. 173.

95. July 11th, 1846.

96. BRETON, *Memoires du Marquis de Boissy*, p. 8.

97. Ibid., p. 19.

98. *I Guiccioli*, II, p. 90.

99. Malmesbury, op. cit., I, p. 35.

100. *I Guiccioli*, II, p. 88. Teresa's new grand manners were no doubt partly due to the snubs she had received in the past, – as when, in 1836, Lady Blessington's sister Lady Canterbury, had declined the pleasure of her acquaintance, unless she should meet her 'at any house where I visit'. Lady Blessington commented that 'all this worldly-mindedness is so wholly at variance with my feelings and experiences that it disgusts me', but was obliged to communicate the message.

101. *Athenaeum*, April 5th, 1873, p. 439.

102. This story is told by the Principessa di Belgioioso in her *Souvenirs dans l'exil*.

103. MARY R. DARBY SMITH, *My reminiscences of Madame la Marquise de Boissy*, in the *Victoria Magazine* for November 1873, p. 12. This magazine is among Teresa's books at Settimello. Miss Smith's reminiscences were later reproduced in a little book entitled *The Marquise de Boissy and the Comte de Waldeck*, which Miss Mayne considered 'the silliest book that has ever been written'.

104. Ibid., pp. 5, 11 and 24. Mr. Harold Nicolson has observed that it is remarkable that these messages should have been in French – a language which Byron, when alive, firmly refused to speak.

105. Unpublished note, among Teresa's papers, 'on the importance to be attached to biographical works'. 'I have never given any importance', she adds, 'to this sort of compilation because I soon discovered that among foreigners it is the custom to speak every day of people in such a way, without injuring the highest reputation (see the Court Journal) and that among Italians, where persons and public morals are more respected, *only the initials of the names were given.*'

106. She had written to Murray that the 3rd and 4th volumes contained 'some words which I should be infinitely obliged to you if you could suppress in the next edition', and shortly afterwards she had sent him the volumes, 'where I have marked in the margin the words which offend in a particular manner the delicacy and truth, putting instead some others which I think more convenient'. Especially she begged that five lines from Byron's letter to Murray of June 1st, 1820 might be entirely suppressed. 'This passage is the most *indelicate* and *unjust* too, though written it seems by poor Ld. Byron himself. But he wrote sometimes under the impression of the moment – without examination – and frequently for the same reason he was sorry.'

107. June 2nd, 1858. Unpublished letter in French, belonging to Sir John Murray.

108. A copy of this book, together with Moore's *Life*, is still in Teresa's bookshelf at Settimello, with her marginal notes.

109. Letter referred to in note 107.

110. Leigh Hunt reproduced a facsimile of one of Byron's verses, from *English Bards and Scotch Reviewers*, in which almost every word had been amended – and, immediately below it, a verse in Shelley's hand, without any corrections.

111. In this Teresa was right. Lamartine's estimate of Byron was considerably affected by Leigh Hunt's portrait, and Stendhal described it as 'très ressemblant'. And even Lady Blessington is said to have remarked 'that Leigh Hunt gave in the main a fair account of him' – a remark, if true, greatly to her discredit. (H. C. ROBINSON, *Diary*, II, p. 132.)

112. In his Diary, a few months after Byron's death, Hobhouse himself recorded the following conversation between Byron and Stanhope: 'Talking one day of his [Byron's] eventful life, Stanhope said, "Why do you not write your life?" Byron replied that his friends could do it as well: Gamba knew all his later years, and Hobhouse his early ones.' BROUGHTON, op. cit., II, p. 61. But there, as far as Hobhouse was concerned, the matter ended.

113. February 16th, 1836.

114. GUILLAUMIN, op. cit., p. 373, quoting from a letter of Teresa's written in 1856.

115. Ibid.

116. This serial never appeared in book form, nor is it included in LAMARTINE's *Collected Works*. It appeared in *Le Constitutionnel*, September-December 1865.

117. TERESA GUICCIOLI, *Lord Byron jugé par les témoins de sa vie*, vol. I, p. 321. *Lettre à M. de Lamartine.*

118. JERNINGHAM, *Reminiscences of an Attaché*, p. 108. The author translated Teresa's book into English.

119. In *Lord Byron jugé*, etc.

120. JERNINGHAM, op. cit., p. 99.

121. MALMESBURY, op. cit., I, p. 33.

122. The Black Book of the Ravenna Police for 1843, contains the following note: 'Count Ruggero Gamba, patriot and Freemason, who, owing to the shameful relationship with Lord Byron, was exiled in 1821, and condemned by His Eminence Rivarola to 20 years of imprisonment.' MAIOLI E ZAMA, *Patrioti e Legittimisti delle Romagne*, p. 87.

INDEX

INDEX

The page numbers referring to the footnotes are in *italics*. Where the notes have been grouped together (pp. 493-521) the page number is followed (in brackets) by the number of the note.

523

MELBOURNE, Lady
  21, 236, 341
MENGALDO, Cavaliere Angelo, 14,
  33-6, 91, 92, 93, *93*, *494* (n 24, 26)
MENICHINI, don, 201-2
METAXATA
  Byron at, 358-67, 369-73
MEZZOFANTI, Cardinal Giuseppe,
  111, 287, *499* (n 27)
MILBANKE, Lady, 131, 328
MILLINGEN, Dr. Julius, 383
  Memoirs, 376, 386
MILTITZ, Baroness, 193
MISSIAGLIA, Giovanni Battista, 91, *91*,
  140
MISSOLONGHI, 18, 358, 360, 371, 373
  Byron at, 373-83
MONTENERO, Byron at, 309, 318
MONTEVECCHI, Monsignor Do-
  menico, 253, *506* (n 53)
MONTGOMERY, Colonel, 34, *34*
MONTI, Vincenzo, 157, 209, *209*, 319
MOORE, Thomas, 30, *39*, 127-8, 297,
  330, 357, 397, 406, 420, 421, *499*
  (n 35), *519* (n 72)
  Life of Byron, 17, 73, 111-2, 117, 127,
  129, *136*, *183*, 297, 312, 314, 315, 323,
  343, 344, 346, *500* (n 90), *506* (n 68)
  Letters (or passages from letters)
    From Byron, 10, 128, 143, 179, *181*,
    187, 192, 211, 212, 227, 252, 283,
    286, 316, 328, 330, 345, 386, *394*
    Contessa Guiccioli on Life, 187-8, 416,
    521 (n 106)
MORANDI, Antonio, *515* (n 1)
MORANDI, Rosa, 195
MORELLI, Luigi, 91, 166, 173, 174,
  190, 193, 196, 207, 210, 228
MORGAN, Lady, 106, 182, 303, 406,
  506 (n 53)
MORNING HERALD, The, 405
MOUNTCASHELL, Lady, 293-4
MURRAY, John, 8, 56, 111, *116*, 142,
  398, 400, 402, 407, *502* (n 22)
  Letters (or passages from letters)
    To Contessa Guiccioli, 407, 408,
    508-9 (n 23), *513-4* (n 81)
    From Byron, 10, 34, 56, 78-9, 103,
    114, 129-30, 131, 142, 143, 161,
    162, 164, 167, 169, 173, 173-4,
    182, 186-7, 200, 201, *218*, 222,
    224, 238, 239, 240, 243, 313, 321,
    330, 335, 400
    From Contessa Guiccioli, 7, 139, 407,
    408, *508* (n 23), *513-4* (n 81), *521*
    (n 106)
MURRAY, John, Jr., 408, 417, *520* (n 76)

NAPIER, Colonel Charles, 355, 358, 371,
  515 (n 13)

NAPLES, 201-2, *202*, 225-6, 247, 251,
  336
NEAPOLITANS
  Rising of, 16, 201-2, 247, 251, 252
  Byron's letters to, 225-6
  Byron on, 201, 250, 251, 252
NEWSTEAD ABBEY, 7, 120, 397, 407,
  407, 421
NORTON, Caroline, 409, *520* (n 83)
NOTT, Dr., 293, *293*

ODYSSEUS (Andritzinos), 357, 381
ORSELLI, Conte Giuseppe, 205
OSBORNE, Lord Sydney Godolphin,
  366, 385, 386, *516* (n 40)

PADUA, 117, 118
PAPI, Vincenzo, 317
PARRY, William, 377, *377*, 379, 383,
  386, 418, 420, *517* (n 63, 67)
PASQUIER, Etienne-Denis, Duc, 415
PASTA, Giuditta, 148, 156, 163
PATTERSON BONAPARTE, Eliza,
  395, *518-9* (n 41)
PELLICO, Silvio, 16
PELZET, Maddalena, 108
PEPE, Guglielmo, General, 202, 225, 226,
  247, 251
PERELLI, don Gaspare, 44, 50, 51, 66,
  69, 78, 101
PERTICARI, Conte Giulio, 208-9, *208*
PIGOT, Elizabeth, *519* (n 72)
PIGOT, Dr. John, M.B., 408, *519* (n 73)
PIO VII, Pope, Gregorio Chiaramonti,
  26, 168, *168*, 171, *171*, 186, 187, 189,
  190, 192, 193, 246, 251, 284, 285,
  308, 309, 335, *505* (n 54)
PISA, 15, 266, 274, 275-6, 278, 279, 282,
  283, 290, 291, *309*, 325, 327, 359
  Byron in, 292-306, 318-24, 369
PRATO, 274, 275, 276

QUIROGA, Antonio, General, 209,
  504 (n 23)

RAMPI, Conte, 260
RAMPI, Madre Margherita, 23, 29
RANGONE, Conte Francesco, 32, 33,
  41, 62, 107, 108, 111
  Papers of, 32-3, 41, 62, 68, 85, 101,
  107-8, 110, 147, 251-2
RANGONE, Conte Giuseppe, 33, 38,
  97, 98, 118, 270
RASI SANTE, Dr., 206, 310
RASPONI, Conte Cristino, 153, 154
RASPONI, Conte Giulio, 68, 156, 197,
  206